Taking on the Superpowers

Collected Articles on the
Eritrean Revolution (1976-1982)
Vol. 1

[handwritten inscription: To Alganesh, With best wishes for the future (signature) 2004]

Taking on the Superpowers

*Collected Articles on the
Eritrean Revolution (1976-1982)*
Vol. 1

Dan Connell

**Introduction by
Basil Davidson and Lionel Cliffe**

The Red Sea Press, Inc.
Publishers & Distributors of Third World Books

11-D Princess Road   P. O. Box 48
Lawrenceville, NJ 08648   Asmara, ERITREA

The Red Sea Press, Inc.

Publishers & Distributors of Third World Books

| P.O. Box 1892 | P.O. Box 48 |
| Trenton, NJ 08607 | Asmara, ERITREA |

Book Design: Dan Connell with Debbie Hird
Cover Design: Debbie Hird
Cover Photo: Sarah Errington

Library of Congress Cataloging-in-Publication Data

Connell, Dan.
    Taking on the superpowers : collected articles on the Eritrean
    revolution, 1976-1982 / Dan Connell. p. cm.
    "vol. 1."
    Includes bibliographical references and index.
    ISBN 1-56902-188-0 – ISBN 1-56902-189-9 (pbk.)
    1. Eritrea–History–Revolution, 1962-1993. I. Title.

DT397 .C677 2003
963.507'1–dc22   2003019850

To the martyrs

*All author's royalties
from the sale of this
book will be donated to
charitable organizations
to help the people of Eritrea.*

Acknowledgments

Over the twenty-seven years that I wrote these articles, hundreds of Eritreans helped me in ways too numerous and too varied to recount without stretching this into a full-blown memoir. But for their assistance, their insight, and their personal support, little of the material between these covers would have seen publication in the first place.

This is their legacy. I was fortunate to be there at certain crucial moments and to have had the opportunity to communicate what I saw, heard and learned of what they, the people of Eritrea, did for themselves. It is to them that I owe the greatest debt and for them and those who will follow that I compiled this collection.

I am also grateful to the many working journalists—reporters, photographers, editors, and others—who unselfishly taught me how to craft this experience into forms suitable for publication or broadcast to a diverse audience, often because they, too, were moved by what they saw and simply wanted others to know about it. You know who you are. Thank you.

Several institutions deserve thanks for providing me the resources to pull this collection together. Among them are the Research and Documentation Center and Sabur Printing Services in Asmara, Simmons College and Boston University's Mugar Memorial Library in Boston, and the Blue Mountain Center, a writers' and artists' retreat in the wilds of northern New York where such projects as this gestate in an extraordinarily nurturing environment.

And special thanks to my wife and partner Debbie Hird, whose support and encouragement, even when all seems unrelentingly dark, keeps me going.

Contents

***

Introduction

By Basil Davidson and Lionel Cliffe

Dan Connell's work is undoubtedly the most complete chronicle in English of the long struggle of the Eritrean people for nationhood and statehood. He has followed events in the country for almost thirty years and covered all the key phases in that struggle: the gains of the 1970s, the strategic withdrawal, the switch from defence to attack in the late 1980s, liberation and reconstruction in the 1990s, and then the drift again into war.

The collection of all his press stories and longer articles in these two volumes is a boon to ordinary readers keen to get a feel for the dynamics of the Eritrean revolution and to future historians. In the first volume, he records the public services and the reform measures in land and the way people governed themselves in liberated areas. The second volume covers the decisive last few years of the liberation struggle — including the dreadful famine of the 1980s, induced as much by war as drought — and provides a record of many of the initiatives that followed Independence.

Connell's concern throughout has been not just with the armed struggle but also with the conditions of the people themselves as they struggled to survive as well as to build new lives. His reports enable us to see unfolding events from the viewpoint of ordinary Eritreans — rank-and-file fighters, refugees, women heads-of-households, the famine-affected — and that is where his commitment lies. His links have all along been with the main and ultimately victorious liberation movement, the Eritrean People's Liberation Front (EPLF), and his identification has been with that movement and with its successor, the People's Front for Democracy and Justice (PFDJ), now the ruling party.

That perspective of sympathy with the people and the identification of the EPLF as an exemplary movement have been shared by

many foreign commentators and activists, not least the two of us. But
Connell has also seen at close hand the disheartening events of the
last five years. The descent into war with big brother Ethiopia
brought again many casualties, widespread displacement, a general
mobilization of the young and other scarce resources, for destructive
rather than reconstructive purposes. But it was more than just
tragedy; it was avoidable and thus a crime.

The final section of volume two brings out the tragedy of war-
revisited but also offers fresh insights as to how that drift was inte-
grally linked with the emergence of a style of leadership that was
becoming more and more remote and centralized — and divided. We
recall with sadness how a couple of days after the formal
Independence ceremony in 1993, Basil — who had long argued that
the Eritrean struggle for self-determination was a just cause — was
asked to address a distinguished audience of senior EPLF officials,
government personnel and intellectuals at Asmara University on the
lessons to be learned from comparative African experience.

The main thesis of that address was that if Eritrea wanted to
avoid the institutional crises that were at the heart of the failures in
much of Africa, it had to narrow the gap between leaders and the
people by encouraging participation and ensuring answerability. This
it could best do by building on the legacy of the liberation struggle,
but this would also need 'mine detectors' that would give early warning of shortfalls in participatory practices.

In the following years it is now clear there was unease within the
movement and the general population about the increasing tendency
for decisions to be taken at the top, without discussion, and to be pronounced by decree. There was concern about the long delay in implementing the Constitution that had been ratified in 1997 and in drawing up a legal basis and concrete plans for promised elections. But
these worries were not expressed, and they fermented within as well
as outside the ruling party, eventually leading to the statement of
protest by the G-15 group of senior PFDJ members in 2001. The
excuse of pre-occupation with the war with Ethiopia has been challenged in Bereket Habte-Selassie's new book *The Making of the
Eritrean Constitution* (Red Sea Press, 2003), wherein he points out
that the commission to prepare electoral laws and plans met only
twice over several months and with little urgency or clear focus —
even before the war.

A related worry was the increased reliance on repressive measures
without due process: the constituting of a Special Court outside the

judiciary — initially justified by the need to get quick action on corruption — and the use of extra-judicial detention, torture and even killings, as documented in Amnesty International reports. One noble stance, sadly taken alone in 2001, was the statement of the then Chief Justice, Teame Beyene, expressing his view that the Executive and particularly the President's Office was interfering too much in the activities of what was supposed to be an independent judiciary. The regime immediately confirmed fears that the rule of law was being infringed in its desire to control when it sacked him for this — and by decree, not through the procedures laid down in the (inoperative) Constitution.

When we were trying to understand this decline in a recent conversation, Basil posed the question: "What did we, the 'friends' of Eritrea, the observers of the liberation struggle, overlook?"

Well, it is now being recognized, not least in the new prologues to this collection, that what we are seeing is an accentuation of authoritarian tendencies, which were always one characteristic of the old EPLF. Yet perhaps attention needs to be given not just to the issue of power and its centralisation but to the policies and strategies being pursued by that power. Misjudgements have been made, crucially, in the drift into war, but also in the approach to land, in tackling the reintegration of fighters and refugees, in unrealistically pursuing the 'Singapore model' and turning away from self-reliance, in seeing the pastoralists as a 'problem,' and, recently, in joining the U.S.-led coalition in the conquest of Iraq.

In those heady days of the Independence celebrations, when we were both among the non-diplomatic, official guests, there was an informal party for these foreign 'friends of Eritrea.' We were encouraged by a short 'thank-you' talk that President Isaias gave in which his first remark was, "What Eritrea will now need most from its 'Friends' is criticism." With hindsight one wonders whether he meant it, but it sounded the right note at the time. However, what has increasingly characterized official reactions since then has been an extreme defensiveness by him and other core members of the regime, which makes them unable to listen to the mildest forms of criticism, whether from Eritreans or outsiders, or to respond to them without vitriolic denunciation.

This is the antithesis of Basil's post-liberation advice. But it is more than timely now to remember Isaias's words and to assert that criticism of the regime like Dan Connell's is the true mark of commitment to Eritrea's people. Indeed, there is little that foreign friends can do but condemn a process of authoritarian rule, which is for the moment seemingly impervious to reasoned argument but that will ultimately prove unable to resolve real contradictions by commandism rather than dialogue — with the people as well as opponents.

Bath, United Kingdom, September 2003

Enough!
An author's statement

One political party cannot be the solution—this is a very dangerous and risky game. The only alternative is a pluralistic political system, though there are many questions about how this should work.

Isaias Afwerki[1]

[T]here must be the seeds of difference in this broad-based movement. It will be constructive as long as it allows the free discussion of different political opinions, as long as it creates a political culture of tolerance. Otherwise, if there is a suffocation of this process, there will be a reaction outside it and the appearance of destructive options.

Haile Woldetensae[2]

In April 1976, I slipped into Eritrea's besieged capital, Asmara, where I witnessed the assassination of a high-ranking Ethiopian official and its bloody aftermath — the summary execution of dozens of innocent civilians. My eyewitness account of the massacre appeared on the front page of *The Washington Post*, breaking Ethiopia's long-standing blockade of information on the war for Eritrea's independence, then in its fifteenth year.

Soon afterward, I flew to Sudan, contacted the two liberation fronts through their offices in Khartoum, and traveled into guerrilla-held Eritrea to see the conflict from the other side. What I found,

---

[1] Dan Connell, *Against All Odds: A Chronicle of the Eritrean Revolution* (Trenton, NJ: Red Sea Press, 1997), p. 272.

[2] Dan Connell, *Rethinking Revolution: New Strategies for Democracy & Social Justice: The Experiences of Eritrea, South Africa, Palestine & Nicaragua* (Trenton, NJ: Red Sea Press, 2002), p. 375.

particularly with the Eritrean People's Liberation Front (EPLF), moved me deeply: not just their military strength, though it was certainly impressive, but rather their wide-ranging efforts to unify and transform Eritrea's diverse society as they were liberating it.

This was far more than a war of national liberation. It was a revolution: thoroughly restructuring the power relations of a complex society onto a far more inclusive, egalitarian basis. It was nation-building in its most profoundly democratic sense: tackling the great social divides of clan, ethnicity, religion, gender and class and knitting together a common identity as Eritreans.

Over the next twenty-seven years, I wrote hundreds of articles on the Eritrean Revolution: on the bold experiments with radical social transformation underway in 1976, on the near defeat of Ethiopia's American-backed army in 1977, on the intervention of the Soviet Union and the liberation movement's strategic retreat in 1978, on the famine that swept the region in the mid-1980s, on the final Eritrean victory in 1991, on the effort to reconstruct and develop the war-ravaged new state later in that decade, on the renewal of war with Ethiopia in 1998-2000, and on the economic and political reverses that followed and flowed out of this latest conflict.

The idea for collecting these articles for publication came initially from Zemhret Yohannes, with whom I worked in 2001 and 2002 to produce a country handbook for Eritrea when he was the acting Minister of Information. I had been organizing my old news stories, photographs and color slides to donate to Eritrea's Research and Documentation Center, the precursor of a national archives. Zemhret suggested I assemble the written material for publication by a press in Asmara owned by the People's Front for Democracy and Justice — the EPLF's successor — and he arranged for the transcription of many of the yellowed newspaper clippings. As they were typed into computer files, I proofread, formatted and laid them out in publishable format. Later, I added pieces that I uncovered in my personal archives, in microfilm libraries in the U.S., and in other collections.

There is much to be learned from the Eritrean experience. The EPLF united its diverse society — half Christian, half Muslim, from nine distinct ethnic groups — into a highly-motivated, well-disciplined national movement that was able, with almost no outside support, to bring successive U.S.- and Soviet-backed Ethiopian governments to their knees. This was in itself a remarkable achievement — the more so when contrasted with the dismal experience of nation-building among Eritrea's neighbors. At the same time, the front worked to liberate women, workers and peasant farmers from centuries of grinding poverty, chronic hunger and unspeakable oppression. In fact, it was experiments with land and marriage reform and the provision of services like agricultural extension, primary education, adult literacy and village-level public health in the liberated areas, implemented in a highly participatory manner, that motivated such large numbers of peasant farmers, workers, women and youth to join the struggle. The synergy between these two projects — national liberation and social transformation — is the most important lesson to take from the Eritrean experience. Accounts of how this was done make up much of this collection.

However, the amassing of these articles for publication coincided with dramatic and far-reaching changes in the postwar political situation in Eritrea — steps that undermined the very popular democracy project that had drawn me into Eritrea so tightly and for so long. Prominent among them were the closing of public political space, the shutdown of the private press, the arrest and indefinite detention of key figures from the liberation struggle, many of whom are quoted in the articles here, and the imposition of a coercive regime on the population at large. These chhanges transformed me from a stalwart supporter to a dogggged critic.

As unique as Eritrea's accomplishments have been up to this point — the integration of ethnic and religious minorities, the elevation of women's status, the suppression of crime and corruption —the country's current trajectory follows a disappointingly familiar path, what is often termed the "crisis of the postcolonial African state": the concentration of power within the executive branch of government, the marginalization of nominally independent parliaments and judiciaries, the imprisonment or exile of vocal critics, the sharp restriction of independent media and autonomous civil society institutions, the outlawing of rival political parties, and, through this, the consolidation of power under a single leader who justifies his extended stay in office by the fragility of the nation over which he presides. In short, the corruption of the political process and with it faith in the institutional foundation of the society itself.

As I watched this pattern unfold within Eritrea, more than a decade after it had been discredited elsewhere on the continent, I knew that this represented a giant step backward for the objectives, the values, and the vision that I chronicled in my news articles throughout the liberation struggle and that I so strongly argued for in my analytic writing in the post-independence period. To publish a book that suggested otherwise, even if only by omission, would be dishonest. In December 2002 I broke off the arrangement to publish the collection with the PFDJ and set about organizing an alternative, as I remained convinced both of the value of the front's earlier experience and of the importance of analyzing how it could be so dramatically derailed later.

———

Like many of those involved in this movement over the past several decades, I held off as long as I could from such a decision, with all its implications and consequences, but it has become impossible to stand apart from these events. Why it took so long to get to this is another matter — partly political, partly personal, and all the more difficult because the two were so thoroughly intertwined.

I can only echo what many EPLF veterans have said when they, too, became public critics of the movement they helped to build: that the promise was so great, the achievements so impressive, the possibilities so humbling that it took an enormous act of will to face the fact that the Revolution was in jeopardy, that silence in the face of this was complicity, and that open criticism was the only option.

But it was also deeply personal. I had been in the trenches under withering enemy fire with people on both sides of this divide — remarkable, courageous individuals who risked everything to free their nation and whom I loved and respected as my own family, whatever they did or said to each other. Breaking with any of them was like cutting off a part of myself.

The tangle traces back to three political activists who met in Kassala, Sudan, in 1965 to share their disillusionment with the parochial, deeply corrupt liberation army they found there — the Eritrean Liberation Front — and to dedicate themselves to the creation of a truly revolutionary nationalist movement, whatever the cost. To cement their commitment, each carved an "E" in his upper arm and took a blood oath. Today, Mussie Tesfamikael is dead, Isaias Afwerki is Eritrea's president, and Haile "DruE" Woldetensae languishes in prison.

I never knew Mussie; he was killed in questionable circumstances before I became involved in Eritrea. But Isaias was a friend and mentor to me through much of the liberation struggle. He danced at my wedding. Haile, who ran the EPLF's political program, sat with me for hours upon hours to explicate the front's political evolution during and after the liberation struggle. We always laughed about the morning we careened out of Keren together, hours ahead of

Ethiopia's reoccupation of the city — Eritrea's second largest — in 1978. I last saw him three weeks before he was arrested in September 2001. The same is true with others now in detention and with the PFDJ officials who prepared the ground for their arrest — foes now but heroes of the Revolution and personal friends to me only yesterday.

Nor does it stop there.

The Eritrean Revolution has defined me for most of my adult life. At times, this has entailed personal sacrifice. Also risk. But it has been an enormously enriching experience, too, in terms other than monetary — not least for showing me (and through me, others) the sheer power of the human spirit and the capacity of entire societies once conscious and organized to change themselves for the better. I have drawn on this experience to compare, understand, and analyze other revolutions, and I have broadcast the Eritrean experience as widely as I could in the hope that people of good will, revolutionary or not, would learn from and support it.

How hard then to say: Enough! This movement is no longer what it was, nor what I hoped it would become, and it is taking down too many others — along with the dream — to stay silent.

Once I reached this conclusion, however, I had also to admit that there were disquieting signs for some time.

———

I recall that I was taken aback upon my first postwar visit in October 1991 to learn of the dismantling of the entire popular political apparatus as the front transformed itself into a government — the EPLF's Department of Mass Administration with its corps of cadre who lived and worked among the people was folded into an Asmara-bound Ministry of Local Government; the dynamic mass organizations of women, youth, peasants, and workers were at that time either dormant or reduced to service providers; the EPLF itself was virtually absent as a political force until reorganized and renamed the PFDJ in early 1994. I thought this hiatus in grassroots mobilization a mistake, and said so many times, but I was swayed by those who insisted they would revive the bottom-up popular movement once the institutional framework for the new state was in place.

The government's forced closure of the country's first nongovernmental organization in 1993 — the Regional Centre for Human Rights and Development, which had overnight attracted generous start-up funding from donors eager to work with anyone not affiliated with the state or the party — was also disturbing. But the argument that this was not the time for such an initiative when the front's mass organizations were struggling to establish themselves as self-financing, autonomous social movements won me over.

An alarm I could no longer ignore sounded several years later when I learned that the popularly elected village assemblies — a hallmark of the movement since the 1970s — had been replaced by a system of party appointees who presided over village forums that no longer had political power of their own. The announcement shocked me, as I had been writing for years that this was an essential building block for the new popular democracy.

Village self-government was where the people learned how to express themselves, identify their interests, make decisions, choose and hold accountable their leaders, and much more. This was the country's school for democracy, where the mechanisms of popular governance would be developed and tested and out of which a genuinely democratic national culture could grow. Told that these assemblies were not functioning "efficiently" enough, I nearly gagged. The argument that the people are not suited to govern themselves is as old as Plato. And what it leads to — rule from the top, whether by one man or a few, in the name of the people or not — is well documented.

On the other hand, there was the uniquely participatory constitution-making process that drew in most of the Eritrean population at home and abroad from 1995 into 1997. The document that came out of this extended national seminar, though tilted too heavily toward executive power, was an impressive and promising start. (By the same token, the failure to implement it upon ratification — fully a year before war broke out with Ethiopia — was the clearest sign yet that the regime's commitment to democratization was compromised.)

And there was the evidence everywhere of the continuing commitment to egalitarian social and economic development — the new schools, the training centers for women, the village health stations, the new rural roads, and much more. Material life was improving for large numbers of people, and structural social inequities were being continually challenged, if not wholly overcome.

Eritrea was (and remains) a contradictory reality.

———

When war broke out with Ethiopia in May 1998, I continued to defend Eritrea and its leaders in public, as I remained convinced that the war was in the main the result of Tigrayan political and territorial ambitions. But from day one I also felt that the Asmara leadership was squandering opportunities to avoid armed conflict, and I was appalled at the potential cost of such misjudgments to the people of Eritrea and to the fragile experiment in revolutionary social change and democracy-building underway across the country.

After the war, these concerns proved well founded. The government quickly signaled its intention to pick up where it had left off with its ambitious infrastructure projects. But popular democracy — the political scaffolding of the new state, as Eritreans themselves had defined and designed it — was no longer on the agenda. Nor was a critical assessment of the causes and consequences of the recent war. Even a long overdue party congress was on indefinite postponement. What was going on?

By the early part of 2001, the fact that a highly charged power struggle was taking place within the leadership had become widely known, if not officially acknowledged. Residents of the capital — Asmarinos — followed every twist and turn through the local rumor network. When this contention burst into public view in the spring, the private press picked it up and ran with it.

I voiced my concerns over the need for vigorous political dialogue to resolve outstanding differences in a June 2001 interview in one of Eritrea's more outspoken new papers, *Maqaleh*. Once the door to such discourse was slammed shut with the arrest of the leading dissidents and the closure of the private press, I articulated my dismay in an October interview with the Eritrean Web site Asmarino.com (included in Section 8).

I came late to this position, and I regret that. But make no mistake: I have no second thoughts about the attention I brought to this extraordinary revolution in the years before this cruel reversal. The events and achievements these articles chronicle remain as impressive and inspiring today as they were then, as do the people who made them.

I publish this collection precisely to spotlight the rich revolutionary legacy on which those who rule Eritrea are now trampling in the name of "nationalism." The women and men who struggled and died so that Eritrea might be independent and truly free deserve more than this. I dedicate this collection to them.

———

Volume 1 covers the period from my first visit to Eritrea in March 1976 through the liberation movement's near victory in 1977 and the return to guerrilla warfare in the early 1980s. Volume 2 starts with the famine that wracked the Horn of Africa in 1984-85 and continues through liberation and postwar reconstruction to the renewal of conflict and the closure of the country's emerging "democratic space." The two volumes are further divided into eight sections (four in each) that are organized both by time frame and theme.

Space considerations dictated the place where the first volume breaks off and the second begins — I wrote more news articles about the liberation war than I did about the postwar period, when I shifted toward lengthy report formats and full-length books — but there is a thematic logic to this, too.

The first volume covers the EPLF's most highly politicized, most socially revolutionary period. The turn toward "moderation" came in the mid-1980s, as several factors combined to push the front toward a more nationalist, less revolutionary posture. Among them were the abandonment of the Eritrean cause by most of the international left, the demise of the rival Eritrean Liberation Front (ELF) in a brief but bitter civil war and the spread of the EPLF's scarce cadre throughout the country, the need for the EPLF to gather in a broader social base at home and among the diaspora now that it was the sole fighting force, and the impact of the famine on the ability to mobilize people around a political agenda — issues and events that I take up in the articles in the later sections. There was also a power struggle within the movement — about which I only learned later — that led to a militarization of the core leadership around the front's dominant personality, Isaias Afwerki, which I describe in the Prologue to Section 8.

Brief prologues appear at the start of each section in order to set the historical and political context for the articles that follow, to describe my up-and-down relations with the media, and to fill in gaps not covered by the articles themselves. I have also included some references to my personal travails — changing childcare responsibilities, marriage and divorce, financial difficulties — as they help to explain the ebb and flow of my output. But I have not attempted to turn this collection into a memoir, and such personal details are not explored.

I began my reporting for *The Washington Post* and the New York-based *Guardian* in 1976 and 1977. As I learned the trade and expanded my contacts, I added the BBC, then Reuters news service, and finally a long string of national and regional newspapers. These included at various times: *Aftenposten* (Oslo), *The Boston Globe*, *The Christian Science Monitor* (Boston), *The Financial Times* (London), *The Guardian* (London), *The Irish Times* (Dublin), *The Miami Herald*, *The Observer* (London), *La Repubblica* (Rome), *Le Monde* (Paris), *The Toronto Globe and Mail*, *The Washington Star* (before it folded in

1981), and a few others. I also filed for the Associated Press via their Cairo bureau and the Voice of America via Nairobi without using any bylines, and later for both Pacifica radio and Monitor radio. And there were the odd publications in the Philippines, East Africa, Australia, and Europe, as well as special assignments.

I wrote under five pennames during my first five years, mainly to protect my ability to write in Sudan when its government sought to curtail my movement or, at one time, even my presence in the country. I have not included any of the articles filed for radio broadcast or any of the news briefs filed for the wire services, though I have reproduced a small number of longer news analyses and features from Reuters. Nor have I included articles in languages other than English, of which there were many, or, with few exceptions, articles from English-language papers that duplicate stories appearing elsewhere. However, I have listed as many of these as I know of in the Appendix, along with longer broadcast documentaries, reports, and books, so that a researcher can find them if need be.

A few pieces are reproduced that roughly mirror one another — see for example the articles appearing in early October 1980 in the London *Guardian* and *The Irish Times* — mainly to illustrate the phenomenon of simultaneous publication and to draw attention to the subtle editorial differences that appear in the published product. I also did so a few times to demonstrate that stories that accurately reflect the reality on the ground can, if devoid of strident political rhetoric, appear in outlets at opposite ends of the political spectrum. See, for example, the articles in the New York-based *Guardian* on January 1, 1979 and *The Boston Globe* four days later.

―――

My role as a journalist changed dramatically when I was ousted from Sudan under pressure from Ethiopia in 1981 (described in Section 4). This was also a time when the economics of freelancing changed, making it far more difficult to sustain such a mode of information production, especially without consistently living in the place where I worked. And it coincided with changes in my personal life — the reason for my episodic reporting — when my alternating custody arrangement broke down, and I made the decision to spend more time at home. This marked the end of my prolific news reporting.

I spent much of the winter of 1981-82 organizing and drafting a book on the liberation struggle, a project I had decided to undertake in 1977 but which had until then eluded me, as I raced to keep up with current events. But my first try was a frustrating failure. I produced a rough draft of nearly 100,000 words, but I was unable to interest a publisher, and I set the project aside.

In June 1982, under growing financial pressure, I took a short-term assignment with the Boston-based charity Oxfam America to go to Lebanon to assess relief needs during Israel's invasion. This was extended to a full-year contract, during which I sought to convince the aid agency both to commit to a continuing program in Lebanon and to take on famine-prevention work in Eritrea. When the agency declined to do either, as I describe in the Prologue to Section 5, I resigned to start a new nonprofit agency, Grassroots International. This marked another turning point in my writing, as I went from reporter to full-time campaigner — penning funding appeals, commentaries and opinion pieces rather than hard news stories and often working behind the scenes to influence the coverage of other writers.

I left Grassroots International after seven years to take another shot at writing the long-delayed book on Eritrea's liberation. The result was *Against All Odds*, which I drafted in 1991-92 and which appeared with Red Sea Press in 1993 (revised and reissued with a new Afterward in 1997). At that point, I returned to freelancing but not hard news reporting, which was no longer viable in the way I had practiced it in the 1970s. Instead, over the next decade I took consulting contracts with international aid and human rights organizations, and I received two writing grants from the MacArthur Foundation, mainly for work in the Horn of Africa. (The reports and books that came out of these assignments and grants are listed in the Appendix.) During this time, I also wrote articles for magazines and journals, and I did several opinion pieces for daily newspapers, most of which appear here. In September 2002, I began teaching journalism and African politics at Simmons College in Boston.

I have not edited or revised the articles included here, though I have certainly been tempted to do so while rereading them, as much for tone and style as for content. But these pieces reflect the language and atmosphere in which this revolution was fought and won. They need to be read within that historical framework — not only that of Eritrea but also that of the world as it was in those cold-war years, in particular the Left, which set the terms for the global discourse on national liberation struggles and with which I identified as a political actor.

That said, this collection also records my development as a writer

and an activist and my struggle to combine these sometimes contradictory vocations. I grew as a journalist as I learned how to present
my material in a form and a language that readers could take in wherever they sat on the political spectrum. Though my passion never
waned, I sought to manage it so it did not get in the way of others
seeing, understanding, and appreciating what I experienced up close.
If this book has value beyond its contribution to the historical record,
it is in the extended illustration of how to practice such "advocacy
journalism" to a diverse global audience — how to organize and
disseminate information from a "popular" standpoint to make a
difference in the way others understand and respond to unfolding
political events.

I often use the term advocacy journalist to describe myself, so let
me add a word or two on what I mean. Throughout these twenty-
seven years, I was always both a journalist and an advocate — a
chronicler of events (not *neutral*, but as *objective* as I could be) and
also an actor trying to influence those events. It was and remains a
difficult balance, yet, if we are honest with ourselves, few writers in a
similar position will deny that they struggle with this tension. It
comes with being human.

Journalism is inherently subjective, whatever the pretense of
detachment. Its practice is very like the child's game of "telephone,"
in which a story is whispered to another player, and then to the next,
and so on down the line in as close an approximation of the original
as possible until it gets to the last person and is repeated aloud in
what is invariably a far different form than it started.

Reporters, especially Americans, routinely pack their stories with
quotation marks and descriptive details to disguise this, implying that
we are merely recording devices transmitting exactly what we witness. But we are fallible in our perceptions, and we are affected by our
values and experiences. We select what we report, whom we quote,
which quotes we use, what questions we ask to get these quotes, and
how we organize it all to present it to you. This does not mean we
intentionally manipulate or falsify the truth (though some clearly do)
— only that we make judgments on what we report and how we do it.

All journalism comes with such baggage. If you are serious about
getting a full, all-sided picture of events or issues, you must gather
multiple perspectives and make your own judgments. Or at least be
aware of those being made by the reporter to whom you turn and factor that into your perceptions.

I did not present all sides of every issue or event I covered — nor did I pretend to — though I referenced other perspectives when appropriate and tried to make it explicit when I was expressing opinions I could not substantiate. But much of what I wrote redressed a crushing imbalance in the perspectives and reportage of others, conveying a reality that was hidden from public view, a truth not otherwise known. I took the task of relating this truth to be both my journalistic and my political mission.

This collection is the Eritrean Revolution from where I sat, stood, or crouched over nearly three decades. It includes the lows and the highs, the retreats and the advances. It contains the disheartening moments when the work and the sacrifice of so many was turned to dust and the ecstatic instants when the prospect of fashioning a new world of economic and social justice dangled at our fingertips, and all things seemed possible. And it does so as fully and as accurately as I was able to capture and present it.

Throughout my extended encounter with Eritrea, I have continued to believe that the truth will in fact set us free — if we know how to recognize it when we see it, if we understand how to interpret it, and if we are willing to process its consequences. When respect for truth died a public death in Eritrea in 2001 and 2002, my role as a journalist there came to an end, but my responsibility as a truth-teller did not.

—

The last articles in this collection, together with the prologue for section in which they appear, sum up my views today: "Eritrea and the International Media" critiques the Eritrean government's approach to public information, the Asmarino.com interview elaborates my criticisms of the 2001 crackdown, "Inside the EPLF" begins to unpack the role of the secret party within EPLF whose postwar legacy shapes the contemporary political context, and "New Strategies for Democracy and Justice" summarizes my theoretical approach to these issues in a comparative political framework.

I have come to conclude that the radical experiment in popular democracy that I chronicled through these many pages is at risk today not from external sources but from its own leaders, despite the fact that commitments to social and economic egalitarianism persist under the regime's paternalistic stewardship.

The schools and clinics for all Eritreans, the roads and bridges that link the most remote areas of this diverse country, the new dams, the millions of freshly-planted tree seedlings, the extension of electrification, the construction of new industries and agricultural schemes

— all this and more make magnificent monuments to the liberation ethos that powered this movement for decades. But that is all they will be — monuments — if the fundamental respect for the people who nurtured this ethos is lost, if the conviction that it is the people who drive this revolution is reduced to a hollow slogan.

During the decade since independence, the president and his closest allies have squeezed the "liberty" out of liberation and left only the seductive shell of a top-down egalitarian development project. Even this may not survive long without deep roots among the people such as those so carefully cultivated during the liberation struggle. The coercive regime that now rules Eritrea is severing those roots. As a consequence, Eritrea and the movement that liberated it will never be the same.

What then to do?

The answer is deceptively simple: Trust the people — now, as before.

What happened to the Eritrean Revolution at the dawn of the twenty-first century is a tragedy, but it does not cancel the remarkable advances that are chronicled in the bulk of this narrative. Nor does it foreclose the possibility that the Revolution will revive and blossom under new leadership.

Dan Connell
Gloucester, Massachusetts, August 2003

Eritrea's modern history: A chronology

1890	Italians claim the colony of Eritrea during the European "Scramble for Africa."
1896	Italians invade Abyssinia but are repulsed.
1896-1910	Abyssinia quadruples in size by conquering peoples to its south; changes name to Ethiopia.
1936-41	Italians occupy Ethiopia and British Somaliland and administer them, with Eritrea, as "Italian East Africa."
1941	British-led forces defeat the Italians; Ethiopia regains independence, Eritrea falls under British administration; the U.S. establishes strategic communications facilities in Asmara.
1952	Over protests by independence parties, Eritrea is federated to Ethiopia under a UN plan that gives Eritrea a separate flag, constitution and parliament; Italy's other colonies—Libya & Somalia—prepare for independence.
1953-58	The U.S. arms Ethiopia in exchange for military bases in Eritrea; Haile Selassie regime arrests Eritrean nationalists, imposes Amharic language, takes down Eritrean flag; troops fire on protesting students and workers; nationalists form underground Eritrean Liberation Movement (ELM).
1960-61	Eritrean Liberation Front (ELF) founded in Cairo, fires first shots of independence war on police units in western Eritrea.
1962	Haile Selassie regime forces Eritrean parliament to dissolve itself and annexes Eritrea as Ethiopia's 14th province.
1970-72	ELF splits, core of Eritrean People's Liberation Front (EPLF) is established, ELF declares war on EPLF.
1974	Haile Selassie is overthrown by a military committee (the Derg); ELF and EPLF agree to a truce and turn their guns on Ethiopia.
1977	ELF and EPLF capture all but a handful of Eritrean towns; the Derg breaks with the U.S., realigns Ethiopia with the USSR.
1978-79	Ethiopia mounts a series of massive, Soviet-backed offensives and reoccupies Eritrea's major towns and cities; EPLF withdraws to mountain base area.

1980-81	EPLF's offer for referendum to end the war with Ethiopia is rebuffed; renewed fighting breaks out between EPLF and ELF, ELF splinters and scatters in Sudan.
1982-85	EPLF repels repeated Ethiopian attacks on Sahel base area; war- and drought-induced famine sweeps the region.
1988	EPLF breaks ten-year stalemate and encircles Ethiopian forces in main cities.
1990	Massawa is liberated, placing Ethiopian forces in Eritrea under total ground siege.
1991	EPLF defeats Derg forces in Eritrea on May 24, establishes Provisional Government, helps Ethiopian opposition topple the regime there; new governments end 30-year war.
1993	Independence declared on 24 May, after April referendum on Eritrea's political status.
1994	EPLF transforms itself into the People's Front for Democracy and Justice (PFDJ); Government of Eritrea announces universal national service, establishes independent Constitution Commission.
1995	Government of Eritrea proclaims national agrarian reform.
1996	Regional & local governments are streamlined to decentralize administrative authority.
1997	Constitution is ratified in May, but not implemented.
1998-2000	Ethiopia caps a series of provocative border incidents with declaration of war on Eritrea, expels 76,000 Ethiopians of Eritrean origin, and displaces 600,000 Eritrean civilians in three rounds of fighting before a ceasefire is reached and the border dispute goes to international arbitration.
2001	A postwar political crisis in Eritrea leads to the arrest of critics and the forced shut-down of the private press. National elections are indefinitely postponed.
2002	Border dispute resolved, but implementation of abitrators' decision delayed and relations with Ethiopia remain tense.

Appendix

A Master List of Publications on Eritrea by Dan Connell 1976-2002

Note to the reader: Some publications are missing from this list, particularly among those issued outside the U.S. If you notice any, please contact Red Sea Press with the details (title, publication, date) and the information will be added to future editions.

Books and Special Publications

1981

"Six Million Dispossessed in the Horn: A White Paper." Editor and Main Contributor. Special issue, *Horn of Africa Journal*, vol. 4, no. 1.

1997

Against All Odds: A Chronicle of the Eritrean Revolution. Trenton, NJ: Red Sea Press.

Foreign Policy In Focus: Eritrea. Albuquerque, NM: Interhemispheric Resource Center & Institute for Policy Studies, vol. 2, no. 45 (September).

2001

Foreign Policy In Focus: Ethiopia-Eritrea Disengagement Proceeds Slowly, Civilians Watch & Wait. Albuquerque, NM: Interhemispheric Resource Center & Institute for Policy Studies (February).

2001

Getting Home Is Only Half the Challenge: Refugee Reintegration in War-Ravaged Eritrea. Washington, DC: U.S. Committee for Refugees (August).

2002

Eritrea: A Country Handbook. Editor and principal writer. Asmara: Ministry of Information.

The Proceedings of the 20th Anniversary Conference of the National Union of Eritrean Women: November 1999, Asmara, Eritrea. Editor and contributor. Asmara: National Union of Eritrean Women.

Rethinking Revolution: New Strategies for Democracy & Social Justice: The Experiences of Eritrea, South Africa, Palestine & Nicaragua. Trenton, NJ: Red Sea Press.

Articles in Books

1980

"The Changing Situation in Eritrea" in Basil Davidson, Lionel Cliffe, Bereket Habte Selassie, eds., *Behind the War in Eritrea*. London: Spokesman Books.

1985

"Introduction" in James Firebrace and Stuart Holland, *Never Kneel Down: Drought, Development and Liberation in Eritrea*. Trenton, NJ: Red Sea Press.

1995

"Eritrea: An Island of Stability in Strife-Filled Africa" in *Global Studies: Africa*. Guilford, CT: Brown & Benchmark.

2000

"Strategies for Change: Women in Eritrea and South Africa," in Diana Fox, ed., *Women's Rights as Human Rights: Activism and Social Change in Africa*. Lewiston, NY: Edwin Mellen Press.

2002

"Introduction" in Alemseged Tesfai, *Two Weeks in the Trenches*. Trenton, NJ: Red Sea Press.

Radio Documentaries (excluding spot news reports)

1978

"The Eritrean David Meets the Soviet Goliath" (30 minutes), BBC Africa Service (London)—aired November 15

1979

"Long March in Eritrea" (30 minutes), BBC World Service (London)—aired January 3

"Behind the Lines in Eritrea" (30 minutes), BBC World Service (London)—aired August 8

"A Generation Born to War" (45 minutes), Australian Broadcasting Corporation (Sydney)—aired August 14

1980

"Stalemate" (30 minutes), BBC Africa Service (London)—aired September 5

Articles in Journals & Magazines

1977

"Ethiopia, Eritrea & U.S. Policy," *The Nation* (New York), March 19

1978

"The Cubans Move In," *The Nation* (New York), May 6

"The Battle for Massawa," *SUDANOW* (Khartoum), February

"Mengistu Goes For Broke," *SUDANOW* (Khartoum), August

"Dreams Become Despair," *SUDANOW* (Khartoum), September

1979

"Eritrea: The Politics of Refugees," *Horn of Africa Journal* (New Brunswick, NJ), Vol. II, No.4

"Eritrean War Goes On," *SUDANOW* (Khartoum), August

1980

"Life and Death on the Horn of Africa," *The Boston Globe Magazine,* July 13

"The Birth of the Eritrean Nation," *Horn of Africa Journal* (New Brunswick, NJ), Vol. III, No.1

"Repression as a Way of Life," *Horn of Africa Journal* (New Brunswick, NJ), Vol. III, No.2

"Report from the Eritrean Front," *The Nation* (New York), October 25

1981

"The War That Won't Go Away," *Africa Today,* Vol. 28, No.4

1982

"War Crisis Escalates," *MERIP: The Middle East Report* (Washington, DC), June

1987

"The Next African Famine," *Dollars & Sense* (Boston), November

"Alignments in the Horn: Famine Reshuffles the Deck," *MERIP: The Middle East Report* (Washington, DC), March-April

1991

"The Battle for Eritrea," *Midweek* (Manila), February 6

1992

"Eritrea: A New Country Emerges," *Links* (New York), Spring

1993

"A Revolution in Process," *Monthly Review* (New York), July-August

"Eritrea Turns from Guns to Hoes," *African Farmer* (New York), October

1994

"The Greening Of Eritrea: Famine Unlikely Again," *African Farmer* (New York), October

1995

"Engendering the Left: The Rise of Third World Women's Movements," *Dollars & Sense* (Somerville, Mass.), November

"Beyond Famine, *In Context* (Bainbridge Is., Wash.), Fall

"Eritrea: Starting from Scratch," *Monthly Review* (New York), September

"Eritrea: Starting from Scratch," *Pulsang Bayan* (Manila), January-February

1997

"New Challenges in Postwar Eritrea, *Eritrean Studies Review* (Trenton, NJ), Spring

"After the Shooting Stops: Revolution in Postwar Eritrea," *Race & Class* (London), Spring

1998

"Africa's New Bloc," *Foreign Affairs,* March-April

"From Alliance to the Brink of All-Out War: Explaining the Eritrea-Ethiopia Border Crisis," *Middle East Report* (Washington, DC), Fall

"Strategies for Change: Women & Politics in Eritrea & South Africa," *Review of African Political Economy* (London), No. 76, June

1999

"Against More Odds: The Second Siege of Eritrea," *Eritrean Studies Review* (Trenton, NJ), Summer

"Behind the Eritrea/Ethiopia War," *Middle East International* (London), March 4

"Shootout in the Horn of Africa: A View from Eritrea," *Middle East Report* (Washington, DC), Spring

"Letter from Eritrea: At Issue Is Not Just Borders...," *The Nation* (New York), March 29

"Libérer l'Erythrée, un processus inachevé," *Vivant Univers* (Belgium), January-February

2000

"The Importance of Self-Reliance: NGOs and Democracy-building in Eritrea," *Middle East Report* (Washington, DC), Spring

"Confronting FGM in Eritrea," *The Women Today* (Nairobi), March-April

"Eritreans Try to Control NGOs," *The Women Today* (Nairobi), March-April

2001

"Inside the EPLF: The Origins of the 'People's Party' & its Role in the Liberation of Eritrea," *Review of African Political Economy* (London), September

2002

"Eritrea and the International Media," *Eritrean Studies Review* (Trenton, NJ), [delayed]

Articles in Newspapers, Newsletters & Web sites

[does not include spot news for wire services or broadcast media]

1976

The Washington Post

"War Signs Seen in Ethiopia," May 13

"Death, Hunger and Fear in Asmara," May 14

"U.S. a Puzzle for Eritreans," May 18

"Ethiopia Losing in Eritrea," May 20

"Eritreans Claim to Win Clashes With Peasants," June 1

"Eritreans Fill Squalid Camps in Sudan," July 11

"Peasants Learn 'Truth About Eritrea'," August 1

"Eritrean Rebels Say They Hold Four," August 4

"Revolt Hailed at Eritrean Rally Here," August 22

"Behind Rebel Lines in Eritrea," October 10

1977

The Guardian (New York)

"Roots of Eritrean Struggle," March 2

"Two lines in Eritrean movement," March 9

"Eritrean liberation struggle pushes Ethiopian revolution," March 16

"Eritrean liberation struggle escalates," July 6

"Ethiopia organizes peasant militia," July 6

"Eritreans flee massacres," July 13

"Eritrean struggle nears final victory," July 20

"Behind Ethiopia's 'socialist' mask," July 27

"Eritreans stage new offensive," July 27

"Shift in Eritrean liberation forces," August 31

"Eritrea's EPLF consolidates gains," September 28

"POWs become allies in Eritrea," October 5

"Eritreans prepare to liberate Asmara," October 12

"EPLF sets example in liberated Eritrean city," October 19

"Eritreans dissect Ethiopian division," October 26

"How the EPLF organizes in Eritrea," November 2

"Liberation in an Eritrean village," November 9

"Vanguard militia safeguards Eritrea," November 16

"Eritrean groups take unity step," December 7

"Another front launches war on Ethiopia," December 14

The Washington Post

"Israelis, Out of Favor in Africa, Still Find Home in Ethiopia," October 1

"Besieged Ethiopian City is Pictured in Despair," November 17

1978

Africa News (Raleigh-Durham, NC)

"Ethiopia: Tigre nationalists in the fray," June 26

Aftenposten (Oslo)

"Avgjorende styrkeprove pa trappene i Eritrea," August 1

"Frykt for trefninger Etiopia-Sudan," August 2

"Stategiske byer i Eritrea frivillig oppgitt av geriljaen," August 3

"Eritriesk utholdenhet," September 2

"Kubanske styrker i kamp i Eritrea?," September 11

"Hoy moral hos EPLF," October 10

"Eritrea-offensiv stanset, etiopisk moral svikter," October 26

The Baltimore Sun

"Quiet pervades embattled Asmara after failed Ethiopian offensive," November

"Eritrean rebels report executions are being ordered by Colonel Mengistu," November

"Eritrean rebels' capital continues life at night," November

"Eritrean rebels run refugee camp," November

The Boston Globe

"Ethiopia reportedly readies drive in Eritrea," March 26

"Eritrean rebels falling back," November

The Christian Science Monitor (Boston)

"Ethiopian jets use napalm on besieged Eritrean port," January 25

The Financial Times (London)

"The Horn of Africa: The Coming battle for Eritrea," February

"EPLF quits two key towns," August 2

"Ethiopian troops take major town," August 13

"Ethiopian move on Keren repulsed," August 21

The Guardian (New York)

"Eritreans hold Massawa," January 11

"Fighting intensifies in Asmara," February 1

"Life in an EPLF camp," March 8

"Ethiopia prepares Eritrea attack," March 29

"Eritrean fighting forces forge united front," April 19

"Eritrean struggle enters crucial stage," May 10

"Eritrean struggle nears turning point," May 24

"Eritrea support mounts in Europe," May 31

"Ethiopia poised for Eritrea drive," June 21

"Ethiopia military drive fails," July 12

"War strains Ethiopian economy," July 19

"Eritreans plan new offensives," Aug 16

"Eritreans block Ethiopia," August 30

"EPLF repulses Ethiopian attack," September 6

"EPLF keeps city, takes offensive," September 13

"Ethiopia prepares Eritrea offensive," November 22

"Eritrean factions spur civil war," November 29

"Social struggle in an Eritrean village," December 6

"Life in Keren before offensive," December 13

"Eritrea: EPLF girds for protracted war," December 20

The Miami Herald

"Breakthrough by Ethiopians is Reported in Eritrean Hills," July 23

"Cuban Force Reported in Eritrea," September 14

"Ethiopians Move North On Eritrea," June 1

Le Monde (Paris)

"Des Sovietiques participeraient aux combats contre les maquisards erythreens," February 4

"Les maquisards erythreens paraissent en mesure de resister a la contre-offensive," March 9

"Les Ethiopiens assurentavoir repris a ville d'Agordat," March

"Uma luta contra o tempo," March 20

"Plusiers brigades d'Addis-Abeba se dirigeraient vers les frontiers de l'Erythree," June 13

"Le lieutenant-colonel Mengistu joue son va-tout dans l'offensive en cours," July 25

"L'offensive ethiopienne progresse en Erythree," July 27

"L'armee d'Addis-Abeba continue su progression en Erythree," August 3

"Le F.P.L.E reconnait a son tour avoir perdu du terrain," August 4

"Les Ethiopiens assurentavoir repris la ville d'Agordat," August 11

"Les fronts de liberation font etat de 'replis tactiques'," August 11

"Des pilotes cubains participeraient a l'offensive ethiopienne contre Keren," August 15

"Le F.P.L.E fait etat d'une victoire au sud d'Asmara," August 18

"L'offensive Ethiopienne contre Keren marque le pas," September 9

"M. Fidel Castro se rend a Addis-Abeba," September 12

"Les maquisards erythreens auraient repris le controle des routes autour d'Asmara," September 16

"Les Troupes gouvernementales restent bloquees a Asmara et a Massaouah," October 26

The New York Times (via Reuters)

"Militia Units Set Up by Eritrean Rebels," January 23

The Observer Foreign News Service (London)

"Russian Troops Join in Eritrea Battles," February 10

"Eritrean Movement Revives Guerrilla Tactics," August 1

"Eritrea's Guerrillas Set a Trap," August 14

"We're Holding Ethiopian Attacks, Say Guerrillas," September 8

"Red Flowers of War," October 10

"Ethiopian Guerrillas Hold U.S. Pilot," November 23

"Russians Join Eritrea Battles," December 21

La Repubblica (Rome)

"Dove Israele si allea allo Yemen," February 15

"Mengistu deciso a domare la ribellione in Eritrea," May 30

"Sul fronte dell'Eritrea i cubani frenano Mengistu'," June 3

"Forze etipiche verso l'Eritrea," June 13

"Respinto dai partigiani l'assalto all'Eritrea di centomila etiopici,"
July 9

"Vicino al tracollo uno dei Fronti eritrei," July 26

"Sovietico il "cervello" dell'offensiva etiopica contro gli eritrei,"
July 27

"Mosca non crede piu a Mengistu forse una nuova svolta etiopica,"
July 28

"La riconquista e solotano cominciata," July 31

"Ora gli etiopici puntano su Asmara," August 3

"Mengistu e formo in Eritrea," August 10

"L'Eritrea as una svolta I cubani in primi linea," August 15

"Bloccata ad Asmara l'offensive etiopica," August 19

"Duemila cubani ad Asmara," September 12

"I partigiani eritrei ripendono una cita," October 10

"Ad Asmara e tornato il terrore," October 14

"Cosi Mosca s'e arenata in Eritrea," November 10

"Mengistu sta per sferrare un nuovo assalto all'Eritrea," November 12

"Ora l'Eritrea si batte contro i sovietici, la guerra e cambiata," November 30

The Toronto Globe & Mail

"Ethiopia near major victory in war against Eritrean guerrillas," July 22

The Washington Post

"Deserters Say Soviets in Eritrea War," February 2

The Washington Star

"Soviets, Cubans Help Ethiopia/Lack of Outside Aid Angers Eritrean Radicals," November 7

"Ethiopia Rebels Claim Capture of American," November 11

1979

Africa News (Raleigh-Durham, NC)

"Eritrea: Guerrilla morale 'very high'," March 2

"Ethiopia/Eritrea: Military setbacks, political repercussions," August 31

"Africa News special: Glimpses of a war zone," November 9

Aftenposten (Oslo)

"Tilbakeslag i Eritrea for Etiopia tross Kreml-stotte," August 14

The Boston Globe

"Eritrean guerrillas boost attacks," January 14

"Eritrea: Modern war for an ancient land," August 7

The Guardian (New York)

"Eritrean forces resume guerrilla attacks," January 3

"Eritrean guerrillas counter third offensive," January 10

"Eritrea: Radio Liberation," January 31

"Eritrea: London symposium," February 7

"EPLF thwarts latest Ethiopia attack," February 14

"Eritrea and self-determination," February 21

"Mengistu represses dissent," February 28

"Colonialism and Eritrean nationalism," March 7

"Eritrea's anticolonial struggle," March 14

"Eritrea: from national to social revolution," March 21

"Eritrea: EPLF reorganizes," March 28

"Eritrea: Ethiopia offensive," April 18

"Eritrea: Guerrilla offensive," July 4

"Eritrea: War tide turning," July 18

"Eritrea: Ethiopian attack," July 25

"Eritrea: Ethiopian setback," August 15

"EPLF persists after Ethiopia drive," November 7

"Liberation movements," August 22

"Eyewitness view of Eritrean struggle," November 14

"Eritrean rebels launch offensive," December 12

"Eritrea: Guerrilla offensive," December 19

The Miami Herald

"Ethiopians Too Strong Head On, Eritreans Revive Hit-Run Tactics," January 5

"Eritreans Predict They'll Win As Ethiopia Readies Offensive," June 27

"Eritreans Fear Return of 'Red Terror'," July 5

"$10-a-Month Soldiers Desert Ethiopia," July 15

"Endless War Drags Ethiopia Into Abyss," August 2

"Ethiopia's Offensive Might Appears Severely Crippled," August 3

"Peasants Want War to End—But Only With a Victory," August 4

The Observer (London)

"Ethiopia steps up war on Eritrean guerrillas," July 29

The Observer Foreign News Service (London)

"Eritreans Go Back to Guerrilla War," January 10

"Guerrillas Ring Asmara," July 30

"MIGs Against Nomads," July 31

The Washington Star

"Visit With Rebels Shows Ethiopia's failure," August 4

1980

Africa News (Raleigh-Durham, NC)

"Eritrea/Ethiopia: Alliances shift among government foes," Spring

Aftenposten (Oslo)

"Partene lader opp til et nytt oppgjor," May 3

"Jerngrepet strammes om et urolig Etiopia," May 14

"Russiske gifteksperter nytt vapen i Eritrea?," July 4

"Russiske leger tatt i Etiopia," July 4

"Indre strid i Eritrea-geriljaen," August 18

"Fredsplan fremlagt for Eritrea," November 25

"Etiopisk offensiv i Eritrea," December 12

"Etiopisk tilbakeslag i Eritrea," December 19

The Boston Globe

"Secessionist Eritrean guerrillas open major offensive," January 10

"Big Soviet arms lift to Ethiopia," June 11

"Civil war threatens in Eritrea," September 1

"Nationalist groups pose direct threat to Ethiopian regime," September 6

"Ethiopia seeks end to fighting," November 9

"Eritrean leaders offer plan to end 19-year war," November 27

"Sudan expels 2 newsmen; crackdown seen in coverage of Ethiopian rebels," November 27

The Christian Science Monitor (Boston)

"Ethiopian Army poised for new Ogaden guerrilla assault," July 29

"Embattled Ethiopia faces insurgents on two fronts," October 8

The Financial Times (London)

"Eritrean guerrillas back on offensive," April 28

The Guardian (London)

"Ethiopia bombing 'will lead to famine'," October 17

"Eritrean allies at war with each other," October 28

"Eritrean front may concede," November 6

"Guerrillas may shift alliance," November 14

The Guardian (New York)

"Eritrea: EPLF counteroffensive," January 16

"Eritrea: EPLF counteroffensive," January 23

"Ethiopia tries to blunt EPLF gains," February 20

"Eritrea: Lull before the storm?," May 7

"U.S. eyes strategic Horn of Africa,," June 18

"Signs of Eritrean civil war mounting," September 10

"Eritrea: Women make gains," September 17

"Fighting rages in Ethiopia province," October 1

"Eritrea: People's radio," October 8

"Ethiopia: Famine looms," October 22

"Eritrea's EPLF faces war on two fronts," November 5

"Eritrea: Critical juncture," November 12

"Eritrea: ELF cadre desert," November 19

"Eritrea: Radical realignment," November 26

"Eritrea: Peace plan," December 3

"Eritrea: Ethiopian offensive," December 10

"Eritrea: Guerrilla victory," December 24

The Irish Times (Dublin)

"Eritrean groups turn on each other," October 25

The Miami Herald

"Soviet Arms Influx Points to Renewal of Eritrean Conflict," June 12

"Guerrillas Capture 2 Soviet Doctors as Ethiopia's Little-Known War Rages," July 18

"Ethiopia May Cost Soviets Their Grip on Horn of Africa," September 21

"Rival Eritrean Rebels Giving In to Ethiopia?," November 6

"Sudan Seeks to Expel 2 Western Reporters," November 27

La Repubblica (Rome)

"Dan Connell espulso dal Sudan," November 28

1981

Africa News (Raleigh-Durham, NC)

"Eritrea:Nationalist forces renew unity effort," April 27

"Eritrea: Changed line-up for next round of fighting,"
November 16

Associated Press (Cairo)

"Guerrilla Group Calls for Boycott of Aid to Ethiopia," February 2

The Guardian (New York)

"Ethiopia: United front?," February 18

"Eritrea: Famine looms," March 25

"Eritrea: Unity move," April 22

"Eritrea war near turning point?," August 19

"Eritrea: ELF betrayal?," September

"Tigray minority presses attack on Ethiopian government," October 7

"Eritrea: 20 years of struggle," October 14

"Eritrea: Long history of struggle," October 21

"Eritrea: New Ethiopian offensive?," November 4

The Toronto Globe & Mail

"Aid seen as threat by Eritrean rebels," August 11

"Relief heads for tense region," November 18

1982

The Boston Globe

"Rebels say heavy fighting is underway in Eritrea," February 19

"Eritrean guerrillas reportedly attack key supply facility," February 27

The Guardian (New York)

"Eritrea: EPLF attacks Asmara," February 3

"Eritrea rebels claim significant victories," March 3

The Miami Herald

"Ethiopia to launch a major offensive, Eritrean rebels say," January 17

"Eritreans charge Ethiopia is using gas as new offensive spills over
into Sudan," February 21

"Ethiopian leader, Soviet generals hurt in battle, guerrillas claim," March 7

The Toronto Globe & Mail

"Ethiopia uses gas in war, rebels say," February 19

"Eritrean guerrillas claim major victories," February 23

1984

The Boston Globe

"Ethiopia's hidden victims" [editorial opinion], November 26

The Christian Science Monitor (Boston)

"Famine and politics" [editorial opinion], November 25

The Orlando Sentinel (Florida)

"Famine victims used as pawns in Ethiopia," November 25

1985

The Boston Globe (Focus)

"Hunger is a way of life—and death," February 3

In These Times (Chicago)

"Starvation is on the upswing in Eritrea," February 13

The Miami Herald (Viewpoint)

"Slaves of the Night," December 15

The Wall Street Journal (New York)

"Millions May Starve, but Ethiopian Regime Bids to Control" [editorial opinion], January 10

1987

The Boston Globe (Focus)

"Profiting from Africa's misery," August 16

The Boston Globe

"Facing political issues of Ethiopia's famine"[editorial opinion], December 27

1989

The Boston Globe (Focus)

"Witness to Eritrea's struggle," March 12

The Guardian (New York)

"War-torn Eritrea closes in on victory," March 29

"Mengistu beset by coup attempt, Eritrea gains," May 5

"Georgia peace talks probably won't stop new round in war,"
October

1990

Africa News (Raleigh-Durham, NC)

"Eritrean War Grinds Toward End," November 12

The Christian Science Monitor (Boston)

"Eritrean Rebels Prepare for Life After War—And After Marxism,"
November 15

"Eritrea's Other War—Against Famine," November 15

The Guardian (New York)

"Eritrean rebel attack batters Ethiopian army," February 28

The Independent (London)

"Appointment in Asmara," November 11

1991

The Canberra Times

"The hard road to building a new Eritrea," December 27

Green Left Weekly (Sydney)

"After war, new problems for Eritrea," December

The Independent (London)

"On the hard road to a new Eritrea," December 30

1992

The Christian Science Monitor (Boston)

"Eritrea's Path to Independence," January 15

"Drought, Landmines, Greet Refugees Returning Home," January 15
"Reviving a National Church," January 15
"Long Drought Threatens Eritrea's Recovery," January 29

Green Left (Sydney)
"Eritrea: Out of the Ashes," January 29

The Guardian (New York)
"Eritrean Independence: Not By War Alone," April 1

In These Times (Chicago)
"The echoes of war in Eritrea," January 29

1993

The Christian Science Monitor (Boston)
"An Opening for Democracy in Eritrea," April 30

In These Times (Chicago)
"Eritrea: Birth Pangs," June 28

The Miami Herald
"Out of Africa, A Promising New Nation is Born," May 9

Oxfam America News (Boston)
A New Nation Shapes Its Future, Fall

1994

The Christian Science Monitor (Boston)
"Eritrea: An Island of Stability in Strife-Filled Africa," November 30
"Eritrea's recent past," November 30
"One major change: Women's right to own land," November 30
"The greening of Eritrea: Famine unlikely to recur," November 30

Eritrea Profile (Asmara)
"Taking Health Care to the People," October 8
"Letter from Orota: Where have all the fighters gone?," October 15
"Famine Unlikely Again," October 22

1995

The Miami Herald
"Eritrea: A new country that works," February 12

The Progressive Response (**Albuquerque**)
"Thoughts on East Timor & Eritrea," September

1998

The Seattle Times
"Eritrea: Poised for economic growth on its own terms" [syndicated editorial opinion via Knight-Ridder], March 29

2000

The Boston Globe
"Reining in Ethiopia [editorial opinion]," May 31

The Guardian (**London**)
"Ethiopia Shatters Ceasefire," May 5
"Ethiopia Puts Its Puppets into Eritrea," May 29

The Los Angeles Times
"Lasting Peace Remains Elusive "[editorial opinion], June 2

2001

MERIP Press Information Note (Washington, DC)
"Ethiopia-Eritrea Peace Process Creeps Forward," February 10

Eritrea Profile (**Asmara**)
"Going Home to Gash-Barka," March 10
"Eritrea's Liberation Revisited," May 6

2002

MERIP Press Information Note (Washington, DC)
"Eritrea-Ethiopia Verdict Due Out This Week," April 12

Section 1

First Impressions
1976

Prologue

When I first traveled to the Horn of Africa in the autumn of 1975, Ethiopia was in the midst of a profound transition whose outcome was yet undetermined. Emperor Haile Selassie was gone, trundled off to prison in the back seat of a VW beetle after decades of cruel and often whimsically despotic rule. The "socialist" military dictatorship of Mengistu Haile Mariam was not yet in place. In the interim, the kingdom was under the control of a 120-member military committee, known only as the *derg* (Amharic for committee), whose membership and political orientation were not clear. Meanwhile, the superstructure of the feudal society was collapsing and the economy was virtually paralyzed.

The new regime had arrested leading members of the nobility and officers of the imperial Army, executing dozens. It had also hastily nationalized rural and urban land, along with major financial institutions and manufacturing and assembly plants, but it had done little to return them to productive activity. In the meantime, the country struggled to recover from a terrible famine, itself a factor in the upheaval that swept Selassie out of power. No one was quite sure what would come next.

The unsettled political and economic situation was punctuated by rising urban protest against military rule by cadres of the ultra-'left' Ethiopian People's Revolutionary Party and other clandestine opposition groups of divergent political persuasions. Among them were several ethnic nationalist movements challenging the long-standing Amhara domination of the empire. Secondary schools and universities — hotbeds of radical political activity — were closed, with the students called-up for a hastily mobilized national literacy campaign whose tacit aim was to defuse the opposition. By September 1976, however, protest turned to political assassination, and the regime responded with ruthless ferocity, launching what it called the campaign of "Red Terror." Over the next twelve months, the regime and a host of vigilantes acting in its name slaughtered more than 10,000 people, most of them young urban intellectuals.

Far to the north, the war in Eritrea heated up. The feuding rebel movements — the Eritrean Liberation Front (ELF) and the Eritrean People's Liberation Front (EPLF) — reached a truce after battling each other for three years. Together, they placed the occupation forces in a state of siege in the contested territory's main towns and cities. This, coupled with the unresolved situation in Addis Ababa, fostered an accelerating decline in the Ethiopian army's morale, organizational coherence and fighting capacity, enabling the rebels to make steady gains. But the conflict was largely invisible to the outside world — and to most of Ethiopia — due to a strict travel ban on journalists. Despite this news blackout, its impact was felt across the land, as resources were methodically redirected to the war front and as repression aimed at Eritrean nationals grew in frequency and intensity.

Oddly, under these circumstances, the United States supported the new Ethiopian military regime, seeking to demonstrate that it could work with such radical nationalists. Embassy officials justified the derg's adoption of state-centric development strategies to me by citing the need for a strong hand in these unconsolidated postcolonial societies to offset the chaos and inter-ethnic conflict there. Coups d'etat were sweeping Africa and much of the Middle East, often resulting in ruptures with the West and realignments with the Soviet Union. Somalia and Sudan were two recent instances. Washington did not wish to see its oldest African ally, Ethiopia, follow the same path.

This produced an intriguing anomaly: a self-declared "socialist" military regime backed by the U.S. The prospect of unraveling this enigma was what initially drew me to Ethiopia.

———

I was not a professional journalist in 1975. I was a political activist with roots in the American civil rights and anti-war movements of the 1960s and early 1970s who aspired to write about freedom struggles in Africa. I had no commitments from prospective publishers, only the force of my own curiosity and conviction. For credentials, I carried a letter of introduction from a journalist-friend long active in Southern Africa solidarity — Danny Schecter, the "news dissector" at Boston's alternative rock station, WBCN. I traveled with a friend, photographer Bruce Parkhurst.

We passed through Ethiopia for the first time in October 1975 at the start of a year-long journey intended to run from Cairo to Cape Horn. We rode third and fourth class trains across Egypt and Sudan.

We had to fly from Khartoum to Addis Ababa due to the unsettled situation along the border, but we took buses to Kenya's northern frontier and hitched to Nairobi and then Tanzania. We got as far as Dar es Salaam.

My hope was to explore newly-independent, socialist Mozambique and apartheid South Africa — and to write about the freedom struggles there. But arranging this proved more difficult than I anticipated. Tanzania was a bureaucratic nightmare. I met interesting people, had fascinating political discussions, thoroughly enjoyed the ambiance, but got nowhere with my project. Mozambique, seized by the exigencies of state-building after the collapse of the Fascist dictatorship in Portugal and its abrupt disengagement from its African colonies, had no functioning embassies. I couldn't get in. South Africa, a complex garrison state, appeared more difficult to infiltrate than I had imagined.

Ethiopia beckoned.

I went back to Addis in January 1976 to see what I could ferret out on the changes taking place there and on the peculiar role of the U.S. in this explosive political environment. I met local activists in and out of the transitional government. I also met the Africa bureau chief for *The Washington Post*, David Ottaway. I proposed to him that I write something on famine-relief programs in the countryside, which I saw as a way to explore how the Ethiopian Revolution was affecting the empire's destitute and long-disenfranchised rural population.

Ottaway was encouraging but made no commitments, which was the norm for such freelancing. Next, I parlayed my WBCN letter into a travel permit from the deputy director of Ethiopia's Relief and Rehabilitation Commission, Maj. Dawit Woldegiorgis, to go to the southeastern Ogaden. With this in hand, I hitchhiked through the parched desert region with RRC reps and other local aid workers for a month to see what was going on there.

The trip was eye-opening in ways I had not anticipated. What was most striking in the face of the chronic and pervasive suffering we witnessed was the lack of direct government involvement in the recovery, most of which was sub-contracted to international aid agencies. For its part, the army — everywhere evident — did nothing. Over the course of this month, I was also bombarded with the anger that Ogadenis of wide-ranging social status (as well as many lower-level Ethiopian bureaucrats) felt toward the new "revolutionary" regime. I returned to Addis with more questions than I had when I started.

Once in the capital, I had several chance encounters with Eritreans, one of whom was beaten senseless on a downtown street corner by security thugs who suspected him of talking politics with me. This further whetted my interest in the hidden war in the former Italian colony whose annexation in 1962 gave landlocked Ethiopia access to the Red Sea. An intuitive sense that it held a key to the contradictory character of the Ethiopian Revolution convinced me to go see it for myself.

Bruce and I secured another travel permit from the RRC vice chair — this time to tour the feeding centers in Wollo province, halfway between Addis Ababa and Eritrea. Once on the road, we caught a series of rides to Tigray, the province that bordered Eritrea. The last lift was with a pair of Eritreans driving home from Dire Dawa where they'd watched the Africa Cup football games. When I explained my interest in Eritrea, they offered to take us with them. In the Tigrayan city of Makele, they got us permits to travel by convoy to Asmara. We were described to authorities as tourists, which was consistent with our visas.

The account of this journey — and the spate of political killings I witnessed in the besieged Eritrean capital over the following week — would provide the material for my first published stories on Eritrea in *The Post* and for the first chapter of the book I wrote fifteen years later, *Against All Odds*.

———

Once back in Addis again in early April, I took my tale to David Ottaway. He said to write it up. He'd send it to Washington.

I set out to craft a coherent narrative from my chaotic notes and recollections, but it was not easy. I felt a haunting responsibility to my informants and a terror of not getting it right. I had a classic case of writer's block. How to let the stories of these shattered lives speak for themselves? How to keep myself and my strong personal reactions in the background?

I wanted desperately to open a window onto what was happening there, but I was ill-equipped to do so. I struggled for ten days with this experience, writing and rewriting until I was knee-deep in crumpled paper.

Meanwhile, a contact at the American embassy told me the derg was organizing a massive military campaign to end the war, using waves of untrained peasant conscripts to overrun rebel strongholds. He took me into the embassy vault one night and showed me classified reports on Ethiopian preparations for the offensive. He told me where troops were prepositioned, where food and fuel were stockpiled, where doctors and nurses were preparing to treat the wounded, and more.

I was boggled by the disclosure, but unsure what to do with it. I was not a breaking-news reporter. I had nowhere to go with the information with any confidence it would get published, but I was determined to try. In the end, I wrote up my notes on the coming assault and mailed them to a friend in New York in public relations, urging her to get the information to someone who would know what to do.

She passed my letter to a contact at *The New York Times*, which assigned a Washington reporter to check it out. He did so, confirmed the basic thrust of it, and promptly ran a story on page one announcing the coming crusade — under his byline and with no mention of me as a source. By a fortuitous coincidence, my lengthy account of life under siege in Asmara, topped by more information on the forthcoming peasant campaign, landed on the desk of the foreign editor for *The Washington Post* that very afternoon. *The Post* ran my story the next day on page one. Which is how and when I broke into journalism.

When I landed in Khartoum, Sudan, a week later on a mission to meet the guerrillas whose presence I had felt but not encountered throughout my foray into Asmara, I found telexes waiting for me at the American embassy from both *The Times* and *The Post*, asking for more files. They were competitors. I had to choose between them.

I opted for *The Post* and set out to gain access to the rebel-held areas, while poking around Sudan and filing more stories on what I found there. But going to the guerrilla zones was both more difficult and more complicated than moving about within Ethiopia, where the chaos of the current political situation offered cracks through which one could slip if he were creative — and persistent. Not so in this case, where deeply rooted suspicions of Americans asking probing political questions, combined with more mundane factors, produced one delay after another.

The ELF said "maybe" — but come back tomorrow (and tomorrow and tomorrow...). The EPLF was more forthcoming but also more wary. Their representative asked me for a political biography, which — unbeknownst to me — they sent to Washington to have their supporters vet me. Once I passed this hurdle, I was quickly cleared to go. The approval came six weeks after I arrived in Khartoum. When I told ELF officials that I was headed in with EPLF, they quickly agreed to give me a tour, too.

In the event, I traveled inside Eritrea for nearly five weeks in July and August 1976, finishing the journey with the ELF on foot after their truck broke down in the Barka lowlands. Despite the hardships,

I was so bedazzled by what I observed of life in liberated Eritrea, particularly with the better-organized and more politically developed EPLF, that I submitted more than twenty pages of narrative to *The Post*. Much to my chagrin, however, the editor scoffed at my treatise and asked me, did I think I was writing for a newspaper or a sociology class?

It was a shocking comeuppance. Some weeks later, I came back with a more compressed account, which, after more editing, appeared in *The Post*'s Sunday Outlook section in early October. The experience was dispiriting, however, and this was the last story I wrote for six months.

War Signs Seen in Ethiopia

The Washington Post, May 13, 1976

Addis Ababa, Ethiopia

The signs here indicate that the Ethiopian army will soon open a major offensive against rebellious Eritrean guerrilla forces.

Relief officials returning from the secessionist province of Eritrea report large scale troop buildups there; foreign missionaries have been withdrawn from the countryside into Asmara, the provincial capital, and journalists have been barred from entering the province, a former Italian colony.

Five hundred doctors, nurses and medical aides have been drafted from this area and sent to key towns and cities in Eritrea; a local factory and women prisoners in the penitentiary here have been put to work packaging native foods in plastic bags for combat rations; and the government is forming a "volunteer army" and arming it with pre-World War II Italian rifles.

[Despite the indications of a war footing, there are some signs that there may be dissension within the Dergue, the ruling military council, about an offensive in Eritrea, according to reports reaching Washington.]

[Almost daily flights of officials between Addis Ababa and Asmara have led observers in the Ethiopian capital to speculate that negotiations may be continuing between the government and the Eritrean rebels.]

To supplement the almost 20,000 police and troops the government has in Eritrea—of slightly more than 40,000 in the country as a whole—it is recruiting a peasant force. Reportedly, more than 30,000 peasants have volunteered in Begemdir, a northwestern province, alone.

Authorities here in the Ethiopian capital say that filling stations along the road to Asmara have been ordered to keep full inventories of diesel fuel and at least 50 per cent stocks of gasoline, while bus companies and truckers' unions have been put on alert for possible emergency service to ferry the voluntary force to Asmara.

With a photographer, I joined a convoy of more than 400 supply trucks on a three-day journey to Asmara at the end of March. That experience and 10 days of interviews in the provincial capital suggest that a force of untrained regulars will meet stiff resistance. The general population seemed to be almost universally in sympathy with the Eritrean guerrillas, largely because of the Addis Ababa government's use of undisciplined military force and its policy of brutal counter-terrorism measures.

The staging area for our journey through guerrilla infested territory was Adowa, a sleepy and semi-deserted town on the border between Eritrea and Tigre Province, only about 90 miles from Asmara.

The last previous convoy had gotten through to Asmara six weeks earlier, and since then trucks had been pouring into the area for the next run.

At 5 a.m. we began to line up, and trucks laden with grain, firewood, construction materials, spare parts, cotton, gasoline and other raw materials jockeyed for position as the army vehicles rolled past to secure the road ahead. They carried soldiers of the recently reactivated Territorial Army, a kind of reserve force called up to cope with the protracted emergency in Eritrea.

Unsmiling conscripts looked out at us from between the wooden slats of World War II surplus American trucks. Some of the soldiers cradled U.S. made M-14 rifles in their laps, others had them slung casually over their backs.

Most wore bandoliers of bullets across their chests like Hollywood-style Pancho Villas. On each truck there was a heavy machine gun mounted over the cab, manned by a soldier scanning the road ahead.

In mid-morning, we passed through Rama, a town that had been overrun by the Eritrean Liberation Front. The guerrillas had come and gone swiftly, knocking out communications facilities and government buildings. A crippled tractor stood in front of the ruins of a government office; another partially blocked the road.

To our surprise, a carnival-like atmosphere prevailed and children lined the streets to wave. We saw few men and no signs of injury to the people of Rama. Women sold home-made beer to the thirsty drivers, and we were later told that the raiding Eritreans had taken 35 students off for a week of "ideological training" and returned them unharmed to their town.

At our stops, there was little interaction between the soldiers and the drivers, many of whom were Eritreans who displayed resentment at being forced to carry supplies for the troops in Asmara rather than for the civilian population.

About six miles into Eritrea we reached the first blown-out bridge, and detoured through the dry riverbed below, a soldier walking ahead and probing the sand for mines with a thin metal rod.

An hour later we had detoured around the shattered remains of another bridge and arrived in Adi Quala. It took six hours for all the trucks to reach the town for the night.

At dawn we were awakened by the sound of army trucks moving out to secure the road to Adi Ugri, less than 20 miles away. Four hours later we got the word to move out.

The terrain was barren rock hills and sand, with occasional thickets of eucalyptus trees that offered little shelter for a large force, but seemed ideal for guerrillas.

Halfway between Adi Quala and Adi Ugri, as we climbed a steep rise, our accordion-like line of trucks met a convoy going the other way—more than 300 trucks loaded with beer, soft drinks, bicycles, bed frames, automobiles and other industrial products.

The last day we had to travel bunched together, rather than strung out over 5 or 10 miles, and by noon we were only about a mile out of town, inching along while soldiers spread out on foot to comb the hostile countryside.

Our driver took a place in line behind a bus, saying the Eritrean guerrillas concentrate their file on military vehicles and leave the civilians in convoys alone. He told us of an attack he had been through on this same stretch a year earlier, adding that two days after that attack the soldiers had returned to destroy the two nearest villages.

Since the army holds the local population responsible for guerrilla attacks, the villages along this section of the road were deserted. As people learned of our approach, they melted into the desert to avoid trouble.

We saw the rubble of stone huts, empty shells that testified to the army's retaliation. On distant hills there were open huts and corrals with neat stacks of dried cow dung and hay nearby, but there were no signs of life.

Here and there were traces of recent battle. The blackened hulk of a trailer truck beside the road. A gaping hole in the road indicated that it had hit a landmine.

When we made it to Asmara without further incident, the drivers agreed that the credit belonged to Col. Beshu Gebre Tekla, who commanded the convoy.

He had created a diversion by first sending several military trucks from Asmara to Keren, where they had engaged a guerrilla force, and then ordered the convoy from Asmara that we had passed on the road. His tactic apparently caught the guerrillas off guard.

Eritrean by birth, commanding impressive loyalty from his troops, Col. Beshu was dead the day after he got us to Asmara safely.

Sunday, as the colonel and his bodyguard sat in a car in front of a café, a taxi reportedly drove by with two passengers, a man and a woman, who killed the two men with three shots.

That night, eight persons were killed in what seemed to be random reprisals. The following night, another 37 or more suspected "sympathizers" were rounded up one by one and shot. A dozen bodies were stacked in the sunny square where the colonel had been killed, and left there until noon.

Death, Hunger and Fear in Asmara

The Washington Post, May 14, 1976

Asmara, Ethiopia

This graceful tropical city, a unique mélange of Eritrean, Italian and Arab cultures, is also a blend of hunger, emergency restrictions and jitters.

The city buses run, and the dark olive green military trucks and cars cruise the streets restlessly, but bicycles have been prohibited under the state of emergency proclaimed last year and the yellow Fiat taxicabs have been banned, so most of the people move on foot.

Young children chatter in several languages on their way to school, but most of the men walking to work sit idly at their desks or in their factories, with little or nothing to do. Women still head for the market, but in these times of shortages and strict rationing they find little to buy.

Asmara's population is estimated to have dropped from 300,000 in January 1974 to 175,000 in 1976, but these figures mask a significant shift in the makeup of the city.

Young people, especially males between the ages of 15 and 25, are conspicuously absent. In their place, we saw the very young, the old and the indigent. With stepped-up bombings of the rural areas and the clearing of a ring five miles deep around the city, Asmara has had to absorb many refugees.

Death seldom strikes singly here, and with darkness there is often what Asmarans call *la musica della notte*—the staccato bursts of automatic weapons, the steady rhythm of semiautomatic rifles, and occasional cannon blasts usually aimed out of the city at one of the surrounding villages.

One night, as we huddled with two young Ethiopians who had stumbled across the body of a colonel who had presumably been killed by guerrilla sympathizers, we heard the shots of reprisal rising in intensity as jeeps raced by, their heavy machine guns aimed at the roofs for snipers.

But we heard no human sounds—no shouted commands, no challenges, no cries of protest—only the sounds of motors and of guns.

The two young men paced about, too agitated to sit, repeatedly describing how the dead colonel and his bodyguard, slumped over a submachine gun, had looked, and telling how they walked the three blocks back to the hotel, frightened that by running they would call attention to themselves.

Huddling in the semidarkness, the two talked of their fears. As members of the Amhara tribe, the dominant ethnic group of Ethiopia, they felt themselves to be aliens in Eritrea, distrusted and with few local friends. But occupying Ethiopian soldiers occasionally mistook them for Eritreans, threatening and harassing them.

With dawn came a temporary truce, and we learned that eight persons had been shot during the night and their bodies left in the square where the colonel was killed; the next night 37 more were killed, a dozen bodies being left in the square and the rest spotted at strategic points around the city.

During the first night of reprisals, one of the two Ethiopians told me about leaving a café with a friend one night three months earlier. He heard two quick shots, and his friend fell dying at his feet. He never know who did it, he said, or why.

The war has unbalanced the economy as well as the social structure, and little of the corn, sugar, coffee and grain that one sees on trucks around the city reaches the open market. The goods show up on the black market, where food intended for the military filters down to the civilians. On the black market, grain sells for double or triple its usual price and onions for nearly a dozen times the open market price.

With money, one can buy almost any exotic or imported food, but the staple Ethiopian grain called *teff*, used to make the flat bread that is eaten three times a day in most homes, has not been seen in Asmara for months.

Both sides have used food as a weapon. Last October, before the harvest, the Ethiopian government ordered a halt to all international relief efforts in Eritrea to increase the pressure on the rural population, on whom the guerrillas depend for support.

Following a bumper harvest, the Eritrean Liberation Front retaliated by cutting off all food supplies to the cities.

Until 1974, 8,000 Americans were stationed at the Kagnew communications base inside Asmara. There were also thousands of Italians, those who had stayed here after the fascist defeat and their children and grandchildren, born here.

Now, the American presence at Kagnew has shriveled to a staff of 35, many Italians were repatriated, and most other Europeans evacuated the city as the war intensified. Many educated Eritreans left the city to join the guerrillas or fled to neighboring Sudan.

A photographer and I wandering the tree-shaded avenues were very nearly the only foreigners in town—certainly the only tourists—and became the objects of much curiosity.

People repeatedly stopped us, praising the Americans who had lived here. But these warm memories seemed to be severely strained by current associations with the brutal repression by the Ethiopian military forces.

Homes and shops in a nearby Moslem quarter were pockmarked from hundreds of rounds of ammunition, and our host told us that the soldiers often came to this neighborhood when they wanted revenge for an attack because they assumed that all Moslems were supporters of the guerrillas.

We also heard stories about the guerrillas, usually of vehicles being captured but returned undamaged to their owners after completion of some guerrilla mission, of government troops being taken for re-education and later released, of explicit warnings to collaborators and informers before punishment or of Robin Hood-like acts of theft and redistribution. The stories may have been exaggerated or embellished, but they showed clearly the sympathies of those who told them.

U.S. a Puzzle for Eritreans

Warm Feelings for Americans
Clouded by Arming of Ethiopians

The Washington Post, May 18, 1976

Asmara, Ethiopia

As this lovely tropical city waits uneasily for the expected opening of the Ethiopian army's major offensive against secessionist guerrillas of the Eritrean Liberation Army, many of its residents express a
mixture of fondness for the Americans they have met and bewilder-
ment at the U.S. government's role in the war here.

A few weeks ago, for example, two visiting American free-lance
journalists were invited to lunch at the home of a 26-year-old clerk in
a government office who has been the sole support of his parents,
three brothers and one sister since his father lost his job a year ago.

The seven live in a small, two-room house set back from the street
by a narrow entry way that opens into a cement courtyard where they
often take their meal. Two beds in each room cover much of the floor
space, but there is a sitting area in one and a charcoal stove in the
other. Family photographs decorate the bare, white-washed walls.

The meal consisted of *shiro*, a spicy dish traditionally eaten during the Lenten fast, and an *injera* or flatbread made from wheat
rather than *teff*, the local grain. The clerk apologized for the lack of
teff, showing the visitors unused and expired ration coupons and
explaining that the family could not afford the black market prices
since his father had been laid off without a pension by the factory
where he had worked all his life.

Over lunch he pointed out the chipped plaster above his parents'
bed and described the night a year earlier when a rifle-grenade landed in front of the house.

Sporadic fighting had been going on for a couple of months, he
said, since the Eritrean Liberation Front had tried to take the city in
February 1975. Since the Ethiopian army did not know who the guerrillas' supporters were, he went on, it blamed the general population
for supporting the front and reprisals were largely random.

At 10 one evening, guerrillas attacked a nearby army base, and
the government forces responded by raining fire on the neighborhood. The family was asleep when a violent explosion in the courtyard blew open the doors, perforated the water tank and sprayed

water and shrapnel in all directions. Two chunks of shrapnel flew through the open window, hitting the back wall and nearly wounding the elderly couple in their bed. The next morning, the clerk said, he found a fragment of metal casing from a rifle-grenade, inscribed "U.S. 1954."

The lunch and the story illustrate the ambivalence toward America that one finds here. In contrast with the more aloof Europeans, one is told, Americans are known for eating the unusual local food, learning at least the basics of the difficult language and meeting Eritreans on a common level, but these warm feelings are severely strained by the U.S. government's current association with the Ethiopian army's often brutal repression in the province.

American airplanes, supplied by Washington to the Ethiopian government, bomb Eritrean villages; American advisers train Ethiopian soldiers to use American rifles, machine guns, tanks and an apparently unlimited supply of other weapons.

Eritreans who knew Americans during the years when 8,000 U.S. personnel were stationed at the communications base at Kagnew ask whether the American people support the war Addis Ababa is waging to prevent the Red Sea province from seceding and why the United States has turned against them.

The Addis Ababa military government has bought large supplies of small-arms ammunition from Italy, Turkey and, reportedly, Israel, but an effort to convert C47s into gunships is moving slowly and a light infantry unit called the "Flame Brigade," armed and equipped by the Israelis, reportedly will not be combat-ready until July.

The presumption is that the offensive must be before or after the rainy season, for although the Eritrean guerrillas operate year-round, the government forces are road-bound and vulnerable to the heavy downpours that come to the highlands in the summer months.

Two weeks of interviewing Eritreans suggests that the Ethiopian offensive will meet with stiff resistance. Nearly everyone expressed support for the guerrillas and resentment for the brutal counter-terrorism eforts and undisciplined use of military force. While Western observers offered complex analysis of factional politics within the guerrillas' camp, the people of Asmara spoke of "the front" and tended to identify with it.

"You don't save your life by staying out of the front," one slightly drunk man said almost hysterically. "I might die tomorrow or next week. Why shouldn't I fight with the front? What are we doing sitting here while our brothers are dying all around us?"

A tour of the checkpoints around the city limits—manned by Ethiopian veterans of the Korean War, known as "Father Warriors"—shows the edge of the five-mile deep no-man's-land the army has cleared around Asmara.

Turning from that view, toward Moslem neighborhoods, one sees row after row of pockmarked homes and shops their walls scarred by hundred of rounds of ammunition.

The guide, an Eritrean, explains that the soldiers often come to these neighborhoods for revenge after an attack, on the presumption that all Moslems are members or at least supporters of the guerrillas.

On the road to the northern roadblocks, he points out a waste-land of eucalyptus stumps, what remains of Massawa Park. The large carefully-tended tract was deforested by soldiers in search of fire-wood, he said.

On palm-shaded Haile Selassie Avenue, the cafés and pastry shops, shoe and clothing stores, photo studios, souvenir stands, jewelry and hardware and book and stationery stores all appear well stocked, but there are few customers.

And behind the stone walls in the gardens flashing with the reds and oranges of bougainvillea and shaded by lavender-blossomed jacaranda, Asmara waits for the war.

Ethiopia Losing in Eritrea

The Washington Post, May 20, 1976

Gedaref, Sudan

The Ethiopian army in the strategic Red Sea province of Eritrea is being slowly driven by secessionist guerrillas into a few isolated positions, most of which can be supplied only by air, according to Western diplomats in Ethiopia and Sudan.

The number of military bases under Ethiopian control in Eritrea has shrunk from 60 to 17 in less than 18 months, according to Eritrean guerrilla spokesmen.

Heavy fighting is reported around bases at Nacfa and Af Abet, where 500 Ethiopian soldiers are surrounded and receiving supplies by parachute, according to guerrillas interviewed during a tour of the

Sudanese border area near Eritrea.

The rebels and the Ethiopian government have presented conflicting versions of the situation with both expressing confidence that
their forces are about to achieve victory.

There have been similar "brink of victory" predictions from both
sides during the course of the 14-year-old civil war, but this time they
come amid reports that the government plans an all-out offensive
using tens of thousands of peasant "volunteers" starting next month.

Ethiopian government officials have predicted that the offensive
could wipe out the guerrilla threat in Eritrea within two or three
months.

Conversely, the guerrillas say they can defeat the road-bound
Ethiopian troops in the same time-span, taking advantage of the rainy
season starting next month, which will limit the government advantage of air cover and heavy armament.

If the guerrillas take some of the most hard-pressed Ethiopian
positions, it would give them control of the entire northwestern corner of Eritrea, Western diplomats say.

The rebels are digging in around the Sudan border area and
expect other guerrilla groups to prevent government forces from
entering Eritrea. They are also arming large numbers of civilians to
help in the fight against government positions:

• In the lowland area along the border with Sudan, the government controls the towns of Tessenei, Agordat, Keren and Om Hajer;
but diplomatic and guerrilla sources alike say that the road connecting these towns with Asmara, the provincial capital, has been under
siege for more than a week.

• In the highlands, there are government base camps at or near
Adi Ugri, Adi Quala, Segeneti and Decamere. Last month I saw that
the road from Decamere to Asmara was cut, and guerrilla fighters say
that the American-built radio station at Mai Adaga, two miles from
Decamere, has been taken.

In Khartoum, capital of Sudan, a spokesman for the Eritrean
Liberation Front pointed out that such mass campaigns, or *kitet*, are
traditional for Ethiopians. They aim at overwhelming the opposition
by sheer weight of numbers.

"The same thing happened between October 1966 and March
1967," he said. "Everything was against us: Our army was small, we
lacked ammunition and arms, yet we still resisted.

"Ethiopia was well-prepared for that campaign. She armed
35,000 soldiers with new weapons from the United States. But the

soldiers were tricked into attacking us. They were given ropes and told they were going to capture a few bandits. Instead they found our army.

"For the coming campaign, all our military bases are prepared. The number of our fighters is high, and we have all the ammunition we need. Their forces are poorly equipped and untrained, and again they are being tricked with talk of bandits and Arab invasions. How can we possibly lose such a campaign?"

Sunday night, Gen. Teferi Bante, chairman of the ruling military council in Ethiopia, broadcast a nine-point proposal for regional autonomy and negotiations with the "progressive forces" of Eritrea.

Asked about their willingness to negotiate, the guerrilla official noted that President Jaafar Nimeiri of Sudan had tried before to bring about a peaceful solution, and that the Eritrean Liberation Front had accepted his offer a year ago.

Nimeiri had suggested three conditions for negotiations: a cease-fire, release of all political prisoners and no further preconditions.

The guerrilla spokesman insisted, however, that the only matter for discussion is the evacuation of the Ethiopian troops.

As for access to the Red Sea, which is crucial to Ethiopia, the guerrilla official stated that the coast belongs to Eritrea, but Ethiopia would be able to trade through it.

"For the mistakes that the government is committing, we do not want to harm the people," he said.

"We would not close the border to them nor would we in any way prevent their access to the sea."

An official of the other guerrilla faction, the Popular Liberation Forces, took a harder line, demanding the acceptance of two preconditions for any talks with the Ethiopian government: Evacuation of all Ethiopian armed forces and full recognition of Eritrean independence.

Negotiations could then begin, he said, under auspices of a mutually acceptable third party.

Meanwhile, fighters from both movements are conducting their own discussions with each other and are mounting joint operations. If the leaderships proceed too slowly, the guerrillas and events in the field may settle the issue.

Unconfirmed reports reached Khartoum Tuesday of air raids along the Sudanese border by Ethiopian planes. Several wounded Eritreans and Sudanese nationals were reportedly rushed to Khartoum for treatment, but no casualty figures were available.

Eritreans Claim to Win Clashes With Peasants

The Washington Post, June 1, 1976

Khartoum, Sudan, May 31

Radio reports from guerrilla units inside the Ethiopian province of Eritrea claim that secessionist Popular Liberation Forces have defeated Ethiopian peasant volunteers in several clashes within the past 10 days.

Guerrilla spokesmen here say that these field reports describe heavy fighting near Adigrat, Asmara and Agordat and skirmishes with Ethiopian regular troops.

Today, however, Ethiopian government representatives here for talks with Sudan's President Jaafar Nimeiri categorically denied that the Addis Ababa government has begun an offensive against secessionist guerrillas in Eritrea or that there is a large-scale peasants' march into the strategic Red Sea province.

Maj. Berhanu Baye, ranking member of the Ethiopian delegation, became visibly angry at repeated questions about reports of a massive peasants' campaign in Eritrea.

"There is no march," he said, saying that the peasants near the border between Tigre and Eritrea Provinces were responding to guerrilla attacks on their villages and theft of their crops. The Ethiopian government, he added, is not involved in that fighting.

Maj. Berhanu denounced British and American reports of a mass peasant march organized by the Ethiopian government to spike secessionist elements in Eritrea as propaganda by the "imperialist press."

In what appeared to be a major departure from past policy of identifying the guerrillas only as bandits, the major said the Addis Ababa government is prepared to meet with any "progressive forces," including the two guerrilla organizations—the Eritrean Liberation Front and the Popular Liberation Forces.

"We don't discriminate," he said.

Meanwhile, guerrilla spokesmen here told of radio reports from the field describing successful guerrilla ambushes at Zal Embessa and Tokor.

In the first clash, May 21, the guerrillas said a column of 8,000 to 10,000 men armed with pre-World War II Italian rifles, spears, swords and farming implements were routed by guerrillas armed with automatic weapons.

The Popular Liberation Forces unit claimed to have taken an undisclosed number of prisoners and to have captured large quantities of arms and food, as well as mules used for transport. Four days later, the guerrillas claim, another force, of about 5,000 men and led by about a hundred Ethiopian commandos, was attacked at Tokor, 12 miles from Asmara.

After two days of fighting, the guerrilla spokesmen say, their forces destroyed a tank and captured a quantity of M-14 rifles and ammunition. During the battle, they say, a guerrilla force turned back an Ethiopian reinforcement column on its way to help the peasants at Tokor.

Reports reaching Khartoum also speak of heavy fighting near Agordat after Ethiopian regulars attacked a guerrilla camp at Tekrerat, five miles west of the city.

Refugees reaching Sudan say that troops are being moved around by road and by air at night under tight security, but it has not been possible to confirm these reports.

Although the Ethiopian military government denies that it initiated the peasant campaign, calling it a spontaneous volunteer uprising, Western intelligence sources have been reporting government preparations for the campaign for more than two months.

In today's press conference, Maj. Berhanu—head of an Ethiopian delegation that included representatives of Ethiopia's Foreign Ministry and the Ethiopian ambassador here—refused to evaluate the military situation in Eritrea.

"That is not the issue now," he said. "The issue is the Ethiopian government's offer"—a nine-point program for a settlement released two weeks ago.

In the program, Addis Ababa proposed a form of "regional autonomy" for Eritrea, release of a number of political prisoners and an end to the 16-month-old state of emergency in the province.

An Italian colony for half a century, Eritrea became federated with Ethiopia in 1952, and has since seen its autonomy taken away by Addis Ababa. Secessionist sentiment still appears to run high there.

Maj. Berhanu said his government has not yet received a response from the Eritreans to its offer. If they reject it, he said, "We will ask them again to accept."

He did not elaborate on details of the "regional autonomy" proposal, saying that that is a matter to be worked out in negotiations, but he said that independence is "unimaginable" even if Eritrea would guarantee Ethiopian use of its ports of Massawa and Assab, which are Ethiopia's only outlets to the sea.

Eritreans Fill Squalid Camps in Sudan

The Washington Post, July 11, 1976

Wad El Heleiwa, Sudan

Eight trucks bearing medical supplies arrived two months ago at this camp, which houses more than 40,000 refugees from Eritrea. The refrigerators, generators, beds, blankets, tables and medicines they brought doubled the medical treatment capacity of the settlement.

Only two humanitarian organizations are active here in the southeastern Sudan, and their total personnel amounts to one doctor, two medical students, two nurses and two assistants.

Wad el Heleiwa, a Sudanese village of 3,000, absorbed its first major influx of Eritrean refugees in 1967—3,000 of them, officials here say.

After February 1975, when Eritrean Liberation Front forces clashed violently with troops of the Ethiopian government, another 20,000 refugees arrived, these officials say. Now they put the refugee population here at more than 40,000, about half of them children and more than half of the adults women.

Most of these refugees are pastoral nomads from the lowlands of western Eritrea, and ill equipped to stay long in what amounts to a small city.

Here they live in cramped straw huts, each holding five or six people. In some sites, as many as 10 people share one hut, which means that some of them are forced to sleep outside. This leads to infections and illness, especially, during the rainy season from June to October.

The rainy season also creates a problem of muddy floors in the huts, and cuts the camp off from wheeled vehicles. During those months one can reach the settlement only by helicopter or on foot.

The huts have jars for water and grain, a stone fireplace and simple beds of sticks and straw mats. The refugees gather firewood from the surrounding area, and officials say that the nearest source of wood requires a day's round-trip by camel. Those who do not have camels must pay for transportation.

The U.N. High Commission for Refugees has supplied food through the Sudanese government for the past year. Local administrators say that each person's daily ration is 400 grams of dura, a regional type of sorghum; 300 grams of soybeans and 20 grams of milk powder.

Many refugees claim, however, that they receive only dura, and irregular quantities of that. Furthermore, they argue that this ration is their sole income, and they must sell some of it to pay for getting the rest ground, as well as for cash for all other purchases.

Water, for instance, can be bought from a pump in the village; but most of the refugees get their water from the Setit River, a mile from the camp. The Setit is badly polluted by sewage from villages upstream, which a medical team in the camp blames for the high rate of gastroenteritis, and diarrhea among the refugees.

These medical workers also point to the lack of latrines or other sanitary facilities, and the filth of the huts, as offering favorable conditions for infectious diseases. But they have no time for preventive care or health and hygiene education because they are so occupied with daily emergencies.

Health officials here doubt that even the recent reinforcement of medical help will be enough to take care of the refugees' burgeoning needs, and the two Eritrean liberation movements' own relief agencies say they do not have the resources to help the refugees in Sudan, who are believed to number 110,000 or more.

Bitterly, they point to the millions of dollars in aid pouring into Ethiopia each year while the Eritrean refugees are left begging—evidence, they say, of an "imperialist conspiracy" against Eritrea.

One of the Eritrean groups has started two schools in the camp here but together they can handle only about 200 of the 20,000 or so children in the camp. About 30,000 more refugees are spread out among several villages near Sim-sim and Quala en Nahl. The United Nations and the Sudanese government are working on plans for aid.

Not as badly off as the refugees in camps are those with some education or skills who settle in the cities. In Khartoum, Sudan's capital, for example, several hundred Eritreans have congregated seeking work or passage to Europe or America to continue their education.

Although the U.S. embassy receives a daily stream of hopeful applicants, few are able to find the sponsors needed to meet the strict visa requirements.

A few work in international hotels or one of the many bars and restaurants, where their command of several languages gives them an edge over the Sudanese but the Eritreans complain that they are paid about half what a Sudanese gets for the same work.

The rest live off savings or the earnings of those lucky enough to find work. On most days they can be found at the U.S. Information Service American Center or the British Council Library, devouring the

latest newspapers and magazines as fast as they arrive, in an attempt
to stave off boredom and despair.

While the urban refugees struggle to keep busy, those in the
camps fight to stay alive. Some of them have been in the settlements
for two years, some as long as nine years, and they all seem to share
a fatalistic skepticism about prospects of any substantial improve-
ment in their situation.

The only genuine solution, they say is for peace and independence
in Eritrea, so they can return to their homes.

Peasants Learn 'Truth About Eritrea'

Ethiopian Captives Tell of Regime's Deceit,
Literacy Training by Rebel Captors

The Washington Post, August 1, 1976

Hamasien District, Ethiopia

Deep in the arid mountains in the Sahel district of northern
Eritrea, the strategic and secessionist Red Sea province of Ethiopia,
we were taken by rebel forces to see two quite different groups of
prisoners captured during the "peasants campaign" that the Addis
Ababa government began in May and called off in June.

The first group consisted of 45 peasants from Wollo and Tigre
Provinces, taken prisoner in raids and clashes as they awaited orders
to march into Eritrea—orders that never came, as it turned out.

The peasants—the youngest 16, the oldest 60 and most in their
mid-40s—seemed cheerful and spoke of expecting to be freed to
return to their homes.

By contrast, the 42 regular Ethiopian soldiers we were shown
seemed deeply depressed and expressed doubt—and some fear—that
they would be released. They said that their government would have
them killed to keep them from telling what they had seen, and they
seemed to be in the process of resigning themselves to never seeing
their homes or families again.

The Ethiopian government will not permit journalists to visit
Eritrea now. We were touring with the Eritrean People's Liberation

Front—one of two liberation groups fighting against the Ethiopian government's rule in the province.

To reach the captured peasants, the guerrillas drove us along a crude dirt road they said their troops had built through the rocky volcanic terrain, and told us that the Toyota land cruiser we rode in had been captured from the Ethiopians.

We had driven by night, to avoid being spotted by Ethiopia's American-supplied F-86 and F-5 jets, and stopped a few hours before dawn.

With the first light we had a breakfast of sugary tea and set off on foot, scrambling for four or five miles along a maze of mountain trails and rocky streambeds. Finally we halted, in the sparse share of some thorn bushes, while the prisoners were brought out.

In a few minutes the prisoners, escorted by half a dozen guerrillas, walked down the steep slope toward us.

They chatted among themselves as they came, seeming at ease with their guards. A few had long pants on, but most wore the patched shorts and tattered shirts and jackets that are the universal dress of Ethiopian peasants.

When they got to the dry stream bed, their escorts told them to sit in the shade while we prepared for the interview. At no time were guns pointed at them. The guards and the prisoners talked back and forth. The guards knew many of the peasants by name, and I saw no sign of force or coercion.

We were told that we could ask any of the peasants anything we wanted. Moving up and down the line, I asked the same questions of several of them, varying my choice among those who spoke Amharic and those who spoke Tigrinya, to get a fair sampling.

None, they said, had ever served in the armed forces or had any training or experience in war. Asked why they had volunteered for the offensive against Eritrea, they spoke angrily and emphatically of deceit, trickery and kidnapping. While one spoke, others raised their hands to answer next or called to one of the guards to make sure of getting a chance to talk.

A middle-aged peasant from Tigre's Enderta region said a representative of the Ethiopian military government had demanded five "volunteers" from each village in the district, and his neighbors had elected him to go.

Several said they had been told they were going to a rally and would be brought back home afterward; one said that peasants who had been resisting the government taxation system were told that they would be pardoned if they turned themselves in. Those who did so were put in trucks and sent north, he said.

A 42-year-old peasant from Woldiya, in Wollo Province, said he was walking to the coffee house when he was forced into a police wagon and later transferred to a truck that brought him north. Another said he had been having his pants mended when he was kidnapped. He stood up to show that all he had to wear was a sack around his waist, because he had not been allowed to wait for his pants.

Some who volunteered took primitive bolt-action rifles with them. Others were given British .303 rifles or old Italian rifles left over from World War II and 15 to 20 bullets, but many were not armed at all—they were told they could take the guns from dead enemy soldiers. None of the peasants was given any kind of training or instruction.

One morning in late May, they were marched out of Zal-Ambassa, a pass north of Adigrat on the road to Eritrea, with Ethiopian troops behind them and a few regular troops among them to lead and give orders.

When they engaged the Eritrean guerrillas, the peasants said, the Ethiopian troops remained behind them to shoot any peasant who tried to retreat. All those captured told stories of panic and confusion.

They spoke animatedly, competing for my attention, about their friends who had died, the farms they had left behind at planting time and about the misconceptions they had had about Eritrea.

Instead of a horde of foreign invaders threatening Ethiopia, they said, they had found a native army of people very like themselves who told them they only seek national independence for Eritrea. Their captors were giving them daily education in the history and aims of their revolution—and teaching the captured peasants to read and write in their native languages, to insure that the political education stuck.

This seemed to impress the prisoners deeply, and they spoke of how they would go back to "tell their countrymen the truth about Eritrea."

They said that they received showers in a nearby waterfall once a week and that they were getting enough to eat. No one looked undernourished or ill. A man who had been wounded in the leg and shoulder was set apart, and we were told that he had been treated with antibiotics and bandaged after the bullets were removed. He appeared comfortable and willingly posed for photographs. All the prisoners had been examined by a doctor upon arrival, we were told.

Asked what would happen to them next they replied almost en masse that they knew they would be freed and sent home. A woman guard said that the plan was to release them once they had mastered their letters, and that the prisoners had been told this to encourage them in their studies.

As I prepared to leave, a very old man demanded my attention. He said he had a lot to say but that I had not given him a chance. He sat up straight with a cane in his hand and boomed out his story.

He was 60 and had been recruited and captured with his 30-year-old son who sat nearby, smiling shyly at the ground as his father spoke. Neither he nor his son had volunteered, the old man said. When they had resisted the call-up together, the young man's house had been burned and both men were forced to go. They were not told their mission until they were sent out at gunpoint from Zal-Ambassa to fight, he said.

He went on to say that he had known nothing about Eritrea before, but now he saw that the Ethiopian government was trying to join it to Ethiopia by force and that was not right. The military rulers of Ethiopia are worse than the old feudal landlords, he said, and he would tell that to anyone who would listen, here or at his home village.

He said the Eritreans had been good to him: He was receiving all the food and water he needed, he had been examined by a doctor for the first time in his life and—proudly displaying his exercise book on which the Amharic alphabet was crudely scrawled—he said he was learning to read and write. He was eager to go home to see how his family was, but he had no complaints here, he finished.

After we thanked them and walked away for rest and more tea, we could hear the prisoners talking with each other and laughing loudly.

Among the regular soldiers we saw in captivity—22 in a camp near the peasant prisoners, another 20 at a second camp 100 miles to the south—there was not laughter and little hope.

The 22 represented a fairly broad cross-section of Ethiopia's ground forces: one from the elite airborne battalion, four each from the commandos and bodyguard, and 13 from the army.

A few were educated, and one spoke English, but most had been—like the captured peasants—made literate since their capture, and a few were helping to teach the peasants.

The man who spoke English said he had been in the army for 13 years, except for a brief stretch of unemployment in Addis Ababa, and had been trained in Israel in 1962 as a commando.

He said his unit had been moving by road from Asmara to Segheneiti a year earlier when it was attacked by guerrillas. He was the sole survivor, he said, adding that if he returned to Ethiopia he would be killed. He seemed resigned to staying in Eritrea.

Several displayed bullet wounds that they said had been treated by guerrilla doctors. One showed seven scars and said he had recovered in the guerillas' central hospital from partial paralysis. He stood up to show that he was fully recovered.

A hundred miles to the south in the mountainous Semhar district east of Asmara on the Red Sea coast, we interviewed a group of 20 POWs captured by guerrillas a week earlier inside Tigre, in northern Ethiopia.

Eighteen soldiers and two wives traveling with them, one of whom was now a widow, had been captured in an ambush at Soro, a village on the main highway that connects eastern and western Ethiopia between Axum and Enda-Selassie.

According to their accounts, a force of between 175 and 200 soldiers had been escorting three buses and one large truck loaded with food and supplies for the garrison at Enda-Selassie when they were encircled and attacked with machine guns and hand grenades. These 20 were the only survivors, they said, and several of them had been wounded.

Asked what he had been told by his superiors about the war in Eritrea, he looked at the ground and said that he was just a simple soldier of peasant origin, that it was not for him to understand politics. His leaders had told him nothing about Eritrea, he said. All he knew, he said, was what he had been hearing on the radio about bandits and Arabs. Nor did he know about the peasant campaign except that he had seen five truckloads of peasants riding south to Makalle.

All the POWs looked to be in fair to good physical health. The two women were distraught and kept their faces covered throughout the interview.

Eritrean Rebels Say They Hold 4

The Washington Post, August 3, 1976

Barca, Ethiopia

Four Westerners reported lost in the Danakel region of north-eastern Ethiopia are being held by the Ethiopian [should be Eritrean—D.C.] Liberation Front pending negotiations for their release, a spokesman for the front said.

The spokesman gave the names of three of the four as Ian Machesney, Brian Hazlehurst and Bruce Thompson. Two are said to be British and one American. The fourth prisoner, whom the spokesman did not identify, is thought to be an Ethiopian citizen of Polish origin.

The four appear to have crossed the border between Wollo Province and the strategic, secessionist Red Sea province of Eritrea during the second week of June. Their land rover was confiscated and they were questioned at length.

Officials of the front who have visited the men say they are no longer suspected of being spies and are being well treated while negotiations for their release go forward.

In early July, when I visited this area, I was shown photographs of the four, who appeared to be in good health with no signs of wounds or injuries.

There do not appear to be any specific demands attached to their release, but the front leadership is said to be working to define conditions.

Revolt Hailed at Eritrean Rally Here

The Washington Post, August 22, 1976

[Washington, DC]

One thousand Eritrean students and their supporters from as far away as Boston, Miami and San Francisco gathered in Washington this weekend to commemorate the 15th year of Eritrean insurgency.

Speakers hailed the heroism and determination of the people for liberty and independence. Slides and films depicted Eritrean military and political history and young people performed traditional dances and songs under flags and patriotic banners.

The Eritrean revolt is still going on. A former Italian colony, the strategic Red Sea territory of Eritrea was federated with Ethiopia by the United Nations in 1952 and was later absorbed into Ethiopia as its 14th province.

Guerillas split between two factions—the Eritrean Liberation Front and the Eritrean People's Liberation Forces—have been fighting against the Ethiopian government since 1961 to form an independent state.

At the anniversary rally held at George Washington University's Marvin Theater Friday evening, members of a student organization called Eritreans for Liberation in North America assembled to denounce U.S. support for the Ethiopian government. They also celebrated recent successes by the insurgent forces who have gained control, according to EFLNA leaders, of more than 95 percent of the Eritrean countryside.

Banners condemning "U.S. imperialism, Israeli Zionism and Ethiopian colonialism" and saluting Eritrea, Oman and Palestine hung from the walls of the auditorium as Hasam Rahman, the featured speaker and the deputy permanent representative to the U.N. of the Palestinian Liberation Organization, spoke.

Asserting the Palestinians would join Lebanese leftists in a Vietnam-style people's war, Rahman said that his organization would not negotiate with the Syrians or the Lebanese Phalangists until all Syrian forces were withdrawn from Lebanon and a "secular democratic state" was accepted.

The Eritrean students came to Washington for a five-day conference to study the situation in their home country and map out a strategy of support. Many have been in the United States for three to four years, fearing to return to their homes, they say, because of the likelihood of violent reprisals from Ethiopian authorities.

Behind Rebel Lines in Eritrea

The Washington Post Outlook, October 10, 1976

Outside Asmara, Ethiopia

Asmara's streets lay empty beneath their bright lights. The guerrillas stood within a mile of the provincial capital. The nearest Ethiopian army outpost was within rifle shot.

A lone pair of headlights moved along a side street on the edge of town, turned and vanished. There was a security curfew in Asmara.

Behind, by contrast, the highways and makeshift roads crisscrossing the rebel countryside were busy with guerrilla traffic, moving with dimmed headlights to avoid attack by the American-made jets of Ethiopia's air force.

The guerrillas were an escort, not a fighting band, and they did nothing but look. But the fact that they could with impunity bring a pair of journalists—an American photographer and this writer—so close to Asmara was an indication of their growing strength.

According to Western intelligence estimates, there are between 25,000 and 30,000 Eritrean guerrillas and about 20,000 troops of the Ethiopian army in the strategic Red Sea province. The guerrillas claim to control about 90 percent of the land, home to about 70 percent of Eritrea's people, and to have restricted the government's control to about a dozen cities.

The Ethiopian regime, for its part, minimizes the guerrillas' impact, although its forces are mainly supplied by air and by heavily armed convoys. The fact that U.S. supplied tanks, armored personnel carriers and jet planes defend these convoys testifies to the frequent ambushes.

The government also refuses to allow journalists into the province to report on the war. But after some weeks of negotiating with guerrilla representatives in neighboring Sudan, we were able to cross the border into rebel areas of Eritrea.

For the next five weeks, we moved about freely without escorts, visiting small villages and towns where the rebels' control appeared to be unchallenged.

The only strictly military activity seen during this time was the strafing of a village by a government F-86 Sabre jet. The guerrillas did not seem particularly concerned about the strafing, saying such attacks appear to be intended mainly to frighten peasants.

The trip to the edge of Asmara was a typical experience. We rode part of the way in a Land Rover taken, the driver said, from an

Ethiopian officer. Five miles from Asmara we passed three loaded Fiat trucks bearing the markings of the Ethiopian Relief and Rehabilitation Commission. The trucks, the guerrillas said, had been captured several days earlier.

At about 11 that night we left the jeep in a field and set out on foot along a rutted path, following two teams carrying Russian-made Kalashnikov automatic rifles.

At the last village overlooking the desolate approach to Asmara we stopped to talk to the guerrillas on guard. We had passed within 200 yards of an Ethiopian outpost, so we spoke softly. The guerrillas laughed at our caution and said no shots had been exchanged in months because the Ethiopians wanted to avoid battle.

For their part, the guerrillas seemed to be putting off any major push on the government-controlled cities until after the two rival guerrilla movements could forge some sort of unity. Guerrillas repeatedly stressed the object lesson of Angola, where a decade-long war against the Portuguese turned into a bitter civil war among three guerrilla movements, each with outside backing.

So an uneasy stalemate continues in Eritrea, with the guerrillas dug in and concentrating, for the most part, on local political organizing and social and economic development projects.

War and Peace

During those weeks with the guerrillas, we were driven along hundreds of miles of dirt and gravel roads built, the rebels claimed, within the past year. We walked more than 150 miles through remote mountain hamlets and nomadic settlements in the tropical lowlands.

We had to skirt the major cities, with a member of the guerrillas' engineers to guide us around mines planted beneath the paving, but nowhere in the countryside did we see any sign of Ethiopian troops.

We did see the remains of burned-out villages, the bullet holes and bomb craters of past air raids, the crumbling buildings and faded signs of old government offices—and abundant evidence of guerrilla-directed reconstruction and development.

The guerrillas did not display their most powerful military hardware—which, according to Western intelligence, includes B-10 rockets, antitank weapons and heavy artillery. But we did see many units armed with automatic weapons and plenty of ammunition. Some individual fighters carried as many as 450 bullets. And we saw a shop for the repair of captured weapons.

But the guerrillas—or those we saw—were not fighting or guarding fortified positions, rather, they were operating hospitals and small factories, distributing food or hanging up their weapons to help peasants in the fields, building roads, running political education programs or caring for refugees. These thousands of trained and armed men and women were functioning less as a military force than as a sort of Eritrean Peace Corps—or, rather, as two rival Peace Corps.

In the parched desert hills of northwestern Eritrea, we spent two days in a base camp of the Eritrean People's Liberation Forces, an offshoot of the Eritrean Liberation Front.

We ate what the fighters ate—*kitcha* and *taita*, flatbreads of roughly ground wheat and millet flour, with peppery sauces of lentils and onions. These were occasionally supplemented with eggs and pots of rice, foods usually reserved for the sick and the wounded. We slept on the ground in a cave-like sunken stone house covered with dirt and thorn branches as camouflage from the periodic Ethiopian bombing raids.

We were introduced to Ethiopian POWs who, we were told, were undergoing literacy training as well as political orientation in captivity. The prisoners appeared to be on good terms with their captors, but expressed gloom about the future. They could never go home again, several said, because the government would kill them rather than let them tell what they had seen.

We also were taken to settlements run by both guerrilla movements for refugees from the fighting. Most of the refugees we met spoke of raids on their villages by Ethiopian forces—usually reprisal or vengeance raids, we were told.

The stories were depressingly similar. After some event that humiliated the government forces—a meeting of rebels, an ambush, the loss of an outpost to guerrilla attack—Ethiopian troops would come to a village, herd together as many of its residents as they could find, kill many as an object lesson to the survivors, set fire to the huts and leave.

In the northwestern Sahel district, some 200 miles from Asmara, there was a tent settlement in a thickly wooded area next to a small stream—almost hidden from the ground and, presumably, from the air.

The village leaders were in a tent on the river bank, and their voices mingled with the sounds of children playing outside.

The settlement, they said, then had 800 inhabitants. But in the year and a half of its existence, they said, the village had been in three different locations and as many as 30,000 refugees had passed through, most on their way to neighboring Sudan.

"They come by foot and by lorry with the fighters," one elder said, "often in large groups from a town recently attacked by the Ethiopians. With most of the young ones joining the front, those who come here are the old, the very young and the sick."

Each arriving family, he said, is assigned to a settled family for temporary shelter, then sent to the camp's small clinic for a physical examination and an evaluation of the family's nutritional needs to determine the ration of grain, sugar, coffee, salt and canned vegetables.

All the tents in the camp were the same: 10-by-12-foot canvas affairs without floors, but with heavy flaps against the anticipated seasonal rains. In most cases, the interior was reserved for sleeping. Cooking was done in a clearing nearby.

One of the main efforts now, the guerrillas say, is to try to persuade the refugees who have crossed into Sudan to return to Eritrea, to the camps and villages where the fronts are trying to build a new society.

Less than 20 miles from Asmara, there was a meeting with the village committee formed after the Eritrean People's Liberation Forces took over. A wrinkled old man, sitting on the dirt floor with his knees pulled up to his chin, described the committee's aims.

"When we were elected, the main target of our work was to bring down the ones who were floating on the top and to raise up the ones who were oppressed at the bottom, to create fraternity and equality in our village."

Pressed for examples, a second peasant said: "Formerly, when we used to build houses, some of the rich peasants took more area than the rest. But now we have a specific rule that allows 30 meters by 8 meters for each house—and we have made them (the rich peasants) take down the extra. Those with smaller houses were helped to expand theirs."

Grass Roots Action

In mobilizing the population politically and fostering village self-government, the two movements have adopted different approaches.

The ELF is trying to meet immediate wartime needs, postponing more radical change until after the hoped for victory, while the EPLF is setting up an elaborate system of interconnected cells.

In one EPLF-controlled village, there is a regular weekend meeting. At one session the problems handled included a dispute between two half-brothers over inheritance rights, a woman's charge that she had been insulted by a neighbor, a boundary quarrel and a claim for compensation for bodily injury. After the cases were heard and decided, the session turned into a general discussion on how to stop roving cattle from walking on young crops. A subcommittee was assigned to come up with recommendations by the following week.

The five-man committee in a village in ELF-controlled territory was organized along areas of responsibility. One member was the police force, though when necessary he could call on militia help. Another collected taxes and controlled prices in the local markets. A third supervised that essential, the wood supply. A fourth made sure the guerrillas passing through the village had food and shelter. And there was a chairman, a distinguished looking elderly man who had been village chief before the war.

Both movements have set up health care and hospital systems. They are also acting like governments in other ways, establishing supply and distribution systems to prevent profiteering and offset an Ethiopian embargo on food distribution in the countryside, caring for some of the half-million or more refugees in the province, administering Italian-owned farms and plantations, nominally nationalized by the government but actually under peasant control; and—most significant, perhaps—setting up small industry to reduce dependence on the Ethiopian economy.

One "factory" in EPLF territory was hidden against air attack in a dense thicket. Ten people were there, busily making fruit crates. In an underground workshop, carved out of a mountainside, more than a dozen people with hand tools were making a variety of wooden products. The workers included an elderly man, several young women and two children perhaps eight years old. In a leather workshop sheltered by an outcropping of rock, a crew of nine men and three women turned out cartridge holders for the Kalashnikov automatic rifles all EPLF fighters carry.

A metal workshop provided sharp contrasts. In one section there were welding machines for repair of captured weapons. In another a boy chopped tin cans apart to make sheet metal squares.

The ELF region boasted a garage and auto repair shop. It sprawled beneath a dense umbrella of towering *zagla* trees. High in one of the tallest trees there was a rifleman with binoculars.

Below, 18 mechanics toiled over an assortment of trucks, buses, Land Rovers and sedans. The shop boss said he ran his own garage in Addis Ababa until two years earlier, when he decided to "lay my head for the people."

Eighteen months earlier, the guerrillas said, the ELF had only five vehicles and no formal repair facilities. Now, the claim was, it had two garages and 144 vehicles, including captured equipment. Two Scania trucks being fitted with spare fuel tanks had been donated, we were told, by the Iraqi government.

Child Revolutionaries

Predictably, both guerrilla movements have undertaken large-scale literacy campaigns. We saw groups of peasant children learning the alphabets in Tigrinya and Arabic, the two "official" languages of Eritrea. We were told of plans to open elementary schools, and we saw mimeographed curricula that included math, science, social studies and English. Children in both territories are taught revolutionary songs, and one—"Where Is My Comrade Fighter?"—was whistled or sung wherever we went.

The EPLF has established a special unit of 8-to-15-year-olds called the Vanguards. At a training camp in Sahel we watched them on military maneuvers. They were receiving both political and military training, we were told, although the younger ones would be assigned only to support roles in the rear areas.

One 13-year-old said that one day he and his young comrades would lead the revolution, because—having been brought up under it—they were "the most revolutionary of all."

Section 2

Life in the Liberated Areas 1977-78

Prologue

In March 1977, the EPLF captured the hilltop town of Nakfa, kicking off a round of nationalist victories that in six months left the two liberation fronts in control of most of Eritrea. Both rebel armies established civil administrations in the cities and towns they held, demonstrating competing visions and giving the people a glimpse of what their accession to state power might mean. The U.S.-armed and -trained Ethiopian Army was on the ropes. The end of the war was on the horizon.

However, Ethiopia's sudden break with the U.S. and its realignment with the Soviet Union — agreed upon in Addis Ababa in December 1976 and announced in March 1977 — turned this situation on its head. The Russians quickly insisted that the Eritrean fronts bury their aspirations for independence and join a regional *Pax Sovietica*. They refused.

The upshot was a new war.

Massive Soviet military aid to Ethiopia helped the derg resist Somali incursions in the southeast during the summer of 1977. After this campaign, the Addis Ababa government shifted men and materiel to Eritrea. In September, new Soviet artillery and T-54/55 tanks participated in battles outside Asmara. The drivers were South Yemenis. Rumors flew of imminent Cuban involvement.

By December, the growing Soviet intervention started to turn the tide of battle. An EPLF effort to capture the strategic port of Massawa was stymied, and the war ground to a stalemate. Over the next four months, the Eritreans captured several government garrisons on the Asmara-Massawa road, but a steady buildup on the Ethiopian side signaled that the two-year run of unanswered rebel victories was over.

During the lead-up to these events in the winter of 1976-77, I worked as a carpenter, not a writer. I set up housekeeping with my two daughters (Joanie, 11, and Laura, 9) in Cambridge, Massachusetts.

I had custody for the school year. I hoped to return to Eritrea the following summer, if I could find a way to cover travel costs.

In February, I was invited to appear at an Eritrean community event in Boston. The featured speaker was Irwin Silber, a columnist for the New York-based *Guardian*, an independent-left weekly newspaper that supported the Eritrean cause. Afterward, Silber asked me to write a series that laid out the roots of the war, analyzed the rival liberation movements and critiqued Ethiopia's new military regime. I was intimidated, as this called for a level of historical knowledge and analytic depth for which I felt unprepared, but I took it on and set out to remedy my deficiencies through further study.

The articles came out in March under a penname, Jonathan Kendrick, which I adopted out of concern that public association with the Marxist-oriented *Guardian* could jeopardize my ability to write for mainstream media. (Many *Guardian* contributors routinely used pseudonyms.) I also published an article in *The Nation* on U.S. policy in the Horn, using my own name. But bylines were the least of my worries. I was not a trained journalist and did not know how to write like one. I struggled as much with format as with content. Each article took me a week to draft.

———

As the spring wore on, I grew closer to *The Guardian*. In June, when my daughters moved across Cambridge to live with their mother for the 1977-78 school year, I went to New York to work directly with the radical newsweekly. The month of July served as an accelerated apprenticeship.

The Guardian was a "movement" operation. The paper's executive editor, Jack Smith, was a politically-astute, former UPI reporter who, along with a dedicated cadre of editors, writers and production workers, sought to bring professional standards to an otherwise seat-of-the-pants political project. Much of the copy came from activists who called in their reports. Few had journalistic skills. Their prose was laced with stilted rhetoric and unintelligible jargon. It fell to the underpaid and overworked staff and a corps of volunteers to translate this material into accessible news stories. I was one of them.

Jack sent me to Barnes & Noble to buy a used journalism textbook, and he put me through the paces on interviewing techniques, lead-writing, inverted pyramids, sourcing and attribution, narrative structure and more. I immersed myself in these studies in the mornings, over lunch, late at night — whenever I had a free minute. Foreign editor Karen Gellen assigned me short informational articles on issues the paper covered regularly — liberation movements in Africa and the Middle East, changing alignments in Asia, repression and resistance in Latin America, whatever came across her desk. I also rewrote national and regional stories that came in the night the paper went to press.

The deadline pressure was excruciating, and we sustained ourselves on a diet of pizza and adrenalin, coffee and cigarettes. But the thrill of producing a paper we hoped would change the world was exhilarating.

This was better than school ever was.

———

In August, I set out for Eritrea, but it was not a simple matter.

I departed New York on a complimentary Air Canada ticket owed *The Guardian* for tours to China the paper had organized for many years — until the Chinese broke-off the arrangement in a pique over *The Guardian's* support for the MPLA in Angola against Jonas Savimbi's pro-Chinese (and pro-American) UNITA movement. This was the last of *The Guardian's* Air Canada freebies, and it was good for any place to which the airline flew. Unfortunately, Africa was not one of them. The closest I could get was Greece. I planned to charge the next leg — Athens-to-Khartoum — and pay it off by writing stories once in the field.

On arrival in Athens, I bedded down on the roof of a low-cost hostel, curling up in my sleeping bag with my backpack for a pillow after drinking far too much Metaxa with a rag-tag group of other budget travelers. I carried a small tape recorder, a dozen cassettes, several notebooks and pens, a borrowed camera, ten rolls of film, a few hundred dollars in travelers' checks, and three changes of clothes. It was all tucked beneath me.

Disaster struck the next morning. I awoke to find that my passport and checks were gone!

Fortunately, the catastrophe proved fleeting: I got a new passport in two days. American Express quickly replaced the checks. And the Amex travel agent promised to get me to Khartoum, despite the fact that all flights to Sudan were fully booked for three weeks. He confided that he was a Greek communist and a long-time supporter of the Eritrean struggle. He told me not to worry, and I left his office with a round-trip KLM ticket, the departure details left blank.

Almost as soon as I arrived at the airport the next day, I heard myself paged. Clutching my tattered backpack, I presented myself at the ticket counter where I was handed a first class boarding pass for the next flight to Sudan. I was as surprised at this as the KLM agent was when he saw whom the ticket was for, but I managed somehow to take it in stride.

As it turned out, this was the last bit of luxury I would experience for nearly eight months.

———

Once in Khartoum, I went straight to the EPLF office.

I'd decided to immerse myself in EPLF areas for an extended period. I'd arranged to file for *The Post* and for *The Guardian*. The EPLF had agreed in advance to take me in and to courier my stories to Khartoum, from where they would be sent via telex to the newspapers, which would pay the transmission costs.

After more than two weeks haggling with Sudanese authorities for travel permissions (from the police to leave the capital, from the security forces to cross the border), I departed for the field. I arrived in Port Sudan on a sweltering day in August with British photographer Sarah Errington and an EPLF escort. We spent a restless night in the stultifying mid-summer humidity of the country's only major seaport before setting out early the next morning in a banged-up land rover the guerrillas had captured in a recent battle.

It was a harrowing ride along what was once a two-lane tarmac road, built by the British more than thirty years earlier but left to disintegrate in the scorching desert heat. Jagged chunks of black asphalt and gravel jutted out of the sand as we tracked a meandering row of rusted metal telephone polls through the dunes, snippets of wire dangling randomly like long-abandoned May poles. This was the easternmost corner of the Sahara; it felt like the end of the earth.

At Tokar, we were forced to halt by a huge seasonal flood, the product of heavy rains in the faraway Eritrean highlands. The murky brown expanse stretched across the plains as far as the eye could see. We switched to camels and trudged through the knee-deep water for more than five hours, picking our way among stands of partially-submerged sorghum, around sunken ravines, and past tangles of acacia branches and other debris swept there by the torrent spilling off the plateau (see the photo on the cover of this volume).

At Marafit, there was another EPLF depot. We stopped to rest.

Around midnight we were awakened to ride across the unmarked border under cover of darkness, when Ethiopia's U.S.-supplied F-5 jet fighters, lacking night vision capability, were grounded. The road was in better shape than the year before — a path through the partially dry riverbeds had been cleared of large boulders — but the journey was exhausting.

Shortly before dawn we reached the EPLF base camp at Fah. There, we joined a three-person Italian film crew from Lotta Continua, one of three small parties to the left of the Italian Communist Party and strong supporters of the EPLF. They were in the field to produce a documentary on the revolution. We would all travel together for two weeks, ending our tour in the highlands at Decamare. (This mix of freelance journalists and left-wing solidarity activists [mainly from Europe] was fairly typical of the visitors then.)

In my case, I was to proceed from there on my own, carrying a letter from EPLF politburo member Sebhat Ephrem that allowed me to move about at will. It was the only time I would have such liberty, for the procedures governing press visits soon tightened up as more and more mainstream journalists made their way to the war zone to record the guerrillas' growing success.

I planned to stay inside Eritrea at least six months — to gather material for a book and to file news stories and features. During the first ninety days, I took full advantage of the front's openness and crisscrossed EPLF-held territory in guerrilla vehicles and civilian buses, even traveling on foot and mule into neighboring Tigray with the Tigray People's Liberation Front to glimpse the early stages of a regional upheaval that would one day lead to the derg's ouster in Addis. I filed stories on everything I saw.

My relationship with *The Post* was problematic from the outset, however — at both ends of the telex.

In their view, I sent too much copy, and I was too close to the Eritreans. As I saw it, they altered my writing for content as well as style and used me to score editorial points with which I disagreed. The exchanges grew increasingly strained.

What irritated me the most was that *Post* editors kept inserting politically-charged epithets for the main players — the Eritreans were always "secessionists," the Ethiopians "Marxists." And they did so under my byline.

I understood this to be an anticolonial struggle, not a war of secession. The difference was basic. I did not call the Eritreans "freedom fighters," but I insisted on a neutral term, such as nationalist guerrillas or independence fighters. And I was not out to discredit Marxism either, only the demagogues in Addis, whom I characterized as "self-described 'socialists.'" But this didn't do it for *The Post*.

Through the autumn, the editors took a dozen or so of my files and produced two heavily-edited "Letters from Eritrea," personalizing my accounts from the field while continuing to inject their own spin. Eventually, I severed the relationship.

Meanwhile, I filed a fresh account of life behind guerrilla lines nearly every week for *The Guardian*. At $25 per story, this would not pay the bills, but it was enormously energizing. (In any case, I donated this to the paper to cover the cost of subscriptions airmailed to the EPLF via Port Sudan.) Yet I was all-too-aware that *The Guardian* on its best days only reached 25,000 readers, many of them political activists but hardly the social base for shifts in U.S. foreign policy or for substantial material solidarity for the liberation movement. And it was impact that I was after, not just passing attention.

One evening in early October — before my rupture with *The Post* — I sat in an EPLF bunker in the hills outside the government garrison at Adi Caieh, listening to the BBC's evening news program, "Focus on Africa." There were lengthy accounts of what this or that bureaucrat said about one of his counterparts, what political intrigue marked this or that meeting, what aid project was or was not working, what prospect there was for peace talks in this or that low-level armed conflict. But, as usual, nothing about Eritrea.

This got me thinking.

The BBC was the one media outlet that covered Africa in depth. It did so on a relatively modest budget by tapping into a continental network of unsalaried stringers who were paid for the stories they submitted to London by telex from their country's communications hub (nearly always the capital), and that were read over the air waves by Focus staffers.

There was rarely anything on Eritrea because there was no foreign journalist in Eritrea. Politics played a part in this — notably Ethiopia's effort to isolate the war zone from reporters — but logistics were also a factor. Getting there was difficult, as I have indicated, and it took considerable time to get a story that few people were following. Once inside, there was no place for a journalist to set up shop, no means to send copy, no way to even contact the home office. And daily life in the field was no picnic.

Yet there was a story unfolding of a growing military and political challenge to a brutal military regime that presided over one of the largest countries in Africa and was (still) the oldest U.S. client state on the continent. Beyond this, there was a radically egalitarian, multicultural society emerging through this war — the new Eritrea — whose story cried out to be told.

The next day I penned an account of conditions near Adi Caieh, where government and rebel forces confronted one another in trenches reminiscent of World War I. There was no breaking news there, but the situation typified that of the territory's few urban enclaves still in Ethiopian hands.

I packaged the report with a brief cover letter saying who I was, where I was, that I had reported for *The Washington Post*, and that I would be pleased to send the BBC more frontline stories if they wished. I addressed my hand-written missive to "BBC London" and asked an EPLF comrade to arrange for it to be hand-carried to Khartoum, given to someone on a British Airways flight to the UK, and then handed over to BA personnel at Heathrow for onpassing to BBC headquarters. It was a long shot, but I had time on my hands.

Three weeks later, I tuned into Focus and heard my piece read on the air by Robin White. This was a turning point. Shortly afterward, I traveled to Khartoum to straighten out my media relations — breaking with *The Post* and establishing a direct link with the BBC. I also met the Rome bureau chief from Reuters news agency. He was on his way to Eritrea.

At this point, the guerrilla victories were attracting more and more reporters, mainly from Europe. Most came in for a week or two, wrote a situation analysis and a handful of features, then left. I briefed several of them: orienting them to the geography of the war zone, suggesting where the conflict was headed, offering ideas for sidebars, explaining the logistics, offering tips on EPLF personalities. Initially, I did this to get the story out, as the Front had no organized public relations program, but the upshot was often an arrangement to report for the paper if something broke. Once I grasped this pattern, I pursued it relentlessly.

Reuters was the first. I helped plan the visiting reporter's trip. He invited me to file after he left. We signed a contract, and I went on a modest retainer. He told me to file as often as several times a day if the war escalated, and he tutored me in Reuters style and drilled me on the agency's rigorous attribution policy. We practiced together in what amounted to my second, brief field apprenticeship.

After Reuters came *La Repubblica*. Then *Le Monde*. I also began writing longer pieces for the Khartoum-based monthly *Sudanow*, a publication of Sudan's Information Ministry under the direction of a prominent southern politician, Bona Malwal.

With these arrangements in hand, I asked the EPLF to relay short news stories by radio to Khartoum for Reuters and the BBC. They agreed to code them in the field and decipher them in Sudan before taking them to the Sudan News Agency, SUNA, for telexing. It was a cumbersome arrangement but the only option I had, and it reduced my communications time to a single day, sometimes two.

This may seem an eternity today, with the wonders of satellite phones, streaming video, instant messaging and so forth, but it was a major breakthrough at the time, and it enabled me to function as a breaking-news reporter, not simply a writer of timeless features and overviews. It also put Eritrea into the news in a manner and with a frequency it had never had before.

The high point of my journalistic output that year came after the EPLF cut the strategic Asmara-Massawa road in December and threatened to move against both key cities. The Eritreans looked to be on their way to a final victory. I spent nearly six weeks on or near the frontlines around Massawa watching the drama unfold and recording everything I could on paper and on film.

For much of this period, I was thrown together with freelance British photographer Mike Wells and BBC-TV reporter Simon Dring, who were collaborating on a book project. This cost me the ability to write for BBC radio, as Simon did it himself, but I got valuable mentoring from each of them — in radio production and in photojournalism — and it was a heady and extremely productive time. However, it was also an extremely disheartening one from the standpoint of the story itself, as the prospects for an end to the war steadily receded.

My most frustrating point as a writer came in a chance encounter with a reporter from Agence France Presse (AFP), who passed through Eritrea in the midst of the heaviest fighting of the war and stole my innocence along with my story. We met in Keren, after the EPLF's unsuccessful effort to capture Massawa. I had just come from the trenches. She had just visited a group of rural villages to compile a feature on civilian life. We sat together through the evening, exchanging tales of what we'd seen — mostly me running on about my war experiences, happy to have an avid audience, and her taking copious notes without my noticing.

After she left, I settled down to write my story, tapping out the tale unhurriedly on my flimsy Olivettti portable. By the time I finished, however, my account was old news. She had told it in riveting detail under her own byline, describing herself as filing from "Outside Massawa." This was a claim that was hard to dispute on its face, though how far outside Massawa was an issue. I heard the report on the BBC before I sent mine off. Lesson learned. (Maybe two or three lessons learned.)

———

Journalism is often a matter of chance — being at the right place at the right time and getting the story of this encounter to the right outlet in a timely manner. I got another chance a few weeks later.

From the Massawa battle onward, the war underwent rapid and far-reaching changes. The EPLF captured a string of towns along the Asmara-Massawa road in January, but the tide was turning. The Soviets were coming. Ethiopia was building a new army. It would soon be a new war. This much was already obvious, though precisely how it would play out was hard to forecast.

I prepared to leave the field at the end of the month, stopping in the Sahel base area to gather my thoughts, block out my last stories, say my goodbyes. Still, it was my practice to observe and record anything or anyone when the opportunity arose, so when I heard there were Ethiopian prisoners in the vicinity, I asked to speak with them before I headed out. In the course of questioning them, I was surprised to hear from one officer that there were Soviet advisors with them on the frontlines.

I pursued this, and it yielded a major scoop. Russian advisors were for the first time directly engaged in combat in Eritrea: firing the artillery, directing the tanks, participating in command decisions at the highest levels.

I filed some of this material from Khartoum in early February and then flew to London to flog the story. I met with editors at *The Observer* and *The Financial Times*. Each wanted a piece. *The Observer* asked for one on what I'd seen in Massawa and on the growing Soviet involvement. The *FT* asked for a broad overview of the conflict and what was likely to come in the next round.

In the next few weeks, I placed versions of the *FT* overview in several papers in continental Europe and North America, including my hometown paper, *The Boston Globe*. (Multiple submissions were accepted practice at the time, so long as the markets did not overlap.)

The ability to sell and resell essentially the same story — self-syndication — is what made freelancing like this viable. Without it, I could barely have paid the airfare with what I recouped from writing. In this case, the stories I wrote and distributed at the end of my trip created the possibility for me to go home, meet my obligations there, and come back within a year to pick up the story again.

Roots of Eritrea's Struggle
The fight for freedom
The Guardian (New York), March 2, 1977

[Byline: Jonathan Kendrick]

The Eritrean struggle for national liberation is forging an independent nation after centuries of feudal and colonial domination, most lately by Ethiopia.

Some of the country's long history, the emergence of the modern liberation movements and some of the difficulties confronted by the Eritreans—background not widely known outside the country—are summarized in this article.

Eritrea is a relatively small country among the giants of eastern Africa. Covering 43,000 square miles, approximately the size of Pennsylvania, it has a population estimated at 2-4 million persons. Located between Sudan in the west and the French territory of the Afars and Issas (Djibouti) to the southeast along the Red Sea, its strategic location has played a significant role in its modern history. First colonized by the Ottoman Turks in the middle of the 16th century, Eritrea has been occupied by a succession of African and European empires for over 400 years.

Endowed with striking natural beauty and geographical diversity, the Eritrean landscape has palm-studded subtropical lowlands, gently rolling hills and slopes, flat fertile plateaux, towering mountain ridges and a scorched sub-sea level desert that is reputed to be the hottest place in the world.

Abyssinian Empire

The Ethiopian claim to Eritrea rests on the argument that it is an historical extension of the ancient Abyssinian empire that began with the legendary Queen of Sheba in 1000 B.C. and which lasted until about 1000 A.D. The empire's center was in the city of Axum near the present border between Eritrea and the Tigre administrative region of Ethiopia. The empire included most of Eritrea, Tigre and northern Shoa—perhaps one third of modern Ethiopia—and at its peak it also extended west to Sudan and across the Red Sea into Yemen and south Arabia.

This empire was crushed by a succession of invasions and forced to retreat into the mountainous highlands to the south, leaving the coastal plains of Eritrea to be colonized eventually by the Ottoman Turks in the middle of the 16th century. After a brief conquest by the Egyptians in the 19th century, the Italians seized Eritrea in 1883. Ethiopia only resisted the Italian conquest when it was threatened in the highlands. In the famous battle of Adowa in 1896, Ethiopian Emperor Menelik defeated the Italian invaders, but he signed a treaty recognizing Eritrea as "a legitimate possession of Italy."

It was only in 1950, when the UN was deciding the future of former Italian colonies, that Ethiopia claimed Eritrea was an integral part of the Ethiopian empire. Even then emperor Haile Selassie was willing to accept a British plan to divide the colony between Sudan and Ethiopia.

The British plan was finally scrapped after losing in the General Assembly, while Ethiopia abstained. The UN then approved a U.S. proposal to link Eritrea with Ethiopia in a vaguely defined federation, which granted Eritrea control over internal affairs, a provisional parliament subject to the ultimate power of the Ethiopian emperor and a constitution guaranteeing civil liberties and cultural autonomy. The arrangement gave Ethiopia two ports on the Red Sea, the rich agricultural highlands of Eritrea and the highly developed industry around Asmara. It gave the U.S. Kagnew station in Asmara, then the largest military communications base in the world, to facilitate global military communications and to monitor broadcasts throughout Africa and the Middle East. Later, Israel acquired a naval base in the Dahlak Islands off the Eritrean coast.

In a unique political arrangement, colonial control of Eritrea was transferred from the British, who occupied Eritrea during World War 2, to the Ethiopian empire, although Ethiopia was less developed socially and economically than its northern neighbor. Under Italian rule Eritrea had undergone sweeping changes: introduction of irrigated plantation farming, construction of roads to connect the burgeoning towns and the growth of internal trade. Industry developed, especially around Asmara, and an Eritrean proletariat began to form.

During the British occupation from 1941-1950 trade unions were organized and political parties were formed, institutions entirely alien to the feudal agrarian cultures of the rest of the Ethiopian empire. Although Italian colonialism had destroyed the traditional ruling groups in Eritrea, Ethiopia's ruling class had remained intact strengthened by its opposition to the Italian invaders. With the connivance and support of the U.S., the Ethiopian empire was easily able to dominate Eritrea.

After 10 years of association with Ethiopia, the Eritreans had lost their flag, trade unions, political parties, newspapers, constitution and finally their parliament. Whole industrial plants had been dismantled, machine by machine, and moved to the Ethiopian capital of Addis Ababa. Through sheer military might, Ethiopia suppressed Eritrea's more advanced social development and appropriated its technological advantage. In 1962, the federation was dissolved without a murmur from the UN, and Eritrea was incorporated into Ethiopia as its 14th province.

Today the military junta that overthrew the emperor over two years ago is offering an undefined regional autonomy to Eritrea as the basis for a settlement to the war for independence that was launched in 1961, but the Eritreans reject this out of hand.

A compromise which might have been possible immediately after the overthrow of the emperor is now opposed by Eritreans who have suffered continuous barbaric repression that has included use of free-fire zones and napalm, arbitrary arrests and torture, My Lai-style massacres, strangling of children, mass-raping of young girls and a host of other unspeakable crimes and atrocities, that all remain unpunished by the martial law administrators.

Strategic Importance

The Eritrean independence struggle is also impeded by imperial interests outside of Ethiopia. Eritrea is strategically located at the narrow southern entrance to the Red Sea and is a prime concern to Israeli and U.S. commercial and military interests in the area. It borders the French territory of Afars and Issas to the south and could be a key factor there in a confrontation between Somalia and Ethiopia. It is Ethiopia's principal connection with the outside via the ports of Massawa and Assab and is therefore crucial to any international trade.

When the U.S. obtained Kagnew in 1953, it agreed to arm and train the Ethiopian army and air force. Three divisions were organized and equipped. Many of the officers were trained in the U.S., but specialists from the Military Advisory and Assistance Group (MAAG) came to Ethiopia in the 1960s to instruct Ethiopian forces in counterinsurgency operations. The Israelis sent specialists who trained a commando force known as the Special Strike Force Police.

During the past 20 years, more than one-half of U.S. aid to Africa has been given to Ethiopia, principally in the form of military grants and credits.

Until 1974, Israel also maintained a naval base in the Dahlak Islands off the coast of Eritrea, but since the 1973 war it has been forced to keep a lower profile. The latest Israeli training mission in Ethiopia created a new commando unit known as the "flame brigade."

Since 1974, the military junta has also obtained arms from Yugoslavia, Turkey, Italy and several other European nations but its principal supplier is still the U.S.

In 1975, Ethiopian purchases in the U.S. included 22 M-60 tanks, 12 M-109 self-propelled howitzers and six TOW missile launchers with 120 missiles. In 1976, Addis Ababa bought 16 F-5E jet fighters and ordered six coastal patrol boats developed for Vietnam. In December 1975 an agreement was signed for a modernization of the entire armed forces over five years at a cost estimated at $300 million.

American policy has consistently supported the "territorial integrity" of the Ethiopian empire. With few exceptions, most African countries have sought to avoid involvement in the Eritrean question, calling it an internal affair of Ethiopia. Aid to the Eritreans has been mostly from friendly Arab countries, and even this has been uneven and irregular.

Liberation Forces

The Eritrean liberation forces are divided into two separate organizations, the Revolutionary Command of the Eritrean Liberation Front (ELF) and the Eritrean People's Liberation Forces (EPLF or simply PLF). At one time these rival movements practically destroyed each other in a bitter civil war, but today they are allied together against the military government of Ethiopia in the struggle for national independence and popular democracy.

The Provisional Military Advisory Council of Ethiopia, known as the dergue, claims to be putting down a nationalist secession movement in Eritrea, which it says is "unnecessary" in the context of the Ethiopian revolution instituted in 1974 when the emperor was deposed.

During the four months of traveling inside Ethiopia, I saw that the revolution barely extends beyond the capital city of Addis Ababa. The regime does not control the countryside. The directives it sends out to the provinces have almost no effect. There is organized armed resistance to the government in at least six provinces.

Almost all the schools beyond the 6th grade were closed through most of 1976 because of student opposition to the dergue. Protests are met with repression or arrest and often death. And the war in Eritrea is draining the limited resources still in the hands of the military.

What keeps the dergue in power today is a massive input of aid—both military and economic—from the U.S. and Western Europe. Forces have been unleashed in Ethiopia which may well lead to an authentically democratic and socialist revolution, but the military regime currently in power lacks a popular base, is incapable of leading a revolution and would collapse completely without Western support.

The struggle of Eritrean liberation fighters against the U.S.-backed Ethiopian government has lasted two decades. Only the leaders of the Addis Ababa regime have changed.

In 1958, after the massacre of several hundred Eritreans striking in Asmara to protest the suppression of their flag by Emperor Haile Selassie, the Eritrean Liberation Movement (ELM) was founded. Initially it was an underground political organization for national independence, but did not advocate armed resistance. In 1961, when it had become obvious that the federation with Ethiopia was on the verge of being dissolved, the ELF was organized and it began armed struggle.

At first the fighting was sporadic and almost at random. The forces were organized along religious and tribal lines, and lacked a common ideology or military strategy. But after 1966 two tendencies began to emerge, one that sought to build a progressive political movement on a national basis, the other to protect entrenched class interests. By 1969 internal fighting had broken out between the two factions as the ELF leadership sought to crush the growing challenge to its power, and over 200 fighters and agitators were liquidated.

Finally in April 1970, three groups from within ELF broke away and formed a united front which eventually became the PLF. The remaining ELF forces convened a congress in 1971 to which the PLF forces were invited but not recognized as a separate force or permitted to participate in the planning stages. The PLF declined to attend, and the split was thereby finalized. In February 1972, the ELF formally declared war on the PLF and three years of fratricidal civil war followed.

In early 1974, the feudal regime began to collapse as a result of spontaneous strikes by teachers, students and workers; a severe drought in the Wollo and Tigrai regions, which took the lives of over 100,000 peasants; and mutinies in the armed forces. At the same time, democratic and progressive forces had arisen inside the ELF which opposed the fight with the PLF, and there was growing pressure from the civilian population to unify the guerrilla forces.

At a mass rally in November 1974, two months after the

Ethiopian military deposed Haile Selassie, 50,000 people marched out of Asmara to demand that the two fronts settle their differences and take advantage of the chaos in Ethiopia to advance Eritrean independence. Since then a tenuous alliance has been in effect while the two organizations move toward a formal unity.

The ELF holds that the PLF wrongly formed a separate organization and the ELF was wrong in declaring war, but now there are no substantial ideological differences, so the two organizations should unify and forget the past.

The PLF contends that there are still secondary contradictions between them, that the past must be analyzed and that certain people must be punished for their crimes before all can be forgotten. It favors a gradual merger through the intermediate stage of a united front prior to the national congress which has been called for by the ELF.

Two lines in Eritrea's movement
ELF, PLF seek unity

The Guardian (New York), March 9, 1977

[Byline: Jonathan Kendrick]

Two people's armies are battling the Ethiopian ruling junta for national liberation in Eritrea. What does each stand for—and is there a basis for unity between them?

Contradictions between the organizations—the Revolutionary Command of the Eritrean Liberation Front (ELF) and the Eritrean People's Liberation Forces (PLF)—have in the past led to armed conflict. Now they are fighting together, while struggling on the political level to determine principles and conditions for formation of a single united Eritrean liberation movement.

In the early stages of the armed independence struggle, the ELF was a loose-knit alliance of Moslem nationalists, divided by tribal and regional allegiances and lacking a united political line or even a common military strategy. Later, after the split into ELF and PLF, religious and regional tendencies declined in importance as political and military developments including a massive influx of recruits during

1975 and the growth of the liberated areas blurred the old lines between the two fronts. Now, with the question of a principled basis for unity in the forefront, political differences have again assumed a greater significance.

Intense Political Struggle

During a recent extensive tour of the areas of Eritrea being administered by the ELF and the PLF, I heard the internal political struggle repeatedly referred to as primary by regular fighters and the leadership alike, although the emphasis varied from one organization to the other.

The PLF stressed its efforts to organize the peasant masses and lay the groundwork for a social revolution that would follow independence. The ELF, for its part, constantly emphasized the need to bring about political unity with PLF in order to first defeat Addis Ababa and then to initiate economic and political change.

The campaign to win the support of the Eritrean people is being waged principally by political cadres of the two rival organizations. They are trained for three to six months in cadre schools in the liberated zones held by each front and then sent to do mass work among the civilian population.

Both Eritrean movements say they are national fronts representing the interests of all classes opposed to Ethiopian rule. The actual contradictions between them are more to be found in their concrete practice than in their stated political lines.

The ELF is a classic patriotic front, which includes within it a broad array of class interests united against a foreign oppressor. While the ELF leadership articulates a program modeled in some respects after Soviet theories of "noncapitalist development," its overriding aim is for military victory against Ethiopia, with the social revolution to follow chronologically.

Under the ElF political umbrella, there are well-to-do merchants whose sole concern is independence and there are fighters whose consciousness is muddled with contradictory fragments of theory unconnected with practice. There are also dedicated Marxist-Leninist cadre who openly question the priorities of their leaders.

In contrast to this unevenness in the ELF, the PLF exhibits a consistently high level of consciousness and discipline, the only weakness of which is an occasional suggestion of left dogmatism among newer recruits.

The PLF is of course also committed to victory against the Ethiopian colonialists, but they define themselves in theory and in practice as social revolutionaries whose armed struggle is laying the basis for the class struggle.

In the Liberated Zones

Evidence of this contradiction between ELF and PLF was obvious everywhere. With the PLF, I always stayed in the homes of the poorest peasants, with whom the fighters had warm and affectionate relations. I spoke with many in Italian, and I discovered a sophistication in their questions as well as in their personal accounts of struggle that bore eloquent witness to the efforts of the PLF mass mobilization.

With the ELF I stayed often in the homes of rich peasants and merchants who charged my escorts for the food which they demanded and who displayed more of a penchant for complaint than for analysis.

Impressions such as these were borne out by more detailed observations of the practice of political mobilization in the villages and the establishment of contrasting forms of self-government.

For the old colonial administrators, the ELF has substituted a state system of 5-member committees with specific duties such as security, tax collection, forestry conservation and the feeding of visiting fighters. Lacking any significant political preparation, village meetings have tended to elect the old chiefs and the more influential townspeople to these committees which were then responsible to the nearest ELF military unit.

The PLF works more slowly but more thoroughly to overturn the old order. It begins by sending cadres of the Armed Propaganda Squad—a military unit with a political assignment—into a town to organize on a house-to-house, family-to-family basis, evaluating the responses and classing the people according to their economic status in the village.

A member of this squad in the Hamasien region explained that certain people are chosen at this stage principally from the poor peasant class and privately politicized to help organize the village. At the same time, mobile medical teams and agricultural workers come in to provide services and to discuss politics.

Mobilizing the Peasants

When the cadres determine that the village is ready, he continued, they call for a mass meeting to initiate land reform. In contrast to Ethiopia's feudal land-holding system, the traditional form of land-tenure in Eritrea is known as *diesa*, meaning a village owns all land communally and divides it equally among its members. The land is recirculated every seven years to insure fairness. Colonial occupation and war have disrupted this system, however, and many villages haven't redistributed land for 30 to 50 years. The initial aim of the PLF, therefore, is to get the *diesa* process functioning again.

I learned that while this redistribution is being carried out, deeper political organization continues in the area. Women who are most receptive are organized into women's associations and up to a dozen secret cells are formed among the men. The PLF cadre work primarily among those who are landless or otherwise impoverished and forced to sell their labor power because these people are considered more receptive to an analysis of their economic and political circumstances based on social class differences.

The leaders of these cells form a separate group with its own leader who is in turn associated with the leaders of other villages in a branch which is directly linked to the nearest PLF unit in the area. In the village meanwhile, when the circulation of the land is completed, another public meeting is held at which a 15-member village committee is elected. Further elections are encouraged every four to five months, I was told, to sift out "the less progressive elements and to avoid entrenching personalities."

One rainy afternoon as I sat in the main room of a poor peasant's house less than 20 miles from Asmara, the Eritrean capital, in a PLF-controlled village, the local village committee filed in to visit us. One wrinkled old man sitting on the floor with his knees pulled close to his chin began the discussion. "When we were elected, the main target of our work was to bring down the ones who were floating at the top and to raise up the ones who were oppressed at the bottom, to create equality and fraternity in the village.

"We decide on certain cases not because someone can talk well or somebody can talk badly, but by knowing the truth and trying to point out the just solution to the problem which oppresses one or the other. Not only in the assemblies but also on the daily activities of the people, we oppose the exploitation of man by man and any opportunistic tendencies in the village. We are putting maximum effort into practicing democracy which can prepare us and our country for a true people's revolutionary government."

The extent to which the entire population is involved in the liberation struggle was brought home again and again. Children sang songs of the revolution as they worked in the fields, young girls and boys trained with the PLF Vanguards to assist on the battlefield and in the many reconstruction projects, women and men served side by side in combat units and elderly peasant proudly served with the people's militias. But here, too, the differences between the ELF and the PLF were striking.

The ELF armed the peasants as quickly as it captured weapons. Hundreds were inducted into militia units in the spring of 1976 when the ELF captured large stocks of guns and ammunition. Many leaders of the ELF militia whom I interviewed had been armed and trained in a previous Ethiopian effort to develop a militia and had simply changed sides when the ELF took military control of the area.

A People's Army

In contrast, the PLF put politics first and armed only those peasants who demonstrated a clear understanding of the history and goals of the revolution. Ten or a dozen of the poorest peasants from a village were chosen for a militia through the same lengthy political process used to elect the village committees except that here the peasants were picked by the political cells rather than the whole village assembly.

Outside Asmara I met the militias from two neighboring villages. Twenty-three peasants clad in patched cotton shirts and loose trousers with thin blankets wrapped around their shoulders and armed with British .303s and American M-1s captured from the Ethiopians marched into the village meeting area and sat on the ground to take turns telling me about their role in the revolution.

The first to speak summarized the history from Italian colonization through the Ethiopian occupation. "During that period," he concluded, "our children came to understand the need for independence without thinking about their own interests, they went into the field to fight for their country. Following their footsteps we ask for our country's independence, and we will fight for it."

Asked what they did in their villages, one rose to tell me, "We are not usually in combat, but we bring food and help the wounded when there is fighting. Our main jobs are security in the village and support in battle." After he described this work, an old man in a frayed green sweater and shorts declared, "We have realized the revolution fully and we are going to work toward its victory until the end. We are ready to defend our village and to die like martyrs for our country."

Both ELF and PLF are active in many areas of reconstruction in the liberated areas, but here again the contradictions in the ELF's political leadership were glaringly evident. Repair shops, small-scale production units, farms, medical clinics and schools were being organized to serve the civilian population, but their success or failure appeared to depend upon the strengths or weaknesses of the individuals running them.

PLF projects consistently reflected a higher level of political development and organizational discipline. Wherever a person practiced an important skill, she or he was surrounded by up to a dozen people who were in training. All production units sought balances of women and men, young and old, masters and apprentices within the limits of who was available. They engaged in political study as a collective unit and shared in decision-making with regard to their immediate and long-term production goals.

ELF and PLF have been officially committed to a truce aimed at joining forces to oust the Ethiopians since November 1974. The two movements are at the same time each deeply involved in a race to win the allegiance of a majority of the peasantry to strengthen their ability to lead an independent Eritrea. A key issue here is how to achieve unity between the two contending fronts.

One such attempt was made in March 1976, but ended in failure. At that time, leaders from the ELF and the foreign mission of the PLF signed an agreement to merge at the top levels. The pact was subsequently denounced by the PLF field command, however, sparking a split within that organization.

Today both groups say they favor unity—but their approaches and proposed timetables for realizing it are quite different. The ELF has launched a campaign throughout Eritrea under the slogan, "One organization, one army, one leadership." There are "Unity Teashops" in many villages under ELF jurisdiction and the traveling ELF Band and Drama Group, as well as the monthly publications of the ELF Information Section, echo this theme.

The official position of the ELF since its 2nd Congress in May 1975 favors "unity with the PLF through democratic dialog." Ibrahim Totil, head of the Political and Organizational Office of the ELF and a member of its executive committee told me, "The way to achieve this target is to hold a unifying congress for the two organizations which should be preceded by a coordination period not exceeding one year, during which the corresponding political and information organs should concentrate their efforts to create a suitable atmosphere for unity."

Sebhat Efram, speaking for the leadership for the PLF in a separate interview in which he cited "ideological differences and a long history of contradictions in the political and armed struggle of Eritrean people," called for a longer coordination period that would begin with the establishment of an alliance under a temporary united front. He suggested that initial steps might include reassignment of military forces to share responsibility for all areas under mutual administration, coordination of medical and social services for the fighters and the civilians and a committee to draft a common political program.

While the ELF leaders say they agree with this kind of step-by-step approach, they express fears that a united front, maintaining the separate identity and the right to secede of each front, might be a ploy by the PLF to try to take control of the ELF. The PLF leaders for their part express reservation about a speedy unification that might dilute their political program and weaken their strict discipline.

Eritrean liberation struggle pushes Ethiopian revolution

The Guardian (New York), March 16, 1977

[Byline: Jonathan Kendrick]

What is the relationship of the national liberation struggle in Eritrea to the revolutionary movement in Ethiopia, the oppressor nation?

As the vanguard of the Eritrean revolution, the Eritrean People's Liberation Front (PLF) is leading not only the armed struggle against Ethiopian rule, but also the political struggle to implement the national democratic revolution. At the same time, the PLF emphasizes the need to analyze the class contradictions of Eritrean society in order to mobilize the workers and peasants for class struggle.

And for the past two years, they have been sharing their practical and theoretical knowledge with Ethiopian revolutionaries so as to help them build their military and political struggle. The Ethiopian movement is rapidly gaining momentum, partly as a result of this connection, but the two struggles remain at decisively different stages of historical development.

Both are directed at the ruling military junta in Addis Ababa, which is fighting desperately to defend what it considers to be the allied interests of the incipient Ethiopian bourgeoisie, U.S. imperialism and Israeli Zionism. But the roots of each struggle are not identical, and the growth of the progressive movement in each country has proceeded along related but independent courses.

The national liberation movement in Eritrea arises out of a century of occupation and exploitation by Italy, Great Britain, Ethiopia, the U.S. and Israel. Nearly 16 years of armed struggle have given the Eritrean liberation forces the test of practice, during which they have forged a highly developed theoretical analysis from Marxist-Leninist principles applied to their particular historical conditions. This analysis is now serving as the basis for the PLF to sink its roots deeper among the Eritrean people and to raise the movement for national independence to a higher level of class struggle for social as well as political revolution (Guardian, March 9).

The differing development of the progressive forces in Ethiopia has to be understood in the context of its recent history. While Eritrea was being shaped by the Italian colonial experience at the turn of the century, the Ethiopian feudalists were doubling Ethiopia's territorial frontiers by gaining sovereignty over what is now called southern and southeastern Ethiopia and expanding their hegemonic control over the nationalities which inhabited these areas. Class and national oppression were intertwined in various forms as feudal relations were strengthened where they had already existed and initiated where they had not.

Classes in Ethiopia

Following the violent disruption brought by the Italian conquest between 1935-41, the traditional Ethiopian ruling classes of highland nobility and Coptic clergy resumed control of the empire under the leadership of Haile Selassie I. Some of the best lands were taken by Selassie and his family and by foreigners for plantation farming. The burden on the peasants throughout the empire grew steadily heavier. Oppression of many nationalities was intensified through cultural domination, linguistic restriction and religious persecution thus feeding traditional antagonisms between regions and nationalities.

Simultaneously, a sizable new middle class of intellectuals, government bureaucrats and military officers grew via the American-designed general education system and a variety of civilian and military training programs here in the U.S. The kernel of a multinational proletariat also began to form in Addis Ababa and two or three other towns where light industry was established by foreign capital.

By 1974 the rising expectations of the petit bourgeoisie—frustrated by the emperor's autocratic resistance to the development of a national bourgeoisie and to bourgeois democratic reforms—had combined with the increasing dissatisfaction of the urban workers and the explosive anger and desperation of the suffering peasantry, literally dying by the tens of thousands in the central highlands as the result of a drought which Haile Selassie refused to recognize. This gathering fury erupted in spontaneous uprisings against the emperor.

By February students and teachers all over Ethiopia went on strike to demand among other things radical changes in land tenure for the peasants. In March the trade unions walked out in a general strike demanding sweeping political changes as well as improvements in their immediate working conditions. Discontent in the military showed itself in a series of revolts against higher officers beginning in the Ogaden and spreading to Massawa and Asmara, the Eritrean capital, over issues of pay raises, reform and the growing war in Eritrea.

No outside force, no organized liberation movement or party brought down Haile Selassie and his feudal retinue. Instead, internal conditions caused an accelerating collapse which left a vacuum at the top. Into this political vacuum stepped the Provisional Military Advisory Council (PMAC)—made up of 100-200 junior officers and enlisted men—who began in late spring to arrest members of the emperor's cabinet. Finally, in September, when the PMAC had firmly taken power, Haile Selassie was unceremoniously deposed.

For the next three months the proclaimed revolution seemed to stand still. But inside the Dergue—as the PMAC came to be known—there was a scramble for power which climaxed in November 1974 in the execution of Dergue chairman Gen. Andom Aman (an Eritrean by birth), in a partial coup d'etat which was obscured by the simultaneous execution of 59 feudal leaders. The move served to bring Maj. Mengistu Haile Mariam and his nationalist following to prominence within the Dergue.

In December 1974, the Dergue began to respond to the impatient cries of the people for the antifeudal revolution to be carried through. Official proclamations declared Ethiopia to be on the road to socialism, albeit a nationalistic variety to be patterned after Tanzania under the slogan "Ethiopia First." In this context the new leaders called for the long-awaited land reform to begin.

Having thus attempted to step out in front of the tide rushing across the empire, the Dergue moved quickly to consolidate its rule. Students and teachers who threatened to revolt if the promised revolution lagged were scattered across the countryside in a hastily conceived rural development campaign. In February 1975 a military campaign was mounted in Eritrea to eradicate the national liberation forces. Minor benefits were offered to the Ethiopian workers, but by mid-1975 their protests were being met with the arrest of trade union leaders. And in September, 15 members of the airline workers union were gunned down at the airport for handing out anti-Dergue leaflets.

While the Dergue had maneuvered itself into a coincidence with the popular will in early 1975, by the end of the year a yawning gap had opened up between the junta and the people. An underground movement known as the Ethiopian People's Revolutionary Party (EPRP) was growing among the students, workers and progressive petit bourgeoisie. The army had suffered major defeats in Eritrea and was trapped inside fortified enclaves in perhaps a dozen towns. Regional movements were developing among several of the nationalities. Opposition to the Dergue was springing up everywhere.

By the spring of 1976 the Dergue reacted to this mounting pressure once again with a combination of empty leftist-sounding rhetoric and brutal repression. A National Democratic Revolution was announced in April, followed in May by a program of "regional autonomy" for the provinces including Eritrea. In late May and early June the forced march of Ethiopian peasants known as the Wodezemach was launched against Eritrea. Dozens of workers and students who protested the campaign in several towns and cities were arrested or killed.

Today the position of the Dergue has deteriorated still further. On the inside, Mengistu Haile Mariam—now Lt. Col.—has finally consolidated his power by staging a series of coups and liquidating his opposition. In the country at large the feudalists of the Haile Selassie era are for the most part dead, imprisoned or exiled, but the land reform has yet to be fully carried out because the Dergue has not been able to mobilize even the army to implement its high-sounding program. Other announced goals such as regional autonomy and equality for the nationalities are similarly stalled, although the religious domination of the Coptic Christian Church has been at least lessened.

Rightist Opposition

Meanwhile, opposition has coalesced around several organizations. In the north, where hostility toward the central imperial regime had a long history, two movements have developed. A coalition of feudal landlords, exiled generals and disaffected bourgeois elements is leading the Ethiopian Democratic Union (EDU). It is an army of peasants and refugees who have been recruited on the basis of appeals to traditional loyalties, fears of religious persecution by the Dergue and promises of booty upon victory. The EDU recently made news when it took over the town of Humera near the tri-national border with Ethiopia, Sudan and Eritrea. They are a classic Ethiopian army which depends wholly on military force for its strength. Thought by many observers to be aided by the CIA, it is known to be well-armed and equipped.

Elsewhere in the Tigre Administrative Region, the Tigre People's Liberation Forces (TPLF) are expanding in less dramatic but more substantial form. With meager material resources but with the power of historical materialist theory, the TPLF is less engaged in military combat than in mass mobilization of the peasantry. (There is no industry and no proletariat in this region).

Consciously patterned after the PLF, many of the leading cadre of the TPLF were trained in Eritrea and initiated in armed political struggle against the Dergue there. During the so-called Wodezemach in May-June 1976 the TPLF mounted joint military actions with the PLF in northern Tigre and, with the allied forces of the Eritrean Liberation Front (ELF), a second Eritrean fighting force, stopped the abortive invasion before it even crossed the Eritrean border.

In the urban areas the opposition has centered around the EPRP, a fledgling Marxist-Leninist party. Last year the group initiated armed struggle in the central highlands as the Ethiopian People's Revolutionary Army and has opened a campaign of political assassination in Addis Ababa. The only multinational party in Ethiopia, it has attracted a broad backing among anti-Dergue progressives but has singularly failed so far to unite with the oppressed nationalities, a precondition for a successfully revolutionary movement. Recent attempts to demand hegemony over all anti-Dergue forces have been met by sharp resistance from even the TPLF.

Against this historical backdrop and in the context of the substantial differences in the levels of socioeconomic development of the two countries (see Guardian, March 2), the policy of the PLF to ally with but not merge into the EPRP, the TPLF or any aspiring all-Ethiopia movement must be evaluated. Sharing the same enemy, PLF points out, does not necessarily call for merging unevenly developed progressive forces, nor for an identity of tactics.

While committed to national independence for Eritrea, the PLF has developed into a principled political vanguard whose deeper commitment to social revolution calls forth an internationalist solidarity with the neighboring Ethiopian people. This solidarity takes concrete form in the PLF's practice of giving military and political training as well as material support to the TPLF and EPRP.

The TPLF and the EPRP reciprocate in the same spirit of internationalism by declaring their firm support for Eritrean independence. In March 1976 representatives of the PLF leadership and the EPRP central committee signed a joint statement unconditionally supporting Eritrean independence and calling for military and material cooperation in their two struggles to implement the national democratic revolution in both Eritrea and Ethiopia.

The Dergue's days in Addis Ababa are clearly numbered. The key to Ethiopia's future, however, lies not with the inevitable collapse of the junta but rather with the development of the Ethiopian progressive forces around a leadership which can apply a proletarian ideology to the particular forms of exploitation and national oppression in Ethiopia.

The future in this region may well see a voluntary confederation between Eritrea and Ethiopia, perhaps between Eritrea and several autonomous states constituted out of the ashes of the Ethiopian empire. However, such a confederation would not be possible before the achievement of genuine independence for all parties so that any union can be one between equals and on the basis of a common ideology tested and proven in social practice.

ETHIOPIA, ERITREA & U.S. POLICY

The Fifteen-Year War

The Nation (New York), March 19, 1977

In Ethiopia, a military junta known as the Dergue (Amharic for "committee"), composed of nationalists and self-proclaimed Socialists and heavily dependent on American military and economic assistance, is increasingly threatened by civilian protest in the towns, armed revolt in the countryside, and a bitter fifteen-year-old war for independence in the ex-Italian colony of Eritrea.

At the same time debate is underway within the new administration in Washington over whether or not to maintain the high levels of aid to the ailing Ethiopian military regime in the face of a chronic instability and mounting evidence of widespread political repression that call into question the Dergue's ability to govern. This debate threatens to go public soon with the release of at least three major reports of massive human rights violations in America's longest standing client-state in Africa.

The first report will come from the State Department itself, in accordance with a new law that requires such reports to accompany any requests for Security Assistance (a euphemism for arms). Sources who have seen the embassy's December report, on which State is basing its evaluation, say that the situation is acknowledged to be appalling. In spite of this, the study recommends that, because of overriding interests in the region, we should maintain a "wait-and-see" approach with continued aid.

The other two reports—one prepared by a delegation of Senators who recently visited Ethiopia and one produced by an independent human rights organization—will probably dispute these conclusions, since they reportedly document consistent patterns of flagrant denials of human and civil rights which journalists have been describing sporadically over the past two years.

A bizarre series of alleged coups, counter-coups and assassinations has recently called international attention to this situation. The shoot-out in early February among top leaders exemplified their ruthless desperation. Knowledgeable observers have long speculated that Lt. Col. Mengistu Haile Mariam was striving to be the most powerful member of the Dergue, but there have been repeated efforts by contending forces to divert some of his power to themselves. A recent attempt to set constitutional limits on the various elements of the ruling group resulted in such a curb on him. Within weeks, an attempted "coup" was discovered and leaders of Left and Right factions, including Gen. Teferi Bante, nominal chairman of the Dergue, were killed. Mengistu—described as a strong nationalist who arrived at his "Socialist " politics opportunely after assuming power—survived the takeover.

Elsewhere in the fragile empire, however, the challengers are less easily disposed of. The Ethiopian Democratic Union, a rightist army of old landlords and generals from Haile Selassie's imperial court, is challenging the Dergue in the northwest. The Tigrai People's Liberation Front, a tightly disciplined guerrilla army patterned after the Eritrean People's Liberation Forces (EPLF) in the north, is escalating its activities in the northeast. Somali-backed guerrillas periodically harass Ethiopian forces in the southeast. An Oromo

Liberation Front has begun an armed uprising in the southwest. The Ethiopian People's Revolutionary Party, advocating a program of civilian rule, has developed a broad constituency in towns and cities in nearly all the provinces. And the allied forces of the Eritrean Liberation Front (ELF) and the EPLF have very nearly won a military victory in Eritrea by gaining control of all but perhaps a dozen government bases in the larger cities and towns.

The response of the Dergue has been to unleash a fog of revolutionary rhetoric that has thoroughly obscured the political landscape, and at the same time to use the massive military assistance provided by the Nixon/Ford administration to stonewall its opposition. Unable to implement its programs in the rural areas, where 95 percent of the people live a precarious feudal existence, the regime has turned increasingly to policies of terrorism and coercion to hang onto its power.

Nowhere is this more clearly and brutally illustrated than in Eritrea, where a two-year military campaign by the Dergue has united virtually the entire population behind the two guerrilla armies of the EPLF and ELF. And nowhere is the American role in propping up the Dergue more evident. Last spring I rode into Eritrea with government forces bringing relief supplies to the besieged capital of Asmara. These monthly convoys are protected by sizable Ethiopian military units against ambush by the Eritreans. We were preceded by American-supplied armored personnel carriers, covered from the air by F-86 and F-5 fighter bombers, and surrounded on all sides by Ethiopian soldiers who rode in surplus World War II American vehicles and carried M-1 and M-14 rifles. The final ironic detail was provided by the canteens and web belts where "U.S." was inscribed in 4-inch letters for all to see.

It did not surprise me that Eritreans in the countryside described these troops as American surrogates whose main mission was to protect the National Security Agency base at Kagnew Station in Asmara. While only thirty-five American personnel remain to oversee the operations of this "communications monitoring base," it once housed more than 3,000 who were assigned to listen in on telecommunications as far away as West Africa, the Middle East and Southern Africa. This, our last military base on continental Africa, remains for the Eritreans a powerful symbol of what they are really up against in their bitter struggle for national independence.

Eritrea's strategic location along the southwestern coast of the Red Sea has made it a target for a succession of outside interests. Inheritors of a colonial past that reaches back to the middle of the

16th century, when they were conquered by the Ottoman Turks, the Eritreans were under the domination of Italy in this century until, after Mussolini's defeat, a U.N.-sponsored federation with the Ethiopian Empire was initiated in 1952. Ten years later, its "autonomy" dissolved along with its Parliament and constitution, Eritrea was forcibly annexed by the Ethiopian Emperor and a war for national independence began.

The sequence that followed is a familiar one. Strategic interests, which included the Kagnew Station in the heart of Eritrea and control of the Red Sea, led the United States to send several hundred American advisers from the Military Advisory and Assistance Group (MAAG) to train the Ethiopian army and air force in counterinsurgency techniques. Paralleling the situation in Vietnam, "strategic hamlets" were created with wholesale economic and social disruption in the countryside of Eritrea. Planes furnished by us rained terror onto the civilian population, in order to punish those who might have supported a resistance movement that grew stronger daily in reaction to the coercive and brutal policies of the Ethiopian Government.

The absence of American troops from the front lines and a virtual news blackout by the Ethiopian Government have combined to keep most Americans ignorant of the situation in Eritrea and of our country's deep involvement there. The one notable exception came during the "February War" of 1975 when the Dergue, in one of its first major acts after overthrowing the Emperor, attempted an all-out offensive to crush the independence movement.

Whole villages were leveled as Ethiopian forces took revenge on those suspected of aiding the guerrillas. A corridor 11 miles wide was cleared around the capital city of Asmara and thousands of peasants were forced to flee their homes, evading marauding units of the Ethiopian army and hiding from the ever-present F-5 and F-86 fighter jets which cruised the skies. Nearly 50,000 made their way into crowded, unsanitary camps in neighboring Sudan, while many thousands more remained in improvised shelters or with relatives in other villages.

Several members of the Western press managed to enter Eritrea at this time. One of these, Dial Torgerson of the *Los Angeles Times,* reported on February 14, 1975, that "Government troops have killed hundreds of civilians in an orgy of bloodletting and looting." Among the examples he cited was a massacre of 100 peasants in the village of Woki Deba after they had been rounded up by soldiers and herded into the church where they were assured they would be safe. As the priest begged for mercy, the troops opened fire.

Over the next few months, the occupying Ethiopian army was severely defeated and forced into fortified enclaves in the major population centers, where they remain today. In retaliation for losing control of the rural areas, however, they cut off all humanitarian relief and have barred potential donor nations and organizations from investigating on the scene charges of indiscriminate bombing of civilians, wholesale destruction of crops, well and spring poisoning, and the seizure of donated grains and medicines. Nor are agencies or nations that operate in Ethiopia permitted to assist the civilian population of Eritrea.

Such tactics convinced Commander Assefa Seifu, head of the Eritrean Red Cross Society, to flee in December 1975 to England, where he charged that relief money was being appropriated for military uses while the Eritrean people's needs grew ever more serious. A *Times* of London article on December 21 quotes him as saying, "The money is spent on military supplies and arms which are then used to kill the very people for whom the aid was intended."

With the banning of foreign journalists from Eritrea and the restrictions placed on the few reporters permitted to remain in the Ethiopian capital of Addis Ababa, public documentation of conditions is sketchy. Reports on Eritrea, however, have been chillingly consistent over the past two years, the accounts telling of civilian massacres, martial law, executions without trial, widespread political arrest and torture of suspected dissidents, and random atrocities apparently designed to instill fear in the general populace.

During a seven-month tour that took me to all sides of the conflict I saw dozens of examples for myself. In the government-held city of Asmara I spoke with residents and foreigners (including American officials) who told me of two years of unrelenting terror under the martial law of the Ethiopian army, and I witnessed the execution of more than forty civilians in reprisal for the shooting of one Ethiopian officer. In Asmara and in Sudan I spoke with Eritreans and Ethiopians who had been arrested and tortured for suspected sympathy with the Independence movement. In Addis Ababa, an Eritrean was beaten and arrested as I watched, simply for speaking to me in public. And, finally, in the Eritrean countryside I saw the burned-out remains of villages, the bullet-riddled hulks of clinics and schools and the wounds and scars of the survivors, all of whom asked—"Why, Why does America wage war on us? Why do the American people support the war?"

American involvement in Ethiopia goes back to the end of World War II when the defeat of Italy left a power vacuum in the region. With Britain and France retaining title to most of the rest of Africa, Ethiopia offered us a kind of wedge into the continent. On the heels of a decade of British occupation in Eritrea, we engineered a U.S.-sponsored federation between Eritrea and Ethiopia, followed closely in 1953 by a bilateral agreement with Emperor Haile Selassie whereby we undertook to "guarantee the territorial integrity of Ethiopia"—i.e., to maintain Ethiopian claims on Eritrea—in exchange for a twenty-five-year lease on the base in Asmara and use of the port facilities of Massawa. Since the signing of that agreement we have poured more than $600 million in aid—half of which has been military—into Ethiopia as payment for the base.

Figures for fiscal 1976 show aid to Ethiopia under the Military Assistance Program (MAP) to be $22.9 million out of a total package for all of Africa of $46 million. What is more significant, though, is that the Dergue, using foreign reserves from the takeover of the Emperor's fortune and from the sale of coffee grown on the newly nationalized plantations, has begun to purchase substantial arms for cash. In 1976 they paid $125 million for hardware that included sixteen new F-5Es for use in the war on Eritrea.

State Department spokesmen say privately that Kagnew Station is on the way out. A "gap-stopper" communications satellite is already in place, although there is some lag in the installation of ship-borne transmitters and no official target date has been set for closing the base. The agreement runs out in 1978, however, so some decision must be reached by next fall.

What is perhaps more noteworthy is the substantial presence of the Soviets in neighboring Somalia, a legacy of the Kissinger era. Somalia and Ethiopia have a long history of antagonism based principally on Somali irredentist claims to the Ogaden region of southeastern Ethiopia which the Emperor Menelik conquered at the turn of the century. With the steady growth of the Ethiopian military, the Somalis, after a snub from the United States, turned in the late 1960s to the USSR for economic and military aid. Today this very aid has evolved into the primary American argument for continued assistance to Ethiopia.

Fears of a confrontation between Somalia and Ethiopia over the imminent independence of the French Territory of Afars and Issas, and Israeli fears of Arab influence in Eritrea were also cited by the last administration as justifications for maintaining support for the

Dergue, regardless of its internal political difficulties.

It is here that the Carter administration must meet head-on the challenge of living up to its campaign promises. The situation which the Carter people inherit is one in which geopolitical considerations of Soviet/American parity have consistently overridden local factors. America's relations with other peoples of the Third World have largely been determined on a global checkerboard of Soviet and American squares seen so abstractly as to blend one into another. Will this change radically under Carter? Will we now evaluate each situation according to criteria that include respect for a basic level of human rights?

Ultimately, of course, the question is political, not simply moral. The Kissinger strategy was one of short-term goals based upon the ability of American and third-party efforts to inhibit change, to reify a particular circumstance and then to hold on as long as possible in the knowledge that we could not ultimately win. Carter's somewhat evangelical vision, on the other hand, suggests the possibility of final American victory if only we behave ourselves and encourage the forces of good over evil. In the Carter scheme of things internal conditions become the starting point for determining policy, even if it must still be evaluated within the context of geopolitics.

A major realignment of forces may therefore be getting underway in Ethiopia. With Sudan nuzzling up to the United States behind Egypt and with Saudi Arabia willing—according to Ambassador Akins's testimony before the Senate Foreign Relations Committee last summer—to open up channels of aid to Somalia and thereby reduce its dependence on the Soviet Union, the Dergue's instability takes on a different light.

They are losers; no amount of aid or advice at this stage will alter that simple fact. Although they once coincided with a national rising against the corrupt feudal regime of Haile Selassie, they no longer command a popular following. Growing more desperate and more erratic with each day, they will fall in the end, though to whom it is not yet so easy to say. The question, then, is whether we reduce our support and thereby hasten the process, hoping to pave the way for friendly relations with the government or governments which follow, or we hang on to the last moment with Kissinger-like attempts to manipulate the situation in our favor.

A pullback would be accompanied by a shift of attention toward the Sudan, a move already underway at the end of 1976 with the reopening of economic aid and the sale of military transport planes after a five-year hiatus in our relations with the Nimeiri government.

And more attention would probably be paid to the autocratic Kenyatta regime in Kenya, and our Diego Garcia base in the Indian Ocean would continue to grow. By thus surrounding Eritrea, Ethiopia and Somalia, any risks we run by releasing our shaky grip on the Dergue would fade in importance and allow for maneuvering through the Saudis, while we credited ourselves publicly with being motivated by moral considerations.

Before us lie two clear options if we choose to back off: the dismantling of the base in Eritrea and the suspension of military assistance and cash sales to the Dergue. What might follow is considerably less obvious. What kinds of guarantees can we give or solicit from others to protect Ethiopia from Somali attack? What of our sizable economic assistance? And what of the more than 100,000 Eritrean refugees in Sudan, homeless there as the direct result of our arms assistance to the Ethiopian army and air force?

These and many other questions regarding our responsibility for the consequences of the Kissinger policy in Ethiopia and Eritrea will have to be raised on the way to an overall re-evaluation of policy, but the clock is running out on the Dergue and there is little time left for American initiatives of any sort. Today, the lesson of the American defeat in Indochina lies heavily over the Horn of Africa. National liberation forces there too are inflicting a decisive military defeat on unpopular forces backed by the United States since 1953. With the writing so clearly on the wall, a strategic withdrawal to a broad encirclement of the area appears to be the only viable option left. Pragmatists that they are, Carter's strategists cannot have failed to perceive this between the lines of the spate of reports of human rights violations in Eritrea and Ethiopia.

Eritrean liberation struggle escalates

The Guardian (New York), July 6, 1977

As the U.S., the USSR and regional governments in the Horn of Africa maneuver and realign, the Eritrean war for national liberation appears to be gaining strength.

Eritrea's struggle for independence from Ethiopia has been going on for 16 years: The area constitutes Ethiopia's only access to the Red Sea.

Honed to a sharp edge by more than a decade of armed struggle against the combined forces of Ethiopian feudal reaction, U.S. imperialism and Israeli Zionism, the Eritrean revolution continues to cut through new obstacles to liberation concocted by the opportunistic military junta that deposed Emperor Haile Selassie in 1974 and now seems to be allying itself with the Soviet Union.

The support received by some elements of the Eritrean struggle from conservative Arab regimes clouds the picture. But the clarity of the Eritrean People's Liberation Front (EPLF) line on self-reliance and nonalignment leaves little room for genuine confusion. Misunderstandings arise because of the mistakes by those on the left as well as the right who lump together all anti-Dergue forces under the heading of the Eritrean Liberation Front (ELF), which is only one of two organizations fighting for liberation. (The Dergue is the name of Ethiopia's ruling body, led by Col. Mengistu Haile Mariam, who has promised to "crush" the Eritrean movement.)

The Eritrean struggle is further complicated by the activities of the former foreign representative of the EPLF, Osman Saleh Sabbe, who identifies himself as the leader of the "Eritrean Liberation Front-People's Liberation Forces," a term that arose from an abortive attempt on Sabbe's part to merge the leaderships of the ELF and EPLF, resulting in his expulsion from the EPLF leadership in March 1976.

Sabbe's intimate relations with many of the reactionary regional regimes on the Arabian peninsula give him access to the bourgeois media, which repeat his wild claims and declarations uncritically.

Sabbe actually speaks for little more than a small clique of cronies whose hold on funds contributed—but not passed along—to the EPLF prior to their expulsion (estimates run as high as $2.5 million) provides them with the means to exaggerate their strength by subsidizing an expatriate force of untrained refugees numbering about 1500 which has yet to see combat inside Eritrea.

Sabbe's willingness to collaborate with the same forces of imperialism against which the Eritrean struggle has been fighting for years makes him a prime target for U.S. manipulation—but the effect in the field is minimal. It is only in the area of world opinion that he is potentially dangerous.

Political Differences

More of a problem within and without Eritrea is the contradiction between the two liberation fronts: ELF and EPLF. The political differences between them are basic and ideological, having to do with the class line which dominates in each front and which defines the revolutionary practice of each organization.

The ELF's principal tactic in its propaganda battle with the EPLF has been to deny these differences, but their unwillingness until now to accept the EPLF's proposal to form a United National Front since calling off their war to exterminate the EPLF two years ago belies their public statements.

The ELF leaders have in fact played upon anti-Ethiopian feeling in the Arab world to garner support from Syria, Iraq and the Sudan. Recent reports indicate that money from Sabbe which comes from Persian Gulf states and from Saudi Arabia among others is also finding its way into ELF coffers.

Since the break with Sabbe in 1976, the EPLF has had very little material support from any external sources. Political support comes from a number of organizations and liberation movements and from the People's Democratic Republic of Yemen across the mouth of the Red Sea. The PDRY also maintains diplomatic relations with Ethiopia but has no relationship with the ELF. Principal among other EPLF supporters are Polisario in the Western Sahara, the PFLO in Oman and the PLO in the Middle East.

Sudan's new policy of supporting all opposition to the Dergue has fueled the impression of neocolonial backing for the Eritrean struggle, but a closer look reveals the complexities of this view, too.

A traditional hostility between Sudan and Ethiopia had always encouraged a sympathy for the Eritrean struggle, but Sudanese fears of an independence movement in southern Sudan had offset any inclination toward outright support until quite recently. Ethiopian air attacks on targets inside the Sudanese border and a huge influx of refugees from Eritrea and Ethiopia over the past year put increased pressure on Gen. Jaafar Nimeiry, the Sudan's chief of state. A recent coup attempt against him, which he alleges was aided by Ethiopia and Libya, pave the way for Nimeiry to strengthen his power internally by suppressing opposition elements and externally by allying himself more closely with Egypt, Syria, Saudi Arabia and the U.S.

He came out publicly for Eritrean independence last December, but his actual support consisted only of permitting supplies to pass through Sudanese territory on their way to Eritrea, a policy which had been tacitly in effect for years, and in offering anti-Dergue forces access to radio facilities.

Of five organizations which were offered invitations to beam broadcasts over the border by Nimeiry, only the ELF and the reactionary forces of the Ethiopian Democratic Union accepted the opportunity. The three main progressive organizations in Eritrea and Ethiopia—the Ethiopian People's Revolutionary Party, the Tigrai People's Liberation Front and the EPLF all declined.

In the early 1970s, when Sabbe was soliciting funds for the EPLF, support had come also from Libya (which now supports the Dergue) and from several Arabian states which have held up aid since the break. The main source of supply for the EPLF, however, is and has always been the enemy itself through captured weapons. Recent victories of the EPLF in Sahel province have accentuated their slogan, "Defeat the enemy with his own guns and bullets."

The EPLF emphasizes mass mobilization and self-reliance as the keys to victory, but it has welcomed material assistance from outside when there were no strings attached.

Pressure Resisted

Ba'athist influence has also been a problem. In September 1975 a representative of the Iraqi government went to Eritrea to push for acceptance of the "Khartoum Agreement" which Sabbe had negotiated with the ELF to "merge" with the EPLF. The EPLF was told that if it accepted, it would receive a large quantity of weapons. It if refused, there would be "dangerous consequences." The EPLF refused.

Some thought the EPLF would be hard-pressed without external support, but more than a year has passed without it and the EPLF continues to gain strength militarily and politically. Recent events in the field demonstrate this clearly.

After a six-month siege, the provincial capital of Sahel in northwestern Eritrea was finally taken with a minimal loss of EPLF forces. Two weeks later, the EPLF took the Ethiopian base at Af-Abet, the last remaining enemy outpost in the province. With that, the second-largest province in Eritrea was entirely returned to the Eritrean people.

The EPLF lost 30 fighters at Nacfa to Ethiopia's 420 dead and 170 captured. Several American-supplied planes were reported shot down and reinforcements were all turned back with substantial losses. In the end, the besieged garrison had to be supplied wholly by air, all of which is now in the hands of the EPLF.

At almost the same time, the EPLF held its first national congress else where in liberated Eritrea. The congress passed resolutions on critical internal and external issues and adopted a "National

Democratic Program" which called for the establishment of a people's democratic state with a "self-reliant, independent and planned
economy."

Tentative Unity

The EPLF congress also reaffirmed the organization's call for a
National United Front with the ELF in which the two lines of the
Eritrean struggle could engage each other in democratic dialogue. For
two years the ELF has resisted this offer, calling instead for a merger
of leaderships in order to retain control of their wing of the movement. But the increasing success of the EPLF both in the military field
and in the political field where they have concentrated their resources
on deepening their roots among the Eritrean peasantry appear to have
broken the ELF's resistance to uniting with the EPLF.

For three months representatives of the ELF and the EPLF have
been meeting in the field. Early this month an announcement was
made that they had reached agreement on forming a coordinating
committee to work for national unity that excluded Sabbe as a third
force from all such discussions, a point which the EPLF had also
insisted upon over the past year. The first joint policy announcement
of the committee was to reject the Soviet-backed Ethiopian proposal
for regional autonomy in a new federation with Ethiopia, a proposal
offered also a year ago in slightly different form with U.S. backing at
the time.

Ethiopia organizes peasant militia

The Guardian, New York, July 6, 1977

Ethiopia's military government last week unveiled a newly trained
peasant militia of 100,000 troops who marched through the streets of
Addis Ababa chanting "Death, death!" The militia will reportedly be
used against a variety of forces which oppose the regime, ranging
from the reactionary army of the Ethiopian Democratic Union in the
northwest of Ethiopia to the Somali-backed Western Somali
Liberation Front in the southeast to the national liberation forces of
the EPLF and the ELF in Eritrea.

Government propaganda lumps all of these forces together with the leftist urban guerrillas of the Ethiopian People's Revolutionary Party (EPRP) and the regional armies of several Ethiopian nationalities as counter-revolutionaries "who are making a frantic attempt to throw the Ethiopian broad masses back into the repugnant (feudal) system."

The first action of this militia was reported two months ago when more than 300 students sympathetic to the EPRP were rounded up in Addis Ababa and slaughtered in mass executions. Parents were later charged $100 to retrieve the mutilated bodies.

Almost exactly a year ago behind a similar propaganda campaign, a peasant army known as the "Wodezemach" was thrown together by means of imposing quotas on villages in several northern Ethiopian provinces. Following a call for 100,000 "volunteers," some 40,000 peasants were rounded up and transported to the Eritrean border where they were defeated by the armies of the EPLF and the ELF with support from the EPRP and the revolutionary army of the Tigrai People's Liberation Front (TPLF).

In the year since this abortive march, opposition to the government has increased substantially in the northern part of the country. The TPLF has grown more active militarily and all major roads through the region are closed to regular traffic.

The new peasant militia, better armed and trained, is drawn principally from the southern and central provinces from where junta leader Col. Mengistu Haile Mariam draws his major support. One of the reasons for this is that it is the main region where land reform has been successfully carried out by the Galla peasantry against their Amhara lords, most of whom had settled there at the turn of the century.

With the failure of the regular Ethiopian armed forces to hold back the rising tide of resistance to the junta's brutal rule, this new peasant army is the last card Mengistu has to play.

Rumors of a plan for an Ethiopian accommodation with Somalia over the fighting in the Ogaden region with the WSLF (Western Somalia Liberation Front) and with the Eritreans in their 16-year-old struggle for national independence swept the bourgeois press this spring under headlines of a "Pax Sovetica" said to be proposed by Moscow and apparently supported by Cuban President Fidel Castro on his visit to the region in March.

But subsequent characterizations by the Somalis of the Ethiopian junta as "murderers not socialists" and outright rejection of the proposal by the Eritreans have rendered these last ditch efforts for a "peaceful solution" useless. Castro's recent statements downplaying the Cuban role in Ethiopia seem to suggest a decision to remain at arm's length to see how the conflicting forces resolve themselves— except to support a move by the Ethiopian regime against the monarchist forces of the EDU along the Sudan border.

Eritreans flee massacres
Diary of a visit to an Eritrean refugee camp
The Guardian (New York), July 13, 1977

More than 600,000 Eritreans have been left homeless during the 16 years of fighting between Eritrea and Ethiopia, according to officials of the Eritrean Relief Association (ERA). In addition, more than 140,000 Eritreans are seeking refuge in neighboring Sudan.

Those who have fled Eritrea receive minimal attention from a few international relief groups, including the UN High Commissioner for Refugees and the World Council of Churches, but the plight of the refugees still within Eritrea has reached critical proportions without gaining any response from the outside world.

Because nearly every major international relief organization is involved in aid to the drought-affected areas of Ethiopia, the Ethiopian government has been able to establish a kind of relief-blockade of Eritrea by threatening any would-be assistance group with expulsion from Ethiopia if they offer any help to the Eritreans.

Relief aid to Eritrea for war-related casualties and for a persistent drought and famine which also affected most of northeastern Ethiopia was officially halted by the Ethiopian military government in October 1975. The purpose was to increase the pressure on the liberation forces by striking at the peasant population which supported the fighters. (The Ethiopian government regards Eritrea as a province of Ethiopia. The Eritreans are fighting for their national independence.)

The situation today in Eritrea is similar to that in Ethiopia three years ago when a severe drought struck the central highlands, killing more than 100,000 peasants before the then Emperor Haile Selassie would permit outside agencies to even discuss the problem. His refusal to recognize and respond to that crisis was one of the major factors in his subsequent downfall at the hands of an aroused population.

Once again, the Ethiopian government—now a military junta which claims to be "socialist"—is concealing a crisis and blocking efforts to resolve it with the active collusion of a wide variety of international accomplices. In Addis Ababa, I spoke with UN officials, representatives of private relief agencies and diplomats who acknowledged the situation In Eritrea but claimed they could do nothing without jeopardizing their important programs in Ethiopia.

During a five-week tour of the war-torn countryside of Eritrea, I visited several of the villages wholly or partially destroyed in the fighting, spoke with peasants who had been forced to seek temporary quarters with relatives and friends in neighboring settlements and visited a small refugee camp run by the Eritrean People's Liberation Front (EPLF) in the lowlands of Sahel.

The most seriously devastated area is around Eritrea's capital city of Asmara, where major offensives by the Ethiopian forces in 1967, 1970 and 1975 have displaced over a quarter million people.

In a walking tour, I saw scores of burned-out homes in the now sparsely settled environs of Asmara which suffered most in the "February War" of 1975. The village of Waukie, for example, 20 miles from Asmara and the scene of a mass meeting of the then-warring liberation organizations (EPLF and the more conservative ELF—Eritrean Liberation Front) in November 1974, fell victim to a reprisal raid by Ethiopian ground forces and artillery in early 1975. Two-thirds of the stone houses of Waukie lie in ruin today.

An aging peasant farmer in the village told me that of the 800 people living there before the attack, most had fled when the Ethiopian soldiers came. "But the others of my village," he said, "33 of them, were pulled from their homes and machine gunned here in the village square." He looked around at the piles of stone. "Only 200 live in Waukie now. The rest have gone to villages far away."

Four miles from Asmara and within sight of the outskirts of the besieged city is Woki Deba, a virtual ghost town where one of the worst massacres of the February War occurred.

Mass Execution

I was taken to the village church by several peasants who explained what had happened. They said that government troops rounded up as many of the 300 residents as they could find and brought them to the church, telling them they would be safe. As the local priest begged for mercy, 85 people were executed and left to be buried by the survivors.

All of the villages in this region are now occupied by fighters of the EPLF and the ELF and defended by captured .50 caliber U.S.-made Brown or Chinese-manufactured Dashka machine guns, but fear has kept most inhabitants from returning. Farther from Asmara, however, some of the people have adapted themselves to the exigencies of wartime and resettled near their old homes.

A member of the rapidly expanding militia in the town of Adi Worehi, 30 miles from Asmara, took me through the remains of his decimated village and explained what had taken place. Watching from nearby hills, the people saw Ethiopian soldiers throw gasoline on the grass roofs of every house in the town and then ignite them in one blazing inferno. Over 260 houses were destroyed.

Most of the town's 750 inhabitants were still in the forest or in other villages, he explained, but 150 had come back to rebuild. Scattered among the surrounding hills, with as much as a half-mile between houses, these people had constructed cave-like shelters hidden from airplanes in the natural shelter of the rocky terrain and they were tenaciously holding on to their ancestral homelands.

Two hundred miles away in the northwestern province of Sahel, I was escorted through a refugee settlement run jointly by the EPLF and the ELF for people who had fled the embattled highlands for neighboring Sudan. A spokesman for the EPLF said that efforts were being made to keep the refugees inside Eritrea and to encourage those in Sudan to return to their home country.

When we arrived at the settlement, in a thickly wooded area, we were invited into a tent on the river bank for a rest and tea while a group of village leaders gathered to meet with us. Outside we could hear the sounds of children playing.

According to the elders, there were 800 people in the settlement but in the 18 months of its existence in three locations, as many as 30,000 refugees had passed through, most on their way to Sudan.

"They come by foot and by truck with the fighters," said one of the village leaders, "often in large groups from a town recently attacked by the Ethiopians. With most of the young ones joining the front, those who come here are the old, the very young and the sick."

Upon arrival, he said, a family is assigned to a settled family for temporary shelter and then sent to the small clinic located in the village for a physical examination and an evaluation of the nutritional needs of the family that would determine the size of their ration.

Before going to see the clinic and the food store we toured the living area. All the tents were the same—10 x 12 canvas tents without floors but with sturdy fly leaves and flaps to protect against the rain that would come soon.

The first tent that we approached housed a family of five which had come from a village near the port of Massawa nine months ago after their house had been burned and many of their relatives killed in a reprisal raid by Ethiopian troops.

The woman who lived in this tent with four of her young children told us that her husband and two older sons had gone to fight with the front. "Life in the camp is good enough," she said, "but we'll stay here only until we can return to our village."

The next tent was set back under the trees and covered with loose branches. The area in front was neat and carefully swept but inside the furnishings included only a few blankets and cooking utensils. An 80-year-old man lived here with his wife and granddaughter. They had escaped from the village of Hirgigo a year ago during a massacre that reportedly took the lives of 500 villagers.

According to the old man, the Ethiopian soldiers came at 4 in the morning. First they fired artillery into the village and then they came on foot, going from house to house to kill those who had not been able to escape at the first explosions of artillery. Some went back the next day, he said, but many fled empty-handed and became refugees.

The Hirgigo massacre is one of several that we heard mentioned again and again. Another one is the Em Beremy massacre of February 1976. On our way to another tent, we encountered two old men lying in the sun who had escaped from Em Beremy where, they said, over 200 were killed in a reprisal raid after an Ethiopian checkpoint near Massawa had been overrun.

A dozen other families with whom we spoke told similar stories of murder and destruction in the towns of Keren, Mai Habar, Belesa, Maya Dega and Asmara. They had left their homes with nothing but the clothes on their backs and what few things they could carry.

In contrast to the crowded and unsanitary conditions reported in the camps in Sudan or the fearful hand-to-mouth existence of many in the highlands, this settlement was a virtual "utopia." But as one member of the Eritrean Relief Association observed, this was only 800 people out of 600,000 in similar straits. "Without massive assistance from the outside," he said, "we cannot hope to care for more than a small percentage of them."

Eritrean struggle nears final victory

The Guardian (New York), July 20, 1977

The 16-year-old Eritrean struggle for national liberation is rapidly moving toward the final stages of victory.

As Ethiopia rushes troops from across its beleaguered empire to reinforce its demoralized forces in Eritrea, the allied armies of the Eritrean People's Liberation Front (EPLF) and the Eritrean Liberation Front (ELF) are intensifying the pressure on the encircled town and cities. They are capturing them one by one.

The failure of the regular troops to hold their positions in Eritrea has led the Ethiopian junta to raise a peasant army of 100,000 men to try a last ditch campaign to hold onto the strategic Red Sea territory. Some 40,000 of these peasant irregulars are reported to be near the Eritrean border, where they are already coming under attack. Like the Ethiopian army inside Eritrea, they are being defeated.

Early last week the EPLF liberated Decamare, the second largest city in Eritrea. By week's end they had taken the town of Keren, thereby severing the link between the few remaining Ethiopian bases in western Eritrea and the Ethiopian headquarters in the Eritrean capital of Asmara.

The ELF is attacking the western base at Barentu and is stepping up attacks on the Ethiopian garrison in the city of Agordat. There are also reports of ELF attacks inside the port city of Assab, far to the south, near the newly independent Republic of Djibouti (formerly French Somaliland).

Carefully developing their strategy of step-by-step people's war, Eritrean liberation forces have moved gradually but steadily to consolidate their control of the rural areas, mobilize the Eritrean masses to support and participate in the struggle, and finally to encircle and attack the Ethiopian forces in the towns and cities.

Political Differences

Political differences between the ELF and the EPLF had retarded the military struggle until recently, when a tentative agreement was reached on forming a united front. Since then the two groups have coordinated their strategies and moved decisively to retake the remainder of their country from Ethiopia. Ethiopia illegally annexed the former Italian colony in 1962 after subverting a UN-sponsored federation that had been in effect since 1952.

During the past two years both fronts have begun to develop communication and transportation networks and social services for the civilian population, while consolidating their military forces.

In order to raise the level of military struggle, certain political objectives had to be reached. Some form of unity between the ELF and the EPLF had to be agreed upon if they were to win independence and form a viable government. And the Eritrean masses had to be mobilized to join the struggle if the revolution to liberate the land and people was to be carried through.

The EPLF and the ELF differed on these key points. The ELF called for immediate unity between the leaderships of the contending liberation armies and emphasized the military aspect of the national liberation struggle. The EPLF favored a united front between two autonomous organizations that would lead over time to a principled political unity that included the Eritrean people.

Meanwhile the EPLF concentrated its main efforts on mass mobilization and political education, broadening and deepening its roots among the exploited workers and the oppressed peasantry. Within the EPLF, Marxist-Leninist forces struggled with backward elements for leadership, winning hegemony in 1976 when the EPLF expelled its reactionary foreign mission led by Osman Saleh Sabbe.

The EPLF Program

The national democratic program approved at the first EPLF national congress in early 1977 solidly reflects the political ascendancy of Marxist-Leninist forces in the EPLF. It concretely outlines a strategy for economic and social development which relies on the strength and initiative of the Eritrean masses led by advanced workers and other progressive elements. This development will lay the basis for the transition to socialism, according to the EPLF.

The EPLF program draws heavily on their experience in organizing the peasantry in the liberated areas. Many national objectives of the program have already been implemented and tested at the village level including plans for democratic village administration, land reform and literacy training.

The ELF, in contrast, has tended to postpone political development. It has a considerably smaller number of trained political cadre than the EPLF, has postponed land reform and relies on old chiefs and merchants for village administration and liaison with ELF units.

The ELF includes a broad array of class interests united loosely around patriotic aims and nationalist goals. There are progressive elements under the ELF umbrella, but petty-bourgeois ideology dominates the front.

The EPLF holds that a united front offers the possibility of democratic dialog to resolve what it considers to be secondary contradictions between the two fronts. Their assumption is that their correct political line and their strength among the Eritrean masses will bring about a political victory.

The EPLF's recent political and military victories, together with changes in Ethiopia and in the international context of the struggle, appear to have convinced the ELF leadership to follow the EPLF line on forming the united front. Last month a tentative unity agreement between the ELF and the EPLF was signed.

The practicality of this strategy has been borne out by dramatic developments in the military struggle.

EPLF Military Victories

A series of smashing victories over the past several months has built up an EPLF momentum which could well carry them into the capital of Asmara before year's end. A half-dozen major towns and cities have been taken, shrinking the Ethiopian ability to strike back and swelling the Eritrean arsenal with captured weapons and equipment.

In January the EPLF liberated the town of Karora, near the western Eritrean border with Sudan. After a 5-month siege, the provincial capital of Nacfa fell in late March, yielding a million rounds of captured ammunition and a large quantity of light and heavy weapons.

The Ethiopians attempted to relocate the capital in Af Abet, but this town fell to the EPLF in early April. Later that month the agricultural center of Ela Bered in Senhit province was taken, and in mid-May the EPLF liberated the copper-mining town of Debarwa.

The liberation of Karora, Nacfa and Af Abet left the entire northern Sahel province in the hands of the EPLF and allowed the release of many fighters to the southern front. The victories this month in Decamare and Keren are the result.

Keren is the second provincial capital to be taken by the EPLF. Decamare, a major industrial center before the war, is the largest city to return to Eritrean control.

Both Keren and Decamare were heavily fortified and well supplied. Their capture demonstrates the EPLF's ability to win conventional battles against the strongest Ethiopian defenses. It also provides sizable additions to the EPLF arsenal, including several tanks and armored personnel carriers.

The ELF has had mixed military successes. In May they liberated the agricultural town of Tessenei in the heart of the liberated zone of Barca province. A precipitous capture of the town of Barentu, however, was turned around by Ethiopian reinforcements from Agordat who drove the small ELF force into the surrounding hills. Today the ELF again has Barentu under siege.

Preparations for Final Campaign

Reports of Ethiopian preparations for a final campaign have indicated large-scale troop movements to Ethiopian bases inside Eritrea. As the number of these bases declines weekly, the Ethiopian forces become increasingly vulnerable.

With Ethiopian morale at its lowest point in the 16-year war, the possibility also increases of internal collapse by the occupying forces. Desertions by Ethiopian soldiers are common and the likelihood is growing of large-scale mutinies such as the one in 1974 that toppled the late Emperor Haile Selassie.

At this late stage, the Eritrean victory appears assured. The question is only how, when, and what will follow. For the EPLF, national independence is only one small step in the long struggle for the liberation of the Eritrean land and people.

Behind Ethiopia's 'socialist' mask
Essentially conservative junta fights on several fronts
The Guardian (New York,) July 27, 1977

Despite its leftist-sounding rhetoric, Ethiopia's military government is essentially a conservative military junta defending the interests of a would-be national bourgeoisie against the revolutionary aspirations of Ethiopian workers and peasants.

Lacking the strength to survive on its own, this class has been maneuvering to align with one superpower or another to prop it up against growing opposition from broad segments of the Ethiopian population. The junta has recently shifted allegiance from its U.S. and Israeli backers and has moved much closer to the Soviet Union, which now characterizes the regime as "socialist."

The government's dual policies of reform and repression, genocidal war against the Eritrean people and opportunism in international relations reflect its basically bourgeois character and its fundamental inability to carry through the Ethiopian revolution.

The Dergue, as the military rulers are called, is comprised mainly of middle echelon officers drawn from the petty bourgeoisie. They have allied with elements of the small comprador bourgeoisie to displace the feudal nobility in the government bureaucracy, thus spawning a new class of bureaucratic capitalists who have shaped the state machinery to pursue their interests.

Poorly developed as these forces were before the 1974 overthrow of Emperor Haile Selassie, they came under immediate pressure from the revolutionary forces of workers and peasants. Before they could carry through the bourgeois democratic revolution, they were placed on the defensive internally and confronted with a highly developed revolutionary situation in the former Italian colony of Eritrea. Selassie had laid claim to Eritrea in 1962 after dissolving a UN-sponsored federation.

Regime Crushes Progressives

The new regime reacted by setting out to crush the Ethiopian progressive forces while co-opting an opportunist element of the student movement to act as its propagandists. In order to achieve these goals, the government first raised its level of dependence on the U..S. and Israel through substantial increases in military and economic aid. When this failed, it turned to the Soviet Union for similar support.

The Dergue leapfrogged into prominence in 1974 over the backs of protesting workers, students and intellectuals and the oppressed masses of rural peasants who were rising up to challenge Selassie's corrupt feudal rule.

In early 1974, there was a series of mutinies within the armed forces, inspired by the wave of civilian protest sweeping the empire. Initial demands were economic and were quickly met by the emperor. But the persistent political uprisings around Ethiopia eventually found their counterparts within the military.

In the spring, military units held secret elections and constituted a 120-member committee of officers and enlisted men known as the Provisional Military Advisory Council (PMAC). This was later tagged the "Dergue," Amharic for committee. Gradually the PMAC emerged as the only organized force with the power to take on the emperor.

While it was the combined pressure of the Eritrean liberation movement and the revolt of Ethiopian students, workers and oppressed masses which broke the back of feudalism and reaction in Ethiopia, it was the disgruntled and ambitious junior military officers, allied with the nascent Ethiopian bourgeoisie, who stepped forward to take state power.

The New Military Rulers

These officers rapidly consolidated their control of the PMAC. Today less than 20 of the original 120 remain in Addis Ababa at the seat of power. Many were sent to the provinces to replace the imperial bureaucracy. Some officers, like Gen. Aman Andom and Gen. Teferi Bante—who held figurehead posts as nominal chairmen of the PMAC—were executed in internal power struggles. Others have been arrested or have simply disappeared.

Throughout, one man has been consistently in the center of power—then Major, now Lt. Col. Mengistu Haile Mariam. An ambitious officer who in 1975 gloated over Ethiopia's role in UN operations in Korea and the Congo, Mengistu was once quoted as saying that communism is totally bankrupt. Today he is chairman of the Dergue and clearly the head of the government.

The apparent transformation of Mengistu's early anticommunist "Ethiopian socialism" to his alleged "scientific socialism" of today is a graphic illustration of the ideological opportunism which characterizes the Dergue. In an effort to fool the people, the military rulers have adapted their political line to the needs of remaining in power.

The Dergue's first proclamation in 1974 called for a "democratic" form of government that would include the emperor himself. Later, in September, popular demands for his removal finally led the military council to arrest him. Even then, an opening was left for the emperor's son to return from England to replace the deposed autocrat.

Immediately, the previously banned literature of Marx, Engels, Lenin and Mao Tsetung began to surface. Socialism was debated in small meetings and mass gatherings across the empire. Demands for land reform and sweeping political change intensified.

In December the Dergue made its move. Land reform was proclaimed and a kind of classless socialism was declared under the chauvinistic slogan of "Ethiopia Tikdem" (Ethiopia First). Before the students could challenge the limitations of these proclamations, they were dispersed into the countryside in a hastily contrived rural development campaign.

Dergue Intensifies Repression

Following a brief period of unrestricted democratic freedoms, the Dergue moved throughout 1975-1976 to suppress militant workers and other political movements and organizations which had been active in the struggle against Selassie's regime. The Confederation of Ethiopian Labor Unions was banned along with the powerful Teachers Union and the University Students Union. Militant leaders were arrested.

Throughout this period, economic aid from the U.S. and Western Europe continued to play a decisive role in the Ethiopian economy. Three-quarters of the coffee harvest still finds its way to U.S. markets. And trade with Israel through the newly independent city state of Djibouti flourishes, much to the consternation of Djibouti's Arab friends.

A key question in analyzing the international line of the Dergue is the Eritrean question.

Shunning political negotiations, the Ethiopian government has twice in as many years organized massive peasant campaigns against Eritrea, after an all-out campaign in February 1975 by regular troops ended in ignominious failure. In 1976 and mid-1977, Ethiopian peasants were fed lies about Arab invasions of the Ethiopian heartland and sent to their deaths with inadequate weapons and training.

A reign of terror has been directed against the rural Eritrea population by U.S. supplied aircraft. Urban Eritreans have been under martial law and subject to arrest, torture, rape and murder by occupying Ethiopian troops. Despite several public statements about "peaceful solutions," the Dergue has consistently depended on genocidal military campaigns to resolve the conflict.

The Land Question

A key internal question for Ethiopia is the land question. By the time the Dergue stepped into power in 1974, land reform had been a central issue for the progressive movement in Ethiopia for a decade. The Dergue's proclamation in early 1975 was therefore basically acceptance of a longstanding demand from the masses.

Land redistribution, even if fully carried out, is not enough to liberate the oppressed peasantry. The primary question remains who holds economic and political power.

The cycle of the peasant is to grow barely enough to feed the family, sell at harvest time when crop surpluses drive prices down, and buy between harvests when supplies are low and prices high.

Operating in a backward subsistence economy, the peasants are always subject to the slightest change in climate. They live at the knife-edge of existence where holding a small piece of land is no guarantee of survival.

Distribution, storage and technical development are all controlled by local bourgeois elements backed by Western interests. If land reform is not linked to the seizure of political power and the end of capitalist relations of production and exchange, the peasant cannot be liberated.

The Dergue has sought to base its power among backward elements of the peasantry in alliance with the small comprador class in the cities. It has created a network of Peasant Associations as the local instruments of its control These associations have been used to recruit for a "people's militia," essentially an extension of the regular army rather than a local defense force.

Some 100,000 recruits in this new militia are today spread from one end of the empire to the other to back up the demoralized Ethiopian armed forces against mounting opposition. Since this is the planting season for the highlands, the absence of these men from their farms will inevitably result in a new agricultural crisis during the coming year.

The Dergue's ideological face has been a composite of hollow socialist rhetoric and high-sounding appeals to the peasantry. But they serve neither the interests of the workers nor those of the peasantry. Opposition to the regime from workers and students is intensifying. The future role of the peasants in the revolution may provide the key to its outcome.

Eritreans stage new offensive

The Guardian (New York), July 27, 1977

The EPLF has launched a major offensive against the last Ethiopian strongholds in Eritrea.

Units of the Eritrean People's Liberation Front last week began shelling the Ethiopian bases in Asmara and the port city of Massawa with heavy artillery captured from Ethiopian forces in recent victories in the cities of Decamare and Keren.

The attack on Asmara provided cover for a daring EPLF raid on Sembel, the largest of several Ethiopian prisons in the Eritrean capital, in which more than 1000 political prisoners had been held. All were freed, according to an EPLF statement.

Sembel prison is less than a quarter mile from the airport, said to be the most carefully defended Ethiopian base in Eritrea, but the operation was accomplished without a casualty.

The EPLF raid appeared to signal preparations for a major assault on the largest remaining Ethiopia-held city. It follows a carefully coordinated series of attacks on surrounding garrisons which have encircled Asmara and trapped 8000 Ethiopian troops, nearly half the total number now in Eritrea. Another 4000 are 40 miles east of Asmara on the Red Sea coast in Massawa, the other city to come under EPLF artillery attack this week.

Heavy summer rains are keeping the much touted Ethiopian peasant militia from coming to the aid of the regular troops, while fighters of the Western Somali Liberation Front are reported to be attacking the Ethiopian city of Dire Dawa 100 miles southeast of Eritrea.

Dire Dawa is located on the railroad halfway between the Ethiopian capital of Addis Ababa and the port city-state of Djibouti through which over 60% of Ethiopia's trade flows. It is one of Ethiopia's largest cities and sits on the slopes of the Abyssinian highlands from which the Ogaden lowlands of southeastern Ethiopia were conquered three-quarters of a century ago. The WSLF is fighting to retake this area today.

Shift in Eritrean liberation forces

Eritrean People's Liberation Front gains upper hand

The Guardian (New York), August 31 , 1977

Khartoum, Sudan

The balance of force within the Eritrean liberation movement has shifted dramatically in recent months with the revolutionary PLF growing in size and strength and the nationalist ELF apparently falling into disarray.

A series of victories against heavily fortified Ethiopian bases has built up a momentum in the Eritrean People's Liberation Front (EPLF) that has carried them to the brink of what they call "the final assault" on the remaining Ethiopian-held positions.

EPLF forces trained and under arms now exceed 20,000 women and men, nearly the total number of Ethiopian troops in Eritrea. Some 3000 more new recruits are currently enrolled in a 6-month program of political education and military training. They are training at bases in the liberated areas of northern Eritrea and being armed with U.S.-supplied M-14 rifles and Soviet-supplied Kalashnikovs captured by the EPLF in the victories at Nacfa, Decamare and Keren.

Keren, the capital of Senhit province and the second largest city in Eritrea, was considered the most heavily defended Ethiopian position in the former Italian colony, now in its 16th year of armed struggle against occupying Ethiopian forces. Taken by the EPLF on July 8, Keren is remembered by Eritreans also as the site of the British victory against Italy in 1941, a "victory" for Eritrea only in that Eritrea went from being an Italian colony to a British protectorate before being passed on to Ethiopia in a sham federation.

According to an EPLF release, "the Battle of Keren...was the biggest and most ferocious battle ever waged by our resolute and heroic People's Liberation Army, hitherto without parallel in the Eritrean Revolution." Ethiopian forces numbered close to 4000 and were spread over 11 fortified camps, one of which was dug into a strategic hillside overlooking the city. About 1500 prisoners were taken. The rest were killed in action.

A report in Vanguard, the official organ of the EPLF, describes the significance of the capture of Keren: "Keren is not only an important agro-industrial center but also an extremely strategic city forming the key to the lowlands and the gateway to the plateau.... The capture of Keren deprives the enemy of all road links to its camps in the western lowlands which it uses to control Barka—the largest province in Eritrea. Thus, its dwindling forces in Barka and the plateau have been cut apart and isolated from each other."

The Ethiopian garrison at Keren was a rear supply base for the lowland region and was heavily stocked with weapons, equipment and ammunition, now all in the hands of the EPLF. Captured were over 100 trucks and a variety of guns, artillery, mortars, tanks armored cars and rifles, including new Kalashnikovs and Dietrofs recently rushed to Ethiopia by the Soviet Union.

The Barka lowlands have for a long time been the principal liberated area of the nationalist Eritrean Liberation Front (ELF), though in recent months the EPLF is reported to have spread into northern Barka from Sahel province, which the EPLF entirely liberated in March and April.

With the EPLF victory at Keren, the ELF has been greatly assisted in this area, and their forces have tightened the sieges around both Barentu and Agordat, but as yet they have been unable to mount the winning attack.

'Third Force'

The ELF is assisted also in this area by a new third force of hastily trained refugees and young recruits under the banner of the "ELF-PLF," a splinter group which broke off from the progressive EPLF. The leaders of this force were expelled from the EPLF in 1975 after trying to effect a merger between themselves and the ELF leadership to gain control of the Eritrean liberation movement. Denounced as traitors by the EPLF leadership, this small clique retained substantial funds collected from conservative Arab regimes in the Persian Gulf and used the money to quickly create a third army.

Taking its name from the abortive merger agreement, the "ELF-PLF" now numbers around 2-3000. Since all the rural areas of Eritrea were already liberated by the time of the formation of this force, the only way it could take to the field was through the cooperation of the ELF in allowing it into ELF territory. A spokesman for the "ELF-PLF" in Khartoum now claims that his army is fighting alongside ELF forces around Agordat.

Meanwhile, ELF and "ELF-PLF" spokespersons last week announced their intent to fully merge the two armies at the leadership and the fighter levels. As the "ELF-PLF" faction is the most conservative of all the forces in the Eritrean movement, identifying itself solely as nationalists and condemning the Marxist trend in the EPLF, this merger signals a further shift of the ELF leaders toward the right.

Conflicts in ELF

At the same time reports are coming from the field of major conflicts within the ELF. Critics of the ELF have long suggested that the progressive-sounding program and public face of the ELF leaders masked a rightist ideology, but these critics have also pointed out that democratic forces within the ELF opposed this line. Today, the democratic forces are in open confrontation with the leadership.

Whole units of ELF fighters are reported to be mutinying against their leaders, and two members of the 40-member Revolutionary

Command of the ELF are dead in the wake of fighting in Danakil, Barka and the neighboring province of Serai. The rebelling ELF units have so far not come to a decision about whether to make a complete break with the ELF or to remain and struggle. Their actions, however, follow a wave of arrests by the leadership of radicals at all levels.

The current trend of radical opposition to an essentially nationalistic leadership in the ELF mirrors the situation from 1969 through 1971 when repression of left elements in the original ELF led to the formation of the EPLF. At that time the ELF leaders declared a civil war and tried to liquidate the fledgling revolutionary army, but after three years of inconclusive fighting were forced to call a halt under pressure from the civilian population.

Today the situation is different in one critical respect. The EPLF exists in Eritrea as the strongest force militarily and politically, so radicals still within the ELF cannot easily be isolated from the overall struggle. Although the EPLF is not in any way involved in the ELF conflict, its growth and military success serve to isolate the conservative ELF leaders within the movement. The move by these leaders to ally with the "ELF-PLF" clique only exacerbates their isolation from the rank-and-file fighters and from the Eritrean masses.

The EPLF victory at Keren, added to an impressive sequence of successful attacks on a half-dozen other Ethiopian-held towns and cities, moves them to the forefront of the protracted national liberation struggle.

Frightened of the rising EPLF prestige among the Eritrean people, the leaders of the rival forces have sought explanations for recent EPLF victories in bizarre theories of "collaboration" with the Ethiopian government. Taha Mohammed Nur, head of foreign relations for the "ELF-PLF," said in an interview that the Dergue (the Ethiopian term for the ruling military junta) intentionally sacrificed Keren to strengthen the EPLF against the ELF and the "ELF-PLF."

Elaborating on this theme, he told me that the Dergue's plan was to liquidate the old Ethiopian army because it was not fully loyal, replacing it with the newly created peasant militia of some 70,000-100,000 men now spread across the flagging Ethiopian empire. The new militia, according to Taha Mohammed, will be used against the ELF and the "ELF-PLF" and following their liquidation, an agreement will be signed between EPLF and the Dergue to give Eritrea regional autonomy.

The Ethiopian junta has on several occasions suggested its willingness to negotiate separately with the EPLF—but the EPLF has turned them down. In 1976, a letter was sent by the Dergue to the EPLF offering to meet privately, but the EPLF leadership immediately passed the letter along to the ELF as a sign of "good faith."

The EPLF position has consistently been no talks without the ELF and no negotiations for anything short of full and complete independence. Recognizing the ideological differences between the two fronts, the EPLF has repeatedly called upon the ELF to join a united front in which political conflicts could be struggled out democratically.

Moscow Backs Federation

The USSR, which is directly supporting Ethiopia with the backing of some progressive countries, is believed to subscribe to the idea of unity between the EPLF and the ruling Dergue, wherein some form of recognition would be given to Eritrean independence but would not result in a severe loss to Ethiopia. The ELF, which is considered to have the backing of conservative neighboring regimes, would be squeezed out of such an arrangement.

Some commentators insist that the new regime in Ethiopia, which took power in February with Mengistu Haile Mariam at the head, is "revolutionary" and "socialist" and that the EPLF—which may have been correct in rejecting overtures from Addis Ababa before—should now treat with the ruling military junta.

The EPLF, supported by a number of other radical forces, does not believe the new regime is progressive at all and holds that the only way to secure the independence of Eritrea is to fight to the end. For EPLF this means working with the ELF.

The situation in Ethiopia is extremely complex, particularly with progressive Somalia backing the swiftly gaining liberation struggle in eastern Ethiopia at the same time. The USSR has long had fraternal relations with Somalia and is in the embarrassing position of being the major arms supplier to both Somalia and Ethiopia, who are virtually at war.

The Soviet objective is said to effect some kind of solution to the question of Eritrea and the Somali land claims that would not destroy Ethiopia in the process or result in the emergence of a new regime in Addis Ababa which would align with the conservative Arab governments in the area. The ideal solution from this point of view would seem to be some kind of "socialist" federation among Ethiopia, Eritrea, Somalia.

Neither the progressive Eritreans nor Somalis have bought the idea up to now. Both have long-term grievances against Ethiopia and neither, at this point, shares Moscow's view that the new Dergue is Marxist and revolutionary.

Eritrea's EPLF consolidates gains
Military, political victories continue
The Guardian (New York), September 28, 1977

Keren, Eritrea

"Awat nehefash!" – Victory to the masses!

The slogan of the Eritrean People's Liberation Front (EPLF) can be heard from one end of Eritrea to the other.

The fruits of the EPLF's increasing success against Ethiopia's occupation army belong to the Eritrean people, upon whose support the EPLF's protracted struggle depends.

Returning to Eritrea a year after my first visit here in 1976, I am deeply impressed by the EPLF's dramatic progress on all fronts.

In the military sphere the EPLF has delivered a series of crushing blows to Ethiopian forces in the first eight months of this year, cutting the number of their remaining bases in half.

This month the EPLF routed the so-called "Red Army" of conscripted peasant irregulars in heavy fighting southeast of the Eritrean capital of Asmara.

In the first engagement with the new militia, which is armed by the Soviet Union with the latest automatic weapons, more than 1000 peasants were killed when troops of the regular army tried to mount an offensive behind the peasants against the EPLF.

On the political front the EPLF has raised the consciousness of large segments of the population and mobilized thousands through the formation of mass associations.

Social services for the civilian population have similarly expanded. Medical facilities have nearly doubled; schools are springing up throughout the liberated areas.

Public transportation has even been instituted, with nightly bus service to the outskirts of Asmara at a price based solely on the cost of fuel.

Lying along the southwestern coast of the Red Sea, Eritrea is

inhabited mainly by settled agriculturalists with a significant minority of nomads and semi-nomads. In such a society the main issue is the
land question.

Land reform tops the EPLF political agenda and is itself a significant material force in the revolution. Slowly but steadily the old
order—compounded as it was by half a century of Italian colonization prior to annexation by Ethiopia—is being overturned.

Land is being transferred from feudal landlords to the tillers of
the soil. Political power is accruing in the hands of the poor and middle peasants as they are organized into peasant associations and self-
governing village committees.

Two Liberation Fronts

The principal complicating factor in the Eritrean revolution is the
existence of two liberation fronts, recently supplemented by yet a
third force.

Alongside the EPLF is the Eritrean Liberation Front (ELF),
formed in 1961 to initiate the armed struggle for national independence. The EPLF derives from a split within the ELF in 1970 brought
about by the ELF leadership's efforts to liquidate radical elements.

Shunning dialog with growing opposition from the progressive
political forces, ELF leaders declared a civil war against breakaway
units which came together as the EPLF. A temporary alliance between
the EPLF and a conservative faction of the ELF leadership which also
broke away in the ensuing power struggle provided the EPLF with
necessary funds raised from friendly Arab countries.

An uneasy truce was called between the warring fronts in 1974
after the current ruling military junta deposed Emperor Haile Selassie
only to intensify the genocidal campaign in Eritrea. A year later a
strengthened EPLF severed its connection with its fund-raising arm
abroad over efforts by the foreign mission to submerge the EPLF back
into the ELF through a rapid merger of the two armies.

The EPLF's line on unity with the ELF had been and remains a
call for a principled united front in which contradictions can be
resolved through democratic dialog.

Today the EPLF is the dominant force in the Eritrean liberation
movement. The ELF is again racked by internal dissension which is
assuming the proportions of a second civil war. And the ex-foreign
minister of the EPLF has hastily raised a small third army in an
attempt to region a foothold in the movement.

The ELF's current problems are a virtual rerun of the 1970 scenario.

Progressive elements who oppose the leadership's support of the right-wing faction purged from the EPLF are being violently suppressed.

Once again ELF leaders are choosing force over dialog to resolve internal contradictions. In the resulting conflict hundreds of ELF fighters are breaking away to form roving bands of armed opposition. Nearly 1000 fighters have come over to join the EPLF.

ELF Split

It appears that the ELF is in danger of disintegrating altogether and the split reaches as high as the ELF leadership itself. Several members of the ELF Revolutionary Command have recently sought refuge in Sudan.

The EPLF's policy has been not to interfere except to send messages to ELF leaders calling for a peaceful resolution of internal problems. ELF fighters who turn to the EPLF are sent to training camps for thorough political education just as any new volunteers.

This influx into EPLF ranks comes on top of a flow of recruits that has reached nearly 1000 a month. Each EPLF advance has accelerated their momentum.

EPLF victories against heavily fortified Ethiopian bases in the large towns and cities have seasoned the fighters in conventional warfare and yielded a clear knowledge of Ethiopian defensive strategies. Organized in battalion strength last year, the EPLF is now in brigades backed by light and heavy artillery captured from the enemy.

The liberation of Keren in July has even provided three tanks and two armored personnel carriers which are being readied for action with parts made from armor destroyed in the recent battle with the peasant army near Asmara.

The first major clash with the new Soviet-equipped supplement to Ethiopia's demoralized regular forces ended in a full-scale rout only 10 miles from Asmara where the Ethiopian offensive began.

The Battle for Asmara

A trip to the battlefield showed the bodies of hundreds of the peasant irregulars dotting the fields and hillsides where the worst fighting occurred in the abortive 2-week campaign. More than 1000 peasants were killed while used, in effect, as a shield for the regular army. Poorly trained, though well-equipped with the latest Soviet and Czech arms, the peasants were virtually slaughtered.

Interviews with some of those taken prisoner by the EPLF disclosed that the so called Ethiopian "Red Army" is but a pathetic caricature of its namesake.

Wearing the insignia of the hammer and sickle on their lapels, the peasants had no notion of what it stood for, had had no political education with their two months of military training and had little idea of why they had been sent to Eritrea at all.

Mobilized under the pretense of becoming a homeguard militia in their own villages, they had been quite surprised to find themselves transported to Eritrea where they were told they would finish off "a few reactionary elements" of the ELF.

Instead they were thrown head-on against the EPLF, about whom they had no knowledge. One of the prisoners said: "We've been cheated. We weren't even taught to fire properly. We were afraid of our own guns, so when the battle started we hid our heads and shot at the sky."

He said that only the most ignorant peasants had been picked for the militia, those who could neither read nor write and who knew nothing about politics.

Forced into combat with the EPLF, he exclaimed angrily, "This was a kind of massacre!"

Letter from Eritrea
Israelis, Out of Favor in Africa, Still Find Home in Ethiopia

The Washington Post, October 1, 1977

Decamare, Ethiopia

The Marxists who rule Ethiopia are arming their forces with Soviet-made weapons but curiously they prefer to have their training conducted by Israelis, who are out of favor in most of black Africa.

Israelis have trained Ethiopian government forces since 1975 and sometimes have taken a more direct hand in things, an Ethiopian brigade commander, a lieutenant colonel, who defected to the Eritrean side in the country's 16 year-old civil war recently told me. Israeli instructors are said to have trained a special force of 400 elite Ethiopian troops in 1975 and 1976 that now serves as the personal bodyguard of the strongman ruler, Lt. Col. Mengistu Haile Mariam.

Twelve Israeli specialists last year trained 75 Ethiopian instructors who in turn trained the Flame Brigade, a force of 20 battalions and 10,000 troops, the defector said.

"These troops are the most savage in our armed force," he said.

The Israeli advisers played a direct role during the five-month rebel siege of the Ethiopian garrison at Naqfa earlier this year, the defector said.

When Ethiopian airmen proved unable to parachute supplies accurately to the encircled government force, he said, Israelis flew with them to direct the operation. These supply drops were more effective, but nonetheless the garrison fell to the rebels in March.

Since the United States halted military aid to Ethiopia in April, Israel has provided spare parts for the U.S.-made F-5 jet fighters of Ethiopia's air force, he said, and it has also sold Ethiopia some Soviet arms, presumably captured from Arab forces in 1973.

The Ethiopian military government has considered establishing full diplomatic relations with its clandestine ally so that the assistance can be increased, he said. The government of the late Emperor Haile Selassie reluctantly broke relations with Israel at the time of the 1973 Arab-Israeli war, as did most of black Africa. Until then the two had close ties with the Israelis providing numerous military and civilian advisers.

Government forces and guerrillas of the rebel Eritrean People's Liberation Front are dug in within sight of each other a few miles from Decamere and often spend days exchanging occasional small arms fire.

During the late afternoon, gray clouds roll in and by early evening, violent rainstorms begin.

The fighters huddle together under makeshift lean-tos as thunder echoes off the surrounding mountains and lightning flickers in the sky. By midnight the rains abate and the two armies sleep restlessly until dawn brings renewed confrontation and the threat of an all-out attack.

Here in Decamare in the rebel controlled portion of secessionist Eritrea province, prisoners from the army speak of their experiences. They come from all over Ethiopia, a broad cross-section of language and culture. The common denominator is that they are poor, illiterate subsistence farmers who say they were recruited to join a militia to defend their homes.

One young peasant from a village in Tigre province near the Eritrean border said he was picked by his village chief to help fill a quota imposed by the government. A hundred others were gathered and were marched toward Addis Ababa, he said, but nearly half escaped along the way.

At the training camp, he said, the recruits from his village were mixed with peasants from other regions. They had no common language, were forbidden to speak their own and had trouble understanding orders, given in Amharic, the language of Ethiopia's traditional ruling ethnic group.

Another prisoner, a peasant from Gojjam province, said "We weren't even taught to fire properly. We were afraid of our own guns, so when the fighting started, we hid our head or shot at the sky."

On this government soldier's collar was a yellow hammer and sickle on a red cloth background.

I asked him what it meant. He said he didn't know. "Maybe it shows I am a farmer," he mused.

Keren, the third largest city in Eritrea, was captured by secessionist forces last summer and residents say that after 10 years of rigid controls under the Ethiopian government forces, life is returning to pre-war normalcy.

Bicycles are back on the streets after a two year ban. A curfew that was imposed in 1966 has been lifted.

Fruits and vegetables from farms are finding their way into the city markets once again. Street vendors have come to life. Generators damaged in the fighting have been repaired and one day in August the city's lights were turned on again for the first time in weeks.

That afternoon the Eritrean People's Liberation Front paraded captured U.S. made tanks and armored personnel carriers through the streets.

The victorious troops organized a rally that night and, for the first time in 11 years, the citizens of Keren were able to walk about the streets after dark. Thousands of the city's 32,000 residents attended the rally, which.lasted until nearly 3 a.m. singing and dancing and music from electric guitars and an organ.

Keren, a major agricultural center, was considered by Western observers to be one of the key Ethiopian military bases in Eritrea, once an Italian colony.

Vascussi Riguardello, 63, is one of about 20 Italians still living in Keren. Before the war there were 3,000. Riguardello owns Keren's first class Riva Hotel, and he like the city, hopes to make a comeback.

Standing on the roof as we surveyed the sprawling urban landscape, he spoke animatedly about the past and future.

Work on the hotel, built in the pretentious style of the Italian fascist period, was completed at the end of 1966, 12 days after the evening curfew was imposed.

Since then, the flow of tourists and vacationers dwindled steadily. On the eve of the final attack by the rebel forces, there was only one guest in the 50-bed hotel—an Ethiopian government official checking Riguardello's tax records.

The prematurely aged hotel owner says he watched the fighting through binoculars from a fourth-floor balcony and he pointed at baseball size shell pocks in the hotel's faux marble veneer.

Now, although he is uncertain of his commercial future as a hotel owner under the new guerrilla administration, he says, "I feel nothing but relief." Last month he reopened the hotel coffee shop for the time when vacationers will return to Keren.

During lulls in the fighting the Eritrean People's Liberation Front works feverishly in the area it controls to organize it politically and socially.

Elections are being held in villages throughout the rebel-controlled territory in preparation for what the front sees as its eventual administration of all of Eritrea.

A network of crude but effective roads has been constructed. Deep in the arid hills of Sahel province, shops and factories have been carved out of the rocky ground. Beneath their carefully camouflaged grass and dirt roofs, rebel workers turn out new uniforms, repair weapons and machinery and manufacture a growing variety of basic products for the rebel army.

Periodic raids into government held towns yield raw materials for their underground cottage industries.

Political organizers of the Liberation Front have been in the area for more than two years, seeking support among peasants and establishing a rudimentary form of self-government based on 15-member village committees and small cells for intensive politically study.

In one village I visited, the Liberation Front is setting up "mass associations" as the basis of grass-roots government. There are to be a peasant association, a women's association and a youth association, for example.

Leaders of each of these associations will sit in a village congress. The village congresses will elect a district congress. Eventually, the rebels hope, this pyramid will be topped by an Eritrean national congress.

POWs Become EPLF allies in Eritrea

Ethiopian prisoners support liberation struggle

The Guardian (New York), October 5, 1977

Keren, Eritrea

The Eritrean People's Liberation Front (EPLF) has taken close to 3000 prisoners during the first half of this year in stepped-up fighting against Ethiopian occupation forces in Eritrea.

The stories of these POWs and their treatment reveal much about this long and bitter struggle and the politics of its participants.

A year ago, with fighting more sporadic and less concentrated— the EPLF's main resources were then directed at political mobilization—there were fewer than 200 prisoners with the front.

With the opening of the current offensive against Ethiopian-held posts in the cities and garrison towns, the number swelled rapidly. More than 1700 were taken at Keren alone in July.

Those held today include regular army soldiers, officers up to the rank of colonel, Israeli-trained commandoes, Ethiopian peasants forced into the new peasant army, and even criminals recently broken out of Asmara's Sembel Prison. All are treated the same.

POWs Receive Education

The higher echelon officers are initially kept separately for intensive debriefing. Many—as angry at their superiors in Addis Ababa as any of the conscripted peasants—are cooperating freely with the EPLF.

The rest are housed at EPLF bases in the rear areas or in former government buildings in the recently liberated towns. There they recover from their wounds with EPLF medical assistance, receive daily political education that includes basic literacy and share their opinions freely with their fellow soldiers.

In the arid, rock-strewn hills of Sahel Province, I spoke with POWs from Af Abet and Decamare who were camped side by side with the recent escapees from Sembel. Together with 350 prisoners taken at Nakfa who were quartered nearby, there were over 600 at this location.

The main concern of the soldiers was for the outside world to recognize their plight. The Ethiopian junta denies their existence, fearing the spread of information that their return would prompt, and refuses to repatriate them.

Conditions for the Prisoners

The men were barefoot, their boots stacked on a sandy hillside to discourage attempts at escape in the rugged volcanic terrain. But EPLF guards were otherwise relaxed in their supervision.

The POWs had no place to go. And if they tried, as a few had, the peasants on the surrounding area were sure to bring them right back.

Several carried firewood and water into the camp as we sat down to lunch. The prisoners ate what we ate—kitcha, a chewy flatbread, and canned vegetables recently donated to the EPLF.

Exercise books lay on the ground. The POWs spoke enthusiastically of their lessons and angrily of the false propaganda they'd been fed by the Ethiopian junta.

Many expressed the wish to join the Ethiopian People's Revolutionary Party (EPRP), a growing underground force in Ethiopia which is challenging the military regime. The EPLF's policy is to release those who choose to fight in the EPRP after they have received minimal education and raised their political consciousness.

The prisoners released from Sembel in Asmara offered a slightly different challenge to the EPLF. Of the 900 inmates who were broken out in a daring July raid into Asmara, most were political prisoners. These were released immediately by their liberators.

One, a gray-bearded old peasant who spent two years in Sembel for suspicion of harboring fighters, is now traveling with the EPLF cultural troupe, singing ballads of his escape and praises of the EPLF.

There were also Eritrean Liberation Front (ELF) and EPLF fighters in Sembel awaiting execution. These were returned to their respective units.

Seventy men were criminals, however—most convicted murderers. An EPLF political cadre who worked with this group said that while they acted under somewhat different circumstances from the soldiers, the underlying causes and therefore the solution were essentially the same.

They were desperate men, he said—products of a violently skewed social and economic environment. Most had acted for pay. All would receive intensive political education. Those on whom it appeared to "take" would later be released. The incorrigible would be held.

In the town of Af Abet, overrun by the EPLF in April, there are 1784 Ethiopian soldiers captured in the battle for Keren. On the day I arrived there, they were sitting in large groups under shade trees, holding broad-ranging political discussions led by EPLF cadres.

Resistance in the Ethiopian Army

Talking about resistance within the army, one told how he had flown supplies to Nakfa during the EPLF attack on the base there but had been unable to land or even drop them because "the war was at a climax."

Back in Keren, he said, the men met and decided to send a delegation of five to the representatives of the government "to say that a solution must be found—either a peaceful solution, a political settlement or a total offensive." They also asked that the truth of the military situation be broadcast to the other troops.

The five were arrested the next day, held for six days in prison and then disappeared.

Most of the POWs said they had been afraid even to speak to each other, but nine announced they had been secret members of the EPRP and had been responsible for smuggling in political literature. Unfortunately, few of the soldiers could read before they were captured.

A lieutenant held in Keren estimated that 20-30% of the army is sympathetic to the EPRP. A member himself, he said that many pamphlets had circulated during the past two or three months and organized discontent was growing.

Another officer, in describing the morale of his former command, said: "I came to get my salary, nothing else. It is our job, We are ordered to come here by our government. If we refuse, we are shot. There was no determination among us."

The most pathetic of all were the poor and ignorant peasant farmers who had been "drafted" into the junta's peasant army. Poorly trained and entirely uninformed about Eritrea, they had been herded like cattle onto the battlefield where hundreds were slaughtered in an abortive attack against the EPLF.

Nearly 200 had been captured in the fighting earlier this month, some because they were unable to retreat past regular army troops who threatened them from behind of they sought safe cover.

Complaints Against Ethiopia

The extent of their political education had been to learn two slogans—"Down with ELF!" and "Down with the [Ethiopian Democratic Union] EDU!" No mention had been made of the EPLF. One said he had been told they would "liberate the Eritrean masses."

His most serious complaint, though, was that under the ruse of being recruited into a village militia, he had been shipped away from home at planting time. Lacking any grain reserves from last year, he feared for the lives of his wife and young baby with no crop this year.

Tens of thousands of peasant families throughout Ethiopia will share this fate.

Another said that he had been told that if he were captured he would be cut up and burned. Instead, he was being fed and was receiving medical treatment. He had met the highly politicized peasants of the EPLF militia and knew now that his countrymen were being sacrificed to crush a popular movement.

"This story," he said, "I will tell my people."

Eritreans prepare to liberate Asmara

The Guardian (New York), October 12 , 1977

Near Asmara

Asmara is a city in chaos. The end is near, but the last days are the most brutal of all. House-to-house searches, mass arrests, random executions and gang rapes are becoming the order of the day.

Demoralized soldiers of the Ethiopian army accompanied by undisciplined peasants of Ethiopia's new peasant militia rampage through the streets by day and retreat to the safety of their camps at night.

Scores of refugees are fleeing the city, but escape is not easy. The peasant army rings the city. Regular troops guard all checkpoints.

One boy who made it out said three in front of him were arrested when they tried to pass the guards. He turned back and waited until dark to slip past the drowsy sentries.

Another escapee said a girl had been with him, but the soldiers wouldn't allow her to pass. "Wait," they said. "We need you." As he walked on, they threw her to the ground and raped her.

The exodus includes Ethiopian deserters as well as Eritreans. The Eritreans come to join the Eritrean People's Liberation Front (EPLF). The Ethiopians ask for passage to their country where they will fight, the ruling junta with the Ethiopian People's Revolutionary Party (EPRP). What was a daily trickle of four or five refugees has become a flood of more than 50. Everyone—civilians and soldiers alike—knows it shouldn't be long now before the liberation forces capture the city.

The spirit of the occupation forces has been completely broken by the strain of the intensifying siege, the recent string of Eritrean military victories, the EPLF rout of the peasant militia and the Ethiopian junta's policy of brutal punishments for military failures.

From Agordat in the western lowlands comes word that the army has set fire to the city and evacuated to the only remaining government base in the area at Barentu after a 5-month siege by the Eritrean Liberation Front (ELF).

The ELF, beset by internal strife which recently brought over 1000 ELF fighters to the EPLF, has also managed to overrun the two small garrisons in south central Eritrea at Adi Quala and Mendefera.

In the far south there is one Ethiopian base at Adi Kieh, though there is also the threat of invasion from Ethiopia by thousands of peasants of the new militia who are massed at the border.

Adi Keih is surrounded by a brigade of the EPLF and all food supplies are cut off. According to a radio operator who fled Asmara, this garrison is desperately calling for help but the junta is unable to respond.

A series of EPLF victories over the past six months liberated eight other key cities and towns. There remain only the ports—Assab and Massawa—and a string of four small bases which protect the 50-mile corridor between Massawa and Asmara.

The move to cut the capital city's lifeline and complete its encirclement cannot be long in coming, the culmination of 16 years of armed struggle for independence.

Coming Independence

But with this step the Eritrean liberation movement enters a new phase. To take Asmara will mean to declare independence.

EPLF cadres have laid the political groundwork for independence through dozens of secret cells inside the city whose task has been to raise mass consciousness about the program of the new democratic revolution.

In this area and in the area of meeting the people's immediate economic, medical and social needs, the EPLF has gained valuable experience in the cities of Decamare and Keren, liberated early in July.

The EPLF has decided to put off a military attack until it is prepared to win the battle quickly and decisively, minimizing the cost to the civilian population.

Therefore, the EPLF is working steadily to reach maximum strength and thousands of new recruits are in a crash training program in the rear areas.

Captured tanks and armored personnel carriers are being repaired. Vast stocks of small arms and light artillery captured from the peasant army are being inventoried and distributed.

Hundreds of poor and middle peasants who have been politicized and trained in clandestine cells in villages around Asmara for up to two years are being armed and inducted into the people's militia.

The EPLF has yet to mount an attack in the current campaign which it has not carried through to victory within days or even hours. The complicating factor is the ELF which has initiated attacks several times this year that it was unable to at first sustain. The consequences for the people were heavy in each case.

At this moment only a handful of ELF fighters are in the immediate vicinity of Asmara, but in this mobile war it takes only a matter of days to move whole brigades into position. A precipitous ELF attack is therefore possible.

There are also the crucial issues raised by independence. Can a coalition government be formed? For two years ELF leaders have resisted the EPLF's call for a united front. Their position on unity is, in fact, the chief cause for the internal conflict that has rent the ELF for the past two months. Although the EPLF is far stronger politically and militarily than the ELF, enjoying broader and deeper support from the masses, to what extent will local and reactionary powers intervene on the side of the ELF?

At the same time, an independent Eritrea will need international recognition and immediate military assistance to defend the cities and borders against possible attack by Ethiopia. (The junta is announcing a new mobilization of up to a million people for its peasant army.)

Problems Inside Asmara

Meanwhile, the people of Asmara face a host of problems intensified by a regime whose grip on its own army is slipping.

One of the problems is that there are two distinct occupation armies, neither mixing with the other except on specified missions.

First, there is the regular army, a beleaguered holdover from the feudal era of Haile Selassie. Then there is the peasant "militia," a band of poorly trained conscripts led by army officers transferred into Eritrea from elsewhere in the embattled empire. They are the junta's last hope.

The regular troops distrust the new army. The regular forces have failed, and the government does not let them forget it. Many of their officers were executed or arrested for their losses. When not on duty, the peasants are kept carefully confined in their overcrowded quarters, unable to learn the true situation in Eritrea from the people, nor does Ethiopia want them to mingle with the regular forces and be undermined by the rock-bottom morale of the veterans.

The enmity between the two forces is undisguised, say the refugees, but it is the people who suffer the consequences.

With the militiamen taking over the defense of the city, soldiers of the old army have taken to donning masks and roving the streets, looting, robbing and raping.

One refugee said he was held up in the street by a gang of soldiers and stripped of his money, his cigarettes and his watch. Another told of a man who was killed in his house when soldiers broke in. When his wife came on the scene and screamed, she too was gunned down.

A week ago the government ordered a house-to-house search for contraband, but refugees claim it turned out to be more an officially sanctioned looting spree.

The people were disarmed of all potential weapons down to cooking knives. Grain, kerosene, gasoline, even typewriters were expropriated as possible aids to the liberation fighters. Over 600 people were arrested in one day on charges stemming from this dragnet.

There followed a proclamation that all young men and women from Asmara will be drafted into the "militia" to fight in Somalia, where the junta is also engaged in military battles. The announcement sparked a wage of arrests and kidnappings of teenagers who were thus "volunteered" for duty. The rumor is that by week's end, every family in Asmara had to produce one recruit.

During the past five days an unbroken stream of young people have risked their lives to escape impressments and to volunteer instead to fight on the side of the EPLF. Most were already politicized through membership in clandestine EPLF cells inside Asmara.

Those who remain behind—primarily the elderly and families with young children—suffer a deepening economic crisis and a growing danger of infectious disease.

Many factories have closed for lack of supplies. Employed workers who earn an average of $50 per month find the price of 55 pounds of grain is upward of $60.

Essential commodities such as charcoal, cooking oil, salt, tea and sugar are in extremely short supply. Black market prices are soaring out of reach of all but the very rich.

With the city literally stuffed with the soldiers of the twin occupying armies, sanitation facilities have been severely overloaded and fears are rising of epidemics of influenza and cholera.

Meanwhile, the EPLF army waits on the outskirts, preparing for the final attack on the city.

EPLF sets example in liberation Eritrean city

The Guardian (New York), October 19, 1977

Keren, Eritrea

The Eritrean People's Liberation Front has taken the first steps toward establishing people's democracy in this newly liberated city.

Against the backdrop of Eritrea's continuing struggle with Ethiopia for independence, the EPLF last month convened public meetings throughout this city of 32,000 people to outline its program. Within days of these discussions, the people of Keren were organized into mass associations along class and social group lines. At the first meetings of these associations, EPLF political cadres began the long process of political education.

The second largest city in Eritrea after the capital of Asmara, Keren represents a major testing round for the EPLF. It is being regarded by the freedom fighters here as a model for the future political development of an independent Eritrea.

EPLF is engaged in a national democratic revolution. It defends the interests of all classes and individuals who are anti-feudal, anti-imperialist and anti-bureaucratic, regardless of whether they also possess capitalist leanings. At this stage of its struggle, EPLF espouses the cause of peasants, workers, petty bourgeoisie and even national bourgeoisie, provided they support the front's democratic program.

EPLF's program differs from that of the Eritrean Liberation Front (ELF) primarily because it is the working class that leads the EPLF. ELF, on the other hand, is conducting a bourgeois democratic revolution which is antifeudal and anti-colonial but ultimately fought for the benefit of indigenous bourgeois elements.

An ELF victory would bring the national bourgeoisie to power in Eritrea. And due to the essential weakness of this class, the ELF would necessarily depend on the international bourgeoisie in order to retain power. A neocolonial state would be the end product of ELF ascendancy.

In contrast, the EPLF is attempting to steer the Eritrean revolution on a leftward course. It aims to bring the working class and its allies to power, thereby laying the foundation for socialist revolution.

EPLF is now the dominant force in the 16-year-old independence struggle, but ELF remains, in the words of an EPLF fighter, "a hindrance to our struggle."

Until recently, Keren had been an ELF stronghold. EPLF began operating here in 1974 at the conclusion of a 3-year civil war with ELF.

Initially, EPLF cadres organized supporters here and in nearby villages into clandestine cells. ELF propaganda had exploited local religious sentiments and political prejudices to portray EPLF as anti-Muslim and communist. Political education and practical experience helped EPLF overcome these early obstacles.

Popular support for ELF is already on the wane because of its high taxation and expropriation of land and animals. EPLF military victories in the Keren area, including a decisive defeat of Ethiopian forces at the River Anseba in early January swung the people further to its side.

By the time EPLF liberated Keren in July, its support came from broad segments of the local population. But there were still divided loyalties among families with members who had supported the other front.

EPLF Practice

The EPLF answered any fears people had with its practice. The conduct of the war itself was the first step.

During the four days of fighting against Ethiopian forces, the EPLF evacuated most of the civilian population to safety. "What gave me great joy," said one Keren resident, "was the discipline of the fighters. When we came back, we found all our houses as we had left them. In other wars there was always looting. Here there was none."

During the following month, EPLF teams worked throughout the city to repair the damage done in the fighting. Electricity was turned back on and the 10-year-old curfew was lifted. Emergency food rations were distributed. Hundreds of bushels of flour were brought in so that the Muslims could hold their traditional Ramadan feasts for the first time in decade.

Life began to return to prewar normalcy. Families long dispersed by the protracted war were reunited. Trade between city and countryside resumed. Most important of all, according to many residents, was the relaxation of tensions which had haunted them for as long as they could remember.

"I used to wonder when I would be killed " one peasant widow told me. "I was just waiting for my death-time. Now we can sleep as we like, freely. We don't worry whether our children are killed or our houses are destroyed. I have never seen days like these."

July and early August were a time of celebration. The EPLF held several evening cultural rallies that ran until near dawn. Traditional dances and revolutionary songs alternated with political presentations on Eritrean history and the EPLF program. In this way the people were prepared for the next stage.

All the city's residents were registered and given identification cards listing their name, the names of their parents, their addresses and their class or identifying social group. On this basis, the people were then organized district-by-district into mass associations which will serve as the basic level of political organization.

Mass Associations

There are to be five mass associations in each of Keren's six districts or "zones": a Peasants Association, a Workers Association, a Petty Bourgeois Association, a Women's Association and a Youth Association for persons age 16-25. These organizations will, in turn, be subdivided into groups of 50 members for political education. The handful of comprador bourgeois in Keren will be worked with separately.

These groups recently held their first meetings which began with explanations of Eritrean history and discussions which sought to identify the real friends and the real enemies of the Eritrean revolution.

After one such session of the Women's Association, a barefoot peasant woman told me emotionally that this was the first political meeting the women of Keren had ever attended. "Now that the fighters have come to us out of the mountains and the forests," she said, "we will never stop coming to political meetings."

A meeting of a Petty Bourgeois Association elsewhere in Keren produced similar enthusiasm—but not without hints of skepticism from some merchants who questioned the system of classification.

One young teacher expressed the sentiments of the progressive segment of his class when he said, "We believe we are the stored energy of the revolution and we will strive to give our utmost to it."

Interspersed throughout these associations are people who had been previously organized into the secret EPLF cells. They continue to meet on a daily basis for intensive political education.

Before the liberation of Keren, cell members had met to study on their own with materials smuggled into them by the Popular Front, as they call the EPLF. At night they had distributed leaflets and pamphlets, brought supplies out to the fighters, gathered intelligence and participated in EPLF raids on the city.

At a recent session in their ongoing politicization, they were discussing a chapter in the EPLF political manual on "why the mass struggle will win." One participant explained to me that he was "learning the philosophy which guides our revolution to victory. Our role will be to educate the mass, to organize the mass, because our struggle is a mass struggle."

The former cell members are being prepared by the EPLF to play leadership roles in the long and difficult political struggle now getting underway. As the vanguard, they are expected to guide the developing mass associations in a progressive direction and insure that the laboring classes—the workers and the poor peasants—are dominant in these associations.

"Working-class ideology will lead the new democratic revolution," according to Sebhat Efrem, head of the EPLF People's Administration and a member of the Political Administration and a member of the Political Bureau. "The political education in all the associations will be left-oriented, and we will be strict in our line.

"It will be culturally anti-imperialist as well as politically and economically," he explained. "For example, rich peasants will never be allowed to dominate the Peasant Associations, nor will we allow the Youth Associations to incline toward imperialism—they will participate in production and we'll not permit Western decadence such as hashish smoking."

Present Tasks

In the present period, he continued, the main task of the EPLF is to raise the level of mass consciousness, to teach the people to identify their class interests and to choose leaders from the advanced segments.

Further steps toward institutionalizing self-government will eventually be taken. Each group within each district mass association will elect a leadership. These group leaders will select an executive body which will join with their counterparts in the other four associations to form a people's assembly.

A 12-member central committee will be elected from this assembly which will include a chairman, a secretary and a treasurer; a

3-member legal commission to hear disputes and "settle contradictions among the people", a 3-member economic commission; one person in charge of security; an overseer of the people's property, e.g., housing; and a social worker responsible for the special needs of the people in the zone.

Out of these committees, a city-wide assembly will eventually be formed with its own executive body which will govern Keren. In this way, the people will assume political power through the vehicle of their mass organizations.

Eritreans dissect Ethiopian division

EPLF continues advance toward liberation

The Guardian (New York), October 26, 1977

The Ethiopian junta's fall offensive in Eritrea appears to have collapsed after less than a week of fighting.

One division of Ethiopia's conscripted peasant army has been decisively defeated by the Eritrean People's Liberation Front (EPLF) outside the Eritrean capital of Asmara.

A second is in retreat toward Ethiopia's Tigre province from the garrison at Adi Kieh. Fighters of the Eritrean Liberation Front (ELF) are reportedly harassing it but avoiding direct contact.

The government's plan had been for the two forces to converge on the EPLF-held city of Decamare in a pincer movement led by an armored column and supported by aerial bombardment.

The Asmara-based division advance 12 miles out of the city before it was routed by the EPLF in three days of heavy fighting late last month. Two tanks were destroyed in the fighting and two captured.

EPLF estimates place enemy dead at over 1000. Some 142 prisoners were taken on the last day and over 500 light arms and machine guns were captured.

The division at Adi Kieh failed to move a step north of their heavily fortified camp. Supply problems and sagging morale brought on by a month-long EPLF siege appear to have led them to withdraw to the south into ELF territory.

The story of the battle near Asmara is a now familiar one of EPLF determination in the face of a numerically and technologically superior but demoralized enemy.

It is also a story of massive popular support for the EPLF by workers, peasants and students who came from as far away as 40 miles to back up their fighters.

The battle also contains another aspect. ELF conduct in the "d-day war," as the EPLF fighters are calling it, is a catalog of intrigue and opportunism.

The Battle Outside Asmara

The battle began early in the morning as an estimated 8,000-10,000 Ethiopian peasants marched out of Asmara behind a column of 30 tanks.

Anticipating the move, the EPLF was dug in along a 15-mile front south and west of Asmara to block several strategic points from which the attack might have been launched.

One gap existed in the EPLF wall. The road south which leads to the ELF-held city of Mendefera was defended by an ELF battalion camped on a key mountain that overlooks a narrow pass six miles out of Asmara.

Offers to share the responsibility for this critical point were spurned by the ELF. "We'll defend it to our last drop of blood," one is reported to have boasted. They lasted half an hour.

When the ELF abruptly retreated, the peasant army poured through the opening behind EPLF lines and advanced another six miles to the village of Saladaro before setting up camp.

Saladaro peasants who fled before the Ethiopian onslaught spoke bitterly of the incident upon returning later to find their homes looted and burned.

"For 30 days, we served the ELF," said one woman. "We brought them food and water. Our children had to follow their orders. If we didn't do it, there was a stick on our heads. Then instead of helping us they ran away."

She said one ELF fighter claimed they had to go to defend the town of Debarwa, a half-hour to the south. Another peasant said he had been told they were retreating because their Dashka, a .50 caliber machine gun, was broken.

Said one toothless old man, "The responsibility for our burned houses and stolen goods lies with the ELF. They ran out and gave our village to the enemy."

Meanwhile, the EPLF was rushing reinforcements to the nearby village of Adi Abzemat. On the morning of the second day, the Ethiopian force moved east from Saladaro toward Decamare and ran directly into EPLF defenses.

By falling back to a previously fortified ridge, the EPLF trapped the tanks and infantry in a steep valley. Flanking them as well, they counterattacked and drove the heavily armed but sluggish enemy two miles beyond Saladaro.

On the third day, the Ethiopian peasant army was routed and driven back to the very edge of Asmara. Panicked, the officers desperately warned by radio that Asmara itself was about to fall. Reinforcements were called out, but the EPLF didn't follow.

"Militarily we were in a good position to enter the city," explained the EPLF commander, "but there are many other factors. We will pick the time for the attack ourselves."

During this last day of close fighting, the ELF reappeared to take a share of the captured weapons. At first they followed the retreating peasant army to scavenge discarded rifles and ammunition, but local villagers blocked them and collected the arms for the EPLF.

Asked to explain ELF actions in the battle, an ELF leader refused comment to this reporter and forbade ELF fighters to talk with me.

Tensions continue to run high among EPLF fighters who suspect the ELF of intentionally allowing the Ethiopian army to gain an early advantage against EPLF defenses.

Support for EPLF

"They are traitors to the revolution," said one man about the ELF.

Popular support for the EPLF is growing by leaps and bounds as the people gain practical experience in the differences between the two rival fronts.

The key to victory in this battle was the spirit and coordination between the EPLF fighters and the civilian population that came forward to maintain and supply their army.

People came by truck, by donkey and on foot from EPLF base areas to the east being food, water, firewood and ammunition and carrying out the wounded.

A steady stream braved a continuous hail of rockets, bombs and exploding shells from a massive Ethiopian air and artillery bombardment.

During the first night they teamed up to construct a 6-mile feeder road over rocky ridges and through swampy valleys to open a vehicular supply line directly to the front.

Some residents of Adi Abzemat remained in their village despite daily air and artillery attacks to cook for the fighters and car for the injured.

With this defeat, say the EPLF leaders, the government will know their peasant army is beaten. Twice they have tried to break out of Asmara and twice the EPLF has sent them back.

EPLF captures Ethiopian battalion

The Guardian (New York), October 26, 1977

The Eritrean People's Liberation Front (EPLF) reported scoring a big victory Oct. 12 as it captured an entire battalion of Ethiopian soldiers on the road between Asmara and Massawa.

The EPLF said it destroyed 260 vehicles in the 300 truck Ethiopian convoy, which was headed toward garrisons in Asmara loaded with arms, ammunition, fuel, medicine and other supplies.

How the EPLF organizes in Eritrea
The Guardian (New York), November 2, 1977

Keren, Eritrea

A tight organizational structure, an effective propaganda campaign and political line are key underlying reasons for the success of the Eritrean People's Liberation Front (EPLF) in its struggle against Ethiopia.

While EPLF's armed liberation forces battle Ethiopian conscripts for control of Eritrean territory, a behind-the-lines political and propaganda operation builds popular support for the independence movement.

The EPLF's office of Mass Administration is composed of trained fighters whose main responsibilities are not on the field of battle, but instead in the political mobilization for national liberation and against internal reaction.

Members of this unit work among the civilian population, both in areas under Ethiopian occupation and in sectors held by the nationalist Eritrean Liberation Front (ELF). Organizing efforts are also conducted in territory already controlled by the EPLF.

Political and propaganda work in those areas held by EPLF is relatively straight forward. Armed units of four to six EPLF cadres establish themselves in a centrally located village and begin organizing the region.

In mass meetings and private discussions, these teams start the long process of political education with presentations on Eritrean history, the origins of the EPLF and the aims of the revolution. Slowly, the most receptive residents are recruited into clandestine cells of up to 15 members. The cells are organized along class and social group lines for more intensive political study.

Secrecy Essential

In those areas dominated by ELF, organizing and propagandizing is more difficult. Secrecy is essential throughout the 6 month to 1 year process of recruiting and training EPLF cell members to become fighters in the People's Militia.

Discovery by the ELF is a constant danger faced by EPLF organizers in the ELF areas.

"The ELF doesn't want the masses to be organized because they know it's against their interest," one EPLF clandestine leader explained. "When the poor and middle peasants get organized, the ELF becomes isolated together with the merchants and landlords and they lose their place in the village."

The ELF has launched a counterpropaganda campaign against EPLF activities, the organizer explained. "They try to sabotage our land reform by saying these things shouldn't be done until after the armed struggle," he remarked. "They say it is ultra-'left'."

In constructing a revolutionary cell, the EPLF stresses political study and encourages mass organization. Cell members are drawn together from one of five categories delineated by EPLF: peasants, workers, petit bourgeoisie, youth and women.

Once a particular cell has reached a level of consciousness that encompasses Eritrean history, the EPLF program and the basic principles of Marxism-Leninism, it is instructed to multiply itself.

Each member of the original cell is expected to organize a new cell of which he or she will become the leader. Like a chain letter, the process continues until the number of people linked together through the cell structure is quite large.

Successful Cell Actions

Cell members participate in intelligence-gathering activities for EPLF forces, propaganda dissemination and sometimes even in elaborate, commando-type raids on an occupied city.

One cell member here described how his group engaged in covert work before the city was liberated by the EPLF.

"We were completely surrounded," he began, "so to make contact [with EPLF fighters] we dressed as shepherds or went out with camels as merchants with goods.

"We took cigarettes, soap, paper and other goods to the fighters," he continued. "We studied the location of the police and the soldiers and we took this information out too."

One of the most successful actions involving a cell occurred in Decamare, a town of 15,000 inhabitants which had nearly 100 EPLF cells at the time of its liberation in July. A 5-member cell of teenagers was instrumental in supplying EPLF forces with Ethiopian materiel.

The boys studied the logistics of the storage compound for weeks. They took notes of the number of soldiers guarding the supplies, the types of weapons they carried and safe access routes for EPLF fighters.

"After studying all these things," one of the boys explained, "we communicated to the mass administration who talked to the army. They picked the time and date, and we met them outside the city to make the plan.

"At 8:30 pm we went to safe places we had identified earlier, checked the location of the enemy and led the fighters in. First, we started getting out the cows. Then we arranged to get the trucks. We loaded them with portable goods and pushed them past the police station.

"We returned for other things we could carry like typewriters, medicines and milking machines," he added. "Some things broke and people were laughing and shouting by then, but no one came. Afterward, we came to know from comrades in the military that the [Ethiopian] soldiers were listening but were afraid to come out."

This benign attitude among some Ethiopian soldiers toward the EPLF is also evident in the independence forces' propaganda work.

During the recent battle at Saladaro, EPLF fighters broadcast directly to Ethiopian military leaders, arguing their cause calmly and analytically to curious and often sympathetic listeners.

Using captured U.S. and Israeli radios, the Eritreans tapped into the main Ethiopian communications system. At first, EPLF broadcasts were greeted with outbursts of profanity by Ethiopian radio operators, but the officers eventually silenced them and began a dialog with their foes.

The first question asked by the Ethiopians was, why should Eritrea be a separate country? The ensuing discussion covered topics like the history of Eritrea, the notion of regional autonomy, the right of nations to self-determination and, finally, the EPLF's analysis of Eritrea as a colonial entity.

Ethiopian Defections

On a less sophisticated but more sustained basis, the same discussion is carried out daily with the more than 3000 Ethiopian prisoners of war currently held by EPLF.

These POWs are taught to read and write and are instructed in political principles. Many will eventually be returned to Ethiopia where they will propagandize for the EPLF and the Eritrean cause.

This kind of reasoned and carefully constructed propaganda is in marked contrast to the distortions disseminated by Ethiopia.

The Addis Ababa line on the Eritrean independence movement until recently consisted solely of denunciations of "shiftas," or bandits. Now the Ethiopian junta claims that feudalists and reactionaries are stirring up discontent in Eritrea.

When mobilizing the 100,000-member "peasant army" of conscripts to fight in Eritrea, the junta warned of an impending "Arab invasion" of Ethiopia by way of Eritrea. Addis Ababa appealed to peasants' religious prejudices and claimed that neighboring Sudan was trying to destroy Ethiopia through Eritrean separatism.

Peasants led into combat under these false impressions often direct their anger at Ethiopian leaders when they discover that reality does not square with the junta's accounts of the situation.

The result is frequently defections to the EPLF or a demoralized "enemy" that has no interest in opposing Eritrean freedom.

Liberation in an Eritrean village

The Guardian (New York), November 9, 1977

Zagur, Eritrea

This village recently marked the 16th anniversary of the opening shots of the Eritrean revolution with an historical moment of its own.

On Sunday morning, only 15 miles from the besieged capital of Asmara, 300 peasant farmers assembled together to hear their village declared "completely liberated."

"This is a new chapter for the village," said Stefanos Afeworke, coordinator of the Eritrean People's Liberation Front (EPLF) propaganda teams assigned to the military zone north of Asmara.

"If we are going to be victorious, we have to organize the masses and raise their consciousness," he continued. "Before our organizations were secret. Now that we have liberated this area, they will be open. In this village, the highest political power will be in the hands of mass associations," he explained. "Through these associations the people will struggle side by side with the EPLF."

The peasants sat on the ground, their knees tucked under their chins, their cotton netselatat (thin blankets worn in lieu of coats) pulled up to their noses, listening in rapt attention as Stefanos outlined the purposes and structure of the new village organizations.

The organizational plan for Zagur follows a pattern already implemented in slightly different form in several liberated towns and cities. It will soon be carried out in all the rural liberated zones.

Three days after the Zagur assembly, propaganda teams from throughout this zone held their bimonthly meeting to sum up their organizing experiences and set the objectives for the next period. On the following Sunday, village assemblies will be held throughout the region to replicate the assembly here.

The current lull in the EPLF military offensive comes at a time when the political offensive is taking a critical leap forward. The remnants of feudal tyranny and colonial oppression are being swept away. The national united front, with the worker-peasant alliance at its core, is formally coming to political power.

Zagur's political history is illustrative of scores of similar villages across Eritrea where EPLF propaganda teams have been educating, struggling and organizing for over two years to prepare for this step

EPLF Provides Medical Aid

A team of five EPLF cadres came to Zagur in 1975. They began by studying village life in order to gain the practical knowledge on which their later organizational work would depend.

It was difficult in the beginning. The peasants were reserved and suspicious. Guerrillas of the rival Eritrean Liberation Front (ELF) had been here earlier and left a legacy of anger and distrust. Said one 65-year-old peasant, "All the ELF ever did here was eat our food."

Gradually the EPLF team won acceptance by their day-to-day conduct, their patient explanations of the EPLF's aims and goals and by concrete assistance they channeled into the village.

Land reform was carried out, a school was set up and medical services were provided. One old man, wracked by the pain of incurable tuberculosis, told me how the EPLF has helped him.

He came down with tuberculosis four years ago and sought help from Ethiopian doctors in Asmara. First they demanded $2.50 from him which he was forced to borrow. Then after a month of confinement, he was charged $5 and dismissed with no medicine.

"After that," he said bitterly, "I aid I prefer to die rather than go back to those people." The ELF did nothing for him, he said. "I waited two years until the Popular Front came to our village." But by then it was too late. He was slowly dying.

The EPLF gave him a series of injections and continues to supply him with quinine. They also provided him with an overcoat and a blanket so he is warm, but he says the coughing keeps him up most of the night.

The most receptive peasants were organized by the EPLF into secret cells for political study. They formed the main link between the EPLF team and the village, bringing the people's ideas and opinions to the cadres who studies them, clarified them and gave them back in the form of proposals for action which the more conscious peasants than carried back to the village.

Feudal Landlords Expropriated

In 1976 the EPLF encouraged the peasants to expropriate a feudal landlord who lived in Asmara and farmed land near Zagur with hired labor. Later that year a village committee was elected with EPLF guidance which has since arbitrated land disputes and managed village affairs.

A 10-member village militia was also constituted by the EPLF out of the most5 conscious peasants in the clandestine cells. They have since played a leading role in organizing the village as well as carrying out specific duties such as village security and enforcement of village committee decisions.

In early 1977 90 plots of land were expropriated from absentee landlords and collaborators and turned over to the village to be farmed collectively. A people's cooperative shop has been set up and a people's grain mill is under construction.

Meanwhile, the village committee has abolished a $60 funeral fee traditionally collected by the church and is considering sweeping changes in a whole range of feudal customs inherited from the past.

The ideas for all these reforms originate with the people themselves. The impetus for the action is provided by the EPLF which plays the role of a catalyst. The poplar leadership that carries through the decisions comes from the cell members of the secret associations.

"So far we have been preparing the objective conditions for organizing the peasantry and the other classes in the villages," Stefanos explained to me. "We've been trying to raise the level of class consciousness through continuous political education and continuous organization of the different classes and groups within the peasantry.

"We want also to change the objective conditions of the masses with land reform, collective farming, the introduction of a cooperative market—in general changing the economic conditions of the village."

To accomplish these objectives, the previously closed organizations and cells will be opened and expanded. In Zagur, there will be three associations: a Peasant Association, a Women's Association and a Youth Association.

Within these organizations, the people will be subdivided along class lines into groups of 20. In Zagur there are poor, middle and rich peasants. The classifications, analyzed over a two-year period by EPLF propaganda squads, are based on ownership of oxen and farm implements and land under cultivation.

Each group in each association will elect a leader who will guide the unit's weekly political study and sit on a village congress which will now replace the old village committee.

Since poor peasants constitute 60% of the village, they will dominate the congress. Men, women and youth (aged 15-25) will also be represented in direct proportion to their share of the population.

An executive body of 12 will be chosen by the congress to administer the village on a day-to-day basis with certain members responsible for settling disputes, managing economic affairs, overseeing security and so on.

As Stefanos stood in front of the peasant assembly and read the EPLF directive on the rights and duties of members of the Peasant Association, the people murmured in agreement. Afterward questions were asked and declarations of support offered.

One rose to say, "We have understood what you have said and we willingly accept the political line and principles of the EPLF. We want to form our groups and continue our political education, but now we have problems with our harvest. How will the associations help us?"

Stefanos answered that the associations will raise the economic level of the poor peasants by providing food and services through the cooperative farm, the store, the mil and other projects yet to come.

One of the objectives of the associations, he explained, will be to develop the productive forces of the village and thereby benefit all the members.

When he finished, registration for the new association began. Peasants were asked for information on family size, land under cultivation, number of animals and other income for purposes of classification. All 312 who attended the assembly signed up.

Later Ababa Haile, the woman fighter who heads the EPLF team in Zagur, spoke to an assembly of women. One of the goals of the Women's Association, she explained, is "to eradicate the double oppression of women in their political, economic and social life."

The significance of these associations and the village congress which will arise from them cannot be overstated. Raising the level of people's organization in liberated Eritrea to a markedly higher level, they also are laying the basis for mass participation in the political affairs of an independent Eritrea.

Vanguard militia safeguards Eritrea

The Guardian (New York), November 16, 1977

Zagur, Eritrea

Thousands of Eritrean peasants armed with captured U.S. weapons marched through the streets of liberated Keren recently to mark a key turning point in the Eritrean revolution.

After more than two years of clandestine political organizing in broad areas of the liberated countryside, the Eritrean People's Liberation Front (EPLF) is arming the people and consolidating the many small village squads into a national people's militia.

Village militias from as far away as the central highland region around the city of Asmara and the arid lowlands of Sahel province in the north assembled in Keren to be coordinated into platoons and battalions on a district and zonal basis.

Parading together through Keren, they carried banners that proclaimed: "The People's Militia Is Born In Struggle," "Political Power Grows Out of the Barrel of a Gun" and "Long Live Proletarian Internationalism."

One slogan atop a recently captured tank pointedly differentiated this highly conscious volunteer corps from the conscripted Ethiopian peasant army declaring: "A People's Militia Is Not the Product of Three Months Training at the Point of a Gun."

But neither is the Eritrean people's militia simply a volunteer army. It is highly selective and includes only the most conscious poor and middle peasants in every village. None but those who are cell members of EPLF mass associations are eligible and then only after a lengthy period of political study.

In their home villages, the militias function as a political vanguard, working with EPLF propaganda teams to organize and politicize the people. They take the lead in initiating cooperative projects and play an active role in production.

Militarily, their primary task is to protect the village from internal and external enemies. They are both an armed security force and a self-defense corps.

Now organized on a regional level, they can also be called into combat at any time the enemy mounts an attack within their particular military zone. They are thus a back-up force for the regular EPLF fighting units.

A year ago there were only 10 or 12 militia members in each village. Now there are between 25 and 40 and the number is planned to reach 60 within the coming two months. In the area around Asmara, this will mean a military force numbering in the thousands.

More important than the military aspect, however, is the militia's political dimension. As the people's own armed force, their main responsibility is to protect the interests of the working class and the peasants. In the words of one EPLF cadre, "The militia is the ultimate guarantor of the masses against class enemies."

If political consciousness is the prerequisite for membership, the determining factors are class origin and dedication. Close to 90% are poor peasants. All but a handful of the rest are middle peasants. This is, in a rural society roughly composed of 60% poor peasants, 30%

middle peasants and 10% rich peasant, based on ownership of means of production.

Militia units meet weekly for political study. Village leaders will meet monthly from now on at the district level to coordinate the common program. The leaders will also spend three to four months at the EPLF cadre school. In this way, these peasants are being developed into civilian political cadres.

Chosen from the secret cells of the mass organizations, the militia plays a leading role in guiding these associations. "They are nearer the mass than the guerrilla," explained an EPLF organizer. "They can translate the language of the progressive into the language of the mass."

When the EPLF initiated the underground associations, the first to be organized were the poor peasant farmers. As a consequence the early militias were comprised mainly of older men.

Since then, the Women's Associations and the Youth Associations have been formed.

Women fighters in the EPLF were a challenge to the traditional patriarchal society but under the daily stresses and strains of war they won their acceptance. Women militia in their home villages face more entrenched resistance.

These women and girls are at the cutting edge of the struggle for women's emancipation in Eritrea. It is a difficult struggle which pits them against the feudal backwardness of many women as well as the deeply ingrained chauvinism of the men. They are supported by the EPLF, but their courage and determination are what sustains them.

The daily work of militia members includes patrolling the village, guarding community projects, gathering intelligence, enforcing decisions of the Village Committee, engaging the people in political discussions, rounding them up for meetings and taking the lead in cooperative village work.

There are several cooperative schemes under development here. Land that was expropriated from absentee owners and collaborators is being farmed collectively by members of the village associations.

With the help of the EPLF, the Youth Association has built a people's cooperative store. The shop will be stocked with goods purchased by the proceeds from the first harvest on the new cooperative plots.

The latest project is a people's grain mill. The EPLF has donated the motor to drive the mill and farmers from the Peasant Association have taken turns on Sundays to construct the building and set up the machinery.

The mill is seen as a major step to liberate women from the drudgery of hand-grinding, a backbreaking task that takes up to three hours every day. The mill will serve the surrounding area and operate at cost.

In all these activities, the militia plays a key role. They patiently explain the aims of every new proposal, mobilize volunteers to help with the work and themselves join in construction and production to serve as model workers.

By observing discipline, participating actively and serving the people, they are steadily building support for the national democratic revolution in Eritrea as well as carrying it forward step by laborious step.

<u>Letter from Eritrea</u>

Besieged Ethiopian City Is Pictured in Despair

The Washington Post, November 17, 1977

Outside Asmara

The streets of Asmara are quiet now, according to reports from traders and deserting soldiers fleeing the besieged Ethiopian city.

Eritrean secessionist guerrillas have completed their encirclement of the provincial capital, and Ethiopian government troops occupying the northern city of 250,000 have become subdued and apprehensive in the expectation of a rebel assault.

A lack of fuel in Asmara has brought about a ban on all but military traffic. Electricity has been severely curtailed, and most factories and businesses have closed as a result.

Although nearly all economic activity in the city has ground to a halt, citizens of Asmara are able to move about freely for the first time in months.

Reports from persons crossing the lines to the rebel side say the troops holding Asmara appear listless and afraid, and they have ceased all acts of repression against the population.

Eritrean rebels give two reasons for this turn of events.

They feel Ethiopian forces were demoralized by the recent surprise announcement that the two main Eritrean rebel groups, which battled each other as well as government troops during the 16-year independence struggle, had formed a united front.

Eritrean leaders also believe their ambush of a government supply convoy last month on the road from the port city of Massawa to Asmara was a serious blow to morale. By cutting this road, which they claim was the last land corridor still open to the besieged city, Eritrean rebels say they left Ethiopia no way to re-supply and reinforce its garrison except by air.

Preparations for the ambush, which took place about 18 miles west of Massawa where the road to Asmara runs through a narrow pass, had been under way for months.

Leaders of the Eritrean People's Liberation Front said they waited until the onset of the rainy season to spring the trap, so that the cloud cover would preclude Ethiopian air strikes on the rebel positions.

When a large convoy came down the road headed for Asmara, the rebels closed off both ends of the pass and systematically annihilated the government troops escorting it.

Three Soviet-supplied armored cars were reported captured, and six armored cars and tanks were destroyed in the three days of heavy fighting.

A contingent of Ethiopia's 30th Infantry Battalion accompanying the convoy was also destroyed, according to the Front, whose reports have generally been accurate.

The rebels said they captured 10 fully loaded fuel trucks, 20 trailer trucks and six army trucks carrying equipment and food supplies. Many other trucks were reported to have burned in the fighting.

The real significance of this battle lies not in the captured equipment and supplies, but in the fact that the Eritrean rebels now control the road to Asmara.

Since Ethiopian forces have been unable in the past two months to break through rebel lines on the western and southern outskirts of Asmara, the cutting of the Massawa road completes the isolation of the provincial capital.

If the rebels can keep the Massawa road closed, Asmara will have to be wholly supplied by air. This poses a logistical problem that the Ethiopian government—already strained to the breaking point by its war with Somali forces in the southeastern part of the country—will find difficult if not impossible to handle.

Because of the significance of the Massawa road, Eritrean rebels say they expect a major new Ethiopian effort to reopen this corridor.

They vow, however, that not one more Ethiopian truck will ever reach Asmara.

One of the major problems that has long plagued the Eritrean independence movement is the existence of two major liberation fronts—the People's Front and its rival, the Eritrean Liberation Front.

Hence, the announcement that the two rebel groups were finally forming a united front set off major celebrations in areas of Eritrea under the control of the rebel forces.

In the city of Decamare, thousands took to the streets to cheer the news, and the singing and dancing continued well into the night.

"They say they have different programs and plans for the future," one resident of Decamare said, "but they are our children, and we want them to stand together to kick out the enemy."

Just how long they will remain together, however, remains an open question.

While open fighting between the two groups officially ended in 1974, the two groups had been unable to reach any kind of alliance until now—and shoot-outs between rival forces in the field have left at least six dead in the past two months.

Rebel leaders suggest that the sudden Eritrean Liberation Front interest in joining a united front may well have a lot to do with the growing strength of the People's Front position.

The Eritrean Front which is estimated to have between 4,000 and 7,000 guerrillas, has suffered several humiliating defeats at the hands of government troops in recent months.

The People's Front on the other hand, signed up thousands of new recruits following a series of victories against government forces in the spring and summer. It now appears to have between 25,000 and 30,000 men under arms.

Organized in brigade strength and operating a sizeable fleet of captured vehicles, including tanks and armored personnel carriers, the People's Front has evolved from a ragtag guerrilla force into a highly disciplined, mechanized army engaging the government in conventional, set-piece warfare.

Sudanese President Jaafar Nimeiri is credited with playing a decisive role in bringing about the agreement to form a united front. In the final analysis, however, the agreement was a simple recognition by both parties of the realities of the situation.

With government resistance collapsing, the two groups were running out of time if they were to avoid an Angolan-type situation in Eritrea.

Another front launches war on Ethiopia

The Guardian (New York), December 14, 1977

Keren, Eritrea

The Ethiopian government is beset on all sides. A sharply escalated war is raging in the Somali-populated Ogaden region, while guerrilla forces control all roads leading to the Eritrean capital of Asmara. And in the northernmost Tigray province, both rightwing dispossessed feudal elements and a progressive guerrilla army are at war with the central government.

The Tigrai People's Liberation Front (TPLF) began an armed struggle in 1975 against what it terms a century of national oppression by Ethiopia's ruling Amharas. During a recent week-long tour of central Tigray province, I visited liberated base areas under TPLF control and saw much evidence that the movement enjoys widespread popular support.

In organizing the people of the province, the TPLF is competing politically with the rural wing of the Ethiopian People's Revolutionary Party (EPRP) in eastern Tigray. In the western region at the same time, TPLF guerrillas are engaged in armed confrontation with the reactionary Ethiopian Democratic Union (EDU), which represents the feudal landlord class.

According to TPLF leaders, the organization's political work includes carrying out land reform in areas under its control, forming mass organizations to mobilize the population and arming the most conscious elements to form people's militias. In contested areas and in towns under Addis Ababa's control, they say they are initiating clandestine cells to win broader support and to carry out intelligence work.

The TPLF was founded in February 1975, five months after a committee of military officers known as the Dergue deposed Ethiopia's feudal emperor Haile Selassie. After an initial wait-and-see period based on hopes placed in the Dergue's revolutionary promises, opposition had begun to develop throughout the country.

Progressive activists in Tigray in 1974 began propaganda and agitation in the towns as the Tigrai National Organization. By early 1975, the group determined that armed struggle was necessary, and 19 militants went into the western Tigray countryside with four weapons among them—one carbine and three antique bolt-action Italian rifles.

Seven of the would-be guerrillas went to Eritrea to train with the then Eritrean People's Liberation Forces (now the Eritrean People's Liberation Front—EPLF). The others remained behind to study a handful of books of Marx and Lenin which they had brought with them.

"It was very difficult starting," said one young fighter. "We had only a few comrades and a few guns. All we did at first was armed propaganda."

When the seven returned from Eritrea with new guns and a more developed political consciousness, they stepped up their efforts to mobilize support and expand their ranks. But their first major military operation didn't come until September when they pulled a surprise daytime raid on the state bank in Axum.

Seventeen fighters with seven rifles and a handful of pistols and grenades took over the police station, the telecommunications office and the bank in a late afternoon attack. They escaped 45 minutes later with $85,000 and a quantity of arms.

This action provided them with both initial funds and widespread publicity in Tigray and across Ethiopia. From here they began moving east and west, rapidly picking up support and strength.

In the first half of 1976 they made three joint military operations with the EPLF against a microwave relay station, a supply convoy and at a base of the government's first abortive peasant campaign aimed at Eritrea.

Beginning in June 1976, the class content of the TPLF struggle became more clear with the start of direct confrontations against the organized feudal forces of the EDU, which had opened an unsuccessful 2-month campaign to enter western Tigray.

In September the EDU came again with fresh arms and new recruits. The fighting this time lasted until January 1977 with the EDU finally being demoralized and dispersed.

The third wave began in March of this year, and is today in its last stages in fighting near the Takazze River along Tigray's border with Begemdir province. The EDU came with a force of 7000, according to the TPLF, armed with automatic weapons, some of which were captured from the Dergue in raids on the Begemdir towns of Humera and Metema.

They advanced in a mass, said one TPLF fighter, with trumpets blaring and guns popping like a traditional Ethiopian feudal army. Undisciplined, untrained and lacking any system of organization or unified political program, they fell easy prey to prolonged guerrilla tactics of hit-and-run ambushes and quick-decision surprise attacks.

Though the EDU lacks popular support for obvious reasons, they are not always opposed by people who have suffered such conduct for centuries. The EDU has intimidated and confused the people with terrorist tactics and feudal propaganda aimed at the peasants' religious and ingrained cultural fears.

As a consequence, the TPLF's main work in the area is not military but political. They work to make the peasants politically aware, and then to organize and arm them to join in the resistance.

The TPLF claims to be active in six of eight Tigray awradjas (the Ethiopian equivalent of a county). They say they have organized 60% of the population and that they administer 50% of the land.

According to Abai, one of a 7-member TPLF central committee, land reform and mass organization have been carried out in 90% of the villages of Adua awradja and in many villages in Shire, Agami and Axum awradjas where their main bases are.

A young front at an early stage of development, the TPLF has recently instituted separate departments for health, economics, mass administration, politics, urban organizations, military affairs, foreign relations, security and intelligence, culture, handicrafts and logistics.

Still top-heavy with a membership drawn mainly from the petty bourgeoisie, the TPLF appears to be composed mainly of students, school teachers and civil servants. There are, however, a growing number of peasant recruits.

As a consequence, perhaps, the initial years of TPLF development saw political deviations to both the "left" and right. At first the small front declared itself led by Marxism-Leninism-Mao Tsetung thought and promptly found itself isolated from an unorganized people already distrustful of intellectuals.

Later, exploiting and tailing the nationalist sentiments of the people in order to build support, it gained followers without arming them ideologically to successfully prosecute the struggle.

Today, TPLF leaders say they are waging a national and class struggle. "Our struggle must aim at double oppression," said Abai, "National struggle is the tactic, but class struggle is the objective and the ultimate liberator of the people."

Citing 100 years of oppression by the ruling Amhara nationality, he said that the national question is one of the burning questions that now face Ethiopia. The failure of the multinational EPRP to adequately address this question, he said, necessitates the independent struggle of the TPLF and other democratic national organizations.

"We are fighting for self-determination for the Tigrai nation," said one fighter, explaining that the TPLF sought to overcome "linguistic, cultural, political and economic oppression."

The TPLF is also critical of what they call the EPRP's "insurrectionist strategy" in the cities which, they say, has provoked massive reprisals without seriously challenging the Dergue.

Estimates of the number of young people killed by the Dergue over the last year range from 10,000 to over 25,000. One TPLF fighter said he had witnessed the slaughter of several thousand youths in Kaffa province before leaving to join the armed struggle in Tigray.

The TPLF favors a strategy of people's war based in the countryside and fought mainly by what they call "proletarianized peasants"- peasants who have been politicized to adopt the working-class standpoint.

Their recruiting process has become more selective than before, and is aimed at the peasantry rather than the petty bourgeoisie. "It depends on political attitudes and class consciousness," said one cadre. "They must have already worked with us and learned clearly who are their friends and who are their enemies. Nationalist feeling is not enough."

They call for a multinational united democratic front of equals to wage the struggle against the government. "It will take a long time," said a TPLF political leader, "but we believe in protracted struggle. In the end, victory will be ours."

Eritrean 'reign of terror as death squads roam streets'

The Guardian (London), December 16, 1977

From Reuter, North of Asmara, Eritrea

Diplomats in Addis Ababa said yesterday that they had reports confirming that Eritrean guerrillas had broken through the defenses of the port of Massawa. The port lies a few miles away from Asmara, capital of Eritrea.

Meanwhile, deserters from besieged Asmara say its Ethiopian defenders have carried out batches of executions of officers and soldiers blamed for military defeat.

More than 150 officers and men were executed in a few days last month, according to Lieutenant Gebremichael Tsadik, who said that he deserted to the Eritrean guerrilla forces surrounding the city because he feared he would soon be caught up in the purge.

Defectors and civilian refugees say the Eritrean capital, with a population of 200,000, is hardpressed.

Civilians are being killed at random every day by a roving death squad called the Afagne—Amharic for stranglers—say deserters and refugees. Sergeant Mohammed Aman-Abdela said that on November 18 he came across a coffee bar in Ras Beraki Street in the center of Asmara strewn with the bodies of 15 people shot by the Afagne.

Defectors also say that combat units from South Yemen, technicians from the Soviet Union and doctors from Cuba, are helping the Ethiopian forces in Asmara. Lieutenant Tsadik said that he had seen South Yemeni tank crews, wearing unmarked uniforms, in action south of Asmara in September.

Since defecting, Lieutenant Tsadik said, he heard a detailed account from two friends, who escaped the slaughter by lying as though dead in a mass grave which had been dug by a bulldozer, then slipping away in the darkness. The friends told him that 10 truckloads of handcuffed military prisoners were taken from Sembel prison to a place near the airport called "Track C." They were made to sit next to prepared mass graves, then shot from behind, the friends told him.

At the time, Lieutenant Tsadik said, he had heard trucks moving and the sound of shooting. Commanders assured him nothing special was happening, but in the morning he learned that between 50 and 60 officers and men had been executed.

The militiamen, he said "are fed up with being here. That's why the Government is shooting them. They want to go back to their homeland."

Tigrai Front consolidates base

The Guardian (New York), December 21, 1977

Keren, Eritrea

"There is constant movement," said the guerrilla of the Tigrai People's Liberation Front (TPLF). "Most of our time is spent walking, going up hills and coming down again."

TPLF fighters are on the move throughout most of Ethiopia's northernmost province, working to organize and politicize the Tigrai minority nationality. The organization, which says it is fighting for "self-determination for the Tigrai nation," is battling on two fronts. While fighting against the ruling military junta in Addis Ababa, the movement is also carrying on a civil war against the feudal landlord-led Ethiopian Democratic Union (EDU).

The main TPLF base area is in the central zone of the province, but the guerrillas are also active to the east and west, and are beginning to make headway in the south, the principal area of government strength.

In a recent week-long tour of Tigray province, I marched with a TPLF column throughout the central zone. The TPLF militants were fed and housed willingly all along the way by peasants who clearly welcomed them as their patriotic sons and daughters.

The TPLF fighters engage in armed propaganda, politicizing and educating the people as they crisscross the countryside. During the harvest time, they carry sickles with their automatic weapons and join the peasants in the fields.

Stopping at a religious celebration at the monastery of Debre Damo, the column I was with distributed leaflets and held discussions with thousands of Tigreans who had come from all over Ethiopia for the annual festivities.

A TPLF cultural troupe performed for the large crowds, playing traditional tunes with revolutionary lyrics for enthralled audiences. Between songs, short presentations were given on the history of Tigray and the program of the TPLF.

TPLF women cadres are especially active in the mass political work, but as one fighter explained, they have special problems initially. "Since the people have a backward culture and a feudal bias against women," she said, "when we tell them to gather, often they don't come."

Male domination in the home and religious and cultural factors especially inhibit women from heeding the calls to meetings, she added. The women cadres thus go to them where they drink coffee, while they are preparing food and at the many religious celebrations.

In the towns, clandestine cells carry out propaganda and agitation and collaborate with the fighters in urban guerrilla operations. They contribute money, clothes and medicine, distribute leaflets and do reconnaissance for surprise raids.

Here, too, women were slow to get involved, but their participation is rapidly growing, according to one young girl organizing in Aduwa: "At first the task of raising their consciousness was undertaken by the boys, but now we have our own cells and are organizing ourselves."

They are recruiting more women and distributing literature on the woman question together with other leaflets, she said, "but we have not concerned ourselves only with questions to do with women. We also paint slogans on the walls, teach political education and we are organizing students, workers, even soldiers."

The intelligence gathered by these cells plays a key role in setting up raids and attacks by the rural-based fighters. Two successful actions during the week I traveled with the TPLF were credited in part to the prior work of internal cells.

On my last day, a radio report came into headquarters announcing that a TPLF column had taken the town of Abiy Adi in the south for six hours and gotten away with several vehicles laden with arms and supplies.

On my way out of Tigray, I was overtaken by a small truck filed with medical equipment which was taken in a midnight raid into the heavily defended town of Aduwa, the government's main base in northern Tigray.

Life in these towns is rife with fear and suffering, according to TPLF cell members from Aduwa where over 4,000 conscripted campaigners from the government's peasant army are quartered.

Mass arrests of students and murders of suspected opposition figures have terrorized the people. Transportation difficulties and a countrywide economic crisis have driven up prices and brought about critical shortages of essential goods.

More than two years after land reform was proclaimed by the military junta, it has yet to be carried out in the areas around the occupied town. Taxes are high and the people are periodically subjected to further call-ups into the militia for service in Eritrea and in the Ogaden war.

Although the TPLF appeared to lack the military strength to challenge the government for control of the towns, they express confidence that by continuing to build popular support, they will in time reach that stage.

They are now expanding their ranks and training their own voluntary militias, many of whose members are dropouts from the central government's peasant army. These recruits say they were impressed into service after being rounded up at market places in the larger towns.

Militias are growing rapidly under the TPLF with 20 or more members in most villages. Under one leader for political and military training, they act as a security force in the villages, carry messages and support the TPLF in battle and play a leading role in mass mobilization.

In one village I saw over 100 Tigrai peasants from that district drilling with TPLF instructors. An elderly man carrying a turn-of-the-century, bolt-action rifle estimated that a fourth of their number had come from the government force.

Two of these militiamen traveled with us during our tour of the province. One said, "We are proud to be militia. We have taken guns to liberate our people and to keep the peace."

Ethiopia executes army officers in Asmara

The Guardian (New York), January 4, 1978

North of Asmara, Eritrea

Ethiopia is turning on its military leaders after sustaining a series of crippling military defeats in Eritrea. The murders of top army officers which began last month continue, while Ethiopian troop morale plummets and the desertion rate soars, according to soldiers and refugees fleeing the besieged Eritrean capital of Asmara.

As army discipline disintegrates in the capital, Eritrean People's Liberation Front (EPLF) forces are close to taking control of the vital port city of Massawa. The capture of Massawa will leave an encircled and isolated Asmara as the only center of Ethiopian power remaining in Eritrea.

And last week, the EPLF was holding every section of Massawa except the island and peninsula of Girar, with battles raging at the Ethiopian naval base near the city's harbor. Some 2,000 Ethiopian soldiers have been killed in the last two weeks of fighting in Massawa, EPLF representatives report.

In the capital, as many as 150 senior Ethiopian officers and enlisted men have been executed in recent weeks, refugees and deserters reaching EPLF lines report. According to former Ethiopian Lt. Gebremichail Tsadik, who went over to the Eritrean side in early December, between 50 and 60 were killed in a single night.

Tsadik also said the random killing of civilians has become common in Asmara, with young people being gunned down on the street every day. "They are massacring people without any reason," the defecting Ethiopian officer told the Guardian. "It is genocide against the Eritrean people."

The occupied city of 200,000 has been under full ground siege since Oct. 12, when the EPLF cut the vital road that links the highland capital with Massawa. Four major attempts to reopen this key supply line have been turned back by the EPLF, which has been holding 12 miles of the 65-mile highway. "The situation in Asmara is now desperate because there is no food, no water, no electricity and no fuel," said Tsadik.

Emergency food supplies and heavy Soviet-supplied military equipment are being airlifted into Asmara and brought by ship to Massawa, Lt. Tassew Sissay—Asmara's airport supply officer, who also deserted in early December—said just prior to the current EPLF assault on the port city.

"Cargo planes bring rations and ammunition every day," said Sissay, who claimed that Soviet technicians, Cuban doctors and South Yemeni military units are also in Asmara.

The mass killing of Ethiopian officers and soldiers by the junta commenced after the third defeat on the Massawa road, according to the defectors now with the EPLF and Eritrean refugees arriving here.

"They began on Nov. 17," said Lt. Tsadik. "Two of my friends were in Sembel prison with 47 other officers and men for various petty breaches of military discipline during the fighting. About 10 trucks took them with some other prisoners to a place near the airport called Track C [a former U.S. army installation].

"I heard the trucks go by our barracks at about 9 or 10 pm, so I called up 18th brigade headquarters to ask what was going on.

"They said not to worry. They were only reinforcements. Later, we heard shooting, so I called headquarters again to ask what was happening. I was told it was nothing, only shooting at suspects. By morning we knew. Between 50 and 60 had been executed."

Lt. Tsadik reported that over 80 soldiers were also killed in Asmara on the nights of Nov. 18 and 19. "Many of them were from the peasant militia," he said. "They want to go back to their homelands. They are fed up with being here. This is why the government is shooting them. They want to go back, but there is no way out."

The peasant conscripts were told by the government that they would be sent home after six months, according to Tsadik. That was in June. Today the peasant irregulars are being offered $20 a month, he added, but most are refusing because they are afraid they will be kept here if they take it.

Ethiopia—Siege (News Focus)

Reuters news service, December 30, 1977

Massawa, Ethiopia

Eritrean guerrillas have tightened their grip on the encircled Ethiopian defenders of this strategic city, under siege for several weeks.

The guerrillas, members of the Eritrean People's Liberation Front (EPLF), which seeks the independence of the Ethiopian province, are still in position in the hills and on the beaches north, south and west of this strategic Red Sea port and naval base.

According to a senior EPLF spokesman it is now "only a matter of time" before the Eritrean city, the major distribution center for all arms and supplies reaching Ethiopia's few remaining garrisons in the province, is captured.

The EPLF view the struggle for Massawa as an important part of their 16 year war for independence.

Its loss, the guerrillas point out, would be a major setback to the Ethiopians who now control only two other cities and two small garrisons in this former Italian colony.

But signs are that the Ethiopians are going to put up a strong fight for the city.

A stepped up Soviet airlift observed here suggests further escalation in the level of fighting which so far has involved Russian-supplied heavy armor, artillery and, for the first time in Eritrea, bombing by new Russian MiG-21 jet fighters.

The fighting started during the second week in December, when the Ethiopians launched an offensive in an effort to reopen the vital highway connecting the port of Massawa with the besieged inland Eritrean capital of Asmara.

The EPLF fought back and in two days of fighting reversed the Ethiopian advance, pushing a column of nearly 8,000 troops supported by armor and artillery back 25 kilometers (15 miles) to the outskirts of Massawa.

The EPLF had planned an attack of its own for the next day, according to Isaias Afwerki, EPLF Assistant General Secretary. "We were ready to attack, and we carried on as planned," Isaias said.

Wedged into a narrow rock crevice with two EPLF machine gunners, I watched the battle unfold.

A column of Soviet tanks and amphibious armored cars covered the Ethiopian infantry as they took up positions on a barren ridge near the asphalt highway.

Jets bombed and strafed the Eritrean guerrillas as they inched toward the encircled Ethiopian defenses.

After five hours, the Ethiopian units began to retreat. By evening they were pinned down at their Dogali base camp five kilometers (3 miles) to the rear.

At dawn on the second day, the EPLF overran Dogali, capturing Massawa's water supply, and then drove the retreating Ethiopian forces to the outskirts of the port city.

Fifteen captured tanks and armored cars were observed in the aftermath of the Ethiopian retreat along with large stores of food and small arms.

Soviet cargo planes were observed during the following week, the voices of the pilots clearly recognizable in Russian over radios on the ground.

Soviet-supplied MiG-21s made their appearance on the fourth day of the Massawa siege, and rockets launched by Russian Katyushkas (known as Stalin organs) were seen in clusters of up to 20 at one time.

EPLF reinforcements were also observed in large numbers moving into place around Massawa for what appears to be shaping up as the largest battle yet to be fought in the turbulent Horn of Africa.

The rapid influx of EPLF guerrillas, however, created a supply crisis for the Eritreans. Some front-line guerrillas say they went without food for as long as four days before replenishments could be moved in from rear bases over 100 kilometers (62 miles) away.

On the Ethiopian side, air and sea shipments have been cut short to Massawa by EPLF mortar and artillery attacks on the port, and the sizable Agyp oil storage area on the southern edge of the city has been destroyed.

Radio reports quoting diplomatic sources say the Ethiopian International Airport at Addis Ababa has been temporarily closed to accommodate a massive new Soviet airlift.

An EPLF mortar attack on the Eritrean airport in Asmara has left the Ethiopians only airdrops as a way of getting supplies into Eritrea, according to EPLF sources here.

Ethiopia—Battle

Reuters news service, January 10, 1978

Massawa, Eritrea, Jan 10 (Delayed)

Soviet-supplied Ethiopian MIG jets are using napalm bombs to try to break the siege of this Eritrean port city. From five miles offshore, six warships, some of them supplied to Ethiopia by the United States in the 1950s, others said by the Eritreans to be Soviet, log shells onto the guerrilla supply lines.

(In Moscow, the official news agency Tass has denied that any Soviet warships or aircraft were involved in the fighting but acknowledged that the Soviet Union was giving Ethiopia "appropriate material and technical assistance.")

A mortar bomb from the Ethiopian-held naval base explodes in the sprawling residential area now under guerrilla control.

Throughout the day the air, sea and land bombardment continues. It is sporadic, random and unsustained, but it takes a steady toll in the crumbling city.

As the battle for the strategic Red Sea Port entered its 34th day (EDS: January 10), the Eritrean People's Liberation Front (EPLF) holds three-quarters of Massawa and its trenches reach to within 50 yards of Ethiopian positions.

Some 6,000 Ethiopians—soldiers, sailors and peasant militia—are cornered in Massawa's coastal naval base and its island port facility.

Most of the city's 50,000 civilians have long since fled to the safety of outlying villages and improvised refugee camps in the arid hills to the west.

The depleted Ethiopian garrison, defeated twice in open battle with the EPLF guerrillas since the campaign began on December 8, appears to be relying on newly-supplied Soviet heavy arms to turn the tide in its favor.

Since the beginning of this year, the MiG-21 fighters have flown up to 30 sorties over the city each day, attacking with bombs and cannon, napalm and anti-personnel shells.

Artillery and heavy mortars and T-54 tanks—all Soviet-made—join in pounding suspected guerrilla positions.

Offshore the ships fire in close support.

The Eritreans, now in their 16th year of war for independence from Ethiopia, answer with periodic barrages of their own, using tanks, mortars and artillery captured from the Ethiopians.

The guerrillas appear to hold the initiative and EPLF military leaders are confident of eventual victory, but they decline to state when it will come.

"We will never retreat," said one EPLF brigade commander, "but we will not attack until we are certain we will win." Walking through Massawa today, the devastation is visible in every corner.

A mosque lies in a heap of concrete rubble, its rooftop loudspeaker crushed under a pile of broken brick and stone. In the next street stand the remains of Massawa's secondary school, its windows blown out and holes gaping in its roof and walls. In the playground lies a metal casing from a bomb.

Two hundred yards away the charred and twisted wreckage of a dozen houses surrounds a 15-foot-wide bomb crater.

The blackened body of a civilian caught in the crossfire lies under a mangled sheet of corrugated iron. Sheep paw the wreckage in search of food.

One EPLF guerrilla estimates that a quarter of the houses in Massawa have been destroyed.

"This is the price of war," says another. "The main task of the revolutionary is reconstruction."

Eighty miles inland; in the town of Keren, the 16-year war is still much in evidence. The guerrillas captured Keren last year, and it now lies far behind their front lines, but it is still within range of the Ethiopian jets.

The guerrillas say Keren and three other towns were bombed and strafed January 1 with anti-personnel and conventional bombs.

A week later, the EPLF says, the aircraft returned and bombed the Keren hospital. They gave no estimate of casualties, but damage was visibly heavy.

Shrapnel from the airburst anti-personnel bomb was observed over a wide area.

In Keren; many people could be seen digging bomb shelters. "This marks a new phase in our struggle," said one EPLF military leader of the attacks on civilian targets. "It is like what the Americans did in Vietnam near the end of their war."

Eritreans hold Massawa

The Guardian (New York), January 11, 1978

Massawa, Eritrea

Ethiopia has intensified its efforts in the last week to regain control of this key Red Sea port city—the only city except the Eritrean capital of Asmara and the port of Assab that is not totally liberated by Eritrean guerrilla forces.

The battle for the city has been continuing for over a month, with the Eritrean People's Liberation Front (EPLF) gradually extending its control. The EPLF now controls three-quarters of the city.

Using U.S. made F-5E bombers, the Ethiopian air force strafed EPLF positions inside Massawa and around the Ethiopian-held naval base and port area Dec. 17. The month-long fight for Massawa has left the EPLF entrenched within 50 yards of the remaining Ethiopian positions.

Ethiopia Drops Napalm

Bad weather over Christmas week provided a perfect cover for the Eritrean guerrillas to move in reinforcements. Additional artillery and ammunition were brought into the city from EPLF base camps in the nearby hills. When the sky cleared, the depleted Ethiopian garrison of approximately 6000 troops called in a helicopter airlift of supplies.

A pre-Christmas napalm attack had severely damaged buildings in Massawa's residential area, with houses still burning when the renewed air attack began last week.

In a statement issued in Rome Jan. 2, EPLF spokesman Ermias Debesai said that Ethiopia had "attacked Keren, which has a population of 40,000 and several villages on Dec 1 and Jan. 1 with bombs and napalm."

At Guardian press time Ethiopian troops at Asmara airport were under heavy siege by guerrilla forces. Reports that the airport had been captured, however, remained unconfirmed.

Women Fighters Attack

Fighting is heavy inside Massawa. I watched a large EPLF force, which included a number of women fighters, make a furious, repeated daylight assault on the naval base. Ethiopian air raids are constant, as is the firing from tanks reported by Ethiopian prisoners to be operated by South Yemeni soldiers.

Casualties are heavy on both sides, but the EPLF still clearly hold the initiative despite the protracted battle and repeated bombardment. And the morale of the Eritrean fighters appears to be high.

Thousands of Refugees

EPLF resources are being severely strained, however, by the nearly 20,000 refugees pouring out of Massawa. The guerrillas are trucking food more than 100 miles from liberated base areas to supplement combat rations and stores of International Red Cross- and European Common Market-donated wheat flour captured from Ethiopian troops.

Civilians still trapped inside the city are being evacuated by the EPLF under cover of darkness as the guerrillas consolidate their hold on Massawa and prepare for the final assault.

MILITIA UNITS SET UP
BY ERITREAN REBELS

Farmers and Youths Help Counter
Expected Red Aid to Ethiopia

The New York Times, January 23, 1978

Keren, Ethiopia, Jan. 22 (Reuters)

Eritrean guerrillas have begun mobilizing their supporters on a large scale to counter growing Soviet and Cuban military involvement on the side of the Ethiopian Government in the battle for the northern province's independence.

Hundreds of Eritrean peasant farmers and teen-age boys and girls are being organized into local militias to defend rear areas and to provide depth in the front lines. Armed with American and Soviet-made weapons captured from Ethiopia, the volunteer military patrols can be seen in towns and small villages throughout Eritrea's Red Sea coastal territory.

Recently, thousands of people assembled in the town of Keren to be formed into platoons and battalions by the Eritrean People's Liberation Front. Small squads marched into Keren from as far away as the Central Highlands region near the city of Asmara, which the guerrillas have put under siege, and from the arid northern lowlands near the Sudan border.

Local residents cheered the volunteers as they carried banners proclaiming such sentiments as "The People's Militia is born in struggle" and "political power grows out of the barrel of a gun." One propaganda statement scrawled on a recently captured Soviet armored car declared, in a pointed reference to Ethiopia's Soviet-equipped Peasant Army, "A People's Militia is not the product of three months' training at the point of a gun."

Engaged on Several Fronts

Guerrillas of the Eritrean front and a second smaller movement, the Eritrean Liberation Front, are engaged with the Ethiopian army in several operations in the former Italian colony, which was annexed by Ethiopia in 1962 after 10 years as a United Nations-sponsored federation. Seeking independence for their province, the guerrillas control all but a few of the larger cities and garrison towns there, and are fighting to capture the strategic Red Sea port of Massawa.

Although they sense a final victory, the Eritreans appear increasingly concerned over the possibility of large-scale Soviet and Cuban intervention on the Ethiopian side. Functioning both as a striking force and a self-defense corps, the militia organization intends to release large numbers of the independence fighters for duty on the front lines, according to Stefanos Afewerke, who is 28 years old and a liberation front political organizer. "The militia is the ultimate guarantor of the people against all their enemies," he said.

The militia units also serve as a "political vanguard," according to Mr. Afewerke. He said they worked with Eritrean propaganda teams to organize and politicize the civilian population. They also undertake village projects such as joint farming plans and cooperative shops and grain mills, he said.

Militia units meet weekly for military and political study, and village leaders meet monthly to coordinate their programs, according to Mr. Stefanos.

Militia Numbers are Growing

A year ago there were only 10 or 12 militia members in each village, he said. Now there are between 25 and 40, and the number is expected to grow to 60 in the next two months. Members are chosen from the front's "mass associations," once organized on a clandestine basis and now open to general membership, Mr. Stefanos said.

When the People's Liberation Front initiated the underground associations, the first to be organized were poor peasant farmers, according to the young official. As a consequence, the earliest militia forces consisted mainly of older men. Since then, he explained, women's associations and youth associations have been formed. Many young people were visible in the Keren parade.'

Their daily work includes patrolling their villages, guarding projects, gathering intelligence, and enforcing the decisions of the committees, which directly administers the community.

The Battle for Massawa

SUDANOW (Khartoum), February 1978

The sun glints off the wings of two MiG-21 jets that streak across the pale blue morning sky over the Red Sea port of Massawa. Nothing moves in the deserted streets of this embattled city of 50,000 residents as the silver birds bank sharply and go into steep, staggered dives toward the abandoned air field.

Screaming out of the east, the brilliant glare of the tropical sun behind them, the supersonic Ethiopian engines of death disgorge their payloads into the open field. Immediately, they lift their gleaming bodies skyward, out of reach of the curtain of the anti-aircraft fire trailing in their wake.

Wheeling about, the new Russian-supplied MiGs—in their second week of operation in Eritrea—execute a second dive, swooping in from the east and south to cross at the nadir of their low paths. One looses an airburst anti-personnel bomb while the second strafes. The crackling of multiple explosions echoes through the nearby city.

A third dive follows, and another airburst. A fourth brings the snort of the MiG cannon, the chatter of anti-aircraft and machine guns close on their tails as they twist and weave up and away from Massawa to return to their home base far to the south in the Ethiopian highlands. Then an eerie silence.

The introduction of the Russian jet fighters—coincident with their widely reported use in the Ethio-Somali war in Ethiopia's contested Ogaden region—marks a new phase in the 16-year Eritrean war for independence from Ethiopia.

With Ethiopia's American-trained and equipped regular army virtually decimated and the new Russian-equipped peasant militia stymies here, the country's military rulers appear to be turning increasingly to massive supplies of Russian heavy arms, Russian and Cuban military advisors and South Yemeni combat troops to turn the tide of war in their favour.

The battle for the deep water port of Massawa, whose strategic location on the southwestern coast of the Red Sea gives its control global significance, is the first major test of this costly new strategy.

The loss of Massawa would deprive Ethiopia of the largest of only two points of access to the sea, for which the late emperor Haile Selassie I annexed the former Italian colony of Eritrea in 1962. Its fall would also further isolate an estimated 25,000 Ethiopian troops currently under guerrilla siege in the Eritrean capital of Asmara, 65 miles inland.

For the Soviet Union, whose gamble on supporting the self-proclaimed Marxist junta that came to power in 1974 has already cost it the use of the Somali port at Berbera, the failure to hold Massawa poses a multi-faceted threat. The Soviets, too, want the deep water port and former American naval facility, but in addition, like the US in Vietnam, their international credibility is at stake here.

The regional implications of an Eritrean guerrilla victory in Massawa further compound the situation. Israeli interest in the Red Sea has led to an unholy alliance with the Russians to back Ethiopia's ruling military council.

Israeli spare parts for previously supplied American equipment continue to flow into Ethiopia, according to guerrilla sources who claim that Israeli advisors and military personnel play a significant role in the conflict. The Israelis are also charged with supplying the anti-personnel bombs now falling daily on Massawa.

The scene of the worst fighting yet in the turbulent Horn of Africa, the city is paying a high price for what might otherwise be considered a quirk of geographical good fortune.

As the smoke clears from the empty airport and the thick brown dust settles into fresh bomb craters, the plaintive bleat of a half-starved goat can be heard over a muted chorus of scrawny tom cats scavenging for food scraps that were once plentiful in the dirt streets. Today, there are none.

Massawa has become a ghost town in the 33 days of fighting in and around the strategic port between guerrillas of the Eritrean People's Liberation Front (EPLF) and Ethiopian government forces. Most of its civilian population, already depleted by a steady exodus that began months ago, has sought a precarious safety in outlying villages and improvised refugee camps west of the city.

The daily bombardment by Ethiopian jet fighters, tanks, mortars and both land and naval-based artillery has wreaked havoc in the sprawling mainland residential area which has been under EPLF control since December 21. An estimated 6000 troops of Ethiopia's regular army, navy and conscripted peasant militia are cornered in the heavily fortified coastal naval base and the island port facility.

A shell bursts a few hundred yards from where this reporter sits. Several minutes pass. A second explosion rips open the tin roof of another house out of sight behind me. The clatter of bits of wood and metal can be heard falling into neighbouring buildings. Soon afterward, there is a loud 'pop' from an outgoing mortar shell aimed at the naval base. And so on throughout the day.

The guerrillas lie low, waiting for the protecting umbrella of darkness to emerge under which they will continue their preparations for what they say will be a final assault on the remaining Ethiopian enclaves.

The opening battle in the Eritrean campaign to capture Massawa was fought 15 miles inland on December 8 within the arid, scrub-covered hills and valleys west of the port. The EPLF was entrenched there, holding 12 miles of the vital highway that links Massawa with the besieged highland city of Asmara.

After an Ethiopian supply convoy of some 300 heavily-laden trucks, packed troops carriers and buses was halted by the guerrillas, a counter attack began that in 26 hours carried the EPLF to the out-skirts of Massawa.

From a hilltop machine gun position, I watched the EPLF infantry repeatedly outflank and charge the retreating Ethiopians, one hill at a time until the orderly withdrawal became a chaotic rout. Over 1000 government troops were killed in the fighting and 15 tanks and armoured cars were captured or destroyed, according to EPLF sources.

Massawa's fresh water supply was also taken and its flow shut off by the advancing guerrillas who rapidly encircled Massawa on three sides before pausing to dig in and consolidate their gains. It was an impressive and perhaps unexpected victory, brought about by the sudden collapse of the Ethiopian defenses.

On the afternoon of December 9, the EPLF found itself within striking distance of one of the most strategic and most heavily defend-ed cities in Eritrea, scattered across an arc some ten to fifteen miles around, exposed and well within the Ethiopian navy, air force and armour, but without having set up supply lines or reinforcements.

For the next twelve days, the guerrillas worked feverishly to resolve their logistical difficulties and to ready themselves for the assault on the port. Convoys of EPLF trucks rolled in each night from all over Eritrea. civilian volunteers from guerrilla-held villages and towns arrived with donated food, bandages and other supplies. Military reinforcements, too, poured in by foot and in trucks.

On the second night, a carnival atmosphere took over the EPLF's rear area when three truckloads of civilians drove in signing 'Eritrea, my Eritrea, your cities become our camps.' Guerrillas surrounded them, joined in their songs, clapping and laughing in obvious relief and joy.

Barefoot peasants in tattered shorts and nondescript cotton dresses stood side by side with shopkeepers and dapper teenagers wearing pressed slacks and fashionable leather shoes. The guerrillas, clad in patched rubber sandals and mismatched uniforms taken off the Ethiopians, formed circles and danced in the road.

For a brief moment the horrors of this long and bitter war seemed forgotten, but after a half hour the civilians were dispersed to camps where they would take over many of the non-combat tasks of maintaining the EPLF army, now swollen to at least four thousand men and women.

In the days leading up to the assault on Massawa, the prevailing mood among guerrillas and volunteers was one of unrestrained optimism. Many expected the city to fall in three or four days once the attack began.

An over-enthusiastic Rome spokesman for the EPLF declared that the fighting had already begun inside the city. The airport had been take4n he said, and the fall of Massawa was only a matter of hours away. It was an announcement that would haunt the guerrillas as a world without any other corroborating contact with the battlefront became increasingly skeptical of the EPLF's claims.

On the night of December 20, a spokesman for Ethiopia was quoted as claiming that the EPLF had been repulsed to a distance of three miles outside Massawa and that the city was now quiet.

At dawn the next day, however, the guerrillas did in fact overrun the airport, advancing deep into the centre of the city and driving Ethiopian forces into the base and port area where they remain today. "It was not actually a battle," said one guerrilla fighter. "They were retreating and we were following."

During the night a flood of refugees began pouring out of the city. Hiwet Tekle, a divorced mother of one child, described the day's fighting in much the same terms. "I live near the market," she said. "All morning we heard shooting. By noon it came near my house. Hundreds of the Zemach [Ethiopia's peasant militia] ran past with their rifles on their backs. I went into my house and stayed under my bed. In the afternoon I heard singing, so I looked out to see the front fighters go by."

Others were not so fortunate. One sobbing woman, a young child in tow, said three of her four children had been gunned down in the street by panicked peasant soldiers.

By the afternoon of December 22, the outer areas of the city were empty of all but the guerrillas and scores of animals left behind in the hasty civilian withdrawal. under a random aerial and artillery bombardment, the EPLF prepared to hit the naval base.

Throughout the evening and late into the night, the streets buzzed with the sounds of departing residents, incoming EPLF supply trucks and columns of guerrilla reinforcements.

The morning of December 23 began quietly enough. There were sporadic explosions every few minutes, but there was no movement on the streets.

At precisely 2.16 pm. An EPLF mortar barrage commenced from hidden positions across the deserted city. The ground shook under the rhythmic, methodical explosions.

Small clusters of guerrillas began milling about restlessly behind the twelve-foot high sea wall that borders the salt flats between the city and the peninsula naval base. At 2.30, they turned as one and scrambled over the top, dashing headlong through 500 km of shallow water towards the base.

A second line appeared on the north side, darting across the sandy peninsula to converge with the first force. Halfway across, the shooting started, first singly and then at once from everywhere.

A jeep rolled up to the sea wall with a 105mm recoilless rifle mounted on the back. In seconds, it added its booming voice to the din of small arms and mortar fire. A loud crack, like lightning, roared over the others. An Ethiopian tank had leveled its cannon at the sea wall.

Twenty minutes later, the shriek of F-5 Starfighters washed over the battlefield as two dived and bombed the tin shacks behind the EPLF frontline trenches. An hour later, a Canberra bomber also appeared. For the remainder of the afternoon, the city rocked under the impact of bombs, bullets and exploding shells.

Near dusk the last of the air-raids brought napalm. As the blue gray hues of twilight appeared, orange and crimson flames licked the evening sky from at least three areas of the city where tumbledown wooden shanties dissolved rapidly into ash and smoke.

The EPLF had established trenches in the sand banks around the naval base, but it was now glaringly apparent that the capture of the base would not be an easy matter. The guerrillas settled in for what was to prove an unexpectedly long siege.

In the weeks since, there has been no troop movement on either side. day after day the two sides hammer each other with mortar and artillery barrages which occasionally stretch deep into the night.

Three days of thick cloud cover kept the planes away for

Christmas, but when the skies cleared, they soon returned. New Year's Day brought the Russian-supplied MiG-21s over Massawa for the first time, coincident with EPLF reports of bombing attacks against the guerrilla-held inland cities of Keren and Decamare.

The protracted battle for Massawa has become a brutal contest of nerves, of mounting stresses and strains which build inexorably toward a final explosive showdown which neither side can afford to lose.

The massive build-up of Russian armaments—which include large numbers of tanks, armoured cars and MiG-21 and 23 aircraft—and a substantial superiority in manpower give Ethiopia the ability to mount coordinated attacks in several directions against the Eritreans.

The chief flaw in the Eritrean defense is the lack of unity between the EPLF and the ELF. The rival fronts have maintained an informal alliance since December 1974, after three years of bitter civil war, but negotiations toward unification began four months ago and have not yet yielded concrete results.

The problem is further compounded by the existence of a newly formed third force known as the ELF-PLF and led by Osman Saleh Sabbe. Though considerably smaller than either the ELF or the EPLF, the Rightwing ELF-PLF is receiving substantial aid from Saudi Arabia and the United Arab Emirates who fear the emergence of the Leftist EPLF as the dominant force in Eritrea.

Time is the key factor. If the Eritreans can resolve their internal conflicts and withstand the impending Ethiopian and Cuban offensive until June when the rainy season engulfs the highland plateau, they would be in a strong position to take Asmara and move south toward Assab where the last and perhaps the most difficult battle awaits them.

Unlike the Ethiopia-Somali war, time also works to the Eritrean advantage by continually increasing the role of the civilian population. The independence of the EPLF from virtually any external support has led them to concentrate heavily on internal mobilisation.

Thousands of volunteers are now undergoing military and political training at secret EPLF camps inside Eritrea, while others are being inducted into local militias in their home villages. EPLF cadres are also organising urban guerrilla units inside the cities still under government control and are arming previously clandestine groups in towns and cities captured in 1977.

At this stage, Ethiopia faces a universally hostile population in Eritrea whose fervent nationalism has reached a level where it appears beyond compromise. Any advance by Cuban and Ethiopian forces would thus be subject to constant threat from within as well as from counter-attack by Eritrean armies.

Fighting intensifies in Asmara
Ethiopian army under siege in Eritrean capital
The Guardian (New York), February 1, 1978

Massawa, Eritrea

Ethiopian forces failed in a Jan. 22 attempt to break through the rebel siege of the Eritrean capital of Asmara. The abortive attack, the most recent of repeated tries at opening supply lines to the Ethiopian-held city, was repulsed by the large Eritrean People's Liberation Front (EPLF) force surrounding the capital.

Inside Asmara itself, conditions are rapidly deteriorating. In this city of 250,000, public water supplies have been cut off, there is no fuel, no electricity and there are critical shortages of food and medicines. The guerrilla armies of both the EPLF and the Eritrean Liberation Front (ELF) have maintained the full ground siege for several months, and are now preparing for a full-scale assault on the government's main Eritrean stronghold.

The battle for the key Red Sea port of Massawa, 70 miles down an EPLF-blocked road from Asmara, continues to rage. With the EPLF holding three-quarters of the city, Ethiopian air force bombing has leveled every significant economic target in Massawa.

[At Guardian press time, the EPLF reported the liberation of two key garrison towns on the Asmara-Massawa road. According to the communiqué, 3500 Ethiopian troops were killed in the battle for Dongolo Jan. 24. The same day, the important agricultural center of Ginda was liberated in fighting that claimed over 1000 army troops.]

From five miles off shore, six warships—some supplied by the U.S. in the 1950s, others said by the EPLF to be Soviet—lob shells onto guerrilla supply lines in Massawa.(

[In Moscow, the official news agency Tass denied that any Soviet warships or aircraft were involved in the fighting, but acknowledged that the USSR was giving Ethiopia "appropriate military and technical assistance."]

A mortar bomb from the Ethiopian-held naval base here explodes in the sprawling residential area now under guerrilla control. Throughout each day, the air, sea and land bombardment continues. It is sporadic, random and unsustained, but it is taking a heavy toll in this crumbling city.

Most of the city's 50,000 civilians have long since fled to the safety of outlying villages and improvised refugee camps in the arid hills to the west. Some 6000 Ethiopians—soldiers, sailors and peasant militia—are cornered in Massawa's coastal base and its island port facility.

The depleted Ethiopian garrison has retreated twice in open battle with the EPLF guerrillas since the Eritrean attack on Massawa began Dec. 8. Addis Ababa now appears to be counting on newly supplied Soviet heavy arms to turn the tide in its favor. Since the start of the new year, USSR-made MiG-21 fighter planes have flown up to 30 sorties over the city each day, attacking with bombs and cannon, napalm and antipersonnel shells.

The Eritreans, now in their 16th year of war for independence from Ethiopia, are answering the attacks with periodic barrages of their own. Entrenched within 50 yards of Ethiopian positions, the EPLF is using tanks, mortars and artillery captured from the army. Last week, the Eritreans reported shooting down both a U.S.-made F-5 fighter and a MiG-21 over Massawa.

Massawa Devastated

As this reporter walked through Massawa, devastation was visible in every corner. A mosque lies in a heap of concrete rubble, its rooftop loudspeaker crushed under a pile of broken brick and stone.

In the next street stands the remains of Massawa's secondary school, its windows blown out and holes gaping in its roof and walls. In the playground lies a metal casing with the inscription: "Bomb-25 kg. Cluster antipersonnel!" About 200 yards away, the charred and twisted wreckage of a dozen houses surrounds a 15 foot-wide bomb crater.

In Asmara meanwhile, an estimated 12-15,000 Ethiopian regular army and peasant militia troops are also apparently counting on a sizable infusion of Soviet-supplied materiel to head off the expected Eritrean assault on the capital.

The steady trickle of Ethiopian army deserters and Eritrean refugees leaving the besieged city describe a situation of military and economic chaos. With the war now on Asmara's doorstep, discipline among Ethiopian troops is said to be breaking down, and there have been reports of rebellions among rank-and-file soldiers.

Military Patients

Asmara's largest private hospital is filled with military patients, the defecting soldiers say, and the luxury Ciaue Hotel has been commandeered to cope with the overflow. The severe economic crisis brought on by the siege is meanwhile being felt most keenly by the civilian population.

Inflation is driving the price of essential commodities out of the reach of many, according to the refugees. Grain prices have increased by 500% and sugar has not been seen on the open market since the Massawa road was cut in mid-October. To aid the civilians, the EPLF has begun transporting fruits and vegetables from farms and plantations under their control to the city's edge, where residents pick them up by night and smuggle them in.

Most factories and businesses are now closed. Medical supplies are running out, sanitation facilities are breaking down, and there is real concern over the possibility of epidemics, according to those escaping the capital.

Unity Eludes Guerrillas

The guerrilla armies outside have long been poised to take the city. The joint siege has however been more successful than the attempts over the past few months to unify the two forces. Two recent rounds of talks between the rival Eritrean fronts—which fought a bitter civil war from 1972-74—have yet to produce more than joint statements of the need for unity. At the end of the year, a terse communiqué was issued, stating only that agreement had been reached on some points, but that further discussion was necessary.

The lack of organizational unity is cited by EPLF leaders as the principal factor in delaying their attack on Asmara, though they say they will not postpone their attack indefinitely. The guerrillas appear to retain the initiative despite the influx of heavy weapons reaching the Ethiopian forces. EPLF military leaders are confident of eventual victory, but they decline to speculate on when.

"We will never retreat," said one EPLF brigade commander, "but we will not attack until we are certain we will win."

EPLF captures more Ethiopian garrisons

The Guardian (New York), February 8, 1978

Khartoum, Sudan

Eritrean rebels continued their string of military victories last week in the fight for independence from Ethiopia.

Eritrean forces captured six Ethiopian government bases and repulsed one Ethiopian attack in separate engagements, according to a spokesman for the Eritrean People's Liberation Front (EPLF).

EPLF guerrillas overran government posts at Dongolo, Ginda, Embatkala, Nefasit, My Haber and Shengireni, the spokesman said here. He reported that more than 5000 government soldiers were captured or killed and large quantities of Soviet arms and ammunition were taken at the outposts.

In addition, four tanks were reported destroyed and hundreds of Ethiopian troops were killed in fighting in the port city of Massawa.

The capture of the outposts, which lie along the vital highway that links Massawa with the inland capital of Asmara, places the entire length of the 69-mile road in the hands of the insurgent forces, according to the EPLF spokesman.

RUSSIAN TROOPS JOIN IN ERITREA BATTLES

Observer Foreign News Service (London), February 10, 1978

With EPLF forces, Northern Eritrea

Russian and South Yemeni military personnel are participating directly in battles between the self-proclaimed Marxist Ethiopian military government and Eritrean independence forces on Ethiopia's northern front, according to deserting Ethiopian officers.

Russian crews operated BM-21 multiple-rocket launchers—"Stalin organs"—during recent fighting in the Red Sea port of Massawa, according to one senior officer who clams to have witnessed the early stages of the battle.

"I saw them firing the BM-21s without any Ethiopian assistance because we do not yet know how to use them," said the officer, who is now with guerrillas of the Eritrean People's Liberation Front (EPLF). He also said that Russian tank and artillery technicians were in Massawa, and South Yemeni combat crews drove Russian-supplied T-54 tanks into battle.

Russian warships were also seen by this reporter firing rockets and guns into Massawa.

South Yemeni pilots are flying Russian-supplied MiG jet fighters which daily bombed and strafed guerrilla positions in Massawa and are reported to have bombed civilian targets in five other Eritrean cities since January, said the officer.

The new Russian fighter aircraft are replacing American-supplied F-5 and F-86 jets acquired by Ethiopia during 25 years of close military cooperation with the United States which ended abruptly in early 1977.

There are three squadrons of Russian MiGs in Ethiopia now, including 24 MiG-21s and 12 MiG-23s with two more squadrons of 12 planes each expected to arrive soon, according to a middle level officer who also deserted recently.

Sixty Ethiopian pilots were trained in the Soviet Union to fly the new fighter planes, but South Yemeni pilots are the only ones yet to use them on combat missions, said the Ethiopian major.

More than 1,000 Russians and 2,000 Cubans are now in Ethiopia, according to Western intelligence sources.

Somali officials have repeatedly warned that these forces were organizing an invasion of Somalia across Ethiopia's south-eastern border where Somali-backed insurgents are engaged with Ethiopian forces.

Eritrean guerrillas, now in their 16th year of war for independence from Ethiopia, claim that the Russian build-up is also aimed at suppressing their increasingly successful rebellion in the north.

Russian interests here, say the guerrillas, center on control of the strategic Red Sea ports which dominate the Persian Gulf oil routes. There have been reports that the Russians are constructing naval facilities on the Dahlak islands off the Eritrean coast and in the port of Assab.

"The Russians are building up in Assab in case they lose Massawa," said the senior Ethiopian officer. "The Dergue (Ethiopia's ruling military council) has assigned $10 million to expand the facilities there, and Russian contractors are already bidding for the job."

The deep-water port of Massawa, also the site of a sophisticated American-built naval base, has been under attack since December 9 when guerrillas of the EPLF surrounded the city.

According to the Ethiopian army major, there are now eight Russian and Cuban military advisors stationed in Asmara, the Eritrean capital, and between 100 and 120 South Yemeni combat troops operating Russians tanks and artillery.

The South Yemenis have the specific responsibility of guarding Asmara's international airport through which the besieged garrison now receives all its supplies and reinforcements. An EPLF mortar attack closed the airport for three days in late December.

A factor in Ethiopia's growing reliance on foreign advisors and combat troops is the declining morale of Ethiopia's own officers and men, whose rate of defection from Asmara alone is now running at 15 each day.

The deserters say that the Ethiopian army has lost the will to fight and has no confidence in its ability to hold out against EPLF attacks. Many have also described macabre mass-murders of soldiers and civilians inside the besieged cities.

The most recent high level deserter to come to the EPLF asking for safe conduct to neighboring Sudan confirmed earlier reports of the November execution of 58 dissident officers and soldiers in Asmara and said that the killings continue in smaller numbers.

"It is becoming a daily occurrence," he said. "Anyone who questions military policy is subject to arrest and death without trial."

The worst incident which he said he knew of was the killing of 260 civilians in Massawa on December 14 and 15. One hundred were rounded up on the first day as fighting continued on the outskirts of the city and another 160 were arrested and killed the next day, said the officer, who cited this incident as the final straw in convincing him to desert.

"They killed teachers—men and women—bar girls, municipality officials, drivers and anyone else they suspected of sympathizing with the Front fighters," he said.

"The deaths are caused by the Government's political cadres who spy on all of us, not by the army commanders, many of whom do not even approve of the war," added the officer.

"You can trust no one but yourself," he concluded. "The only alternative is to escape."

The Horn of Africa:
The coming battle for Eritrea

The Financial Times (London), February 1978

With the current lull in the war between Ethiopia and Somalia, it appears that Cuban-supported Ethiopian forces are preparing for a major offensive in the northern territory of Eritrea. Eritrean guerrillas claim that more than 2,000 Cuban troops have been airlifted into the besieged Eritrean capital of Asmara and heavy fighting is now going on southwest of the city. The Cubans deny any intention of intervening in the Eritrean war, saying that it is an internal Ethiopian matter.

Diplomatic sources in Ethiopia suggest that the much touted Ethiopian offensive in the Ogaden had the limited objective of placing Somali forces on the defensive and re-opening the vital rail link between Addis Ababa and the port of Djibouti, while diverting attention from the build-up in the North.

In this view, the attempt to regain control of the strategic coastal province, with its two key ports on the Red Sea, is the first priority for Ethiopia's beleaguered military government as well as for the Soviet Union, which is playing a major role in directing the overall military operations.

Now in its seventeenth year, the war in Eritrea has reached a crucial stage. Eritrean independence forces have scored an unbroken series of victories against the central government which has carried them to within striking distance of Asmara and almost complete occupation of the central Eritrean highlands.

A steady flow of Russian heavy arms, Russian and Cuban military advisers and South Yemeni combat troops over the past six months has failed to stem the Eritrean advance, and it now appears that large numbers of Cuban troops are being airlifted from Angola to join the Ethiopian counter-attack.

A six month tour of Eritrea showed the guerrillas of the Eritrean People's Liberation Front (EPLF and the Eritrean Liberation Front (ELF) control most of the countryside. The EPLF dominates the north, east and center, while the smaller ELF holds the western lowlands and sections of Eritrea's southern border with Tigray province. The EPLF has also made gains in southern Eritrea, and both fronts overlap in the south-eastern Danakil lowlands that stretch along the coast toward the port of Assab, through which Ethiopia receives most of its arms and supplies.

In early 1977, the EPLF went on the offensive against Ethiopian positions in the larger towns and captured a string of garrisons that run on a north-south axis across Eritrea. March saw the fall of Nakfa. A month later, the EPLF overran Afabet and went on to take Elabaret and Debarwa. In July, the EPLF simultaneously captured Decamare and Keren, two of the most heavily defended cities in Eritrea.

Since then, the EPLF has moved against the towns of Segeneiti and Digsa in the south, the bases at Dogali, Dongolo, Ghinda, Nefasit, Mai Haber and Shegerini in the east, and finally against the coastal city of Massawa, former site of a sophisticated U.S. naval base and Eritrea's most important deep water port.

The attack on Massawa stalled in late December when an estimated 6,000 Ethiopian troops—supported by South Yemeni tank crews, Russian-manned BM-21 multiple rocket launchers and both Russian and Ethiopian warships—retreated to the peninsular naval base and two offshore islands which are connected to the mainland by a mile-long causeway. These enclaves remain under siege today.

The fighting now appears to be concentrating in the mountains south-west of Asmara. The EPLF Rome spokesman reports a major push near the highway that runs through Mendefera to link the capital with central Ethiopia.

The spokesman also says that Ethiopian Airlines flights have for two weeks been ferrying Cuban troops from Luanda, Angola to Asmara to join the Ethiopian offensive. European diplomats in Ethiopia confirm the Luanda-Asmara airlift and say the flights were routed through Addis Ababa.

The Ethiopian position in Eritrea has become critical. The loss of Asmara would not only be a crushing military blow but also a severe political setback, likely to be followed by an Eritrean declaration of independence. Such a move would thrust the long-0ignored war in Eritrea into international prominence just as the Organisation of African Unity (OAU) was holding its annual summit meeting in Khartoum, Sudan, where support for the Eritrean cause is strong.

The current Ethiopian offensive seems to be aimed at re-opening supply lines to Asmara where more than 20,000 Ethiopian troops and 200,000 civilian residents have been completely encircled since mid-October. Refugees and Ethiopian army deserters say that the city is facing acute shortages of food, fuel , water and medicines. Emergency stockpiles have run out and a joint Russian-Ethiopian airlift—disrupted for three days in late December by an EPLF mortar attack—has not been able to keep pace with supply needs.

On the other hand, the rapid advance of the Eritrean guerrilla armies has ;left them with wide areas to defend against counterattack, and divisions between the two liberation movements have so far precluded military coordination between them.

The massive build-up of Russian armaments—which include large numbers of tanks, armoured cars and MiG-21 and 23 aircraft—and a substantial superiority in manpower give Ethiopia the ability to mount well co-ordinated attacks in several directions against the Eritreans.

The chief flaw in the Eritrean defence is the lack of unity between the EPLF and the ELF. The rival fronts have maintained an informal alliance since December 1974, after three years of bitter civil war, but negotiations toward unification began four months ago and have not yet yielded concrete results.

The problem is further compounded by the existence of a newly formed third force known as the ELF-PLF led by Osman Saleh Sabbe. Though considerably smaller than either the ELF or the EPLF, the Right-wing ELF-PLF is receiving substantial aid from Saudi Arabia and the United Arab Emirates who fear the emergence of the Leftist EPLF as the dominant force in Eritrea.

Time is a key factor. If the Eritreans can resolve their internal conflicts and withstand the impending Ethiopian and Cuban offensive until June when the rainy season engulfs the highland plateau, they would be in a strong position to take Asmara and move south toward Assab where the last and perhaps the most difficult battle awaits them.

Unlike the Ethiopia-Somali war, time also works to the Eritrean advantage by continually increasing the role of the civilian population. The independence of the EPLF from virtually any external support has led them to concentrate heavily on internal mobilization.

Thousands of volunteers are now undergoing military and political training at secret EPLF camps inside Eritrea, while others are being inducted into local militias in their home villages. EPLF cadres are also organizing urban guerrilla units inside the cities still under Government control and are arming previously clandestine groups in towns and cities captured in 1977.

At this stage, Ethiopia faces a universally hostile population in Eritrea whose fervent nationalism has reached a level where it appears beyond compromise. Any advance by Cuban and Ethiopian forces would thus be subject to constant threat from within as well as counter-attack by the Eritrean armies.

While the large-scale introduction of Cuban combat forces and heavy arms may prolong the war, it does not appear likely to prove decisive. In the final analysis it may only make a peaceful solution more difficult to attain.

Life in an EPLF camp

Learning lessons to build a new society

The Guardian (New York), March 8, 1978

Debaat, Eritrea

Sadeia, 22, fled her home in Ginda almost two years ago. She left when Ethiopian troops began executing villagers and burning houses in reprisal for a raid by the Eritrean People's Liberation Front (EPLF) on a fuel storage tank in the vicinity.

She, her mother and her two babies began a 250-mile trek across Eritrea with one sheet and a straw basket of clothes. Looking for sanctuary from the marauding Ethiopian army, they found it as Debaat.

Nestled in the arid, volcanic hills of Sahel province in northern Eritrea, Debaat is one of three resettlement camps run by the EPLF for people like Sadeia and her family.

Comprised of refugees from all Eritrea's nine national groups. Debaat provides a unique testing ground for the EPLF's political and social programs. As such, the developing community offers a kind of model for the new society being forged in the shadow of war.

An intensive program of political education and popular organization appears to be the key to Debaat's steady progress. Guided by the EPLF, the people are united in their zeal to support and participate in the Eritrean revolution.

It was not always like this. When Sadeia's family first arrived here in early 1976, it was to an uneasy and uncertain fate. Moved three times to avoid Ethiopian air raids, the Debaat camp resembled something between a gypsy caravan and a welfare ghetto.

Meeting Basic Needs

The EPLF did its best to meet the people's basic needs by providing canvas tents, free medical care and food rations. But there were shortages of both goods and experience in coping with the new economic and social challenges.

Step by step the situation improved. Twenty-four months later, Debaat is much changed, reflecting in microcosm the growth and development of the EPLF itself.

An air of efficient calm now pervades the settlement. Signs of productive activity are visible at every turn. And the residents refuse to be described as "refugees."

"We are no longer escaping from the past," said one. "This is our home for now. We are struggling to meet our needs and to serve the revolution."

As Sadeia put it, "At the beginning, we were thinking only as refugees. We knew nothing. We didn't read or write. We thought only of ourselves.

"But there have been many developments in this camp and for me since then," she added. "We began first to struggle against illiteracy. We had free discussions, woman to woman and with our husbands. Soon we were cooperating together. The difference in our daily lives from then to now is like the difference between the land and the sky."

When I arrived at Debaat, I was ushered into a small stone office. Over the door hung a bright red banner proclaiming, "Victory to the masses!"

The interior walls were decorated with photographs of dancing villagers, an EPLF medic examining a small baby and peasant farmers plowing their fields. A file cabinet contained detailed records of Debaat's 1200 inhabitants. A fighter sat on a bench reading Stalin's "Foundations of Leninism."

Over dinner, I discussed Debaat's progress and its national significance with Askalu, the young woman fighter who heads the camp.

At first a catchall for refugees en route to neighboring Sudan, Debaat came under tighter regulation when the EPLF Social Welfare Department was formed after the front's first organizational congress in January 1977, she explained.

The first step was to reorganize the camp into four zones under direct EPLF supervision. Study and work groups were set up within each area, dividing the women from men. "Until we bring them to the same way of thinking," said Askalu, "it is better for them to take their lessons separately."

Each group elected leaders who together shared administrative responsibilities. An immediate consequence was that numerous women came to political leadership. Within weeks, they christened the four districts, "Equality, Unity, Liberation and Independence."

Political education was systematized with EPLF cadres holding three meetings per week with each small group, after which the local leaders held evening discussions In eight months, the community worked through the EPLF political manual for fighters covering Eritrean history, aims, goals and tactics of the revolution, the handling of contradictions and rudimentary political economy, among other subjects.

Weekly criticism/self-criticism sessions were organized and the entire camp began to meet monthly to exchange suggestions and new ideas. Classes, already in progress, were stepped up to three times a week in Tigrinya and in Arabic to give people common languages, while many small informal groups sprang up to study minority languages. EPLF doctors also began presenting weekly lectures on hygiene and sanitation.

"Slowly, we plan to integrate them into full administrative responsibility," said Askalu, "but we want first to fight their backwardness and feudal ideas. The more we change organization and consciousness of the people, the more we can be sure they can take control of themselves."

Tribal Divisions

One of the principal problems facing Debaat and Eritrean society as a whole were deeply rooted tribal and ethnic divisions. Overcoming them was an early target of the political education.

"We told them that tribalism is a device of the colonialists to sap our strength, and we taught them the history of how the Italians the British and the Ethiopians exploited our differences to their advantage," recounted Askalu.

"We also relocated some families to mix people of various nationalities with each other. The more you put them together the more they lose their bad ideas. They had completely different cultures, but now they share the same one."

More recently, adult volunteers were called for help at the nearby central EPLF hospital. Eighty women went for a month's service, according to Askalu.

Thirty-eight men also spent a month building shelters in Zero, and are waiting to go to a coastal EPLF agricultural project to help gather the grain harvest.

"They want to work," said Askalu. "They enjoy being with the fighters and participating in the revolution. Our problem now is finding enough for them to do."

The hospital has begun to send truckloads of laundry to Debaat for washing. Sixty quintals of chick peas were brought to be roasted before being ground into shirro, a staple in the Eritrean diet. Volunteers in the camp are making food baskets and clay ovens for the EPLF branches in Sahel. Tomatoes and green peppers are under cultivation using hand-carried well water for irrigation.

A recent offer to open a class for 50 people to learn sewing turned up 150 volunteers, forcing the EPLF to send for more machines to set up a cottage industry in Debaat.

Each resident receives millet, wheat flour, butter, sugar, tea and salt in liberal quantities. Canned tomato sauce, vegetables and sardines donated from abroad are given out as available and kerosene and cooking oil as needed. Each child and pregnant woman is also given a can of powdered milk equivalent to 33 1/3 pints of whole milk.

A clinic staffed by two field-trained paramedics and two helpers services the camp's health needs.

Changes for Women

The cooking areas are outside, an innovation which leads to much socializing among women who have been accustomed to spending most of their time alone in their houses. Schools for the children and an impromptu system of communal daycare also freed the women for social and economic activities.

At four o'clock we strolled over to the preschool area where children between the ages of three and five gather twice daily for a kind of "head-start" program of physical training, organized play and national song.

Two rows of chubby-cheeked girls and boys sat on the ground singing, "Let the masses be organized and conscious so their eyes will not be closed by a few individuals."

Standing as we arrived, they went into a medley of songs and dance from six of nine Eritrean nationalities, closing with a rousing "Victory to the masses! I will fight!"

Jumping up and down for more, they were told by the EPLF teacher that they should stay in straight lines and maintain discipline. "We know that," said one precocious 4-year-old. "We're comrades."

The challenge in Debaat seems well in hand. The task now is to extend the lessons learned here—from the mistakes as well as the successes—to similar problems that continue to plague many thousands of other Eritreans.

An estimated 600,000 people have been displaced in Eritrea in the past decade of war. More than 140,000 refugees are now in Sudan living in city slums and squalid rural camps.

Another 20-30,000 Eritreans have fled the barren desert hills around the port of Massawa during the battle for the city that began in early December and continues today. With up to a fourth of the housing destroyed by a continuous Ethiopian air, sea and land bombardment, many Massawa residents will continue under EPLF care for some time.

Debaat has become the center of a national network of cadres who are drawing up plans to deal with them when possible within the local communities themselves according to Askalu.

At this time, Ethiopian forces occupy only the Eritrean capital of Asmara and a handful of surrounding villages a small section of the port area of Massawa, a garrison at Barentu in the western lowlands, a corridor of villages leading to the Adi Keih garrison on the south and the remote southeastern port of Assab. All but Assab are under siege.

Plans are being made to resettle Debaat residents in their previous homelands as they become liberated and organized. "Most of those here will return home as conditions permit," said Askalu. "We see Debaat as essentially a temporary settlement, although there are people such as war-wounded and orphans who will be unable to support themselves. Perhaps this or similar settlements will continue in some form."

Africa News Special: Showdown in Eritrea

Africa News (Durham, NC), April 3, 1978

Having won a victory over Somali forces in the Ogaden, Ethiopia's military regime is turnings its attention to other parts of the former Ethiopian empire in which government authority is challenged. The most serious threat comes in Eritrea, a Red Sea coastal territory once colonized by Italy and Britain, federated to Ethiopia in 1952, then annexed by Emperor Haile Selassie in 1962. There a guerrilla independence movement has established broad popular support. American journalist Dan Connell has recently returned from an extended stay with the Eritrean guerrillas, and AFRICA NEWS reached him for an interview last week.

AN: *When did you first visit Eritrea?*

DC: The first time was in 1976, I had been led into the area by what I had read about the Ethiopian revolution and I went as a free-lance writer to dig around and see what was really happening in Ethiopia. I spent four months in the rural areas of Ethiopia in which I became convinced that very little was actually being carried out under the Ethiopian revolution.

I first went into Eritrea on a government supply convoy to the capital city of Asmara in March 1976. On the second day I was there the colonel who had led the convoy in was assassinated by the Eritrean People's Liberation Front (EPLF), and the Ethiopian troops took their revenge out on the civilian population.

I spent a lot of time asking individual Eritreans about the situation there, [I learned] the people were fighting for independence against a corrupt military regime that had replaced the feudal regime of Haile Selassie.

Then I went to Sudan and made contact with the EPLF and the ELF (Eritrean Liberation Front), and spent five weeks in Eritrea split between the two fronts, in June and July of 1976. At that time it was effectively a guerrilla operation, and we traveled from one area of the countryside to another to the guerrilla bases.

When I went back again in August 1977 and stayed for six months, the situation had developed quite a bit. In fact the EPLF is not really a guerrilla army any more. They are a national army which maintains their own supply lines and raise their own food on farms they set up. It is mechanized: they move from place to place by truck over some highways they've captured and some they have built themselves. They organize in brigade-strength now, concentrating as before on the political and social organization of the people at the same time they are carrying through the military struggle.

Village Democracy

AN: *Can you give us some sense of what it was like to be there?*

DC: I spent a lot of my visit in the towns that the EPLF had taken in the last year. I was able to sit in the city of Keren and have coffee at a café in the center of town. Watching the camels move by with the local traders moving in and out of the city, and the children going to school, one can have the sense that one is sitting anywhere, in a normal city with business going on as usual.

AN: *Are you saying that the EPLF control the towns to the extent that normal civilian life is possible?*

DC: They do. But they haven't set up military bases in the towns. Their bases are still in the countryside. In these towns they have concentrated on organizing the civilians to take over the administration themselves.

They organize civilian associations among the women, youth, peasants, workers and middle classes. These people in turn elect their own leaders. There is close coordination, but the civilian population effectively run their own organizations, and through them elect legislative assemblies which take over much of the administration.

AN: *What is the structure of the EPLF itself?*

DC: The EPLF is a front which is organized along fairly broad lines, to include as many different classes and social groups in the society as are able and willing to participate. It has a collective leadership, with a central committee and a 13-member political bureau at the top of it. All decisions are made collectively by this body, in coordination with a pyramidal structure manned with political and military people.

When you are actually with the Front, though, you can't really tell who's a leader and who isn't. When I was there the first year, I sat down at one point with the whole leadership without realizing it till I came back this year and was introduced to them individually. They dress the same, they eat the same, and they behave the same as the ordinary fighters.

AN: *What about the role of women in the organization?*

DC: Women play an active role in the EPLF and the mass organizations. They didn't start getting really involved in the Eritrean struggle until 1971-72, when the EPLF began to grow. Now, I have seen the women fighting in the front lines of Massawa as part of the battalions in the fighting units. I couldn't give you an exact figure, but I think close to 30% of the fighters are women. More important is the fact that by the work done among the civilian population they are guaranteeing that women won't step back after the war is over. They've banned arranged marriages, they've brought women into the local associations and local militias.

For a woman to carry a gun in her own town is a real shock to some of the people there. I talked with one girl in a small village who had joined the militia. When she came home with a gun on her back, her parents wouldn't let her in the house. All their neighbors and her parents kept saying that a woman should carry a baby and not a gun. She had to sleep outside for four nights, but she stayed with it.

Efforts Toward Unity

AN: *What is the relationship between ELF and EPLF?*

DC: They made a very big step toward unity in October when they set our a formal statement of principles of unity, and they have been meeting privately since.

The problem is that they have different approaches to unity. The EPLF is a much more highly politicized organization. The ELF is made up of a lot of different elements, many of which have as their main concern to postpone social revolution until the military struggle is over. The ELF wants merger at the top level, while the EPLF wants a united front at all levels.

At this stage the ELF is in a very weak position, having suffered several small military defeats at the hands of Ethiopia. There is a split inside with some favoring closer relationships with the EPLF and some moving to the right to support the small third force, Osman Sabbe's ELF-PLF. I think the ELF is getting in a position where it has to accept the EPLF terms. Otherwise it's apt to be destroyed by the Ethiopians.

I think the idea of these two fronts being engaged with each other over a long period of time suggest to the ELF that they would simply be absorbed into the more disciplined and better organized EPLF. My own experience is that when I was with the ELF and I asked questions about their positions, I was always referred to the leaders. There was no trust that the ordinary fighters knew what the position of the ELF was, and in fact when I did talk to them they often had very different opinions.

AN: *What is the expected result of the Ethiopian offensive said to be coming soon?*

DC: There have been offensives against Eritrea for the last three years at this time of year. Each time the offensive has not been successful. I think the view inside Eritrea is that this one also will be turned back, but perhaps at a greater cost in Eritrea. The increase in the weaponry, especially from the Soviet Union, but still some NATO weapons coming in through other sources to Ethiopia, mainly has the effect of raising the level of destruction in the civilian areas.

AN: *What are the prospects of active Soviet and Cuban involvement in Eritrea?*

DC: It appeared to me that the Cubans had held back all through

the fall from getting too involved, with the exception of sending occasional advisers up to visit in Eritrea. There weren't any Cubans permanently stationed except a few medical personnel in Asmara.

The main foreign force has been South Yemeni. They've been in
the tanks and manning artillery ever since September. The Soviet
Union has sent technicians into the area, in Massawa and in Asmara.
It appears they had come in to train the Ethiopians in the use of some
of the more sophisticated weapons, but the war has been proceeding
at a much faster pace than perhaps they could keep up with and they
have been forced into pulling triggers.

Now there have been fairly convincing reports of large numbers
of Cubans being flown into Asmara, reports from the EPLF and from
diplomatic sources and journal;ists in Addis Ababa. I think it is clear
that if they are in Asmara, which is the focus of a lot of military activity, they will inevitably be drawn into the fighting.

AN: *The Cubans used to back the Eritrean struggle. Has the
EPLF tried to do anything internationaly—diplomatically—to put
pressure on Cuba?*

DC: They have, but I think the EPLF is weakest in the diplomatic struggle. I know that when I first learned of the involvement of the
South Yemenis in combat in September, they preferred not to make
any of that information public until they could first talk privately
with South Yemen, but they were very disappointed with the results.
South Yemen, of course, had been one of the EPLF's major suporters.

They have tried through a variety of informal contacts to oppose
the Cuban involvement, and when I was there they were still hopeful
that it wouldn't take place.

A Lack of Allies

AN: *What are their international links?*

DC: They don't have many. They have support from the guerrilla
movement in Oman. They have some links with the POLISARIO and
with some of the Palestinian movements. But because they were a left revolutionary movement, they were isolated from the West. With the large-
scale involvement of the Soviet Union and Cubba in Ethiopia they have
been comletely cut off from the East.

They have had continuing offers of aid from a number of Arab
countries which in the past they've refused because of the strings
attached, the attempts to gain influence. Their concern now is still to
make contact with other liberation movements and with progressive
countries, partioularly in Africa, in order to overcome the picture of

them as an Arab-backed movement. They are also concentrating on trying to raise the issue at the OAU meeting in June in Khartoum.

AN: *Do they now have to depend on some arms frm countries like Sudan and Saudi Arabia?*

DC: Sudan never gives any actual material aid, but simply allows aid to pass through. Saudi Arabia has been placing its aid in the direction of the ELF-PLF, the right-wing movement, and staying away from the EPLF.

AN: *Where does the EPLF get its arms?*

DC: They get them mainly from Ethiopia. They are captured arms. I saw this in the battle for Massawa. I've seen them capture tanks and artillery and turn them right around and use them on the Ethiopians. I've seen them capture mountains of ammunition, small arms, food and medical supplies. They also maintain underground bases throughout Eritrea where they work on these weapons, and they can make a small arm from scratch now.

Pitting Rifles Against Tanks

AN: *What was the military situation when you left?*

DC: The entire countryside is in the hands of the Eritreans. There are no roads or highways open to the Ethiopians at this point. They still hold the remote port of Assab and the capital city of Asmara, a little corner of Massawa, and two small garrison towns, Barentu, sourrounded by the ELF, and Adi Caieh, surrounded by the EPLF.

The last two months I was in Eritrea I spent in the port and around the port of Massawa, where the heaviest fighting of the war had taken place. The main port for Ethiopia, Massawa was the site for a sophisticated American naval base, which was used up to early 1977 and turned over to Ethiopia when the U.S. was evicted. It was also the main port for supplies into Ethiopia up until two years ago when the roads were more or less cut.

The Eritreans cut the road to Massawa in October. The Ethiopians tried unsuccessfully five times to re-open the road from Massawa to Asmara. In the fifth effort, on December 8, they brought a convoy of some 300 heavily laden trucks, troop carriers and buses, led by an armored column of 20 to 30 Soviet T-54 tanks, driven by South Yemenis.

I came down the night before the battle. The EPLF had prepared for December 10 to try to attack the main Ethiopian base at Dogali. But the first shots of the battle were fired by the Ethiopians when they tried to move their convoy through. We were awakened at about 6:45

a.m. with an artillery shell going off in our camp. The EPLF held up the convoy all through the morning. It was an extraordinary sight because the Ethiopians had brought up their heaviest armor. They had tank columns, rockets, heavy artilery; they were being suported by air cover from American-made F-5 jets and even by fire from ships lying off the coast. The Eritrean fighters were armed mainly with hand-held assault rifles, rocket-propelled grenades and supported by machine guns and mortars. But they pinned the Ethiopians down all through the morning, and opend their own attack at about 11:15. Within about 15 minutes, the Ethiopians began to retreat.

AN: *What gives the Eritreans the edge in that kind of situation?*

DC: It was morale and determination to fight.

Another aspect to the EPLF has been the involvement of the civilian population. When I was in Massawa, hundreds of civilian volunteers came down by the truckload to take up positions on the front lines.

AN: *Is there any truth to the view that Ethiopians purged from the government, such as Teferi Benti or Atnafu Abate, were more open to accepting Eritrean demands?*

DC: Atnafu Abate was in Eritrea for two months in September and October 1977, investigating the Eritrean question. He went back to submit a report, saying that there was no military solution possible and there had to be a political settlement with Eritrea. He was asked three times to woithdraw his report by [Ethiopian leader] Mengistu. After the third refusal, he was called in and executed. That information comes from a man named Mengesha Gessassa who was assistant governor of Eritrea until he defected in January.

AN: *Are there any Eritreans prepared to accept anything less than full independence?*

DC: No. There is no possibility of that. They might negotiate over questions of access to the ports and over some relationship to Ethiopia after independence, but they are very firm that they wouldn't raise any of these questions except on the baqsis of full national sovereignty.

AN: *What do you think might have happened after Haile Selassie was overthrown had those who favored a negotiated solution prevailed?*

DC: I think the EPLF would not like to say it, but I think the feeling among the people and even some elements of the front was such that they might have settled at that point. If a genuine peaceful solution had been offered, I think it might have been accepted. Instead, there were major offensives against the Eritreans, beginning in January and February of 1975.

AN: *What about possibilities for the future?*

DC: The Eritreans all the way up to the leadership, of the front feel a close fraternal relationship with Ethiopia. I think it is not possible under the Mengistu government, but if one proceeds first on the basis of nationaal sovereignty for Eritrea, I think there is no question that there would be close linkls between these peoples for generatons to come. The Eritreans very consciously distinguish between the present military government and the Ethiopian people, saying that their natural allies and friends are the Ethiopian masses.

Section 3

Soviet Intervention
&
Strategic Withdrawal
1978

Prologue

The Ethiopian military build-up for an assault on Eritrea continued through the spring of 1978. The regime's propaganda mill warned that they were threatened by an Arab invasion through the former Italian colony, playing on myths and memories of historical conquest to whip up anti-Eritrean sentiment. Shipments of new Soviet tanks and artillery poured into Assab. High-level Soviet military advisors moved from the Somali frontlines to Eritrea. Tens of thousands of freshly trained Ethiopian troops massed in central Ethiopia.

On the other side, the Eritreans watched their limited external support shrivel and disappear. Cuban envoys tried to convince them to give up their demand for independence and join the emerging pro-Soviet entente. Moscow went further, pressuring its allies and supporters throughout Africa and beyond to break with the Eritreans, now characterized as tools of imperialism — witting or not — for their continuing hostility to the new Ethiopian regime. Despite this, the U.S. and other Western powers declined to take up the Eritrean cause, deeming it to be unsustainable (and too "left-wing" for their taste).

These tectonic political shifts triggered wrenching debates within the nationalist movements — particularly the EPLF — but no retreat from their overarching objectives. Unfortunately, neither did they push them to bury their differences in order to unite their heavily outgunned forces.

Thus, the stage was set for the fiercest battles of the seventeen-year liberation war, with all the odds — and most of the world — on the side of Ethiopia. In effect, this marked the start of a second war of national liberation for the Eritreans — one waged against a new political foe, fought against a new army, conducted with new strategies and tactics (on both sides), and carried out on a scale and intensity never before seen in Africa, while the liberation movement was still internally divided.

The Ethiopian campaign unfolded in a series of three major offensives that stretched over nearly eight months into early 1979, during which the two fronts ceded control of all but one previously-captured town, Nakfa. Once the Ethiopians were stalemated outside this small but highly symbolic provincial capital, there was a pause. Government forces tried to break through EPLF lines in a fourth round in April 1979, but were unsuccessful. They launched another assault in July — the Fifth Offensive — which also proved fruitless. There were more such attempts to come in the 1980s, but it was the first three rounds in 1978-79 that decisively altered the positions of these formidable adversaries and, in so doing, reset the terms of the war itself.

———

I returned to Khartoum in May 1978 with my two children, who stayed with me through August. I sublet an apartment for the summer from a professor at Khartoum University and set up shop as a freelance reporter. My ability to travel to the field to cover the war was limited by my familial responsibilities, but I had access to many of the players in the Sudan capital, and I wrote-up a storm.

At the outset, I was on retainer for Reuters to report on the war, and I was assigned to a Reuters team to cover the annual summit meeting of the Organization of African Unity in July. I was also on retainer for *The Financial Times*, and I was stringing for several newspapers for which I had already written — *The Boston Globe*, *The Toronto Globe and Mail*, *La Repubblica*, *Le Monde*, and *The Observer* — and for two new ones, *The Christian Science Monitor* and *The Miami Herald*. By the fall I added Oslo's leading daily, *Aftenposten*, along with *Time* magazine and *The Washington Star*, and I started to file occasional stories for the Voice of America and the Associated Press, though I could not use my own byline with the latter two because I was reporting for rival broadcast and print media. This was the widest range of outlets for which I ever reported.

The Ethiopian offensive got underway in June as the newly trained and equipped Ethiopian brigades drove north through Tigray on three roughly parallel fronts. They were harassed at every step by TPLF guerrillas and repeatedly ambushed by mobile units of the EPLF and ELF, but they kept coming. In early July they pushed into southern Eritrea.

Tessenei was the first major town to fall. The Ethiopians took it on July 19. Within days Adi Quala, Mendefera and Agordat — the remaining ELF-controlled urban centers — followed. The EPLF, now vulnerable on its exposed flanks, withdrew from Massawa and Decamare. At that point the Ethiopians paused. End of round one.

———

Apart from a single unsuccessful journey to the Sudan-Eritrea border with the ELF — whose leaders balked at taking me inside once they realized they were being routed — I covered the initial fighting from Khartoum. After my children flew home in August, I went inside with the EPLF for three weeks to assess the new situation, filing from Sudan when I came out. In October, I went into the war zone a second time and returned to Khartoum again to file. During this trip, I kept an audio diary on my cassette recorder and sent it to the BBC, which used it to produce a thirty-minute radio documentary — "The Eritrean David Meets the Soviet Goliath." The program aired on November 15.

The fighting in Eritrea resumed later in November. I was with the EPLF in Keren as the Second Offensive got underway. The government's full force was focused on the EPLF. On November 17, the front withdrew from the towns along the Asmara-Massawa Road. Nine days later, after heavy fighting north of Asmara, the EPLF pulled out of Keren in a well-planned and executed retreat that left the movement positioned to take up the fight on more favorable terms. Again there was a pause.

The Ethiopians regrouped, resupplied and moved in reinforcements. They launched the Third Offensive in January, advancing to positions just beyond Afabet, but that was as far as they penetrated. The EPLF stopped them in the mountains northwest of Nakfa where they bogged down for the next decade, despite several ferocious and enormously costly attempts to break through.

In the Sahel region, EPLF units controlled the high ground. They used the inhospitable terrain to neutralize the impact of Ethiopia's armor, artillery and air power, and they dug in there to make their stand. This was a brilliant strategic move that no doubt saved the Eritrean revolution from defeat. Yet it took quite some time for those watching the conflict from a distance to grasp it.

I remained in Keren on November 26 into the final hours of this turnabout — the end of the movement's fleeting experiment with urban administration and the return to the bush — and dashed out of the city at dawn with the last of the EPLF forces. But much to my enduring distress I was unable to file anything then to set the event in a comprehensible context. As I relate in an article on "Eritrea and the International Media" in Section 8, I begged the front to give me access to a radio to send this story out immediately, but top EPLF commanders insisted they had more urgent concerns.

Not surprisingly, the Ethiopians announced a crushing victory in

Keren the next day — once they discovered the city was empty — and forecast the imminent end of the war. Many commentators far from the scene believed them. By the time my account got out describing what really happened, it was old news and had little impact. This was not so important in itself, but it shaped subsequent perceptions of the viability of the liberation movement.

For the Eritreans, the question was where to draw the lines for the next stage of this bitterly protracted struggle. EPLF leaders were willing to leave Nakfa and go back to their remote base near the Sudan border, even to abandon the base and resume mobile guerrilla warfare, if that was what it took to live to fight another day. But they would not fight a battle they knew they could not win. Such were the basic tenets of protracted people's war, the Maoist-derived military strategy that guided the EPLF throughout its long struggle.

However, for much of the rest of the world, the dominant image was that of a defeated and largely unsupported Eritrea confronting a major superpower, the Soviet Union, and a foe twenty times its size, Ethiopia. All that was left, said many European and North American writers and policymakers, was the mopping up.

"The 16-year-old Eritrean effort to gain independence from Ethiopia collapsed this week when upwards of 35,000 Ethiopian troops backed by Soviet and Cuban advisors drove the Eritreans from their last stronghold," said Jay Ross in a November 29 *Washington Post* article, forecasting a reversion to "a low-key guerrilla struggle."

"The nasty little war in the Horn of Africa, once on America's front pages, is fading quietly," wrote *Baltimore Sun* reporter Henry Trewhitt a week later in what amounted to a political obituary. "The fall of Keren ended everything approximating organized conflict."

They could not have been more wrong, but it was difficult to argue this at the time. All I could do from my vantage point was to keep reporting what I saw and heard — which I did.

My news shorts were broadcast on the BBC and the Voice of America. My longer stories ran on Reuters and the AP and in newspapers across Europe and North America, reaching other outlets through syndication. My audio account of the withdrawal from Keren aired on the BBC on January 3, 1979 in a thirty-minute documentary, "Long March in Eritrea." Later that month, I traveled to Europe, where I placed stories with *Trouw* and *Vrij Nederland* in Amsterdam and *Algemein Dagblatt* in Rotterdam, as well as other outlets for which I'd written earlier.

Ethiopia reportedly readies drive in Eritrea

The Boston Sunday Globe, March 26, 1978

Khartoum, Sudan

With the collapse of the Somali army in Ethiopia's contested Ogaden desert, the focus of war in the strategic Horn of Africa is shifting to the northern territory of Eritrea.

More than 2000 Cuban combat troops have been airlifted into the besieged Eritrean capital of Asmara, and extensive preparations are under way in northern Ethiopia for a new offensive against Eritrean independence forces, according to Eritrean guerrilla sources.

An airstrip is being built for Ethiopia's new MiG jet fighters under Russian supervision in the city of Makele, 80 miles from Eritrea's southern border, and supply depots are being set up in the cities of Gondar and Axum, these sources say. A smaller airstrip is also being built to accommodate light reconnaissance planes on the Dahlak islands off the Eritrean coast, and army, navy and air force bases are being erected in the Eritrean port of Assab, according to Ethiopian officers, who have recently defected.

Until recently Cuba had refrained from becoming directly involved in the politically complicated Eritrean war, now 17 years old. A decade ago, Cuba aided the Eritrean movement against Ethiopia's Emperor Haile Selassie, but Castro's decision to lend full support to the present Ethiopian regime appears to be leading him, like South Yemen, Libya and other erstwhile allies of the Eritreans, to side against them today.

Diplomatic sources in Addis Ababa suggest that the attempt to regain control of the strategic coastal province, with its two key ports on the Red Sea, is the first priority for Ethiopia's beleaguered military government as well as for the Soviet Union which is playing a major role in directing the overall military operations. The war in Eritrea has reached a pivotal stage. Eritrean independence forces have scored a series of victories that has carried them to within striking distance of Asmara and almost complete occupation of the central Eritrean highlands.

A steady flow of Russian heavy arms, Russian and Cuban military advisers and South Yemen combat troops over the past six months has failed to stem the Eritrean advance, and it now appears that large numbers of Cuban troops are being airlifted from Angola to join the next Ethiopian counterattack.

A separate Italian colony for the first half of this century, Eritrea has been the object of conquest of a succession of empires stretching back to the Turks in the mid-1500s. Forcibly linked to Ethiopia in a UN-sponsored federation in 1952, the territory was annexed a decade later and the war for independence began.

A six-month tour of Eritrea showed that guerrillas of the Eritrean People's Liberation Front (EPLF) and the Eritrean Liberation Front (ELF) control the entire countryside. The EPLF dominates the north, east and center, while the smaller ELF holds the western lowlands and sections of Eritrea's southern border with Tigray province. The EPLF has also made gains in southern Eritrea, and both fronts overlap in the southeastern Danakil lowlands that stretch along the coast toward the port of Assab, through which Ethiopia receives most of its arms and supplies.

In early 1977, the EPLF went on the offensive against Ethiopian positions in the larger towns and captured a string of garrisons that run on a north-south axis across Eritrea. Then they moved against the coastal city of Massawa, former site of a sophisticated American naval base and Eritrea's most important deep-water port.

The attack on Massawa stalled in late December when an esti-mated 6000 Ethiopian troops supported by South Yemeni tank crews, Russian-manned BM-21 multiple rocket launchers and both Russian and Ethiopian warships retreated to the peninsular naval base and two offshore islands which are connected to the mainland by a mile-long causeway. These enclaves remain under siege today.

Apart from Massawa and Barentu, the only Eritrean towns still in Ethiopians hands are Asmara, the remote port of Assab and a small garrison at Adi Caieh in the south. Both Asmara and Adi Caieh are also under EPLF siege.

The latest fighting was concentrated in the mountains southwest of Asmara. The EPLF spokesman in Rome reported a major push last week near the highway that runs through Mendefera to link the capital with central Ethiopia, but said it was turned back after a four-day battle.

The spokesman also says for three weeks Ethiopian airlines flights have been ferrying Cuban troops from Luanda, Angola, to Asmara to join the Ethiopian offensive . European diplomats in Ethiopia confirm the Luanda-Asmara airlift and say the flights were routed through Addis Ababa.

The Ethiopian position in Eritrea has become critical. The loss of Asmara would not only be a crushing military blow but also a severe political setback, likely to be followed by an Eritrean declaration of independence. Such a move would thrust the long-ignored war in Eritrea into international prominence just as the Organization of African Unity (OAU) holds its June summit meeting in Khartoum, Sudan, where support for the Eritrean cause is strong.

The impending Ethiopian offensive seems to be aimed at reopening supply lines to Asmara where more than 20,000 Ethiopian troops and 200,000 civilian residents have been completely encircled since mid-October. Refugees and Ethiopian army deserters say that the city is facing acute shortages of food, fuel, water and medicines. Emergency stockpiles have run out and a joint Russian-Ethiopian airlift – disrupted for three days in late December by an EPLF mortar attack – has not been able to keep pace.

Among the factors favoring the Eritrean forces is the deteriorating morale of the Ethiopian army which has been repeatedly defeated south and west of Asmara in previous efforts to break the EPLF siege. Defectors say that the government has executed more than a hundred dissenting officers and soldiers since November for voicing criticism of the military situation. The rate of desertions from Asmara is now running at 15 to 20 a day, according to EPLF sources.

On the Eritrean side, high morale and the determination to win at all costs appears to be guerrillas' main asset. This is strengthened by broad popular support which takes the form of active civilian participation at the battlefront.

On the other hand, the rapid advance of the Eritrean guerrilla armies has left them with wide areas to defend against counterattack, and divisions between the two liberation movements have so far precluded military coordination.

Superior manpower and the massive buildup of Russian armaments – which include large numbers of tanks, armored cars and MiG21 and 23 aircraft – give Ethiopia the ability to mount coordinated attacks in several directions against the Eritreans.

But while the large-scale introduction of Cuban combat forces and heavy arms may prolong the war, they do not appear likely to prove decisive. And they many only make a peaceful solution more difficult to attain.

[Versions of this article appeared at about the same time in *The Financial Times, The Toronto Globe & Mail, Le Monde, Aftenposten,* and *La Repubblica.*]

Ethiopia prepares Eritrea attack

EPLF forces ready defenses

The Guardian (New York), March 29, 1978

In the wake of the collapse of the Somali army in Ethiopia's contested Ogaden region, extensive preparations are now underway for an Ethiopian offensive in Eritrea.

There are strong indications that Soviet and possibly Cuban forces will play a major role in the impending Ethiopian campaign, similar to that in the Ogaden last month.

The results for Ethiopia, however—with or without increased foreign help—are likely to be quite different in Eritrea where they will face not only the highly disciplined and experienced army of the Eritrean People's Liberation Front (EPLF) and allied antigovernment forces, but also a thoroughly mobilized and conscious civilian population.

According to EPLF, more than 2000 Cuban combat troops have been airlifted into the besieged Eritrean capital of Asmara and a series of bases are being constructed under Soviet supervision in the northern Ethiopian province of Tigray.

In a major battle March 14-16, some 10,000 Ethiopian troops were turned back when they attempted to break out of Asmara and crush the EPLF encirclement. EPLF sources claimed 1500 Ethiopian troops were killed in the clash.

Cuban officials have in the past denied any intention of becoming directly involved in Eritrea, but an EPLF spokesman says that Cuban soldiers were active in the battle.

In support of the campaign against Eritrea, day and night construction work has been proceeding on an airstrip for Ethiopia's new Soviet-supplied MiG jet fighters in the Tigray capital of Makele, 60 miles south of the Eritrean border, with Soviet Antonov-12 supply planes ferrying in materials and equipment from Addis Ababa.

Supply bases for the Ethiopian move north are being built in the cities of Gondar and Axum. An airstrip is also being set up to accommodate light reconnaissance planes on the Dahlak islands off the Eritrean coast, and army, navy and air force bases are being erected in the Eritrean port of Assab.

Thousands of hastily trained recruits of Ethiopia's peasant militia are also reported moving north and reinforcements are expected soon from the more experienced Ethiopian forces in the Ogaden as the war there winds down.

Now in its 17th year, the war in Eritrea has reached a pivotal stage. Eritrean independence forces have scored an unbroken series of victories against the central government which has carried them to within striking distance of Asmara and almost complete occupation of the central Eritrean highlands.

A steady flow of Soviet heavy arms, Soviet and Cuban military advisers and South Yemeni combat troops over the past six months has failed to stem the Eritrean advance, and it now appears that Cuban troops are being airlifted from Angola to join the next Ethiopian counterattack.

A 6-month tour of Eritrea showed that the armies of the EPLF and the Eritrean Liberation Front (ELF) control the entire country-side. The EPLF dominates the north, east and center, while the smaller ELF holders the western lowlands and sections of Eritrea's southern border with Tigray province. The EPLF has also made gains in southern Eritrea, and both fronts overlap in the south eastern Danakil lowlands that stretch along the coast toward the port of Assab, through which Ethiopia receives most of its arms and supplies.

The Battle for Asmara

The protracted battle for the coastal city of Massawa, former site of a U.S. navy base, involved the most substantial outside support yet for Ethiopia with South Yemeni crews driving tanks, Soviet technicians firing BM-21 Katyusha multiple rocket launchers (Stalin organs), South Yemeni pilots flying the new MIG-21 jets and Soviet warships joining Ethiopian naval vessels in shelling the city.

It was geography, however, that in the end forced the EPLF to settle in for a lengthy siege as the Ethiopian forces retreated to the safety of the peninsular naval base and two small offshore islands where they remain today.

Meanwhile, EPLF forces cleared the entire highway between Massawa and Asmara and began concentrating around the key highland capital where Ethiopia appears to be preparing to launch at least one prong of its planned offensive.

Apart from Massawa and Barentu, the only towns still in Ethiopian hands are Asmara, the remote southeastern port of Assab and a small garrison at Adi Caieh in the south. Both Adi Caieh and Asmara are under EPLF siege.

The Ethiopian position in Eritrea has become critical. The loss of Asmara would not only be a crushing military blow but also a severe political setback likely to be followed by an Eritrean declaration of independence. Such a move would thrust the long-ignored war in Eritrea into international prominence just as the Organization of African Unity (OAU) was holding its annual summit meeting in Khartoum, Sudan.

The impending Ethiopian offensive seems to be aimed at reopening supply lines to Asmara where more than 20,000 Ethiopian troops and 200,000 civilian residents have been encircled since mid-October. Refugees and Ethiopian army deserters say that the city is facing acute shortages of food, fuel, water and medicines. Emergency stockpiles have run out and a joint Soviet-Ethiopian airlift has not been able to keep pace with supply needs.

Among the factors favoring the Eritrean forces, according to EPLF, is the deteriorating morale of the Ethiopian army which has been repeatedly defeated south and west of Asmara in previous efforts to break the siege. Defectors say that the government has executed more than 100 dissenting officers and soldiers since November for voicing criticism of the military situation. The rate of desertions from Asmara is now running at 15-20 each day, according to EPLF.

On the Eritrean side, high morale and the determination to win at all costs appears to be their main asset. This is strengthened by broad popular support which takes the form of active civilian participation at the battle-front.

While with the EPLF, I saw the fighters repeatedly rout numerically and technically superior Ethiopian forces outside Asmara and in Massawa. Carrying assault rifles and rocket-propelled grenades, they were able to turn back tank columns, overrun artillery positions and withstand the heavy air and naval bombardment with surprisingly low casualties.

Peasant farmers and townspeople have also been organized and politicized through EPLF mass associations to play support roles in combat, and a growing civilian militia has been trained to join the war if necessary.

Coordinated Attacks

On the other hand, the rapid advance of the Eritrean armies has left them with wide areas to defend against counterattack and divisions between EPLF and ELF have so far precluded military coordination between them. Also, the massive buildup of Soviet armaments and a substantial superiority in manpower give Ethiopia the ability to mount coordinated attacks in several directions against the Eritreans.

The EPLF siege of Massawa is maintained by supply lines extending more than 100 miles into the interior. An Ethiopian landing along the sparsely inhabited northern coast could threaten to cut this corridor and isolate the EPLF in Massawa. However, such an attack would have to be accomplished quickly because the hilly, volcanic terrain around Massawa is ideal guerrilla territory while lacking water or food necessary to support a large army.

There are also a number of little used roads into Eritrea from Tigray which could be followed by armored columns and infantry, but these run through mountains well suited to ambush and defense.

Additionally, there is the guerrilla army of the Tigray People's Liberation Front (TPLF) to contend with. The TPLF has in the past coordinated military actions with its Eritrean neighbors and leaders of the TPLF were recently in Eritrea to confer with the EPLF on joint strategy along their common border.

The chief flaw in the Eritrean defense has been the lack of unity between the EPLF and the ELF. The rival fronts have maintained an informal alliance since December 1974 after three years of bitter civil war. Negotiations toward unification began four months ago. These talks apparently yielded some results last week, the Guardian learned, and may soon lead to military coordination between the two organizations.

Internal Conflicts

The problem is compounded by the existence of a newly formed third force known as the ELF-PLF, led by Osman Saleh Sabbe, a former member of the EPLF foreign mission who was denounced by the EPLF leadership in 1976 for secretly negotiating a pact with the ELF.

Though considerably smaller than either the EPLF or ELF and in position only in a narrow area long Eritrea's border with Sudan, the right wing ELF-PLF is receiving substantial aid from Saudi Arabia and the Arab Emirates who fear the emergence of the leftist EPLF as the dominant force in Eritrea.

The nationalist ELF has also been the recipient of Arab military aid through Iraq and Syria, but internal conflicts have seriously weakened them over the past year with members defecting to both the EPLF on the left and the ELF-PLF on the right.

With the reported agreement on military actions between the EPLF and ELF, there is a growing possibility of a rear area civil war between them and the ELF-PLF which could strain the defenses against Ethiopia.

Time is a key factor here. If the Eritreans can resolve their internal conflicts and withstand the impending Ethiopian offensive until

June, when the rainy season engulfs the highland plateau, they would be in a strong position to take Asmara and move south toward Assab where the last and perhaps the most difficult battle awaits them.

Unlike the Ethiopian-Somali war, time also works to Eritrea's advantage by continually increasing the role of the civilian population. The independence of the EPLF from virtually any external support has led them to concentrate heavily on internal mobilization.

Thousands of volunteers are now undergoing military and political training at secret EPLF camps inside Eritrea, while others are being inducted into local militias in their home villages. EPLF cadres are also organizing urban guerrilla units inside the cities still under government control and are arming previously clandestine groups in towns and cities captured in 1977.

At this stage, Ethiopia faces a universally hostile population in Eritrea whose fervent nationalism, enhanced by their deep-rooted commitment to social revolution under the leadership of the EPLF, has reached a level where it appears beyond compromise. Any advance by Ethiopian forces would thus be subject to constant threat from within as well as from counterattack by the Eritrean armies.

West keeps Ethiopian ties

State Department views Ethiopia's ties with Soviets as shaky

The Guardian (New York), April 5, 1978

Port Sudan, Sudan

Ethiopia appears to have moved into the anti-imperialist camp, but discrete ties with the West still play an important role in propping up the military government.

The ruling Provisional Military Administrative Council (Dergue) had been unable to obtain spare parts for its U.S.-supplied weapons after a mid-1977 embargo. The needed supplies were recently released to Ethiopia by the State Department in what appears to be a U.S. effort to patch up relations with Addis Ababa.

World Bank funds and non-military aid to and from Western Europe are still flowing into Ethiopia, and there is increasing discussion in Washington of renewing direct air programs to Ethiopia.

A significant trend among State Department analysts views Ethiopia's current tied with the Soviet bloc countries as potentially ephemeral—stemming more from the Mengistu regime's immediate military and political needs than from a deep ideological commitment.

Ethiopia's close military and economic ties with Israel were apparently disrupted only a month ago, after Foreign Minister Moshe Dayan publicly acknowledged the continuing relationship. The Israeli admission proved an embarrassment to the "leftist" Lt. Col. Mengistu Haile Mariam, who then ordered scores of Israeli military advisors to leave the country. Arms sales and less visible forms of aid, however, apparently remain in force.

The initial Israeli military presence in Ethiopia followed close on the heels of a U.S. buildup that began in 1953 under the auspices of the late Ethiopian Emperor Haile Selassie. It has survived the ascension of a self-described leftist military regime which came to power in 1974. The relationship has continued in the unlikely context of Ethiopia's realignment away from the U.S. and into the camp of the Soviet Union and its allies.

If Israel, Cuba, South Yemen, East Germany and the USSR make strange bedfellows, it did not appear to phase the Zionist policymakers, who cite their national interests in the Red Sea region as more decisive than ideological differences with the Dergue's other allies.

The common denominator for Israel in 1977 and early 1978, as it was for the U.S. in the 1950s and 1960s, was the commitment to "maintain the territorial integrity of Ethiopia" against what they perceived as an Arab-supported independence movement in the coastal territory of Eritrea.

A former Italian colony, Eritrea was federated with Ethiopia under U.N. auspices in 1952. A mutual defense pact signed a year later between the U.S. and Ethiopia guaranteed the union in exchange for U.S. military assistance and the right to build military bases in the strategic Eritrean port of Massawa and the highland capital of Asmara.

Under a subsequent agreement, Israel also began to provide military aid to Ethiopia and was granted supply bases on the islands of Haleb and Fatima, which lie close to the narrow southern entrance to the Red Sea, east of the Eritrean port of Assab. While the U.S. bases were closed in 1977 during Ethiopia's shift to the Soviet bloc, the Israeli naval supply bases are thought to remain in use.

During the 1950s, U.S. military advisers reorganized Ethiopia's army into three modern divisions and an imperial bodyguard, which later became the fourth army division after an attempted coup d'etat in 1961. Following a decade of political unrest in Eritrea, which climaxed the same year with the formation of the Eritrean Liberation Front, U.S. and Israeli advisers arrived to train Ethiopian soldiers in counterinsurgency warfare.

Israel was at the same time reportedly using bases in southwestern Ethiopia to train and assist guerrillas in southern Sudan as well as antigovernment elements in ... [missing] ... advisers also trained the Ethiopian police.

More recently, as the guerrilla war in Eritrea escalated under the Eritrean People's Liberation Front, Israel was called upon by Ethiopia's military leaders to train regular army units.

In 1976, 40 Israeli advisers organized a 10,000-member force known as the "Nebelbal" (flame brigade) at Arba, 156 miles east of Addis Ababa.

The Nebelbal have since been dispatched to fight in Eritrea and served in the Ogaden war as well. They were initially armed by Israel with captured Soviet weapons taken in the 1973 Arab-Israeli war.

Israel has also been supplying Ethiopia with spare parts for U.S.-made equipment left over from the pre-1977 period of U.S.-Ethiopian military cooperation.

Ethiopian deserters reaching Sudan earlier this year told the Guardian that Israeli military advisers were training Ethiopian commandos at three locations in central and southern Ethiopia in the Awash Valley and near the towns of Leghadadi and Shashemani for duty in Eritrea and in the southeastern Ogaden region.

Whether the Israelis are now pulling out of Ethiopia is an open question. It is perhaps well to remember that Haile Selassie also made a great show of evicting the Israelis and breaking diplomatic relations in 1973.

In any case, it is clear that some of Ethiopia's military leaders are anxious to keep a door open to the West, and the U.S. appears to be waiting in the wings for an invitation.

Eritrean fighting forces forge united front

The Guardian (New York), April 19, 1978

After eight years of intense rivalry, and three years of bitter civil war, Eritrean independence forces have taken concrete steps to establish a united front against Ethiopia.

The Eritrean People's Liberation Front (EPLF) and the Eritrean Liberation Front (ELF) have announced a joint statement of principle and will meet later this month to establish a common program.

According to the EPLF Rome spokesman, the accord recognized unity on the following points: full independence for Eritrea; opposition to all forces which intervene "against the identity of the Eritrean population;" the safeguarding of the democratic rights of the Eritrean masses; and the establishment of good relations with all progressive forces in the world.

A separate Italian colony for the first half of this century, Eritrea was forcibly linked to Ethiopia in a UN-sponsored federation in 1952 and annexed a decade later. The Eritreans have been fighting for their independence since 1961, but the movement has been divided between the EPLF and the ELF since 1970.

The next formal meeting between the two fronts, scheduled for April 20, will implement the unity agreement by laying out a program of coordination in military, economic, foreign and political and propaganda affairs.

The common program and departmental coordination will take place under the direction of a committee made up of three members from each front, according to Ermias Debessai, a member of the EPLF's Central Committee.

The announcement of unity climaxes five months of negotiations which began in Khartoum, Sudan, on October 20 with a joint statement of intent by Isaias Afwerki of the EPLF's Politburo and Ahmed Nassar of the ELF's Revolutionary Council.

The accord is to be known as the Oct. 20th Agreement. Its implementation paves the way for joint military action against the few remaining Ethiopian strongholds in Eritrea as well as for joint defense against a major Ethiopian offensive expected to be launched against Eritrea soon.

The new accord is the latest of a series of attempts to unify the Eritrean movement. Past united fronts have proved to be fragile and have come apart after short periods. The most recent agreement appears to have been concluded on a more solid political and practical foundation than those in the past, however. The terms of the agreement are a political victory for the EPLF, which has been calling for such a plan since 1971, while the ELF insisted instead on an all-or-nothing merger at the leadership level.

The EPLF had proposed a united front in order to allow for a period of internal struggle to resolve the substantial political differences that exist between the two organizations.

The EPLF's political program rests on the principles of New Democracy. Following a strict line of self-reliant development, the Popular Front has concentrated its efforts on mobilizing and politicizing the civilian population, effectively laying the groundwork for class struggle in Eritrea as it prosecuted the war for independence from Ethiopia.

Practically, this has been reflected in the EPLF's implementation of land reform in the Eritrean countryside and the establishment of a network of mass associations of peasants, workers, youth, women and petty bourgeois elements through which the people play a direct role in the revolution.

In the associations, the people study the history of the struggle, the aims and goals of the revolution and the theory which guides it. They learn lessons in the value of political education, how to identify their international friends and enemies and the rudiments of Marxist political economy.

In contrast, the ELF has concentrated its major efforts on military matters, and left pressing economic and social contradictions to be resolved after the victory over Ethiopia.

Not surprisingly, these political differences have been reflected in the military sphere where the EPLF has steadily advanced from hit and run guerrilla war to conventional siege and assault tactics against Ethiopian positions in the larger cities and towns.

At the same time, the ELF has floundered on the battlefield and met with decidedly mixed success against the increasingly well armed and well-equipped Ethiopian army.

Faced now with the prospect of a massive Soviet-supported Ethiopian offensive over the Eritrean border, the ELF appears to have seen the writing on the wall and finally yielded to the EPLF's unity proposals.

As a face-saving gesture, the compact is not being officially labeled a united front, but the effect is clearly just that.

Eritrean Battle Front
The Cubans Move In

The Nation (New York), May 6, 1978

In the wake of the collapse of the Somali Army in Ethiopia's contested Ogaden region, the focus of war in the strategic Horn of Africa is shifting to Ethiopia's northern territory of Eritrea (See Dan Connell: "Ethiopia, Eritrea and U.S. Policy," *The Nation*, March 19, 1977.) There are strong indications that Soviet and Cuban forces will play a major role in the impending Ethiopian campaign there similar to that in the Ogaden during February and March. The results in Eritrea, however, are likely to be quite different both for Ethiopia and for the Russians and Cubans.

More than 3,000 Cuban combat troops have been airlifted into the besieged Eritrean capital of Asmara, and extensive preparations are underway in northern Ethiopia for the offensive against Eritrean independence forces. An airstrip is being built under Russian supervision for Ethiopia's new MIG jet fighters in the city of Makele, 80 miles from Eritrea's southern border, and supply depots are being set up in the cities of Gondar and Axum. A smaller airstrip is being built to accommodate light reconnaissance planes on the Dahlak Islands off the Eritrean coast, and army, navy and air force bases are being erected in the Eritrean port of Assab.

Until recently, Cuba had refrained from becoming involved in the politically complicated Eritrean war. A decade ago, Cuba aided the independence movement against Ethiopia's Emperor Haile Selassie I, but Castro's decision to lend full support to the present Ethiopian military regime appears to be leading him, like South Yemen, Libya and other erstwhile allies of the Eritreans, to side against them today. Cuban officials have in the past denied any intention of becoming directly involved in Eritrea, but State Department officials say that the number of Cuban troops in Ethiopia has now reached 17,000 and they are expected to move against Eritrea soon.

Diplomatic sources in Addis Ababa suggest that the attempt to regain control of the strategic coastal territory, with its two key ports on the Red Sea, is the first priority for Ethiopia's beleaguered military government as well as for the Soviet Union, which is said to be playing a major role in directing the overall military operations.

The Eritrean war is a unique and enigmatic phenomenon in contemporary world politics. The longest running armed conflict in Africa, it is also politically the most highly developed struggle yet to arise on the continent. At the same time, it is the war perhaps least understood. Current maneuvering in the Horn of Africa has complicated the situation, while further obscuring the fundamental issues involved.

Eritrea's seventeen-year war for national independence raises a host of questions. Chief among them is why, in the first place, should Eritrea be independent from Ethiopia and what effect would that have on African politics? Second, what is the nature of the parties involved-where do they stand politically and what are they fighting for, or against?

The Eritreans have long argued that they are a colony of Ethiopia fighting a war of national liberation. Their critics characterize Eritrea as a "nation" within Ethiopia that is waging a secessionist struggle. In this dispute, the Eritreans receive little support. Other African states, fearing a precedent that might encourage separatist movements in their own often-fragile countries, have done their best to ignore the situation.

Still, the question persists. Regardless of the Eritreans' success on the battlefield—and today they are on the verge of driving the last Ethiopian Government forces out of their land—they must secure international recognition in order to declare and sustain their independence. Barring such recognition and the aid that must accompany it, they will find themselves eternally on the defensive against a well-supplied and heavily armed foe, which has demonstrated that it will not hesitate to invade again and again until Eritrea is either vanquished or utterly destroyed.

The Eritreans argue that their situation is the product of a new historical circumstance. Located along the coast of the Red Sea at its narrow southern entrance, Eritrea has been an object of conquest for a succession of imperial powers. An Italian colony for fifty-five years—after being wrested from Egyptian control—Eritrea was briefly occupied by Britain before being federated to Ethiopia by the United Nations in 1952. Ten years later, Ethiopia's aging Emperor Haile Selassie dissolved the ill-fated compact and forcibly annexed the valuable coastal territory to his landlocked empire.

Ignored by the U.N., which was then preoccupied with the continental movement for decolonization from the declining European empires, Eritrean nationalists in 1961 launched an armed struggle for independence. Throughout this period, Ethiopia was generously supported by the United States and Israel, which were granted military bases in Eritrea as early as 1953 in exchange for commitments to arm, equip and train the Emperor's sizable army and air force. Without this support, say the Eritreans, Ethiopia would never have been able to sustain its annexationist claims.

What does it matter, the Eritreans ask, whether they are exploited and oppressed by Italians, Britons, Ethiopians or Americans? In each case, they paid high taxes to a foreign power. Their best lands were taken by foreign landlords. Their economic development was stunted to benefit the dominant country. Their democratic rights were denied; their protests were violently suppressed. The point is that these powers were exploiting and oppressing the Eritreans as a people and as a recognizable economic and political entity.

Today, the Eritreans face a new obstacle and a new argument. The Ethiopian military junta that deposed Haile Selassie in 1974 claims to be "Socialist" and has the backing of the Soviet Union and its allies. Now, say Ethiopia's military leaders to the Eritreans, we are "progressives"—you no longer need independence to settle your grievances. Soviet military aid far in excess of that previously offered by the United States gives ironic force to this argument.

Quoting Marx and Lenin does not make you progressive, the Eritreans answer. Nor does Soviet aid. True Marxists know that unity cannot be imposed by force, they add, and our national rights and aspirations remain unchanged.

If viewed from the Eritrean perspective, the "fallout" from their independence would be minimal in the rest of Africa. No national boundaries would have to be redrawn, no states broken up, with two possible exceptions—Namibia (South West Africa) and Western Sahara (formerly the Spanish Sahara). Few Africans contest black Namibia's right to independence from white-dominated South Africa, though the history of the former German colony's relationship to its apartheid neighbor is similar to that of Eritrea's with Ethiopia. Western Sahara is another question. Annexed jointly by Morocco and Mauritania after being abandoned by Spain, the small but mineral-rich territory forces a challenge upon Africans much as does Eritrea.

Meanwhile, behind the theoretical issues lie the practical realities. During the past twelve months the protracted Eritrean struggle has moved decisively from the stage of mobile guerrilla war to

conventional siege and assault warfare aimed at the handful of
remaining fortified government bases in the larger Eritrean towns and
cities. Independence forces have won a series of impressive victories
and now threaten the main Ethiopian stronghold in Asmara. Over the
past seven months, a steady flow of Russian heavy arms, Russian and
Cuban military advisers and South Yemeni combat troops has failed
to stem the Eritrean advance, and it now appears that large numbers
of Cuban troops are being airlifted from Angola to join the next
Ethiopian counterattack.

A six-month tour of Eritrea showed that guerrillas of the Eritrean
People's Liberation Front (EPLF) and the Eritrean Liberation Front
(ELF) control virtually the entire countryside. The EPLF dominates
the north, east and center; the ELF holds the western lowlands and
sections of Eritrea's southern border with Tigray Province. The EPLF
has also made gains in southern Eritrea, and both fronts overlap in
the southeastern Denakil lowlands that stretch along the coast
toward the remote port of Assab, through which Ethiopia receives
most of its arms and supplies.

In early 1977, the EPLF went on the offensive against Ethiopian
positions in the larger towns and captured a string of garrisons that
run on a north-south axis across Eritrea. In January of this year, the
EPLf overran a half-dozen Ethiopian bases outside Asmara. Before
that, it also moved against the coastal city of Massawa, former site of
a sophisticated American naval base and Eritrea's most important
deep-water port.

The protracted battle for Massawa, begun in mid-December,
enlisted the most substantial outside support yet given to Ethiopia,
with South Yemeni crews driving tanks, Russian technicians firing
BM-21 Katyusha multiple rocket launchers (known as "Stalin
organs"), South Yemeni pilots flying the new MIG-21 jets, and
Russian warships joining Ethiopian vessels in shelling the city. It was
geography, however, that in the end forced the EPLF to settle in for a
long siege as the Ethiopian forces retreated to the safety of the peninsular naval base and two small offshore islands, where they remain
today.

Apart from Massawa, the only towns still in Ethiopian hands are
Asmara, the port of Assab and small garrisons at Adi Caieh in the
south and Barentu in the west. Both Asmara and Adi Caieh are also
under EPLF siege, and Barentu is surrounded by the ELF. Recent
fighting has been concentrated in the mountains southwest of
Asmara. The EPLF's spokesman in Rome reported a major push by

10,000 Ethiopian troops on March 14 to try to break out of Asmara and crush the EPLF encirclement. It was turned back after four days. At the time of writing, the EPLF was reporting an attack of its own on Adi Caieh.

The EPLF spokesman also says that Ethiopian Airlines flights have since February been ferrying Cuban troops from Luanda, Angola, to Asmara. European diplomats in Ethiopia confirm the Luanda-Asmara airlift and say the flights were routed through Addis Ababa.

The Ethiopian position in Eritrea has become critical. The loss of Asmara would not only be a crushing military blow but also a severe political setback, likely to be followed by an Eritrean declaration of independence. Such a move would thrust this long-ignored war into international prominence just as the OAU was holding its annual summit meeting in Khartoum, Sudan, where support for the Eritrean cause is strong.

The impending Ethiopian offensive seems to be aimed at reopening supply lines to Asmara, where more than 20,000 Ethiopian troops and 200,000 civilian residents have been encircled since mid-October. Refugees and Ethiopian Army deserters say that the city is facing acute shortages of food, fuel, water and medicines. Emergency stockpiles have run out and a joint Russian-Ethiopian airlift-disrupted for three days in late December by an EPLF mortar attack-has not been able to keep pace with supply needs.

Among the factors favoring the Eritrean forces is the deteriorating morale of the Ethiopian Army, which has been repeatedly defeated south and west of Asmara in previous attempts to break the EPLF siege. Defectors say that the government has since November executed more than 100 dissenting officers and soldiers who voiced criticism of the military situation. The rate of desertions from Asmara is now running at fifteen-to-twenty a day, according to EPLF sources.

Eritrea struggle enters crucial stage

Guerrilla forces sign unity pact

The Guardian (New York), May 10, 1978

The next few months may prove decisive in the 16-year liberation war in Eritrea.

On the one hand, Ethiopia is intensifying preparations for an all-out offensive-a move expected since the Mengistu regime regained control of the Ogaden region.

But there are apparently rumblings of discontent among Ethiopia's international supporters over the junta's unwavering insistence on a military solution. Eritrea is not the same question as the Ogaden, where international opinion largely backed the junta against the Somali invaders.

And inside Eritrea, the two major liberation fronts signed a formal unity pact April 28, an important step that will bring full military and political coordination to the defense of Eritrea.

With Ethiopia poised for a full-scale military onslaught and with the Eritrean guerrillas now joining forces, it is clear both sides are preparing for a military showdown. And on the diplomatic level, both Eritrean and Ethiopian leaders are on the move across the world, meeting with leaders of a half-dozen involved and interested countries in efforts to win support.

At the heart of the controversy is Cuba, with the question: will Cuban troops join Ethiopia's spring offensive in Eritrea?

The answer is not yet in, but time is running out on the debate with the approach of the summer rain which will seriously handicap Ethiopian military movement, and with the July opening of the annual summit meeting of the Organization of African Unity (OAU) in neighboring Sudan.

The achievement of a viable united front between the EPLF and the ELF has strengthened the movement's military and diplomatic positions. The joint announcement on unity came on April 28 after a week of meetings held in the town of Hagaz in western Eritrea.

Under the terms of the pact, a 6-member coordinating committee made up of three leaders from each front will represent the movement and oversee long-term plans to merge fully the rival organizations.

Subcommittees on military, economic, cultural, foreign and political affairs will also be formed with two leaders from each front to integrate departmental programs.

Military coordination between fighting units of the two fronts is expected to come first due to the imminent threat of invasion from across the Ethiopian border.

Substantial political differences are likely to take longer to overcome. "We have to struggle politically," pointed out Ermias Debessai, EPLF central committee member and foreign mission spokesperson in Rome. "We are independent in our political line, so for a common political program, it will take some time," Ermias explained. "We have to study the whole situation."

The EPLF program is one of national democratic revolution. Lacking major external support, the EPLF has concentrated its efforts on civilian organizations to forge an alliance between Eritrean workers, peasants and other progressive individuals under the leadership of Eritrea's proletariat.

The alliance takes concrete form through a network of separate highly politicized mass associations of peasants, workers, youth, women and petty bourgeois elements. These in turn are the basis for civilian self-rule and the mobilization of material support for the war.

The implementation of sweeping land reform in the liberated zones, price controls in the markets and shops, democratic administrative reorganization and the setting up of cooperative farming projects, shops and mills along with a national system of schools, clinics and hospitals has won the EPLF broad mass support.

The short-term EPLF goal has been to win the war for independence. But, in the words of the front's political manual, "If you fight against imperialism as a united people, led by the workers, you step toward socialism."

The ELF, on the other hand, while putting forward a similar political program has in practice emphasized the need to win a military victory over Ethiopia before proceeding with extensive social or economic changes.

ELF insistence on a rapid and complete merger of the two leaderships without struggling through deeper political differences has blocked unity between the two fronts since the initial division of the movement in 1970. In recent years, several abortive announcements of intent to unify were never followed through.

"We are strongly against the complete merger that the ELF wanted," said EPLF's Ermias in Rome this week, "but this agreement is very different. We now have an agreement based on general political principles which are very progressive," Ermias pointed out.

The current accord recognized unity on the following points:

(1) Full independence for Eritrea; (2) opposition to all forces which intervene against the Eritrean struggle; (3) the safeguarding of the democratic rights of the Eritrean people, and (4) the establishment of good relations with all progressive forces in the world.

"We needed this kind of agreement, and we were struggling to get it for a long time," Ermias added. "It is a great advance for us and for the whole Eritrean people."

A further component of the ELF-EPLF agreement is a call to the small right-wing splinter group known as the "ELF-PLF" to dissolve itself within 30 days or be crushed.

The achievement of unity inside Eritrea has been paralleled by rumblings of opposition to Ethiopia's refusal to enter into negotiations with the Eritreans from within circles once thought to be solidly behind Ethiopia's uncompromising military leadership.

Representatives of the EPLF this week traveled to the Malagasy Republic, Mozambique and Algeria to present their case. Unconfirmed rumors also suggested the presence of Eritrean delegations in Tanzania, China and even Cuba, although EPLF's Ermias Debessai denied that such meetings had yet taken place.

"We are touring East Africa to inform the frontline countries of current developments in our movement," said Ermias.

According to a correspondent for the British Observer, Algeria and Sudan have been playing a leading role in the effort to achieve a negotiated, rather than military, solution. In an April 30 report Robert Stephens states that "in the conflict in the Horn of Africa, Algeria was initially inclined to back Ethiopia, but it considers the Eritrean issue quite different from that of the Ogaden."

A visit to Cuba by Ethiopian leader Lt. Col. Mengistu Haile Mariam aimed at getting a full Cuban commitment to join the military campaign in Eritrea meanwhile appeared to fall short of success. Leaders of the EPLF and the ELF have at the same time continued to express confidence in their people's ability to withstand the impending Ethiopian offensive.

Against such a backdrop, the likelihood of moves to open negotiations has improved slightly, but most observers believe the results of the next two months of fighting in Eritrea will prove most decisive in bringing the two sides to the conference table.

Eritrean struggle nears turning point

The Guardian (New York), May 24, 1978

As the Eritrean war for independence from Ethiopia faces the biggest military showdown in its long history, diplomatic and political maneuvering is intensifying on both sides.

An estimated 80-100,000 Ethiopian troops are now inside or within striking distance of Eritrea, preparing for a major campaign to retake key cities in Eritrean hands and to lose Eritrean supply channels along the border with neighboring Sudan.

Some 40-50,000 Eritrean fighters backed by tens of thousands of militia men and women and civilian volunteers are arrayed against the Ethiopian force.

Behind the scenes of the impending battlefront confrontation the divided Eritrean movement is in the process of establishing a united front, while Ethiopia's international supporters appear to be divided over the Eritrean question.

The Soviet Union and Cuba appear unsatisfied with Ethiopia's complete reliance on military means to settle the struggle in Eritrea, while officials in Mozambique and Algeria, among other countries, are expressing increasing reservations about the course of the war.

Countries such as South Yemen which once supported the Eritrean revolution now actively oppose it. Others, such as Britain, which once occupied Eritrea, now seem to support it.

In its 17th year, the Eritrean revolution is both the longest-running armed struggle in Africa and also the least well understood. Yet despite the confusion brought on by the recent shift in international alignments in the region, there is an internal consistency to the conflict which defines the basic issues.

Centuries Of Struggle

For 400 years the Eritreans have fought a succession of outside powers for control of their lands, and they are determined to continue fighting no matter who the enemy is until they win their full and complete independence.

In the 1880s, Italian imperialism drove the occupying Egyptians (who had succeeded the Ottoman Turks) out of the Eritrean coast and established Eritrea's modern boundaries along the Red Sea, with Sudan to the west, Ethiopia to the south and French Somaliland (now Djibouti) to the southeast.

Over the next half century, the Italian colonial regime transformed Eritrean society. They wiped out the old feudal landholding
class, developed plantation agriculture and small industries and built
an elaborate infrastructure, effectively defining Eritrea as a distinct
sociopolitical entity.

Due to Italy's expansionist ambitions in this area, Eritrea received
special attention. In the 1930s Mussolini was describing the colony as
"the heart of the new Roman empire."

In the late 1930s, the Italians went on to conquer the entire Horn
of Africa, but in 1941 a British-led force defeated them and pulled the
curtain on Mussolini's dreams.

The upshot was a return to independent status for Ethiopia, while
Eritrea-as a colony of a defeated axis power-fell under British occupation for the next 11 years.

In the late 1940s and early 1950s, the victorious Western allies set
out to divide the spoils of World War 2, but Eritrea posed special problems and the issue finally went to the fledgling UN for resolution.

Four proposals were discussed with regard to Eritrea's future:
returning it to Italy, dividing it between Sudan and Ethiopia, giving it
full independence or joining it directly to Ethiopia.

Through a series of compromises, the field narrowed to a U.S.
backed call for a federation between Eritrea and Ethiopia and Soviet-
backed proposals for Eritrean independence.

In 1950, Andrei Vishinsky, chief of the Soviet delegation,
declared, "The colonial system is going through an acute crisis.
Accordingly, in considering the fate of Eritrea-once of the former
Italian colonies-the UN must take a decision which will satisfy the
longing of the Eritrean people for independence and freedom from
national oppression.

"The General Assembly cannot tolerate a deal by the colonial
powers at the expense of the population of Eritrea," the Soviet representative continued. "In the circumstances, the only just solution...is
to grant independence."

Speaking in support of the Soviet resolution and against the proposed federation, the Czechoslovak delegate added, "The federal
form of government which would thus be imposed on Eritrea is not
based on the free, spontaneous and democratic expression of the will
of two sovereign states. It is merely a mask for the annexation of little Eritrea by a larger and more populous state."

While Eritreans demonstrated at home for independence,
Ethiopian diplomats unleashed a fog of mythology and legend to

claim ancient ties with Eritrea in the precolonial era, but what won the debate in the end was U.S. pressure to reward a Western ally with the gift of an outlet on the Red Sea.

The federation was set up in 1952 and within a decade the Czech analysis was proven correct as Ethiopia's emperor Haile Selassie moved decisively, with U.S. backing to dissolve the agreement and annex the territory.

First the Eritrean trade unions and newspapers were suppressed. Later the Eritrean flag was taken down, the emperor's language of Amharic substituted for the Eritrean languages in the schools, and finally the Eritrean constitution and parliament were dismantled. In 1962, the process of annexation was completed and Eritrea was declared Ethiopia's 14th province.

U.S. Guarantees

But these events did not occur in an international vacuum. In 1953, the U.S. signed a bilateral agreement with the emperor to guarantee Ethiopia's control over Eritrea in exchange for 25-year leases on military bases there.

The U.S. soon built a naval facility in the port of Massawa and the highly sophisticated Kagnew Station communications complex in the Eritrean capital of Asmara.

Kagnew served as a listening post to spy on all of Africa and the Middle East as well as a relay station for the U.S. fleet in the Indian Ocean and for U.S. operations in Southeast Asia.

In return for these bases, the U.S. armed, equipped and trained the emperor's armed forces, pouring in $600 million in aid by 1977. Israel, which also received base rights from the emperor, was the junior partner in shoring up the feudal regime and facilitating the annexation of Eritrea.

Inside Eritrea, however, resistance developed rapidly. In September 1961, on the eve of formal annexation, an armed struggle for independence was launched by the Eritrean Liberation Front (ELF).

Over the next 10 years, the guerrilla movement severely disrupted Ethiopia's control over the territory and was met by an escalating U.S. and Israeli-supported counterinsurgency strategy that included Vietnam-style "strategic hamlets" and indiscriminate rural bombing and urban repression.

Although the independence movement generated widespread popular support and was aided at times by Algeria, Cuba and China, it was rent by regional, ethnic and religious divisions and the war floundered.

By 1970 democratic elements inside the ELF were organizing around calls for a long-term military and political strategy. In the ensuing power struggle, the ELF spilt and a second army. Known as the Eritrean People's Liberation Forces (EPLF, later to become the Eritrean People's Liberation Front) was formed.

The next three years saw a civil war between the rival fronts while the imperial Ethiopian army sought to smash them both. In 1974 the inability of the ELF to crush the growing EPLF, together with mounting pressure from the Eritrean civilian population, finally brought an end to the infighting and an informal truce was declared between ELF and EPLF.

The year 1974 also saw the fall of Haile Selassie and the ascension to power in Ethiopia of a military junta known as the Derg (Amharic for Committee).

The coup was the culmination of years of unrest in Ethiopia. Weakened by the Eritrean war, growing protest by a strong leftist movement of students and workers, peasant uprisings and military mutinies, the old feudal order collapsed.

The common demands of the internal Ethiopian opposition groups centered around land reform and democratic rights. When the military, as the only organized force capable of seizing power, deposed the emperor, they quickly proclaimed rural and urban land reform and declared the country socialist. But they took a hard line on Eritrea.

In February 1975 there was the most intense fighting of the war in and around Asmara. But the recently allied liberation fronts turned back the Ethiopian offensive and gained control over broad areas of the countryside.

In May 1976 the military government publicly issued a call for a "peaceful solution" in Eritrea, while at the same time launching another all-out offensive there by a conscripted peasant army known euphemistically as the "Wodezemach" or "volunteer campaign."

With the failure of this offensive, the junta turned to the U.S. and Israel for more help. Israeli advisors trained a 20,000 man force known as the "Nebelbal" or "Flame Brigade" while the U.S. provided the largest dollar amount of equipment in its 24-year aid program, including F-5 Starfighter jets and M-60 tanks.

It was not enough. The Eritreans kept winning.

Finally, in December 1976, representatives of the junta went to Moscow where they were offered a virtual open-ended promise of military hardware and advisory personnel.

Three months later the junta broke its military ties with the U.S. and openly aligned itself with the Soviet Union. The returns were substantial in political as well as military terms.

Close to $1 billion worth of military equipment was shipped and airlifted to Ethiopia by the USSR in the company of over 1000 military advisors up to the rank of general. Some 17,000 Cuban advisors and combat personnel also arrived in Ethiopia, while declaration of support for the junta came from Eastern block countries and former supporters of Eritrea such as Libya and South Yemen.

As China and the U.S. maintained a low-key profile in Ethiopia, keeping up economic aid programs with a view toward the future, the Eritreans found themselves almost completely isolated from outside support, with the exception of a handful of Arab countries and other liberation movements that included the Palestinians and the Polisario Front in Western Sahara.

Ethiopia's 1977 offensive, however, was frustrated by the coincidence of EPLF advances in the spring against a string of government-held garrison towns and cities in Eritrea while Somali forces moved into Ethiopia's Ogaden region.

By the spring of this year, the Somali campaign had been decisively defeated by a joint Soviet, Cuban and Ethiopian force, but the Eritreans had gained control of all but two major Eritrean cities and three smaller bases.

Mass Base Of Support

More significantly, they had mobilized and organized the Eritrean people to provide the base of support necessary to carry the struggle forward in the absence of outside support.

The EPLF, in fact-clearly now the dominant force in Eritrea-had concentrated so heavily on political, social and economic development that they were practically administering Eritrea as a national state.

Drawing on the revolutionary experience of countries ranging from China and Vietnam and Mozambique and Guinea-Bissau, the EPLF developed its own unique strategy of people's war, placing the politicization of the civilian population at the core of its program of self-reliant protracted struggle.

Internally trained political cadre established clandestine cells in the villages and town which served as the building blocks for mass associations of peasants, workers, youth, women and progressive petty bourgeois elements.

People's Assemblies were elected from within the associations and executive bodies were set up to administer the villages and towns.

Land reform was systematically carried out. Agricultural cooperatives were initiated together with cooperative shops and grain mills. Price controls were set in the private sector and large farms were developed under the direct control of the front.

A network of clinics and hospitals was built to serve both the fighters and the civilians; teams of EPLF veterinarians roamed the countryside vaccinating animals; schools were opened through the sixth grade with mimeographed texts printed by the EPLF; a Social Welfare section organized a relief program for the hundreds of thousands of refugees and displaced people and militia units were organized.

Relying mainly on captured weapons, the EPLF carved out underground repair shops and cottage industries. Hundreds of miles of roads were built connecting supply depots hollowed out of the ground.

The arrival in Ethiopia of Soviet and Cuban forces disappointed the Eritreans-the EPLF had supported Cuba's role in Angola-but it did little to dampen their commitment to continue the struggle for self-determination which these countries had once so vigorously supported.

Neither the character of the Ethiopian regime nor the countries which support it alter the Eritreans' view of themselves as a former Italian colony fighting against Ethiopian annexation. It is perhaps also worth noting that the EPLF continues to identify its principal enemies as imperialism, Zionism and colonialism, while adhering to its program of national democratic revolution.

Unlike Somalia, which called for Western aid to counter the Soviet and Cuban presence in Ethiopia, the EPLF has stepped up its diplomatic efforts to secure support from anti-imperialist countries, primarily in Africa, while settling in for what will likely be a period of bitter and prolonged battle with the much-strengthened Ethiopian armed forces.

Eritrea support mounts in Europe

The Guardian (New York), May 31, 1978

Rome

"Eritrea is not the Ogaden," the Italian Communist Party (PCI) newspaper declared in a front-page editorial last week.

Amid conflicting reports of the opening of Ethiopia's long-expected military offensive in Eritrea, diplomatic and political support for the Eritrean struggle is mounting, especially within the European left and trade union movements.

The May 18 editorial in the PCI daily L'Unita appeared as Ethiopian head of state Lt. Col. Mengistu Haile Mariam warned in Addis Ababa that the Eritreans would meet the same fate as the routed Somali invaders of the country's Ogaden region.

The public PCI stand marks the initiation of a party campaign against Ethiopia's insistence on a military solution in Eritrea. It reflects an increasing trend among political parties in Europe and certain governments in Africa who have otherwise been friendly to Ethiopia's self-described "socialist" regime.

In a major speech broadcast over Radio Ethiopia, Mengistu announced that "Soviet, Cuban, South Yemeni and East German comrades" were dying on the battlefield for Ethiopia. This assertion led Western commentators to speculate that the offensive in Eritrea was already underway with direct Cuban and Soviet participation.

Representatives of the nationalist Eritrean Liberation Front (ELF) in Beirut and Rome simultaneously reported heavy fighting in four separate areas of Eritrea, reinforcing this speculation.

However, representatives of the revolutionary Eritrean People's Liberation Front (EPLF) denied that the offensive was in fact underway and suggested that fighting around the besieged Eritrean capital of Asmara was merely another probing action by Ethiopia prior to the beginning of the expected overall campaign.

At this time, noted the Front's Rome spokesman, an EPLF tank brigade has joined ELF infantry forces in a joint attack on the Ethiopian-held garrison at Barentu. This is the first combined military operation by the two fronts since the formal establishment of a united front last month.

Political Offensive

Against this backdrop, important pressure on Ethiopia is building around demands for a political rather than a military resolution of the 17-year war for Eritrean independence.

Current estimates place 115,000 Ethiopian troops in and around Eritrea poised for the forthcoming offensive, while heavy bombing of Eritrean towns and cities in the hands of the liberation forces continues on a daily basis.

Because the overwhelming majority of the Ethiopian force has had link or no combat experience and only limited military training, it is widely believed that the offensive cannot be carried through without foreign direction at the middle and upper leads of command if not also at the front line.

While Ethiopia now possesses an abundance of new Soviet heavy weapons, it is also thought that the lack of trained Ethiopian personnel means that foreign technicians will have to operate them if they are to play an effective role in Eritrea, as they did in the Ogaden earlier this year.

Mengistu's Addis Ababa broadcast is thus being viewed as an attempt to pressure for Soviet and Cuban participation in this offensive.

Much of the current political activity is therefore being directed toward the Soviet Union, South Yemen and Cuba in an international effort to keep them from joining the impending offensive in Eritrea.

An editorial in L'Humanite organ of the French Communist Party, called for an end to the fighting in Eritrea and a solution to the war that recognizes Eritrea's legitimate right to self-determination. The Belgian Communist Party followed suit with a brief policy statement shortly afterward.

The stand announced here this week by the PCI is the strongest and most significant such statement yet to appear in Europe.

The PCI's turnabout from earlier legalistic calls for a settlement in Eritrea based on the 1952 UN resolution that formed the former Italian colony with Ethiopia came as a surprise to many. It follows, however, a long campaign by the EPLF to support within the party and in Italy's powerful trade unions.

The PCI has been one of Ethiopia's strongest European supporter since early 1977 when the USSR replaced the U.S. as Ethiopian's main arms supplier.

Rather than attack head-on the PCI's earlier stand on Eritrea, the EPLF representatives moved to win over the party rank and file and the trade arises from which the PCI draws much of its strength.

Through a series of informational meetings and conferences, the EPLF won widespread support from the General Confederation of

Italian Workers (CGIL) the Italian Confederation of Union Workers (CISL), the Italian Workers Union (UIL) and the Metal-workers Federation (FLM).

The unions are now calling for a political solution in Eritrea and they oppose the introduction of foreign troops into the war.

Parties and newspapers to the left of the PCI such as Proletarian Democracy, Manifesto and Lotta Continua have recently published articles supporting Eritrean independence and opposing foreign intervention in the struggle.

"The question raised by the Eritrean independence movement cannot be confused with Somalia's military intervention in the Ogaden," begins the PCI analysis. "They are questions of radically different quality."

The article, signed by Romano Ledda, chief editor of the PCI's weekly cultural magazine, goes on to describe the Ogaden situation as a threat to African stability.

"Applying the Somali solution to this complex national question would mean redividing most, if not all, national borders in black Africa," says Ledda. The breakup of the Ethiopian state would have a destabilizing effect on the Horn of Africa and on Africa as a whole, he adds.

Ledda argues that because the development of African states was stunted by colonialism, certain national questions must be postponed and the borders inherited from colonialism must be respected or, "Africa could dissolve and the young states not survive."

The state in Africa is not the final product of national formation as in Europe, he points out but, in the words of the late Guinea-Bissau independence leader Amilcar Cabral, "It is the state that must create the nation, unifying the market, the language, etc."

Not a 'Border Change'

However, says the PCI, Eritrea is not such a national question.

"Eritrea was destined, to become an autonomous state," Ledda continues. "Instead, along with the former Spanish Sahara, it is the only case of a former colonial territory which has been annexed by an African state." (The former Spanish colony was annexed by Morocco and Mauritania in 1975.)

Citing Ethiopia's abrogation of the 1952 UN agreement that established Eritrea's autonomy while federating it to Ethiopia, Ledda concludes that "the struggle for the liberation of the Eritrean people is a just struggle adhering to the general principles that govern the political order of this stage of the national life of the African continent."

The justice of this struggle is not lessened by the liquidation of feudalism in Ethiopia, he adds, "Whether there is in Addis Ababa (former emperor) Haile Selassie or young officers of progressive inspiration changes nothing of the legitimacy of the Eritrean struggle."

Rejecting Ethiopia's charge that the Eritrean struggle serves Arab reaction or imperialism, Ledda argues that finding a political rather than a military solution to the Eritrea situation would "diffuse the dirty maneuvers of those who fear a Horn of Africa with a progressive orientation."

The day after the publication of the PCI position, L'Unita ran an article signed by prominent members of the party hat called on Cuba not to intervene in Eritrea. The PCI has also indicated that it will participate officially in a national Eritrean solidarity committee which is being formed by Italian trade union and left organizations.

Elsewhere in Europe support for Eritrea is being voiced within the Spanish, Portuguese and German left, with especially strong statements coming from the Basque movement in Spain.

Motion In Africa

Recent EPLF delegations in Africa have also received marked but less-public support. EPLF central committee members last month met with officials in Tanzania, Madagascar, Mozambique and Algeria and will go on to make a West African tour that will likely include Guinea-Bissau, Guinea (Conakry) Benin and possibly Nigeria.

These countries support Cuba's role in Africa, particularly regarding Angola, but there are indications now that they are also privately taking issue with any Soviet or Cuban involvement in Ethiopia's campaign against Eritrean independence.

These developments can also be seen as marking the failure of Ethiopia's 2-year diplomatic campaign to neutralize opposition on Eritrea from progressive countries and left organizations. The ruling Dergue has been arguing to those sectors that progressive elements inside the military junta favored a "peaceful solution" in Eritrea but needed time to consolidate their positions.

Time and practice have shown that this was a stalling tactic designed to build the military capacity to crush the Eritrean movement. But the pendulum of political support is now swinging to the side of Eritrea.

Ethiopians Move North on Eritrea

Rebels Go On Defense; Full Offensive Begun?

The Miami Herald, June 15, 1978

Khartoum, Sudan

After nearly a month of delays and false starts, Ethiopia's long-expected full offensive to recapture the Red Sea territory of Eritrea appears to be getting under way.

Thousands of Ethiopian troops were reported moving throughout northern Tigray province near the Eritrean border in what appears to be a concentrated action to secure bases in Eritrea and possibly to push north against towns and highways now in the hands of Eritrean nationalists.

Three anti-government movements are massing in Tigray and Eritrea to repel the offensive, according to guerrilla sources.

The Tigray People's Liberation Front (TPLF), the Eritrean People's Liberation Front (EPLF) and the Eritrean Liberation Front (ELF) are preparing to mount joint operations to keep government forces out of Eritrea and to protect TPLF base areas in Tigray, according to a spokesman for the TPLF.

Brigade-size units of the Ethiopian army began on Friday to roll out of the Tigray towns of Ende-Selassie, Adua and Adigrat toward Eritrea in what looked like the largest operation ever attempted in the 16-year Eritrean war, according to the TPLF spokesman.

Radio reports from Tigray indicate that TPLF guerrillas are putting up strong resistance to the Ethiopian advance, using ambushes and land mines on the government's main supply routes. The TPLF is an anti-government guerrilla army that operates in Tigray but cooperates militarily and politically with the independence forces to neighboring Eritrea.

The Ethiopian army is using Tigray as a base for its planned campaign in Eritrea, where the allied armies of the EPLF and the ELF have gained control of an estimated 90 per cent of the 45,000-square-mile territory, according to the TPLF spokesman. The Eritreans seek independence for the former Italian colony, which was loosely federated with Ethiopia in 1952 and forcibly annexed a decade later.

The Ethiopian buildup in Tigray has been seriously disrupted by TPLF guerrillas and the government now is moving in force against TPLF strongholds in the smaller towns and rural areas on their way toward Eritrea, TPLF spokesman Yemane Kidane said in Khartoum.

One brigade has pushed out of the town of Ende-Selassie in western Tigray, going northwest toward the towns of Semama and Adi Daro, now held by the TPLF, Kidane said.

These towns lie along a little-used road to the town of Shambuko on the Tigray-Eritrea border, from which a major push into the western Eritrean lowlands in possible.

Separate mechanize brigades are moving from Adigrat in the east and Adua in central Tigray toward the key town of Intechew, from which another road runs north into Eritrea, the TPLF spokesman said.

More brigades are preparing to push directly northward from Adua toward the Tigray town of Rama, which is just short of the Eritrean border and is along the main highway that leads to Central Eritrea, he said.

It is not yet clear whether these forces will continue immediately into Eritrea, according to the TPLF spokesman, but such movements set the state for a concentrated offensive to retake the Eritrean city of Mendefera; now held by the ELF, and to try to reopen the highway to the besieged Eritrean capital of Asmara.

Observers suggest that the Ethiopian actions may be limited in scope and designed to secure bases in southern Eritrea from which to push forward later.

On the other hand, a quick thrust forward from the west and center of Tigray across the flat plains of western Eritrea might reopen supply lines to the besieged garrison at Barentu and threaten the Eritreans' supply channels from Sudan.

Spokesmen for the Eritrean armies said they had no reports yet of offensive movement by Ethiopian forces inside Eritrea, but they anticipate some action to pin down forces that otherwise might be thrown into combat along the Tigray border.

Ethiopia poised for Eritrea drive

Troops reportedly moving near Eritrean border

The Guardian (New York), June 21, 1978

Khartoum, Sudan

After nearly a month of delays and false starts, Ethiopia's long-expected offensive to recapture the Red Sea territory of Eritrea appears to be getting underway.

Thousands of Ethiopian troops are reported now moving throughout northern Tigray Province near the Eritrean border in what appears to be a concentrated action to secure bases in Eritrea and possibly to push north against towns and highways now in the hands of the Eritrean liberation forces.

Three antigovernment movements are massing in Tigray and Eritrea to repel the offensive, according to guerrilla sources.

The Tigray People's Liberation Front (TPLF), the Eritrean People's Liberation Front (PLF) and the Eritrean Liberation Front (ELF) are preparing to mount joint operations to keep the government forces out of Eritrea and to protect TPLF base areas in Tigray, according to a spokesman for the TPLF.

Brigade-size units of the Ethiopian army began June 9 to roll out of the Tigray towns of Enda-Selassie, Aduwa and Adigrat toward Eritrea in what looks like the largest operation ever attempted in the 17-year Eritrean war, according to the TPLF.

Smaller government units were unsuccessful in similar actions in Tigray earlier this month, but the size and strength of the forces moving against the TPLF now is more than they can handle in face-to-face confrontation by themselves, the representative told the Guardian.

"If they come in such a big force, we can't stop them but they will suffer a lot," said Yemane Kidane, the TPLF Khartoum spokesman.

Radio reports from Tigray indicate that TPLF guerrillas are putting up strong resistance to the Ethiopian advance using tactics of ambushes and land mines on the government's main supply routes.

The TPLF spokesman reported that five trucks and three tanks were destroyed June 10 on the highway between Adigrat and Aduwa, and two buses were hijacked that day from the important government base in the town of Enda-Selassie.

The TPLF is an antigovernment guerrilla army which operates in Tigray but cooperates militarily and politically with the independence forces in neighboring Eritrea.

Military Buildup

The Ethiopian army is apparently using Tigray as a base for its planned campaign in Eritrea where the allied armies of the EPLF and the ELF have gained control of an estimated 95% of the 45,000 square mile territory. The Eritreans are fighting for independence for the former Italian colony which was loosely federated with Ethiopia in 1952 and forcibly annexed a decade later.

Ethiopian army division headquarters and the main forward command post were recently moved from the Eritrean capital of Asmara to the Tigray capital of Makele, and this week to the town of Aduwa just south of the Eritrean border. The total number of Ethiopian forces in Tigray two months ago was about 10,000, but the TPLF says this figure has now been tripled. But the Ethiopian buildup in Tigray has been seriously disrupted by TPLF guerrillas and the government is now moving in force against TPLF strongholds in the smaller towns and rural areas on their way toward Eritrea, Yemane Kidane said here.

One army brigade has pushed out of the town of Enda-Selassie in western Tigray province going northwest toward the towns of Semana and Adi Daro, now held by the TPLF. These towns lie along a little-used road to the town of Shambuko on the Tigray-Eritrea border from which a major push into the western Eritrean lowlands is possible.

Separate mechanized brigades are reportedly moving from Adigrat in the east and Aduwa in central Tigray toward the key town of Intechew, from which another road runs north into Eritrea. More brigades are meanwhile grouping to push directly northward from Aduwa toward the Tigrayan town of Rama, just short of the Eritrean border and located along the main highway that leads to central Eritrea.

'War of Generations'

It is not yet clear whether these forces will continue immediately into Eritrea. But such movements set the stage for the possibility of a concentrated offensive to retake the Eritrean city of Mendefera, now held by the ELF. The army may also be readying a renewed attempt to reopen the highway to the besieged Eritrean capital of Asmara.

Informed observers here suggest that the Ethiopian actions may be limited in scope and designed to secure bases in southern Eritrea from which to push forward later.

On the other hand, a quick thrust forward from the west and center of Tigray across the flat plains of western Eritrea might reopen supply lines to the besieged garrison at Barentu and threaten the Eritreans' supply channels from Sudan.

In a major speech broadcast over Radio Ethiopia earlier this week, Ethiopia's head of state Lt. Col. Mengistu Haile Mariam vowed to continue the war in Eritrea for generations if necessary. Mengistu called for a total mobilization of every able-bodied person in Ethiopia for the war which he said might take a long time and much sacrifice to win. The Ethiopian head of state had just returned from a tour of the army bases in Eritrea and Tigray.

Representatives of the EPLF and ELF here said they have no reports yet of offensive movement by Ethiopian forces inside Eritrea, but they anticipate some action to pin down forces which might otherwise be thrown into combat along the Tigray border.

The Ethiopian presence in Eritrea is now limited to the Asmara capital, the ports of Massawa and Assab and the smaller besieged garrisons of Adi Caieh and Barentu.

ELF and the EPLF have launched a joint action by their forces against the Barentu base. This is the first combined military operation between them since April, when they agreed to establish a form of unity against Ethiopia.

ETHIOPIA
TIGRE NATIONALISTS IN THE FRAY

Africa News (Durham, NC), June 26, 1978

Khartoum

[AN] On June 14, the Eritrean People's Liberation Front (EPLF) revealed that for the first time in years they have launched a major attack outside Eritrea. They say their forces killed some five hundred out of 40,000 Ethiopian troops amassed at a garrison in Ethiopia's Tigre province, just 15 miles from the border with Eritrea.

Tigre, which has its own nationalist guerrilla movement, borders Eritrea, and is included in Ethiopia's Northern Sector Command. In that area the Ethiopian army faces the cooperating forces of the Tigre People's Liberation Front (TPLF), the EPLF, and the Eritrean Liberation Front (ELF).

Two days before the announcement, AFRICA NEWS correspondent Dan Connell spoke with TPLF Central Committee member Seyoum Mussa in Khartoum about the military role of the TPLF and its political goals.

AN: Ethiopia has been preparing for a major offensive in Eritrea for months. How has this affected the situation in Tigre?

TPLF: Two months ago there were only 10,000 government troops in Tigre but now that has increased threefold. The Ethiopian regime is building a new airbase in Makele and it has opened a new training center at Quiha, ten kilometers east of Makele. All these preparations are to take an offensive against the liberation organizations in Eritrea and Tigre at the same time.

According to secret documents which we have discovered, they are considering Tigre as a base area so they want to clear Tigre first before they launch an offensive attack on Eritrea. they want to make sure their supply lines are cleared to guarantee the passage of convoys.

AN: What has been the TPLF response to this buildup?

TPLF: The TPLF has been obstructing transportation and the concentration of troops by ambushes on the main roads and attacks on their garrisons. In the past two months, we captured 300 and killed 200-250. We have made raids in Hauzien, south of Adigrat, in Maikenetal, south of Aduwa, and in Naader, south of Axum, and now that they are trying to move to Eritrea, we are using land mines and ambushes to stop them.

AN: What is the TPLF's relationship to the Eritrean movements?

TPLF: We don't see any separate military movement from that directed at Eritrea because both Eritrea and Tigre are under the same [Ethiopia's] Northern Sector Command, so their total offensive will be on Tigre and Eritrea. What Eritrea will face, Tigre too will face. We have cordial relations with both the EPLF and the ELF, and we give each other mutual political and military support. We are confronting a common enemy, so it is a matter of coordinating our military and political activities to crush this enemy.

AN: The Soviet Union and Cuba gave Ethiopia a great deal of assistance in its recent war with Somalia. What role are they playing here?

TPLF: There are Russians and Cubans in the main towns of Makele, Axum, Aduwa and Adigrat, but we have no evidence they are participating on the front lines. They are training and advising the Ethiopian force.

AN: A year ago, there were three antigovernment movements in Tigre: the TPLF, the rightist Ethiopian Democratic Union (EDU) and the self-described Marxist-Leninist Ethiopian People's Revolutionary Army (EPRA). What is the situation today?

TPLF: The EDU, led by Tigre's former feudal lords, was attacking Tigre from bases in Begemdir province. We had a hard time fighting this army, but we defeated them on January 5th. They tried again in the beginning of March, but we kept them out. The EDU is no longer in Tigre.

The EPRA was in Tigre for three years, mainly in the northeast near Asimba mountain. They were not accepted by the people of Tigre because of their wrong analysis of the Ethiopian situation. They were attacking the TPLF politically and this alienated them from the Tigre people. In the beginning of March, they attacked a small clinic that we had near Asimba for the peasants—we think they coordinated the attack with the EDU in the west—and we fought a civil war with them. Our guerrilla army was engaged with three different forces at the same time— the EDU, the EPRA and the Dergue [Ethiopia's military government]. Due to the strong support of our people, we have crushed these forces. This army, too, the EPRA, is no longer in Tigre.

AN: In the wake of all this fighting and with the increased buildup of government forces in Tigre, how strong is the TPLF and what is the scope of your operations?

TPLF: Our liberation army is strong enough to defend its guerrilla zones and semi-liberated areas. It can freely move throughout the countryside of Tigre, but its main concentrations are in the western, central and eastern parts of Tigre. If the Dergue comes in a big, mechanized force, we can't stop them, but we can make them suffer a lot.

AN: What are the objectives of the TPLF and what are you fighting for?

TPLF: We are true revolutionary nationalists. Our objective is to wage a national democratic revolution for the self-determination of the Tigre people. We have carried through a program of land reform. We have organized the rural people into different social organizations and we are cooperating with the people in establishing small shops, clinics and other social services. The TPLF is mobilizing the whole Tigraen people, especially the oppressed ones, to participate in their national struggle. We are agitating, politicizing and organizing them. To do this we are forming a people's militia.

AN: Are you fighting for an independent Tigre, apart from the rest of Ethiopia?

TPLF: Whether to remain under a united Ethiopia or to establish a People's Democratic Republic of Tigre depends on the overall political atmosphere of Ethiopia. We leave this demand for the people, but our immediate objective is to achieve the right of self-determination. In the meantime, we have also clearly proclaimed the need to establish a united democratic front with the other liberation organizations in Ethiopia. This invitation will open the road for the coordination of the different nations and nationalities in Ethiopia.

Starvation stalks Eritrean refugee camp

The Baltimore Sun, July 1, 1978

Wad el Hilaywa, Refugee Camp, Sudan (Reuter)

"There is starvation here, and it is getting worse every day," said a relief worker at this camp of 25,000 Eritrean refugees.

A food shortage has left 75 per cent of the camp's inhabitants suffering from malnutrition, which has broken down their resistance to the point where they die from simple ailments, said the volunteer, asking not to be identified.

"I have seen four or five deaths this week that I can attribute to these causes, and there are many more whom I haven't seen," the relief worker said.

The immediate cause of the crisis in Wad El Hilaywa can be traced to the ending of relief distribution of food in March. But refugees, relief workers and government officials disagree on the solution to the problem.

Wad el Hilaywa has been officially designated a temporary camp by the Sudan government, as well as by the United Nations World Food Program, which has been supplying emergency food to the refugees.

Food and medicines are available at a dozen permanent resettlement camps, according to the officials who say that the residents must move if they want relief.

The refugees generally refuse to move, though officials say that 4,500 of the poorest ones have left during the last three months.

A three-day tour of Wad el Hilaywa showed the magnitude of the problem.

A Land Rover bounced its way over the crude dirt road that led to the dusty camp, 15 miles from Sudan's border with the territory of Eritrea from which the refugees have been fleeing for the past decade of war with Ethiopia.

Two allied Eritrean movements are fighting for independence for the former Italian colony, which was annexed forcibly by Ethiopia after a 10-year period of United Nations-sponsored federation.

As visitors sloshed across the Atbara and Setit rivers, the driver said that the summer rains would soon make transport to and from the camp impossible.

As the vehicle claimed the dirt hills north of the Setit, the grass huts of the camp spread out. In the full heat of mid-day, with temperatures over 115 degrees Fahrenheit, Wad el Hilaywa appeared almost deserted, but under the conical roofs of thousands of crowded huts, the camp's residents could be seen passing the time in stoical silence.

The family of Mohamed Ali Mahmud is perhaps typical. The father of six children, one of whom was born in the camp in May, Mr. Mohammed is bedridden with chronic tuberculosis.

His wife, Salihah Mohammed, said she starts her day at 5 A.M. by preparing a breakfast of tea and wode-aker (low-grade sorghum). For the rest of the day, she has little to do beyond hand-grinding more sorghum for lunch and dinner.

The family has not eaten meat or dairy products for months, according to Mr. Mohammed.

The oldest son, Siraj Mohammed, 14, attends an elementary school run by one of the Eritrean liberation movements in the camp. In his spare time, he supports the family by transporting water from the Setit River on the family donkey and selling it.

On a normal day, Siraj can manage three trips, according to his father, but on Fridays and Sundays when school is closed he can get five or six donkey-loads.

"I came to find peace," he said, adding that he had just received word that Galug was bombed again last week.

Mr. Mohammed said that he will move to one of the new resettlement camps when he is well, but for now he cannot. He blames the United Nations for his plight.

Officially say the first large influx of Eritrean refugees came to Wad el Hilaywa in 1967, but the flow has slowed to a trickle since July of last year.

The drop-off in refugees coming to the Sudan is generally attributed to the increasing success of the Eritrean independence movements, which

now control virtually the entire Eritrean countryside and all but a handful of the larger towns and cities.

"There are only a few towns left. It can't be much longer," one
young refugee said.

The very success of the Eritrean movements has severely complicated the situation in Wad el Hilaywa, according to government officials, because the refugees anticipating the end of the war will not
move farther away from the border.

The refugees speak of bad weather, disease and lack of housing in
the new resettlement camps, but officials say these are merely excuses.

"The real reason is that they are near the border. If Eritrea is liberated, they will go home, if they move, they fear they will lose their
national identity," said Sayed Ismail Mohammed, Sudan's assistant
commissioner for refugees.

The dilemma for the Sudan is how to cope with a "temporary
emergency" which is now entering its second decade.

Sudan officials cite transportation difficulties and the lack of
either local food supplies or work as factors that make the relocation
of the Wad el Hilaywa camp necessary, but say they have been hin-
dered in efforts to effect the transfer.

With the World Food Program's regular distributions stopped,
the crisis inside the camp appears to be accelerating. But there is no
sign that the people will leave before the summer rains expected to
begin any day now, relief workers in the camp said.

To worsen the problem, 20,000 Eritrean and Ethiopian refugees
living in Khartoum have been told they must leave the capital for
security reasons before the summit meeting of the Organization of
African Unity, scheduled to begin there on July 7. Relief workers fear
that many will come to Wad el Hilaywa.

"If they come here, there is already a lack of food," one relief
worker pointed out. "There is no housing either. They will have to
live only in the sunshine."

Officials in Khartoum say the refugees leaving there will not be
taken to Wad el Hilaywa. Instead they will go to the town of Gedaref
west of the camp where they will be free to choose where to remain.

Officials also say that 800 tons of relief food, enough to carry
10,000 of the neediest people in Wad el Hilaywa through the rainy
season, are soon to be taken to the camp.

For most of those in Wad el Hilaywa, the future appears uncertain, but they seem to think that the real solution to the problem lies
not in Sudan but in Eritrea.

Big Assault by Ethiopia

Reuter news wire, London, July 1, 1978

Khartoum, Sudan

Ethiopian forces directed by Soviet military advisers have launched their biggest offensive in the 17-year war against secessionists in Eritrea province, according to Eritrean guerrilla sources here.

The main thrust of the assault began yesterday when a force numbering many thousands rolled out of the forward government command base at Adua, in neighboring Tigray province, along the highway towards the Eritrean border, the sources said.

The guerrillas said they had intercepted radio messages revealing a Soviet radio messages revealing a Soviet role in planning the attack, but they said that no Soviet or Cuban forces were involved in combat.

Big Attacks

Guerrilla intelligence sources said several thousand Cuban troops were garrisoning government-held towns in Tigray to release Ethiopian soldiers for the offensive.

The sources here said three antigovernment movements-the Eritrean People's Liberation Front (EPLF), the Eritrean Liberation Front (ELF) and Tigray People's Liberation Front (TPLF)-were cooperating under a joint command to repel the attack.

A TPLF spokesman said the main Ethiopian assault was preceded in the last two weeks by three big probing attacks which the guerrillas had managed to contain.

Raid Repelled

First, a force of 8,000 men crossed the Takazze river from a government base at Humera near the Sudanese border and tried unsuccessfully to capture the Eritrean town of Om Hajer, held by the ELF, he said.

Then a similar-sized army occupied the town of Enticcio, in Central Tigray, and attempted to push north but was turned back in two battles fought mainly with the EPLF, he said.

The third and largest drive began a week ago when a force numbering 10,000 to 12,000 left Ende-Selassie, in Tigray, and began to fight its way north to the Eritrean border.

The spokesman said the TPLF had managed to halt its advance for two days before getting reinforcements from both the EPLF and the ELF.

Objective

But he said Ethiopian troops succeeded in reaching the town of Adi Daro, 24 km north Ende-Selassie, last Tuesday and were trying to continue northwards.

Guerrilla sources here said the immediate objective of the force which left Adua yesterday was not yet clear, but it might try to link up with advancing units to the west.

The sources said the Ethiopians were using new tactics, perhaps on Soviet advice. The Ethiopian infantry was preceding the armor in human wave attacks and heavy air-raids were being carried out in Tigray for the first time, they said.

The TPLF spokesman said he thought the Soviet strategists might have underestimated the effect of summer rains, which began four days ago, on the offensive.

He said the Takazze river, which defines the border between Tigray and Eritrea in the combat zone, was running extremely high.

Eritrean guerrillas claim repulsion of Asmara drive

The Baltimore Sun, July 3, 1978

Khartoum, the Sudan (Reuter)

Guerrillas fighting Ethiopian rule in Eritrea province said yesterday they smashed a big drive by government troops trying to break out of Asmara, the besieged provincial capital.

A spokesman in Khartoum of the Eritrean People's Liberation Front (EPLF), one of the main insurgent groups, said the battle was fought all day Saturday.

A big Ethiopian force supported by tanks, heavy artillery and planes was defeated near the village of Adi Gumbolo, south of Asmara, he said.

One Russian-made T-54 tank was captured undamaged and another tank was destroyed.

Spokesmen for another Eritrean group the Eritrean Liberation Front (ELF), and the Tigray People's Liberation Front which is fighting along Eritrea's southern border with Tigray province, also claimed to have halted advancing Ethiopian forces there.

Eritrean liberation forces control an estimated 95 per cent of the strategic 45,000 square-mile territory. Only three major cities and two smaller garrisons are in government hands, the insurgents say.

For the past two weeks the government radio has broadcast forecasts that the fall of guerrilla-held towns and the reopening of Eritrea's major highways was imminent.

Representatives of the liberation movements in Khartoum were jubilant at the announcement of the EPLF victory near Asmara. It follows by a day a statement by the ELF that it had held a large government force from crossing the southern Eritrean border at the Mareb River, north of the Tigray town of Adua.

The guerrillas say the Ethiopian attacks from Asmara and Adua were intended to meet at the ELF held city of Mendefera on the important highway that links Asmara with central Ethiopia.

Under the new plan, the fighters of the two fronts will establish direct contact with each other. Political cadre will crisscross into areas of the country traditionally dominated by one or the other of the fronts. Nonmilitary departments will seek to integrate their programs.

At this time, the EPLF is not only a more disciplined and politicized organization than the ELF, but also considerably larger, outnumbering the declining ELF by a ratio of around three to one.

Ethiopia military drive fails

The Guardian (New York), July 12, 1978

Khartoum, Sudan

Ethiopia has launched its largest military campaign in the 17-year Eritrean war for independence. The first assault was stopped along the Eritrean border and within the handful of besieged government-held enclaves inside the Red Sea territory.

Moving in sequence on five separate fronts, the Ethiopians tried to recapture the southwestern corner of Eritrea. They were turned back or stopped in each case.

On July 5, a second wave of attacks was reported in the same areas. Heavy fighting has resumed on four fronts south of the Eritrean border-at Humera, Adi Daro, Rama and Intechew. A new attack is also in progress southeast of the Eritrean capital of Asmara.

Outside Eritrea, meanwhile leaders of the country's two liberation movements made a joint call for peace talks with Ethiopian's Mengistu regime. Appearing together in Beirut, Eritrean Liberation Front (ELF) Revolutionary Council chairman Ahmad Nassar and Eritrean People's Liberation Front general secretary Ramadan Mohammed Nur said there would be no preconditions for such talks.

The Eritreans emphasized, however, that there would be no compromise on the questions of independence. The Ethiopian response to date has been negative, saying that there is no basis for negotiations on these terms.

The Ethiopian push came as the military government was beset with escalating economic and political troubles. Famine is reported in widespread rural areas and hunger is spreading to the cities as well. There are also reports that Ethiopia's most important ally, the USSR, is considering throwing its weight behind a political rival of Lt. Col. Mengistu Haile Mariam, head of the ruling Dergue.

On shaky grounds at home, Mengistu has invested his personal prestige fully behind the Eritrea campaign now underway. A major defeat there, which the past week shows is likely, will place his government in a severe crisis. And the chances of his riding it out appear increasingly slim.

Joint Resistance

In the current fighting, the two Eritrean armies and the allied Tigray People's Liberation Front (TPLF) in Ethiopia chalked up a series of impressive victories in separate and joint engagements with their common foe. Observers say it was the heaviest week of fighting ever seen there.

The first large-scale Ethiopian troop movement began some two weeks ago from bases in Tigray Province, south of Eritrea. A force numbering an estimated 6000 soldiers tried to push north from the Tigray town of Intechew, but were smashed by the EPLF and small TPLF units that joined in the battle.

Shortly afterward, some 8000 troops with 36 tanks crossed the Takasse River in the far west and took the Eritrean border town of Om Hajer, but they were stopped from further advance by the ELF, according to ELF sources here.

The next move came from the Tigray town of Enda-Selassie in west-central Tigray when 10-12,000 Ethiopian troops supported by heavy armor and air strikes drove north toward the Eritrean border.

They were halted initially by the TPLF until ELF and EPLF forces came to their assistance. The advance was finally stopped in the village of Adi Daro, short of the Eritrean border.

This area is the soft underbelly of the Eritrean defense as the terrain is mostly flat and open and offers a clear route into southwestern Eritrea once a series of small hills is passed.

Late last week, the largest force yet rolled out of the Tigray town of Aduwa which serves as the government's forward command post for the "northern front." They headed up the Tarmac Highway to the Eritrean border.

This force, too, was stopped by the ELF short of the Mereb River which serves as the border with Tigray, according to an ELF spokesman. The ELF claims nine tanks, one armored car and one helicopter destroyed there, with 413 Ethiopians dead. A lieutenant colonel in charge of the Ethiopian attack was also reported wounded.

On the next day, Ethiopian forces tried to break out of the besieged Eritrean capital of Asmara to link up with the Aduwa units, but they were defeated in a daylong battle by the EPLF near the village of Adi Gumbolo. One Soviet-made T-54 tank was reported captured intact and another destroyed, but casualty figures were not available from the EPLF's Khartoum spokesman.

The Ethiopian strategy appears to be aimed at taking areas mainly under ELF control on the premise that the ELF has not fared as well as the larger and stronger EPLF in recent combat. But with the two fronts now operating under a joint high command, representatives here say they are cooperating to defend the entire 45,000 square mile territory. Both Eritrean fronts have commended the smaller TPLF also for their important role in breaking this first phase of the Ethiopian offensive. The TPLF operates only in Ethiopia's Tigray Province, but it supports the Eritrean independence movement and cooperates with both Eritrean fronts.

The current campaign has focused heavily on Tigray, where the government has been massing its forces for the offensive, and TPLF guerrillas have been harassing them for two months there.

When the offensive broke, the TPLF concentrated most of its forces, estimated at 2-3000 women and men (excluding a militia three times that size), to join the EPLF near Intechew and the ELF north of Enda-Selassie.

Mengistu's Troubles

In Addis Ababa, meanwhile, Mengistu is battling for his political life as his no-win military solution falters in Eritrea. Radio Revolutionary

Ethiopia announced this week that a coup planned for June 1 was uncovered only in May. And, the broadcast stated, there have been nine assassination attempts against Mengistu since the first of the year.

Recently there were reports of Cuban and South Yemeni efforts
to bring Negede Gobezi, a leading exiled member of the suppressed
Me'eson Party, back to the Ethiopian capital to share power with the
current military leaders. Now there are new rumors, indicating that
the Soviet Union is backing a Lt. Argo as Mengistu's replacement.
Argo is said to favor regional autonomy for all Ethiopian nationalities who wish it, and a return to civilian rule.

ELF leader Nassar was recently in Moscow for talks. Earlier,
there were reports of contacts between the EPLF and Soviet representatives elsewhere.

But for now, the principal players appear to be remaining in place-
Mengistu going for an unattainable military solution; his allies still on the
fence; and the Eritreans firm in their demand for genuine independence.

Reliable sources say that the ELF delegation to Moscow sought to
convince Soviet leaders to withdraw support from the Mengistu regime.
They were reportedly told that while support for Mengistu himself is
warning, Soviet leaders believe this can be reversed from within the
junta if the Me'eson Party can be brought into the government.

Soviet understanding of the current military and political situation in
Eritrea was sketchy, according to these sources. A re-evaluation of Soviet
policy appears to be taking place, however, although there is as yet no
clear sign of how it will come out.

War strains Ethiopian economy

The Guardian (New York), July 19, 1978

Khartoum, Sudan

Ethiopia's economy is headed for disaster as a result of the strain
of war and internal conflict, according to a confidential report recently submitted to the country's ruling military Dergue.

Drought, poverty and famine threaten Ethiopia, but it is essentially man-made problems which are preventing the implementation
of viable solutions, the report charges.

"Out of a total of three enemies-the external enemy, the internal enemy and famine and misery-war has officially been declared against the first two only," says the report, entitled "Report on Expected Famine in Ethiopia" and signed by Lars Bondestam, a Swedish expert with the Ethiopian Relief and Rehabilitation Commission.

"Side by side with an advanced waging of war, various forms of poverty and lack of food are becoming rampant among certain groups, especially among the poor peasants and pastoralists in conflict-stricken areas, the rural wage laborers and the lower classes of urban people," says Dr. Bondestam.

The report notes the existence of natural problems such as damage to crops from hailstorms and insects, but it concludes that the main danger comes from a general breakdown of the economy due to political and military causes.

The Dergue's single-minded concentration on military matters while giving only token attention to economic questions appears to be at the root of the current crisis.

"Long-term solutions to the Ethiopian food problem will depend on the future economic policy, but at present we do not know whether capital will control economic planning, or a planned economy will control the flow of capital," Bondestam says,

Meanwhile, he points out, it is the poorest and working classes who suffer most

A combination of factors is leading to decreases in both agricultural and industrial production while consumption is increasing in food producing areas and relief supplies are not reaching those in need, according to the confidential report.

The result is "a transfer of hunger from the rural areas to the urban centers," he says.

The report cites a number of "principal man-made factors" it says are exacerbating the current crisis.

Out of a total population of 30 million, 5 million are non-peasants and only 10 million live in surplus producing areas, according to the report.

With the abolition of feudal taxes and tithes and the partial redistribution of land, particularly in central and southern Ethiopia, food intake has increase d by 5-10% (100-200 calories per day), the report says.

At the same time, a half-million people or 5% of the productive peasant work-force (only 40% of the rural population is directly involved in agricultural production) has been withdrawn from active production due to 'local and regional disturbances.'

War disrupts production

The Guardian (New York), [??] 1978

Armed resistance to the government has disrupted production to some extent and distribution to a larger extent. Many peasants have fled these areas, others have been recruited into the "new peasant bureaucracy" and tens of thousands have been conscripted into the "national militia."

The regions most adversely affected by wars and revolts, according to the report, include Eritrea, Gondar, Tigray, Sidamo, Bale, eastern Arusi and Harrarghe. This area covers two-thirds of Ethiopia claimed territory.

"The problem is that people become separated, not only socially but in many cases also geographically from their land and means of production, which makes even greater demands upon the organization and transportation of food," says Bondestam.

Furthermore, he points out, many of the militia forces are being killed or badly wounded and will be permanently out of the workforce. No provisions are being made for them, and no steps are being taken to compensate for the loss of labor power.

Hunger Spreads to Cities

In addition, economic relations between country and town are also breaking down, due in part to the decrease in surplus agricultural produce, but also to a general disengagement of the peasant s from the national economy.

There are also labor problems in state-controlled industry and on the large nationalized plantations. These sectors are being squeezed between the profit demands of the government to finance the war fronts on the one hand, and the wage demands of workers caught in an inflationary economy on the other. This is causing shortages of manufactured goods which would otherwise serve as incentives to peasants to market surplus grain supplies, according to the report.

The decrease in industrial production in the towns also means less purchasing power for urban workers and the poorest urban dwellers, thus aggravating he growing imbalance between town and countryside.

In any case, says the report, given a constant rural labor productivity, the peasants would have to increase their labor time by 1-1.5 hours per day to compensate for the overall decrease in agricultural production and the increase in their own subsistence consumption in order to supply the towns. This is not possible, as they are already working 10-12 hours each day.

But instead of developing the rural economy or seeking political solutions to the many conflicts which rend Ethiopia, the military government continues to mobilize for war while seeking relief aid from abroad to solve its economic problems.

However, says the report, official priority for transport is so heavily weighted in favor of the military that adequate transportation is not available for relief or imported grain arriving at the port of Assab.

The report notes that there has been a decrease in the overall number of trucks (many have been captured by Eritrean independence forces during the past two years). Also, many civilian trucks are now being used for military transport which increasingly means traveling in large escorted convoys.

Fertilizers have a particularly low priority despite the fact that the lack of fertilizers last year brought about an estimated production decrease of 90-100,000 tons of grain. This amount must now be imported or donated.

The rapidly declining grain stocks are resulting in a lack of food for non-peasant consumption and increasing grain prices. The hardest hit by this are the lumpen proletariat, permanent, seasonal and day laborers and the poorer sector of the petty bourgeoisie, according to the report.

The upper-and high-middle classes get by through hoarding grain, thus aggravating the problem of the urban poor.

Warning Ethiopia's self-proclaimed "socialist" military government of dire consequences if these problems are not soon addressed, the Swedish report advises that purely technical solutions are not enough.

"As the conflicts which contribute to deteriorating economic and food conditions are of a political nature, it obviously follows that solutions to alleviate these problems are also basically political," concludes the report.

The massive military buildup in and near Eritrea under the slogan "Everything to the war front" while government leaders are pleading for international relief assistance does not suggest, however, that recommendations in the report are being implemented.

'We surprised them'

Guerrillas describe battle in Ethiopia

The Baltimore Sun, July 26, 1978

Near the Eritrean border, Ethiopia (Reuter)

Rain pelted the palm-front roof of a makeshift clinic as the wounded guerrilla fighters of the Tigray People's Liberation Front (TPLF) told a reporter about their last battle with Ethiopian government forces.

The guerrillas appeared to be in good spirits. The TPLF men were recuperating in the clinic. Outside, a diesel-powered generator sputtered as guerrilla mechanics kept working.

"One brigade tried to come out from Adi Daro with multiple rocket launchers and 10 tanks, but we surprised them and annihilated the whole force," said Abraha Desta as he lay across a mattress on the dirt floor with a bullet wound in his leg.

Adi Daro is in northeastern Ethiopia's Tigray province, where the TPLF operates in opposition to the country's military government. In recent weeks the TPLF has been coordinating its activities with two liberation movements from neighboring Eritrea against a massive offensive there by government forces.

Mr. Desta watched the young field trained medical orderly dip cotton in bottled water and carefully wash the surface of an 11-inch strip of exposed muscle from a shrapnel wound in another fighter's leg before continuing his narration of the Adi Daro battle.

"The Eritrean Liberation Front was on one side and we were on the other," the 28-year old Mr. Desta said. "More than 300 of the peasant militia were killed and their tanks became useless."

He said the TPLF men knocked out one tank with a B-10 rocket and two others with rocket-propelled grenades. Then they were ordered not to hit the other tanks because the Ethiopians were abandoning them in hasty retreat.

"Reinforcements came with heavy artillery," the wounded guerrilla continued. "They were Nebelbals (Israeli-trained regular Ethiopian troops). They fought well."

A spokesman said the TPLF is a 3 year-old organization which engages mainly in partisan tactics of hit-and run ambushes against moving convoys and small government outposts.

To have defeated an entire armored brigade in the first stage of this battle was a big victory for them, the spokesman said. Some of his comrades joked and exchanged anecdotes as he spoke.

There were several TPLF guerrillas here with leg wounds from the Adi Daro battle, which took place June 28.

"The ones with bullets in their arms are still fighting," one guerrilla said.

Tsehaiay Alem lay in pain as the orderly worked the cotton swab into his pitted wound, "red like the inside of a ripe watermelon," as one of his comrades remarked.

With the others kidding him, the 21 year-old Mr. Alem broke into a Tigray revolutionary song through gritted teeth. He leaned forward on his elbow and grinned.

As his leg was being re-bandaged, he told the story of one guerrilla who was examining the Ethiopian dead and shouting "Awat!"(Tigrinya for "victory") when he took a bullet in his shoulder from the advancing government reinforcements.

Mr. Alem said the fighter, on his way down, raised his fist and again yelled, "Awat!"

As the orderly cut away the blood-soaked bandage from Abraha Desta's leg where the bullet had passed through the calf, Mr. Desta praised the Tigray peasant volunteers who fed the guerrillas during the battle and later carried off the wounded.

He winced, however, as he recounted his own evacuation.

"When I was shot," he said, "it felt like being hit with a stick, but when I looked down and saw my leg wide open, I wondered if I would lose it."

Several peasants picked him up to take him to the rear, he said, but one slipped in the thick mud and they dropped him.

"It really hurt worse than when I was hit," he said.

The other guerrillas burst into laughter.

The TPLF spokesman said many peasants had come forward to join the rapidly expanding guerrilla army after the passage of the government force through their villages. The spokesman predicted that the recent combat would significantly strengthen the TPLF for future battles.

The wounded guerrillas say they will recuperate here until they are able to walk again.

Breakthrough by Ethiopians
is reported in Eritrean hills

The Miami Herald, July 1978

Khartoum, Sudan

Ethiopian forces have broken through Eritrean insurgents' front lines in Eritrea's heavily populated central highlands and are driving deep into guerrilla-held territory, according to informed sources in Khartoum.

The large, mechanized Ethiopian force Friday captured the town of Adi Quala, which was held by the Eritrean Liberation Front (ELF). The Ethiopians now threaten the ELF-held city of Mendefera, 37 miles inside the strategic Red Sea territory, the sources say.

Ethiopian units also are reported thrusting into southwestern Eritrea on two fronts from government bases in Ethiopia's Tigray province and from Gondar after overrunning ELF positions along the border last week.

ELF resistance appears to be crumbling throughout the areas under its control because every major city in its hands is under immediate threat by the advancing Ethiopian forces.

A spokesman for the Eritrean People's Liberation Front (EPLF), the larger of the two Eritrean independence movements, says that all is quiet in EPLF controlled areas after a series of major assaults, which he says were repulsed by the EPLF.

Now in the sixth week of the largest military offensive ever launched in the 16-year Eritrean war, the Ethiopian government appears to be concentrating its efforts on winning back the central and southwestern areas of Eritrea from the ELF.

However, government victories in ELF areas soon will threaten the more successful EPLF with further attacks against their formerly secure rear areas.

The EPLF occupies the northern Eritrean lowlands, much of the central highlands, including the Red Sea coast and the southeastern regions of the 40,000 square-mile province, a former Italian colony.

The EPLF spokesman says that Ethiopia has committed almost 200,000 troops to the present offensive from bases along Eritrea's southern border and from government-held garrisons inside Eritrea.

With ELF defenses apparently collapsing, the EPLF will bear the full brunt of the military campaign over the coming weeks. However, the EPLF spokesman said that EPLF forces will defend its areas and prepare to try to take back territory lost by the ELF.

The initial Ethiopian breakthroughs came against the ELF in the border towns of Om Hajer and Shambuko in the southwestern lowlands. These forces are reported to be driving toward the ELF-held city of Tessenei and toward the Ethiopian government's garrison at Barentu.

The latest government victory came against ELF forces at the Mereb River border in south-central Eritrea, where the ELF reportedly had concentrated its strongest force to defend the densely populated highlands.

Ethiopian capture of Tessenei in the southwest and Mendefera in central Eritrea will pose immediate threats to the EPLF-held cities of Keren and Decamare and force it to open two more battlefronts.

The EPLF has four fronts to defend, including the west-central border with Tigray at a placed called Gehrusinia; the southeastern region at Adi Kaieh; the Red Sea coast at the port of Massawa and the entire periphery of the Asmara capital.

Three of these government base areas threaten the city of Decamare. With Mendefera in government hands, Ethiopia could open a fourth front against Decamare. Heavy fighting is expected there soon by the EPLF.

The EPLF spokesman said that the real test of the offensive will come here. He pointed out that the western lowlands are a rolling flat area difficult of defend, but the highlands, where the war now is focusing, are mountainous and ideally suited to defensive warfare.

The spokesman said that an exodus of displaced persons coming to EPLF areas was straining the front's economic and social resources, but he said that EPLF military strength was at its highest point in the protracted war.

Diplomatic sources in Khartoum suggest that Ethiopia may try to crush the ELF and offer to negotiate with the Marxist EPLF from a position of increased strength, but the EPLF spokesman discounted the possibility.

Ethiopian Army Thrust in Eritrea

The Financial Times (London), July 1978

Ethiopian forces have broken through Eritrean Liberation Front (ELF) lines in Eritrea's heavily populated central highlands and are driving deep into guerrilla held territory.

The large mechanized Ethiopian force yesterday captured the ELF-held town of Adi Quala and now threatens the ELF-held city of Mendefera 60 kilometers inside the strategic Red Sea territory, according to reports reaching the Sudanese capital.

Ethiopian units are also reported to be thrusting into South-western Eritrea on two fronts from government bases in Ethiopia's Tigray and Gondar provinces after over-running ELF positions along the border last week.

ELF resistance appears to be crumbling throughout the areas under their control as every major city in their hands is now under immediate threat by the advancing Ethiopian forces.

A spokesman for the Eritrean People's Liberation Front (EPLF), the larger of the two Eritrean independence movements, says that all is quiet now in EPLF-controlled areas after a series of major assaults by the Ethiopians which he says were defeated by the EPLF.

Sixth Week

Now in the sixth week of the largest military offensive launched in the 17-year Eritrean war, the Soviet and Cuban backed Ethiopian Government appears to be concentrating its efforts on winning back the central and south-western areas of Eritrea from the ELF.

Government victories in ELF areas will soon threaten the more successful EPLF with further attacks against their formerly secure rear areas.

The EPLF occupies the northern Eritrean lowlands, much of the central highlands including the Red Sea coast and the south-eastern regions of the 100,000 square kilometer former Italian colony.

The EPLF spokesman claims that Ethiopia has now committed close to 200,000 troops to the present offensive from bases along Eritrea's southern border and from government held garrisons inside Eritrea.

A lengthy period of intense battle will have a profound political impact on the parties involved which may well prove the determining factor in the eventual outcome of the war.

More than mere territory is at issue. Both sides have staked their political existence on their ability to bring about a military victory.

EPLF quits two key towns

The Financial Times (London), August 2, 1978

Khartoum

The Eritrean People's Liberation Front (EPLF) says it has voluntarily withdrawn from two key Eritrean towns in order to mount offensive operations against Ethiopian government forces, according to the EPLF's Khartoum spokesman.

The EPLF pulled out of the Red Sea port of Massawa and the important inland town of Decamare as well as other smaller positions in the face of a massive Ethiopian build-up.

This is the first time the EPLF has yielded territory won from the government in more than three years. It follows a series of Ethiopian victories against the other main independence movement, the Eritrean Liberation Front (ELF), over the past two weeks.

The EPLF spokesman insisted that the withdrawals were not taken under direct Ethiopian military pressure, but he conceded that Ethiopia's penetration of ELF areas had substantially increased the pressure on EPLF defences.

The spokesman termed the moves "tactical withdrawals" and said that they would permit the EPLF to concentrate its defence of its main base area while freeing large mobile forces to attack the government's now extended supply and communications lines.

Ethiopia claims to have driven the EPLF out of Massawa and Decamare, and last night announced it had taken Adi Caieh from the EPLF.

Ethiopian troops take major town

The Financial Times (London), August 13, 1978

Khartoum

Ethiopian government forces rolled into the city of Agordat this week, taking the last major town from the Eritrean Liberation Front (ELF) and setting the stage for a showdown with the Eritrean People's Liberation Front (EPLF).

The fall of Agordat has been a foregone conclusion since Ethiopia overran a series of ELF-held cities and towns during the past three weeks of what has become the largest military campaign ever fought in the 17 year Eritrean war for independence from Ethiopia.

Its main significance lies in the fact that the Government is now in a position to launch a two-pronged assault on the Eritrean city of Keren, which is held by the EPLF, the stronger of the two main Eritrean guerrilla movements. Informed sources here say that such an assault may already have begun with substantial backup support from Cuban forces on the ground and in the air.

Agordat, nestling in the foothills of western Eritrea, is the gateway to the Red Sea territory's highland plateau, which rises rapidly to 2,500 metres (8,000 feet) above sea level and is the most densely populated area of Eritrea.

The Ethiopian strategy in the current offensive breaks down into three stages. In the first, the Government set out to mobilize and deploy its forces inside Eritrea and along Eritrea's southern border with Tigrai and Gondar provinces.

State one began officially on June 5, according to the Government's own official statements, but it was substantially delayed by attacks from the EPLF, the ELF and a third anti-Government movement in Tigrai, the Tigrai People's Liberation Front (TPLF).

Stage two called for the opening of three principal highways running from Tigrai and Gondar to the encircled city of Asmara and the capture of all cities and towns along these roads. To date, this has been only partially successful.

Stage three, which involves Government strikes on rural guerrilla bases in the vicinity of the newly reoccupied towns and highways has yet to be implemented except in the western lowlands against the battered remnants of the ELF. Instead, Ethiopia appears to be concentrating its full strength for the confrontation with the EPLF between Agordat and Asmara. Diplomatic sources say that the Government plans a pincer attack west from Asmara and east from Agordat toward Keren with fully mechanized units and a heavy reliance on airpower.

Eritrea's Guerrillas Set A Trap

Observer Foreign News Service (London), August 14, 1978

Khartoum, Sudan

After Ethiopian forces had taken former guerrilla strongholds in Eritrea without firing a shot, Ethiopian officials announced a major victory and expressed confidence that Government troops could now begin to consolidate their position by establishing control over the surrounding countryside and isolating the guerrillas.

Spokesmen for the main Eritrean movements disagree, saying that Ethiopia has over-extended itself too quickly and walked into a well-laid trap which will give the guerrillas the military initiative after two months of the heaviest fighting in the 17-year Eritrean war for independence. "The Ethiopians have taken what they are capable of taking and that is the end of their advance so far as we are concerned," said the Khartoum spokesman of the Eritrean People's Liberation Front (EPLF).

Ethiopia's Russian-and Cuban-backed army has reoccupied three large cities and a score of smaller towns and villages from the EPLF and a second smaller movement - the Eritrean Liberation Front (ELF) - during the past three weeks.

Driving into western and southern Eritrea against the ELF, the Government took the towns of Tessenei and Adi Quala and the important city of Mendefera by the end of July. At this point, the EPLF appears to have voluntarily withdrawn from the Red Sea port of Massawa, the central highland city of Decamare and a series of other positions in central and southern Eritrea, lifting the siege of the Asmara capital which had been in effect since last October.

Ethiopia immediately rushed in to fill the vacuum, spreading its forces out over a wide area, which is exactly what the guerrillas say they wanted.

"We abandoned our permanent positions in the east and south not out of weakness, but to preserve our strength," said the EPLF spokesman. "We are now in a position to attack any of their re-established camps one at a time."

Having the advantages of mobility and popular support, the Eritreans say they can now pick the time and place to resume the surprise tactics which won them control of most of the strategic Red Sea territory during the previous three years.

More than 150,000 Ethiopian troops were mobilized for the current government offensive which began in June. They were armed with Russian small arms, T54 tanks, armored cars, "Stalin organs" and heavy artillery, while Ethiopia's new Russian-supplied MiG jet fighters flew air support and Russian and Cuban advisers and technicians directed the campaign.

Reliable sources say that the next stage of the Ethiopian strategy involved striking out at rural guerrilla bases from the recently reoccupied garrisons and securing the western Eritrean border with Sudan against further infiltration of supplies by means of helicopter patrols and supporting infantry units.

Such tactics will place increasing demands upon the Russian and Cuban technicians who are responsible for key logistical and communications functions, and they will also threaten to create border incidents with Sudan.

Ethiopia Held Preparing Attack On Secessionists

The Baltimore Sun, August 14, 1978

Khartoum, Sudan (Reuter)

Ethiopian government forces are preparing for a heavily armored pincer attack against a key town held by rebels seeking the secession of Eritrea province, Western intelligence sources here said yesterday.

They also said Cuban troops, until now restricted to support roles, appeared to have been drawn deeper into the fighting as the Ethiopian forces prepared for a crucial clash with the guerrillas.

The intelligence sources believe Cuban troops will back up Soviet-equipped mechanized units advancing northwest from the provincial capital of Asmara and east from the town of Agordat, which fell to government troops Thursday.

They said the assault on Keren, Eritrea's second largest town with a civilian population of about 50,000 would be the most highly mechanized attack in the two-month offensive, in which Ethiopian forces have advanced across the southern and western parts of the province, retaking town after town captured by the guerrillas last year.

Agordat was the last town held by the Eritrean Liberation Front (ELF),which took the brunt of the offensive and which informed sources said has been battered and demoralized after a string of defeats.

Keren is held by the other major movement, the Eritrean People's Liberation Front (EPLF), which still controls several towns in the north of the province and along the main road from Asmara to the Red Sea port of Massawa 72 miles away down the mountains.

The EPLF withdrew from several towns around Asmara last month to conserve their own forces after they saw the ELF suffer heavy defeats and the government troops break a 10-month rebel siege of Asmara.

Keren, 70 miles northwest of Asmara, was captured relatively easily by guerrilla forces in July 1977, after a long siege which thoroughly demoralized the government troops. Its fall was considered one of the most important victories for the guerrillas when they launched their own offensive against the towns after occupying the Eritrean countryside for years.

At that time the defending Ethiopian government garrison in the hilltop town, which is linked by road and rail with Asmara, was estimated at between 4,000 and 8,000 men.

Keren is in the heart of EPLF territory and the group's spokesmen are confident they can stave off the impending two-pronged attack, saying the steep mountainous terrain is far more suited to their style of fighting.

But diplomatic sources say morale is high among the troops of the Marxist military Ethiopian government and their position only can be strengthened if the Cubans play a more active role.

Eritrean Movement Revives Guerrilla Tactics

The Natal Mercury (Durban, SA), OFNS, August 15, 1978

Ethiopia's recent successes against the Eritrean Liberation Front in a string of Eritrean towns and cities are causing the ELF to shift back to the rural-based guerrilla tactics that characterized the movement two years ago.

Spokesmen for the Elf and the rival Eritrean People's Liberation Front say that close to 200,000 Ethiopian troops are now mobilized for the campaign to recapture Eritrea, including reinforcements and logistics personnel in adjoining provinces.

No Cubans

Thousands of Cuban combat troops are also reported behind Government lines, but the Eritreans say there is as yet no evidence of Cuban participation in the fighting.

Ethiopian strategy and tactics in the Eritrean offensive of the past two months show a marked similarity to those used in the successful Russian and Cuban backed campaign against Somali forces in the contested Ogaden region earlier this year, with the one significant difference being the absence of Russian and Cuban forces from the front lines in Eritrea.

Technical Aid

But the Russians and Cubans are playing an important role in planning the present offensive, and they are providing key technical assistance, according to both diplomatic and guerrilla sources.

"Even if they do not take a direct part in the fighting, they are actively supporting the Ethiopians," said an EPLF spokesman.

The spokesman noted that South Yemen appeared to have made a political decision to pull out of Eritrea after taking part in battles near Massawa and Asmara against the EPLF, but the large Cuban presence near Eritrea continued to leave open the possibility of their coming to the aid of Ethiopian forces should the war take a sudden turn for the worse for the Government.

Meanwhile, Ethiopia's sudden success is posing problems. The penetration into Eritrea necessitates extended supply lines against which the ELF is already moving.

The ELF's transition to guerrilla tactics began even as they were mounting their last-minute defense of Tessenei and Mendefera. ELF units removed or destroyed supplies and equipment considered of use to Ethiopia, and a demolition squad blew up the only bridge over the swollen Gash River in the west between Tessenei and Barentu, thus separating two of the Government task forces from each other.

Corridor

Ethiopia does not appear to have maintained a supply corridor behind the Tessenei force, where ELF guerrillas still control the countryside, but convoys are said to be transporting supplies by road to the Mendefera force. These convoys are likely to be subject to continual guerrilla attack.

Eritreans plan new offensives

The Guardian (New York), August 16, 1978

Khartoum, Sudan

Ethiopia's sudden military advances recently in the Red Sea territory of Eritrea and neighboring Tigray province may prove to be more of a liability than an asset in the long run.

Using overwhelming force, Ethiopia recaptured over two dozen towns in Eritrea, including the strategic Red Sea port of Massawa and the important inland town of Decamare. Ethiopia also said it had finally broken the 3-year siege of Asmara, the capital of Eritrea.

At issue now is whether the military government of Lt. Col.

Mengistu Haile Mariam will be able to retain the territory its forces now hold. Three liberation movements, led by the Eritrean People's Liberation Front (EPLF), are preparing to mount counteroffensives and they are superbly equipped to cause enormous problems for the Ethiopian occupiers.

Two weeks ago Ethiopian government forces appeared to be rolling toward victory in Eritrea and in Tigray province. Guerrilla spokesmen here, however, say this was in some part an illusion created by their own tactical decisions to withdraw from certain defensive positions in order to switch to offensive actions once the government spread out its forces and exposed its weak points.

"Ethiopia has taken what it is capable of taking and that's the end of its advances as far as we're concerned," according to the Khartoum spokesman for the EPLF.

Spokesmen for the Eritrean Liberation Front (ELF) and the Tigray People's Liberation Front (TPLF) say they have already begun guerrilla actions behind Ethiopian lines.

In June, Ethiopia launched the largest military offensive yet in the 17-year Eritrean war for independence, mobilizing between 150,000 and 200,000 men and large quantities of Soviet-supplied heavy arms for the campaign.

Soviet and Cuban strategists and technicians played a key role in the planning and execution of the offensive, according to informed sources, but guerrilla spokesmen say there is yet no evidence of a frontline Soviet or Cuban combat role. By late July, Ethiopian forces occupied a number of large Eritrean and Tigrayan towns and several key highways previously in the hands of liberation fronts.

In some cases they overran Eritrean and Tigrayan positions, but in others, the insurgents simply pulled back and allowed the government to advance. While the ELF suffered serious battlefield losses in Eritrea's western lowlands and southern highlands, the larger EPLF yielded territory without a fight and then moved in to surround the new government positions and retake the roads necessary for overland supply.

"The military situation has now stabilized," said the EPLF spokesman, "and we are in a position to attack any of their reestablished camps one at a time."

A major side effect of the recent shifts in Eritrea has been a further increase in the leftist EPLF's dominance over the divided Eritrean independence movement as well as a strengthening of the TPLF in Tigray which was used as a staging area for the Eritrea campaign.

A recent visitor to EPLF-and ELF-held areas of Eritrea says that morale is extremely high within the EPLF while the ELF appears badly demoralized following defeats which cost it the control of all but one city under its control.

No figures are available on the ELF's actual losses, but reliable sources say they were high, and the ELF is known to have lost the core of its infrastructure and large quantities of supplies and arms. The EPLF, on the other hand, retains large and well-defended base areas including several urban centers in the north and east.

Forces Intact

"The only significant change for us that has come about is that we made tactical changes on the eastern and southern fronts, but on the other fronts it remains the same," said the EPLF spokesman. "Our forces are intact," he added. "If anything, they have been strengthened by all the arms we captured during this time and by all the young men and women who have now volunteered to fight and are in our training camps today."

The EPLF spokesman conceded that Ethiopia has a significant superiority in manpower and arms, but he said that the EPLF has the advantages of tactical and strategic superiority and the support of the Eritrean people. These factors, he said, make it impossible for the EPLF to fight a defensive war of attrition against the Ethiopian government but they give the EPLF the edge in a situation where the front can maintain the military initiative by adopting flexible and mobile offensive tactics which he predicts will now be the case.

"The Ogaden will not be repeated so long as we have the determination to be free and the support of our people," he said. "Our main task now is to mobilize and arm the whole population of Eritrea," he added in apparent reference to the disintegrating morale in the former ELF-held areas. Reliable sources say that the EPLF may now begin to mount offensive actions in the ELF's lost territory using large mobile forces which were previously tied down in southern Eritrea and in the 8-month siege of the capital, Asmara.

A spokesman for the beleaguered ELF also said here that ELF units will now begin to mount small-scale guerrilla operations. "We feel that after getting reorganized, a process which we have already started, we can also begin to take the initiative," he said.

With Ethiopian forces continuing their buildup in the newly reoccupied ELF areas, the next few weeks are likely to prove decisive for the survival of the ELF.

'Heavy casualties' In Eritrean battle

The Scotsman (Edinburgh), August 18, 1978

Khartoum, Sudan (Reuter)

The Ethiopian Government have sent waves of peasant militiamen against Eritrean rebels fighting to hold the mountain town of Keren, the last of the Red Sea province's main towns under rebel control, according to a rebel spokesman here today.

The Eritrean People's Liberation Front official said that 700 Government militiamen and troops had died in four attempts to smash through rebel lines on Monday. The attacks had been made on the road leading north from Asmara, the Eritrean capital, to Keren.

After the drive towards Keren had been blunted, Government forces had thrust west of Asmara with a heavy mechanized force on Tuesday, the spokesman said. One tank had been captured and three destroyed in the first clash and fighting was still going on.

"We are holding our positions," the spokesman added.

Diplomatic sources said that the EPLF appeared to be making progress against the Government forces, who have so far recaptured a score of towns and villages in a month-long offensive. The rebels have admitted making several tactical withdrawals.

The EPLF's main base areas are north of Asmara and Keren, and if the Government recaptured Keren it would greatly restrict guerrilla activity in Southern Eritrea. It would also make possible a Government operation to clear the last major road still held by the rebels, the road from Asmara to the Red Sea port of Massawa, according to diplomatic sources here.

The EPLF spokesman said that guerrilla units who had pulled out of towns as the Government forces had advanced into Eritrea last month had returned to rural bases and resorted to their old strategy of living in the mountains and controlling or harassing roads.

A Government convoy had been ambushed on the main road south from Asmara this week, the spokesman added, without giving details. Western intelligence sources said a large Cuban force had just been driven to Asmara along this road from the Ethiopian heartland.

The EPLF spokesman said he had no report of Cubans being directly engaged in the current campaign.

According to diplomatic sources in Addis Ababa, Cuban troops have taken over garrison duties to free Ethiopian units for front-line roles.

Ethiopian move on Keren repulsed

The Financial Times (London), August 20, 1978

Khartoum

Ethiopia's third attempt in five days to reach the guerrilla-held Eritrean city of Keren has been repulsed with heavy losses, according to the Eritrean People's Liberation Front (EPLF).

The EPLF claimed that 350 Ethiopian troops were killed, 600 wounded and 20 captured in 14 hours of heavy fighting outside the Eritrean capital of Asmara on Friday. This brings the total reported Ethiopian losses in the campaign to capture Keren to almost 2,000 last week. The guerrillas say that 15,000 Ethiopians have been killed so far in the 10 week offensive to regain control of the strategic Red Sea territory.

The EPLF would not give figures for its own losses, but claimed they were low.

EPLF units also have begun attacking Ethiopian supply lines in recently reoccupied areas of southern and western Eritrea in order to force the government to commit large forces to defensive positions, a spokesman said.

The guerrillas mounted their second ambush in a week near the new Ethiopian base at Seganeiti on the highway linking Asmara with central Ethiopia, according to the spokesman, who said that 70 soldiers were killed there, and 14 captured.

Eritreans Block Ethiopia

Guerrillas Holding Line Near Keren; Many Casualties

The Guardian (New York), August 30, 1978

Khartoum, Sudan

Ethiopian forces were crushed last week in an all-out attack against the Eritrean city of Keren. The Eritrean Peoples' Liberation Front (EPLF) turned back a series of Ethiopian assaults on the key EPLF held city, killing close to 2000 government troops and destroying 15 tanks.

"It was a massacre," said the EPLF's Khartoum spokesman, amid widespread reports that Cuban combat forces were poised to enter the important battle. However, there is no evidence of their participation on the frontlines in what may become the turning point of Ethiopia's current offensive to regain control of the strategic Red Sea territory.

Meanwhile, EPLF units also attacked government positions in Ethiopia's vulnerable rear areas. There are signs that the EPLF will soon begin major counteroffensive actions.

The showdown battle with the EPLF for Keren began on Aug. 14, within days of Ethiopia's successful reoccupation of the city of Agordat in western Eritrea, the last town held by the Eritrean Liberation Front (ELF). Informed sources say that Ethiopia's plan was to roll through Agordat east toward Keren and launch a 2-pronged pincer attack in conjunction with a large force coming west from the capital city of Asmara. The initial phase of the operation was foiled when the EPLF blocked the advance from Agordat and moved in behind the city to cut the government's supply lines from the nearby garrison at Barentu.

Large Ethiopian Loss

When the second phase opened north of Asmara, EPLF forces were ready along a broad defensive front. Between 13,000 and 15,000 government troops charged out of long-besieged Asmara behind a wall of Soviet-supplied tanks and armored vehicles, supported by an exceptionally heavy aerial and artillery bombardment. But they do not appear to have gotten far.

The EPLF representative said that the assault came near the village of Embaderho, where the Ethiopians tried four times to break through EPLF lines before they retreated in disarray to Asmara. Early the following day, the Ethiopians tried again, this time coming out of Asmara on the western side near the village of Adi Yacob, but after two days of continuous fighting, the results were the same.

More than 1500 Ethiopian troops were reported killed in these three days. One tank was captured and 13 destroyed, along with four army vehicles. EPLF losses were described as light.

Two days later, on Aug. 18, Ethiopia attempted again to break through the Embaderho lines but after 14 hours of intense combat the attack was broken. This time, the EPLF reported 350 Ethiopian dead, 600 wounded and 20 captured. Two tanks were also destroyed and 112 pieces of light and heavy arms taken. Western intelligence sources based in Ethiopia's capital confirmed the size of the government's losses.

"It is going to be a war of attrition in this area," said the spokesman for the EPLF. "They are going to attack and we are going to smash them again and again. Then we are going to attack."

The EPLF also announced that guerrilla units had ambushed an Ethiopian supply convoy on the southern highway linking Asmara with central Ethiopia for the second time in a week. The ambush came between the towns of Decamare and Segeneiti on Aug. 16, according to the EPLF spokesman.

The EPLF victories are the first fruits of a daring strategy they implemented early this month by discreetly withdrawing from towns held in this region and lifting the 6-month siege of Asmara. Government forces rushed into fill the vacuum left by the retreat and Ethiopian officials rashly declared victory. Such claims are now proving to have been premature.

Eyewitnesses to the EPLF evacuations say that they were carefully planned and announced to the civilian population in advance. Those people who were visibly associated with the EPLF, such as members of the People's Assemblies and the militia, were moved to the countryside with their household goods. Detailed explanations of the withdrawal were then given to other residents and all those who chose to leave were given transit to safe areas.

Ethiopia's subsequent "triumphal" reoccupation was therefore an anticlimax, Government troops found a handful of elderly residents in towns stripped clean of supplies and goods. When they tried to move their own supplies in, they were attacked and isolated.

"Ethiopia is now getting into a quagmire with no way out," said the EPLF spokesman here. "We still control the countryside and the roads. How are they going to capture them? We can hit them wherever we want."

ELF Areas Taken

In the EPLF strategy, military actions follow political conditions. The population in southern Eritrea is fully organized and essentially secure except for these few positions. However, western Eritrea—where the ELF was based—has yet to be fully mobilized. Hence, the EPLF's military attention has shifted in this direction.

While defending the northern base area (where Keren, among other EPLF-held towns, is located) and controlling movement in the south, the EPLF is beginning to take the offensive in the west. The likelihood is that EPLF units will move to retake some of the ELF's lost territory soon, beginning perhaps with the city of Agordat.

The ELF has been hurt badly. Last week Ethiopian forces are reported to have made a surprise attack against Tekeraret, the site of the ELF's headquarters in the west. EPLF mobile units are already operating in this area against government supply convoys, while political cadre start their work organizing and politicizing the local population.

In overall terms, the EPLF has never been in a stronger position in Eritrea. Tensions have built up again with the ELF after a break that followed the signing of a unity pact last April, but the lopsided disparity between the two forces now renders such problems peripheral to the struggle with Ethiopia.

The key arena of conflict is now Asmara, where the battle for Keren will likely resume soon. Ethiopia's whole strategy hinges on the reconquest of Keren and the reopening of the western road to Asmara. It is here that the government has concentrated its maximum strength, and heavy fighting may continue for several weeks before the final results are in.

Two important questions remain to be answered: How long can Ethiopia sustain the kind of losses it experienced this week, and will the Cubans join the fray?

EPLF tactics are designed to force the government to commit larger forces to defensive positions across Eritrea, and it is not likely that Ethiopia can substantially increase the size of the Asmara attack force in the immediate future. Western intelligence sources say there is slightly less than one Cuban mechanized brigade now in Asmara to back the Ethiopians should they run into trouble, but there is still considerable doubt as to whether the Cubans will actually participate in the battle on the ground. In the view of some observers, the Soviets and Cubans are trying to walk a tightrope between backing Ethiopia's ruling military Derg and preventing their own full commitment to the battle in Eritrea.

Change In Addis Ababa?

In this view, the Soviets and Cubans are waiting for a major Ethiopian defeat in order to bring about a change in the leadership in Addis Ababa which might negotiate a peace to bring the 17-year Eritrean war for independence to an end. The viability of such a strategy depends, however, on several unstable factors, including Derg leader Mengistu Haile Mariam's ability to stay in power and the possibility that Cubans may be drawn into the fighting in Asmara whether they plan to or not.

Soviet bombers could also be called in to fly missions around Asmara should the Ethiopian defenses suddenly collapse. Another uncertain factor is the outcome of the increasing diplomatic pressures on all parties to seek a peaceful solution to the conflict.

Any number of scenarios are possible as long as the situation remains fluid, and as long as the Soviets and Cubans continue the sizable rear support for the Derg in the offensive without taking a clear political stand on the Eritrean question. What is certain is that they must make their decision soon, if it is to have any effect, because the initiative is rapidly passing to the EPLF.

Eritrean Fighting

Reuters news service, September 2, 1978

Khartoum, Sudan

Ethiopian forces fell back Friday, after losing 1,500 men killed in three days of human wave assaults on rebel lines north of the Eritrean capital of Asmara, a rebel spokesman said in Khartoum.

The official of the Eritrean People's Liberation Front (EPLF) said Ethiopian commanders formed up waves of troops and militiamen 16 times Thursday alone. The massed infantry attacks were on rebel lines on the road to the EPLF stronghold of Keren and in surrounding mountains.

In a final counter-attack the guerrillas drove the government troops back through the village of Adi Yacob to the positions from where they began the latest breakthrough bid on Wednesday, the spokesman said.

The Ethiopians lost eight tanks, the spokesman said. He added that 700 Ethiopians were captured and an estimated 2,000 were wounded.

EPLF losses were not given.

EPLF repulses Ethiopian attack

The Guardian (New York), September 6, 1978

Khartoum, Sudan

Ethiopia's all-out offensive in Eritrea ground to a temporary halt this week following significant victories by guerrilla forces in Eritrea.

Meanwhile, informed sources say that Ethiopia plans to announce the formation of an official Ethiopian political party Sept. 12, the fourth anniversary of the Provisional Military Administrative Council's (the Derg) takeover from the late emperor Haile Selassie. This is reportedly to be followed by the formal establishment of a "Democratic Republic of Ethiopia."

In two weeks of heavy fighting around the Eritrean capital of Asmara, the Eritrean People's Liberation Front (EPLF) successfully repulsed repeated Ethiopian attempts to advance toward the EPLF-held city of Keren far to the south.

The battle for Keren has become the crucial test of strength for both sides over the outcome of Ethiopia's 3-month offensive, the largest military campaign ever fought in the strategic Red Sea territory of Eritrea.

The Ethiopian strategy in Eritrea was apparently timed to bring a decisive government victory by the Sept. 12 anniversary. But the EPLF has upset this timetable; it appears likely now to hold out near Asmara while moving into other parts of Eritrea to take the offensive against Ethiopia's newly reoccupied garrisons.

The goal of the Ethiopian campaign has been to capture the main Eritrean towns and highways and then to press for negotiations on its terms while striking out at rural guerrilla bases with infantry attacks and concentrated aerial bombardments.

EPLF Frustrates Ethiopia Strategy

Government forces have been only partially successful in the early stages of this plan against guerrillas of the Eritrean Liberation Front (ELF). But the EPLF's tactic of withdrawing from certain fixed positions in southern Eritrea and around Asmara to make a stand for Keren is frustrating the campaign strategy. The prospect of negotiations on any terms appears as far away as ever, according to informed sources.

Two weeks ago, Ethiopian forces began a series of fully mechanized assaults on EPLF positions north of Asmara. These were aimed at breaking through to Keren, after capturing or reoccupying more than a score of towns and small villages, mainly from the ELF.

Close to 2000 Ethiopian troops were killed in heavy fighting that continued over four days in this area. The government renewed its attacks last week under unusually heavy aerial and artillery bombardment, but the EPLF again repulsed them with heavy Ethiopian losses. At Guardian press time the battlefield appeared quiet while Ethiopia regrouped for another try.

Continuous fighting is reported to have taken place during Aug. 21-23 near the village of Quazien, with 400 Ethiopians killed.

A second assault launched on Aug. 23 near the village of Embaderho, the scene of fierce fighting the previous week, brought much the same results with the EPLF holding its ground.

The EPLF's Khartoum spokesman said that fighting has also been reported southeast and east of Asmara in the direction of EPLF positions along the key highway linking Asmara with the Red Sea port of Massawa. But he termed these attacks "diversionary" and said the EPLF was holding there also.

Meanwhile, in Tigray province, which borders on southern Eritrea, Tigray People's Liberation Front (TPLF) guerrilla units are stepping up counteroffensive actions against Ethiopia's lengthy supply lines to Eritrea and against Ethiopia's dwindling bases there.

The TPLF last week captured the important district capital of Abiy Adi, only 40 miles from the Tigray capital of Makele, which is the government's main base in the province. The town also controls an important secondary road running north toward Eritrea.

Ethiopia's military government cannot long sustain such losses without moving to reinforce their rear areas in Tigray, a move which will also limit their ability to continue the costly Asmara fighting with the EPLF But any let-up in the fighting there will signal a major turn in the overall Eritrea campaign, with the likely result of follow-up offensive actions by the EPLF.

Against this backdrop political developments in Ethiopia take on increasing significance, centering around the future of Derg leader Lt. Col. Mengistu Haile Mariam.

Intense maneuvering is now in process in the Ethiopian capital of Addis Ababa to complete reported preparations for the declaration of a political party. The unanswered question is whether Mengistu will emerge as its chairman and go on to become president of a new government.

Five political organizations once vied for leadership within

Ethiopia's ruling circles: Meísone (All-Ethiopia Socialist Movement); Echat (Revolutionary Organization of Oppressed Ethiopia's United Struggle); Seded (Revolutionary Flame); Malerid (Marxist-Leninist Revolutionary Organization); and Waz League (Proletarian League).

Once the strongest of these pre-party formations, at least among the civilian population, Meísone was suppressed by the Derg last year and has since gone underground. Echat was later suspended for inclining toward Meísone, leaving the other three to form a common front that is apparently going to merge into a national party.

Seded is far the largest of the remaining organizations and is thought to be under the personal control of Mengistu. Placing him in a strong position for the future. Mengistu has tenaciously clung to a hard line on Eritrea and the national question, while the two suppressed parties are thought to have put forward more conciliatory lines on these and other questions.

Significantly, the common front recently announced an identity of views on a series of points, including dropping the phrase "up to secession" from their stand on the rights of nationalities to self-determination. This is sure to have an effect on reported attempts at negotiations over the Eritrean struggle for independence.

Reports Of Negotiations

Ethiopian diplomats here say that contacts were made between the Derg and the EPLF last winter and spring but with no tangible results. Yilma Tadesse, Ethiopia's ambassador to Sudan, said three meetings took place between the two sides in January, March and June in East Berlin. He said that the EPLF's uncompromising stand on independence prevented any progress and the talks were broken off.

"They were not serious," he said. "The more we talked about peace, the more they thought we could not fight a war."

The EPLF denies that formal discussions ever took place, saying that the EPLF delegation in East Berlin was part of a worldwide effort to spell out its stand on the Eritrean question.

Regardless of how these meetings are depicted it is clear the two sides are holding to opposing views of grounds for a settlement.

Against the EPLF stand on full self-determination for Eritrea, the Derg continues to advance its 1976 9-point peace plan for regional autonomy for nations within Ethiopia. By extension this plan calls for restricted cultural autonomy for tribal groups which overlap between Eritrea and neighboring Ethiopian provinces, a strategy for breaking up Eritrea as a recognizable social and political entity.

Such a plan is predictably as unacceptable for the EPLF as full independence is for Mengistu, leaving the solution for the time being to be decided on the battlefield where the EPLF is now regaining the initiative in the bitter struggle.

We Are Holding Ethiopian Attacks, Say Guerrillas

Observer Foreign News Service (London), September 8, 1978

While the battle rages between Ethiopian Government forces and the Eritrean People's Liberation Front (EPLF) for the guerrilla-held city of Keren, eyewitness reports say that life within the important city appears little affected, and there is no sign of preparations for evacuation.

Ethiopia appears to have concentrated its full military strength for the effort to take Keren, and the past three weeks have seen some of the heaviest fighting of the three-month Ethiopian offensive in Eritrea near the city of Asmara, but the EPLF has so far held its positions and Keren residents seem confident that their city will not fail.

"Nobody was afraid that the Ethiopians would reach Keren," says Walter Michler, a freelance German journalist who has just visited the city. "Life was quite normal. You couldn't imagine that the frontlines were only 50 kilometers (30 miles) away at Agordat and 70 kilometers (40 miles) away toward Asmara."

The Ethiopian campaign to take Keren opened on August 14 with a major assault by mechanized units and human wave infantry attacks from Asmara north toward Keren against EPLF positions, but the EPLF claims to have repulsed this and five subsequent attempts with heavy Ethiopian losses of men and arms.

A pincer attack was also expected from the government-held city of Agordat, taken from the rival Eritrean Liberation Front (ELF) along with a series of other ELF-held towns and villages in western Eritrea during July, but there has yet been no sign of movement there.

EPLF units are also reportedly dug in just outside Agordat and guerrilla forces are said to be operating behind government lines in that area to head off the second prong of the Keren campaign.

Michler, who was in Keren for nine days, said here that the only sign that the battle was in progress were daily overflights of MiG jet fighters.

Only once did the jets dip below a height of 6,000 meters (20,000 feet), though every appearance was met by heavy EPLF anti-aircraft fire. At no time did the planes try to bomb the city, he added, giving rise to speculation there that these missions were either for drawing fire to photograph future targets or for demoralizing the guerrillas and the civilian population.

But, said Michler, the people generally seemed undisturbed. Although daytime activities were curtailed, the city bustled with life in the evenings. Schools were in session from 6 to 10 p.m. Electricity was turned on during the same hours, and nightly buses carried passengers from Keren to the outskirts of Asmara, he said.

"In the evenings the tea shops and cafes were full of people having small casual discussions," said Michler, adding, "I was very surprised by this. For me the days in Keren were like holidays.

"There was no doubt that everybody I talked to was on the side of the fighting. I could not find anyone who favored a compromise with the Ethiopians."

Eritrean forces repulse Ethiopian assault on Keren
EPLF keeps city, takes offensive
The Guardian (New York), September 13, 1978

Khartoum, Sudan

The Eritrean People's Liberation Front (EPLF) this week beat back Ethiopia's sixth consecutive attempt to reach the liberated city of Keren, inflicting heavy losses and capturing territory in the exchange.

In three days of continuous battle outside the Eritrean capital of Asmara, EPLF forces defeated two simultaneous Ethiopian assaults aimed at reopening the key highways to Keren on the north and to the Red Sea port of Massawa on the east, while launching an offensive action of its own against government positions west of Asmara.

Eyewitness reports from inside EPLF-held Keren, now the target of Ethiopia's full military strength, say that life there continues as usual with no sign of discouragement on the part of either EPLF fighters or the civilian population.

The latest military action marks the first time EPLF has launched a full-scale conventional attack since the beginning of the 3-month Ethiopian campaign to regain control of Eritrea and it indicates the EPLF may now be regaining the overall military initiative.

EPLF guerrilla units also ambushed a government supply convoy in southern Eritrea on the highway between Adi Kaieh and Segeneiti for the third time since Ethiopia reoccupied three former EPLF towns in this region, while Tigrayan guerrilla units overran an important district capital in neighboring Tigray.

With the tide of the war seeming to turn in favor of the allied Eritrean and Tigrayan revolutionaries, there are signs that Soviet military assistance to the now demoralized Ethiopian government forces is increasing.

Just returned from Keren, Walter Michler, a freelance German journalist reported: "The population has a big trust in the EPLF. Life was quite normal. You couldn't imagine that the front lines were only 31 miles away at Agordat and 43 miles toward Asmara."

'Human Wave' Assault

The heaviest fighting of the offensive has been taking place for the past three weeks near Asmara as Ethiopian forces have launched repeated mechanized assaults with human wave infantry attacks in an effort to break through EPLF lines, much as they did in July against the Eritrean Liberation Front (ELF) along Eritrea's southern border.

After five straight defeats in mid-August, Ethiopia renewed its offensive against Keren Aug. 29 with an all-out attack near the village of Adi Yacob, which coincided with another breakout from Asmara aimed at the Massawa road, also under the control of the EPLF.

The eastern battle, termed a "diversion" by the EPLF's Khartoum spokesman, lasted a single day with government forces crushed at the village of Seidicci.

The northern battle, directed at Keren, lasted three days with Ethiopia launching 16 separate assaults on the final day, all with the same results. By sunset Aug. 31, both sides were back in their previous positions.

Meanwhile to the west, EPLF units hit Ethiopia's flank and recaptured three villages—Deki Shehai, Mekera and Adi Worehi—previously taken by Ethiopia from the ELF. The EPLF drove on five miles to the village of Adi Gebru, where the fighting also continued for three days.

When the smoke cleared, the EPLF counted 1500 Ethiopian dead, 2000 wounded, 700 prisoners, eight tanks and six military vehicles destroyed and three tanks and four vehicles taken, along with large quantities of light and heavy arms.

"This is the most strategic victory we've won against the Ethiopians since the campaign against Keren began," said the EPLF spokesman here. "We are very confident they're not going to enter Keren," he added.

The significance of the EPLF advance to Adi Gebru, along with the simultaneous victories at Adi Yacob and Seidicci, is twofold. In military terms, it substantially narrows the government's front line and limits its ability to maneuver, while also moving the front out of the western plains into rugged mountainous terrain, which gives the EPLF a further advantage.

At the same time, it strikes another blow at sagging Ethiopian morale, which had been high after the advances against the weaker ELF. And it boosts the spirit of the EPLF, which has been on the defensive for months and has had to voluntarily pull back from several hard-won positions in order to make the current stand for Keren and the EPLF's northern base area.

The EPLF capture of former ELF areas will also hasten the already accelerated shift of popular support away from the disintegrating ELF and toward the EPLF, thus in the long run settling Eritrea's principal internal contradiction and foreclosing the possibility of any future civil war.

EPLF guerrilla units are reported moving into the western Eritrean lowlands in the wake of the ELF's defeats there, as well as into the southern highlands near the former ELF-held towns of Mendefera and Adi Quala. The main work of these units now is to politicize and organize the civilian population. But offensive EPLF military actions there are expected soon.

In the southeast, where the EPLF recently yielded the towns of Decamare, Segeneiti and Digsa, EPLF guerrillas have so far prevented a single Ethiopian supply truck from reaching these towns.

"They have the towns in this area, but we control the roads. And we will not permit any supplies to pass," said the EPLF spokesman.

The latest attempt last weekend cost the Ethiopians 150 dead and an undisclosed number captured, according to the spokesman, who said: "They were all wiped out. None escaped."

Business As Usual

According to an official EPLF statement released here this week, close to 12,500 Ethiopians have been killed by the EPLF since the current offensive began in June, 22,000 wounded and almost 2000 taken prisoner.

The EPLF has scaled down earlier estimates of the total number of Ethiopian troops involved in the offensive to 100,000 saying that 40,000 are now committed to reopening the Asmara-Keren road and taking the important city.

Walter Michler was in Keren Aug. 14-22 when the first five Ethiopian assaults from Asmara were launched. He said that daily overflights by Ethiopian MiG jet fighters were the only sign of war in the otherwise peaceful city.

"Nobody was afraid that the Ethiopians would reach Keren," said Michler, adding that he was quite surprised by the way the people carried on business as usual.

Keren schools were in session in the evenings; there was electricity every night between 7 and 10 PM and nightly bus service was available to the outskirts of Asmara, according to the visiting journalist.

Michler also said that 3000 people who were evacuated from Massawa last December were in Keren and receiving clothing from the EPLF's social welfare department, a boarding school was being set up for orphans and street children and a veterinary medical laboratory was being relocated into larger quarters-all signs that the EPLF expected to remain in Keren indefinitely.

The only indication the war was close by were the meetings of the mass associations in which donations were being collected for the fighters on the front lines, he said.

"They were ready to give the last that they had for the fighters," Michler said, adding: "There was no doubt that everybody I talked to was on the side of the fighters."

With the battle for Keren intensifying near Asmara and Ethiopian losses increasing, there have been reports from Asmara refugees reaching Sudan that 1000 Soviet advisers and technicians are now in the Eritrean capital operating the long range artillery and taking on a greater role in directing the government's military operations.

Meanwhile, in Tigray province guerrillas of the Tigray People's Liberation Front (TPLF) are also scoring major successes against the government, which in turn puts added pressure on the now extended forces in Eritrea.

With Ethiopian forces increasingly on the defensive throughout Eritrea and Tigray, the largest military campaign ever launched there appears to have been initially broken, but renewed attacks aimed at Keren are expected soon and heavy fighting is expected to continue for an indefinite time before the offensive is over.

Cuban Force Reported in Eritrea

Ethiopia Using Pilots, Troops, Refugees Say

The Miami Herald, September 14, 1978

Khartoum, Sudan

Cuban combat forces are participating directly in Ethiopia's military offensive against Eritrean independence forces and have suffered casualties in fighting around the Eritrean capital of Asmara, according to Eritrean refugees reaching Khartoum.

Cuban pilots are flying Ethiopia's Russian supplied MiG jet fighters, and Cuban troops are operating Ethiopia's artillery in support of infantry attacks launched from Asmara against the Eritrean People's Liberation Front (EPLF), the refugees say.

Three young Eritrean men - two industrial workers and one student - who fled from Asmara in early august say they saw at least 2,000 Cubans in Asmara with the large occupying Ethiopian force and on the battlefield during July, which was marked by heavy fighting near the city limits.

(Meanwhile, the Eritrean rebels Tuesday claimed to have killed, wounded or taken prisoner 00 Ethiopian soldiers in repelling a government attack on the Eritrean town of Cohayen. No figure for rebel casualties was given.)

The Refugees also said that Ethiopia's "Red Terror" was being carried out widely against civilian residents of the Eritrean capital while severe shortages of food, fuel and medicines had reached extreme proportions. The population by July had shrunk from 20,000 to less than 100,000 during a ground siege of the city, which Eritrean guerrillas began last October.

The siege was lifted in August after Ethiopian forces broke through the lines of the Eritrean Liberation Front (ELF) in southern Eritrea and the EPLF withdrew from its positions south and southeast of Asmara. However, intense fighting between the EPLF and the government has continued since then on the western, northern and eastern sides of the city.

Western intelligence sources have been reporting the presence of Cuban and Russian advisers and technicians with the Asmara garrison, including pilots for the MiG aircraft that are bombing guerrilla positions near the city, but the refugees said they were unable to distinguish between the two foreign contingents.

"We saw white men with the Ethiopians," said one 26-year old

Eritrean worker. "There were so many. Most of them were Cubans."

He said that he saw the white enter a battle in mid-July in the village of Bileza on the northern outskirts of Asmara.

"I saw them firing," he said. "The Ethiopian militia was in front, and the white were behind them firing the big weapons which were on heavy trucks."

The white troops were firing field artillery, mortars and "Stalin Organs"(Russian-supplied multiple rocket launchers), according to the refugees.

REFUGEES DREAMS BECOME DESPAIR

SUDANOW (Khartoum), September 1978

As the fighting gets heavier in Eritrea, the number of refugees fleeing over the border has risen dramatically. This new influx has brought new strains to already overloaded services—and new hardship to many refugees, as Dan Connell reports.

The life of a refugee is one of fear and uncertainty. Uprooted from his homeland, he depends entirely on the goodwill of others for his livelihood, his security and his day to day survival while clinging to dreams of a change which is often out of his control.

For the tens of thousands of Eritrean refugees in Sudan, the dream has been to m home to a free and independent land after close to two decades of war and three quarters of a century of foreign colonisation, but Ethiopia's current military offensive there has dampened camps many hopes.

Sudan has long held a reputation of liberality and generosity towards the refugees from Eritrea, but the growing economic and social pressure of the sheer numbers still coming appears to be finally taking its toll.

New regulations are being promulgated that may force thousands of urban refugees out of the towns and into rural agricultural settlements. At the same time, a new influx of refugees in the East is severely taxing existing resources for the refugees already there.

Kassala province has been flooded with more than 7,000 new refugees, many of them wounded or injured, who are fleeing

Ethiopia's Russian- and Cuban-backed campaign to retake Eritrea's liberated towns and cities. Many of these people are back in Sudan for the second time after returning home only to be displaced again.

The effect on their mental state and on Sudan's social resources is devastating. Anxious relief officials are trying to move the new refugees away from the immediate border to temporary while they draw up plans for long term resettlement, and close to 4,300 are now being housed in tents and school buildings in Khashm el Girba, 90 km south of Kassala.

Entering one of the three sites at Khashm el Girba through a cordon of barbed wire, the visitor is immediately struck by the counterpoint of chaos among the throngs of children and animals and the listlessness of the adults in the tightly-packed camp.

One mother struggles to grind her ration of dura between two rough stones, her whimpering child strapped to her back. An old man lies shivering with malaria on the concrete veranda of the elementary school where 40 people are crowded into a single classroom. Goats and chickens pick their way between the tents, leaving their dung piled along the children's pathways.

Some families escaped Eritrea with beds, personal belongings and their precious animals, but others came with nothing.

Mr. Mohammed Ali, in his late fifties and the father of eight children, was sitting in a tent donated by the United Nations High Commission for Refugees (UNHCR), with nothing but his prayer mat and his Koran.

Mohammed said that he and his family rushed across the border from the village of Teletasher when they heard Ethiopian artillery close by. 'We were afraid, so we could only bring enough food to get to Sudan,' he explained.

The UN World Food Programme (WFP) is distributing sorghum, vegetable oil and milk powder to the refugees, but doctors say this is not enough because of the precariously low level of health in which the refugees are arriving. Malnutrition, overcrowding among people and animals poor ventilation, a lack of latrines and fast breeding of insects due to the heavy rains are encouraging the spread of infectious diseases, according to Dr Melassie,who heads the Kassala hospital.

'The main disease problems – apart from war injuries — are tuberculosis, malaria, dysentery, gastro-enteritis and most recently, measles among children,' the doctor said. A large number of refugees and some Eritrean guerrillas have had to be hospitalised, creating a medical crisis in Kassala and other border area hospitals.

'These are war conditions,' said one doctor as he escorted relief officials from the UN and voluntary agencies through the Kassala hospital where as many as our patients share a single bed.

'We are frustrated,' he went on. 'We have a shortage of resources, we are overworked and overcrowded, and we have many new medical problems such as war injuries, psychological problems and malnutrition. We have a shortage of space, equipment and personnel.'

Officials of the government and the UNHCR say they have chosen a new temporary site for these refugees outside of Khashm el Girba, but that they are also pushing ahead with plans to get the Eritreans to settlements on agricultural schemes where they can find work as wage labourers once the rains stop.

However, these officials concede that new permanent village sites are not yet prepared and that they have not discussed the plan with the refugees themselves, many of whom are town-dwellers unsuited for farm work. Once UNHCR official said that they are contemplating a social survey among the refugees, but he added that there are few programmes and no additional money budgeted for rehabilitation in the towns.

Since the Eritrean war began focusing on the towns and cities in early 1977, a large percentage of the refugees coming to Sudan have been townspeople who gravitate towards the towns and shy away from the rural agricultural schemes.

'Our main problem is the people in the towns,' said Mr. Omar Mohamed Ismail, Commissioner for Refugees. 'Most of the urban refugees are young men and women seeking school, work or a way out of Sudan to the Middle East, Europe or America, but often they are disappointed. Employment opportunities for educated but unskilled people are scarce, school places are few and many countries are not accepting large numbers of the refugees. The result is often despair, and a despondency which is often misunderstood by local residents as careless lethargy, as the refugees are I reduced to hanging about.

One young Eritrean refugee walked into the UNHCR office in Khartoum this month looking for help. We will call him, Amde. He is 21 years old and grew up in Asmara where he attended secondary school.

Amde wants to go to the United States to continue his studies. He has been trying to get his papers in order for more than a year, but he finds himself shuttled from one office and embassy to another without seeming to get any closer to leaving.

In July, he was sent from Khartoum to Gedaref along with

hundreds of other Eritreans. When he came back, he covered that a fire had destroyed the room where he had been staying, so he spent his first night in the capital sleeping outside. During the night his luggage—with his school—was stolen.

The next day he began again, trudging from police station to court to report

his problem, and then going to the UNHCR for emergency help. He stands nervously in the outer office, thumbing through a wad of notes and papers that catalogue every interview he has had during the previous year. Scraps of paper spill onto the floor as he struggles to keep from letting his despair overcome him.

He worries that new government regulations will force him into a rural camp before he can reassemble his documents. His case is by no means unique.

Amde plans to study business administration, a course which he has been preparing for since he was a young boy, but which now seems starkly irrelevant to the protracted war which has engulfed Eritrea He talks wistfully of going home some day, but he is caught by a current that is sweeping him steadily farther away.

His future extends a day at a time to the next appointment, the next paper to procure. Drifting, alone, lost, guilty about not going back to fight but by now almost paralysed by the sheer weight of his efforts to get away.

In the absence of answers or alternatives the government appears to be for the refugees that they will be farmers or farm labourers, as preparations seem to be underway to limit the refugees living in the towns to those who are either working or in school.

Under such pressure, some can be expected to go back to Eritrea to join the war—and a small number did during the forced evacuation of refugees from Khartoum during the OAU summit last month. But the urban refugees appear to be as psychologically and physically unsuited to war as they are to farming, as if their very education has become a burden that narrows rather than expands their choices

Meanwhile,inside Eritrea the problem of displaced people has also increased considerably due to Ethiopian military actions which are now utilising massive bombardment by air and by land against the guerrilla-held towns.

Spokesmen for the Eritrean Relief Association (ERA) and the Eritrean Red Cross and Crescent Society (ERCCS) say that the number of refugees coming to Sudan is only a fraction of the displaced population in Eritrea itself—where international assistance is decidedly more scarce.

Red Flowers Of War

Observer Foreign News Service (London), October 10, 1978

Fah, Eritrea

While Ethiopia's Russian and Cuban-backed army has been carrying out the largest military offensive in the 17-year Eritrean war, life in the northern base area of the Eritrean Peoples Liberation Front (EPLF) appears to have been largely unaffected.

Schools, hospitals, farms and cottage industries run by the EPLF are carrying on as usual. Thousands of fresh volunteers can be seen in military training camps. Supply depots bustle with activity, and at night the roads are crowded with guerrilla convoys winding their way into the central highlands where the EPLF faces the stalemated Ethiopian armed forces.

The only sign of war are the anti-aircraft guns pointing up into the pale blue desert sky and the new camps for Ethiopian prisoners of war taken in the recent heavy fighting near the Asmara capital, far to the south.

Throughout the period of the recent offensive, the immediacy of the war was being carried to the people and the guerrilla fighters here by a travelling troupe of youngsters, known as the Red Flowers with a spirited presentation of songs, dances and political theatre.

The Red Flowers are the latest civilian political organization to take root in Eritrea, according to an EPLF spokesman, who said that they arose spontaneously among children in the EPLF-controlled areas as boys and girls began forming their own military units with homemade wooden guns in imitation of the EPLF fighters.

Comprised of children between the ages of nine and 15, they are now said to be formally organized in villages and towns throughout Eritrea. "The Red Flowers have been so named because they are the flowers of the plants that have been watered by the blood of our martyrs," the spokesman added.

The performers, in traditional peasant garb, moved on to center stage. A cluster of women gathered around a small cooking fire, children played off to the side and two men drove pairs of oxen (Red Flowers on their hands and knees) in nearby fields, swearing at their stubborn beasts.

Suddenly, Ethiopian troops rushed on the stage and set fire to a hut. Within minutes EPLF fighters charged in and routed marauding soldiers to wild applause from the audience. During the next hour they acted out the capture of half-a-dozen towns taken by the EPLF in 1977.

It was a simple uncomplicated piece of political theatre - propaganda to the outsider - but it seemed to stir the audience deeply.

"This activity of the young Eritrean boys and girls provides a vivid picture of the Eritrean People's fiery patriotism and iron determination to sweep away the Ethiopian aggressors and establish an independent, democratic State," said EPLF man.

Which is one way of saying this show will run and run.

Big Purge In Ethiopian Forces

The National Review (Reuter), Bangkok, October 30, 1978

Ethiopian commanders have executed officers and soldiers and carried out a drastic reorganization of their forces in Eritrea since the government's latest offensive stalled a month ago, according to officials of the Eritrean People's Liberation Front (EPLF).

The officials confirmed earlier reports from diplomatic sources in the Ethiopian capital Addis Ababa which said head of state Mengistu Haile Mariam flew to Asmara in the first week of October to personally order executions and restore discipline. Government deserters from the area, where Ethiopia is fighting Eritrean rebels, also spoke of the executions.

Morale in Asmara, capital of the Red Sea province, was low in the last week of September when guerrillas scored two direct hits on the government's main ammunition dump at the former US base at Kagnew.

Tadessa Gibichew, a supply officer with the Ethiopian 83rd Brigade, who deserted a week later, said bomb's rockets and millions of bullets exploded in a 90-minute inferno and sprayed the surrounding area with sporadic bursts for the next three days.

He and a group of recent deserters, talking in EPLF positions a few miles from the city, said Lt. Col. Mengistu surveyed the damage, assessed the problem of getting supply convoys through guerrilla ambushes to replace the dump, ordered the arrest of a score of officers and condoned earlier executions of militiamen ordered by the ruling military council's man in Eritrea, Lt. Dirma.

Reports reaching diplomatic sources in Addis Ababa said some 300 militiamen had been executed from all the units which retreated after five attempts between August 14 and 23 to break through secessionist lines across the road leading north from Asmara to the rebel stronghold of Keren.

Tadessa said 44 militiamen-two from each company- of the 31st Brigade were ordered on Aug. 3 to dig their own graves at the site of the 1969 industrial exposition in Asmara before being shot dead.

Another militiaman, 18 year-old Dughe Tajura, said 500 men from his brigade, the 116th were sent to the front line in August where human-wave assaults on secessionist positions were mounted.

He said he was among only 31 who survived the carnage. All 31 who returned were detailed off to different brigades which were being constantly reorganized now with army and militia being put into 14,000-man divisions with their own armor and artillery elements.

The sources in Addis Ababa said this fusion of the two forces had led to difficulties as the newly raised militia was still on only a quarter of the pay of regular army soldiers.

Dughe and four other deserters, wearing new tan colored uniforms, crossed the lines on the night of Sept 12 carrying their AK-47 Kalashnikov rifles.

The EPLF escorts said they would be allowed to go to Sudan as refugees or cross back into Ethiopia at a point on the Eritrean border of their choice as they were determined not to fight against the Eritreans.

Beshura Meta, 22, also of the 116th Brigade said: "At the beginning I was told I would get military and political training to be a militiaman for my village.

"Later they brought me to Eritrea saying that Arabs were invading. But for three months I could not see Arabs, only Eritreans."

Getahun Teshome, 20, said he was press-ganged into the militia from the market place of his village and driven to the big Tatek training camp outside Addis Ababa.

"Since the beginning I was afraid and my plan was to escape. I was just waiting for the day to die or hold up my hand," he said.

According to the sources in Addis Ababa, there has also been a movement across the lines in the other direction as the loss of life has mounted in the battles in the rugged mountain region.

The sources said about 1,000 Eritreans appear to have crossed to the government side and some quite well-known individuals had set up a new Marxist group which has called on the secessionist groups to stop fighting.

Quiet pervades embattled Asmara
after failed Ethiopian offensive

The Baltimore Sun, November 3, 1978

Ghinda, Ethiopia (Reuter)

Only 2 miles separate Eritrea's guerrilla fighters from the Ethiopian soldiers guarding the entrance to the beleaguered city of Asmara.

Asmara, Eritrea's capital city, is also headquarters of Ethiopian government forces in the embattled Red Sea territory. Its population is estimated to have shrunk from 250,000 to less than 100,000.

In the war being waged in Eritrea, the Eritrean People's Liberation Front (ELF) claims to have liberated the area nine months ago.

Several miles east of Asmara, EPLF soldiers crouch in trenches and stone fortifications.

From their positions, one can see Ethiopian soldiers with the naked eye.

Repeated attempts by the Ethiopian army to break out of Asmara during the government's three-month summer offensive seem to have failed, and an uneasy quiet has descended upon the battlefield.

"Nothing has changed," said 28-year-old Berhane Gebre-Xavier, a member of the EPLF's 13-strong Political Bureau stationed on Eritrea's eastern front. "We hold the same positions now as we did nine months ago when we liberated this area."

The EPLF army is dug in to the parched desert hills surrounding the Red Sea port of Massawa, 60 miles to the east, and it controls the region between the two cities that includes seven towns and former Ethiopian army and naval bases, according to Mr. Berhane.

A tour of the front lines suggested there had been no recent movement by either side.

"The eastern front is the most strategic zone in Eritrea, stretching from Massawa to Asmara," Mr. Berhane said. "This area was the main economic lifeline for our enemy a year ago."

A frontline EPLF fighter in the trenches outside Asmara said the last Ethiopian attempt to break through the guerrilla defenses was on August 28.

"They came at ten past five in the morning," he said. "They tried at first with their heavy artillery and aircraft, and then the military came on foot. We pushed them back and they tried again. We pushed them back again. After that no enemy came."

The morale of the fighters there appeared to be high, despite the bitter cold on top of the mountain ridge, 2,700 feet above sea level, from which they looked out on Asmara.

In the evening a truck arrived from the town of Ghinda in the rear with fresh injera (a soft flat bread) and lentil stew, said by the EPLF spokesman there to have been prepared by volunteers from the Ghinda women's association.

The main activities of the front in Ghinda and the other towns on this area appear to be social and economic. Political cadres mobilize the civilian population while non-combatant EPLF personnel oversee the operation of several agricultural plantations now in the hands of the front and offer social services to the local inhabitants.

Bombing by Ethiopia's Air Force has increased since the halt in the ground fighting, according to an EPLF spokesman, but the civilians sang while they worked.

New refugees arriving from Asmara say that worsening conditions inside the city are likely to produce an increased flow of people to the EPLF-held towns.

Eritrean rebels report executions are being ordered by Colonel Mengistu

The Baltimore Sun, November 4, 1978

Outside Asmara, Ethiopia (Reuter)

Ethiopian commanders have executed officers and soldiers and carried out a drastic reorganization of their forces in Eritrea since the government's latest offensive staled a month ago, according to officials of the Eritrean People's Liberation Front (EPLF).

The officials confirmed earlier reports from diplomatic sources in Addis Ababa, the Ethiopian capital, that said head of state, Lt. Col. Mengistu Hale Mariam, flew to Asmara in the first week of October to order executions and restore discipline personally.

Government deserters from the area, where Ethiopia is fighting secessionist Eritrean rebels, also spoke of the executions.

Morale in Asmara, capital of the Red Sea province, was low in the last week of September when guerrillas scored two direct hits on the government's main ammunition dump at the former United States base at Kagnew.

Tadessa Gibichew, a supply officer with the Ethiopian 83rd Brigade who deserted a week later, said bombs, rockets and millions of bullets exploded in a 90-minute inferno and sprayed the surrounding area with sporadic bursts for the next three days.

He and a group of recent deserters, talking in EPLF positions a few miles from the city, said Colonel Mengistu surveyed the damage, assessed the problem of getting supply convoys through guerrilla ambushes to replace the dump, ordered the arrest of a score of officers and condoned earlier executions of militiamen ordered by the ruling military council's man in Eritrea.

[Reports reaching diplomatic sources in Addis Ababa said about 300 militiamen have been executed from all the units that retreated after five attempts between August 14 and August 23 to break through secessionist lines across the road leading north from Asmara to the rebel stronghold of Keren.]

On August 32, Mr. Tadessa said, 44 militiamen—2 from each company—of the 31st Brigade were ordered to their own graves at the site of a 1969 industrial exposition in Asmara before being shot to death.

Another militiaman, Dughe Tajura, 18, said 500 men from his brigade, the 116th, were sent to the front lines in August where human-wave assaults on secessionist positions were mounted.

He said he was among only 31 who survived the carnage. All 31 who returned were detailed off to different brigades, which were being reorganized constantly now with Army and militia being put into 14,000-man divisions with their own armor and artillery elements.

[The sources in Addis Ababa said this fusion of the two forces has led to difficulties as the newly raised militia was still on only a quarter of the pay of regular Army soldiers.]

Mr. Dughe and four other deserters, wearing new tan-colored uniforms, crossed the lines on the night of September 12 carrying their AK-47 Kalashnikov rifles.

The EPLF escorts said they would be allowed to go to the Sudan as refugees or cross back into Ethiopia at a point on the Eritrean border of their choice as they were determined not to fight against the Eritreans.

Beshua Meta, 22, also of the 116th Brigade, said, "At the beginning I was told I would get military and political training to be a militiaman in my village.

"Later they brought me to Eritrea saying that Arabs were invading. But for three months I could not see any Arabs, only Eritreans."

Getahun Teshome, 20, said he was press-ganged into the militia from the market place of his village and driven to the big Tatek training camp outside Addis Ababa.

"Since the beginning I was afraid, and my plan was to escape. I was just waiting for the day to die or hold up my hand," he said.

Eritrean rebels' capital continues life at night

The Baltimore Sun, November 5, 1978

Keren, Ethiopia (Reuter)

Keren, an ancient mountain city and religious center, has reacted to the threat of government bombing by shutting its doors during the day and living by night.

Its 35,000 residents have rarely ventured out in daylight since Keren became the shadow capital of the Eritrean secessionists and the main target of the latest government counter-offensive in Eritrea's 17-year war for independence from Ethiopia.

Since June, when the counter-offensive began, the Ethiopian government claims to have lost 30,000 dead and 12,000 wounded in its campaign in the rugged rebel-held mountains of the former Italian colony on the Red Sea, diplomatic sources in Khartoum, Sudan, said.

Although Keren has not suffered many direct hits during the conflict, it has been profoundly changed.

When the sun goes down, the city starts bustling with activity. The market opens for business and cafes and restaurants are crowded. Buses run by the Eritrean People's Liberation Front (EPLF) set off for distant corners of Eritrea. As the electricity is switched on, shops open and factories begin to work. The city comes alive again.

An unexploded bomb lies partially buried in a dirt side street, covered with thorn bushes, apparently to keep children away. But the most striking impression on the visitor is the absence of children and teenagers.

Some young people could be seen working on a small farm at the edge of town run by the EPLF.

They were members of the "Red Flowers," a civilian political association. The children worked at the farm during the day and attended school at night, he said.

"We are born in the struggle and we grow up in it," said one 9-year-old girl, wielding a shovel in a tomato patch.

"It is we who are going to take the place of our sacrificed comrades and continue until final victory.

"It is a very, very long struggle, so we are preparing now," she added.

The older children have left Keren to join the EPLF army, the spokesman said. And the city is now mainly inhabited by the old, families with very young children and people displaced from other areas of Eritrea by the recent Ethiopian offensive.

Eritrean rebels run refugee camp

The Baltimore Sun, November 5, 1978

Deba'at, Ethiopia (Reuter)

As a lone Ethiopian MiG jet fighter buzzed high overhead, nothing stirred in the forest of acacia trees and desert scrub along the dry riverbed.

Minutes later people began to appear from their underground houses and from canvas tents hidden in the brush, and normal activity resumes in this rural resettlement camp run by the Eritrean People's Liberation Front in northern Eritrea.

More than 1,100 persons have made their home in the arid, volcanic mountains of Eritrea's Sahel province after fleeing their towns and villages in the central Eritrean highlands, where the wear between Ethiopia's military government and Eritrean independence groups rages on.

EPLF leaders admit that this is a small beginning—they estimate there are 750,000 refugees and displaced people in Eritrea and neighboring Sudan. This camp, they say, provides an example of what could be done with more assistance from outside.

"We have the organization to do more, but there are so many displaced people also in our towns and our material resources are very limited," said Askalu, the young woman who administers the Deba'at settlement.

"It is very hard for us to support all these because we do not get much help from foreign humanitarian organizations," she added.

In Deba'at, the EPLF provides the residents with shelter, food, clothing and medical care, and the people are called upon to work on EPLF projects, according to Askalu.

"The most important thing is to keep the people busy with productive work."

A walking tour of the settlement revealed storage tents stocked with grain donated by a Norwegian church relief group, sacks of used clothing and blankets and a clinic with 12 beds and seven EPLF medical personnel.

The nurse in charge said an average of 30 persons a day were treated, mainly for malaria and dysentery.

There were also two schools for small children, but the EPLF spokeswoman said that school-age children from the camp attend a "revolution school" nine miles away.

Women could be seen making straw baskets for sale and a group of men were sinking a new well for the settlement. There were also several small gardens and a poultry project that were said to be run co-operatively to provide food for the settlement.

The main problem in administering the camp came from the ethnic and tribal differences among the residents who spoke eight different languages and tended to separate into rival groupings, according to the EPLF spokeswoman.

This was overcome, she said, by political education that stressed the unity of the Eritrean people in their war for independence from Ethiopia.

The camp is now organized into four zones called equality, unity, liberation and independence, and the people have been mobilized into political associations of women, youth, peasants and workers that meet regularly for political discussion, Askalu said.

"At the beginning there was a big problem, but we really worked hard, and now they know they are one people," she said.

A literacy program is run for the adults. More than half of them now read and write.

However, the EPLF is not encouraging the growth of the settlement or the formation of similar camps, according to the spokeswoman, who said the goal of the front is to resettle the refugees on land of their own where they can become self-supporting.

More than 100 families were recently moved out of Deba'at to eastern Eritrea where they were given land and tools or jobs on the large commercial farms run by the EPLF in that area, she said.

Four months ago, 35 families arrived from a refugee camp in the Sudan and they were also quickly passed along to other areas for permanent resettlement, according to Askalu.

Soviets, Cubans Help Ethiopia

Lack Of Outside Aid Angers Eritrea Radicals

The Washington Star, November 7, 1978

Keren, Ethiopia

In this shadow capital of the radical wing of the Eritrean liberation movement, the guerrilla leaders vow to crush the next Ethiopian offensive, which is expected at any moment. And they express bitterness over being rejected by the Soviet bloc, the West and virtually all of the neighboring Arab world.

Russian and Cuban military personnel are deeply involved in Ethiopia's current military offensive in the Red Sea territory of Eritrea at every level but front-line infantry operations, according to leaders of the leftist Eritrean People's Liberation Front.

"The Russians are not only supplying arms to Ethiopia, they are also participating in battles. The Cubans and Russians are distributed on all fronts," charged Issayas Afwerki, the EPLF's assistant general secretary and key figure in the front's military command. "They are commanding the battle," he said.

Yet while Eritrean guerrilla leaders now acknowledge the extent of the Russian and Cuban participation in the bloodiest fighting of the 17-year Eritrean war for independence, breaking a long official silence on the question, they stop short of an outright condemnation of either the Soviet Union or Cuba while continuing to denounce the United States for its past and present role in the conflict.

In a carefully worded statement released this week, the EPLF's central committee criticizes Soviet and Cuban actions in Eritrea and "reminds them to correct their erroneous stand, stop their military participation and take a stand on the side of the just cause of the Eritrean people."

The Eritreans have been battling Ethiopia for their independence since 1961, when then-Emperor Haile Selassie annexed the former Italian colony.

The EPLF, together with a second guerrilla movement, the Eritrean Liberation Front (ELF), had gained control of an estimated 95 percent of the Pennsylvania-sized territory before the governments current offensive began in June.

"Every civilian Eritrean living within the military positions of the enemy on all fronts is daily seeing Cubans and Russians training soldiers, participating in the planning of military operations," said Issayas.

While Cubans experts operate heavy artillery behind the front lines, they are not yet involved in an infantry capacity, according to Issayas, who also said Ethiopians are the only ones now flying Ethiopia's Russian supplied MiG jet fighters.

A decade ago Cubans trained Eritrean guerrilla fighters. And while the Soviet Union never has directly supported the Eritrean independence movement, many of the arms coming into Eritrea in the past have been of Russian manufacture - given by Arab intermediaries such as Syria, Iraq and South Yemen. At that time, the United States and Israel were Ethiopia's main backers.

In 1977 the Derg, the military clique that deposed the aging emperor, abruptly terminated its military relationship with the West and turned to the Soviet Union for aid.

But, Issayas insists, "American imperialism has been our enemy, is our enemy and will remain to be our enemy as long as it exists as imperialist force in the world."

While the moderate ELF has continued to receive aid from Arab countries that include Syria and Iraq, the leftist EPLF has virtually been closed off from sources of outside supply except for small amounts of ammunition coming from the radical wing of the Palestinian Liberation Organization.

The Eritreans vow they have no intention of settling for anything short of full independence.

One day last week, the lights of an Ethiopian army division base inside Asmara, the capital of Eritrea province, could be seen glimmering in the cool night, easily visible from the trenches of the EPLF, which surrounds the city on three sides.

The swollen bodies of Ethiopian soldiers and the random debris of war litter the no man's land between the two opposing positions, but there has been no movement by either side for two months.

Ethiopia's latest offensive appears to have stalled after a mixed record of victory and defeat, but both sides are mobilizing for renewed fighting which is expected to break out soon.

Major preparations are now under way for a three-pronged Ethiopian campaign to reopen the highway between Asmara and the Red Sea port of Massawa, which has been under EPLF control since last year, according to Western intelligence sources. They say an attack is planned for Friday.

A month-long tour of the guerrilla positions found them in high spirits after halting the first phase of the Ethiopian offensive and confident they will defeat the coming attacks despite Ethiopia's overwhelming military superiority.

"We are not fooling ourselves that we have crushed this offensive and it's over, but the next round will not be any different from the first, and we will crush it, too," said Issayas.

Keren, the EPLF's fortress headquarters, survived the offensive's three-week onslaught.

The surprising turnabout in the campaign highlights the fact that there are two parallel wars being fought here, one by the EPLF and another by the ELF. The government has concentrated on one at a time.

The two fronts signed an agreement in April to seek unity, but guerrilla leaders concede that there was no military coordination between them during the offensive to date.

The ELF lost all major towns under its control during the recent fighting, and while the EPLF held all but one, from which it later was forced to withdraw, it will now face the full force of the Ethiopian army virtually by itself in the next phase of the fighting.

The EPLF-held areas include most of northern and eastern Eritrea.

In Keren, deep trenches and bomb shelters line the streets.

The EPLF's main difficulties appear to stem from its lack of outside assistance. The Soviet bloc has thrown its weight behind the Marxist Ethiopian military government, while the West has shown little interest in the leftist EPLF and the Arab world has generally supported the ELF and a third small rightist Arab nationalist group called the ELF-PLF.

Situationer: Ethiopia-West

Reuters news service, November 8, 1978

Outside Agordat, Eritrea

The day passes slowly. It is hot in the Western Eritrean Lowlands.

The only sign of activity is the crackle of the radio with which a guerrilla of the Eritrean People's Liberation Front (EPLF) keeps in contact with other units which surround Agordat on three sides.

There are more than 6,000 Ethiopian troops in Agordat now. They recaptured the city from another Eritrean independence movement, the Eritrean Liberation Front (ELF), in early August, according to a young man identified only as Tekelai, Brigade Commander with the EPLF which moved into the area after the ELF defeat.

A network of steep ridges comes together here with a single pass opening to the Eritrean Highlands. There is a highway through the pass. It leads to the EPLF-held city of Keren, the main target of Ethiopia's Russian and Cuban-backed offensive to regain control of this strategic Red Sea territory.

Although a series of Ethiopian assaults aimed at Keren from northern government-held capital of Asmara failed to reach Keren in August and September, EPLF leaders say they expect further attempts to be launched from here.

Later in the afternoon, when the temperature begins to dip from the middle 30s centigrade (mid 80s F), we leave our positions in the abandoned village of Engirnai to drive to the back side of the wall of mountains which rings Agordat.

It is an hour's climb to the peak where Agordat can be seen below, obscured by a thin blanket of low clouds.

EPLF units are dug in to the mountain side within seven kilometers (four miles) of the city, and mobile guerrilla units patrol up to the city's edge, according to the frontline commander.

As in most of the rest of Eritrea, the government has come to a stalemate against the EPLF after making substantial advances against the weaker ELF. And there does not appear to be any sign of movement from either side today.

"Since they arrived here, they have not moved from the places they took from the ELF," said the EPLF commander.

There are periodic artillery exchanges and there is bombing by Ethiopia's Russian-supplied MiG jet fighters, but even this has tapered off in recent weeks, he said.

Meanwhile, the main activity of the EPLF appears to be political with teams of cadre going about the villages behind the lines to mobilize support among the civilian population.

The guerrilla organizers hold assemblies in the villages to explain their programme, and the frontline fighters also go among them to win them over not only from any loyalties to the government but also from the rival ELF, according to an EPLF spokesman here.

The remnants of the earlier ELF presence in the area remain with small groups of ELF fighters in many of the villages, adding one more element of tension to an already delicate situation between the two loosely allied fronts, so this organizing goes slowly, he said.

Eritrea: Battle Stalemate

The Guardian (New York), November 8, 1978

Ghinda, Eritrea

The guns on Eritrea's eastern front are silent now, after three months of the heaviest fighting in this 17-year war. The battle lines remain essentially unchanged.

Repeated attempts by Ethiopian forces to break out of the highland Eritrean capital of Asmara on the Red Sea port of Massawa were blocked by the Eritrean People's Liberation Front (EPLF), and today the two sides face each other in trenches and fortifications within gunshot range on the outskirts of the two cities.

"Nothing has changed," said EPLF political bureau member Berhane Gebrexavier. "We hold the same positions now as we did nine months ago when we liberated this area."

The eastern front covers the strategic mountain slope region between Eritrea's central highland plateau and the Red Sea coast. It includes as its core the 70-mile paved highway connecting Asmara and Massawa. In the region the EPLF holds seven towns and former Ethiopian naval and army bases.

This road is the economic lifeline to Eritrea's interior and provides Ethiopia with its only access to the sea aside from the remote southeastern port of Assab, connected by road to the Ethiopian capital of Addis Ababa.

The EPLF cut the Asmara-Massawa road in October 1977, and went on to capture all the towns and bases along its length by January of this year. They dug in at the edge of Asmara, where an estimated 50,000 government troops are now quartered.

EPLF Troops Supplied By Civilians

A tour of the front lines found EPLF fighters nine miles along the highway in trenches on the steep mountains ridges that overlooks Asmara. From this strategic point they appeared to control all movement out of the city. "These mountains are the army that never moves," said one EPLF fighter.

To reach the front lines we walked along a dirt road. The road was carved out of the mountainside by EPLF fighters and peasant volunteers explained a spokesperson for the EPLF. A captured army truck laden with food supplies followed under cover of darkness.

Fighters huddled in their blankets against the bitter cold of this altitude, waiting for rations of soft flatbread and lentils prepared by women volunteers in the towns below. They would carry the food on foot and by donkey to their fortifications on the peaks above us.

The last of a series of Ethiopian attempts to break through the EPLF lines came on Aug. 28, according to one of the fighters.

Ethiopian Attacks

"They came at ten past five in the morning," he said. "They tried at first with their heavy artillery and aircraft, and then the military came on foot. We pushed them back, and they tried again. We pushed them back again. After that no enemy came."

The morale of the front line fighters appeared to be high, and they expressed confidence that they could hold this line indefinitely. The situation around the port of Massawa is similar, with the EPLF dug in along the parched desert hills on the outskirts of the city. They also are supplied nightly from the towns in their rear.

The only military action here seems to be in the air, as Ethiopia's Russian-supplied jet fighters bomb the front lines and the EPLF-held towns on a daily basis. But this has had no noticeable effect on either the military situation or on civilian morale.

The main activities on the EPLF area appear to be social and economic, with political cadre mobilizing the civilian population. Noncombatant personnel oversee the operation of several large agricultural plantations now in the hands of the EPLF and offer social services to the local inhabitants.

In Ghinda, the largest of the guerrilla-held towns, the telephones are working, electricity is turned on at night and normal economic activity can be observed in the market place, where ample supplies of grain, meat and vegetables are being sold.

There is paid agricultural work available on a large citrus plantation originally developed by an Italian. Eritrea was an Italian colony prior to Ethiopia's annexation of the Red Sea territory after World War 2. The plantation was nationalized by Ethiopia's military government in 1975, before being captured by the EPLF.

The residents of Ghinda appear to be well-organized into political associations of peasants, workers, women, youth and middle classes, with each association mobilized to contribute to the war effort.

Women could be seen working in round-the-clock shifts preparing food for the EPLF army, while the young people were maintaining the roads, digging bomb shelters and working on an EPLF-run vegetable farm.

The main problem for the EPLF here appears to be the influx of displaced people from other combat areas and from the city of Asmara. The population of Asmara is said by the EPLF to have shrunk from a prewar level of more than 250,000 to less than 100,000 now.

A spokesperson for the EPLF said that supplies of food, clothing and medicines for these refugees are scarce, but that the EPLF attempts to provide them with a basis for subsistence. A visit to the EPLF's social welfare, department showed a line of people in tattered clothes receiving rations of grain, sugar and vegetable oil.

New refugees arriving from Asmara say that worsening conditions inside the city are likely to produce an increased flow of people to the surrounding countryside.

Russians & Cubans 'in Ethiopia offensive'

The Observer (London), November 12, 1978

Outside Asmara, Eritrea

Last minute preparations for the second round of Ethiopia's campaign to crush the Eritrean guerrillas' 17-year war for independence are being made amid charges by guerrilla leaders that the Soviet Union and Cuba are deepening their involvement in the fighting.

After a two-month lull in the war, Ethiopian forces are mobilising for renewed attempts to take positions held by the Eritrean People's Liberation Front (EPLF) along the key highway linking the inland cities of Asmara and Decamare with the Red Sea port of Massawa. An Ethiopian pincer attack is also expected from Asmara and Agordat against the EPLF-held city of Keren.

EPLF leaders charge that Russian and Cuban military personnel are involved in the Ethiopian offensive at every level except frontline infantry operations, and a massive mobilisation is taking place in EPLF areas to counter the Ethiopian build-up.

Thousands of Cuban-trained Ethiopian troops have been airlifted to the Government-held cities of Asmara and Massawa for the new offensive expected to begin this week. Large quantities of Soviet heavy arms and equipment, including napalm bombs and chemical defoliants similar to those used by the United States in Vietnam, are reported to have been stockpiled for the assault.

Ethiopia's tenth militia division was airlifted to Massawa from the city of Jijiga in the south-eastern Ogaden region after being relieved by 1,500 Cuban troops, swelling the Massawa force to over 20,000, according to European intelligence sources.

Six brigades have been shifted from positions north of Asmara to the southern city of Decamare for the three-pronged assault on the Asmara-Decamare-Massawa highway, the economic lifeline for Eritrea's interior, which has been under EPLF control for the past year.

One European source said that defoliation operations had already begun along the road in advance of the attack. The chemical spraying was being done by Soviet-piloted aircraft, because Ethiopian pilots had resisted using the new weapons.

A recent visit to this area showed that the road had been stripped clean of trees by the Ethiopian Army last year, but that large citrus orchards remained. This suggests that the purpose of the defoliants is to destroy food supplies in the guerrilla-held areas.

After the bloodiest three months of fighting in the history of the politically-complicated Eritrean war, Issayas Afewerki, the EPLF assistant general secretary, spoke bitterly about the increasing Soviet and Cuban intervention.

"The Russians are commanding the battles," he told me. "There is nothing to hide now. Their direct participation in this war is known to everybody here."

At its semi-annual meeting last month, the EPLF central committee for the first time criticised the Soviet and Cuban role in Eritrea and called upon them to "correct their stand" and get out of the war.

Feudal army

EPLF leaders, however, stopped short of an outright condemnation of their former communist supporters, while continuing to denounce "US imperialism" for its past and present role in the conflict.

The Soviet and Cuban presence in Ethiopia and in Eritrea has built up steadily since March of last year, when the Ethiopian military regime, the Dergue, ousted the last of the US and Israeli advisers who had spent 25 years arming and training the feudal army of Emperor Haile Selassie.

Throughout the earlier stages of the war, Moscow vehemently condemned Ethiopia's designs on Eritrea—a former Italian colony federated to Ethiopia in 1952 and annexed a decade later—and Cubans trained Eritrean guerrillas in the 1960s.

But when the Dergue deposed the Emperor and announced it would build a "socialist" Ethiopia, Eritrea's erstwhile allies abruptly changed sides.

Soviet and Cuban military personnel are manning the heavy Soviet artillery, planning the tactics and strategy of the campaign, and taking responsibility for logistics and communications, according to Issayas Afewerki. "The Russians and Cubans are distributed on all fronts," he said.

During a month-long tour of the guerrilla positions, I found them in high spirits after halting the first phase of the Ethiopian offensive and confident that they would defeat the coming attacks.

"We are not fooling ourselves that we have crushed this offensive, but the next round will not be any different from the first, and we will crush it soon," said Issayas Afewerki.

The 32-year-old EPLF leader said Ethiopian morale was declining. After a series of defeats by the EPLF in August and September, economic and supply problems were worrying the now extended Government forces and combat efficiency among the conscripted peasant army was low.

Six Ethiopian deserters who reached EPLF lines outside Asmara with their Russian-supplied Kalashnikov assault rifles in hand confirmed this analysis in interviews here.

"The soldiers are fed up," said Dughe Tajura, a 20-year-old peasant who deserted from Ethiopia's 116th Brigade. "Always we lose, and we only see militia being killed," he added.

The six claimed that the Government was routinely executing officers and soldiers for "unrevolutionary activities" such as retreating in battle or voicing criticisms of the war.

The EPLF's main difficulties appear to stem from its lack of outside assistance. The West has shown little interest in the leftist EPLF, and the Arab world has generally supported the rival ELF movement and a third small rightist Arab nationalist group called the ELF-PLF.

Eritrea: Ethiopians desert to EPLF

The Guardian (New York), November 15, 1978

Ghinda, Eritrea

In the face of disintegrating morale, Ethiopia's military leaders are stepping up executions of officers and men among the 50,000 Ethiopian troops defending the Eritrean capital of Asmara. The high command is also transferring large numbers of troops from one unit to the other, according to deserting soldiers arriving here.

"The soldiers are fed up," said Dughe Tejura, a member of the 116th brigade of Ethiopia's peasant militia. "Always we lose, and we see only the militia being killed."

Dughe is one of five militiamen who last month arrived behind the lines of the Eritrean People's Liberation Front (EPLF) on the outskirts of Asmara.

The deserting militiamen said that the entire garrison in Asmara is now composed of the peasant militia, with the regular army either destroyed or dispersed among militia units. They added that they had seen no foreign troops involved in combat, although they had seen some foreigners acting as advisers inside Asmara.

Earlier this summer there were widespread reports of a growing Cuban presence in Asmara. Cuban involvement appears to have declined since then, with the Cubans refusing to be drawn further into the politically complicated war.

Economic Deterioration

The five deserters described a general condition in Asmara of economic deterioration and rising opposition to the military leadership. There was a brief period of euphoria in early August when government forces overran all the towns held by a second guerrilla movement, the Eritrean Liberation Front (ELF). The Ethiopian regime managed to run two convoys of supplies into the city from central Ethiopia before the EPLF began guerrilla operations along the road.

The reversal in the war was highlighted by a series of Ethiopian failures in August to break out of Asmara and retake the northern and eastern towns held by the EPLF. The failures generated a wave of repression within the Ethiopian army, the deserters said.

The five men were joined by a sixth soldier who had come four days earlier from inside Asmara, where he served as supply officer for the army.

"It is a daily program to kill militia or officers for 'antirevolutionary activities,'" said Tadesse Gibichew, the supply officer. He added that he saw 45 soldiers killed for retreating in battle Aug. 31.

Tadesse said that the military commanders assembled two men from every company to witness the executions. "Those to be killed had to dig their graves and then they were shot," he explained.

Some 500 men were assembled from different brigades on Sept. 26 to watch brigade commander Captain Telahun described as a reactionary in contact with the guerrillas. He was then executed. "They brought him there and they shot him in front of us," Dughe Tejura said.

Since early August soldiers of the militia have often been shifted from one unit to another to avoid growing disaffection in the ranks, according to the six deserters.

"Whenever we make friends and begin to discuss things together, they separate us into different companies and battalions," Dughe said.

The militiamen said that they were forced to join the army against their will. One said that he had been kidnapped in the market place in his home village and taken in an armored vehicle to a training camp near Addis Ababa. There Cuban and Ethiopian officers instructed him before he was sent to Eritrea three months ago.

"Since the beginning I was afraid and my plan was to escape," said Getahun Teshome, adding, "Always we were losing. I was waiting for the day I die or I give up my hand."

The deserting soldiers said that morale inside Asmara plummeted two weeks ago when the main ammunition and storage depot at Kagnew Station was blown up. The explosion of the former U.S. communications base destroyed an estimated $100,000 worth of food and military supplies. The blazing inferno, they said, lasted for three days.

"I saw Kagnew burned to ashes with all the supplies and ammunition for Eritrea, including bombs for the planes, rockets and millions of bullets," said Tadesse Gibichew.

"We felt happy at first because we thought the battle was finished and we would go home to our villages," added Dughe Tejura. But, he said, when many more soldiers were arrested and 15 were executed, he decided to make his escape.

Pre-teen Eritreans act out raid on village

The Baltimore Sun, November 19, 1978

Fah, Eritrea (Reuter)

In a pool of light cast by electric lamps at a dried-up river bed in the mountains of northern Eritrea, a revolutionary drama is taking place.

Children, many of them the sons and daughters of guerrillas fighting for the independence of this northern Ethiopian province, act out an attack by Ethiopian soldiers on an Eritrean village.

In the play, children, dressed in traditional clothes of the region's peasants, stand around a cooking pot.

Suddenly, into the ring of light bursts a troupe of actors dressed as Ethiopian soldiers. They set fire to a hut. Within minutes another group representing the Eritrean People's Liberation Front (EPLF) routs the invaders.

The audience of about 2,000 women who are training with the EPLF applauds wildly.

The children are members of the latest mass civilian association, the Red Flowers. The movement, consisting of children between 9 and 15, grew up spontaneously among boys and girls in EPLF-controlled areas. They began forming units playing with home-made guns in imitation of the real fighters, according to EPLF officials.

The scenes they depict for their audiences, after night blankets the mountainside and the fear of air raids and Army attacks diminishes, have become a reality on the province where fighting this year has been as intense as at any time during the 17-year struggle for independence.

The Red Flowers troupe can perform almost anywhere. They require a minimum of props.

At the wadi near Fah, they played beneath lights powered by a sputtering diesel generator.

One youngster played the traditional Eritrean guitar, the karar, another used an electric organ and a third drummed on a tin trunk with wooden sticks. A chorus stood behind them, wearing the green uniforms of the fighters, with red berets and neck scarves.

After singing revolutionary songs, the group acted out several incidents, including the capture of towns in the province last year which are still held by the guerrillas.

It is uncomplicated political theater, but it stirred the audience deeply.

"This activity of young Eritrean boys and girls provides a picture of the Eritrean people's fiery patriotism and determination to sweep away the Ethiopian aggressors and establish an independent state," an EPLF spokesman said.

The Red Flowers are a younger version of the Vanguard units, which consist of youngsters from 13 to 18, who receive full military and political training before serving with the fighters in noncombat roles, the spokesman said.

"They have been called the Red Flowers because they are the flowers of the plains that have been watered by the blood of our martyrs," he said.

They are organized on military lines, with squadrons, companies and battalions, each with its own military commander, doctor and political commissar.

Sebhat Efram, chairman of the EPLF department of mass administration and a member of the political bureau, said: "The fighters who have brought our revolutionary struggle to this stage will pass away either on the battlefield or from old age.

"It will be the sacred task of the new generation—today's children—to continue and deepen the decades-old revolutionary process in this country."

Ethiopia prepares Eritrea offensive

The Guardian (New York), November 22, 1978

Near Asmara, Eritrea

Last-minute preparations are now underway for a second round in Ethiopia's campaign to extinguish Eritrea's 17-year war for independence.

After a –month lull in the fighting, Ethiopian forces are mobilizing for renewed attempts to take Eritrean People's Liberation Front (EPLF) positions along the highway linking the inland cities of Decamare and Asmara with the Red Sea port of Massawa. They also seek to take the EPLF-held city of Keren.

A massive popular mobilization is also taking place within the EPLF's liberated areas to meet the next phase of the offensive. And EPLF leaders express confidence that it, too, will be stopped.

Open civil war, meanwhile, has broken out between two smaller factions of the divided Eritrean independence movement-the Eritrean Liberation Front (ELF) and the right-wing "ELF-PLF"-in the western Eritrean lowlands, remote from the current area of battle.

The steady escalation of the war and the mounting evidence of Soviet and Cuban participation in the planning and execution of military operations has prompted the EPLF to break a long official silence on the subject. EPLF Assistant General Secretary Issayas Afwerki spoke bitterly about the increasing Soviet and Cuban intervention here.

"The Russians are commanding the battle," he charged. "There is nothing to hide now. Our political position is something else, but their direct participation in this war is known to everybody here."

Soviet and Cuban Role

Last month's semiannual meeting of the EPLF Central Committee for the first time criticized the Soviet and Cuban role in Eritrea and called upon them to correct their stand get out of the war.

EPLF leaders, however, stopped short of an outright condemnation of either the Soviet Union or Cuba while continuing to denounce
U.S. imperialism for its past and present role in the conflict.

Both Cuba and the Soviet Union have denied any direct role in
the Eritrean conflict. At the meeting of nonaligned foreign ministers
in Belgrade last August, Cuba called for a negotiated solution to the
question of Eritrea's status.

The Soviet and Cuban presence in Ethiopia and in Eritrea has
built up steadily since March of last year when the ruling military
Dergue ousted the last of the U.S. and Israeli advisers who had spent
25 years arming and training the feudal army of Haile Selassie and
suppressing the growing Eritrean movement for independence.

The build-up of a Soviet and Cuban presence in Eritrea began
gradually at first, says the EPLF. But in September 1977, South
Yemeni tank crews were leading charges against the EPLF, and by
January of this year Soviet and Cuban advisers were reported in the
cities of Asmara and Massawa.

When Yemenis were captured by the EPLF in the Massawa fighting, they were quietly released to their government with strong but
discreet protests by the EPLF. Months later, South Yemen pulled its
forces out of Eritrea.

Similar tactics have been used to bring pressure on Cuba. While
Cuban infantry troops have yet to enter the battlefield here, as they
did in the Ogaden war against Somali aggression, Cuban and Soviet
military experts appear to have virtually taken over the direction of
the fighting, say EPLF sources.

Soviet and Cuban personnel are manning the heavy Soviet
artillery, planning the tactics and strategy of the campaign and taking
responsibility for logistics and communications, according to Issayas
Afwerki.

"The Cubans and Russians are distributed on all fronts," Issayas
said. "Whenever there is any offensive from the Ethiopian side, it is
sure that there are Russians and Cubans participating."

Coming Battles

Ethiopia's dramatic advances against the ELF in July and August
were due largely to the use of artillery and air superiority in the flat
open lowlands, but the coming battles will be fought in rugged mountainous country against the stronger EPLF.

Deserters from Asmara say that the Ethiopian army's morale is low, and EPLF leaders say that its combat efficiency is so poor as to render it ineffective without direct assistance from more seasoned and experienced soldiers.

In sharp contrast, the morale of the EPLF fighters is extremely high, and the civilian population is almost totally mobilized behind the EPLF.

"We are not fooling ourselves, that we have crushed this offensive and it's over, but the second round will not be any different from the first, and we will crush it, too," said Issayas Afwerki.

At the front lines, EPLF fighters cite the tactics of withdrawing from their southern positions in early August as the key to their present strength. And they say they can hold the positions they now defend while stepping up the costs to Ethiopia by guerrilla-style operations in the rear areas.

The main strength of the EPLF has been its commitment to self-reliance, which has led it to concentrate heavily on winning local popular support through programs of economic and social reform among the mainly peasant population. The EPLF's Marxist character has at the same time alienated it from lucrative sources of aid within the conservative Arab world.

A Third Force

At the same time, there is a growing third Eritrean force known as the ELF-PLF which is Western oriented in its politics. It bases its internal support on a straight-forward Arab nationalist appeal to the predominantly Moslem lowlanders of Western Eritrea. Headed by Osman Saleh Sabbe, this group is concentrated in a remote area of Western Eritrea and has managed to stay out of the recent fighting altogether while receiving a steady supply of aid from Saudi Arabia, the Arab Emirates and Iran who fear the emergence of the leftist EPLF as the dominant force in Eritrea.

Both the ELF and the EPLF oppose the third force, and last week open civil war broke out between it and the ELF over control of supply lines into the small area in which both are now concentrated due to the recent Ethiopian advances.

Skirmishing between them has been reported for nearly two months but on Oct. 28, the ELF launched major attacks on two ELF-PLF camps after ELF-PLF forces reportedly ambushed an ELF patrol.

Meanwhile, Sudan's government has stepped up pressure on all three organizations to bury their differences and unite and diplomatic sources say that President Gen. Jaafar Muhammad al-Nimeiri this week demanded a meeting of the three in Khartoum under the threat of cutting off support if they refused.

With Ethiopia resupplying its troops for the next wave of attacks, a civil war between the two smaller factions could well leave the Addis Ababa government and the EPLF to fight it out on their own.

Eritrean Factions Spur Civil War

Osman Sabbe's Third Force Attacks ELF

The Guardian (New York), November 29, 1978

With Ethiopian forces on the verge of launching a major second round assault against the Eritrean People's Liberation Front (EPLF), infighting among two smaller guerrilla factions has reached the level of a full-scale civil war.

A ceasefire was declared last week between the Eritrean Liberation Front (ELF) and the Eritrean Liberation Front-Popular Liberation Forces (ELF-PLF) after two weeks of heavy fighting. But there is no sign of letup in the life and death political struggle between them, and neither factions is expected to play a role in the imminent fighting between the EPLF and Ethiopia.

While the immediate cause of the battle appears to have been territorial-the control of supply lines into their overlapping base areas in the Western Eritrea-the root cause is the groups' opposition to the EPLF's growing domination over the Eritrean independence movement.

Superficially, these groupings cover a political range from "left" of the EPLF to the extreme right. But there is an increasing trend toward a consolidation under the umbrella of the avowedly right-wing Arab Nationalist ELF-PLF. The immediate goal seems to be eliminating the centrist ELF to sharply polarize the movement into a simple contradiction between EPLF and ELF-PLF.

Sources close to the ELF-PLF say that the recently formed third Eritrean armed force has the support of conservative Arab regimes including Saudi Arabia and the Arab Emirates, as well as Iran. It is also allied with a dissident group within the ELF known as the "Falloul" (anarchists).

The ELF-PLF strategy is to bring about the internal collapse of the ELF, now demoralized from recent losses to Ethiopia. While the EPLF is weakened by the strain of fighting alone against the government in the next phase of the offensive, according to these sources.

In this scenario, the ELF-PLF can then emerge as the sole representative of the predominantly Muslim Western Eritrean lowlands to demand from the EPLF a Lebanon-style division of Eritrea along religious and tribal lines as the price for an alliance against Ethiopia, postponing a direct confrontation with the EPLF until a later time when Ethiopia has returned to the defensive and foreign support can be consolidated behind the ELF-PLF.

The ELF-PLF is headed by Osman Saleh Sabbe, a shrewd politician who was an original leader of the ELF in the 1960s and later chief of the EPLF foreign mission after the second front broke away from the ELF in 1970.

During this period he formed strong contacts in the Arab world. When he was jettisoned by the left-wing core of the EPLF Field Command in 1976, along with the EPLF's right wing, he rapidly set about establishing a third front with funds from his oil rich foreign allies. His membership was made up of dissidents from the other two fronts, along with refugees recruited from camps in neighboring Sudan.

Aiming at United Front

At this time the EPLF and the ELF were involved in irregular negotiations to form a united front after three years of civil war which had ended in late 1974. ELF leaders sought to take advantage of the new force by giving it access to their liberated areas in Western Eritrea and then demanding its inclusion in unity talks with an eye toward gaining an ally against the rapidly growing EPLF.

When EPLF leaders refused to recognize the Sabbe force, the ELF declared its intention of effecting a preliminary merger with it prior to unity with the EPLF. But the plan backfired within the ELF ranks and generated a grassroots mutiny among guerrillas who foresaw the possibility of renewed civil war with the EPLF in the event of such a realignment.

The summer of 1977 saw wholesale defections of the ELF's left wing with an estimated 1500 going over to the EPLF and another 3000 fleeing to Sudan to reorganize as the Falloul. Rather than fielding yet a fourth army in Eritrea, the Falloul sought to strengthen it support within the ELF while outwardly criticizing both the EPLF and the ELF and biding its time.

When in October 1977 the ELF leadership reversed itself to agree to unity with the EPLF without the ELF-PLF, the lines of political demarcation began to sharpen, and the ELF experienced further defections of its right wing to the Sabbe group.

Gradually, the labyrinthine politics of the Eritrean movement began to resolve into two camps with the Falloul gravitating toward the ELF-PLF, and the EPLF and the ELF making halting progress toward a loose but formal alliance that finally came to pass in April 1978.

However, the opening of Ethiopia's military campaign in June intervened to stir up old rivalries between the EPLF and the ELF as the two failed to coordinate their defenses and the ELF lost all the towns and cities under its control.

ELF-PLF elements within the ELF attempted a series of coup d'e-tats and mutinies which were put down by that front, but the result-ant disarray forced the bulk of the ELF's fighting forces to withdraw to bases in the western lowlands to reorganize.

Meanwhile the Falloul became increasingly vocal in its critiques of the two major fronts, keying on their field losses (which for the EPLF amounted to voluntary withdrawals from several positions rather than battlefield defeats but were characterized as unnecessary capitulation) and their refusal to take an anti-Soviet and anti-Cuban stand.

With the EPLF preparing for the imminent showdown with Ethiopia, it has tended to ignore the intrigues and maneuverings of the rightist forces, but in late October, the ELF struck out at ELF-PLF bases near the city of Agordat. According to several independent sources, they managed to overrun at least half of the ELF-PLF's base area before accepting a ceasefire.

Whether the EPLF and the ELF can now resume the unsteady process of establishing unity, and whether the various other dissident groups will manage to cement their alliance remains to be seen. But what is clear is that the ingredients exist for an ultimate confronta-tion between the two polar Eritrean forces and there is less and less room for either a simple solution to their differences or a third way for those still on the sidelines.

Eritrean rebels falling back

The Boston Globe, November 1978

"This is our long march," quipped Eritrean guerrilla leader Haile Woldetensay, but the mood was somber as the guerrillas worked through the night to dismantle their offices here last month before the city was reoccupied by the Russian-backed Ethiopian army.

Small fires illuminated the moonless night where papers and records were being destroyed as the Eritrean nationalists loaded up their equipment.

In the distance, a low rumble rolled off the hills from the battle-field 12 miles to the south.

The second-largest city in this 42,000 square-mile Red Sea coastal territory, Keren had functioned as the "shadow capital" for the Eritrean people's liberation front (EPLF) since it was taken by the guerrillas in July 1977. Now it was the last of the major Eritrean towns to be evacuated in the face of a massive Ethiopian government offensive that began six months ago.

Though a bitter disappointment, the guerrillas seemed to bear the evacuation calmly, and they carried out the withdrawal systematical-ly, leaving nothing of value behind for the enemy. School desks, hospital beds and cooking utensils were piled up with heavy machinery and food stocks to be transferred to rural caves and underground shelters where the front would base itself from now on.

The view generally held and often expressed by the EPLF guerrillas was that the rapidly escalating role of the Russians on the Ethiopian side had created a new situation to which they must adapt. It was, they said, not the first setback in their 17-year war for independence.

Among the civilian residents, the reaction to the fall of the city was less confident and often less coherent as well. Many appeared to have expected the EPLF to hold Keren, and they seemed deeply dis-couraged when they discovered otherwise.

The actual evacuation came spontaneously after Ethiopian MiG jets carried out six hours of nonstop bombing close to Keren. People appeared to panic, and that evening they began an exodus north to a more secure EPLF's base area and, in many cases, beyond to the Sudan border.

Almost 40,000 people streamed northward, carrying small bun-dles, occasionally a battered leather suitcase on their heads. Men and women wept as they were forced to discard pieces of luggage in order to pick up their bedraggled children.

Not all the residents of Keren fled. Some 1000 to 2000 remained barricaded in their homes, including the handful of Italians who had been in Keren since the end of Italy's colonial rule in 1941.

Later captured by the British, he escaped to Keren and remained to build two hotels, one of which was nationalized by Ethiopia's military government three years ago. In 1977, he watched from his fourth-floor balcony as the EPLF captured Keren from the beleaguered American and Italian-trained Ethiopian regular army. Now he waited for the arrival of Ethiopia's new Russian and Cuban-trained peasant militia.

Some who fled are likely to trickle back into Keren once the shooting stops, but the tragedy of the Keren exodus was that it placed the majority of the civilian population square in the path of the advancing Ethiopian forces although there was no combat in the city itself.

Once the evacuation was complete, EPLF forward units quietly withdrew from their positions nine and 12 miles west and south of the city to regroup.

The fall of KEREN appears to signal a new phase in the protracted Eritrean war, a phase that will pit the technological superiority of the Russian-backed Ethiopian government against the ingenuity and determination of the guerrillas.

Whatever the results, it is already clear that the civilian population, caught in the crossfire, will bear the brunt of the increasing cost of this, the longest running conflict in Africa.

Social struggle in an Eritrean village

The Guardian (New York), December 6, 1978

The MiGs came at 10:30 in the morning, circling high overhead before they bombed the nearby village of Kwazien. As they roared off, the low "whump, whump" of artillery could be heard from the battlefield on the outskirts of Asmara.

Only 12 miles from Asmara, Eritrea's capital, Zagur has been the most advanced in the EPLF's liberated areas.

As the war for independence from Ethiopia grinds on, the

struggle to transform the old colonial and feudal social relations here continued unabated.

After more than four years of patient mobilization and political education by the EPLF here, the people have organized themselves into political associations of peasants, women and youth. A People's Assembly governs the village. And, most important for this rural agricultural settlement, repeated stages of land reform have led to collectivization of the farming here.

When I first visited Zagur in early 1977, the more advanced peasants and the women were being organized into clandestine study cells by a team of five EPLF cadres living among the villagers. A village committee had been elected, and basic land reform that roughly equalized land holdings had been carried out by the committee, with EPLF guidance. The main task of the cadre at that time was broadening the base of support and developing a revolutionary village leadership.

By the time of my second visit to Zagur in the fall of 1977 there had been marked progress. Mass associations of peasants, women and youth had been formed from the cells. The elected cell leaders together formed a People's Assembly which had replaced the village committee.

The People's Assembly had expropriated land owned by collaborators and by people known to have left Eritrea. A cooperative shop and a cooperative grain mill were being established.

The most conscious members of the association had been given military training and were part of a growing EPLF militia, which played a leading political role in the village as well as policing and defending it.

A year later, I saw even more progress in all fields. As I walked through the village, Eden Fasil, one of the EPLF cadres, explained to me what changes had taken place in my absence.

"About 10 months ago we had another land reform, " he began. "Now one-third of the village land is farmed cooperatively and the plots have been consolidated together." While this move stopped short of complete expropriation, Eden explained, it effectively ended tenant farming and individual sharecropping. "Now the village is the only tenant," he said.

"Furthermore, all private holdings are now organized so that the plots of each peasant family border on those of the other members of their cell. This sets the stage for further collectivization," he pointed out, adding that the militia has gone ahead to fully collectivize their land, except for small plots reserved for day to day needs.

The peasant association is subdivided along class lines, with 14 cells of poor peasants, eight of middle peasants and five of rich peasants. "And that is how they're represented in the People's Assembly, so the majority rules," said Eden.

"They (members of the peasant association) say they are going to allocate some of it to the cells of poor peasants in times of need because no poor peasant can live on his own produce for the whole year," said the EPLF cadre. "They are also going to put some on reserve for replanting, and they are going to put some aside for capital," Eden explained that during the past year there had been grain shortages and the association had used its capital to buy grain from a surplus area and sell it at cost in Zagur.

Asked if there had been any major mistakes so far, he said, "not really, because we are careful to go slowly. We try to put into account other people's experiences as well-the Chinese and the Vietnamese experience of setting up cooperatives and collectivizing."

"We have seen that it has to be voluntary as much as possible. You can only teach them, try to make them understand, and show them in practice. You can't push them into cooperatives because the consequences would be devastating, especially in Zagur. This is a model village."

As we strolled through Zagur, we came upon a fenced-in area with more than 50 chickens inside. It was a new poultry project run by the Zagur women's association, one of the first in Eritrea where chickens have traditionally run wild and fed on waste material.

We also came upon two large bomb craters which had destroyed one house and taken the roofs off several others. I was told that Zagur had been bombed a month ago with four large conventional bombs and three months earlier with napalm.

"It is merely done to terrorize the people," he said, "but I have observed that the more the Ethiopians terrorize them, the stronger the morale of the people and the more they feel that they have to fight."

When the two MiGs buzzed over us that day, the adults looked up casually and went on about their work. The children ran into the streets raising sticks into the air as if to fire at them. Then they too went on about their business.

Life In Keren Before Offensive

The Guardian (New York), December 13, 1978

The following report was written shortly before the current Ethiopian offensive and the recapture of Keren, the last major city held by the Eritrean People's Liberation Front (EPLF).

Backed by more than 45,000 troops, tanks, jet fighters and helicopters, the Ethiopian have launched a full-scale attack on the liberated areas in Eritrea. In response, according to EPLF representatives, the liberation front has made a tactical retreat and is resorting to classical guerrilla warfare.

As the following report demonstrates, the EPLF has made great strides in politicizing and organizing the people of Eritrea, advances which will be the basis for supporting the protracted struggle ahead.

Keren, Eritrea

More than a year after liberation, Keren has become a showpiece for the social and economic reforms of the Eritrean People's Liberation Front (EPLF).

The residents are highly organized in mass political associations; the city is jointly administered by elected civilian People's Assemblies and a Provisional Administrative Council of the EPLF; economic activity has returned to its prewar norm and steady development in the economic and social fields is the order of the day.

The second largest city in Eritrea, Keren was liberated in July 1977 by the EPLF in a general offensive that netted the front all but five of the major Ethiopian-held towns. Efforts began immediately to acquaint the people with the EPLF's national democratic program and to begin the process of organizing and politicizing them through associations of workers, peasants, women, youth and other patriotic forces.

As the associations grew in size and experience, People's Assemblies were established in the four zones of Keren. Twelve-person civilian People's Councils were elected from within the assemblies to oversee the day-to-day running of the city.

There were, however, problems. The struggle to organize the women was particularly difficult at first as backward elements in the city opposed their participation in political life.

The EPLF persisted in its organizing efforts, and in November 1977 the Keren Women's Association held a massive street demonstration after which the association steadily grew to the point today where 75% of the women here are members.

At the same time, the overall transition to people's power was not as simple a matter as it first appeared. There have been adjustments made to slow it down and deepen the political base upon which it must rest.

"At the beginning, the majority of the people didn't have a full idea of the importance of the People's Council," according to Mohammed Nur, who heads the EPLF's office of Mass Administration here. He added that some who were elected were transient and not always there.

New elections were held in March; 70-80% of the first-termers were reelected. One of those chosen again in the second round said, "For those of us who suffered all our lives under the oppressive rule of successive colonizers and were shut out from the light of freedom and independence, the People's Assembly was a totally new and invigorating experience."

Further Changes Instituted

This first experience for the people of Keren and the EPLF with urban government was itself an education, and changes followed soon.

Two cadre schools were set up for civilians in March and April and a number of the newly elected representatives attended them. Later, an EPLF Provisional Administrative Council (PAC) was also constituted out of officials from the front's departments of Mass Administration, Finance, Internal Trade, Social Welfare, Housing and Water Supply, Electricity and Mills, Medicine and Security. Under the leadership of a member of the EPLF Political Bureau, they worked with the People's Council in coordinating services and general administration.

The People's Councils distribute all basic commodities at set prices in coordination with the EPLF, which has taken over the role of citywide wholesaler of items such as grain, sugar, salt and vegetable oil. They are also developing cooperative people's shops in each zone to deal in other goods, collecting rents from the nationalized houses, caring for the needy, raising money for the war and balancing distribution of goods.

In the economic sphere, the EPLF in July raised the minimum wage of workers across Eritrea to a level at least twice that of what it was before liberation of the towns from Ethiopia. Under the new wage scale, a worker is also entitled to pay increments based upon the size of his or her family.

The main problem here is the continual influx of the displaced and the homeless who come often with little more than the clothes on their backs. EPLF departments in Keren have rebuilt 300 houses and made them available at low rents, provided jobs and given out food and clothing to the neediest.

A spokesman at the Social Welfare Department said that 3000 people are now regularly under their care, receiving millet, sugar, milk, clothes and shoes when they are available.

Pointedly absent in Keren are the young people who used to congregate on the sidewalks and in the cafes and bars. The children are now organized as the Red Flowers and are busy in the day on a small farm at the edge of town and at school in the evenings, but the teenagers are gone. When Ethiopia opened its all-out offensive this past spring, Mohammed Nur said, the youth left almost en masse to join the front.

Although the EPLF does not maintain a major military presence in the city, there are a growing number of offices and embryo projects here, including a workshop where fighters make custom-fitted wooden legs for disabled fighters, a small research chemistry lab where EPLF technicians are experimenting with local materials to produce soap for future cottage industry and pure alcohol for hospital uses and a veterinary medical section where medics are working with 1500 mice to produce vaccines against prevalent animal diseases.

The work in these projects goes slowly-it takes three nights in the chemistry lab to produce a half liter of alcohol-as in politics, but the Eritreans appear as patient as they are determined to win, and it is perhaps this attribute that insures their eventual victory for full independence and people's democracy in Keren and in Eritrea.

Eritrea: EPLF girds for protracted war

Massive foreign assistance changes nature of Ethiopia's war

The Guardian (New York), December 20, 1978

Outside Keren, Eritrea

The fall of Keren, the last major town held by the Eritrean People's Liberation Front (EPLF), has opened a new phase in the long and bitter struggle for Eritrean independence.

According to the EPLF, it was large-scale direct Soviet participation in the Keren campaign and in Ethiopia's retaking the key Asmara-Massawa road in late November that changed the basic character of the war.

"The face of the war has changed," said EPLF assistant general secretary Issayas Afwerki as we stood near a temporary camp for refugees from Keren which had been bombed that day by two MIG-23 jets.

"We are not fighting the Derg any more," he explained. "Now it is the Soviet Union." Cuban troops in Ethiopia appear not to have been involved in the massive counterinsurgency drive.

There is a lull now on the battlefront after the heaviest fighting in the 17-year war. After retreating from Keren, the EPLF turned back an Ethiopian push toward the crucial guerrilla base area in the arid northern Sahel mountains. The highly mechanized Ethiopian forces were driven back to the recaptured city, where they remain at Guardian press time.

Direct Soviet Role

EPLF fighters say that Soviet military personnel directed the entire Ethiopian operation, commanding and planning battles, flying MiG jets, operating heavy artillery and driving some of the hundreds of armored vehicles which spearheaded the antiguerrilla drive. This was the decisive factor, according to the EPLF. That finally gave Ethiopia the major military gains it had for years been unable to achieve on its own.

But the Eritreans declare that the struggle which was launched in 1961 against the U.S. and Israeli-backed government of Emperor Haile Selassie and continued unabated against the military government that took power in 1974, is continuing nonetheless, although in a new and much more difficult form.

The offensive opened on Nov. 17-18 with simultaneous Ethiopian drives on five fronts. Each was subdivided into multiple fronts. The objectives were EPLF positions along the highway linking the inland capital of Asmara and the Red Sea port of Massawa and the EPLF-held city of Keren on the northwestern slopes of the central highland plateau.

While the initial thrusts were repulsed by the EPLF, an evaluation was made of the relative balance of forces involved. The EPLF based its conclusions not so much on the numerical superiority of the massive Soviet-equipped Ethiopian army as on the sharply increased efficiency with which the weapons were being used by the hundreds of Soviet experts on the battlefield. The result was an EPLF decision to retreat from the Asmara-Massawa road on Nov. 21 to consolidate the defenses around Keren.

It was a new war, demanding new tactics. Until now, Ethiopia had depended mainly on brute force and numbers to pound away at the EPLF in human-wave frontal assaults that had been again and again crushed by the sheet determination and the tactical superiority of the EPLF army.

The steady increase in the size of the Ethiopian arsenal had raised the cost of the war to both sides but had failed to change its course. Now, however, with the sizable Ethiopian air force, artillery and armor-beefed up with outside help, the nature of the fighting changed.

Sophisticated intelligence gathered by Soviet-piloted helicopters and MIG jets along with satellite photographs provided the Ethiopians with the means to orchestrate a complex campaign of flanking attacks. This was done in combination with straightforward drives to divide the EPLF over wide areas on every major front, according to EPLF leaders.

Skilled coordination between air and ground forces also added a new element to the military equation giving Ethiopia the edge in open field conventional battles.

EPLF positions were subjected to a punishing bombardment by waves of up to 10 MIG-23 jets, long-range rockets and 122mm and 160mm artillery aimed at carefully selected weak points in the guerrilla lines. Armored columns numbering some 40 vehicles each, then attempted to drive a wedge there to open the way for the tens of thousands of infantry troops massed for the battles.

Systematic Retreat

Early on it became obvious that the EPLF, lacking sophisticated antiaircraft or antitank guns and possessing only limited numbers of captured field artillery pieces, could not sustain such battles without enduring unacceptable losses.

A steady but systematic-retreat began northward from Asmara and eastward from Agordat toward Keren, the city which had become a kind of shadow capital for the Eritreans.

The Ethiopians made grudging progress, but they suffered heavy losses of troops and arms as the EPLF maintained an iron discipline. The Eritreans continually reformed to strike at the advancing forces while falling back toward more advantageous positions in the mountains nearer to Keren.

After a week of such fighting, Ethiopia had come to within 15 miles of Keren from the south and nine miles from the west. Here they were finally halted and smashed by the EPLF in the most intense two days of fighting in the entire war.

Having learned that they could not fight effectively at long range, the EPLF set ambushes for the armored columns. This permitted them to fight at close quarters where the effect of the heavy arms was at least partially neutralized. The guerrillas also had the advantage, as before, of their determination and discipline under fire.

The battle of Elaberet was fought on Nov. 25-26. Elaberet is an agricultural plantation developed during the Italian colonial period in Eritrea, nationalized by the Derg in 1975 and captured by the EPLF in early 1977. It lies in a long, narrow valley 12 miles south of Keren.

At dawn on the first day, 90 tanks and armored cars rolled down the road into the heart of the valley without meeting any resistance. According to the accounts of guerrilla fighters interviewed later, the line of armored vehicles stretched the length of the valley. The 35,000 strong infantry force was not yet in sight when the EPLF struck from hidden positions.

"It was humans against tanks," said one fighter of the hand-to-hand combat that followed. The tanks immediately broke formation and tried to retreat, but in the initial confusion some 25-30 were cut off and abandoned, he added.

For the next 48 hours the battle raged up and down the surrounding hills with the Ethiopians almost breaking through to Keren early on Nov. 26 only to be pushed back and finally surrounded by day's end.

Another fighter who came to Elaberet on the second day of fighting said, "it was full of tanks, dead bodies and trucks from edge to edge. All the dry grass was burned totally and rows of trees were down from the tanks."

"The planes never stopped coming. They were dropping different types of bombs including napalm and at times the valley was so filled with smoke you couldn't even see. On the road just behind us," he continued, "I counted 25 tanks and seven trucks captured and about five more burned. We pursued them from all the hills into the valley, and they were surrounded.

"We heard them on the radio saying they had no way out and didn't know what to do," the EPLF cadre told me, "then two helicopters landed with Soviet officers, and soon they tried another counterattack, but that movement was crushed and we pushed them back. Then the sun set and the battle was over."

Accounts of the fighting west of Keren are much the same with veterans of the battle claiming emphatically that they were winning when the order to retreat came on Nov. 26.

By this time, unknown to the guerrillas engaged in the Keren battles, a third Ethiopian front had opened up on the east along the Red Sea coast. This force threatened to cut the EPLF's crucial supply lines and drive into the heart of the guerrilla's base area in the north.

Ethiopia had virtually emptied out the other towns and areas under its control to mount a surprise flanking assault by land from Massawa toward the EPLF-held town of Afabet, 135 miles north of Keren. They also approached by sea to Marsa Gulbud toward the key town of Karora on the Sudan border.

Once again the EPLF chose to contract its fixed point by pulling back to a point where it could gain a tactical advantage rather than risk winning one battle only to lose the campaign.

"We don't have enough army to fight on three fronts at the level they could, and we don't have the means to destroy all their airplanes and tanks," said Ibrahim Afa, commander of the EPLF's northeastern front, after the campaign.

The Ethiopian plan was to lure the EPLF into major battle in defense of Keren, cut them off from behind and then to crush them as an effective fighting force, according to Ibrahim.

Though Keren appeared to be the main target, it is now clear that the Soviet-led Ethiopian forces intended to continue their blitzkrieg tactics through Keren to the north. The aim was to carve up the Sahel base, and with the EPLF in disarray the Ethiopians would continue to have the initiative and mop up the remnants of the front at will. Ethiopian prisoners interviewed later confirmed this, and captured tanks bore the inscription "Karora or death."

The EPLF for its part sensed the danger, saw the developments on the Red Sea coast and decided in the week prior to the Elaberet battle to withdraw from Keren and redraw its lines.

By Nov. 23 the Keren pullout was in full swing with EPLF trucks mobilized to carry out all useable goods and equipment north to the base area. The next day, the civilian population evacuated en masse.

The Elaberet battle, then, was fought not so much to defend Keren as to deal the Ethiopian force a heavy enough blow to weaken it before it moved into position to drive on toward Afabet and Karora. In this respect, it was successful, for when the Ethiopians did thrust north the following week they were stopped and forced to pull back to Keren. Thus while the drive in the East was a brilliant tactical maneuver that in effect won Keren for the Derg, it failed in its larger objective of penetrating the EPLF base area.

The exact number of casualties on both sides will never be known, but it clearly runs into the thousands. EPLF losses were relatively heavy, possibly running as high as 2000 on all fronts. Ethiopian dead were said to number several times higher. A walking tour of one of the battlefields in the east showed hundreds of Ethiopian corpses spread over the hillsides and clustered in groups of 10 and 15 in a single place.

The valley floor was so torn up by crisscrossing tank tracks that it looked like corrugated cardboard. Trees and shrubs were ripped out by their roots. Burned tanks rusted in the blistering tropical sun and the stench of death was overpowering.

The EPLF captured more than 25 tanks and armored cars intact, while destroying over three times that many, in several cases because they could not be moved off the battlefield after being taken in the fighting.

In the aftermath, the most striking phenomenon at the frontlines was the extremely high morale of the rank-and-file guerrillas who continually sought me out to explain the necessity of the retreats while stressing their successes in each individual battlefield confrontation.

When word came of two ambushes made on Dec. 5 along the Asmara-Massawa road, there was elation among them, and I was told again and again that this was only the beginning of the EPLF's counteroffensive.

The other topic that invariably came up was the role of the Soviet Union in the war. The direct Soviet participation in the fighting ushers in a new era for the Eritrea war, but there is no sign that the very serious military setbacks have affected the EPLF's will to fight and determination to win. As Issayas Afwerki told me, "We have to now change our tactics and prepare ourselves for a more protracted war."

Russians Join Eritrean Battles

Observer Foreign News Service (London), December 21, 1978

Outside Keren, Eritrea

"The face of the war has changed," said Eritrean People's Liberation Front (EPLF) leader Issayas Afwerki as we surveyed the casualties in a temporary refugee camp north of Keren bombed that day by two Russian-piloted MIG-23 jet fighters. "We are not fighting the Derg any more. Now it is the Soviet Union."

Along the road were 65 wounded civilians from the city of Keren evacuated only a day earlier in the face of a massive Russian-led Ethiopian offensive against the Eritrean nationalists who had held the key city for more than a year.

Among the injured was one family of five. Berhane Gerejesus lay on a canvas stretcher as an EPLF paramedic tended the shrapnel wound in his leg. His wife and three children, also wounded, huddled around him, his 18-month old baby shivering with shock from a head wound that would claim his young life the next morning.

Ten had been killed outright in the late afternoon raid, and 30 more would not survive the next 24 hours.

This is Eritrea's darkest hour in its 17-year war for independence, which began against the US-and Israeli-backed regime of Haile Selassie and is now entering a new phase against the Russian and Cuban military junta that seized power in 1974.

Six months ago the EPLF and a second smaller nationalist movement - the Eritrean Liberation Front (ELF) - controlled 95 per cent of the strategic Red Sea territory and former Italian colony, but between June and September, the Government reoccupied all the towns previously held by the ELF, only to be finally repulsed by the stronger EPLF in a series of battles near Keren. EPLF leaders then claimed that Russian and Cuban advisers and logistics experts played a key support role in the fighting.

Now, however, Russian military personnel appear to have taken over the planning and execution of the war from top to bottom to alter the balance of forces in favor of Ethiopia for the first time. "The Ethiopian command, everything, is under the Soviet Union," said Afwerki, the 32-year-old assistant general secretary of the EPLF.

At the same time, he noted, the Cuban role appears to have stabilized or even receded. While 13,000 Cuban troops are still reported in Ethiopia, there is no sign that they were directly involved in the current fighting here.

Ethiopian prisoners of war interviewed after one battle said that though Cubans trained them they refused to come to Eritrea to fight. The Russians, on the other hand, now number almost 1,000 men, including front-line combat officers, according to EPLF leaders and Ethiopian POWs.

General Petrov, who ran the Ogaden campaign last year, was the top commander of the Ethiopian ground forces - infantry, armor and artillery - while another unnamed Russian general commanded the air force, these sources say.

Eleven Russian officers of the rank of Lieutenant Colonel commanded the field units when the campaign opened in mid-November, and lower echelon officers commanded the smaller combat units, with between 150 and 250 officers deployed on each main front, according to EPLF intelligence sources.

EPLF leaders name Lt. Col. Alexi Alexandrov as the commander of Russian and Ethiopian forces on the western front, Lt. Col. Vassily as the eastern front commander and Lt. Col. Eduard as the northern front commander. Eduard was fatally wounded in a battle at the town of Elabared on November 26, and he died later in Addis Ababa, according to the EPLF.

The new Russian presence changed the character of the war, not only through the introduction of massive quantities of armored vehicles, heavy artillery, rockets and air power, but more importantly by raising the level of efficiency with which the weapons were used.

Sophisticated intelligence, gathered by Russian-piloted helicopters and MiG jets as well as satellite photographs, provided the Soviet strategists with the means to plan the complex campaign, according to EPLF leaders.

In contrast to earlier human wave attacks by the ill-trained, largely peasant militia and random aerial and artillery bombardment with tank support, the current battle saw complicated tactical maneuvers on multiple fronts preceded by intensive pinpoint bombing and shelling.

After two hours of such punishing bombardment, columns of up to 50 tanks would open a wedge for the waiting infantry to pour through behind guerrilla lines.

The EPLF was forced to retreat steadily from its fixed positions and shift back to more mobile tactics that allowed them to fight at close range. This meant leaving the trenches and the cities and returning to the countryside.

The retreat was accomplished smoothly and systematically, with EPLF units peeling off one at a time to reform again and again over a ten-day period between the cities of Asmara, south of Keren, and Agordat in the west.

The heaviest fighting of the war took place at the Elabered plantation on Saturday and Sunday, November 25 and 26, where the EPLF ambushed a column of ninety T-54 and BTR-60 tanks. The 35,000-man Ethiopian infantry force was not yet in the narrow valley when the EPLF struck from hidden positions on both sides of the road.

A young fighter who arrived the second day said, "When we reached Elabared, it was full of tanks, dead bodies and trucks from edge to edge. All the dry grass was burned and rows of trees were down from the tanks. The planes never stopped coming. They were dropping different types of bombs including napalm and at times the valley was so filled with smoke you couldn't even see.

"On the road just behind us I counted 25 tanks and seven trucks captured and about five more burned. We pursued them from all the hills into the valley, and they were surrounded. We heard them on the radio saying they had no way out and didn't know what to do. Then two helicopters landed with Russian officers, and soon they tried another counter-attack, but the movement was crushed and we pushed them back. Then the sun set, and the battle was over."

Eritrean forces resume guerrilla attacks

The Guardian (New York), January 3, 1979

Khartoum, Sudan

The protracted Eritrean war for independence from Ethiopia has sustained serious military setbacks in recent weeks, radically changing the nature of the fighting. But the Eritreans say the struggle is far from over.

They conveyed this message to Ethiopia Dec. 21 with simultaneous guerrilla attacks on 11 separate military posts along the key highway linking the Eritrean capital of Asmara with the Red Sea port of Massawa. The strategic road, long held by Eritrean People's

Liberation Front (EPLF) forces, was retaken by Ethiopia last month.

Diverse countries and movements meanwhile have set off a flurry of diplomatic and political maneuvers aimed at taking advantage of the much-altered military situation. Heavy pressure is apparently being exerted by conservative Arab regimes to carve out a significant political role within Eritrea for the rightist ELF-PLF, a splinter group led by Osman Saleh Sabbe. At the same time EPLF leaders met here this week with leaders of the smaller Eritrean Liberation Front (ELF) in a renewed attempt to unite the two forces.

The coordinated guerrilla strikes along the recaptured highway came less than three weeks after the close of a strong Ethiopian offensive against Eritrean positions. Addis Ababa's military push, carried out with direct Soviet support according to the EPLF, forced the Eritreans to retreat from Keren, the last major town under guerrilla control.

In last week's fighting EPLF units totally destroyed the newly established Ethiopian garrisons, capturing 37 prisoners and large quantities of arms and ammunitions in lightning attacks, according to an EPLF representative here.

"While these victories are important in themselves," he told the Guardian, "their main significance lies in the signal they send to the fascist Ethiopian junta and their foreign backers that their fleeting successes will not last. They will get no rest from us from now on."

In the aftermath of Ethiopia's reoccupation of the remaining large towns and cities in EPLF hands during the last round of conventional open field battle, the movement is reorganizing its forces to shift to more mobile guerrilla warfare. This they say will give them a renewed military initiative.

Ethiopia meanwhile is mobilizing for an assault on the three smaller towns of Afabet, Nakfa and Karora, still under EPLF control within the front's northern Sahel base area. Ethiopia had failed to reach these objectives in the massive military push that ended in early December.

These new conditions have given an impetus to the meetings between the EPLF and ELF here in the Sudanese capital. A key objective of the talks will be the establishment of military coordination between the rival fronts in the coming phase of guerrilla counterattacks. Earlier efforts at such coordination broke down last spring, enabling Ethiopia to exploit the division by concentrating its main strength against one front at a time.

Sudan and other sympathetic but vacillating Arab states are

pressing the Eritreans to consolidate their forces in the political arena under a single umbrella leadership that would also include Sabbe's reactionary ELF-PLF. The stated goal is to bring all the warring parties to the conference table.

Iraq recently announced plans to try initiating negotiations between the Eritreans and Ethiopia's ruling military Derg. Also, Sudanese President Jaafar Nimeiri this week revealed plans to meet with Ethiopian head of state Lt. Col. Mengistu Haile Mariam. The meeting would take place following the conclusion of the Khartoum talks between the Eritrean organizations.

The EPLF says, however, that the recent battlefield reverses have done nothing to dampen its determination to win full independence for the former Italian colony. Thus, there appears little chance that such negotiations will take place in the near future.

EPLF leaders add that they will not now or in the future compromise with the ELF-PLF, which has been lobbying heavily with rightist Arab regimes. Sabbe's aim is to block the leftist EPLF from receiving any external aid unless it recognizes the tiny nationalist clique as a legitimate third Eritrean force. (Sabbe had originally headed the EPLF's foreign department, where he used his position to establish links with countries such as Saudi Arabia, while refusing to build ties with the progressive world. He was ousted from the movement in 1976).

Initially based in a narrow corridor of western Eritrea near the Sudan border, the 3000-member ELF-PLF avoided any involvement in resisting the recent Ethiopian offensive. A small-scale civil war broke out between the ELF-PLF and the ELF in November, and by Guardian press time Sabbe's forces were reportedly pushed entirely out of Eritrea across the Sudan border. There they are under Sudanese army protection.

The renewal of efforts by the ELF-PLF and its supporters to win a political position inside Eritrea apparently stems from the view that the progressive wing of the movement, led by the EPLF, has been so weakened by Ethiopia's military advances that it can be forced into compromises with imperialist interests in the region.

But the EPLF is still intact and remains militarily strong. During a recent month-long visit to EPLF control-led areas it was apparent that the morale of the rank-and-file is also surprisingly high, in view of the latest events.

Massive Soviet assistance to Ethiopia, including direct battlefield involvement has dramatically altered the military balance of forces in favor of Addis Ababa. And politically, pro-imperialist forces in the region are stepping up attempts to use the Eritrean struggle for their own purposes. The EPLF says, however, that this has not had any significant effect on its own uncompromising political line of self-reliant, protracted people's war.

"If there is anything at all that pleased us in this last offensive, it is the firm determination of our people and fighters to stand and fight this huge army with its sophisticated arms from the Soviet Union," EPLF political bureau member Ali Sayed told me after the latest round of major battles.

"We are willing," the EPLF leader added, "to continue no matter how long it takes and no matter what the zigzags of progress, because we are assured of our final victory and we will settle for nothing less."

Eritrean guerrillas counter third offensive

The Guardian (New York), January 10, 1979

As the countdown continues for Ethiopia's third offensive round against Eritrean liberation forces, the guerrillas are stepping up counterattacks of their own against the government's newly established garrisons and supply lines.

Units of the Eritrean People's Liberation Front (EPLF) this week overran 11 Ethiopian garrisons on the key highway linking the inland Asmara capital with the Red Sea port of Massawa, according to the EPLF's Khartoum spokesman.

These bases had just been reestablished by Ethiopia following a similar assault by the EPLF just one week earlier (Guardian, Jan. 3) The actions mark the fourth such series of attacks in this area since Ethiopia reoccupied the important highway a month ago.

More than 500 Ethiopian troops were killed or wounded in the Dec. 28 guerrilla raids which netted the EPLF large quantities of small arms and antiaircraft guns, the front's spokesman reported.

This increase in mobile guerrilla activity reflects a pronounced shift in the character of the 17-year Eritrean war for independence from Ethiopia. It is indicative of the course the fighting is likely to follow in the coming year.

During the past seven months of sharply escalated fighting,

Ethiopian forces reoccupied all the major Eritrean towns and high-ways formerly held by the EPLF and a second smaller movement, the Eritrean Liberation Front (ELF).

EPLF leaders charge that Soviet combat personnel played a key role in the planning and battlefield execution of the campaign. The offensive pitted more than 150,000 Ethiopian troops and massive quantities of Soviet-supplied armor, rockets, artillery and aircraft against the lightly armed guerrillas.

The Ethiopian offensive to date has been only partially successful, however. Though the invasion forces took the large towns, they failed to reach the three smaller northern towns of Afabet, Nakfa and Karora or to penetrate the EPLF's guerrilla base area in this region.

This will be the objective of the next phase of the campaign for which Ethiopia is now remobilizing and which is expected in the near future.

More importantly, from the perspective of the war as political strug-gle, Addis Ababa has utterly failed to win popular Eritrean support in its military advance. The reoccupation of the large towns was accompanied by a mass civilian exodus to the countryside which remains almost entire-ly under guerrilla control.

During a month-long tour of EPLF-controlled areas which coin-cided with the latest phase of the offensive, it was apparent that the manner in which the EPLF withdrew from the towns left the govern-ment in possession of a string of urban islands in a hostile sea.

No town was actually taken by military force. Instead the EPLF fought outside the towns and pulled back after they were fully evac-uated. The retreat of the large military units was carried out system-atically to contract the fixed base area to a third the size it had been seven months ago. Today the EPLF's fully liberated base is in the arid Sahel mountains, bordered on the east by the Red Sea and on the north by Sudan, while defended on the west and south by entrenched brigade-strength units.

Within this area the mechanized supply lines remain fully opera-tive. Food, medicines, ammunition and infantry reinforcements could be seen nightly shuttling back and forth from one battlefront to another. Heavy machinery and equipment removed from the urban centers and heavy arms taken in the fighting were meanwhile being trucked to the rear.

In the 3-week series of major battles, the EPLF captured more than 25 Soviet-supplied T54 tanks and BTR60 armored cars as well as an undisclosed number of large field artillery pieces to bring the number of armored vehicles in their hands to more than 80. This is more than Ethiopia itself possessed under the U.S.- and Israeli-backed regime of Haile Selassie only four year ago, and it gives the EPLF a better equipped armed force than most established African states.

Guerrilla losses on the battlefield appeared to be relatively high under a punishing bombardment by long-range artillery, rockets and MIG jet aircraft using napalm and cluster antipersonnel bombs. The weapons were operated in part, according to the EPLF, by Soviet experts. But the civilian evacuation also brought thousands of fresh volunteers to the EPLF's reinforcements that appeared sufficient to maintain the front's infantry strength at between 25-30,000 men and women.

Still, the EPLF clearly lacks the overall strength now to defeat the Ethiopian army in multiple open field confrontations. Despite charges to the contrary, the EPLF lacks sources of outside arms supply and has no effective defense against the artillery, rockets and aircraft.

Nor do the Eritreans have enough ground forces to match those of Ethiopia, which in the latest fighting was able to spread the war over at least three simultaneous battlefronts before the EPLF pulled back to its present positions.

Battle for battle the Eritreans scored well against the numerically and technically superior Ethiopian forces. In the long term, however, the high rate of attrition on both sides works to the latter's advantage as Ethiopia has an apparently limitless reserve of manpower and a seemingly open-ended commitment from the Soviet Union to resupply lost arms.

In response, the EPLF has begun a rapid transition to the mobile guerrilla tactics that characterized the early years of the war. The movement is demobilizing brigade-size units into companies and battalions which are being assigned to loosely defined guerrilla zones throughout the Eritrean countryside.

This organization will in its turn weaken the EPLF's fixed defenses around their shrunken northern base area. This area is still vulnerable to attack not only from Ethiopia's newly occupied position in the town of Keren but also along the 180-mile stretch of coastline to the east. EPLF leaders say they will stand and fight here, but it seems likely that a further retreat from the towns of Afabet and Nakfa may result from the next round of fighting.

Regardless of the outcome, however, the dispersal of the guerrilla forces elsewhere in Eritrea will shift the focus of the war and the nature of the fighting over a wider area. With this move, the EPLF believes the advantages of popular support and the ability to choose the time and place of battle will give them back the military initiative in what promises to be a long and drawn-out test of will between the two sides.

Halting progress can also be expected in moves to unify the EPLF and the ELF under an EPLF-dominated united front. The rightist ELF-PLF, which is led by Osman Saleh Sabbe and has the backing of the imperialist interests in the region, would be excluded from such a front. EPLF leaders insist that they are unwilling to trade their independent Marxist orientation for assistance from the pro-Western, rightist Arab regimes currently supporting Sabbe's group-an organization with no forces in the field. There is therefore little likelihood of any dramatic new influx of weaponry on the Eritrean side.

The EPLF's main diplomatic efforts are now directed toward winning political support from African and other third world countries. This they hope will pressure the USSR and Cuba-which has apparently not been directly involved in the recent offensive-to limit their role on the Ethiopian side. Such support would also help make it possible to raise the Eritrea issue at the United Nations, which is responsible for the initial linkage of the former Italian colony to Ethiopia in a 1952 federation.

The prospect then, is for the war to continue without decision for the foreseeable future. The military map of Eritrea has been dramatically altered in recent months, and a further escalation of the conventional war may produce additional short-term setbacks for the guerrilla forces. But the dogged determination of the Eritreans to take to the hills and height indefinitely gives them the long-term edge.

Eritrea guerrillas boost attacks

The Boston Globe, January 14, 1979

Khartoum, Sudan

As preparations continue for Ethiopia's third offensive against Eritrean nationalists, the guerrillas are stepping up counterattacks of their own against the Soviet-backed military government.

The increase in guerrilla activity reflects a pronounced shift in the character of the 17-year Eritrean war for independence from Ethiopia, and it indicates the course the fighting is likely to follow in the coming year.

The Eritreans are fighting for the independence of the former Italian colony, which was annexed by Ethiopia in 1962 after a 10-year UN-sponsored federation.

A Khartoum spokesman for the Eritrean People's Liberation Front (EPLF) for example recently announced the destruction of 11 small Ethiopian military camps on the key highway linking the inland Eritrean capital with the Red Sea port of Massawa.

These bases had just been re-established by Ethiopia after a similar assault the previous week, according to the EPLF spokesman. The actions were the fourth in a series of attacks on this area since the government reoccupied the important highway a month ago.

Meanwhile, diverse countries and movements have set off a flurry of diplomatic and political maneuvers aimed at taking advantage of the altered military situation.

During the past seven months of sharply escalated fighting, Ethiopian forces reoccupied all the major towns and highways formerly held by the EPLF and a second smaller movement, the Eritrean Liberation Front (ELF).

EPLF leaders say Soviet combat personnel played key roles in the planning and execution of the sophisticated military campaign, which saw the heaviest fighting yet in the turbulent Horn of Africa.

The offensive pitted more than 150,000 Ethiopian troops and massive quantities of Soviet-supplied—and in some cases

Soviet operated armor, artillery, rockets and aircraft—against the lightly armed guerrillas.

The Ethiopian offensive has been only partially successful, however. Though government forces retook the large towns, they failed to reach the three smaller northern towns of Afabet, Nakfa and Karora or to penetrate the EPLF's heavily defended guerrilla base area in this region.

This will be the objective of the next phase of the campaign, for which Ethiopia is now mobilizing, and which is expected in the near future.

In a month-long tour of EPLF-controlled areas during the latest phase of the offensive, it was apparent the guerrillas remain militarily strong and enjoy widespread popular support. The manner in which they withdrew from the large towns left the government in possession of a strong of urban islands in a hostile sea.

No town was taken by military force. Instead, the EPLF fought outside the towns and pulled back after they were evacuated, systematically contracting their fixed base area into the rugged northern Sahel mountains and dispersing smaller military units into the countryside around towns and highways.

Within the guerrilla base area, the mechanized supply lines remain fully operational. Food, medicines, ammunition and infantry reinforcements were shuttled nightly back and forth from one battlefront to another. Heavy machinery and equipment removed from the urban centers and heavy arms taken in the fighting were trucked to the rear.

In the three-week series of major battles, the EPLF captured more than 25 Soviet-supplied T54 tanks and BTR60 armored cars, giving them more than 80 armored vehicles. This is more than Ethiopia itself possessed under the previous US-backed regime of Emperor Haile Selassie only four years ago, and it gives the guerrillas a better equipped army than most established African states.

Guerrilla losses appeared to be relatively high under a punishing bombardment by long-range artillery, rocket launchers and Russian-piloted MiG jet aircraft using napalm and cluster antipersonnel bombs, but the civilian evacuation of the towns also brought thousands of fresh volunteers that appeared sufficient to maintain the front's infantry strength at between 25,000 and 30,000 men and women.

Still, the EPLF clearly lacks the overall strength to defeat the Ethiopian army in multiple open field confrontations. Fighting mainly with captured arms, the guerrillas have no effective defense against the artillery, rockets and aircraft. Nor do they have enough ground forces to match those of Ethiopia, which continues to conscript peasants into its army by the tens of thousands.

In response, the Eritreans have begun a rapid transition to the guerrilla tactics that characterized the early years of the war, shifting the focus of battle and the nature of the fighting over a wider area.

EPLF leaders say the advantages of popular support and the ability to choose the time and place of battle will give them back the military initiative in what promises to be a long test of will for both sides.

Meanwhile, these new conditions have given an impetus to current meetings in Khartoum between leaders of the EPLF and ELF. A key objective of the talks will be to establish military coordination between the rival fronts.

The Sudan and other sympathetic Arab countries are also pressing the Eritreans to consolidate political forces under a single umbrella leadership that would include the right-wing Arab nationalist ELF-PLF, a splinter group led by former EPLF foreign mission chief

Osman Saleh Sabbe. But leaders of the two leftist fronts refuse to sit with him.

Against this backdrop, the Soviet Union appears to be stepping into a Vietnam-like quagmire of an unwinnable guerrilla war.

The prospect is for the war to continue without decision for the foreseeable future. The military map of Eritrea has been dramatically altered in recent months by the massive increase in Soviet aid to Ethiopia, and a further escalation may produce additional short-term setbacks for the guerrillas, but their dogged determination to take to the hills and fight indefinitely would appear to give them the long-term edge.

Eritrea: Radio Liberation

The Guardian (New York), January 31, 1979

Radio Liberation is now on the air in Eritrea.

The clandestine broadcasts by the Eritrean People's Liberation Front (EPLF) began in late December. They carry news, political education and cultural programs in the Tigrinya and Arabic languages to the people of Eritrea and their nearest neighbors within a 700-mile radius, according to Andemikael Kahsai, the EPLF's Rome spokesman.

The nightly 3-hour broadcasts will soon be extended to include Amharic language programs aimed at the Ethiopian army and people when two relay stations are set up, the EPLF leader added.

The launching of the radio station, based in the EPLF's liberated zone inside Eritrea, climaxes three years of often frustrating struggle to gain access to the air waves.

It also marks a major development in the EPLF's overall campaign to bring accurate information on the day-to-day national liberation war against Ethiopia's military government (the Derg) as well as its long-term revolutionary goals to the Eritrean people and their regional friends.

Importance of Radio

The vast majority of Eritreans, Ethiopians and other peoples in Africa's Horn are illiterate and get news from the radio. Soldiers and civilians alike, including poor peasants, often gather around a portable radio to catch programs in their language broadcast by West Germany, the U.S., and the Soviet Union and by Ethiopia, which maintains two full-time radio stations.

The story of how the EPLF engaged in the war of words epitomizes the general pattern of the struggle and it reflects the front's deep commitment to protracted self-reliant people's war.

The EPLF did a series of half-hour radio programs on alternating days from Sudan last year, but political difficulties caused the front to abandon this outlet.

The Sudan government in 1976 offered broadcast time to all anti-Derg forces. When the rightist ELF-PLF and the feudal Ethiopian Democratic Union (EDU) accepted, the EPLF declined the offer.

In October 1977 the two right-wing organizations were taken off the air, and the EPLF began producing and airing shows every other day along with the Eritrean Liberation Front (ELF).

These broadcasts were halted by the Sudan government during last July's OAU summit meeting in Khartoum and subsequent political differences and questions over the factual content of the ELF shows caused the EPLF to close down the Sudan-based broadcasts.

The ELF and the ELF-PLF meanwhile found air time on Iraq and Somalia's national radio, but the EPLF set out to provide its own facilities.

Late in 1977 the Association of Eritrean Students in North America (AESNA) launched a campaign to raise $50,000 to build-Radio Liberation.

However, after most of the money had been collected, AESNA in mid-1978 broke with the EPLF. This was done on the ultra-"left" grounds that the Popular Front, then battling the largest Ethiopian offensive in the 17-year history of the war, was "capitulating" to the Derg and its Soviet supporters.

Back at square one, the EPLF turned to its other expatriate organizations which unanimously rejected AENA's stand. Within three months Eritrean workers in Europe came up with the equipment and Radio Liberation was born in Eritrea.

Eritrea: London symposium

The Guardian (New York), February 7, 1979

London

"The Eritrean national liberation struggle lies in the midstream of Africa's revolutionary trend and perspective," declared Basil Davidson last month. The noted author made the remarks as he opened a 2-day symposium here on the controversial Eritrean war for independence from Ethiopia. The gathering was sponsored by the British charitable organization called War on Want.

Davidson drew on his long experience with the liberation struggles in former Portuguese colonies to outline the development of African nationalism, from its early anti-colonial stage to a modern revolutionary movement against neocolonialism.

Davidson called on people who have supported the struggles in Mozambique, Angola and Guinea-Bissau to give "close attention and active support" to the Eritrean liberation movement today.

"The case against Ethiopian possession of Eritrea was and is...qualitatively no different from the case against any other colonial enclosure," he said in his keynote address to hundreds of European progressives gathered in here for the meeting.

"If it was right for the European colonial powers to be thrust from their possessions overseas, then it is similarly right for the Ethiopians to be denied possession of Eritrea," Davidson continued in his hour-long address.

"With the growth of a movement of and struggle for national liberation, and above all the crystallization within that struggle of the Eritrean People's Liberation Front (EPLF), the people of Eritrea have begun to make their own history again," he said.

"To the very obvious limits and frustrations of the neocolonial model, the Eritreans through the EPLF reply with a revolutionary perspective: the building of social, cultural, political and economic structures 'from the base,' through which, by the processes of evoking and promoting mass participation in self-rule, the people of Eritrea....take power within their own hands and govern themselves."

Other speakers on the program presented papers on Eritrean history, the emergence of the national liberation movement, the social revolution under the EPLF and superpower intervention in the 17-year struggle.

Among the panelists were French author Gerard Challiand,

Belgian sociologist Francois Houtart, EPLF Central Committee member Amdemikael Kahsai and this reporter.

Challiand pointed out that the EPLF's gradual encirclement and capture of Eritrean towns and cities was without military parallel in the history of African liberation struggles. He said that the EPLF's development of liberated areas inside Eritrea was also unique. Most African liberation struggles operate mainly from bases in neighboring countries.

The Belgian Marxist, Francois Hourtart, who has written mainly about the struggles in Southeast Asia and in Angola till now, went on to analyze the impact of successive colonialisms on Eritrean society. He also traced the EPLF's social practice in advancing the class struggle within the context of the war with Ethiopia and the internal struggle with reaction.

"We cannot forget that the task of the liberation movement has to be accomplished under very adverse conditions: war with Ethiopia, difficulties with the divisions in the liberation struggle (not without relations with the class structure), intervention of the USSR on the battlefield, etc." he said.

A recurrent theme throughout the conference was the need to begin the analysis of the Eritrean question with an examination of national and social struggle within Eritrea, rather than with external alignments.

At the same time, many of the speakers expressed the view that the Soviet Union and Cuba should be criticized, especially by their international friends, for their opposition to the Eritreans.

This reporter, just back from the front lines in Eritrea, said that Cuba appeared to be playing a less direct role in military opposition to the EPLF than the Soviet Union which, he said, was actively and directly involved in the latest Ethiopian offensive against the EPLF.

EPLF leader Amdemikael Kahsai closed the conference with a reaffirmation of the EPLF's commitment to self-reliant, protracted people's war. This, he said, was the key to eventual victory in both the military and political struggles, regardless of the extent of foreign intervention on the Ethiopian side.

Amdemikael said that the EPLF was winning a hearing from countries such as Mozambique, Tanzania, Guinea-Bissau and Algeria which had recently invited EPLF delegations to present their views. They are also presenting their views to liberation movements such as Polisario and the major Palestinian fronts and to many progressive parties and organizations in Europe.

For further information or copies of the papers presented at the symposium, contact War on Want, 467 Caledonian Road, London, England.

EPLF thwarts latest Ethiopia attack

The Guardian (New York), February 14, 1979

An estimated 90 Ethiopian soldiers were killed and 1,000 wounded last week in five days of fierce fighting around the northern bases of the Eritrean People's Liberation Front (EPLF). The Ethiopian assault was finally broken and government forces were driven back to the coastal plains, an EPLF spokesman said. The EPLF claims it has destroyed four Ethiopian tanks and five armored personnel carriers in the process.

The Ethiopian military regime, known as the Derg. Launched a major offensive against EPLF forts last Nov. 18. More than 45,000 troops backed up by tanks, jet fighters and helicopters attacked the liberated areas of Eritrea, including the city of Keren. As a result, the EPLF announced a tactical retreat into its mountain stronghold, where it began to prepare for a prolonged guerrilla struggle.

Meanwhile, in Khartoum, Sudan, leaders of the PLF and the smaller Eritrean Liberation Front (ELF) last week announced final agreement on a program to achieve greater military and political unity between the two fronts.

The joint declaration signed by EPLF and ELF criticized the failure to realize the goals of a similar agreement drafted in October 1977. The declaration went on to outline concrete procedures for bringing the two rival organizations together in the military field and for struggling out their political differences.

"We are confident that this time it will work," the EPLF spokesmen said.

The new agreement calls for a single national military strategy, deploying mixed units under a single centralized command against the Ethiopians. It also proposes regular political seminars and an ongoing program of political education within the two organizations, in order to resolve the still substantial differences in political line that divide them.

EPLF-ELF cooperation

In separate points, the agreement goes on to call for one single liberated base area inside Eritrea, joint bureaus in related social, political and economic fields and the establishment of a joint monthly organ to be known as "Unity."

A joint committee is to be assigned the task of preparing for a full merger through a national congress of both fronts.

The so-called "third force," headed by Arab nationalist Osman Saleh Sabbe, is again condemned in the joint declaration for its efforts to divide the Eritrean people.

The agreement renews the demand that Sabbe's rightist Eritrean Liberation Front Popular Liberation Forces (ELF-PLF) dissolve itself and cease its disruptive actions against the other two fronts.

Sabbe's group now has no military forces inside Eritrea but it retains the backing of Western powers and of rightist regimes in the region who oppose the leftist EPLF's domination of the Eritrean independence movement.

Despite the Sabbe force's insignificance inside Eritrea, its existence continues to have a major impact on the regional and international scene.

The EPLF points to the ELF-PLF as evidence that U.S. imperialism and internal reactionary forces are the primary enemies of the Eritrean revolution. The enemies of the EPLF use Sabbe's presence to portray the Eritrean struggle as a reactionary one directed against the self-proclaimed "socialist" revolution in Ethiopia.

According to EPLF spokesperson, an undisclosed number of Soviet military advisers landed with a mechanized force of 12,000 Ethiopian troops at the Red Sea port of Marsa Teklai early last week, to launch an attack aimed at cutting EPLF supply lines into neighboring Sudan.

An EPLF representative in Khartoum also said that 1,000 Cuban military personnel withdrew from the Eritrean capital of Asmara last month, and that Cubans were not involved in the current round of fighting, which broke out in January. He added, however, that Cuba's political position on the Eritrean war does not appear to have changed, and that Cuba still supports the Ethiopian Derg. He also charged that Cuban personnel still give the Ethiopians rearguard support.

Section 4

Behind the Lines
1979-1982

Prologue

In the aftermath of the Soviet-backed Ethiopian offensives in 1978 and early 1979, Addis Ababa controlled all the significant Eritrean towns but Nakfa, a small provincial capital in the Sahel mountains. Repeated Ethiopian aerial and artillery bombardments coupled with massive but unsuccessful infantry assaults almost completely emptied the community of civilians, yet government forces were unable to break through Eritrean defenses no matter what they threw into the effort. Thus, Nakfa became synonymous with the frontlines in the conventional conflict for the next decade (though large battles were fought elsewhere) and remained a potent symbol of Eritrean resistance throughout the rest of the long war.

North of Nakfa lay the EPLF's sprawling Sahel base, with its warren of underground workshops, hospitals, schools, training centers, arms depots, garages, repair shops, camps for displaced-people and POWs, and much more. These installations were supplied from Sudan and linked together by a network of mountain roads built by the guerrillas during the siege. Holding such an enclave allowed the EPLF to support its forces elsewhere in Eritrea without leaving itself open to external manipulation — no small achievement in this contentious region whose location on the fringes of the Middle East attracted an array of powerful interests eager to manipulate the movement for their own ends. It also gave the front the capacity to act as an independent economic, social, political and cultural force inside Eritrea and in the Eritrean diaspora.

Despite the withdrawal of its conventional forces, the EPLF retained substantial strength in the central Eritrean highlands and along the Red Sea coast, where it had re-infiltrated mobile military and political units, set up caches of arms and other supplies, and re-established social services for the civilian population. In fact, by mid-1979 the front operated in a wider geographical area of Eritrea than ever before due to the shrinkage of the rival ELF, though it did so at a lower level of organization than had been the case during the previous two years due both to the security situation and to a shortage of cadres.

Little of this was visible to (or acknowledged by) the outside world, however. Most commentators wrote off the Eritrea war as done but for the clean-up. The nationalists might fight on as itinerant guerrillas but the fall of Keren marked the end of their capacity to challenge the regime, wrote *New York Times* reporter Michael Kaufman, echoing the widely-held view that history had left the Eritreans behind.[1] Nor was this position confined to the mainstream. Much of the left, particularly that identified with the Soviet camp or for other reasons sympathetic to Ethiopia, shared Kaufman's assessment. In *The Ethiopian Revolution*, authors Fred Halliday and Maxine Molyneux argued: "[T]he choice facing the Eritreans in the period after 1978 was not whether to exercise the right to secession but whether to continue to fight the Ethiopians indefinitely, with no realistic expectation of victory, or to negotiate for whatever measure of autonomy the PMAC [the derg] was willing to concede."[2]

For my part, I was confident that the nationalist movement would rebound, based upon the way the EPLF organized its strategic retreat, the depth and breadth of its popular support, and the clarity of its long-range strategy. But, as a journalist, the question for me was how to make that case? The challenge was all the more vexing because the EPLF was coming under attack from among its own doubting members and erstwhile supporters.

———

In the Eritrean community and the mostly left-wing political circles in which it moved, ideologically-driven perceptions of what was happening in the field grew steadily more divorced from reality, as I discovered as soon as I left Eritrea in early 1979. I recall one public presentation I gave in Delft where representatives of two Dutch communist parties — one pro-Soviet, the other pro-Chinese — shouted slogans at one another as I tried unsuccessfully to interject accounts of what I had observed on the ground. It was no use — neither cared to listen. But this was child's play — truly — compared to the mindless infighting I encountered when I got to the United States.

In the summer of 1978, during the first of the EPLF's carefully executed withdrawals, an extreme 'left' clique within the American-based Eritrean community — heavily influenced by a pro-Albanian

———
[1] Michael Kaufman, "Eritrean Defeat Portends Revival of Guerrilla War, *The New York Times*, Dec. 1, 1978.
[2] Fred Halliday and Maxine Molyneux, *The Ethiopian Revolution* (London: Verso, 1981), p. 192.

communist sect in the U.S. and Canada — engineered a split with the liberation movement over its stance toward the Soviet Union, which the group described as a "rising imperialist power."

Terming the EPLF "capitulationist" because it declined to characterize the Soviets as a greater global danger to the international proletariat than the U.S., the zealots set out to convince Eritreans in the diaspora that the front was retreating out of ideological weakness, not military choice. Many Eritreans — horrified by what they were seeing in their country and misled by a welter of false rumors — believed the lies they were fed or were too cowed to contest them. The formal break with the front occurred at an August meeting of EPLF mass organizations. By the time I arrived in the States six months later, the community was so deeply divided that family members were not speaking to one another, and there were pitched battles at public forums.

I had a small cadre of bodyguards when I gave a reportback on the war at the Roxbury Community College in Boston, and a fight ensued in the hallway as anti-EPLF Eritreans sought to disrupt the presentation (see *Guardian*, Feb. 28). A few weeks later in Washington the police were called to a talk I gave, and the event collapsed. It was brother-against-brother, sister-against-sister — the worst communal conflict I had ever seen in what had always been a highly volatile social group — and the worst I would see until political repression in Asmara in 2001 triggered another bitter schism.

However, for all the passion and cynical manipulation that attended the 1978 rupture, the extremist faction began to collapse within months of its launch. Individuals dropped out of the captured student association (the largest Eritrean organization in the U.S. and the main vehicle for support to EPLF), as word filtered back of what had really happened in Eritrea. Then whole chapters folded, and a new organization — less politicized but eager to rebuild a relationship with EPLF — emerged. Finally, a key organizer of the split took his own life, signaling the death throes of the renegade 'leftist' sect.

Meanwhile, the EPLF also came under attack from the segment of the international left identified with the Soviet camp, and I quickly got swept up in that war of words, too. When I got back to the U.S. in February 1979, I was confronted with an eleven-part series of pro-Ethiopia articles by veteran Australian journalist Wilfred Burchett that was running in *The Guardian*. Burchett was a long-time contributor to the paper; his reporting from Vietnam had turned him into a legend on the left. Now he was glorifying the derg, and *The*

Guardian felt bound to publish his polemics based upon their historical relationship with him. I, in turn, was bound to reply (and was urged to do so by Guardian editors). Once settled in, I wrote my own polemical series [see *Guardian*, Feb. 21 – March 21].

Burchett was one of many left organizations and individuals who broke with the EPLF over the altered geopolitical alignment. Pro-Soviet Palestinian parties that had been among Eritrea's most ardent supporters suddenly grew cold, if not overtly hostile. The African National Congress opened offices in Addis and condemned the Eritreans, as did the ANC's strategic partner, the South African Communist Party. Even the Polasario Front in the contested Western Sahara — coming from a similar circumstance (a former European colony claimed by an African power as the world stood by) — sidled away from their former friends to curry favor with the Soviets.

There were hard lessons to digest here regarding the tension between principle and self-interest, internationalism and nationalism — lessons that cried out for serious study and reflection. But as a journalist, my main immediate challenge was to force those doing the debating to acknowledge the reality on the ground and to factor that into their arguments. I knew that my most effective contribution to this war of words was not counter-polemics, however satisfying they feel at the time, but rather frontline journalism. I decided to go back to document life in the contested areas and the EPLF's powerful continuing presence there.

———

Through the spring I talked incessantly with friends and comrades about this challenge — how to do it, how to finance it, and, above all, where to publish the results. One person with whom I discussed it, a freelance photographer long interested in the Eritrean struggle, proposed that we team up on an assignment for a major magazine. He offered to scout the prospects if I would draft the proposal. I did so, and he wangled a contract with the U.S. edition of the high-gloss European magazine *GEO* for a trip in June and July, all expenses paid.

I spent much of that winter and spring in New York preparing myself for the project. Knowing the physical rigors that faced me, I stopped smoking, ran several miles each morning, and roller-skated around and around Central Park in the afternoons. I volunteered at *The Guardian* again, too, while cultivating contacts at *Time* magazine and at the agency now carrying my photographs, Gamma-Liaison. And I worked on my journalistic skills.

In early June I flew to Khartoum via Beirut, where I stopped briefly to meet members of the EPLF's foreign office. The Lebanese capital teemed with revolutionaries from nearly every imaginable political tendency. It was a headquarters for some groups, a branch for others — and a global arms bazaar for all.

This was my gateway to the byzantine world of Middle East politics, to which I returned in June 1982 after Israel's invasion of Lebanon. On this, my first visit, I made contacts with several social and political organizations on the Palestinian and Lebanese left, but the 1979 stopover was mainly to gauge the extent of the EPLF's political isolation from its former friends and allies in the wake of the Soviet intervention in the Horn. I didn't write about what I saw of Lebanon until much later.[3]

Entering Eritrea from Sudan entailed the usual obstacles and delays with security officials and local transport. But the real hurdles surfaced once the photographer and I were inside. Despite extensive efforts to set up the trek in advance with EPLF contacts outside, there was no apparent acceptance of the plan in the field. I say "apparent" because it was, typically, very difficult to ascertain what decisions had or had not been taken and by whom.

My colleague and I were stranded in a small tent in the base camp for two weeks, while we pleaded with our handlers for permission to start our trip — or at least to meet with someone who had the authority to send us on our way. In the meantime, we toured the hidden workshops, social service centers, repair facilities, POW camps and other quite remarkable but by now over-reported guerrilla institutions there. This was the proverbial cook's tour that most visiting journalists made, though the numbers of such visitors were dwindling as the Eritrea war drifted into obscurity.

But in the course of this limited political sightseeing, with daytime temperatures in the volcanic hills hovering between 115 and 120°F, it came clear that my partner — a heavy smoker out of his element in the East African bush — was just not up to the rigors of the desert climate. The unrelenting heat and dust undid him. After a week or so, he and I determined that walking hundreds of miles behind guerrilla lines under these conditions was just not on for him, and he packed his equipment to return home.

---

[3] See Chapter 3, "Palestine: Symbols Before Substance," in my book *Rethinking Revolution* for an account of my 1979 tour of Palestinian refugee camps.

When he left, he gave me more than fifty rolls of Kodachrome slide film in the hope that we might salvage something from the project, which I was still determined to carry through on my own. By now I had acquired a pair of second-hand Nikon cameras, a 35mm wide-angle lens, and an 80-200mm zoom. I was no more an accomplished photographer than I was a trained journalist — but I was learning on the fly, with help from colleagues in the field and through my own study. This, however, was the first time I had the resources — the film and prepaid processing — to really experiment.

Perhaps these early weeks were a conscious EPLF test of our stamina, perhaps not. I never knew. But as the days passed and as my own deadline for departure loomed — I was committed to take my children for the last half of the summer — I grew desperate to get started. One day I came across a friend traveling about the base camp in his Land Cruiser and slipped him a note to Isaias, begging for a meeting to discuss the project before I, too, was forced to abandon it. A day later I received a summons, met Isaias, and got the okay. The following night, I set out on foot toward Asmara with my frequent guide and translator, Goitom Asgadom.

This was both my most difficult and my most rewarding journey into Eritrea, not only for the opportunity to assess the strengths and weaknesses of the combatants in this new period but for the insights it gave me into the people behind the struggle and their unshakable will to be free. I traveled where no journalist had gone, interviewed people utterly without guile or pretension on their life experiences and their views of the conflict, and witnessed the relations between fighter and civilian up close and personal in ways I never had before and have not done since.

There were amusing, if disconcerting, moments when young children shrieked at the sight of this pale-faced foreigner, wondering if I were an apparition, or when angry peasants approached with threatening countenances until reassured that I was not after all a captured Russian fighter pilot. There were frightening ones, too, as when a pair of Ethiopian MiG-21s streaked out of nowhere to strafe the river valley through which we were walking, or when a flash flood nearly washed us away. And again when we arrived back at Nakfa the very day the Ethiopians launched the fifth round of their offensive. All of this, of course, was material for the stories I would write afterward.

In the event, there was no *GEO* article — my photographs were just not up to their standards — but I on-passed my pix and a story to *Time*, which indicated interest in coverage. They edited, fact-checked and rewrote the article, laid out a page of photos, and had the piece ready to go to the printer on Friday, deadline day, when the news came in that President Jimmy Carter had launched an abortive mission to Iran to free U.S. hostages. Carter's failure crowded me — and Eritrea — out of the magazine, and in the peculiar logic of the American media, the entire experience immediately became old news. However, stories and photographs from the trek appeared in the *Time*-owned *Washington Star* and in numerous other daily newspapers in North America and Europe (some of which are reproduced here) and a full year later in *The Boston Globe Magazine*.

I also carried a small Sony cassette recorder with me on this trek and collected audio "actuality," spontaneous narratives of my experiences, and bits of scripted commentary. The BBC edited this into my third thirty-minute radio documentary, "Behind the Lines in Eritrea," which aired on August 8. The Australian Broadcasting Company then re-cut it with new studio interviews for a forty-five-minute program, "A Generation Born to War," that aired six days later.

———

Money and time were always issues for me. Each trip to Eritrea was a challenge, and there were only so many *GEO*s to cover costs. I had long-term child-care responsibilities, too, which sharply restricted my travel options and made it impossible to remain in place as a working journalist. As a result, I had to hustle each time to underwrite the venture and to fit it into my domestic schedule. This got harder and harder as the regional political situation impinged upon me, as my domestic obligations became more complicated, and as the news industry itself changed.

My next travel opportunity came in March 1980, when the Middle East Research and Information Project, publishers of a monthly magazine called *MERIP: Middle East Report* with which I was developing a growing affinity, got an all-expenses-paid invitation to a conference on Palestinian issues in Baghdad. I had become the group's contributing editor for the Horn, which enjoyed occasional coverage, and I was given one of the three slots. The conference coincided with my children's spring break, so I had two weeks to travel. I used it to piggyback a stop in Khartoum.

Once there, I again ran into difficulty with Sudanese security officials, but this time they were adamant. There would be no permission to go to Eritrea. Ethiopia was putting strong pressure on them to curtail media access to the war zone, and, with their internal political landscape heating up, they were not going tangle with their neighbor over this issue.

Neither I nor the EPLF was ready to accept this information blockade, however, so, with precious little time, I flew to Port Sudan under another name. Once there, I was bundled into the back of an EPLF Land Rover and disguised as a shivering malaria victim. Driving at night, we skirted the police posts along the coast and threaded our way across the border to the base area, where I made another quick round of the high spots, including the frontlines at Nakfa. I returned much the same way, quickly slipped out of Khartoum, and filed a series of features for Reuters, the BBC and several newspapers under the penname John Currie.

This did not fool anyone for very long, and I paid dearly for the ruse later. Nevertheless, it kept Eritrea in the news and demonstrated again that this was a political movement that would not go away.

———

I came back to Eritrea once more in 1980 as a freelancer. This time, I had an assignment to assess the refugee situation for the quarterly *Horn of Africa Journal*, for which I had written several topical pieces on Eritrea. The editors planned to run a special issue on the regional humanitarian crisis with articles on Kenya, Somalia, Djibouti, Ethiopia, Eritrea and Sudan. They tapped me to put it together and funded my travel.

The central premise was that the multiplying conflicts within Ethiopia — exacerbated by superpower intervention — were steadily destabilizing the region's social structures and economies. A catastrophe was on the horizon if remedial measures were not taken soon, starting with a stepped-up aid effort that directly involved the beneficiaries themselves. However, to succeed, these measures had also to include an international effort to promote a durable peace, without which no amount of aid, however well-meant, could resolve the crisis. I was asked to document this.

I flew to Somalia in June, after picking up agreements to file for *The Christian Science Monitor* and *The Irish Times*. Once there, I attended an International Somali Studies Conference in Mogadishu — presenting a paper on the EPLF's strategy for socio-economic and political transformation as experienced in the village of Zagur[4] — before touring refugee camps in both the south and the north and crossing into Ethiopia's still contested Ogaden region with the

---

[4] This paper, not included here, became the basis for a chapter on the EPLF's rural organizing strategy in my book, *Against All Odds*.

Western Somali Liberation Front. [Stories from this trip are not included in this collection.] I arrived in Khartoum via Djibouti in late July where I rendezvoused with an activist from Oakland, California — Chappell Hayes — with whom I planned to travel into the field.

We had trouble with Sudan security, but we managed to get in legally, in part due to the humanitarian nature of my assignment, and we had a successful, if, for me, somewhat prosaic, tour of the base and the Nakfa frontlines. I did another series of features for my main print outlets, this time under the penname James Donaghue in an effort to placate Sudanese officials who feared a backlash from Ethiopia over the appearance of my byline. I also recorded a tape-diary of the trip for another thirty-minute BBC documentary, "Stalemate," that ran on September 5, and I did several long news reports and features for the World and Africa Services [none of which appear in this collection].

The main output from this trip was the *HOAJ* special issue "Six Million Dispossessed in the Horn: A White Paper."[5] While in Sudan, I developed a working relationship with three other writers, all of whom were involved with humanitarian aid agencies there — John Bennett, Gayle Smith, and Kirsty Wright — and each drafted major sections for the project, which I edited, along with the sections I wrote myself. Because the others were at risk for their ongoing work if published under their own names and because I, too, was under pressure from Sudanese authorities, we put the publication out under the penname of Susan Santini.[6]

During this time, media interest in the Eritrea story steadily diminished, not only due to the political considerations I've already cited but because the story seemed not to vary. Though huge battles took place in the early 1980s that involved more than 100,000 troops on both sides and produced casualties of as many as 3,000-5,000 in a single encounter, little changed in the positions of the two sides or in the likelihood of a final resolution. For an international media hungry for spectacle or for the digestible sound bite, there was little to report, unless one happened into Eritrea in the midst of a major battle and if the EPLF, ever wary of putting visitors at risk, would allow a journalist to get close enough to do a combat story. As one result,

---

[5] "Six Million Dispossessed in the Horn: A White Paper," Special issue, *Horn of Africa Journal*, vol. 4, no. 1, 1981.
[6] For those seeking arcane significance in the name, let me add that Gayle Smith chose it on a whim after seeing the film "The Great Santini."

for its last thirteen years the conflict produced no compelling first-person war stories until the combatants themselves began to write them after the shooting stopped.[7]

Throughout the 1980s, apart from a spurt of famine-related coverage in the middle of the decade, it became *de rigueur* for major papers and broadcast outlets in Europe and, occasionally, in North America, Australia and Japan to send a reporter to do the well-trod tour of the base area, visit the Nakfa trenches, and report that the Eritrean national movement was alive and well with remarkable creativity and deep-rooted popular support but little prospect of success. *The New York Times*, for example, sent a reporter to the field only once (in 1988).

For those who followed it, Eritrea became the sort of story that one checked in on now and then but did not cover regularly. For the rest, it was a sideshow. Under these circumstances, I became more and more hard-pressed to generate interest in future files, even though I was paying my own travel expenses. And it got even more difficult as economic considerations led several of the papers for which I was stringing to slash their budgets for freelance writing. (*La Repubblica* stopped taking any.)

This was the backdrop for the long-building confrontation I had with Sudanese authorities upon my return to Khartoum that autumn.

———

I flew home at the end of August 1980 expecting to take charge of my daughters for the coming school year only to find that my alternating custody agreement – unusual enough to start with but made more and more difficult by my lengthy absences — had finally broken down. One of the children wanted to stay with her Mom and the other was swept up in the change-of-plans, leaving me without any childcare duties for the fall. Henceforth, I was to be a part-time Dad.

In late September, cut loose from the tenuous moorings I had maintained at home and in a state of emotional turmoil over these changes, I returned to Khartoum. Once again I charged the airfare to my credit card, planning to pay as I wrote. I also hastily put together arrangements to file news stories for the BBC, Reuters, and the New York-based *Guardian* and to write features for a handful of newspapers whose interest was piqued by the threat of civil war in the nationalist movement.

---

[7] See, for example, Alemseged Tesfai's graphic personal account of life on the frontlines, *Two Weeks in the Trenches* (Trenton, NJ: Red Sea Press, 2002).

But I had not been in the Sudan capital more than six or seven weeks when I was accosted on the sidewalk by a member of the security forces who politely apologized for what he was about to do — and then announced that I had twenty-four hours to leave the country. I had just been PNG'd [designated *persona non grata*].

Those twenty-four hours stretched to seventy-two, as I filed stories on my ouster, solicited protests from around the world, threatened to publish exposés on Sudan, and leaned on everyone to whom I had access to reverse the order — all to no avail. My immediate dilemma was that I could not get through to the security official who had issued the directive, as he remained stubbornly unavailable behind the wall of barbed wire that ringed his compound. However, the larger problem was that regional politics and my many ruses had finally caught up with me.

In the end, I did penetrate the official's defenses and secure an agreement to stay in Sudan so long as I did not write under my own name — this was to assuage Ethiopia's Mengistu Haile Mariam, who had leaned on Sudanese president Jaafar el-Nimeiri to oust me — and so long as I remained within the confines of Khartoum.[8]

I hung about for another five months, living in a small house on the Nile with fellow writer and activist Gayle Smith — whom I married that October early in a stormy relationship that ended in less than four years — and filing stories on the Eritrean civil war, the EPLF's peace initiative, and other developments seen and analyzed from a distance. Gayle hand-carried my articles to the Sudan News Agency (SUNA) and filed them under her name — the sixth name I wrote under (including my own) during the Eritrea war. But the newly imposed constraints on my travel ended my ability to function as a frontline correspondent.

Blocked from going to the field, I decided to run a series of seminars on the nuts and bolts of journalism to enable my comrades to improve their own efforts to disseminate information. The workshops took place in January and February 1981. Those attending included fighters from the Tigray People's Liberation Front and the Oromo Liberation Front and branch representatives of the relief organizations associated with these Ethiopian resistance movements. There were even a few Europeans and Americans active in solidarity work and eager to pick up reporting skills. To my enduring disappointment, however, and for reasons never made explicit — but

---

[8] For a fuller elaboration of this experience, see Chapter 12, "The Dispossessed," in my book *Against All Odds*.

which undoubtedly sprang from their go-it-alone approach to all such undertakings — no Eritreans participated.[9]

Over two months, those who did show up studied the basic news story, the news analysis, and the news feature. We took information on their struggles, some of which had been relayed over great distances and lengthy intervals, and crafted it into press releases that were organized in a format that allowed a reporter to simply add attributions and file them as news. My "students" then handed the releases to local wire-service stringers, and we watched as they were picked up and printed by regional newspapers throughout East Africa and the Middle East. (I also filed a few of these stories for *The Guardian*, AP and elsewhere [under Gayle Smith's byline] — see the articles in late February 1981 in this section for examples.)

If nothing else, we demonstrated that it was possible to get news of the struggles into the international press if we played the information game by its rules. The EPLF was not willing to do so.

Convinced that I could do little to affect the media strategy of my Eritrean comrades, unable to overturn the embargo on my movement, and anxious to repair the rupture within my family, I finally packed up in March and went home, not knowing when (or if) I would be allowed to return.

Once out, I filed several pieces on the situation in Eritrea. I also wrote a series of critical stories on Sudan (not included here), which I had long held back from doing to avoid precisely what had just happened — my expulsion. At first I used the penname Susan Santini, but I soon switched to my own as it seemed likely to make little difference. As the months wore on, I wrote less and less often as I focused instead on repairing my damaged family relations and on writing my long-delayed book on the liberation struggle.

---

[9] See my paper "Eritrea and the International Media" presented at a conference in Asmara in February 2001 and reproduced in Section 8 of this collection for a fuller elaboration of this failure and of the wider issue of Eritrea's chronic difficulties with the media.

Eritrea and Self-Determination

The Guardian (New York), February 21, 1979

Nearly a year ago, the Guardian published a series of articles supporting the struggle of the Eritrean people for liberation from Ethiopia and questioning whether the Ethiopian military leadership was actually pursuing a socialist course. These articles were preceded and followed by correspondent Dan Connell's reports from the Eritrean battle zone. Beginning in November, the Guardian published an 11-part series by staff correspondent Wilfred Burchett. These articles judged the Ethiopian government to be socialist and were critical of the Eritrean liberation struggle. Following is the first of several articles by Connell replying to Burchett.

Eritrea's more than 17-year struggle for national independence from Ethiopia is one of the most complex political questions facing the international progressive movement today.

Less than a decade ago the already protracted Eritrean war was widely recognized as a just, popular and revolutionary struggle for national liberation. As far back as the early 1950s, when Eritrea was first linked to Ethiopia under a UN federation, the Soviet Union loudly proclaimed the former Italian colony's right to independence.

Once the war started in the early 1960s, Algeria, Cuba, South Yemen and China were among many progressive states that actively trained and aided the Eritrean guerrillas while the U.S. and Israel backed the Ethiopian government of Haile Selassie.

Then came the 1974 military coup against Selassie and two years later the whirlwind of international realignments in the strategic Horn of Africa, which found the USSR backing Ethiopia's new self-proclaimed "socialist" government against the Eritreans. South Yemeni troops entered the war late in 1977 on Ethiopia's side; Cuban forces followed in 1978, albeit in a less direct form of involvement, advising and assisting Ethiopian forces but not joining the frontline battles.

Suddenly, the Eritrean struggle became, to its former friends, a "reactionary secessionist" movement against "revolutionary, socialist" Ethiopia.

Dilemma For Left

Many honest revolutionaries and progressives reject the new characterization of the Eritreans, but they are also troubled by the choice forced upon them between what they perceive as two socialist-oriented parties warring with each other while imperialist forces maneuver to take advantage of the situation.

Some ask, should Eritrean nationalism, even if just and legitimate, now be subordinated to larger class and international interests? Should Eritrea accept Ethiopian sovereignty and the political leadership of the Derg (as the Addis Ababa military regime is called) in order to present a solid front against imperialism? And if the Eritreans refuse, does this make them objective allies of imperialism?

The answer, in the opinion of this writer, who has spent much time with Eritrean liberation forces over the past few years, is a resounding no. But the question itself is misleading and starts the debate off on a wrong track.

Though national self-determination is an uncompromisable goal of the Eritrean struggle, it is not the end or sole objective. The Eritrean struggle is a deep-rooted, mass-based revolution whose internal aim is to transform Eritrean society into one free from oppression and exploitation. Externally, it is an integral part of the world revolutionary movement, and its victory will constitute a major blow to imperialism.

The Eritrean People's Liberation Front (EPLF) is the vanguard of the movement and without qualification the dominant political and military force in Eritrea. Through nationalists, they are also deep-going internationalists.

Despite carrot-and-stick offers from enemies and potential backers of all political stripes, the EPLF has consistently refused to compromise its political principles to either achieve a premature military victory or end the fighting short of its final objectives.

In the long term, EPLF leaders say they will consider linking up with any country (Ethiopia) if it is in the interests of peace, freedom and social progress. They are not averse to federations, confederations or full mergers, so long as they are based upon revolutionary principles that safeguard the interests of the workers and oppressed peoples involved and so long as they proceed voluntarily from initiatives taken by the people themselves on the basis of full recognition of each other's sovereignty.

This is clearly not the case in the present relation between Ethiopia's ruling Derg and the EPLF, between the Ethiopian and Eritrean peoples-so the EPLF fights on.

The EPLF, in my view, is politically and militarily the most highly developed liberation movement in Africa, perhaps in the world. To oppose the EPLF, to try to crush it by military force, is to set back the world revolutionary movement and to objectively aid the forces of imperialism and reaction.

The character of the Ethiopian regime or its backers is not the issue, though it is certainly open to serious question. The key questions are whether or not Eritrea has a legitimate historical right to national self-determination and whether or not the EPLF is a genuine revolutionary movement.

Derg supporters recognize this. Though they raise other questions for tactical reasons-to neutralize past or prospective supporters of the EPLF-their main blows are aimed at discrediting Eritrea's demands for self-determination and the EPLF's political credentials.

Wilfred Burchett has laid out the Ethiopian argument in his lengthy Guardian series perhaps as well as could be done based upon a single, short visit to the Ethiopian capital and access to a wealth of background material.

Yet his case is riddled with inaccuracies, laced with unsupported innuendo and tied together with wishful thinking rather than scientific analysis that raises more questions than it answers.

On the one hand we are asked to believe that the Ethiopian revolution is "unique" because by a "political miracle" revolutionary forces arose inside a feudal U.S.-and Israeli-trained army to lead the Ethiopian people to socialism without a party while a spontaneous popular civilian movement was unable to produce any legitimate Marxist-Leninists.

At the same time, Burchett suggests, a popular revolutionary movement in Eritrea after 14 years of war (through 1975) against feudalism, colonialism, Zionism and U.S. imperialism overnight turned reactionary by allegedly executing its progressive leaders and compromising with rightist forces.

To begin with, Burchett's sources are weak and open to doubt. The opening article is a simple but incomplete chronology of events. Subsequent articles on the situation in Ethiopia are based almost entirely on government documents and official interviews rather than extensive on-site investigation. The two principal exceptions are the article on the Derg's left opposition-which rests upon interviews with a handful of former EPRP members whose lives depend on their answers-and the dispatch on Derg chairman Mengistu Haile Mariam, which is a paraphrase of Cuban author Raoul Valdes Vivo's book, "Ethiopia: The Unknown Revolution."

His 4-part treatment of Eritrea is similarly based on secondary sources, but it completely ignores the extensive firsthand reports of visitors to Eritrea and all concrete questions relating to the social practice of the EPLF. Instead, he reduces the life and death struggle of 3.5 million people to a political abstraction.

In Burchett's first article (Nov. 15), he outlines key events of the upheaval in Ethiopia, concluding that it was "during those fateful first two years when fundamental policies were hammered out."

Burchett begins by showing that a massive upsurge by peasants, workers, students and soldiers created a revolutionary situation, but in the ensuing chronology we soon lose track of mass actions in a list of high-sounding proclamations issued by the junta which stepped in to seize power in September 1974.

What role did the civilian opposition to Haile Selassie play during this time and what were the actions of the new military government toward the widespread and deep-rooted popular movement?

A superficial reading of these proclamations does, as Burchett says, suggest an impressive tempo of events, but a closer look reveals a sharp inconsistency within the analysis that he brings to them.

Burchett himself points out in his second article that land reform was a primary demand of the student left from the early 1960s. What happened to the student left? It appears in article three as ultra "left" opposition to the Derg.

The April 20, 1976, Program of the National Democratic Revolution and the May 16, 1976, 9-point proposal for peace in Eritrea are cited by Burchett as evidence of the revolutionary character of the new government. These were both drafted by the civilian Me'isone party. What happened to it? It, too, reappears in article three as ultra-"left" opposition to the military rulers.

To Burchett's credit, he observes several times that the base was ahead of the leadership, but if that is so how then are we to interpret the consistently repressive actions taken by the military against the civilian left?

It is also significant that Burchett entirely ignores the Eritrean revolution in his initial chronology of factors in pushing the Ethiopian upheaval to the left even though half of Haile Selassie's imperial army was engaged in trying to suppress it at the time of the emperor's fall.

It is only in his last article that he touches on this point when he observes, "The 1974 overthrow of the Haile Selassie regime did not lead to the hoped-for resolution of the Eritrean problem."

However, what he doesn't say is that the only moves toward peace from the Ethiopian side were taken by Gen. Andom Aman, briefly the chairman of the Derg, who was executed in November

1974 as a counterrevolutionary. Nor does he mention the stepped-up repression in Eritrea in December that included a series of piano-wire stranglings of young people suspected of sympathizing with the independence movement or the new government's military offensive launched in Eritrea the following January.

Peasant Army

The Derg's actions toward Eritrea, in contrast to its pronouncements, are a constant thread through these years that exposes its true nature. While Me'isone was putting forward its 9-point Eritrea plan, the Derg was in the midst of launching its first major peasant army against the Eritrean fronts. Known as the "Wodezemach," this campaign actually opened during the same month that the Me'isone plan was published.

Over a year later, Col. Atnafu Abate, the Derg's second in command made a fact-finding trip to Eritrea only to return with the recommendation that a peaceful rather than a military solution be found. The result? In November 1977 he was executed as a "counterrevolutionary."

Burchett repeats Vivo's contention that Mengistu, who instituted the so-called "Red Terror" campaign against internal opposition, who masterminded an annual series of military offensives in Eritrea and who executed all opposition to his policies from within the Derg, supposedly "insisted upon the revolutionary idea that troops and police should no longer fire on people in the continuing demonstrations."

This is in reference to the Derg's early years. How then do we explain the killing of striking airlines workers in September 1975, the killing of striking theater workers in April 1976, the killing of student demonstrators at the May Day rally in 1976 and so on?

Mengistu represses dissent

Leader of Ethiopia's derg

The Guardian (New York), February 28, 1979

Nearly a year ago the Guardian published a series of articles support-
ing the struggle of the Eritrean people for liberation from Ethiopia and
questioning whether the Ethiopian military leadership was actually
pursuing a socialist course. These articles were preceded and followed
by correspondent Dan Connell's reports in the Guardian from the
Eritrean battle zone. Beginning in November, the Guardian published
an 11-part series by staff correspondent Wilfred Burchett. These arti-
cles judged the Ethiopian government to be socialist and were critical
of the Eritrean liberation struggle. Following is the second of several
articles by Connell replying to Burchett.

The claim that Lt. Col. Mengistu Haile Mariam is a peace loving
man in the midst of unreconstructed militarists is perhaps the most
ludicrous distortion of facts in Wilfred Burchett's 11-part Guardian
series on Ethiopia and Eritrea.

Mengistu's rise to power as chairman of Ethiopia's ruling military
Derg has been marked throughout by attempts to wipe out his opposition and by the absence of democratic political struggle.

The pattern has been consistent whether dealing with external
opposition or with individuals from within the Derg itself: label them
rightists and counterrevolutionaries no matter what their actual political line, then shoot first and ask questions later, if at all.

The two key issues that have occasioned the most bloodletting
have been demands for civilian participation in the all-military government and a negotiated settlement in Eritrea. It is more than ironic
that Mengistu-and Burchett-have claimed that the opposite is true,
but a survey of the evidence reveals what actually happened.

To begin with the main opposition to the Derg within Ethiopia
and Eritrea has always come from the left, and the Derg's main blows
have consistently been aimed in a leftward direction.

Rightists Disorganized

The principal rightist opposition in Ethiopia came from the
Ethiopian Democratic Union (EDU), a loose agglomeration of former
landlords, government officials and high-ranking army officers displaced with Haile Selassie in 1974. Though the Derg forces made a

half-hearted effort to crush the EDU in the spring of 1977, the rag-tag EDU army never posed a serious threat to the seat of power and were never treated as if they were, outside the realm of propaganda.

It was in fact the left-wing Tigray People's Liberation Front (TPLF) which finally decimated EDU forces last year in the third round of an all-out war between the two armies that saw the Derg sitting on the sidelines.

The main threat from the right in Eritrea since the Derg's ascension to power has come from Osman Sabbe's ELF-PLF-a bogus front supported by the reactionary Arab regimes. The Derg and the ELF-PLF have yet to confront each other on the battlefield, choosing instead to direct their attacks at the leftist Eritrean People's Liberation Front (EPLF) and the petty bourgeois Eritrean Liberation Front (ELF).

Last November, the ELF finally pushed the ELF-PLF out of Eritrea into neighboring Sudan, while the Derg threw all its military strength against the EPLF.

The reason for this is obvious and simple: the Derg needs the rightist forces to give it credibility as a "revolutionary" government. The existence of Sabbe's tiny and inconsequential rightist movement provides a foil for the Derg, a flimsy justification for claiming that the Eritrean struggle is an imperialist plot. The EDU plays the same role in Ethiopia.

Both the internal politics of the Eritrean movement and the Derg's complex relations with the Ethiopian left—Ethiopian People's Revolutionary Party (EPRP) and Me'ison—need through explication in order to be understood and will be subjects for later articles.

For the present, it should be noted that the Mengistu faction of the Derg has not permitted the development of any organized civilian left despite the widely recognized fact that it was a popular left-oriented upsurge that swept Haile Selassie out of power.

Whatever the EPRP's errors-and they were many-it was the first organized civilian Marxist-Leninist party and as such it was the target of a liquidation campaign from the onset of Mengistu's efforts to consolidate his power. Long before the outbreak of assassination-counter assassination by the EPRP and the Derg in the year 1977-78, Ethiopia's military leaders were set on the course of crushing the party.

Not a single demonstration passed without students and workers being shot for openly criticizing the junta. The turning point came in May 1976 when, after the publication of the Derg's National Democratic Program. EPRP leaders approached the government to discuss proposals for a united front as suggested in the program. They were rejected out of hand.

Burchett suggests that the EPRP was split over whether or not to cooperate with the Derg (an incorrect assessment-the main split inside the EPRP was between those who favored the strategy of rural-based people's war and those who followed a strategy of urban-centered insurrection) but in fact the choice was never there.

Instructive here is the fate of Me'ison, the civilian Marxist party that served as the architect of the Derg's political and social policies throughout this period. So long as Me'ison accepted the Derg's absolute power at the top, it was allowed free rein to propagate its views. When in the spring of 1977, Me'ison leader Haile Fida proposed a sharing of power with the party, it too was violently suppressed.

Army Dissidents Shot

Burchett also lists a number of Derg leaders who were executed during this period as "counterrevolutionaries," but a closer look reveals that their main crime was simply challenging Mengistu's single-minded militarist approach to his opposition.

The July 13, 1976, executions of Air Force Maj. Sissay Habte and Chief Administrator of Eritrea Brigadier-General Getachew Nadew are cases in point. Sissay Habte was the head of the Derg's political committee and widely known to favor a return to civilian rule, while Getachew Nadew had submitted a series of reports calling for an end to the fighting in Eritrea.

Burchett hedges on these points by repeating the official version that they "opposed the majority Derg line for a negotiated settlement in Eritrea...."

Or take the case of the February 1977 execution of Derg chairman Gen. Teferi Bente for supposedly plotting a coup. Bente favored some kind of rapprochement with the civilian left, particularly the EPRP. The official explanation for his death: he was charged with being a CIA agent and a counterrevolutionary.

Burchett argues that the charges against Bente were reinforced by the subsequent reduction of U.S. military said to Ethiopia and then the closing of U.S. bases by Mengistu.

These events, too, are subject to different interpretations. What Burchett calls a "drastic" reduction in aid was in fact a shallow ploy by Carter to boost his so-called "human rights" campaign. Only a few million dollars in outright grants were cut in conjunction with a worldwide phasing out of U.S. grant programs, while credits and ceilings on military sales were unaffected.

As to the closing of what Burchett calls "the huge U.S. base at Kagnew" in Eritrea, by early 1977 there were only a handful of U.S. personnel there. Satellites had replaced the functions of the once important spy station, the lease for which expired in 1978.

In other words, though Mengistu's actions were a propaganda victory, they had little substance, like most of the other pronouncements and proclamations used by Burchett to bolster the claim that the Derg was and is a revolutionary government.

The list of those from within the military executed for raising their voices in opposition to the Eritrea war could fill pages. Over 150 officers and soldiers were executed in the besieged Eritrean capital of Asmara in November 1977. Hundreds were shot in Massawa in December 1977. Another 35 were executed in September 1978 and over 250 died a month later. All were members of Mengistu's army who expressed doubts about the Eritrea war policy.

Traitors exist in any war, and executions are sometimes necessary. But the numbers involved here and the unwillingness-or inability-of Mengistu to find any means other than the firing squad to deal with criticisms has become a distinct hallmark of his regime.

Mengistu has resorted to various devices to cover up his policy of continued military rule. Burchett describes the Yekatit School of Politics, set up in 1976 as the "embryo model of a Marxist Party." Speaking of the "paradoxes" and "miracles" of the Ethiopian revolution, he notes, that "it would have been easy for the Derg to form an official single party...and pin a 'Marxist-Leninist'-or any other-label on it." Instead, he says, this is happening slowly while socialism is still being constructed.

What he doesn't say is that the Yekatit School was set up by Me'ison before the Derg suppressed it. And a steady process of selection and exclusion now leaves Mengistu's own Seded organization, based almost solely inside the army, as the only major officially recognized political organization in Ethiopia.

The Eritrean Question

When Burchett gets to the Eritrea question in his last articles, the contradictions become even more glaring. While he admits that Eritrea and several internal Ethiopian national minorities suffered severe oppression under Haile Selassie, nowhere apart from the recitation of official proclamations does he show evidence that things have changed under the Derg. In practice, they haven't changed and his is one of the reasons that national movements are continuing to develop throughout Ethiopia today.

Burchett attempts to portray the struggle of revolutionary elements in the Eritrean movement to gain control of what began as an essentially nationalist struggle as a negative aspect rather than as an inevitable historical development.

Yet he turns around and tries to suggest that when the Marxist EPLF won hegemony in the movement, it immediately executed its Marxist leaders. How then does he explain that the EPLF leaders today are the same people who led the front in the early 1970s, with the sole exception of rightists like Osman Sabbe?

In article 11, Burchett cites the unity agreement signed by EPLF and ELF in October 1977. Osman Sabbe took part in the conference, according to Burchett.

The fact is that Sabbe was pointedly excluded from the conference and all subsequent EPLF-ELF meetings on unity. His organization was roundly condemned and told to disband. However, its members were encouraged as patriotic Eritreans to join the two other fronts where they would be under the military and political leadership of those fronts. Is this different from the tactics followed by any other revolutionary movement? It is different, at least, from the tactics of the Derg toward its opposition.

Burchett next tries to discredit the EPLF by showing that it is seeking aid from Saudi Arabia. The truth is that it vehemently opposes the EPLF, is arresting EPLF sympathizers in Saudi Arabia, does not permit supplies to pass through its airspace en route to the EPLF and actively aids the EPLF's internal enemy-the rightist ELF-PLF.

Ethiopian officials know this well, as their ambassador to Sudan admitted to me last fall in a private interview, yet they continue to try to confuse outsiders about it.

Clearly there has been intense struggle for leadership of both Ethiopia and Eritrea. The question is-struggle between whom and for what ends?

In Ethiopia we have seen a small faction within the army battling workers, peasants, students, intellectuals and even rival factions in the armed forces to consolidate its power. Burchett brings no class analysis to this struggle. Instead he ducks the issue by merely identifying the ruling army faction as the "revolutionaries."

In Eritrea, 17 years of war have more clearly delineated the class forces which today take the concrete form of three separate organizations: EPLF, ELF and ELF-PLF. Yet Burchett would lump them all together as "counterrevolutionaries."

The Derg's undifferentiated and undemocratic suppression of all opposition is an inevitable consequence of its narrow social base in the petty bourgeoisie and bureaucratic bourgeoisie. 'The EPLF's consistently democratic approach to struggling with internal Eritrean opposition flows directly from its worker-peasant base and its genuine commitment to national democratic revolution.

Eritrean meet disrupted

The Guardian (New York), February 28, 1979

A tiny group of Eritrean students and their supporters opposed to the Eritrean Peoples Liberation Front (EPLF), attempted unsuccessfully last week to disrupt a pro-EPLF meeting in Boston.

Three Eritreans, members of the Eritreans for Liberation in North America (EFLNA) tried to enter a meeting sponsored by the Association of Democratic Eritreans in Boston (ADEB). Guardian correspondent Dan Connell was presenting slides from his most recent visit to Eritrea with the EPLF.

The three were joined by a half-dozen members of the dogmatist sect, The Central Organization of U.S. Marxist-Leninists (COUSM-L). The ADEB had learned of the plan to disrupt the program and blocked the EFLNA-COUSM-L group from entering the conference hall at Boston State College where 200 people had gathered for the presentation.

EFLNA and COUSM-L have denounced the EPLF for "capitulating" to Ethiopia's ruling military Derg and to the Soviet Union despite the fact that the EPLF is today engaged in all-out war against the Ethiopia regime.

GUERRILLA MORALE 'VERY HIGH'

Africa News (Durham, NC), March 2, 1979

[AN] Dan Connell, who has regularly reported from Eritrea and Sudan for AFRICA NEWS and other publications, returned to the U.S. recently, but still keeps in close touch with events in the Horn of Africa. In an interview last week he gave AFRICA NEWS an update on Eritrean developments:

AN: The Ethiopian Government has been claiming victory in Eritrea—just what is the military situation there?

Connell: In general there is a shift from the conventional face-to-face confrontations to a smaller-scale guerrilla war spread over a fairly wide area. At the same time, there have been a series of large battles up in the northern part of the country where the Ethiopians have been trying to get into the EPLF [Eritrean People's Liberation Front] base area, and two weeks ago the EPLF retreated from the small town of Afabet to further consolidate its position.

AN: Has the EPLF had any military success in defending the territory it controls?

Connell: To the best of my knowledge they have been able to thwart a series of attempts to get in, both from the Red Sea coast and inland. Less than two weeks ago there was a three-day battle between the towns of Afabet and Nakfa. [Nakfa is held by the EPLF.] Troops of the EPLF were able to turn back that offensive with very heavy casualties to the Ethiopian side, capturing four tanks and over 20,000 rounds of ammunition. A week or two earlier there were battles along the Red Sea coast where there was a sea landing in an attempt to penetrate the base area from that side, which was also unsuccessful.

AN: What is the morale of the Eritrean forces?

Connell: When I left Eritrea at the end of the last major offensive, the EPLF had given up the largest towns under their control. Still, the morale was very high, because in individual battles they had done well against the Ethiopians, even though in the overall situation they were forced to withdraw from some positions because they simply lacked the manpower and the weapons to keep up that kind of a battle. They seemed generally to hold the view that they were up against a better equipped enemy and a more sophisticated enemy, in that Ethiopia was receiving much more direct aid from the Soviet Union.

AN: What's the state of unity and organizational contact between the EPLF and the ELF [Eritrean Liberation Front]?

Connell: The EPLF and the ELF signed a Procedure for Unity last April, some six months after the initial October 1977 unity agreement. But the heavy fighting that went on during this whole period interfered with the process and nothing was really done. In January they signed a new agreement with a much more practical program of establishing co-ordination between them. Concretely what it calls for is an integration of military units, which means that in any given battalion you may find two companies of the EPLF and one of the ELF, or vice versa, under a unified military leadership. The thing that's important about this is that it means that the fighters in both fronts at the lower levels are exposed to each other, so the political differences that separate them will now be struggled out between the members of the front itself rather than argued over negotiating tables by the leadership.

AN: What have been the relative levels of Soviet and Cuban involvement over the last few months?

Connell: At the beginning of the Ethiopian offensive, in late June and early July, there were reports from a lot of different sources that both Cuban and Soviet advisors were playing a discreet background role in setting up the offensive in terms of strategic planning, communications and logistic support. Then, in October-November there appears to have been a fairly substantial change on both their parts, so that when the next round of fighting took place the Cubans seemed to be absent from direct involvement while the Soviet presence had increased dramatically. Soviet officers apparently numbered from one to two hundred in each battle front—advising the Ethiopian troops, directing the campaigns down to the level of the battalions on the battlefield itself. so the Soviets had a quantitative and a qualitative leap in their involvement, while the Cubans backed off.

I talked to some Ethiopian prisoners who had been trained by Cubans. They said that Cuban officers and soldiers had told them they would not serve in Eritrea. so there seems to be some widespread feeling both within the Cuban forces in Ethiopia and at some higher level of backing off from direct military involvement.

AN: Has there been any new talk at all of compromises or negotiations?

Connell: There has not to my knowledge in the last year been any indication from the EPLF or the ELF that they are willing to settle this question with anything short of independence, although there have been numerous tactical decisions about whether or not to negotiate and on what basis to sit down for talks.

A variety of other countries have also attempted to get these talks started. The latest instance was an attempt by Sudan's President Numeiry, who met with Ethiopia's leader, Lt. Col. Mengistu, in Freetown, Sierra Leone, in mid-February. Apparently Mengistu refused to talk about Eritrea, saying that it was an internal matter for Ethiopia. Numeiry insisted that the Eritrean question had to be taken up because he has 300,000 refugees and there have been border incursions into Sudan. They were unable to break that deadlock, and the talks didn't go anywhere.

Colonialism and Eritrea nationalism

Eritrea never a part of Ethiopia

*The Guardian (*New York), March 7, 1979

Following is the third of several articles replying to a series of reports by Wilfred Burchett on the Ethiopia-Eritrea question.

"By all, we were oppressed and exploited," said Comrade Fana, as we sat on the mud floor of her house in Zagur, 18 miles from the occupied Eritrean capital of Asmara.

"The Italians said, 'We'll peel your skins to make our shoes.' The British were better. They built some schools and they left peacefully. The Ethiopians are the worst. They killed our people, they stole our donkeys and they steal our properties. Our sons and daughters who studied 16 classes were hung. The peaceful civilians go out to Asmara to buy some clothes, some foodstuffs. On their way out or in they're killed with their children on their backs."

Fana is a member of the Zagur women's association, her husband a participant in the local peasant association, her 10-year old daughter a "red flower," her 15-year old a member of the Eritrean People's Liberation Front (EPLF) which has organized the other civilian political associations in Zagur over the past four years.

To this 40-year-old Eritrean peasant woman, as with hundreds of thousands like her, Ethiopia's current Soviet-backed efforts to conquer her homeland differ little from those of the European imperialists which came before.

Ethiopia's ruling military Derg and its later-day supporters use a range of sophistic arguments to claim ancient ties with Eritrea. But in three years of visits to Eritrea and Ethiopia the only Eritreans I met who identified themselves as Ethiopians were a handful of merchants and government bureaucrats in Addis Ababa.

The ordinary Eritrean worker or peasant traces his/her history as a nation to the Italian colonization in the late 180s and recalls only local feudal rulers before that, though the oral history includes many tales of battle with Amhara and Tigrayan lords from what is today called Ethiopia as well as with Sudanese sheiks and Turkish warriors.

Eritrea has never been a part of Ethiopia. What is now called Ethiopia was also established as a political entity at the turn of this century.

Wilfred Burchett, in his history of Eritrea (Guardian, Jan 3, 10), acknowledges Eritrea's long legacy of foreign conquest. But using phrases like "the Red Sea coastal area, of the ancient Ethiopian empire" and "the Ethiopian section of the Red Sea coast," he implies a past union of the two countries which is contrary to fact.

Ethiopia's claim to Eritrea rests on the existence of the precolonial Axumite Empire which included most of modern Eritrea, the northern Ethiopian province of Tigray and at its height parts of southern Arabia. The Axumite empire dissolved in the ninth century AD.

After the breakup of the Axumite kingdom, the Bejas invaded Eritrea from the north and occupied the Eritrean highlands for three centuries. From the 15th through the 19th centuries Abyssinian kings intermittently controlled small parts of modern Eritrea, excluding the Red Sea coast which was then subject to the conquest of the Ottoman Turks.

At this state, the debate is purely academic. To assert an identity between the Axumite and Ethiopian empires is like equating the ancient Ghanaian or Congo empires with modern Ghana or Congo (Brazzaville), like arguing an Italian claim to France based upon its conquest by imperial Rome.

Axum Heritage

In fact the heritage of Axum belongs not to the Amhara-dominated Ethiopia of the 20th century but to the peoples of Eritrea and Tigray, who retain cultural, linguistic and historical ties distinct from those of the Amhara who rose to power in central Ethiopia only 100 years ago.

The close fraternal relations between the Eritrean and Tigrayan peoples manifest themselves today in the working alliance between the Eritrean and Tigrayan liberation struggles against the Amhara-ruled empire state of Ethiopia.

This state took its contemporary form at the turn of the century when the Shoan Amhara emperor Menelik II collaborated with French, Italian and British imperialists, having participated in the infamous Berlin Conference of 1885 alongside the Europeans, to triple the size of his mountainous, landlocked empire by expanding south and westward.

That he should also have coveted the Red Sea coastal area then known as Medri Bahri (land of the sea) is hardly inconsistent with his expansionist ambitions, but it does not constitute a legitimate territorial claim, as Burchett suggests.

When one talks about states and national boundaries in Africa, one is referring not to ancient kingdoms shrouded in myth and legend but to the lines drawn by the imperial powers of England, France, Portugal, Germany and Ethiopia less than 100 years ago.

Eritrea was then defined by Italian conquest and colonization, much as the rest of Africa was carved up, often arbitrarily, by external forces. The Italian colony of Eritrea lasted from 1890 through 1941, and Eritrean demands for independence date from this period.

Under Italian rule, the Eritrean were robbed of their culture, their land, their natural resources and their labor, but at the same time their shared oppression and exploitation gave them a new sense of national identity. In these respects, their experience was no different from that of most other colonized African peoples.

Like all other African colonies, Eritrea contained people of diverse ethnic and tribal backgrounds. Under Italian rule, however, a multinational working class began to emerge first to build extensive infrastructure projects to open Eritrea to Italy's settlement schemes and later to labor on massive public works projects and in factories established between 1930 and 1941 in conjunction with fascist Italy's moves to expand in the region.

The settler colonialist policies led to the expropriation of vast areas of fertile land and the displacement of the feudal landlord class in the highlands, along with the impoverishment of large numbers of peasants who inevitably moved into the towns and cities.

This period is characterized by the emergence of distinct social classes, multinational in composition, which began to develop a sharp sense of national identity, following a pattern common to other African colonies.

The change came when Italy lost World War 2. As with the case of Germany in World War I, the defeated colonial power lost its African possessions to the victors. Eritrea then came under British "protection," as Tanganyika had fallen to the British crown a quarter of a century earlier.

But the British were in no position to take on added colonial responsibilities, and the problem of how to dispose of Eritrea fell to the newly formed, U.S.-dominated United Nations.

The brief period of English rule was marked by several subtle but insidious actions against the Eritrean people under the guise of a benevolent stewardship. Italian-built industries were dismantled and stolen, gold was extracted from mines in the highlands and carried out. But worse than that was the deception perpetrated upon the Eritreans by British administrators.

During the fighting with Italy, the British had air-dropped leaflets promising the Eritreans freedom. Later, they shifted to promises that Eritrea would not return to Italian rule while simultaneously maneuvering to divide the colony between Anglo-Egyptian Sudan and imperial Ethiopia, effectively dispensing the spoils of war among loyal British allies.

The British did at the same time build schools and allow a measure of political freedom. This was with the ironic result that open agitation began for full Eritrean independence from within the newly organized multinational working class as well as from the urban petty bourgeoisie.

Colonial Judgement

Incredibly, Burchett cites the chief British administrator of Eritrea as a valid source of proof that Eritrea was not "entitled" to independence. The judgement was a familiar one for that period.

The 10 years of British occupation were marked at first by an industrial boom coinciding with the last years of the world war and then a steady economic collapse as the British set out to ruin the Eritrean economy in order to prove their point about its economic unviability.

During the early years there was a tremendous increase in the size of the working class which organized at the factory level and began asserting both economic and political demands increasingly centered on independence.

The Italian colonial structure was left intact in the countryside and these years were also marked by the further impoverishment of the peasantry and a growing number of peasant uprisings. The most notable occurred in the predominantly feudal lowlands where for eight years (1942-49) an anti-feudal movement held sway.

In the towns, a discontented petty bourgeoisie and an embryonic Eritrean intelligentsia began agitation that included open publication of anti-colonial newspapers and organized demonstrations.

The movement for Eritrean independence thus gained its first solid backing from these social groups in opposition to an alliance of feudal landlords. Coptic church leaders (also landowners) and colonial collaborators who soon tied their fortunes as an incipient national bourgeois class with the transfer of power to Addis Ababa.

Eritrea's anticolonial struggle

Workers and peasants lead the fight

The Guardian (New York), March 14, 1979

Following is the fourth of several articles replying to a recent series by Wilfred Burchett on the Ethiopia-Eritrea question.

Eritrea's 17-year war for independence from Ethiopia is an anti-colonial struggle for national and social liberation.

Its development reflects the classic anti-colonial pattern of protest, spontaneous resistance, repression, underground organization and armed struggle. At first fundamentally nationalist in content and aims, the struggle deepened to become a revolutionary force for social liberation as well.

Wilfred Burchett has attempted to discredit the struggle by first denying the anti-colonial aspect and then distorting the internal class struggle within the movement.

Neither argument holds up under historical examination, though there is no denying that the complexities of the situation make such an analysis difficult.

Burchett never confronts the anti-colonial aspect directly.

Referring to the "decolonization" of Eritrea in the 1950s, Burchett sets up the struggle as a national rather than an anti-colonial one-which he then shows does not meet Stalin's criteria-motivated only by the repressive policies of the Haile Selassie regime.

Hence, the argument goes, with the fall of Selassie, the justification for the Eritrean struggle evaporates and at this point the war becomes a counterrevolutionary one against the new regime.

Case For Self-Determination

A scientific case had been made for Eritrea's right to self-determination by none other than the socialist countries themselves.

"The colonial system is going through an acute state of crisis. Accordingly, in considering the fate of Eritrea-one of the former Italian colonies, the UN must take a decision which will satisfy the longing of the Eritrean people for independence and freedom from national oppression."

The time was 1950. The speaker: USSR delegate to the UN General Assembly Andrei Vishinsky.

"The General Assembly cannot tolerate a deal by the colonial powers at the expense of the population of Eritrea," the Soviet representative continued. "In the circumstances, the only just solution....is to grant independence."

Italy had lost World War 2 and forfeited the "right" to colonial possessions in Africa. But decolonization was not yet on the imperialist powers' agenda; the national aspirations of the Eritrean people counted little in the big power debate over how to redistribute the spoils of war.

"From the point of view of justice, the opinions of the Eritrean people must receive consideration," rejoined U.S. Secretary of State John Foster Dulles later in the UN Security Council, summing up the U.S. view.

"Nevertheless, the strategic interests of the United States in the Red Sea basin and considerations of security and world peace make it necessary that the country has to be linked with our ally, Ethiopia," he continued.

With the lines thus drawn between the Eritrean people and the socialist countries on the one hand and the Ethiopian emperor and U.S. imperialism on the other, the strategic Red Sea country was transferred from Britain-which temporarily occupied Eritrea from 1941-52-to Ethiopia in the form of a sham federation.

Remarked the UN delegate from Czechoslovakia. "The federal form of government....is merely a mask for the annexation of little Eritrea by a larger and more populous state."

History soon proved the Czech analysis correct as Haile Selassie moved with U.S. and Israeli backing to abrogate the UN instrument and consolidate its colonial control.

Resistance To Ethiopia

Burchett's account of the growth of resistance to Ethiopia's U.S. and Israeli-backed efforts to consolidate the colonial enclosure of

Eritrea is a subtle attempt to rewrite history. He emphasizes the participation of indigenous feudal, bourgeois and middle class element and all but ignores the key role of the workers, the peasantry and the lower petty bourgeoisie.

The opposition to union with Ethiopia, according to Burchett, was centered in the "Blocco di Independenzia," headed by Italian colonials. Conveniently left out are the Moslem, League and the Liberal Progressive Party which were the leading Eritrean proponents of independence in the UN debate and which had widespread support among the rural peasantry and the urban workers and lower petty bourgeoisie.

Here, too, he twists history to suggest that resistance came only from businessmen and intellectuals who formed the Eritrean Liberation Movement (ELM) in the early 1950s and was followed by the appearance in 1961 of the Eritrean Liberation Front (ELF) which he says was formed by feudal elements and émigrés from Egypt and Sudan.

No one can deny that the Eritrean struggle began as an essentially bourgeois nationalist movement in opposition to semifeudal Ethiopia's imperialist-backed colonial rule. But neither can one liquidate the role of the workers and peasants at this stage or their eventual rise to leadership of the struggle.

Origins Of Resistance

To begin with, the ELM was not formed until 1958, and then in response to a massive upheaval by Eritrean workers and students whose protests and organized resistance actually laid the basis for the national liberation struggle.

In 1952 the workers, already organized at the factory level, formed the General Union of Labor Syndicates in order to carry their political struggle forward.

In 1958 events climaxed in a general strike which was almost 100% effective throughout Eritrea for several days before the army attacked a rally in Asmara and killed or wounded over 500 people.

By this time the workers had been joined by students and others in condemning Ethiopia's campaign to destroy the Eritrean economy and in calling for independence, but the absence of an organization to lead the resistance coupled with the force of the repression yielded a serious setback to the movement.

In the countryside, especially in the lowland areas, feudal landlords and traditional chiefs served as the instruments of Ethiopian colonization with a resulting degradation of rural subsistence life for the peasantry.

Thus the 1961 opening shots of the armed struggle under the Eritrean Liberation Front (ELF) were fired at a time when the Eritrean working class, the urban petty bourgeoisie and the peasantry stood in sharp contradiction to the cabal of Eritrean feudal and bourgeois classes, Ethiopian colonialism, U.S. imperialism and Israeli Zionism.

Burchett likewise ignores the U.S. and Israeli role in carrying through the Ethiopian colonization of Eritrea.

If backward Ethiopia's colonization of Eritrea appears to run counter to the classical model, the missing link in the equation is U.S. imperialism. Without U.S. actions on Ethiopia's behalf, Eritrea would not have been denied its independence in 1952. In the absence of the ongoing neocolonial relationship between the U.S. and Ethiopia, the subsequent annexation would have been impossible to carry out or to sustain.

The colonization of Eritrea was, in fact, a joint venture between the U.S. and Ethiopia with the spoils divided between them. The U.S. share of the bargain was the unlimited right to build military bases in Eritrea.

The granting of military bases off the Eritrean coast to Israel in the late of 1950s brought Zionism into the struggle as a junior partner alongside the U.S. The first 16 years of the war (through 1977) then saw the U.S. and Israel training, arming and equipping the Ethiopian neocolonial army to wage the counterinsurgency war.

Burchett then goes on to portray the Eritrean armed struggle as a corrupt, "feudal-oriented" movement split into contending factions and lacking in genuine revolutionary content (Guardian. Jan 17). History forces Burchett to acknowledge the emergence of a revolutionary line within the struggle that took organizational form in the Eritrean People's Liberation Front (EPLF), but he abstains from a class analysis of this internal struggle and thus thoroughly misrepresents it.

The existence of contending class forces within a national liberation struggle is a common feature of all revolutions. To obscure this in the case of Eritrea by reducing it to competition among leaders, ethnic groups or ties to external forces, as Burchett does, is to abandon Marxist analysis.

A close and honest look at the origin, programs and social practice of the various Eritrean organizations reveals clearly the forging of an alliance between the working class and the peasantry under the EPLF to win leadership of the struggle today.

Eritrea: from national to social revolution

The Guardian (New York), March 21, 1979

Following is the fifth of several articles replying to a recent series by Wilfred Burchett on the Ethiopia-Eritrea question.

Eritrea's 17-year anticolonial war for independence from Ethiopia has been characterized from the beginning by fierce class struggle.

The history of the movement is replete with political and social contention taking the form of splits, realignments, temporary alliances and even civil wars.

The armed phase of the struggle was launched in 1961 by the Eritrean Liberation Front (ELF). Today there are three separate armed Eritrean organizations: the Eritrean Liberation Front Revolutionary Council (ELF-RC, but usually referred to as ELF), the Eritrean People's Liberation Front (EPLF) and the Eritrean Liberation Front-Popular Liberation Forces (ELF-PLF).

Under the lens of a class analysis, the apparent organizational maze unravels into a movement divided into clearly defined class forces. The interests of the workers and peasants are represented by the EPLF, which now dominates the movement. The interests of the petty bourgeoisie guide the ELF. The interests of the Eritrean bourgeoisie, such as it is, find their voice in the tiny ELF-PLF.

Efforts At Unity

At this stage of the Eritrean revolution, the workers and peasants seek an alliance with the petty bourgeoisie under worker leadership. Hence, the EPLF efforts at unity with ELF. Given the past role of the bourgeoisie in the struggle and the present political and military conditions, no alliance is now sought with this class. Hence, the refusal of EPLF and ELF to include ELF-PLF in the current unity process.

Wilfred Burchett obscures these facts by lumping all the organizations together as factions of a "feudal-oriented" movement whose main internal support supposedly comes from disgruntled sections of an ill-defined "middle class."

Burchett never explains the existence of the three organizations. He presents efforts to bring them together as motivated solely by the desire for outside aid and as proof of the overall reactionary nature of the movement. His technique is to misrepresent the ELF-PLF as the representative force in Eritrea and then to damn the others by association.

His case virtually rests on a game of who-supports-whom, in which he falsely portrays the Eritreans as undifferentiated puppets of Saudi Arabia and Ethiopia's ruling military Derg as a shining example of socialism.

Leaving aside for the moment the important questions of the nature of the Ethiopian regime, the first point to be made-and tested-is that a scientific analysis of the Eritrean movement begins in Eritrea with the identification of the various organizations and the class forces behind them.

Burchett goes to great lengths to show that the first nine years of war were marked by serious errors, even atrocities, committed by the ELF leadership against the peasantry and the fighters themselves.

No one contests this. In fact, Burchett uses EPLF sources to document the nonargument. But this is only part of the picture.

The early ELF was dominated by a small segment of the right wing of the upper petty bourgeoisie and a handful of feudal warlords, as Burchett says. But it also enjoyed the broad support of Eritrean workers, peasants and elements of the lower petty bourgeoisie.

In this respect, the movement differed little from any comparable nationalist force emerging in a colonial context characterized by semifeudal social relations, which was the case in the Eritrean lowlands, where the ELF got its start.

The class character of the ELF leadership limited the independence movement to strictly national aims with no social content. It also inevitably lacked a correct political and military strategy for the conditions in which the war was being fought, not only against Ethiopia but also-by proxy-against U.S. and Israeli imperialism.

Burchett recounts the events of 1969-70 (the rise of democratic forces against the corrupt leadership and the split into ELF-RC and EPLF), but he attempts no explanation of their class content. He says only that civil war broke out between the two rival organizations, and he offhandedly remarks, "Who was being 'liberated' during that period still remains to be identified."(Guardian, Jan. 17).

Burchett then makes much out of the role of the Eritrean middle class in the liberation struggle but he does not elaborate, as if to say their presence is enough to discredit the movement.

The Petty Bourgeoisie

The importance of the petty bourgeoisie in any third world liberation struggle is widely recognized. At the same time, it has its negative aspects.

The question is what role did the class play in Eritrea? It is true that the petty bourgeoisie was instrumental in overthrowing the backward leadership of the ELF. It is also true that this class seized control of one wing of the movement-the ELF-RC. But though it sought to control the emergent EPLF then and since, it has not succeeded.

From its inception, the EPLF's political line has clearly reflected that front's working class orientation. A 1971 draft of the program formally adopted in January 1977 spells out the organization's commitment to the alliance between Eritrean workers and peasants under working class leadership to form the core of the struggle.

But words are sometimes cheap. The ELF-RC also adopted a program in 1971 which on the surface sounded progressive, as did the Derg in 1976.

The test, as always, is practice. While proclaiming progressive goals, the ELF-RC sought to postpone their implementation until after the war was won. The EPLF, meanwhile, set out at once to lay the political groundwork for sweeping social and economic changes.

Today, their many ongoing accomplishments are incontestable in the fields of popular mobilization and political education on a mass scale, in land reform, in the restructuring of rural and urban social relations, in economic and military self-reliance.

Burchett carefully abstains from even referring to these accomplishments. But they have been so often documented by firsthand experience within the pages of the Guardian and elsewhere in the European press that they need not be related again here.

What Burchett does instead is attempt to cloud the issue by relating spurious tales of anti-Marxist EPLF purges in 1974. He claims that the collapse of the Selassie regime "left the middle classes horror-stricken," and that the Derg's nationalization of urban property hit them so hard that they turned to the liberation fronts as the only saving hope.

"Among the fairly immediate consequences was that the civil war between EPLF and ELF quickly calmed down, and the EPLF quickly got rid of its Marxist leadership," Burchett says.

The so-called "decapitation of the most progressive elements within EPLF leadership" was in fact nothing of the kind. In 1972 and 1973 there had been an influx of volunteers from the towns. Among them were petty bourgeois intellectuals who sought in the classic manner to take over leadership of the front based upon their advanced education and book-learned political theory.

It is more than ironic that Burchett, who so casually condemned the Ethiopian People's Revolutionary Party (EPRP) as ultra-"leftists" earlier in his series here puts forward the ultra-"left" Menka ("bats") as the most progressive elements in EPLF.

Menka's disruptive actions in 1973 forced the EPLF to withdraw from the central Eritrean highlands, where they had been clandestinely organizing the peasantry while defending against the ELF-RC's efforts to destroy them. The ensuing internal struggle took eight months and lasted into the spring of 1974.

This experience re-alerted the EPLF to the dangerous negative tendencies of this class. One consequence was the decision to set quotas on its enrollment in the cadre school to prevent its domination of the party then (and now) in formation. Meanwhile, the end of the civil war with ELF-RC came in late 1974 as the result of the consolidation of the EPLF, the failure of the ELF-RC to quash it and massive pressure from the civilian population.

EPLF Political Consolidation

The political consolidation of the EPLF's revolutionary leadership and line also resulted in the jettisoning of the externally based Osman Sabbe circle which had turned to the ELF-RC and tried to manipulate a merger of the two fronts that would leave Sabbe in a position of power.

Sabbe and his followers represented the interests of the upper petty bourgeoisie and the small comprador bourgeoisie. His consistent efforts to oppose the EPLF leadership, his formation of an ELF-PLF in 1976 out of politically underdeveloped Muslim peasants and semi-nomads, his close ties with Saudi Arabia and Iran (under the shah) all lend themselves to Burchett's charges against the Eritrean movement as a whole.

Eritrean reactionaries did turn to the independence movement after the Derg's nationalizations, but it was Sabbe to whom they went, not EPLF or ELF.

ELF-RC, meanwhile, demonstrated its petty bourgeois character in this period by first allowing the new ELF-PLF into its liberated areas and then proposing a merger prior to linking itself with the EPLF. The result, however, was a massive upheaval inside the front, another brief civil war within ELF-RC and the eventual splintering off of thousands of left-oriented guerrillas.

Over 1500 joined EPLF, but another 3000 fled to neighboring Sudan, becoming known as "falloul" (Anarchists). Eschewing a connection with EPLF. This "left" movement is now organizing as the Eritrean Democratic Movement. It has already established ties with

Sabbe's ELF-PLF.

When the ELF-RC then did an about face in October 1977 and signed a unity agreement with EPLF, it lost thousands more right-oriented fighters, this time either directly to ELF-PLF or again to Sudan as refugees.

The trend is obvious. At this moment there are two major contending class forces in the Eritrean liberation struggle: the worker-peasant alliance of the EPLF and the bourgeois-dominated ELF-PLF, with the declining petty bourgeois-led ELF-RC in the middle. No one, not even Burchett, denies that the EPLF is now clearly dominant.

Burchett falsely claims that the EPLF has "asked Sabbe to return to the fold" when the record is quite clearly the opposite. Sabbe has been repeatedly excluded from EPLF-ELF unity talks. He and the class interests which he represents have no place in the Eritrean revolution under the present conditions, no matter how much aid such a tactic would yield. Only his followers, the rank and file of ELF-PLF, have been invited to join EPLF or ELF.

The history of the Eritrean liberation struggle is one of a bourgeois nationalist movement transformed through internal class forces and the pressure of imperialist attempts to crush it into a classic national democratic revolution.

No one should be surprised that reactionary class forces in Eritrea oppose it. That the Derg opposes it raises basic questions not about Eritrea but about the junta itself and its claim to socialism.

Eritrea: EPLF reorganizes

The Guardian (New York), March 28, 1979

The Eritrean battlefield is quiet this week as both sides in the protracted war mobilize for renewed fighting.

"It is very calm now," noted Eritrean People's Liberation Front (EPLF) Central Committee member Ermias Debessai this week in Rome, in reference to the 9-month Soviet-backed Ethiopian offensive. "The Ethiopians are getting weaker and weaker. It is a good time for reorganizing our forces for the counteroffensive."

Following a series of strategic retreats from most of Eritrea's major towns and cities during the recent Ethiopian offensive, the

EPLF has been reorganizing its military and political activities for a return to rural-based guerrilla war.

The main EPLF guerrilla base in the northern Eritrean province of Sahel has been dismantled and redistributed into smaller, separate installations within the labyrinthine valleys and volcanic mountains of the region, still under EPLF control, according to Ermias.

"Now we have mobilized everything," he said. "The workshops are producing again, the schools are open, our hospitals and clinics are functioning, and our infrastructure remains fully intact."

There have also been parallel developments in the EPLF's military and political reorientation, Ermias added, with most brigade-sized units divided into battalions now operative throughout the rest of Eritrea. Village-level mass political associations have been broken down into underground cells in the face of Ethiopian terrorism, he said.

"This reorganization at the military and the political level is necessary to safeguard our social and economic reforms which the Derg (Ethiopia's ruling military junta) is trying to destroy," said the EPLF leader.

According to the EPLF, major military actions against the invading Ethiopian forces must await the transformation of the political and economic base to conform with the new military conditions. However, recent EPLF communiqués indicate a pattern of stepped up counterattacks.

EPLF units last month recaptured the two key towns of Ghinda and Dongolo along the important highway linking the Red Sea port of Massawa with the inland Asmara capital. The EPLF retreated from these towns in November, yielding control of the highway, but on two occasions in December the guerrillas overran several small Ethiopian camps there.

In the Feb. 22 attack on the two towns, EPLF forces claim to have killed, captured or wounded 2000 Ethiopian troops and maintained control of the area for six hours. The towns are 45 minutes away from Massawa and Asmara, where Ethiopia's main troops are concentrated. There were no available reports of EPLF casualties.

Another EPLF action was reported Feb. 25 farther inland near the Ethiopian-held town of Mendefera. Ethiopian units were forced to retreat and a supply convoy was turned back, Ermias said.

The main significance of these actions is that with the successful defense of its northern base area against repeated Ethiopian attacks from December through early February, the EPLF is now shifting the focus of the war to the central highlands. This is the first step in placing Ethiopia on the defensive and setting the stage for the EPLF counteroffensive, likely to begin within the next two months.

The EPLF has also broadened its military and political actions to include large areas formerly dominated by the rival Eritrean Liberation Front (ELF).

Eritrea: Ethiopia offensive

The Guardian (New York), April 18, 1979

Fierce fighting broke out in Eritrea last week as Ethiopian government forces launched a fourth phase of their 9-month offensive there amid stepped up guerrilla attacks on the occupied towns.

More than 40,000 Ethiopian troops supported by heavy bombing and both naval and land-based shelling launched attacks April 2 against the base area of the Eritrean People's Liberation Front (EPLF), according to the EPLF's Rome spokesman.

"There have been four big attacks so far, but we frustrated them all," said EPLF Central Committee member Ermias Debessai. "All their attempts have failed, and they are now retreating."

The Ethiopian assaults were launched from the Red Sea port of Marsa Teklai and the government-held town of Afabet, Ermias said. He added that Soviet military advisors accompanied the Ethiopian forces and Soviet warships provided logistical support.

Three Soviet-supplied MIG-21 jet fighters were shot down in this period, two on the northern Eritrean battlefront and a third near the central Asmara capital where the EPLF is currently carrying out numerous smaller scale guerrilla actions, according to Ermias.

Meanwhile, unity talks between the EPLF and the smaller Eritrean Liberation Front (ELF) concluded in Khartoum last week with major agreement reached on the implementation of coordinated military action by the two fronts and a long term plan for resolving their political differences, the EPLF spokesman said.

Details of the agreement were not yet available at Guardian press time, but Ermias suggested that a joint EPLF-ELF delegation may soon launch a diplomatic offensive to win international support.

Africa News also reported this week that the small rightist ELF-PLF, long excluded from the unity talks of the two major Eritrean independence fronts, has dismissed its leader, Osman Saleh Sabbe. Since the opening of the armed struggle in 1961, Sabbe has been identified with reactionary interests in the Eritrean movement.

One of the early members of the Supreme Council of the ELF in the 1960s, Sabbe broke with that front in a major upheaval that split the movement into the ELF-RC and the EPLF in 1970. Temporarily allied with the EPLF field command, he was ousted from the EPLF in 1976 and denounced as a traitor and a reactionary.

He went on to found the ELF-PLF later that year with funds from rightist Arab countries who opposed the left orientations of the EPLF and ELF. A spokesman for ELF-PLF said Sabbe was now being jettisoned by the newest organization for "dealing with suspicious circles, administrative corruption" and opening a secret bank account in London.

EPLF sources confirmed the report of Sabbe's dismissal and termed it "a positive development for our movement." They also warned, however, that ELF-PLF leaders who seized control of the organization from Sabbe have long associations with rightist interests and may prove to be no better.

Eritreans Predict They'll Win As Ethiopia Readies Offensive

The Miami Herald, June 27, 1979

Sahel, Eritrea

As Russian-backed Ethiopian forces mobilize to renew their year-long military offensive in Eritrea, Eritrean guerrillas predict a defeat for the heavily armed foe that will turn the tide of war in their favor.

Ethiopia also may be planning an armed incursion into neighboring Sudan in an effort to internationalize the protracted guerrilla war and to punish Sudan for its tacit support for the Eritreans, according to Issayas Afwerki, the assistant general secretary of the Eritrean People's Liberation Front (EPLF).

"The Ethiopians, despite all their weaknesses, are doing their utmost to mobilize their forces, reorganize them, reinforce them, to take another round of their offensive," Issayas said in an interview near the front lines where the two entrenched armies now face each other.

"We are prepared to face that, and we feel that this round will be the last," Issayas said, adding that "the next round will lead to the collapse of their military institution."

The EPLF Leader also said that the guerrillas had evidence of an Ethiopian buildup accompanied by a large number of Russian military advisers in western Eritrea, near the border with Sudan.

This move may be aimed at opening a battlefront with Sudan in order to drive a wedge between that country and the guerrillas, who use Sudanese territory to transport supplies into their rear bases, Issayas said.

Issayas, a 33-year-old military strategist, described the current military situation in Eritrea as a "stalemate" after four successive Ethiopian campaigns that involved 120,000 troops, thousands of Soviet combat advisers and hundreds of Russian-supplied armored vehicles, heavy artillery, "Stalin Organ" multiple rocket-launchers and MiG jet aircraft.

With battles nearing proportions of those of World War II, Ethiopian forces were able to advance deep into guerrilla-held territory, recapturing all but two towns and cities previously held by Eritrean forces.

Confronted with a numerically and technically superior enemy, the Eritreans gradually fell back to their mountainous northern base area in a systematic effort to whittle down their opposition while avoiding heavy losses for themselves, according to Issayas, who claims that Ethiopia lost 40,000 to 50,000 men during this period.

The guerrilla leader said that Eritrean losses were less than one tenth this number due to their tactics of ambush and retreat until they reached the harsh volcanic terrain of Sahel, where the utility of Ethiopia's heavy armor and artillery effectively was canceled.

"Our main strength is flexibility and we have exploited this to the maximum in successfully working to demolish the enemy forces, in maintaining our military initiative and in maintaining our manpower," Issayas said.

"Our strategy was to withdraw if it was necessary from all liberated towns to preserve our strong points," he continued. "Now they (the Ethiopians) have reached a stage where they cannot advance farther from their present positions and their morale and combat efficiency are very low."

Issayas conceded that Ethiopia still held the advantage of heavier arms. However, he cited logistics and supply problems due to guerrilla actions in the Ethiopian rear and dissension within the Ethiopian army and between Ethiopian officers and their Russian advisers as among the factors giving the Eritreans an advantage.

But the Ethiopian and the Russian officers had anticipated a quick resolution of the 18-year Eritrean war in the recent series of offensives, according to Issayas, who said that guerrilla intelligence sources indicate that the Russian battlefield presence has decreased lately because their strategy failed. He also cited diplomatic pressure from the outside, declining to be specific.

"Maybe they have to reassess their position because of their underestimation of the Eritrean revolution," he added. "The war is becoming costly to them."

Issayas also charged that Western countries are collaborating with the Soviet Union by providing economic aid to the ruling Ethiopian derg, which helps to keep the present regime in power despite widespread internal opposition, and despite its strong military and political ties with the Eastern bloc.

"The Derg is doing its best to improve its relations with Western European countries and with the U.S. to resolve its economic crisis," Issayas said, adding that the Soviet Union did not appear to be giving Ethiopia any economic help while at the same time demanding full payment for the massive supplies of arms sent to Ethiopia over the past two years.

While the guerrilla leader expressed confidence that the coming months would see the Eritreans once again advancing militarily against Ethiopian forces, he pointed to the deepening economic and political problems in Ethiopia itself as the key long-term factors that would being that country to the conference table to negotiate an end to this war, the longest-running armed conflict in Africa.

Eritrea: Guerrilla offensive

The Guardian (New York), July 4, 1979

Sahel, Eritrea

Nationalist Eritrean guerrillas opened a series of major offensives against Ethiopian garrisons here June 4.

And on the night of June 21 the Eritrean People's Liberation Front (EPLF) captured the city of Decamare and held it for three hours while removing or destroying large quantities of Ethiopian Army food and arms, according to EPLF leaders. Decamare is a major Eritrean city less than 25 miles south of the capital of Asmara. The town was evacuated by the EPLF during last year's Ethiopian offensive.

In Decamare EPLF spokespeople report that an Ethiopian brigade of 1200 soldiers was defeated and grain storage areas holding about 660,000 pounds of grain were burned down. Three Ethiopian army officers were arrested and taken to liberated areas. In addition large stores of arms were seized.

Spokesmen for the Eritrean Liberation Front (ELF) also say that the ELF has over-run two Ethiopian-held villages in the western Eritrean lowlands.

These actions may signal the opening of these guerrilla counteroffensive. The main Ethiopian forces appear tied down on two 12-mile long conventional battle front here in Sahel. One force is near the Red Sea coast east of the EPLF base area, while the other is between the Ethiopian-held town of Afabet and the EPLF-held town of Nakfa.

The Ethiopian forces here are estimated to number 43,000. Some small ELF units are operating with the EPLF, a sign of the new move toward guerrilla unity.

Large mobile EPLF units are also increasingly active in the central Eritrean highlands, with these forces reportedly now large enough to capture any town but Asmara or Massawa. The EPLF is also mounting guerrilla operations in the Ethiopian rear here in Sahel, destroying Ethiopian supply trucks by land mines or ambush.

The EPLF says that its strategic retreat last year to positions of strength and its resumption of classical guerrilla warfare tactics has now changed the balance of forces and given them the military initiative.

Eritreans Fear Return Of Red Terror

The Miami Herald, July 5, 1979

Sahel, Eritrea

The war in Ethiopia's Eritrea province has dragged on for 18 years, the longest-running war in Africa today. Here is a report on Asmara, the provincial capital held by the Ethiopians.

Eritrean civilians fleeing the Ethiopian-controlled city of Asmara say they fear a renewal of the government's "Red Terror" campaign after several months of apparent calm there.

The refugees cited the recent step-up of guerrilla actions near the Eritrean capital, which serves as Ethiopia's main military base in this contested Red Sea territory, along with a large number of arrests last month as evidence of deteriorating relations between the military government and the civilian population.

The group of 23 boys and men between the ages of 16 and 43 sat together in a rural training camp of the Eritrean People's Liberation Front (EPLF), awaiting acceptance as volunteers to join the war for independence, now in its 18th year.

They began by saying that Asmara had calmed down on the surface late last year after Russian-backed Ethiopian government military advances had lifted a year-long siege around the city. The supply of electric power and fresh water had been restored, security was more relaxed and the overt "Red Terror" campaign of arbitrary arrest and execution of dissidents seemed to have abated, they said.

The population of the city, now down to near 100,000 from a high of almost 300,000 was increasing for the first time in years. However, the refugees insisted that underneath this facade things are worse than ever.

The refugees said that old people are entering the city to escape the insecurity of the contested countryside, where there is constant skirmishing between government and guerrilla forces, and that the young still are making their way out.

The men complained of rampant inflation and increased taxes while they said there had been no salary increases since 1975. "It is worse for workers now than it was under (Emperor) Haile Selassie," muttered one 23-year-old man.

When asked for specific examples, Sebhatu, a 43-year-old worker and father of six, answered through a translator that he had labored in a shoe factory for 25 years. He said that under the original Italian owner he had earned $12 (Ethiopian) per day, on which he paid a 4 per cent tax to the Selassie government. Since the self-described socialist military junta came to power in 1974, he said he still made $12 each day, but now he paid monthly taxes of $22.50 for drought relief in Wollo province, $12 to a pension fund, $12 to support the government militia, $18 for normal taxes, $4 for education and $4 for health, for a total of $72.50 or about 25 per cent of his salary.

Sebhatu added that education and health taxes existed previously, but they were paid by his employer before the business was nationalized. He also said that he now was required to attend weekly meetings in his factory, but he said that when the subject of taxes was raised, the questioner was accused of subversion or sympathy with the guerrillas.

"When you see a man asking critical questions, you will not find him around your factory after three days," added another man.

A 28 year-old teacher named Asbaha said that he spent seven months in prison through this past January for suspicion of collaborating with the EPLF.

Asbaha said he had been repeatedly tied with his arms outstretched around a long stick and hung upside down.

"They put a rag in my mouth and a cover on my eyes," he recounted in English. "There are 15 youngsters who stand around you with sticks and other things to beat you continuously in all corners of your body for three hours, especially on your feet. It is few who survive."

Asbaha said he also had been forced to stand on hot asphalt. "For one month I could not walk without help."

Among other torture techniques that Asbaha said he witnessed were the dipping of prisoners' fingers in the hot asphalt, the extraction of fingernails, electric shocks and the firing of a pistol close to the ear after threatening death.

Another man added that 130 persons had been arrested in Asmara on May 5 and there was a general fear that this signaled the reopening of the terror. Refugees also said that the government is stepping up efforts to force civilians to join the militia to fight the guerrillas.

Sebhatu, the shoe factory worker, said that on May 1 a government official came to his factory and asked for 25 men and 25 women volunteers. "Everybody kept silent," Sebhatu said.

$10-a-month Soldiers Desert Ethiopia

The Miami Herald, July 15, 1979

Sahel, Eritrea

"I hate fighting," said the 24-year-old soldier. "I said to myself, 'let it be.' When my chance came, I left the front line."

The speaker was one of 16 former soldiers of the Ethiopian army who had left their posts in the embattled Red Sea territory of Eritrea within the past three weeks.

Two lay shivering with malaria under a tree. The others sat in a semicircle on the sandy bank of a dry riverbed in the heart of the guerrilla base area of the Eritrean People's Liberation Front (EPLF).

The soldiers spoke ruefully of the costly victories won by the Russian-backed Ethiopian government against Eritrean guerrillas late last year, followed by a lengthy stalemate that has left the rank-and-file of the army frightened and discouraged.

Most of the deserters had been members of Ethiopia's peasant militia. They said they were conscripted through local peasant associations and sent to fight for $20 per month, half of which, one added, was taken from them as compulsory contribution to the "call of the Motherlands."

They came from all over Ethiopia and had been on the front lines of Eritrea's dogged war for independence from Ethiopia for the past 11 months, since the opening of Ethiopia's all-out campaign to regain control of the strategic coastal territory.

The men calmly described spectacular and sometimes tragic military exchanges in which hundreds, and occasionally thousands, of their countrymen were killed by the guerrillas. A 19-year-old peasant from Tigray province told of his experience in the Battle of Elabared last November when his 400-man unit met an EPLF force.

Using a thorn-covered branch, he draw lines in the sand to show how he saw the guerrillas in front of them and then groups of herdsman with their sheep and goats on both sides. By the time their unit was encircled, the Ethiopians realized that the "shepherds" were guerrillas, he said.

"They started firing, to," he said. "We were surprised and we ran to a small hill." Less than 150 were left alive after two hours, the peasant concluded.

A peasant from Wollega told of the virtual annihilation of the 508th Task Force in fighting three months ago near the EPLF-held town of Nakfa. He said he watched a 500-man force of the elite Flame Brigade and a 500-man militia force enter the battle, but only 80 of the Flames and 14 militia returned.

The Ethiopian deserters predictably complained about their treatment and complimented the EPLF, but the specifics of their individual statements were at the same time convincing.

They spoke of seeing many of their fellow soldiers suffering anal bleeding from severe diarrhea, for which they received no medication. They also said they had seen others die of thirst in the sun-baked Red Sea coastal plains while their officers scoffed at requests for water and insisted that they sacrifice themselves "for the Motherland."

When asked why they had left their posts, four referred to listening to the EPLF's new radio, "Voice of the Masses," which broadcasts in the Ethiopian language of Amharic as well as in three Eritrean languages.

"It was forbidden, but I listened when I could," said a 19-year-old peasant from Wollo province. "They were explaining the bad deeds of the Derg (Ethiopia's ruling junta) and the positive developments of EPLF. I was impressed. When I compared, I preferred to be with EPLF."

Another said that after being overhead criticizing the government he was relieved of guard duty and told to rest for the day. By coincidence, he added, a battle began then.

"It went on for the whole day," he said. "When it was finished I slept, but I understood that they were going to kill me so during the night I blindly escaped."

The deserters said they had been told that the EPLF would kill them if they were caught.

"Not by the gun but by fire, and then we would be left to the wild animals," said one, who added that what persuaded him to desert was an Eritrean civilian in a bar who whispered that he would be cared for by the EPLF.

None, however, had a clear idea of what the future might hold. One said that he had seen 14 former POWs released by the EPLF killed by the Derg in the city of Decamare earlier this year.

"We cannot go back. We cannot stay here. I don't know what I will do," he concluded.

Eritrea: War tide turning

The Guardian (New York), July 18, 1979

Sahel, Eritrea

As Ethiopian forces mobilize for an imminent renewal of their year-long military offensive here, nationalist Eritrean guerrillas predict a defeat for their heavily-armed foe. And they say that defeat may turn the tide of war in favor of the Eritreans.

"The Ethiopians, despite all their weaknesses, are doing their utmost to mobilize their forces, reorganize the, reinforce them," said Issayas Afwerki, assistant general secretary of the Eritrean People's Liberation Front (EPLF) in an interview near the front lines.

"We are prepared to face that, and we feel that this round will be the last," Issayas said. He added that "the next round will lead to the collapse of their military institution."

The EPLF leader said the guerrillas had evidence of an Ethiopian buildup accompanied by Russian military advisers, in Western Eritrea near the border with Sudan.

The 33-year-old military strategist described the current military situation here as a "stalemate" following four successive Ethiopian campaigns. These pitted 120,000 troops and hundreds of Russian-supplied armored vehicles, heavy artillery, rocket launchers and MiG jets against Eritrean guerrillas. In their offensive last year, the Ethiopians were able to advance deep into guerrilla-held territory, recapturing all but two towns and cities previously held by the Eritrean independence forces.

Strategic Retreat

Confronted with a numerically and technically superior enemy, the Eritreans made a strategic retreat to their mountainous northern base area, reverting to classical guerrilla warfare. They then began a systematic effort to whittle down their opposition while avoiding heavy losses for themselves. Issayas claims that Ethiopia lost 40,000-50,000 troops during this period.

The guerrilla leader said that Eritrean losses were less than one tenth of this, because of their ambush-and-retreat tactics. When they reached the harsh terrain of Sahel, the utility of Ethiopia's heavy armored artillery was effectively cancelled out.

"Our main strength is flexibility and we have exploited this to the maximum in successfully working to demolish the enemy forces, in

maintaining our military initiative and in maintaining our manpower," Issayas said.

"Our strategy was to withdraw, if it was necessary, from all liberated towns to preserve our strong points," he continued. "Now
they have reached a stage where they cannot advance further from
their present positions and their morale and combat efficiency are
very low."

Issayas conceded that Ethiopia still holds the advantage of heavier arms. But he cited the logistic and supply problems which plague
the Ethiopians due to guerrilla actions.

The Ethiopians had anticipated a quick resolution of the 18-year
Eritrean war after the series of offensives, according to Issayas. He
said that Eritrean intelligence suggests that the battlefield presence of
Soviet advisers has decreased lately, due to the failure of their strategy. "Maybe they have to reassess their position because of their
underestimation of the Eritrean revolution," he added. "The war is
becoming costly to them."

The EPLF leader also charged that Western countries are providing economic aid to the ruling Ethiopian derg, which helps to keep
the present regime in power despite widespread internal opposition.

"The derg is doing its best to improve its relations with Western
European countries and with the U.S. to resolve its economic crisis,"
Issayas said. He pointed to Ethiopia's deepening economic and political problems as the long-term factors which would bring that country to the conference table eventually.

Elsewhere in Sahel, the EPLF maintains a large repair workshop
which services the armed struggle. The workshop, the size of a town,
is located in a narrow valley in the heart of the remote EPLF base
area. All over the walls of the main office and the workshops, slogans
remind people that "Self-reliance is the key to our victory" and
"Today's small factories are tomorrow's big industries."

The shops themselves are operating on a smaller scale than last
year, when the guerrillas were forced to retreat from their positions in
the Red Sea area's larger towns. Now the repair shops work only at
night, and mainly use hand tools. Heavier machinery has been hidden
because there is an ever-present danger of air attack from Ethiopian
jets. "There is something under every tree, so if a plane came and
threw a bob here it could not help hitting something," said Goitom,
the EPLF fighter in charge of the workshops.

In one shop a dozen guerrilla workers are using heavy mallets to flat-
ten pieces of corrugated iron. The metal sheets, taken off government

buildings during the retreat, are fashioned into oven covers, water and fuel containers and light shades.

The largest and most important shop is that for weapons repair. Here light, medium and heavy arms are strewn across reinforced work tables, as guerrilla technicians hunch over machine tools that shower sparks on the dirt floor. "We make three kinds of repairs," explained one worker, sliding up his protective goggles to talk. "We replace the missing parts thrown away by the retreating Ethiopians. We repair the damaged ones, and we fix the mechanical defects."

In front of him lay the black barrel and casing of a U.S.-made heavy Browning machine gun. Next to it lay a U.S.-made 57 mm recoilless rifle and a .50 caliber Russian-made Dashka heavy machine gun. Along the walls rows of smaller arms reflected the checkered history of foreign involvement behind Ethiopian efforts to crush the Eritrean independence movement. All, according to EPLF officials, were captured on the battlefield.

Eritrea: Ethiopian attack

The Guardian (New York), July 25, 1979

Sahel, Eritrea

Ethiopian forces have launched a major attack on Nakfa, a town held by the forces of the Eritrean Peoples Liberation Front (EPLF).

The 3-pronged attack, anticipated by the liberation forces of Eritrea for several weeks, opened July 14. On July 16, more than 2000 Ethiopian troops were killed and 4000 wounded in fierce hand-to-hand fighting outside Nakfa, according to EPLF leaders.

The Eritrean people have waged an 18-year struggle for independence from Ethiopia. The last five months have seen a stalemate following a strategic retreat by the EPLF during an all-out Ethiopian offensive last year.

Ethiopians Trapped

Last week, an attempted Ethiopian advance was trapped in a small valley, where the EPLF counterattacked. "Nearly all their artillery and mechanized equipment was paralyzed. This was decisive," said one EPLF leader. His forces claim they have captured three Soviet T-54 tanks with 650 light arms as well as other machine guns and a large quantity of ammunition.

Heavy artillery and air bombardment is reported taking place on the northeastern coastal front, but there is no troop movement, while troops at a third Ethiopian front are bogged down in the Sahel mountains without armored and mechanized supply lines.

Meanwhile, the Tigray Peoples Liberation Front reported from Tigray, a neighboring province which is also the scene of armed resistance to the Ethiopian government, that they captured two Ethiopian government garrisons and several vehicles.

A recent visit to the eastern front, where the Eritrean guerrilla fighters have faced the Ethiopian army since Jan. 26 shows that resistance there has been unflagging. The Ethiopians drove inland in January from the Red Sea in an offensive designed to penetrate the EPLF's heavily defended base area, according to Chinetti, the brigade commander of the guerrilla forces there.

This drive followed a successful campaign by Ethiopian forces to regain control of this Red Sea territory's main towns and highways, which had for almost two years been under guerrilla control.

Stalemate Since January

The Ethiopian forces have tried twice in major drives to push beyond this point since January, but they have been stopped each time, according to Chinetti.

The Ethiopian army has been supported by armored personnel carriers, tanks, rocket launchers, and an undetermined number of heavy artillery pieces, according to EPLF estimates. The Ethiopian forces have also occasionally been supported by naval barrages and by daily aerial attacks from Ethiopia's MiG jet fighters dropping cluster antipersonnel bombs, 250 kilogram conventional bombs and an unidentified "fike" bomb, according to Chinetti.

The EPLF also uses heavy mortars and a variety of artillery including some mounted on tanks, all of which they claim was captured from Ethiopia in earlier battle, though some of the ammunition is likely to come from outside sources.

Ethiopia steps up war on Eritrean guerrillas

The Miami Herald, July 29, 1979

Nakfa, Eritrea

The sounds of war were clearly audible above the rustle of the pre-dawn breeze on the ridge.

At daybreak the percussion of the artillery was joined by the whistle of MiG jets. A new round in Ethiopia's offensive against Eritrean guerrillas had begun.

It is the climax of a war that has already left tens of thousands dead or wounded and made some 100,000 civilians homeless.

The Eritreans are fighting for independence for the former Italian colony, annexed by Ethiopia almost two decades ago. The Ethiopians-with huge Russian military assistance-are determined to hold on to Eritrea and to its two strategically placed ports on the Red Sea.

In the battle for Nakfa, two of black Africa's largest armies are locked in a contest to decide Eritrea's fate. Each proclaims that the battle will be decisive, if not for the 18-year-old war, at least for the immediate future. They prepared for it for nearly four months. The decision will not be long coming.

As we approached Nakfa's mountain citadel, the din grew louder. Small arms fire was punctuated by the tinny explosion of shells, and by the deep rumbling of rocket barrages from Ethiopia's 'Stalin organ' multiple launchers.

At dawn the first Ethiopian MIG-23s arrived. They soared high above in sweeping circles, then swooped to disgorge their Russian-made anti-personnel canisters on the trenches of the Eritrea People's Liberation Front (EPLF).

By 5.30 a.m. close to 15,000 Cuban - trained Ethiopian peasant soldiers were charging forward on two flanks, east and west of Nakfa, behind lines of Russian T-54 tanks and BRDM-2 armored cars. An hour later they were forced to pull back, the bodies of their comrades littering the scrub-covered plains. A knocked-out tank lay smoking; another had been taken by the EPLF.

At 10 the Ethiopians came on again, only to be repulsed by the entrenched guerrillas supported by fire from previously captured mortars.

Late in the afternoon the Eritreans debarked from their trenches to make a two-mile deep foray towards the Ethiopian lines before returning to their original positions under cover of darkness.

At Nakfa the shooting ceased two hours after dark and I went into the town. It was empty of all but a handful of EPLF fighters, the 4,000 inhabitants having long since left to escape daily bombardment.

Later I was taken in a battered Land Rover with a single shaded lamp to meet two members of the EPLF's 13-man Political Bureau. Ali Sayid and Petros Solomon were waiting.

They were tired but exhilarated by the day's events. 'We are sure the Ethiopians will fail this time,' said Petros.

He added that the campaign differed little from preceding ones except for Ethiopia's much heavier reliance on artillery. He insisted, 'the effect is limited because of our underground system of trenches.'

Guerrillas Ring Asmara

Observer Foreign News Service (London), July 30, 1979

Outside Asmara, Eritrea

A veil of gray-brown size haze lay over Asmara as we peered through a thicket of evergreen trees on the crest of a mountain ridge overlooking the Eritrean capital.

Kneeling behind a two-man stone fortification with the commander of a battalion of the Eritrean People's Liberation Front (EPLF), I surveyed the vacant landscape directly in front of us. Less than a mile away, across a shallow valley of uncultivated farmland was the deserted village of Waukie.

"That is where their artillery is," whispered the guerrilla fighter, pointing to a small hill, adding that there were only 350 Ethiopian soldiers stationed there, with their ammunition and supplied loaded aboard a truck in case of a sudden retreat.

On either side of us, an unbroken chain of primitive EPLF blockhouses, constructed of stone and dirt, stretched along the spine of the hills ringing Asmara. It is interrupted only by the main highways linking the city and its 10,00 man Ethiopian occupation force with other Government held towns in four directions, according to EPLF leaders.

With the exception of a handful of villages on the plains surrounding Asmara, the countryside appeared to be entirely under guerrilla control.

In a three-week tour of the area on foot, the only signs I saw of the Ethiopian army were a network of abandoned trenches and four burned Russian and East German vehicles on the road between the Ethiopian occupied towns of Afabet and Keren.

Crossing the Ethiopian lines from the EPLF's besieged base area in the northern Sahel mountains was a relatively easy matter. We walked around them under cover of darkness with a caravan of a dozen camels bound for the central highlands with food and medical supplies.

We threaded our way along a network of centuries-old footpaths, worn ankle deep into the jagged volcanic peaks, and we followed the winding courses of dry riverbeds in two-to four-hour stints from one small EPLF camp to the next.

Each guerrilla station was well-stocked with grain and ammunition. South of Afabet, a Battalion of 600 men and women guarded our passage across the road then being used by Ethiopian convoys to reinforce and supply their troops around Nakfa. The assignment of this guerrilla force was to disrupt the Ethiopian movement with ambushes and landmines.

During the past six months, EPLF "engineering squads" have destroyed 560 trucks and put out of action over 150 armored vehicles, according to EPLF statistics.

Though the Ethiopian Government claims to control the Asmara region, it appeared that the elaborate infrastructure - developed by the EPLF two years earlier during their military ascendancy - remains intact but for mechanized transport links with the Sahel base.

EPLF military units were much in evidence. Early one morning we met a silent file of 400 guerrillas carrying automatic rifles and RPG7 grenade launchers, their ammunition belts slung across their chests.

They were returning from a clandestine overnight raid into a nearby Ethiopian-occupied village, according to the young bearded leader. The purpose of the mission was, he said, primarily political: to keep the Ethiopians off-balance and to build the morale of the civilians.

There have been 17 Ethiopian attempts to penetrate this area over the past six months, all repulsed, according to EPLF Central Committee member Habte Giorgis. The guerrilla leader also said that the EPLF has, in the same period, overrun 15 Government camps and attacked 13 convoys there.

These actions were aimed at interfering with Ethiopia's extended supply and logistics operations, he said, but he stressed the otherwise low profile of the day-to-day guerrilla activities.

Small commando teams make nightly incursions into the outlying Government-held villages and the larger towns to distribute propaganda, make off with supplies and to punish "collaborators," Giorgis said, citing the recent kidnapping of Shirba Woldezion, the appointed administrator for Zagur village. He would not comment about Woldezion's fate.

Habte also claimed that simultaneous bomb explosions in all Ethiopian occupied towns had prevented the Government from holding elaborate May Day rallies, and he said that he pad participated in a recent night action in the city of Decamare, where 350 tons of grain were burned and nine collaborators captured without a shot being fired.

"The Ethiopians ran away," he said. "They didn't even give us a chance to kill them."

"The enemy is incapacitated here," added Stephanos Afeworki, another Central Committee member stationed near Asmara. "It cannot even take small moves against us here any more.

"What you have to understand is that the whole of the Ethiopian force is in Sahel. Here, in the cities and the countryside, they are completely isolated. They are in pockets with no control of the people.

"When they are defeated in Sahel the whole thing will crumble."

The steady build-up of guerrilla units, supplies and ammunition around the towns and along the roads between them during my tour indicated that they are preparing to take advantage of this situation as soon as the results are in from the northern Sahel battlefront.

The likely course such action would take is an initial cutting of the highways to block supplies, the encirclement of the towns and then siege and assault of one of them at a time, such as took place during the EPLF's 1977 offensive.

But the possibility of an Ethiopian collapse also brings with it the risk and chaos and terror aimed at the captive civilian population, according to Afeworki. "You see these aspects when they are on the offensive. Imagine what will happen when this army is defeated," he said.

MiGs Against Nomads

Observer Foreign News Service (London), July 31, 1979

Ayn, Eritrea

After 18 years of war, Eritreans are as determined as ever to win their independence. Russian bombs and rockets won't stop them, reports Dan Connell.

At the 7 a.m. we unpacked our two camels and spread out under the sparse shade of a thorny acacia tree to brew tea and to rest for the day.

During the next two hours a series of camel caravans plodded past in the dry river bed, laden with the curved wooden poles of the Eritrean nomads' huts and topped with brilliantly colored, mated straw canopies decorated with bright red or blue crosses to announce recent marriages.

The nationalist guerrillas of the Eritrean People's Liberation Front (EPLF) with whom I was travelling make it a practice not to move by day due to the ever-present threat of bombing by Ethiopia's Russian-supplied MiG jet fighters.

But the families walking before us - with the women perched precariously on the heavily loaded camels and the small children running alongside to herd the oxen, goats and sheep - were migrating inland from the parched Red Sea coastal plains to seasonal farms in the interior highlands, where rain is now falling.

Shortly after 9 o'clock we heard the two fighter aircraft buzz overhead. "They're going to bomb the people," said Goitom Asghedom, my 29-year-old guerrilla escort on this seven-week tour o the Eritrean war zone.

I was skeptical. There was no mistaking the processions for anything but civilians. The semi-annual population shift through this area is well known. The practice dates back to an era long before this strategic territory was colonized by the Italians in 1890 and centuries before Ethiopia laid claim to it after the Second World War.

Again the high-pitched whine of a MiG 21 shattered the stillness as it raced up the twisting, scrub-covered valley, the second warplane in its wake.

Seconds later we heard the first explosion. Then, close behind, another sharp blast echoing off the barren rocky hills. For six to seven minutes we listened to the sudden, shrieking dives as bombs and rockets peppered the dry wash ahead of us.

Abruptly they were gone and the only sound was the whisper of a hot, dry wind.

When we reached the site of the attack, we found a pool of blood in the sand. Nearby lad a twisted steel bomb fragment with Russian letters engraved upon it.

But the toll was surprisingly light: two women and a seven-year-old boy with minor shrapnel wounds, five camels hurt, one of the beasts in its death throes.

"They were on us in a moment," explained Saleh Mohammed Ali, the 20-year-old bridegroom of one of the wounded women. "They passed us on both sides and turned around to bomb us before we could hide."

Asghedom tore cloth strips from the sheet he carries on his webbed belt and first bandaged one woman's leg to cover a hole the size of a gold ball. As he wrapped the gash in the other's neck and swabbed the child's bleeding head, he instructed the nomads to go directly to the nearest EPLF field clinic, a three-hour walk from there.

"Why bomb civilians?" I asked my companions afterward. "To terrorize the people, to turn them against us," he said. If this is so, the opposite effect appears to result.

Again and again on a journey that took me on foot through remote peasant villages, temporary nomadic settlements and small towns crowded with refugees in the guerrilla-controlled areas of Eritrea, I questioned civilians on this point.

"Wouldn't you rather see the war come to an end after these 18 years of fighting, no matter who wins?" I asked.

"No!" one man told me. "The fighters are our children. It is our war, too."

"This is our land," said Nur Humedai, a 75-year-old peasant who pounded the ground with his hand-hewn walking stick. "We don't want anyone else's land, just our own. Even if Russia and Cuba help Ethiopia, we will fight until there is only one man left."

Struggle For Victory In Eritrean Camp

The News Line (London), August 2, 1979

Chalhanti, Sudan (Reuters)

The sun beat down with ferocious intensity at nine in the morning as we drove into the secluded refugee camp, nestling in the Red Sea coastal hills.

The camp houses 9,750 people, mostly women and small children, driven from the fighting three hours' ride away where Ethiopia's Russian-backed army is battling guerrillas of the Eritrean People's Liberation Front (EPLF).

The guerrillas are fighting for the independence of the former Italian colony of Eritrea; annexed by Ethiopia almost two decades ago.

Strategic

The Ethiopian regime is determined to hold on to Eritrea and its two strategic ports on the Red Sea.

Chalhanti is one of more than a dozen refugee camps in Sudan where over 300,000 Eritreans have gathered during the last ten years of war, according to Sudanese government figures.

But this one is different because it is administered and supplied by the EPLF, not Sudan. This poses thorny political problems and EPLF leaders here say there are rumors that the Sudan government may try to move the camp in November to a new location further from the Eritrean border in order to take control of the refugees themselves.

For the present, however, Chalhanti is run as though it were an Eritrean island, much in the way the guerrillas administer villages within Eritrea behind their front lines.

The camp is divided between an EPLF Revolution School for close to 2,000 children, a section for handicapped guerrilla fighters and a third area for adult civilian refugees and another estimated 4,000 young children.

The students live a spartan life together in the burning hills as they attend classes in reading, writing, math, geography, science, health, politics and current events.

The juvenile trainee guerrillas wear plain green military uniforms and under EPLF supervision maintain their part of the camp. Small boys and girls can be seen carrying water from a well in the otherwise dry river bed, washing their clothes and cooking the traditional flatbread over scattered fires.

Many are the sons and daughters of refugees and of fighters now on the battlefronts in Eritrea and about 250 are orphans according to my guerrilla escort, Goitom Asghedom.

Near the school is another camp for the 1,650 handicapped fighters, war victims who have lost eyes, arms and legs, and who are here to learn a simple skill to allow them to continue to participate in Eritrea's struggle for independence, Goitom said.

There are small metal, carpentry and electronics workshops camouflaged under thorny acacia trees in ease of Ethiopian air attack, but severe shortages of equipment and materials appear to limit the possibilities for rehabilitation on a large scale.

The 29-year-old guerrilla walking with me said there were also three-month typing courses offered to those with leg injuries. But he added that there were only a handful of typewriters.

"Our main problem is finding ways to keep the people busy," he said as we toured the civilian refugee area. There were 400 men there kept occupied with house construction, he said, but he conceded that there was little to do for the 2,140 women.

Seminars

Adults and children in this part of the camp attended political seminars three times a week plus daily literacy classes, he said. But the blistering heat which was then over 120 degrees Fahrenheit discourages outdoor activity in the daylight hours. Most of the inhabitants spend the days in their canvas tents occupied with household chores among their meager belongings.

One problem is medical care. There are, for instance, 70 outpatients a day in a single clinic and with shortages of medicines and medical equipment, the camp's limited resources are badly strained.

But Chalhanti residents are in extremely good spirits, regarding themselves not as refugees but as people only temporarily forced out of their homeland who will speedily return.

"We will not be here long", insisted one wrinkled elderly woman who fled from the city of Decamare ten months ago. "The enemy will be defeated soon, we know this." And these sentiments were echoed by many other camp residents interviewed throughout the day.

Endless War Drags Ethiopia Into Abyss

The Miami Herald, August 2, 1979

Sahel, Eritrea

The war for Ethiopia's northern province of Eritrea has waged for 18 years—Africa's longest, biggest and almost forgotten battle. It is a war that few Western newsmen have witnessed. Correspondent Dan Connell, traveling on foot with guerrillas, spent eight weeks at the front and behind Ethiopian lines and filed this report.

Ethiopia's mercurial dictator, Col. Mengistu Haile Mariam, appears to be in serious trouble, and with him Russia's boldest-and most expensive-African adventure. The Ethiopian government is facing its most acute crisis since the self-proclaimed socialist military junta seized power in 1974.

Against a backdrop of seemingly insoluble economic difficulties, political instability and continuing outbreaks of armed opposition in far-flung areas of the fragile empire, Mengistu's Soviet-equipped and Cuban-trained army is taking a major trouncing in the northern territory of Eritrea.

Ironically, the licking is coming at the hands of a left-wing guerrilla movement that the Soviets once supported against the America and Israeli-backed regime of Emperor Haile Selassie.

Two weeks into the fifth round of its year-long series of military offensives against nationalist guerrillas who seek independence for Eritrea, a former Italian colony, there is a growing likelihood that the campaign will backfire into a major counter-offensive whose political repercussions could threaten Mengistu's brutal and tenacious grip on power.

For weeks Ethiopia's official radio has been predicting that the current drive, under preparation almost four months, would sound the death knell for the "Eritrean bandits." Forecasts have announced the imminent fall of Nakfa, the last major guerrilla-held town, in what both sides term the decisive test of this campaign.

Yet in these two weeks, Ethiopian forces have been unable to advance and have suffered casualties claimed by the guerrillas to number as high as 15,000.

The pressure is on Mengistu from many directions to end the 18-year-old war. The Ethiopian economy is in a shambles, with rampant inflation, nearly exhausted foreign reserves, a breakdown in trade between city and countryside, falling agricultural production, unrest in the industrial work force and soaring foreign debt for arms purchases from the Eastern bloc, according to Western intelligence sources.

An eight-week tour of guerrillas-controlled areas behind Ethiopian liens to within sight of the Eritrean capital of Asmara showed that the government's military position in Eritrea has deteriorated substantially since its dramatic advances last year, while the Eritrean guerrillas appear much strengthened.

By the opening of the present offensive only 70,000 Ethiopian troops remained from the 120,000 who invaded Eritrea, a strategic Red Sea territory a year ago, according to Issayas Afwerki, 33, field commander of the Eritrean People's Liberation Front (EPLF).

The EPLF also claims to have destroyed more than 560 Ethiopian trucks and about 150 Russian-supplied armored vehicles in this period while capturing more than 120 of the modern T54 tanks and BTR60 armored cars.

Ethiopia opened the present Eritrea campaign on July 16, with 40,000 troops almost equally divided between two main fronts in the northern Sahel mountains, according to Issayas. One front lies three miles-south Nakfa. The other stretches 20 miles along the north-eastern cost of the Red Sea.

A third new front also was opened between these, with 10,000 men of the 503rd Task Force, drawn from bases in the central Eritrean highlands, Issayas said.

Less than 10,000 largely inexperienced peasant militiamen remain stationed in Asmara, where an unknown number of Russian advisers and technicians are based, according to EPLF intelligence sources. The rest are said to be spread thin among the other occupied towns and in small garrisons along the key highways linking Asmara with the port of Massawa and with Keren, where there are barely 3,000 government troops defending Eritrea's second-largest city.

With Ethiopian control limited to the towns and the narrow corridors between them, EPLF units have positioned themselves in the surrounding countryside to defend large islands of liberated territory. A second smaller allied guerrilla force-the Eritrean Liberation Front (ELF)-also is active in the western lowlands near the Sudan border.

The EPLF has grown considerably over the past six months, with thousands of previously organized civilians from towns now occupied by the Ethiopians joining the guerrilla army and much of the local EPLF village militias called up for regular duty. The guerrillas now appear to have in excess of 40,000 men and women under arms, possibly as many as 60,000.

The ELF claims nine brigades, but reliable sources place their number at 4,000 to 5,000. However, of more political importance is that the long-standing rivalry between the two guerrilla fronts appears to be diminishing, and small, halting steps are taking place toward unifying them. The overt propaganda battle between them has ceased, and two battalions of the ELF are with the EPLF on the northeastern Sahel front line.

The EPLF also appears to have resolved its earlier ammunition shortages from undisclosed sources. It now is using dozens of previously captured heavy mortars, Russian 122mm, long-range guns and T54 tanks in battle.

Thus two highly sophisticated conventional armies now face each other in the battles raging in northern Eritrea. The rugged, volcanic terrain, long familiar to the Eritreans, cancels the Ethiopian superiority in armor and artillery, according to EPLF leaders, although they concede that they have little to counter the Soviet MiG fighter bombers.

The EPLF now claims to have broken the back of the present Sahel offensive, and it appears to be readying for a major counter-offensive there and in the highland plateau where its troops are positioned around government-occupied towns and along main highways.

Renewed heavy fighting was reported in the north last week, but guerrilla leaders say that the Ethiopian objective now is mostly defensive.

"Militarily speaking, the next step will be some sort of retreat or change of their positions in the Sahel area," the EPLF's Issayas said. "On our side now we have made sure that they will never be able to advance further from their present positions.

"If we get the chance to re-mobilize our forces, then the initiative will be in our hands. It is very difficult to predict what will happen next."

Meanwhile, the beleaguered Ethiopian government also is coming under attack in the neighboring province of Tigray, where guerrillas of the Tigray People's Liberation Front (TPLF) last week claimed to have overrun four small government garrisons and cut the key highway linking the capital of Addis Ababa with the northern battlefront.

The stepped-up actions of the TPLF effectively double the size of Ethiopia's northern front and jeopardize the vulnerable supply lines to Eritrea.

The combination of economic difficulties, political repression and the government's failure of adequately address the demands of other ethnic groups appears to be spawning more such guerrilla movements, with an Oromo Liberation Front (OLF) reporting military operations in the south and southwest. A resurgence of guerrilla activity also is reported in the southeastern Ogaden region by the Western Somali Liberation Front (WSLF).

With the apparent demise of the ultra-'left' Ethiopian People's Revolutionary Party (EPRP) in the towns, opposition there appears to be shifting to elements within the army itself, in what some observers liken to the period prior to the 1974 mutinies that brought down Haile Selassie's government.

The promise by Ethiopia's ruling military Derg to turn power over to a Communist political party appears less likely than ever after the collapse of a "common front" of five recognized left-wing organizations earlier this year. All but one-Col. Mengistu's Abyotawi Seded (Revolutionary Torch) since have been banned, although a new "Communist Union" has been announced for Marxist individuals loyal to the regime.

Mengistu's personal grip on the reins of government seems to be slipping today as power is said by reliable sources to be now evenly divided between him, Derg Secretary General Fikray Selassie and Lt. Legesse Asfaw, in charge of the political orientation of the army and therefore in direct control of the paramilitary cadre distributed throughout the armed forces.

There is increasing speculation that the Russians and Cubans have become disenchanted with Mengistu and his Eritrea policy. They are reported to favor Legese Asfaw as Mengistu's replacement.

A major Ethiopian defeat in Eritrea, as now seems likely, would have substantial political repercussions in Addis Ababa. Whether the Russians will stand by passively remains to be seen.

Among the possibilities for a military response are an escalation or the aerial bombing and the introduction of Cuban troops. However, while the EPLF reported a year ago that Cuban combat forces were in Eritrea, the guerrillas now say that all but a few have been shifted out again.

It is perhaps too late anyway for this round of the war as the EPLF can be expected to make its move within the next two to three weeks, providing Ethiopia and the Soviets with their worst setback yet in this seemingly interminable war.

Ethiopia's Offensive Might Appears Severely Crippled

The Miami Herald, August 3, 1979

Nakfa, Eritrea

The war for Ethiopia's northern province of Eritrea has raged for 18 years—Africa's longest, biggest and almost forgotten conflict. It is a war that few Western newsmen have witnessed. Correspondent Dan Connell, traveling on foot with guerrillas, spent eight weeks at the front and behind Ethiopian lines.

The thin, sparkling rim of a waning moon barely illuminated the rock-strewn valley floor as I rolled over to ask the guerrilla fighter on the blanket next to me, was it thunder or artillery that I heard.

"It is only the wind," he answered groggily, arising to load the camel.

But by the time we climbed to the crest of a high ridge, the sounds of war were clearly discernible over the gentle rustle of the predawn breeze, a syncopated percussion played at a steady if irregular rhythm, soon to be joined at daybreak by the shrill whistle of MiG jet fighters.

The fifth round of Ethiopia's year-long offensive against nationalist Eritrean guerrillas had begun, the climax of months of fierce and intense combat that had already left tens of thousands dead or wounded and an estimated 110,000 civilians homeless.

The Eritreans seek independence for the former Italian colony, annexed by Ethiopia almost two decades ago. The Ethiopians-with massive Russian military assistance-are determined to hold on to the strategic territory and its two key ports on the Red Sea.

The battle for Nakfa, under way today, pits two of the mightiest armed forces in Black Africa against each other in a contest to decide Eritrea's fate. Both sides say that it is to be decisive, if not for the overall protracted conflict, at least for the immediate future of the 18-year war. They have prepared for nearly four months. The results will not be long in coming.

As we approached the mountain citadel, the muffled din grew louder. The crackle of small arms fire was punctuated by the explosion of bursting shells and by the barrages of ground to ground rockets from Ethiopia's Russian launchers.

At dawn the first of a seemingly endless aerial parade of Ethiopian MiG 23s arrived overhead. They soared high above us in broad, sweeping circles, then swooped almost straight down to disgorge their Russian-made bombs on the trenches at the Eritrean People's Liberation Front (EPLF).

By 5:30 a.m., close to 15,000 Cuban-trained Ethiopian soldiers were charging forward on two flanks west of Nakfa behind phalanxes of Russian T54 tanks and armored cars. An hour later they were in retreat. The bullet-riddled bodies of the fallen littered the scrub-covered plains. One tank lay in smoking ruin, another taken by the EPLF.

At 10 o'clock, they came again in massive human wave only to be repulsed once more by the entrenched EPLF guerrillas who were themselves supported by a hall of artillery fire from previously captured heavy mortars, 122mm Russian guns and the long range cannon from T54 tanks secreted in the mountains behind them.

Late in the afternoon, the Eritreans left their underground fortifications and drove forward two miles to press their advantage only to withdraw to their original positions under cover of darkness to await the next day's combat.

Simultaneously, an estimated 20,000 Ethiopian troops surged forward and were also driven back on a 20 mile-wide front near Alghen in the Red Sea coastal foothills farther north. And a third new front was opened when 10,000 Ethiopian soldiers attempted to thrust inland between the two major fronts along a crude road previously constructed by the EPLF from the sea coast toward Nakfa. It, too, was stopped, according to EPLF military leaders in Nakfa.

Promptly at 8:05 p.m., as if the curtain had been drawn over this the first act of the campaign, the shooting near Nakfa ceased but for an intermittent burst of heavy weapons fire.

The town itself was empty of all but a handful of EPLF fighters. The 4,000 civilian inhabitants had long since departed to escape the daily air and land bombardment.

Late in the evening, I was taken in a battered Land Rover to a rendezvous on a sandy hillside with two members of the EPLF's 13-man Political Bureau, Ali Sayid and Petros Solomon.

The two commanders of the Nakfa front appeared tired but exhilarated by the day's events. "We are sure they will fall this time," said Petros.

The lanky 29-year-old military leader added that this campaign differed little from those that had come before but for a decidedly heavier reliance on the heavy artillery.

Still he insisted, "The effect of the heavy weapons is limited because of our hard work in building the underground system of trenches."

The next day brought renewed and save hand-to-hand fighting with EPLF claiming 2,000 Ethiopian dead and 4,000 wounded and only "light" casualties on their side. At nightfall, the positions remained the same.

By week's end the carnage had reached proportions that boggled the imagination - 15,000 Ethiopian soldiers killed, wounded or captured, according to the EPLF-and still no measurable advance.

The new third front had been trapped at Agat, a former EPLF transport depot prior to their retreat six months earlier. A surprise guerrilla attack early on the sixth day of the campaign "liquidated" an entire force of 6,000, according to EPLF spokesmen who claimed that 2,500 bodies had been buried in mass anonymous graves, over 550 captured. The numbers continue to rise as mopping up operations roll on.

A midnight visit to the Alghen front found the fighters in high spirits, regaling each other with accounts of the score of battles along the extended coastal battle lines.

"The infantry movement has been completely paralyzed now. What remains is the tanks, the artillery and the planes," said Central Committee member Teklai Aden later.

Sporadic but reduced fighting continues on the Nakfa and Alghen fronts, but Ethiopia's offensive capacity appears now to be severely crippled.

Meanwhile, the presence of guerrilla reserves and the movement of heavy arms and ammunition-including the captured Russian armor-behind EPLF lines indicates the Eritreans will not wait long to take the initiative into their own hands.

Peasants Want War To End—
But Only With A Victory

The Miami Herald, August 4, 1979

Ayn, Eritrea

At 7 a.m., we unpacked out two camels and spread out under the checkered shade of a thorny acacia tree to brew tea and to rest for the day.

During the next two hours a series of camel caravans plodded past in the dry riverbed, laden with the curved wooden poles of the Eritrean nomads' huts and topped with matted straw canopies decorated with bright red or blue crosses to announce recent marriages.

The nationalist guerrillas of the Eritrean People's Liberation Front (EPLF) with whom I was travelling make it a practice not to move by day due to the threat of bombing by Ethiopia's Russian supplied MiG jet fighters.

The families walking before us-with the women perched on the heavily loaded camels and the children running alongside to herd the oxen, goats and sheep-were migrating inland from the parched coastal plains to seasonal farms in the interior highlands where rain was falling. Shortly after 9 a.m., we heard two fighter aircraft buzz over head.

"They're going to bomb the people," said Goitom Asghedom, 29, my guerrilla escort.

I was skeptical. There was no mistaking the processions for anything but civilians. The semi-annual population shift through this area was well known. The practice dates back to an era long before this strategic territory was colonized by the Italians in 1890 and centuries before Ethiopia laid claim to it following World War II.

Again the high-pitched whine of a MIG21 shattered the morning stillness. The second warplane followed.

Seconds later we heard the first explosion. Then, close behind, another sharp blast echoed off the rocky hills. For several minutes we listened in silence as the sleek-birds of war circled above us and made sudden dives to pepper the dry wash with bombs and rockets.

Abruptly they were gone and the only sound was the whisper of a hot, dry wind.

Once again, the parade of camels, cattle, goats, sheep—and people—began to wander by our hillside vantage point as if nothing out of the ordinary had happened.

By the time we reached the site of the attack, the only sign of what had transpired was a pool of blood in the sand. Nearby lay a twisted steel bomb fragment with engraved Russian letters.

The toll was surprisingly light; two women and a 7-year-old boy with minor shrapnel wounds, five camels hurt, one in its death throes.

"We listened only one minute. Then they came behind us," explained Saleh Mohammed Ali, the 20-year-old bridegroom of one of the wounded women. "They passed us on both sides and turned around to bomb us before we could hide."

ERITREAN WAR GOES ON

SUDANOW, Khartoum, August 1979

In the middle of last month Ethiopia launched the fifth round of its year-long offensive in Eritrea, but within days Eritrean forces appeared to be gaining the upper hand. This campaign was likely to prove decisive and may provide a major turning point in this bitter and protracted war. Dan Connell, a frequent contributor to Sudanow on conditions in Eritrea, has just returned from a two-month visit to the area with the EPLF which took him behind Ethiopian lines up to the Asmara capital, and back to the EPLF's Sahel base area for the opening of the current offensive.

Two delta-winged MiG-21s knifed through the morning sky to awaken me at 730 on my first day in Eritrea with the Eritrean People's Liberation Front (EPLF). They circled high over the Sahel base area and then went into screeching dives above our hidden camp, each loosing a single bomb harmlessly into the rocky hills as EPLF anti-aircraft fire chattered in their wake.

From dawn to dusk Ethiopia's Russian-supplied — some say Russian-piloted — MiG 21 and 23 jet fighters patrol the Eritrean skies They search for signs of the armies of the EPLF and the Eritrean Liberation Front (ELF), which together occupy the arid northern mountains of Eritrea and the subtropical western lowlands. But apart from the entrenched guerrilla positions to the east and south of the base area, the Eritrean fighters offer few visible targets.

By day they are hidden from view beneath the scrawny

flat-topped acacia trees, in the thick underbrush alongside the now dry river beds or in underground caves and carefully camouflaged shelters. But when darkness falls over this inhospitable but strategic corner of Eritrea,the barren hills come alive.

Campfires flicker in the night, diesel-powered generators begin to splutter and chug as electric lights blink on and chains of headlights can be seen winding through the mountains from the EPLF supply convoys.

If it has proven difficult for Ethiopia's ruling military Dergue to search out and destroy the Eritrean guerrilla armies, so too has it been hard for the rest of the world to comprehend what is really going on here. Although the 18-year Eritrean war for independence has faded from the world news, the conflict continues to grind on at a pace and a scale difficult even for the eyewitness observer to grasp.

Six months ago the EPLF retreated from its former base area in the Red Sea coastal foothills to reestablish itself in the more rugged and defensible Sahel mountains. Today things seem little changed in the new location with workshops, hospitals, training camps, supply depots and transport garages functioning as before. And now there is also Dimtsi Hafash — EPLF's radio Voice of the Masses — broadcasting daily from the base in three Eritrean languages and the Ethiopian language,.Amharic.

A five-minute walk from my tent there were also 16 Ethiopian peasant soldiers who had recently deserted their posts to surrender to the EPLF. They described spectacular — and sometimes tragic — military exchanges in which hundreds, sometimes thousands, of their countrymen were killed by the elusive EPLF guerrillas.

A 19-year old farmer from Tigray told me of his experience in the battle of Elabared last November when his 400 man unit met an EPLF force. He said that groups of herdsmen with sheep and goats then appeared on both sides. Soon his unit was surrounded and the shepherds took out guns to join the attack. Within two hours, he added, only 140 of his comrades remained alive.

Another, a 30-year old peasant from Wollega told of the virtual annihilation of the 508th Task Force in fighting four months ago near the EPLF-held town of Nakfa. He said he watched a 500-man force from the elite Flame Brigade and a 500-man militia battalion enter the battle. Only 14 from the militia and 80 from the Flame Brigade returned. But little did we know then that within weeks Ethiopian peasants would be massacred around Nakfa in numbers that would dwarf even these staggering figures.

At that time the frontlines were generally quiet. Early one morning I journeyed in a captured landrover to the eastern front where EPLF forces—joined also by units of ELF—were defending against a 20,000-man Ethiopian force spread along a line 20 miles long.

The dawn came rapidly, as if a curtain were drawn open above our heads to reveal a pale blue swath of sky, dotted with tiny puffs of cottony white clouds. The harsh volcanic walls of the narrow river valley glowed a deep copper-colour in the first light as I crawled under a broadleaf tree and dropped off to sleep.

By nine o'clock the temperature had already reached the mid 40s—more than 100 degrees Fahrenheit—and it was still climbing. Six ringing concussions from heavy Ethiopian artillery shook the ground under my feet, but it was little more than a signal that the other side was still there. It was hard to imagine soldiers climbing up and down those jagged mountains in the blistering heat, as they did weeks later, and for the time being there was no movement, but for the MiGs high above us

A few days later I arrived in Nakfa, the main frontline town today. Nakfa lies cradled in a shallow dish behind the lip of a mountain ridge that drops off to the plains where the decisive battles of the current campaign have since raged. A mountain citadel, the town has been almost bereft of its civilian inhabitants for months as the people sought escape from the daily bombardment by Ethiopian planes and artillery that have reduced whole sections to mud and rubble.

One street, entirely deserted—its neat rows of tan-coloured buildings closed and locked—was almost divided in two by a pair of bomb craters over 15 feet deep. Whole sections of houses were missing. Twisted shards of iron from destroyed roofs littered the ground, a mute testimony of the ferocity of the recent year's fighting.

Crossing the Ethiopian lines from there was a relatively easy matter. We simply walked around them on one of several trails followed by EPLF camel caravans to the highlands in central Eritrea. Walking in two- to four-hour shifts we moved from one EPLF camp to another around the Ethiopian-held town of Afabet on to the slope areas of the plateau and finally to the highlands northeast of Asmara.

At each stop we were fed from apparently ample stocks of food stockpiled for the fighters and for civilian refugees. Whole battalions of EPLF fighters were observed moving in the night near the roads ostensibly under Ethiopian control. But no Ethiopian forces were to be found anywhere outside the towns themselves.

Much to my surprise I found the On our eight-day walk back toward the eastern coastal front and a third new situation in the densely populated highlands quite different from what I had been led to expect b the EPLF's characterisation of the area as a 'guerrilla' zone. Within a mile or less of the villages around Asmara occupied by Ethiopian forces, there were entrenched EPLF positions. A chain of stone and wood blockhouses stretched from near the Asmara-Massawa road around the key capital city to the Asmara-Keren road, which, according to the EPLF, continues in both directions across from these highways.

Behind these lines, operations of the Front seemed as I had left them eight months ago, but for the transport system. I visited flourishing EPLF citrus farms, coffee plantations, field hospitals, schools, a training camp, a grain mill and a series of supply stations. But more importantly, I went into towns and the villages where the civilian population maintained their mass associations of peasants, women, youth and workers, and their self-governing People's Assemblies and their armed militias.

Despite the increased economic difficulties brought on by the Ethiopian advances late last year and the subsequent outflow of refugees to the remaining liberated areas, the spirit of these people was unwavering, along with their patience.

In scores of interviews, 'Ethiopian socialism' was derided by people who recounted stories of the confiscation of produce from village-owned farming cooperatives set up earlier with EPLF help.

by their own accounts more hardened than ever against the Ethiopian occupation. They told of how the Ethiopians chose rich peasants who had opposed the EPLF s land reform to be the new governing Kebele chairmen of the occupied villages, and they described how rows of land mines had been planted in their fields, stripping them of their livelihood.

In contrast, they insisted, they had tasted freedom under the EPLF and now they would settle for nothing less, no matter how long it took to regain it. 'This is our land, declared one 75 year old peasant in Fische, pounding the ground with his walking stick for emphasis. 'We don't want anyone else's land, just our own. And even if Russia and Cuba help Ethiopia, we will fight until there is only one man left.'

When I asked a 45-year old widow if she wouldn't rather see the war end, regardless of who won, she responded indignantly: 'As far as I am concerned, I want to finish it now, thus night. But I don't want the war to stop if the enemy does not go out from our country. I want a victory.'

On our eight-day walk back toward Nakfa, where the decisive battles of the year-long Ethiopian offensive were about to be fought, I had one more graphic occasion to witness the Dergue s principal tactic in its efforts to win the Eritrean people to its side: terror.

At 7 o'clock one morning, we unpacked our camel near a water hole in another dry river-bed and spread out under the sparse, check-ered shade of a spiked acacia tree to brew tea and to rest for the day. During the next two hours,I watched a series of camel caravans pass laden with the curved wooden poles of semi-nomad huts and topped with brilliantly coloured, matted straw canopies which bore bright red crosses to announce recent marriages.

Shortly after nine, I heard the two MiGs fly over us. 'They're going to bomb the people,' said Goitom Asghedom, my EPLF escort. But I was doubtful. There was no mistaking the procession for any-thing but civilians with their goats and sheep being herded along by small children as they migrated inland.

Seconds later we heard the first explosion. Then close behind, a second. And then a third and a fourth. By the time we reached the site of the attack the only sign of what had happened was a crimson pool of blood in the sand.Nearby lay a grotesquely twisted steel bomb fragment with Russian letters engraved upon it. Two women and a seven year old boy were wounded. Five camels injured, one dying. Five families by their own accounts more hardened than ever against the Ethiopian occupation.

A week later, when I awoke at 4 a.m. outside Nakfa once again, I asked the fighter on the blanket next to me was it thunder or artillery that I heard. 'It is only the wind,' he answered, arising to load the camel. But by the time we climbed out of the valley to the crest of a high ridge, the sounds of war were clearly discernible over the rustle of the pre-dawn breeze, a syncopated percussion played at a steady if irregular rhythm, soon to be joined at daylight by the throaty whistle of MiGs.

The offensive that both sides said was to be decisive had begun.

The muffled din continued as we approached the town, with the MiGs remaining in the air late into the afternoon despite a thick cloud cover, but it was to no avail. The first Ethiopian assault started at 5.30 in the morning, but it was turned back within an hour by the EPLF. A second Ethiopian push was broken at ten o'clock and at 5 pm the EPLF counter-attacked to drive forward over two miles.

Simultaneous assaults were launched on the eastern coastal front and a third new Ethiopian front was opened between the other two as a force of 10,000 tried to drive inland toward the rear of Nakfa on a road previously constructed by the EPLF. By the weekend of Friday, July 20, the Ethiopian toll had climbed to figures that boggled the imagination with over 15,000 casualties and no ground gained. The third front was already liquidated entirely, with thousands of peasant soldiers dead and rotting in the blazing sun as EPLF fighters buried them in mass, anonymous graves and continued to round up stray prisoners and collect discarded arms.

The fighters sang and danced late into the night around hundreds of scattered campfires as they celebrated the climactic and apparently definitive defeat of Ethiopia's massive mechanized army. More battles remained to be fought there, but the long-awaited opportunity for the Eritreans to turn around and resume the offensive for themselves seemed finally at hand. In the highlands, far to the north, the peasants patiently awaited the EPLF's return.

Visit With Rebels Shows Ethiopia Failure

The Washington Star, August 1979

Sahel, Ethiopia

Correspondent Dan Connell has just completed an eight-week tour of guerrilla areas in Eritrea, Ethiopia's secession-minded northeast province. This is the first of two articles.

With the latest offensive to crush the guerrilla movement in its strategic Red Sea province grinding to a halt, the government of Col. Mengistu Haile Mariam appears to be in serious trouble.

Under pressure to bring the long guerrilla war to an end, Mengistu just over two weeks ago launched a new drive against the Eritrean rebels, who fought for independence first when the territory was an Italian colony, and are now fighting to free it from the status of an Ethiopian province.

An eight-week tour of rebel-held areas began with the simple act of crossing the Sudan border and walking around the flank of the Ethiopian lines at night with a camel caravan headed for the central highlands. What the tour revealed was the failure of the Ethiopians to make any significant advances in their offensive.

And with that failure, the frustrations that have built up in since the self-proclaimed "socialist" military junta seized power in 1974 threaten to explode, according to U.S. and other sources in the Sudan and sources in Eritrea itself.

An unraveling of authority in Addis Ababa would come as a heavy setback for the Soviet Union, which switched clients on the Horn of Africa to back the Ethiopian regime after first supporting Ethiopia's arch enemy, Somalia.

A military setback would come against a backdrop of seemingly insoluble economic difficulties, ongoing political instability and continuing outbreaks of armed opposition in far-flung areas of the fragile state.

Rebels Also Leftists

Ironically, Mengistu's Marxist-oriented, Russian-equipped and Cubans trained army is now undergoing a major trouncing in the northern Eritrean territory at the hands of a leftist guerrilla movement once supported by the Soviets against the U.S. and Israeli-backed regime of Haile Selassie.

For weeks Ethiopia's official radio has been predicting that the current drive, under preparation almost four months, would sound the death knell for the "Eritrean bandits."

Forecasts have announced the imminent fall of the last major guerrilla-held town, Nakfa, in what both sides term the decisive test of this campaign.

Yet in these two weeks, Ethiopian forces have been unable to advance and have suffered casualties claimed by the guerrillas to number as high as 15,000.

The pressure is on Mengistu from many directions to wind up the 18-year war. The Ethiopian economy is in a shambles with rampant inflation, near exhausted foreign reserves, a breakdown in trade between city and countryside, falling agricultural production, unrest in the industrial work force and soaring foreign debts for arms purchases from the Eastern bloc, according to Western intelligence sources.

The tour of guerrilla areas showed that the government's military position here has deteriorated substantially since the dramatic advances in a similar offensive launched last year, while the guerrillas appear much strengthened.

Occupying Forces Dwindle

By the opening of the present offensive only 70,000 Ethiopian troops remained from the 120,000 that invaded the strategic Red Sea territory a year ago, according to Issayas Afwerki, field commander of the Eritrean People's Liberation Front.

The Front also claims to have destroyed over 560 Ethiopian trucks and some 150 Russian-supplied armored vehicles in this period, while capturing more than 120 modern, Soviet-built T54 tanks and BTR60 armored cars.

Ethiopia opened the present Eritrea campaign July 16 with 40,000 troops almost equally divided between two main front in the northern Sahel mountains, according to the 33-year-old EPLF leader. One front lies three miles south of Nakfa. The other stretches 20 miles along the northwestern sea coast.

A third new front was also opened between these with 10,000 men drawn from bases in the central Eritrean highlands, Issayas said.

Few than 10,000 largely inexperienced Ethiopian peasant militiamen remain stationed in Asmara, the Eritrean capital, where an unknown number of Russian advisers and technicians are based, according to EPLF intelligence sources.

The rest are said to be spread thin among the other occupied towns and in small garrisons along the key highway linking Asmara with the port of Massawa and with Keren, where there are barely 3,000 government troops defending Eritrea's second largest city.

Strength in Countryside

With Ethiopian control limited to the towns and the narrow corridors between them, guerrilla units have positioned themselves in the surrounding countryside to defend large islands of "liberated territory."

A second, smaller allied guerrilla force-the Eritrean Liberation Front-is also active in the western lowlands near the Sudan border.

The EPLF has grown considerably over the past six months, with thousands of previously organized civilians from the now occupied towns joining the guerrilla army and much of the local village militias called up for regular duty. They now appear to have in excess of 40,000 men and women under arms, possibly as many as 60,000.

Thus, two conventional armies now face each other in northern Eritrea.

The rugged, volcanic terrain, long familiar to the Eritreans, cancels the Ethiopian superiority in armor and artillery, according to Front leaders, though they concede that they have little to counter the

Russian-built MiG fighter bombers.

The EPLF now claims to have broken the back of the present Sahel offensive, and it appears to be preparing a major counteroffensive there and in the highland plateau, where they are positioned around the government occupied towns and along the main highways.

Meanwhile, in Addis Ababa the possibility of Ethiopia's ruling military Derg turning power over to a Communist political party appears less likely than ever after the collapse of a "common front" of five recognized left organizations earlier this year.

Mengistu's personal grip on the reins of government seems to be slipping as power is said by reliable sources to be evenly divided between him, Derg Secretary General Fikray Selassie and Lt. Legesse Asfaw, in charge of the political orientation of the army and therefore in direct control of the paramilitary cadre distributed throughout the armed forces.

Guerrilla leaders report that the front-line presence of Russian advisers and Technicians in Eritrea has decreased recently.

But the question is whether the Russians will stand by passively if their clients face a major military defeat in Eritrea.

Eritrea: Ethiopian setback

The Guardian (New York), August 15, 1979

Sahel, Eritrea

The Eritrean battlefronts were quiet last week after three weeks of fighting that has left thousands of Ethiopian troops dead and wounded, according to Eritrean guerrillas.

The Ethiopians were held at bay on three fronts by Eritrean People's Liberation Front (EPLF) forces defending their northern Sahel base area in the fifth round of the government's yearlong offensive in Eritrea. While Ethiopian forces this fall launched, a major offensive and recaptured major cities, they were unsuccessful in their ultimate aim defeat of the EPLF. The guerrillas reverted to classical guerrilla warfare, retreating in order to strike back later.

The likelihood is that the EPLF will aim its main blow at the lines south of the town of Nakfa where some of the heaviest fighting took place during the last weeks. The objective will be to drive the demoralized Ethiopians back to the government-held city of Keren.

Such a push would not only relieve the pressure on their base area but would also reopen their mechanized supply lines to guerrilla positions in the densely populated central highlands where the EPLF is poised to move against the main Eritrean highways and the scattered Ethiopian garrisons there.

The war thus appears to be reaching a turning point. After a year of steady retreats in the face of Ethiopia's superiority in arms and manpower, the EPLF has apparently achieved a balance of force in its favor.

For weeks Ethiopia's official radio has been predicting that the latest drive, under preparation for our months, would sound the death knell for the "Eritrean bandits" and their 18 year war for independence. Forecasts have announced the imminent fall of the last major EPLF held town-Nakfa in what both sides termed the decisive test of this campaign.

Yet in the past three weeks, Ethiopian forces were unable to advance at any point.

"They have totally failed," said EPLF Assistant General Secretary Issayas Afwerki. "This last trial was the final and decisive one for them. They have done all they could. Militarily speaking, the next step will be some sort of retreat or change of this positions in the Sahel area."

An 8 week tour of guerrilla-controlled areas that took me behind Ethiopian lines to within sight of the Asmara capital showed that the government's military position here has deteriorated substantially since their dramatic advances last year. The Eritrean guerrillas, however, appear much strengthened.

By the opening of the present offensive only 70,000 Ethiopian troops remained from the 120,000 that invaded the strategic Red Sea territory a year ago, according to Afwerki.

Ethiopia opened the present Eritrea campaign on July 16 with 40,000 troops almost equally divided between two main fronts in the northern Sahel mountains according to the 33-year-old EPLF leader. One front lies three miles south of Nakfa. The other stretches 20 miles along the northeastern sea coast.

A third new front was also opened between these with 10,000 men drawn from bases in the central Eritrean highlands, Afwerki said.

Less than 10,000 largely inexperienced peasant militiamen remain stationed in Asmara where Soviet advisors and technicians are based, according to EPLF intelligence sources. Remaining troops are said to be spread thin among the other occupied towns and in small garrisons along the key highways linking Asmara with the port of Massawa and with Keren, where there are barely 3000 government troops defending Eritrea's second largest city.

With Ethiopian control limited to the towns and the narrow corridors between them, EPLF units have positioned themselves in the surrounding countryside to defend large islands of liberated territory. A second smaller allied guerrilla force-the Eritrean Liberation Front (ELF)-is also active in the western lowlands near the Sudan border.

The EPLF has grown over the past six months with thousands of previously organized civilians from the now occupied towns joining the guerrilla army. Much of the local EPLF village militias have been called up for regular duty. They now appear to have 40,000 men and women under arms.

The ELF claims nine brigades, but reliable sources place their number at 4-5000. However, of more political importance is the fact that the long-standing rivalry between the two appears to be diminishing, and small halting steps are taking place toward unifying them. The overt propaganda battle between them has ceased, and two battalions of the ELF are with the EPLF on the northeastern Sahel frontline.

Thus two highly sophisticated conventional armies now face each other in the battles raging in northern Eritrea.

The EPLF has now broken the back of the present Sahel offensive, and they appear to be readying for a major counteroffensive there and in the highland plateau where they are positioned around the government occupied towns and along the main highways.

ETHIOPIA/ERITREA
MILITARY SETBACKS, POLITICAL REPERCUSSIONS

Africa News (Durham, NC), August 31, 1979

[AN] The three-pronged attack launched by Ethiopian troops on July 16 was intended to dislodge stubbornly entrenched Eritrean guerrillas from their last strongholds in Eritrea's northern Sahel province, and at blocking renewed guerrilla actions behind Ethiopian lines. But it is now apparent that the effort has failed, and, instead,

400 Collected Articles on the Eritrean Revolution

the new military setback may accentuate political problems for Ethiopia's rulers.

By February this year the Ethiopian army had reversed most of the previous year's gains by the Eritrean People's Liberation Front (EPLF and the smaller Eritrean Liberation Front (ELF). But the EPLF had preserved its forces largely intact by a "strategic retreat," and, after stepping up military cooperation with the ELF, had in recent months prepared to go on the offensive. In a July military confrontation, reports correspondent Dan Connell, recently returned from eight weeks in Eritrea, three Ethiopian task forces tried in vain to overrun the dug-in Eritrean positions. In one prong of the attack a force of 20,000 with tanks and armored cars struck from the south at Nakfa, the last major Eritrean-held town, but were thrown back with thousands of casualties. Along two other fronts 30,000 more Ethiopian troops similarly proved unsuccessful in penetrating the rugged mountains which house the EPLF base area.

Ethiopia's army is equipped and trained with the aid of the Soviet Union and Cuba. But although Cuban advisors were reported to have been on the front lines last year, their role in Eritrean fighting this year has apparently been minimized. And in the latest offensive, EPLF leaders told Connell, even the frontline presence of Soviet advisers has decreased.

Cuba has long been said to favor a political solution to the Eritrean question, in spite of its backing for the Ethiopian government, and the Soviet Union as well is thought to have some questions about Ethiopian leader Mengistu's intransigence. The EPLF, however, attributes the lower Soviet profile primarily to fear of capture and to the fact that more Ethiopians have by now learned to operate the new weaponry.

Even more striking than the results of the battle for Nakfa are Connell's reports on his walking tour, which took him some 100 miles south of Nakfa, within sight of Eritrea's capital, Asmara. His conclusion: since last year the government's military position has deteriorated substantially, and Eritrea's strength has been bolstered by large numbers of civilian recruits who fled Ethiopian-occupied towns. The result, according to EPLF estimates, is that Ethiopia's 70,000 troops in the area only slightly outnumber Eritrean forces. The EPLF and ELF do lack effective anti-aircraft capability against the Ethiopian MiG fighter bombers, but the guerrillas' familiarity with the terrain largely cancels out Ethiopian superiority in armor and artillery.

In the countryside through which he traveled, Connell reports, the EPLF presence, civilian as well as military, was intact—with citrus farms, field hospitals, schools, grain mills, supply stations and training camps. Transport is by foot or camel caravan rather than by motorized vehicles. Ethiopian garrisons are confined to population centers along the roads, and are apparently spread thin.

In February Ethiopia's head of state Lt. Col. Mengistu Haile Mariam, launched a new economic development campaign saying that with military difficulties virtually over, new attention could be given to unmet economic needs. The military situation now is hardly as desperate as in 1977 and 1978, but it falls short of Mengistu's optimistic projection. In addition to the setbacks in Eritrea, Somali-backed guerrillas remain active in the east and south, the Tigre People's Liberation Front harasses Ethiopian garrisons in Tigre province, just to the south of Eritrea, and again there is talk of an Oromo Liberation Front in the south.

Ethiopia's rural economy, no longer under the control of rural landlords, is still unable to produce enough food to supply the urban areas and to protect against periodic drought. The production of collective farms has been disappointing, while individual peasants have been slow to respond to government cooperative plans. International agencies have provided aid which has reduced the risk of famine, but financial stability has been elusive, remaining dependent on the price of coffee, which provides more than 70% of export earnings. Coffee prices have increased in recent months, and production, according to U.S. Department of Agriculture forecasts, is expected to remain stable, but structural changes which could lessen Ethiopia's dependence on the crop are a remote prospect.

On the political front, Ethiopia's rulers have been expected to announce the creation of an "Ethiopian Workers' Party" this September. But there have been rumblings of discontent within the military over the degree of centralization planned for the party by the dominant Mengistu group. A resolution at an armed forces meeting in June called for "crushing all those who have an anti-centrist stand," and a recent Addis Zemen editorial likewise condemned "anti-centralism elements."

The significance of the debate lies in the accusations of the government's opponents that it has been unable to deal with the Eritrean question or with demands for greater rights for non-Amhara nationalities other than by military suppression. Each new military debacle since the military government took power in 1974 has stimulated fresh doubts within government circles, but each time Mengistu's hard-line faction has won out.

Liberation movements: Eritrea

*The Guardian (*New York), November 7, 1979

At dawn, the first of a seemingly endless parade of Ethiopian fighter jets appeared outside Nakfa to drop incendiary and antipersonnel bombs on the EPLF trenches. Shortly afterward, close to 15,000 Ethiopian peasant soldiers charged forward behind lines of tanks and armored cars.

Beaten back, they returned some hours later. Again they were repulsed by the entrenched Eritreans, supported by artillery fire from previously captured mortars and cannon hidden in the mountains behind their lines. At the end of the day one Ethiopian tank lay a smoking ruin. Another had been captured by the Eritreans.

The same day, the EPLF repulsed an estimated 20,000 Ethiopian troops along a 20-mile wide front around the town of Alghen in the Red Sea coastal foothills to the north. And a third new front was opened behind Nakfa when a further 10,000 Ethiopians tried to advance along a crude road constructed by the EPLF. That advance, too, was stopped according to EPLF commanders in Nakfa.

The town of Nakfa itself was empty except (for a handful of EPLF) fighters. The 4000 civilian inhabitants had long since fled to escape the daily land and air bombardment. The orderly rows of packed mud buildings along the wide main street were securely closed and locked, their doors and windows sealed shut with bricks and mortar.

Late that evening two members of the EPLF's 13-member political bureau gave an interview on a sandy hillside outside Nakfa. Ali Sayid and Petros Solomon were tired but exhilarated by the day's events.

"We are sure they will fail this time," said Solomon.

The lanky 29-year old added that this campaign differed little from previous ones, except for a greater Ethiopian reliance on heavy artillery. Still, he insisted, "the effect of the heavy weapons is limited because of our hard work in building the underground system of trenches."

Outside Asmara

A gray-brown haze lay over the capital of Asmara, visible from the EPLF lines on the mountainsides above. Lines of primitive EPLF blockhouses constructed of stone and dirt stretch along the spines of the hills ringing Asmara. The line of blockhouses is interrupted only by the main highways linking the city and its 10,000 strong Ethiopian occupation force with other government-held towns in four directions.

But with the exception of handful of villages on the plains surrounding Asmara, the countryside appeared to be entirely under EPLF control. In a 3-week walking tour of the area, the only signs of the Ethiopian army were a network of abandoned trenches and four burned vehicles along the road between the Ethiopian-held towns of Afabet and Keren.

On the slopes of the northeastern plateau around Asmara, the EPLF runs a field hospital, a citrus farm and a number of acres planted with grain and coffee. There is also a diesel-powered grain mill, a military training camp and a transport garage. There are also numerous secluded supply depots.

Though the Ethiopian government publicly claims to control this region, it appears that the elaborate EPLF infrastructure, developed by the guerrillas two years ago during their period of military ascendancy, remains intact. The only thing it lacks is mechanized transport links with its Sahel base.

Although the EPLF guerrillas keep a generally low profile, small commando teams make nightly raids into nearby government-held villages and towns. There they distribute propaganda, capture supplies and punish collaborators. Habte Giorgis, member of the EPLF central committee, also claimed that the EPLF had managed to set off simultaneous bomb explosions in all Ethiopian-occupied towns, to prevent the government from holding elaborate May Day rallies.

Stephanos Afeworki, another central committee-member stationed near Asmara, explained, "What you have to understand is that the whole of the Ethiopian force is in Sahel. Here in the cities and the countryside they are completely isolated. They are in pockets, with no control of the people."

The steady buildup of guerrilla units, supplies and ammunition around the towns and along the roads between them indicated that the EPLF is preparing to take advantage of this situation. But the possibility of an Ethiopian collapse also brings with it the risk of chaos and terror, aimed at the helpless civilian population, according to Afeworki.

"You see these aspects when they are on the offensive. Imagine what will happen when this army is defeated," he said.

Ethiopian Bombing Raid

As if to underscore Afeworki's prediction, we encountered an Ethiopian bombing raid while traveling by camel back to Nakfa.

A series of camel caravans plodded past us along the dry riverbeds, laden with the curved wooden poles of the Eritrean nomads' huts. The loads were topped with brilliantly colored straw matting, many bearing bright red or blue crosses announcing recent marriages. The families walking by, or perched precariously on top of the loaded camels, were making their annual migration from the parched Red Sea coastal plains to seasonal farms in the wetter interior highlands.

The high-pitched whine of an Ethiopian jet shattered the morning stillness. It raced up the twisting scrub-covered valley, closely followed by a second Soviet-supplied plane. In a few seconds, there were two sharp explosions, then the planes circled for a few minutes before vanishing.

By the time we reached the site, there was only a pool of blood in the sand. Two women and a 7-year-old boy had been hut by shrapnel. Five camels were wounded, and one was dying.

"They passed us on both sides and turned around to bomb us before we could hide," said Saleh Mohammed Ali, the 20-year-old bridegroom of one of the wounded women. After bandaging up the injured, he urged them to go to an EPLF field clinic, three hours walk away.

"They do it to terrorize the people, to turn them against us," explained the EPLF guide, with a kind of tight-lipped calm.

But if this is the Ethiopian intention, it seems to be having the opposite result. Again and again, in peasant villages, temporary nomad camps and small towns crowded with refugees, people expressed their faith in the guerrillas.

"The fighters are our children, it is our war too," exclaimed a small shopkeeper who had fled from the town of Afabet last February, as it was reoccupied by Ethiopian troops. He now runs a small store in the EPLF-held mountains.

In the town of Fische, 20 miles from Asmara, Dahab Zereghaber, a 48-year-old refugee, expressed similar feelings. Zereghaber lost a thriving restaurant business and now supports herself by baking bread and braiding other women's hair in a tiny, windowless I-room house.

"As far as I am concerned, I want to finish it now, this night," she said matter-of-factly as she served freshly roasted coffee. "I want a victory." Like many others interviewed, Zereghaber announced that she was a member of EPLF-sponsored civilian political associations.

Hundreds of guerrilla cadre, in teams of four and five, are dispersed in the Eritrean countryside to mobilize the civilian population to support the 18-year war for independence from Ethiopia. They have initiated programs of land reform, social services-including free medical care and village schools-agricultural and livestock development projects, and administrative reorganization of villages and towns under locally elected "people's assemblies."

Though both sides in this long and bitter war profess socialist ideologies, the Eritrean peasants tend to judge them not by the rhetoric of their leaders but by the impact each has on their daily lives.

Fana Ghebrezghi, the 45-year-old mother of eight children, fled her home village of Zagur three months ago, after it was reoccupied by Ethiopian troops. Two sons and a daughter are with the EPLF.

She recalls the EPLF's establishment of associations for women, for peasants and for youth. These associations selected the delegates to the assembly that governed the village, with large sectors of the population finding a political voice for the first time. She also remembers the construction of a cooperative farm, a shop, a grain mill and a poultry raising project underwritten by the guerrillas and run by the civilian associations.

But Ghebrezghi derides the government's brand of "Ethiopian socialism," under which the village cooperatives were confiscated, the people's assembly was replaced by a peasant association chairman appointed by the Ethiopian officer in charge of the garrison. And landmines were planted in her fields, striping her of her livelihood.

Throughout repeated interviews, a fierce Eritrean nationalism seemed to eclipse all yearnings for a quick peace. These feelings seem to cross all ideological and class lines.

"This is our land," said Nur Humedai, a 75-year-old peasant who pounded the ground with his hand-hewn walking stick, "We don't want anyone else's land, just our own."

AFRICA NEWS SPECIAL:
GLIMPSES OF A WAR ZONE

Africa News (Durham, NC), November 9, 1979

[AN] *The battlefields of Eritrea, where guerrillas bent on independence have confronted successive Ethiopian governments equally determined to keep the Red Sea territory under their control, have witnessed much bloodshed through almost two decades of war. And still the fighting continues, in spite of massive offensives in 1978 and 1979, which restored Ethiopian control over most urban centers and major transportation links. Dan Connell, an American journalist who has visited Eritrea repeatedly since 1976, was there during the latest major offensive in July, and his personal account of more than two months in the country, excerpted here, is intended to give a feel for life in the war zone on the Eritrean side.*

Two silver MiG-21s knife through the morning sky to awaken us at 7:30 on our first day in Eritrea. They circle high over our hidden camp as I crawl sleepily out of the tent to watch them from the shade of a spiked acacia tree. Banking sharply, first one and then the other drops toward us into a steep dive from the east, the blinding sun glinting off their sleek delta wings. Each looses a single bomb harmlessly onto the protective cradle of rocky hills that encircles us as Eritrea anti-aircraft fire chatters in their wake.

In minutes, the shrill wine of the departing jet fighters fades to a whisper, and a young guerrilla fighter appears with a steaming thermos of hot tea and kitcha, the doughy flatbread that is the staple food for the Eritrean fighters. It is the beginning of a typical day in the Sahel mountains where the guerrillas maintain their rear base area.

From dawn to dusk Ethiopia's Soviet-supplied fighter bombers patrol the skies over Eritrea. But apart from the entrenched positions to the east and south of the guerrillas' base, the Eritreans offer few visible targets. By day they are hidden beneath the scrawny, flat-topped thorn trees, in the thick underbrush alongside the now-dry riverbeds or in underground caverns and camouflaged shelters of dried mud and stone. When darkness envelopes this inhospitable but strategic corner of northeast Africa, the barren, volcanic hills come alive. Scores of small cooking fires twinkle in the distance. Long, broken strings of light bounce off the sheer rock walls as convoys of captured Ethiopian trucks snake their way over crude guerrilla-constructed roads to the front lines, the deep throb of their diesel engines echoing through the mountains. Close by our canvas "guest house," a portable generator sputters and chugs. The valley blinks awake as electric lights strung in the trees flash on, and teams of guerrilla mechanics and technicians crank up their machine tools in a network of weapons repair shops, transport garages and cottage industries in which they manufacture everything from gunstocks to uniforms.

We crossed the Sudan frontier into Eritrea at dusk in a convoy of six captured Fiat transports, two U.S. army Macks, one newly-taken Soviet military vehicle and two buses, all bearing Ethiopian license plates that testified to their origin. The night closed over us, dark and abrupt, as the guerrillas dismounted at the Karora border post to pick up their weapons, Soviet-made Kalashnikov automatic rifles and American M-14s.

The charcoal sky swarmed with glittering stars as we drove along a sandy riverbed for an hour and a half, our lights off, before reaching a mountain pass within sight of Ethiopian battle lines. A fighter trotted in front with a small flashlight as we strained to climb a 45 degree incline carved out of the mountainside by EPLF [Eritrean People's Liberation Front] engineers. A squad of ELF [Eritrean Liberation Front] guerrillas, stationed there alongside the main EPLF units as a sign of the increasing cooperation between the two fronts, waved as we rumbled past.

'David and Goliath'

At two o'clock in the morning we arrived at the base camp, deep in the Sahel mountains. Though jarred awake by the shriek of Ethiopia's jet fighters, we found the rest of the day peaceful. Political bureau member Ali Sayid ambled into our tent to ask how we were getting on, then queried me about current international opinion on the war here. When I responded that some commentators seem to think it is almost over, he tilted his head back and laughed from deep down in his bearded throat, saying, "You will son know better."

The EPLF strategy is one of attrition. They fight a David and Goliath struggle to chip away at their giant neighbor until he is cut down to a size where a final and decisive blow can be inflicted. The conventional military yardsticks do not apply here, according to guerrilla strategists. An escalation in armaments, a quantitative jump in the size of the Ethiopian army, may bring temporary setbacks to the Eritreans, but with time and patience, parity and then guerrilla superiority can be achieved.

Both sides promise sweeping change in nearly identical Marxist language: land reform, peasant political power, equality for women, socialism. Words fly faster than bullets in Eritrea and Ethiopia. But the key to Eritrea's future rests on the actual response of the people living in Eritrea's countryside.

At eleven o'clock on a Saturday night, Goitom Asgadom—my constant companion over the next two months—and I pack our goods and equipment aboard an ornery camel and begin the long trek south from Nakfa. Escorted by a half-dozen guerrillas, we follow a narrow, rocky path west of the town, winding up and over the rim of mountains that ring the battlefront, stopping before dawn to catch a few chilly hours of sleep beside the trail when we are out of sight of Ethiopia's forward positions.

We arise at first light to descend the almost vertical walls of a yawning canyon along ancient footpaths etched deep into the stone by an unending procession of unshod hooves and bare feet. A small caravan of merchants edges past on the way north toward Sudan.

That evening and the next, we walk, walk, walk, stopping only to eat and sleep for three hors at a stretch. Three of us push ahead of the camels on short cuts through slim cracks and crevices in the honey-comb of ridges that partition the labyrinthine river valleys, traversing freshly plowed, terraced farms, where peasants are slicing narrow fur-rows in the dry earth with hand-hewn wooden implements.

Late one afternoon we arrive at our first village, a collection of grass and stick huts bunched together on the bank of the river. A group of men clustered around a campfire at the far end of the set-tlement stand and peer at us suspiciously. First one and then the oth-ers inch closer for a better look. It is me they are curious about, my white skin and wavy brown hair drawing their attention like an alarm bell.

"A captured pilot?" asks one, taking care to remain out of reach, one eye on my face as he questions Goitom. "No," he answers with a laugh. "A journalist from America, a guest of the EPLF. We know him well." The grimaces dissolve, there is handshaking all around and we are invited for dinner. Goitom says that we carry sugar and canned sardines. We need only fire and water. But over his protestations we are seated on dried goat skins and a boy brings us a porridge of boiled sorghum swimming in curdled milk and butter. Gathering into a circle we scoop dripping handfuls out of the blackened pot and trade news.

On the morning of the seventh day we climbed for two hours up a ridge that gave way on the other side to a shallow valley that marked the beginning of the EPLF's island of liberated territory north and east of Asmara, an as yet uncontested zone entirely under guerrilla control. In contrast to the washed-out pastel tones of the desert lowlands, this area is painted in broad strokes of rich forest greens and deep browns, fecund farmland once claimed by Italian colonists and recently redistributed by the EPLF to peasants and semi-nomads. Our journey is slowed by a stream of greetings and invitations from dozens of local inhabitants.

'Shirba Was A Traitor'

As we near Asmara, the Eritrean capital, we encounter Fana Ghebrezghi, an old friend. I slept on the packed earthen floor of her cramped stone house on my first foray into Eritrea in 1976, and we have held tumultuous reunions on every subsequent visit, exchanging photographs and gifts, tears and hugs. Two of her sons and one daughter are fighting with the EPLF. She is a fiery and emotional supporter of the guerrillas, and none of the fighters seem surprised that her outbursts at public meetings in occupied Zagur finally forced her to leave for fear of Ethiopian reprisal. Now she is a refugee, living with her husband on a small plot of land they had used to farm on the outer slopes during the highland dry season.

When the Ethiopians occupied the town, she said, they tried to mobilize support among the people. But of the villager they chose as leader she spoke with scorn:

"Shirba was a traitor," she declares vigorously. "He was a big landowner and he was always against the land reform we had. I remember when it was finished and we set aside a section to farm collectively, he said it was a waste of time, so we had better split it up between those who could plow it, meaning him. When the Derg [Ethiopian government] came in and called us together, he alone stood up and denounced our People's Assembly. The Derg cadre immediately appointed him kebele [association] head and he picked 12 of his friends to be on the committee. I stood up and denounced him, but he interrupted and called me a reactionary. Now he is gone [kidnapped by the EPLF] and there is no one from our village who will replace him."

The return journey to Nakfa proceeded relatively quickly, but there were several unexpected features along the way.

It was 7 a.m. on our second day. We unpacked our two camels and spread out under the scant, checkered shade of an acacia and brewed tea. I watched the parade of nomadic families go by, their camels laden with the curved poles of their portable huts, the women perched precariously beneath brilliantly colored, matted straw canopies which bore bright red or blue crosses to announce recent marriages, the children running alongside, herding the goats and sheep.

Shortly after nine, we heard two fighter aircraft pass overhead. "They're gong to bomb the people," muttered Goitom, but I was skeptical. There was no mistaking the procession for anything but civilians, and the semi-annual migration through that area was well known, dating back centuries.

Seconds later, we heard the first explosion. Then close behind, another loud concussion echoing off the barren rocky hills. For six or seven minutes we listened to the high-pitched whine of the MiG-21s break into screeching dives climaxed by sharp cracks in the near distance. We lay flat on the ground, noses in the sand, the point of attack out of sight beyond a jagged spur that bent the riverbed in a broad, sweeping arc. Then suddenly they were gone, and the only sound was the whisper of a hot, dry wind.

Once more, the train of camels, cattle, goats, sheep and people meandered by our hillside vantage point. By the time we reached the attack site, the only sign of what had happened was a crimson pool of blood in the sand. Nearby lay a grotesquely twisted steel bomb fragment with Russian letters engraved upon it. But the toll was surprisingly light: two women and a seven-year-old boy with minor shrapnel wounds, five camels hurt, one dying.

Murderous Fire

When I awoke at 4 a.m. one morning some days later, I asked the fighter on the blanket next to me, was it thunder or artillery that I heard. "It is only the wind," he answered groggily, arising to load the camels. But by the time we climbed out of the valley to the crest of a high ridge, the sounds of war were clearly discernible over the rustle of the brisk predawn breeze, a syncopated percussion of exploding shells, joined at daybreak by the shrill whistle of jets. The fifth round of Ethiopia's yearlong offensive had begun. We halted for the day at an EPLF camp on the outskirts of Nakfa where Goitom and I scrambled up a hill to witness the first battles.

From six to seven o'clock the muffled din was almost unbroken as 15,000 Ethiopian peasant soldiers surged forward east and west of the town. They were met head on and finally turned around by the murderous fire of EPLF automatic weapons which raked the open plains. At ten another human wave washed the valley in blood, but again the Ethiopian fled the field in chaotic retreat. Throughout the day the MiGs soared high overhead, two by two, in broad sweeping circles, swooping almost straight down to disgorge their bombs before yielding to the next pair minutes behind them.

At our camp everything seemed eerily normal for us, passive spectators to the life-and-death drama being acted out close by. One soldier melted rubber patches onto his torn sandals, another washed clothes. The rest relaxed in the shade gazing casually at the planes as if watching an aerial ballet, as if it were just another ordinary day in their lives—which, in fact, it was.

Promptly at 8:05 in the evening, as if the curtain had drawn over this the first act of the offensive, the shooting ceased but for an intermittent burst of heavy weapons fire that flashed against the black horizon. Thus the stage was set for the players to resume on the morrow. The campaign would then continue on this and two other fronts to the northeast along the seacoast until the offensive collapsed ten days later.

Eyewitness View Of Eritrean Struggle

The Guardian (New York), November 14, 1979

Inside Eritrea

In a recent trip to Eritrea, my sixth in three years, I had one top priority: to visit the contested "guerrilla zones" to determine the difficulties and achievements of the Eritrean people in their 18-year-old war for independence. How well were the Eritreans surviving the massive onslaught of Ethiopian troops, artillery and air fire?

The answers were not to be found in the base areas. One had to travel behind the lines to the guerrilla zones in the highland plateau. And finally, after a few days in he base camps, I was on my way.

After dark-when the Ethiopian planes are grounded-I was taken in a Landrover to the EPLF-held town of Nakfa. There, the guerrillas faced some 20,000 Ethiopian troops along a 12-mile conventional battlefront during the 1978 Ethiopian offensive that forced the EPLF to return to traditional guerrilla warfare tactics.

A kind of mountain citadel, Nakfa is now almost bereft of

civilian inhabitants. They had fled a steady Ethiopian shelling and bombing that had reduced whole sections of the town to heaps of mud and rubble. Twisted shards of metal litter the ground, along with discarded bits of furniture and clothing, the paraphernalia of retreat.

At 11 p.m. the next day, Goitom Asghedom—my 29-year-old guerrilla escort and constant companion for the following five weeks—packed our goods and equipment aboard an ornery camel. We began the long trek southward.

Guided by a half dozen lightly armed fighters, we followed a narrow, rocky path west of the town, winding up and over the rim of mountains that ringed the battlefront. We stopped before dawn to catch a few chilly hours of sleep beside the trail when we were out of sight of Ethiopia's forward positions. We did not properly cross through the Ethiopian lines. Instead, we simply walked around them.

Through that evening and the next, we walked, stopping only to eat and sleep for four hours at a stretch. Three of us pushed ahead of the camels on short cuts through slim cracks and crevices in the honeycomb of ridges that partition the labyrinthine river valleys. We traversed freshly plowed terraced farms where peasant farmers were slicing tight furrows in the packed, dry earth with their primitive handhewn wooden implements.

Late on the third afternoon we arrived at our first village, a haphazard collection of grass and stick huts bunched together on the banks of the riverbed. A group of men clustered around a campfire at the far end of the settlement.

Goitom announced that we carried out own tea, sugar and canned sardines (48 cans of them) and needed only fire and water. But over his protestations we were seated on dried goat skins and served a porridge of boiled sorghum swimming in curdled milk and butter. Squatting in a circle, we scooped dripping handfuls out of the blackened pot and traded news.

When there was a lapse in the animated conversation, I ventured a question which Goitom translated into Tigray, the language of the predominantly Muslim lowland nomads: "After these 18 years of fighting, wouldn't you rather see the war come to an end no matter who wins?"

Support the EPLF

"No," exclaimed one of the men. "You have been here before. You should know better. The fighters are our children, so it is our war, too. And we are also members of the organization."

In an aside, Goitom explained that EPLF cadre-known as "armed propaganda teams"-were active there in mobilizing the civilians into formal associations of women, peasants and youth. Weekly meetings were held for subgroups of 20 people. They elected leaders who in turn served in self-governing "People's Assemblies" that replaced the traditional administrative system of village chiefs.

At dawn the next day we passed within sight of Afabet, the Ethiopian rear base for the frontlines near Nakfa. Afabet is linked by road to the city of Keren and thence to the Asmara capital from where supplied were trucked in to the army.

We were in regular radio contact with guerrilla units in the highlands and the next leg of our trip was carefully coordinated with a battalion of fighters who took up positions on the Afabet-Keren road at 3 p.m. to secure our midnight crossing. From then on until we reached the periphery of Asmara almost a week later, the only signs we saw of an Ethiopian presence were the daily overpasses of MiG jets.

Crossing a region known as the "slopes," we climbed up and down the folds and wrinkles of the shoulder of the plateau which rises close to 8000 feet above the coastal plains. These land features mark a sharp economic and social division between the lowland nomadic herders and seasonal farmers and the settled highlanders, mostly Coptic Christians. Our first stop was at an EPLF field hospital consisting of a series of tents routinely camouflaged from aerial view. An undifferentiated mix of fighters and peasants lay on wire beds recovering from a range of illnesses and wounds from malaria and dysentery to bullet holes and napalm burns.

In the afternoon we passed through a guerrilla training camp where a cloth banner lettered in three languages waved in the breeze-"No Victory Without the Leadership of the Proletariat!" The next day we arrived at a small camp on the mountainside where two members of the front's Central Committee were based.

Radio messages were dashed off in a complex numerical code, and we continued on with a special guide to the frontlines at the edge of the plateau from where we looked down at the slumbering bulk of Asmara, nestled in a shallow dish and enshrouded in a dull gray-brown haze. Some 10,000 Ethiopian soldiers were said to be quartered there, together with several hundred Soviet advisers and technicians who oversee the conventional war in the north as well as the efforts to "pacify" the highland countryside.

My guide pointed across the vacant landscape in front of us to the deserted village of Wauki, less than a mile away. "That is where their artillery is," he said, pointing to a small hill in the center of the hamlet, uninhabited but for the 350 government troops permanently bivouacked there. Row upon row of stone houses lay in ruins, slowly ground down by the shifting fortunes of war over the past four years around the capital.

Behind us the Eritrean fighters were dug into the hills in a continuous chain of classic blockhouses constructed of stone and dirt. The slopes crawled with guerrillas who seemed entirely lackadaisical about the proximity of their enemy.

Dancing and Singing

That evening the hills rang with the dancing, shouting and singing of a cultural group from that brigade, practicing a program to be performed on the weekend for a local peasant audience. We were perhaps a mile and a half from the Ethiopian lines, and I could not but wonder what went on in their minds as they sat in their trenches listening to the whooping and hollering where we were. There had been no action on either side there for months, apparently because they were both awaiting the outcome of the fighting in Sahel.

Shunning large scale military operations, the Eritrean partisans were instead making nightly clandestine incursions into the occupied villages, more to needle the Ethiopians and build civilian morale than to effect any substantive military change.

Central Committeeman Habte Giorgis reeled off a list of recent exploits the next morning; 30,000 pounds of grain carried out of Azien and distributed to the peasants, government-sponsored May Day rallies broken up with bomb explosions in Decamare and Asmara, kebele chairman Shirba Woldezion kidnapped from Zagur, supply trucks blown up with landmines on the highways running out of Asmara. He consulted a tattered pocketsize notebook and added that 560 trucks and over 150 armored vehicles had been knocked out by the "engineering squads" over the previous six months.

When I asked the fate of Shirba Woldezion, there was no comment beyond a slight shrug and a telling grin. The kebele is the Ethiopian military Derg's (Junta's) version of a peasant association-or in the case of the towns, a neighborhood association. It is the basic Ethiopian administrative unit. I learned more about it and about Shirba from Fana Ghebrezghi, a peasant women who had fled Zagur three months earlier after being tipped off to her impending arrest.

"Shirba was a traitor," she declared vehemently. "He was a big landowner, and he was always against the land reform we had under the EPLF. I remember when it was finished and we set aside a section to farm collectively, he said it was a waste of time, so we had better split it up between those who could plow it, meaning him.

"When the Derg came in and called us together, he alone stood up and denounced our People's Assembly. The Derg cadre immediately appointed him kebele, and he picked 12 of his friends to be on the committee with him. Now he is gone, and there is no one from our village who dares replace him."

Fana went on to say that after the appointed kebele replaced the elected assembly, Zagur's cooperative store and farm were confiscated-with the Ethiopians insisting that they had belonged not to the village but to EPLF. Prominent EPLF supporters disappeared and finally the village was sealed off by three rows of landmines "planted" in the peasants' fields.

To the outsider, the similarity in the political rhetoric that emanates from both sides in this war is at best confusing. But to the ordinary illiterate peasant words count less than deeds. The differences, between the Ethiopian Derg and the EPLF are invariably expressed in terms of each's impact on their day to day lives.

Not surprisingly, the tangible effect of the EPLF's redistribution of land; the provision of medical services, schools and veterinary assistance; the abolition of female circumcision and arranged marriages; the elevation of poor peasants and especially women to political power through the elected assemblies means most to these people.

Difficulties of War

Perhaps one of the most memorable discussions we had was in the town of Fische where I met with the local People's Assembly one afternoon. There were declarations of support for the EPLF and undying opposition to all forms of oppression. But I pressed them to describe the difficulties they had faced since the previous year's Ethiopian military advances.

Under Goitom's gentle prodding, they gradually opened up to concede that the large influx of refugees from the newly occupied areas was severely straining their resources. "Now is the time of our harvest," ventured Mehret Teklemariam, a widowed 31-year-old farmer, "but we are going to have a problem in a month after we finish our corn. We don't know what will happen then."

"One of our plans is to help these people with piece of land," offered Gebreberhan Hagos. "And of course the organization has to help with this problem. If the fighters are eating twice, now they have to eat once."

There was a burst of laughter at this, and Goitom explained that the 35 year old farmer had paraphrased a slogan being heard over Ethiopian radio which called on the civilians who were eating twice to instead eat once in order to support the Derg's army.

As we stood to leave, Nur Himedai—who after much debate reckoned himself to be 75—hushed the group with one wrinkled hand and intoned softly, "We have been beaten, we have been imprisoned, killed, cut to pieces by the enemy. But this is our land. We don't want anyone else's hand, just our own."

"Now we have tasted freedom," added a young war widow, "and we will never go back."

Eritrean rebels launch offensive

The Guardian (New York), December 12, 1979

The Eritrean Peoples Liberation Front (EPLF) launched an all-out offensive Dec. 2 on enemy positions in the northern Sahel Province, an EPLF communiqué reports. The EPLF has been waging an 18-year armed struggle for the liberation of Eritrea from Ethiopia.

The offensive was preceded by a series of successful attacks on the kebeles, small garrisons which function on behalf of the Ethiopian military. Since August 1978, when the EPLF made a strategic retreat from liberated territory, the kebeles have been used to spy on patriotic sympathizers in EPLF-organized mass groups, according to the EPLF.

From Nov. 7-Nov. 11, the EPLF destroyed five kebeles inside the capital city of Asmara. The following week, four more were destroyed at Adi-Keih in southern Eritrea. Some 45 people were taken prisoner. Ethiopia claims the kebeles in Eritrea are "mass organizations."

'Military Situation Changing'

In the northern front near Nakfa, where the Ethiopians had attempted to establish a new camp, some 30 enemy troops were killed and more than 30 wounded when the EPLF attacked during the week of Nov. 11-17. In the same front, near Serejaka and Adi Acalome, the EPLF ambushed an Ethiopian encampment, killing six and wounding four.

Also that week, the movement's engineering squad destroyed six Ethiopian trucks, three of which were transporting oil, and seven military vehicles. Since June 1978, EPLF say its forces have knocked 655 enemy military vehicles out of commission.

In addition to these attacks, the EPLF scored an important victory in mid-November when the Ethiopians' third largest outpost in the major transport center of Keren was hit, resulting in 50 casualties for the Ethiopians. A substantial supply of arms was captured.

According to the EPLF communiqué announcing the latest offensive, "the military situation is changing in favor of the Eritrean revolution."

Eritrea: Guerrilla offensive

The Guardian (New York), December 19, 1979

The Eritrean People's Liberation Front (EPLF) this week routed Ethiopian occupation forces in northern Eritrea in six days of heavy fighting.

A 20,000 man Ethiopian force was dislodged from positions it had held near the EPLF-controlled town of Nakfa since last January and forced into a 40-mile retreat, according to the EPLF.

Simultaneous attacks were also launched by the EPLF on the Red Sea coast and at key points in the Ethiopian rear to disrupt supply lines to the Nakfa front.

The coordinated EPLF attacks came at a time when Ethiopia was reported preparing to launch the sixth round of its 18-month offensive to regain control of the strategic Red Sea territory.

"Their plan was to begin before November," said EPLF central committee member Ermias Debessai. "First they postponed it, but now it is completely broken. Things have changed dramatically. The balance of power has changed in our favor."

This marks the largest series of EPLF counterattacks against Ethiopian forces in Eritrea since the stalemating of the offensive early this year. But Ermias declined to characterize it as a general counteroffensive.

"Our aim was to take the military initiative in order to prevent their offensive and to weaken the morale of their soldiers, but it was not an all out offensive on our past," he said.

However, he added, "our fighters are preparing now for another attack in Sahel itself."

Sahel is the northernmost province of the Pennsylvania-sized former Italian colony and has been the scene of the main confrontations between EPLF and the Ethiopian army since the front made its strategic retreat from Eritrea's largest towns a year ago.

The EPLF fought Ethiopia to a standstill on the northeastern coast and in an area south of Nakfa in January and has withstood three Ethiopian offensive rounds since that time with no essential change in either of their positions.

The current wave of EPLF assaults began on Dec. 2 near Nakfa and resulted in the capture of two strategic hills the following day where three Ethiopian brigades were reported crushed.

The fighting continued southward in a region known as Naro, which had been the scene of another decisive battle three years ago when EPLF first captured the Sahel towns of Nakfa and Afabet.

By Dec. 7 the battle lines were again drawn close to Afabet when the EPLF halted its advance to regroup. BY that time the front claimed to have captured eight Russian-supplied 155 tanks and destroyed 10 more.

An EPLF communiqué also listed the capture of 1576mm artillery pieces, 45 military vehicles and over 3000 light and medium weapons including antiaircraft guns, mortars and medium range artillery. More than 9000 Ethiopian casualties were reported.

Meanwhile, three tanks were also reported destroyed and 500 Ethiopians killed, wounded or captured on the coast at Alghena where another 20,000 Ethiopian troops are pinned down in the desert foothills.

The following day, another EPLF unit hit the garrison at Halibmentel, between Asmara and Keren, Eritrea's second largest city and the main rear base for the Sahel fighting.

An estimated 300 Ethiopian troops were claimed killed there and another 300 escaped northward to Keren, leaving the EPLF in control of the base and the road by which Ethiopia moves all supplies to the Sahel area.

All supplies are now reported moving by helicopter and by plane to the besieged forces near Afabet.

EPLF losses in these battles were described as mall due to the low morale of Ethiopian forces who are reported deserting to EPLF in large numbers in Sahel.

Ermias characterized the current military situation to be in "our favor" because of the economic and political crises inside Ethiopia, the stepped-up military actions of the Tigray People's Liberation Front (TPLF) in neighboring Tigray province and the steady weakening of the occupation forces in Eritrea by EPLF military successes and rearguard guerrilla actions.

He said that the TPLF, which stands with the EPLF against the Ethiopian military government but seeks national self-determination rather than independence, last week cut the main highway linking central Ethiopia with Eritrea near the city of Makele.

He added that supplies for Ethiopian government forces in Tigray are also moving only by air today as the TPLF is mounting its own general offensive there.

Stepped-up guerrilla fighting in Ethiopia's southeastern Ogaden region has also been reported recently by the Western Somali Liberation Front (WSLF).

The thrust of the EPLF's conventional assaults on Ethiopian positions in northern Eritrea, combined with its smaller guerrilla actions, appear to be aimed at clearing the Sahel region and linking its rear base there with the highland guerrilla zones around the main cities and town in the center of the country.

This pattern recalls the front's approach in 1977 when first Nakfa and then Afabet fell to be followed by monthly attacks on occupied urban garrisons.

At this time, EPLF's main forces are tied down in the Sahel, south of Nakfa, and on the seacoast. All other fronts are dependent upon what happens there.

"If we break this front, we can release our forces to control the highways in the highlands and encircle the garrisons there," Ermias said.

The key is the front between Nakfa and Afabet. Should this one be destroyed, Ethiopia's coastal force will become isolated and neutralized and it is expected to withdraw on its own. "It is useless by itself," said Ermias.

The current fighting can thus be seen as the precondition for an all-out EPLF offensive. Its success this week suggests that such an offensive may not be long in coming.

Eritrea: The Politics Of Refugees

The Horn of Africa Journal (Trenton, NJ), Oct.-Dec. 1979

"This is our long march," quipped Haile Wold'ensae, a member of the Eritrean People's Liberation Front (EPLF) Politburo, as his comrades dismantled their offices in the city of Keren in November 1978, loading their equipment onto waiting vehicles for the retreat north toward the guerrilla base area. But the mood was somber as throngs of civilians poured out of Eritrea's second largest city in the face of a massive Soviet-backed Ethiopian offensive which was to reoccupy all but two guerrilla controlled Eritrean towns by the end of the year.

Over 20,000 people streamed northward toward the Sudan border to swell the refugee total there to more than 200,000 Eritreans who had sought sanctuary from the war since 1967, and who today number in excess of 350,000. Some carried small bundles in their arms, occasionally a battered leather suitcase on their heads. A flatbed truck cruised back into Keren bearing seven women who had lost their children along the way, their tear-stained faces belying their stoical silence.

A contingent of young girls clad in new jungle uniforms and fresh from a four month military training course filed up the road to offer help in setting up temporary camps where sacks of sorghum and wheat flour were off-loaded to feed the new refugees, several thousand of whom had previously fled to Keren from the Ethiopian-occupied cities of Asmara and Decamare.

On the following day the Ethiopians began an indiscriminate bombardment of the area with long range artillery, Stalin Organ rocket launchers and MiG aircraft. Late in the afternoon, three MiG 23s hit one makeshift refugee camp of 2000 to 3000 people some 40 kilometers (25 miles) north of the battle lines.

Paramedics carried the 65 wounded to the edge of the road and tended them there while awaiting EPLF trucks to carry them out after dark, but shortages of medicine and sterile bandages hampered the first aid efforts. Among he injured was one family of five. Berhane Ghebrejesus lay on a canvas stretcher with a shrapnel wound in his leg while his wife and three children, also wounded, huddled around him. His one and half year old baby shivered with shock from a head wound that was to claim his young life the next morning. Ten had been killed outright in the raid. Thirty more would not survive the next 24 hours.

Meanwhile, in Sudan, local administrators were declaring the latest influx of refugees a major crisis and, one again, appealing to the world for emergency assistance, assistance which was at best slow in coming. In the border town of Kassala, Dr. Melassie, Director of the city's only public hospital, told me, "These are war conditions here. We are frustrated. We have a shortage of resources, we are overcrowded and overworked and we have many new problems such as war injuries, psychological problems and malnutrition."

In the nearby village of Kashm el Girba 3800 newly arrived refugees were being housed in empty school buildings and tents. Entering one of the camps there through a cordon of barbed wire, I found a scene of sharp and agonizing contrasts. Dozens of children roamed about restlessly while their listless parents sat huddled in the shade, staring blankly ahead. A middle aged woman leaned against a doorway with her eyes closed and a tiny child sucking her wrinkled breast, while an old man lay shivering with malaria on the concrete floor.

Up to 40 people were living in a single classroom, blackened with soot from their cooking fires. Animals wandered in and out of the buildings and the tents leaving their dung on the pathways where the children played. More than half the people were young children, the rest older men and women, many with serious health problems and nutritional deficiencies.

One man, Mohammed Ali, in his late 50s and the father of eight children, sat in a tent with nothing but his Koran and a prayer mat. He said that he and his family rushed across the border from the village of Teletasher when they heard the sound of nearby Ethiopian artillery.

"We were afraid, so we could only bring enough food to get to Sudan," he said. His case was typical of tens of thousands. Their lives were secure against the quick and indiscriminate death offered by the war. Now they faced the slower, more debilitating possibility of death from starvation or disease or, at least, the gradual erosion of their spirit while an apparently callous world looked on with a blind eye and scattered crumbs in halfhearted token gestures of relief.

Today the situation is little changed. The Eritreans receive little notice and less assistance. The UN World Food Program is distributing small amounts of sorghum and milk powder to the refugees. A handful of international agencies maintains small clinics in the camps. But doctors say it is no where near enough. It is not a question of need, they readily acknowledge, but a matter of politics.

With most major international and intergovernmental relief agencies and potential donor countries operating programs in neighboring Ethiopia, they say that to involve themselves in aid to the Eritreans would jeopardize their programs there. The largest food assistance program in Sudan is run by the US-based Catholic Relief Services, yet even they shun involvement with the Eritrean problem. The reason is not hard to find: their funding comes from the U.S. Agency for International Development (AID). According to a State Department official who asked to remain anonymous, "Any move toward the Eritrean, even through a third party, would be taken by the Ethiopian government as a hostile act. We cannot risk that."

While the U.S. and the Soviet Union thus jockey for influence in Addis Ababa, the Eritreans continue to pay the price of political independence. Invisibility.

Since the Eritrean war began focusing on the towns in early 1977, a large percentage of the refugees coming to Sudan have been townspeople who gravitate toward Sudanese urban areas and avoid the rural relief camps. Many are young men and women seeking school work or a way out to the Middle East, Europe or the Americas. But they are usually disappointed. Employment opportunities are limited for the educated, school places are few and far between, many countries are not accepting the refugees and there are almost no programs of assistance for them in the towns. The result is often despair and a despondency which is routinely misunderstood by local residents as careless lethargy, as the refugees are reduced to hanging about or turning to prostitution for a living.

One young refugee recently walked into the office of the UN High Commission for Refugees (UNHCR) looking for help. He is 21 and grew up in Asmara, the Eritrean capital, where he completed secondary school. We will call him Amde.

Amde wants to go to the United States to continue his studies as he has been unable to find work in Sudan. He has been trying to get his papers in order for more than a year, but he finds himself shuttled from one embassy to another without seeming to get any closer to leaving. A year ago, he was forced out of Khartoum with hundreds of other Eritreans and trucked to a rural camp. When he managed to return to Khartoum to resume his quest for visa, he discovered that a fire had destroyed the room where he had been staying, so he spent the first night sleeping outside. During the night, his luggage-with his school documents-was stolen.

The next day he began again, trudging from police station to court to report his problem, and then going to the UNHCR for aid. He stood nervously in the outer office, thumbing through a wad of notes and papers that catalogue every interview he has had. Scraps of paper spill onto the floor as he struggles to keep from letting his despair overcome him. He is clearly on the verge of a breakdown. The UNHCR give him two Sudanese pounds and wishes him luck.

There is one dim ray of light in this seemingly hopeless situation, but it is in danger of being quenched. It is a camp for refugees in northeastern Sudan run by the Eritrean People's Liberation Front (EPLF). Hidden in the desert hills near the Eritrean border, the Chalhanti camp is an oasis of hope for close to 10,000 people who are actively and cheerfully doing something about their plight, helping to administer themselves, attempting to produce some of their own food, educating each other and managing to keep up their spirits for the time when they can return home. But this camp, despite its unique success, is under threat of closure by the Sudan government which seems to fear a loss of its sovereignty together with the possibility of Ethiopian air attack because of the EPLF's leading role there.

A recent visit to Chalhanti found the residents in a surprisingly positive frame of mind. "We are no longer escaping from the past. This is our home for now," said one 22 year old woman from the Eritrean town of Ghinda. "At the beginning we were thinking only as refugees. We knew nothing. We didn't read or write. We thought only of ourselves. But there have been many developments since then. We began to struggle against illiteracy. We had free discussions, woman to woman and with our husbands. Soon we were cooperating together. The difference in our daily lives from then to now is like the difference between the land and the sky."

Under the EPLF, the Chalhanti camp mirrors life in the liberated areas inside Eritrea. It is highly organized along social group lines-youth, women, peasants and workers each with their own mass associations-and most of the people are in one way or another directly involved in the day to day responsibility of camp life. There are work teams, literacy classes, political seminars and democratically elected committees to adjudicate disputes and govern the camp. Everyone appeared busy as I strolled the well trod dirt paths through the camp.

The first step was to divide the camp into smaller zones under the EPLF's supervision, according to my guerrilla guide. Study and work groups were set up within each area, dividing the women from the men. "Until we bring them to the same way of thinking," remarked my escort, "it is better for them to take their lessons separately."

Each group elected leaders who together shared administrative responsibilities. An immediate consequence was that numerous women came to political leadership for the first time, much as has been the case in Eritrea under the front.

Political education was systematized with EPLF cadres holding three meetings each week with each small group, after which the local leaders held evening discussions. The initial curriculum was drawn from the EPLF's political manual and covered Eritrean history, the aims and goals of the liberation struggle, the handling of contradictions and basic political economy, among other subjects.

Weekly criticism and self-criticism sessions were organized and the entire camp began to meet monthly to exchange ideas and suggestions for how to improve the camp and relate to the struggle in their homeland. Classes, already in progress, were stepped up in the languages of Tigrinya, Arabic and Tigray to give the people common languages, while many smaller groups sprang up spontaneously to study other minority languages.

"Slowly we plan to integrate them into full administrative responsibility," said my guide, "but first we want to fight their backwardness and feudal ideas. The more we change the organization and consciousness of the people, the more we can be sure they can control themselves."

One of the principal problems facing Chalhanti and Eritrean society as a whole were the deeply rooted tribal and ethnic divisions which linger on from the precolonial era. Overcoming them was an early target of the political education.

"We told them that tribalism, is a device of the colonists to sap our strength, and we taught them how the Italians, the British and the Ethiopians exploited our differences to their advantage," explained the EPLF social worker. "We also relocated some families to mix people of various nationalities with each other. The more you put them together, the more they lose their bad ideas. They had completely different cultures, but now they share the same one."

EPLF doctors and paramedics also present weekly lectures on hygiene and sanitation, and there is a clinic in the camp to meet the health care needs of the inhabitants. But there are extreme shortages of medicines from antibiotics to anti-malarials. Although the organizational structure and the personnel are on hand, the material and equipment, which must come from outside, is sorely lacking.

Food is regularly distributed with each resident receiving rations of flour, grain, powdered milk, sugar, tea and vegetable oil, but shortages exist here too for the same reasons. While there appear to be efforts underway to produce vegetables in the camp, the hot, dry climate and the desert soil make this extremely difficult.

Some outside aid was trickling in. One relief agency that retains programs inside Ethiopia was secretly sending blankets and other goods to Chalhanti, and the United Nations High Commission for Refugees was facilitating the supply of food from the WHO in limited quantities, but by and large the situation remains ignored by the international community. This, despite the fact that UN officials have visited the camp and readily acknowledge in Khartoum that it is a model of successful relief work on the other hand, they just as readily concede that the politics of the situation restrain them from taking a more active role in providing and encouraging more assistance. The Sudanese government, meanwhile, has threatened to move the cam entirely to a location deeper in Sudan where it could be taken over by their own officials and run along the lines of the other camps.

Thus, the Eritrean refugee question, at first look a purely humanitarian problem, brings us inexorably back to the political umbrella which overlays the entire Eritrean struggle. The dilemma of the refugees is inseparable from the dilemma of the entire Eritrean nation in its ongoing fight to win international solidarity and attention.

Demonstrably one of the most highly developed political struggles in the world, the Eritrean national liberation war enjoys a virtual blackout in the Western press, and is, of course, continually slandered in that of the Eastern bloc. Eritrea's people are as a result threatened with a wholesale genocide inside and slow death by attrition outside. The reasons for this are not hard to come by.

Both the Soviet Union and the United States find common interest in suppressing this politically independent movement in a competition for influence in Addis Ababa. Each, in turn, exerts constant pressure on its client states and allies to follow its lead. The upshot is an almost total isolation for the Eritrean revolutionaries.

The principal source of solidarity for the Eritreans comes from other liberation movements in the region, including the Tigray People's Liberation Front (TPLF) in northern Ethiopia, the Popular Front for the Liberation of Bahrain, the Popular Front for the Liberation of Oman and various Palestinian liberation movements. But the material aid from this source is at best meager.

Certain left political organizations and parties in Europe and the U.S. have also offered moral support, but again this doesn't feed refugees or defend the guerrilla armies from the hundreds of millions of dollars worth of arms provided to the Ethiopian Derg by the USSR. Nor does it approach the millions contributed to the Derg by the U.S. and Western Europe to prop up that government's sagging economy.

A handful of European voluntary agencies have made concrete gestures toward the Eritreans-notably the Norwegian Church Relief-but this is only a drop in the bucket. If the Eritreans are to survive as a people, a sleeping world must wake up and take notice, as well as responsibility.

Secessionist Eritrean guerrillas open major offensive

The Boston Globe, January 10, 1980

Leftist Eritrean guerrillas this week launched a major military offensive against Soviet-backed Ethiopian forces occupying most of the towns and highways in this strategic Red Sea territory.

The Eritrean People's Liberation Front (EPLF) on Saturday routed a 20,000 man government force on the northeastern sea coast and began round-the-clock shelling of the inland town of Afabet, front official Ermias Debessai said in a telephone interview from Rome.

This marks the first time the guerrillas, who seek independence for Eritrea, have claimed a substantial advance since June 1978, when Ethiopia opened an all-out offensive there with massive Soviet assistance.

In the first eight months of fighting, the Ethiopians carried out a series of blitzkrieg attacks behind waves of Soviet T54 tanks, Stalin organ rockets and MiG jet fighters, retaking almost all the guerrilla-controlled towns.

Since then the war has been at a stalemate, with the government unable to penetrate the guerrilla-base area in the mountainous northern desert and the guerrillas apparently content to whittle away at their better-equipped foe from behind.

"We have been systematically weakening the enemy's forces and neutralizing its offensive capacity," the Front's Rome spokesman said. "This marks the transition from defensive war to the strategic counteroffensive."

The surprise guerrilla attack came at dawn on Saturday, along

25-mile-battle-front, Ermias said. "The entire enemy frontline was overrun, and all the strategic positions are now in our hands."

The guerrilla spokesman claimed that an Ethiopian mechanized brigade and its 505th Task Force were destroyed.

The coastal fighting follows by three weeks a front attack on the government's other main force in northern Eritrea and sets the stage for attacks on previously secure government garrisons in central Eritrea.

With large numbers of guerrillas released from defensive positions near their base, the likelihood is they will move soon to cut the main highways and lay siege to the towns, much as they did in 1977, before the intervention of the USSR on the Ethiopian side.

Soviet advisers have accompanied Ethiopian forces since November 1978 but they have not been active in large numbers in the battles fought since then.

Eritrea: EPLF counteroffensive

The Guardian (New York), January 16, 1980

The Eritrean People's Liberation Front (EPLF) this week opened a major military counteroffensive against Ethiopian occupation forces in Eritrea.

EPLF units on Jan. 5 routed a 20,000-man Ethiopian force from positions on the North-eastern Red Sea coast and began round-the-clock shelling of the inland town of Afabet, according to the front's Rome spokesman, central committee member Ermias Debessai.

The surprise attack on Ethiopia's coastal enclave followed by three weeks of similar EPLF assaults on the government's main inland positions south of the EPLF-held town of Nakfa.

These two battle fronts were part of a pincer effort by Ethiopia to penetrate the guerrilla base area in northern Eritrea.

With both fronts broken by the EPLF, the threat to their base recedes and the possibility for widespread offensive actions arises.

"We are now in a transition from the defensive to the strategic counteroffensive," Ermias told the Guardian. "We are systematically weakening the enemy's forces and neutralizing its offensive capacity."

This marks the first time the Eritrean guerrillas have advanced against Ethiopian forces since June 1978 when the government launched an all-out offensive with massive Soviet assistance.

The EPLF claims to have destroyed Ethiopia's 29th Mechanized Brigade and the 505th Task Force in the dawn Saturday assault along a 25-mile battlefront, but no specific casualty figures were available for either side at Guardian press time.

"The entire enemy frontline was overrun and all the strategic positions are now under our control," Ermias said. (This is a mountainous semi desert region where control of the foothills is the key to domination of the flat coastal plains to which Ethiopian forces retreated.)

The simultaneous shelling of Afabet, where Ethiopian troops had retreated in December from Nakfa, signals the beginning of an EPLF effort to march southward out of this arid base and back to the central area Eritrean highlands where the bulk of the population lives.

Eritrea: EPLF counteroffensive

The Guardian (New York), January 23, 1980

The Eritrean People's Liberation Front (EPLF) captured the Ethiopian army base and airstrip at Mahamimet in northern Eritrean Jan. 10 after a 5-day battle, according to the EPLF. The EPLF also reported that some 5000 Ethiopian troops were either killed, wounded, or captured in the battle, and about 25,000 more troops were driven back to the Red Sea area.

Meanwhile, at Guardian press time fighting continued last week at the inland town of Afabet. The Afabet fighting represents a continuation of the EPLF's renewed military counteroffensive against Ethiopian occupation forces in Eritrea.

The recent battles follow a Jan. 5 EPLF rout of 20,000 Ethiopian forces in the EPLF-held town of Nakfa. About 8000 Ethiopian troops were killed or wounded in the Nakfa fighting, said the EPLF.

Since their defeat at Nakfa, Ethiopian troops, with the aid of Soviet warships, have been evacuating to the Red Sea port of Marsa Teklay, according to the London Financial Times. Reporters of the scene after the 3-week Nakfa battle say they saw the bodies of hundreds of dead Ethiopian soldiers strewn across the hilltop at Assarai.

Soviet tanks and other artillery were also reported captured in the battle.

The EPLF counteroffensive is the first time the Eritrean guerrillas have attacked Ethiopian forces since the Soviet-backed Ethiopian government offensive in June 1978.

Ethiopia tries to blunt EPLF gains

The Guardian (New York), February 20, 1980

Recent Ethiopian military defeats in Eritrea have sparked new wave of diplomatic maneuvering by the Soviet backed Ethiopian military junta to stop the 18-year war short of its goal of full independence.

Ethiopian diplomats have been dispatched to neighboring Sudan and to Europe in a renewed effort to gain support for their 1976 call for a "peaceful solution" to the Eritrea war on the basis of regional autonomy for the former Italian colony.

The aim appears to be to split the Eritrean liberation forces and to undercut their rearguard political support from Sudan while simultaneously preparing for renewed fighting in Eritrea.

A spokesman for the Eritrean People's Liberation Front (EPLF) this week denounced the Ethiopian proposals offering nothing new. He also renewed the EPLF split for negotiations without preconditions.

The exchange of charges was touched off by a recent Sudanese policy declaration that appeared to echo the Ethiopian terms for a settlement, amid rumors that the rival Eritrean Liberation Front (ELF) is considering separate talks with Ethiopia.

The Sudanese declaration came at a meeting of that counter ruling political party, the Sudanese Socialist Union where a representative of the Ethiopia junta was present. Noticeably absent were members of the Eritrean front.

Both the EPLF and the smaller ELF supply their armies through eastern Sudan.

The stepped-up diplomatic pressure on the Eritreans comes at a time when the EPLF has broken the military stalemate in Eritrea and has resumed a counteroffensive.

Since December, the EPLF has forced Ethiopia's two main inward armies into wholesale retreat and has increased offensive actions in the Ethiopian rear.

However, there are signs that the fragile united front between the EPLF and ELF, reached in October 1977, is under severe strain. Both the Soviet Union and Ethiopia are .....seeking to gain advantage from this by making secret overtures to the weakened ELF to consider the regional autonomy offer on the condition it break with the ELF.

Delegations of the ELF and the Ethiopian junta were in Rome last week. According to reports in the Italian press, there are signs the ELF is considering the Ethiopian offer of regional autonomy.

Relations between the two fronts have been noticeably strained over the past several months with progress toward political and military unity stalled.

Since the summer of 1978 when Ethiopian forces with massive Soviet backing recaptured most of the guerrilla-controlled Eritrean towns, the EPLF has borne the brunt of most of the fighting.

Throughout this period, the Marxist-oriented EPLF has maintained an official silence on the progress of unity with the nationalist ELF.

Political Differences

However, substantial political differences continue to divide the rival organizations. The EPLF upholds a line of "national democratic revolution" based upon mass mobilization and a policy of self-reliance, while the ELF is guided by the pro-Soviet line of "noncapitalist development" despite the role of the USSR on the Ethiopian side.

With the ELF reduced to small-scale guerrilla actions in Eritrea and a secondary role in the EPLF's larger military confrontations, ELF diplomacy has been directed mainly at persuading the USSR to back a compromise with Ethiopia.

The ELF's increasing political isolation and its physical shrinkage from the largest armed Eritrean front in the early 1970s to a minor military force today are contributing factors to its present diplomatic and political policies.

ELF leaders are thought to fear that unity with the EPLF would mean absorption into the more powerful EPLF. The EPLF for its part has been strongly backing the unity plan and refraining from open polemics with the ELF over their political differences in order to concentrate its full strength against the ongoing Ethiopian military offensive.

But the EPLF has also moved to strengthen its relations with the Tigray Peoples Liberation Front (TPLF) in the neighboring Ethiopian province of Tigray where over 30,000 Ethiopian government troops are now pinned down in the steadily expanding guerrilla war. With TPLF and EPLF holding a common general political line and program, their growing alliance can be seen as a further political threat to the ELF.

In a telephone interview with the Guardian, EPLF central committee member Amdemikael Kahsai in Rome acknowledged a lack of progress within Eritrea in implementing the unity agreement. Heretofore the EPLF has been silent on the matter.

While declining comment on reports of ELF contacts with the Ethiopian juntas, Amdemikael confirmed the efforts by Ethiopia and "other forces," to divide the two fronts, apparently meaning the USSR.

He also conceded that relations between them in Eritrea are in difficulty. "There are indications that our relationship with ELF is strained," he said. "The ELF seems to be working so that our agreement will not function."

The EPLF leader called the Sudanese initiative and the apparent Soviet and Ethiopian gestures toward the ELF part of a broader political offensive, "closely related to the problem in Afghanistan. There are forces interested in seeing the Eritrean struggle liquidated one way or the other."

He also noted that the Sudanese declaration appears to be part of an attempt at rapprochement with Ethiopia following Sudan's movement away from Egypt over the latter's treaty with Israel.

But, he said, "Our relations with Sudan are still normal, even if it appears different on the surface."

Meanwhile, fighting continues at a low level inside Eritrea where Ethiopian forces have been pushed out of positions they held for over a year along the Red Sea coast and inland near the EPLF-held town of Nakfa.

Battle For The Horn Of Africa
Eritrea guerrillas back on offensive

The Financial Times (London), April 28, 1980

Afabet, Eritrea

Two years of retreat by Eritrean forces in the face of Soviet-backed offensives by Ethiopia have ended. Since last winter, the Eritreans have been driving back the heavily armed and more numerous Ethiopian army.

Now, with the Eritrean guerrillas enjoying a strong position around Afabet, in northern Eritrea, there is a lull in the fighting. But it may be only temporary. Both sides are mobilizing for renewed fighting which is certain to break the stalemate.

Last December, Russian warships had to evacuate defeated Ethiopian troops from a Red Sea harbor, after Eritrean guerrillas had broken a year's encirclement of their mountainous base area in northern Eritrea.

This humiliating setback, for forces which have received more than $1b worth of Russian arms in the past three years embarrassed the Soviet Union. Moscow wants a secure foothold in the Horn of Africa, with its challenging position close to Saudi Arabia and to Red Sea and Indian Ocean shipping routes.

As a result, the Soviet Union has tried to arrange reconciliation between Ethiopia and the weaker of the two main Eritrean fighting groups, the Eritrean Liberation Front, with meeting in East Berlin, Rome and Moscow. Sudan, whose economy has been burdened with nearly 400,000 Eritrean refugees, is also attempting to find a settlement, believing that a solution in Eritrea will remove Ethiopia's dependence on the Soviet Union and stabilize the region.

Today, guerrillas of the more powerful Eritrean Popular Liberation Front virtually encircle the Ethiopians in the strategic town of Afabet. They surround an estimated 13,000 troops on three sides, leaving one tenuous opening to the Red Sea, through which Afabet is irregularly supplied. From high on the steep ring of arid, volcanic ridges, the Ethiopian can be seen encamped on the broad plain. Each side holds entrenched positions on the innermost circle of hills, sometimes less than 200 meters apart.

Neither side appears close to an easy victory, but a show-down may be imminent. Weekly skirmishes between small units suggest a testing of each other's defenses, in preparation for larger attacks, and there are reports of vast quantities of equipment being flown in to Asmara airport, further south.

The Eritreans are now in the 19th year of their war for the independence of this former Italian colony, annexed by Ethiopia two decades ago.

"Ethiopia is weakening," said Petros Solomon, a member of the Eritrean Popular Liberation Front's political bureau, in an interview behind the Afabet lines. "Militarily speaking, we are gaining he upper hand, but this takes time. There can be actions and counteractions on both sides before 3 decisive changes takes place.:

The front claims to have captured large quantities of Soviet arms in the battles between Nakfa and Afabet, including more than 100 military vehicles, 17 T-54 tanks, and an array of long-range artillery, anti-tank and anti-aircraft guns. All this is put to use by the highly skilled and committed guerrillas.

Among those shown are on a walking tour of the guerrilla positions were 76-85 and 122mm artillery pieces and 20, 23, 37 and 40 mm mobile medium range weapons. Large numbers of T-54 tanks were also present in the rear for use as artillery.

Ethiopia, faced with its seeming inability to crush the Eritreans, recently welcomed moves by President Jaafar Nimeiri of Sudan to end the conflict, having rejected them out of hand in February 1979 when it thought it was winning. Its aim is to persuade Sudan to cut off the Eritreans' supply lines, a step which the front admits would severely hamper its now fully mechanized army.

Mr. Abdul-Majid Khalid, Sudan's Vice-President has visited Addis Ababa twice in the past six weeks, but although Sudan has banned journalists from entering Eritrea, supplies to the front do not seem to be affected. The front is wary of Sudanese pressure, but says it has assurances from the Sudanese Government that it will be consulted before any action is taken.

"The Sudan is trying to bring the two sides to the negotiating table," said Issayas Afwerki, a field commander with the Eritrean Popular Liberation Front, in an interview at Afabet. "But they are not trying to impose a solution. For our part we are willing to talk."

A more serious threat to the Popular Liberation Front's present military advantage inside Eritrea may come from the apparent breakdown of moves to unite with the rival Eritrean Liberation Front, which has been in contact with the Soviet Union.

Repeated fighting between Popular Liberation Front and Eritrean Liberation Front forces has been reported since the beginning of the year. The Eritrean Liberation Front is also said to have mounted major attacks on the Tigray People's Liberation Front, which operates in the neighboring province of Tigray, to the south and has close relations with the Popular Liberation Front in Eritrea.

The Popular Liberation Front and the Tigray Front have increasingly coordinated their military strategies against the Ethiopian Government, and they have, on several occasions, made joint attacks in the border region.

Contacts between these two movements and the Oromo Liberation Front in southern Ethiopia, also appear to be developing. An Oromo Liberation Front spokesman in Sudan indicated his organization is holding discussions with the Western Somali Liberation Front, which operates in southeastern Ethiopia with Somali Government backing.

Although there seems little likelihood of overall coordination between these diverse anti-government forces in the immediate future, such a possibility may be evolving in a broad move to overthrow the ruling military junta.

Against the background of the Labyrinth, the battle shaping up for the Eritrean town of Afabet assumes a pivotal significance. An Ethiopian defeat would not be just a military setback for the government. It could also unsettle the attempts by Col. Mengistu Haile Mariam, Ethiopian head of state to consolidate his one-man rule under a new Communist party.

"It is a question of time," said Ali Sayid, a Popular Liberation Front military leader, of the coming confrontation of Afabet. "They are preparing themselves, and so are we."

Eritrea: lull before the storm?

Transition period

The Guardian (New York), May 7, 1980

[Byline: John Currie]

Outside Afabet, Eritrea

The road to the Eritrean town of Afabet is paved with the random paraphernalia of the Ethiopian army's precipitous retreat.

Guerrillas of the Eritrean People's Liberation Front (EPLF) recently drove invading Ethiopian forces 35 miles through this area from their positions outside the EPLF-held town of Nakfa.

In a dramatic turnabout, the guerrillas are today dug in on three sides of Afabet, looking down on the partially besieged town from trenches and 2-person underground stone fortifications high atop the surrounding hills.

The main armed strength on both sides in the 19-year Eritrean struggle for liberation from Ethiopia-which annexed the former Italian colony two decades ago-is now concentrated around this town. A decisive outcome here could have a major influence on the war.

In related developments:

- Ethiopia and its Soviet backers have escalated their diplomatic efforts to gain support for their side, especially with neighboring Sudan.
- Discord has resumed between the main patriotic force, the progressive EPLF, and its smaller, nationalist ally, the Eritrean Liberation Front (ELF).

Journey to Front

Sudan, which permits supplies to pass to the guerrillas, has lately been discouraging journalists from traveling to Eritrea. This visitor managed to get through, journeying the last miles in a battered Land Rover with the headlights turned off to avoid detection.

Even though a showdown appears imminent at Afabet and frequent skirmishes take place, several guerrilla units moved to the rear for a break in the daily action after I arrived. The rhythmic patter of drums echoed across the barren hills until late at night as the guerrillas performed traditional dances from among the nine native ethnic groups that make up the Eritrean nation. They were led by a cultural troupe drawn from the brigades stationed here.

The first gray streaks of dawn brought a brief exchange of artillery fire. The rocky hillsides reverberated with the shock. Then, again, all was quiet. During the day a pair of Russian-supplied MiG jet fighters bombed guerrilla positions, but the projectiles exploded harmlessly among the scattered stones.

Bitter Fighting

Most of the guerrilla positions are deep under the hard ground. They sit in wait within roofed trenches and randomly arranged stone fortifications, at home here in the forbidding semi-desert along the strategic Red Sea coast where temperatures often exceed 125 degrees.

A walking tour of the frontlines here found the Eritrean and Ethiopian armies facing each other on the innermost ridges, sometimes less than 200 yards apart.

The main land supply route running north from the government-occupied city of Keren is all but cut off. The only break in the guerrilla encirclement is to the east, toward the Red Sea coast where the government maintains a base at the small port of Marsa Gulbub.

"When the Ethiopians came into this area, they entered a trap," said frontline EPLF brigade commander Berhane Tsehaiyay. "They faced not only our concentrated strength, but also problems of terrain, climate and supply."

The steep, scrub-covered mountains have made the effective use of Ethiopia's Soviet-supplied tanks and artillery extremely difficult.

Debris along the network of roads and dry-river beds leading to Afabet is testimony to the bitter fighting so far. On a four mile walk to the frontline, I counted 32 destroyed Ethiopian army vehicles, including three tanks, More than 100 vehicles, including three tanks. More than 100 vehicles were destroyed in the December and January route of Ethiopian forces.

The EPLF pulled back into its base area here to make a stand against the then advancing Ethiopian forces late in 1978, after evacuating most of the larger towns previously under their control.

Invading Ethiopian forces were then estimated to number 120,000. Today less than 40,000 of the forces remain in Eritrea, according to EPLF leaders.

The EPLF pulled back into its base area here to make a stand against the then advancing Ethiopian forces late in 1978, after evacuating most of the larger towns previously under their control.

Invading Ethiopian forces were then estimated to number

120,000. Today less than 40,000 of the forces remain in Eritrea, according to EPLF leaders.

Transition Period

"Ethiopia is weakening," said EPLF political bureau member Petros Solomon in an interview behind the Afabet lines, conducted in an underground house.

"Militarily speaking, we are gaining the upper hand, but this takes time," continued the 33-year-old guerrilla leader. "We are now in the transition from the period of stalemate to the strategic counteroffensive, but Ethiopia still has the potential for large-scale operations. There can be actions and counteractions on both sides before a decisive change takes place."

Ethiopia retains the manpower potential to remobilize large infantry forces and the Soviet Union continues to pour in heavy arms and ammunition to the Ethiopian regime, he noted.

"The supply of sophisticated Soviet heavy arms is continuing," said the EPLF leader. "It hasn't slowed down at all. If anything, it is increasing." Soviet military personnel continue to direct much of the battlefield strategy of the beleaguered Ethiopian forces, he added.

Diplomatic Maneuvering

Faced With a seeming inability to win a military victory, the Ethiopians have lately turned to diplomatic maneuvering to persuade the Sudan to cut off guerrilla supplies. The Soviet Union has also reportedly initiated talks with the smaller Eritrean movement, the ELF in an effort to convince it to accept a settlement based upon limited regional autonomy within the Ethiopian state.

Ethiopian and Sudanese officials have been regularly exchanging high level visits since the first of the year. Ethiopian leader Col. Mengistu Haile Mariam is scheduled to meet Sudanese president Jaafar Nimeiri in May.

Sources here suggest the U.S. may have a hand in the moves toward rapprochement between the two traditionally hostile countries. They point out that Sudanese Vice President and Defense Minister Abdel Majid held closed door meetings last week with the U.S. ambassador to Sudan immediately after his return from visiting Ethiopia for the second time in as many months.

The U.S. has long sought to displace Soviet influence in Ethiopia by maintaining a hands off attitude toward the independent leftist anti-government guerrillas and by discreetly continuing economic aid to the Addis Ababa regime.

EPLF leaders say, however, that little of substance has changed in their relations with Sudan and that no coercive pressure has been put on them beyond requests to enter talks at some future time.

A more serious threat to the EPLF's current military advantage comes from a renewal of fighting inside Eritrea with the rival ELF. A series of minor but persistent clashes has been reported since January between the two nominally allied fronts.

Leaders of both fronts minimize these reports, claiming they are being carried out by disgruntled individuals and small groups. But ELF units are also reported attacking the Tigray People's Liberation Front (TPLF) in the neighboring province of Tigray. Leaders of all three organizations are now said to be meeting in Khartoum, Sudan to resolve these problems.

Both EPLF and TPLF have close political and military relations and have in the past carried out joint attacks against government forces.

The ELF, once the largest of the Eritrean movements, has shrunk to a fraction of its former size since suffering major losses in the 1978 Ethiopian campaign here. Reliable sources indicate that the remaining ELF units have avoided direct confrontations with Ethiopia for close to a year while trying to rebuild.

ELF leader Ahmed Nassar was recently reported in Moscow, where he is said by informed sources to have sought intervention to bring about separate negotiations with the Ethiopian regime. The Italian Communist Party played the role of intermediary in these talks, according to these sources.

Serious Shift

The EPLF, for its part, has long been weak at the diplomatic level, depending upon changes in the internal military situation to gain leverage internationally, but so far having little noticeable success beyond a handful of countries in Africa and the Middle East, including Mozambique and Algeria.

While no one here will predict the impending phase of the war, the next three to four months are likely to witness a renewal of heavy fighting and a possible serious shift in military position.

"It's a question of time whether they are going to start the next round or we are," said EPLF military commander Ali Sayid. "Each of us is working toward this. They are preparing themselves and so are we."

ERITREA/ETHIOPIA
ALLIANCES SHIFT AMONG GOVERNMENT FOES

Africa News (Durham, NC), May 1980

[AN] On the eve of an expected Ethiopian offensive against Eritrean nationalist guerrillas, the first signs of the escalation in the fighting have appeared not in Eritrea itself, but in Tigre, the Ethiopian province immediately to the south.

There last week, according to the Tigre People's Liberation Front (TPLF), three battalions of Ethiopian troops were ambushed only six miles from the provincial capital of Makale. In a battle lasting some six hours the TPLF claims to have killed 300 of the government forces and captured significant quantities of small arms. The troops belonged to Ethiopia's newly-mobilized 18th division, moved into Tigre a month ago as part of an effort to dislodge guerrillas from the countryside.

Although the TPLF seeks autonomy within Ethiopia rather than independence, it has developed increasingly close links with the Eritrean People's Liberation Front (EPLF), which does seek independence for that territory, formerly an Italian colony which was federated with Ethiopia after World War II. Both groups share a common left-wing critique of Ethiopia's government, considering it a military clique rather than a genuine socialist regime.

In December 1979 and January this year the EPLF successfully resisted an Ethiopian military offensive aimed at its base areas near Nakfa and its troops advanced further south toward Afabet. For more than six months there has been a pause in the fighting, but the EPLF now claims Ethiopia is preparing a major offensive. The Ethiopian military is said to be building up major arms supplies, including more than 200 new Soviet tanks, hundreds of artillery pieces, 100 troop-carrying helicopters, and, most threatening to the Eritreans, supplies of nerve gas. While the gas has not been used as yet, the EPLF has launched a major diplomatic campaign against Ethiopia and the Soviet Union because it has been supplied, and in the battle zones EPLF fighters have been constructing home-made gas masks.

The other Eritrean guerrilla movement, the Eritrean Liberation Front (ELF), however, now appears to have definitely broken its united front established in 1977 with the EPLF. ELF units have withdrawn from zones where they fought alongside the EPLF in 1979, and ELF deserters who have joined EPLF have told Africa News correspondent Dan Connell that the ELF has been holding back from combat with the Ethiopian forces in its own zones. Connell, who visited Eritrea recently, says that "the level of tension between the two fronts seemed extremely high. All the signs of any practical working arrangements or unity between them seem to be gone."

The ELF, reports say, has showed openness to some compromise with Ethiopia short of independence, and has held talks with Ethiopian government representatives, most recently in Beirut.

The EPLF accordingly has moved to emphasize cooperation with other opponents of the Ethiopian government. Links with the TPLF are particularly close, involving coordination of military operations through radio contact. The EPLF has also trained several thousand recruits in the past six months both for the TPLF and the Oromo Liberation Front (OLF), which operates in Oromo-speaking areas in southern Ethiopia. A formal united front among the three is possible, one EPLF political bureau member told Connell early this month.

Big Soviet Arms Lift To Ethiopia

The Boston Globe, June 1980

A massive air and sea lift of sophisticated Soviet arms which reportedly includes lethal nerve gas may signal a renewal of fighting between Ethiopia's Russian-backed army and nationalist Eritrean guerrillas.

Soviet helicopter gunships, tanks and armored cars have poured into the embattled Red Sea territory in the last two weeks, according to a guerrilla spokesman contacted by phone in Rome.

"We are expecting the Ethiopian offensive within a few days," said Ermias Debessai, a member of the central committee of the Eritrean People's Liberation Front (EPLF).

Eritrean refugees reaching neighboring Sudan claim the Soviet arms shipments include the deadly nerve gas GA, for which there is no known antidote.

Meanwhile, officials of the Sudan-based Eritrean Relief Association have appealed to the United Nations and the International Committee for the Red Cross to block the introduction of the poison gas in the Eritrea war.

The Eritreans are fighting for the independence of the former Italian colony which was annexed by Ethiopia in 1962.

Since late 1976 the Soviet Union has provided the ruling Ethiopian military junta with over $1 billion in arms in a thus far unsuccessful attempt to crush the Eritrean guerrilla movement. Observers now think the Soviets may be escalating the war in an attempt to end it soon.

A series of Ethiopian offensives that began in June 1978 forced the guerrillas to retreat from many of towns and cities they had previously captured, but substantial Ethiopian loses in 1979 have given the initiative back to the Eritreans in what has become the largest and longest running armed conflict in modern African history.

The current government buildup comes in the wake of dramatic Ethiopian military setbacks early this year and on the heels of a breakdown in talks between Ethiopia and Sudan aimed at blocking guerrilla supply routes across the Sudan border.

The latest shipments of Soviet arms reaching the government held Eritrean capital of Asmara and the Red Sea port of Massawa include 24 Soviet made H1 attack helicopters and 120 helicopter transports capable of carrying 40 persons each, according to Ermias Debessai.

More than 200 Soviet tanks and armored cars and an estimated 200 Soviet military experts also have arrived recently in Eritrea, according to the EPLF spokesman.

The H1 helicopters are similar to those being used by the Soviets in Afghanistan. There have also been widespread reports of the use of an incapacitating gas against the Afghan guerrillas.

The GA gas said to be in Eritrea, however, is a lethal agent that reportedly kills upon direct contact within two minutes. It can be delivered by artillery shells, rockets or missiles, and is capable of lingering up to four weeks after initial impact.

The symptoms are intense sweating, bronchial congestion, uncontrollable vomiting, convulsions, paralysis and respiratory failure. Death comes of suffocation.

Relief officials charge that this gas would have major impact on the 100,000 Eritrean nomads who live near the combat zones.

A spokesman for the Soviet Embassy in Washington has no comment on the reports. Ethiopian officials contacted yesterday neither confirmed or denied the guerrilla charges.

Talks between Ethiopian Head of State Col. Mengistu Haile Mariam and Sudanese President Jaafar Nimeiri failed early this month.

Guerrilla advances in December and January have placed the Ethiopian forces in Eritrea on the defensive. A recent tour of the battlefront revealed the extent of Soviet and Ethiopian loses there. In a 40-mile stretch between the guerrilla held town of Nakfa and the government held town of Afabet the litter of Ethiopia's sudden retreat lay everywhere.

There were burned out tanks, blackened base areas, thousands of spent tank and artillery shells, discarded Soviet ammunition cases, scattered army helmets and boots and collapsed canvas tents.

In one spot 15 charred Ethiopian trucks lay in ruins. Down the road was a Soviet T54 tanks. Nearby, a Soviet BTR60 armored car lay on its side.

More than 100 military vehicles including 17 tanks were claimed captured by the guerrillas in the 10-day battle.

U.S. eyes strategic Horn of Africa

The Guardian (New York), June 18, 1980

Recent U.S. moves in the strategic Horn of Africa suggest the beginnings of a maneuver to gain imperialist hegemony over the region.

U.S. strategists appear to be using strengthened relations with several northeast Africa countries to regain influence in Ethiopia and to oppose the growing power of revolutionary nationalist movements there.

The failure of Soviet military assistance in Ethiopia to crush these struggles is a key factor in these developments. Continuing economic and political instability in the countries that make up this important corner of Africa also contribute to the setting for the U.S. thrust.

Substantial offers of U.S. and Western European economic aid are being used in conjunction with a calculated military buildup to woo Ethiopia away from the Soviet Union.

Changes in Decade

Close to a decade ago the political lines were clearly drawn in Africa's Horn. The U.S. held unchallenged sway over Haile Selassie's anachronistic feudal empire in Ethiopia. The Soviet Union exerted considerable influence over "socialist" Somalia.

To the west, the Sudan was loosely allied with the Soviet Union. To the south, Kenya was close to Britain and the U.S., and the tiny city-state of Djibouti remained a French colony.

The only anomaly in the area was the former Italian colony of Eritrea, then a decade into a war for independence from Ethiopia which had annexed it in 1962. The Eritreans received irregular aid from Soviet allies such as Algeria, Syria, Iraq, South Yemen, and Cuba, but the USSR itself held back from direct assistance.

Then came the collapse of the Ethiopian aristocracy in 1974, the rise to power there of a military junta-known as the "Derg"-and a sudden scramble for position by the U.S. and the USSR that literally turned the old alignments upside down.

The self-described "socialist" Ethiopian junta became a Soviet ally. Overnight, Somalia lined up with the West, and the Sudan-which had been moving steadily to the right since an abortive coup d'etat by the Communist Party there-also aligned itself with the U.S.

Since then, little Djibouti has become nominally independent, though French troops remain there in large numbers, and Kenya has moved solidly into an alliance with the U.S.

Again, the peculiar but consistent exception was Eritrea which continued its battle against Ethiopia and now the USSR but at the same time declared U.S. imperialism to be its main long-term enemy.

Refuse to Flip-Flop

Against all the predictions of both East and West, the leftist Eritrean nationalists doggedly refused to flip-flop into the imperialist camp. Instead they set out to rebuild their shattered alliances with progressive states in Africa and the Middle East.

Today, the Soviet presence in Ethiopia appears to some observers to be on somewhat shaky ground, and the U.S. is again subtly but carefully moving to regain its lost ground there.

Meanwhile, both big powers continue to underestimate the contending nationalisms in the region, opting for short-term alliances that clearly lack the material basis for stabilizing the Horn.

Mirror Image

Current U.S., strategy is almost a mirror image of what the Soviet plan was only three years ago: to contain the various guerrilla movements that now oppose the Ethiopian junta by undercutting their rear areas in Somalia and Sudan.

U.S. diplomats are seeking to persuade Ethiopia that their relations with these key neighboring states give Washington the leverage to win a peaceful settlement of the protracted wars in Eritrea and in the Ogaden region of Ethiopia, claimed by Somalia.

U.S. Military Buildup

The argument is that where Soviet arms failed to crush the guerrillas, U.S. diplomacy can succeed. Millions of dollars in economic aid to Ethiopia now pouring in under the heading of famine relief are intended to sweeten the package.

But the carrot is accompanied by a big stick. The U.S. has accomplished a sizeable military buildup in the region which effectively encircles Ethiopia. Further increases in the U.S. presence are underway.

In the mid 1970s, Washington used the Soviet presence in Somalia to justify the construction of a huge naval base at the Indian Ocean atoll of Diego Garcia (see next page). Today, the U.S. is negotiating to take over the former Soviet base at Berbera in Somalia.

The Carter administration has also used the Soviet presence in Ethiopia and in the broader "crescent of crisis" in southwest Asia to justify establishing naval facilities in the Kenya port of Mombassa to the south.

At the same time, expanded U.S. military bases are being set up to the east in Oman. U.S. land forces and advisory personnel have been increased in North Yemen. U.S. naval forces have been increased in the Indian Ocean. And military assistance is growing in the Sudan.

Thus, while the bourgeois media here have focused much attention on the apparent Soviet advance in Ethiopia, the U.S. has quietly but steadily strengthened its political control of old and new client states behind a substantial military buildup.

Meanwhile, Soviet miscalculations in the region as a whole and wrong policies in Ethiopia and Eritrea appear to be playing directly into U.S. hands.

Moscow's all-out military support for the ruling Ethiopian Derg against the Marxist Eritrean People's Liberation Front (EPLF) and against the various oppressed nationalities inside Ethiopia have helped to shrink the already narrow base of popular support for the regime.

Today the Soviet-backed Ethiopian forces in Eritrea are in difficulty and loosely allied national opposition movements elsewhere in Ethiopia re growing rapidly.

Political Solution Sought

A belated recognition by the USSR of the military threat to the Addis Ababa junta posed by these movements appears to be producing a change in policy aimed at emphasizing some form of political solution. But the absence of an accompanying political recognition of the principles of national self-determination upon which a genuine solution must be base d severely limits the options still open.

The result is that the Soviets are bargaining from a position of close identification with the Derg for a compromise with the opposition movements. Among the concessions reportedly being pushed by the USSR are some form of political autonomy in Eritrea and a policy of limited cultural autonomy for the oppressed nationalities in Ethiopia.

Offers to the Derg

These proposals fall far short of the demands of the armed struggles in Eritrea and Ethiopia, all of which call for national self-determination. In the case of Eritrea, this takes the form of a demand for full independence.

Simultaneously, Washington is matching Moscow's policies with similar emphasis on partial political reforms in Ethiopia which would leave the regime in a position of unchallenged control of both Ethiopia and Eritrea.

The difference, then, is not in either big power's relations with or support for the guerrilla movements, but rather with their offers to the Derg.

In the context of Soviet military setbacks in the wars there, the ongoing instability of the Ethiopian economy and the U.S. buildup in the region. Washington's influence appears here, too, to be on the upswing.

The U.S. has a consistent 19-year record of opposition to the Eritrean independence movement. It has also, like the USSR, publicly continued to uphold the "territorial integrity" of Ethiopia against the national movements that have arisen in Ethiopia since the rise to power of the junta.

Increased Aid

Throughout the three years the Soviet Union has enjoyed a military and political alliance with the Derg, the U.S. has maintained a low profile in Ethiopia while continuing to supply economic aid. In the last 12 months this aid has increased substantially through direct and indirect programs.

After a brief lapse in 1978, U.S. corporations have resumed buying Ethiopian coffee, that country's major export crop and the source of revenue for the purchase of Soviet arms.

Grant assistance and loans have also recently been forthcoming from the European Economic Community, the World Bank and the U.S. Agency for International Development (AID). Private U.S. charities-funded by AID-have also stepped up their help to Ethiopia under the heading of famine relief.

This discrete support appears to have set the stage for the current U.S. diplomatic push in Addis Ababa based upon promises to obstruct guerrilla supply routes in Sudan and Somalia where the U.S. is now firmly established in those countries' economies and increasingly in their military forces.

The clearest sign of U.S. success has been a marked shift in the Ethiopian leadership toward pro-Western factions in the Derg.

The most likely short term effect, however, will be an Ethiopian move toward balancing relations with East and West rather than another dramatic realignment. Soviet influence in Addis Ababa would be undercut but not displaced by such a change.

Ethiopian drive expected in Eritrea

The Guardian (New York), June 18, 1980

A massive air-and-sea-lift of sophisticated Soviet arms appears to signal an imminent renewal of intense fighting between Ethiopia's Soviet-backed army and nationalist Eritrean guerrillas.

Soviet helicopter gun ships, tanks and armored cars have poured into the embattled Red Sea territory during the past two weeks, according to a guerrilla spokesman contacted by phone in Rome.

"We are expecting the Ethiopian offensive in a few days," Ermias Debessai, a member of the Central Committee of the Eritrean People's Liberation Front (EPLF), told the Guardian.

Soviet Ship Nerve Gas

Eritrean refugees reaching neighboring Sudan claim that the Soviet arms shipments include a deadly nerve gas, for which there is no known antidote. Officials of the Sudan-based Eritrean Relief Association have appealed to the UN and the International

Committee for the Red Cross to block the introduction of the gas in the Eritrea war.

The Eritreans are fighting for the independence of the former Italian colony which was annexed by Ethiopia in 1962. Since late 1976 the Soviet Union has provided the current Ethiopian ruling military junta with over $1 billion in arms in its so far unsuccessful attempt to crush the Eritrean guerrilla movement.

A series of Ethiopian offensives that began in June 1978 forced the leftist guerrillas to retreat from many of the towns and cities they had previously captured. But substantial Ethiopian losses in 1979 have given the initiative back to the Eritreans in what has become the largest and longest-running armed conflict in modern African history.

The current government buildup follows dramatic Ethiopian setbacks earlier this year and, more recently, a breakdown in talks between Ethiopia and Sudan aimed at blocking guerrilla supply routes across the Sudan border.

The latest shipments of Soviet arms reaching the government-held Eritrean capital of Asmara and the Red Sea port of Massawa include 24 Soviet-made H1 attack helicopters and 120 helicopter transports capable of carrying 40 persons each, according to Debessai.

More than 200 Soviet tanks and armored cars and an estimated 200 Soviet military experts have also recently arrived in Eritrea, according to the EPLF spokesman. "They have already been distributed to all the battle fronts," he said.

Lethal Gas Used In Eritrea

The gas said to be in Eritrea is a lethal agent which reportedly kills upon direct contact within two minutes. It can be delivered by artillery shells, rockets or missiles, and is capable of lingering up to four weeks after initial impact.

The symptoms are intense sweating, bronchial congestion, uncontrollable vomiting, convulsions, paralysis and respiratory failure. Death is due to suffocation.

A spokesman for the Soviet embassy in Washington had no comment on these reports. Ethiopian officials contacted today neither confirmed nor denied the guerrilla's charges. "Our government's policy is to solve the Eritrean problem peacefully," said one diplomat.

Eritrea's War For Independence

The EPLF Holds On

*The Organizer (*Philadelphia Workers
Organizing Committee), July 1980

*The following article was contributed by Dan Connell, whose on the
scene reporting and analysis of the Eritrean war and the politics of the
EPLF has appeared in the Guardian and elsewhere. Connell will be contributing articles on the Eritrean struggle to the Organizer periodically.*

Thousands of guerrilla fighters of the Eritrean People's Liberation
Front (EPLF) are dug in to roofed trenches and two-person stone fortifications high atop the mountains around Afabet. They surround
13,000 Ethiopian government troops in the valley below.

Daily exchanges of small arms and artillery fire are punctuated
with irregular sorties by Ethiopia's supersonic jet fighter bombers.
Once every week or ten days company and battalion size assaults are
launched for tactical positions in the jagged volcanic hills.

Since the middle of 1978, massive frontal offensives and counteroffensives of near World War II proportions have taken place in
Eritrea at three to six month intervals. Casualties in these battles have
numbered in the tens of thousands. Scores of villages have been razed
to the ground and a quarter of a million civilians made homeless in
Ethiopian attacks. Hundreds of tanks and artillery pieces have been
captured or destroyed by the EPLF guerrillas.

The Little Known Long War

The little known Eritrean war for independence from Ethiopia is
the longest running and the largest armed conflict in the modern history of Black Africa. It is also one of the most politically complex liberation struggles in the world today.

The first shots of the war were fired in 1961 by the Eritrean
Liberation Front (ELF) as Ethiopia's emperor Haile Selassie was moving to annex the former Italian colony of Eritrea. The strategic Red
Sea territory was then part of a loose United Nations-sponsored federation with Ethiopia. Over the vocal protests of the Eritrean population, Selassie had dismantled the federation piece by piece before
sending his troops to Eritrea and forcing the local parliament to vote
itself out of existence.

The United States and Israel firmly backed the emperor with military
aid and advisory personnel during the intense counter-insurgency

campaign which followed. The pay-off was the granting of military bases to both countries in Central Eritrea and on the Red Sea coast.

By 1970 the Eritrean nationalist movement had split into two wings - ELF and EPLF. The former represented a broad coalition of nationalist forces under the leadership of displaced landlords and Eritrean merchants and traders. The latter was a revolutionary alliance of Eritrean workers and peasant which for the first time forwarded a program of social and economic transformation along with a call for national independence.

Since that time, the Marxist-oriented EPLF has grown steadily to become today the dominant political and military force in Eritrea. But this decisive shift to the left in Eritrea has been matched by apparently similar changes in Ethiopia.

In 1974, a military junta, known as the "Derg", deposed the feudal emperor and his aristocratic followers to usher in a self-proclaimed "socialist" revolution. Land reform and sweeping nationalizations were announced in the Addis Ababa capital. Rural and urban neighborhood associations were organized. And finally, a break was made with the US and Israel. In 1977 the Soviet Union and Cuba came on the scene.

Meanwhile, the war in Eritrea ground on with little change. A 1976 proposal for limited "regional autonomy" was rejected by the guerrilla armies who called for negotiations with no preconditions based upon a principled recognition of the right of nations to self determination. Ethiopia refused. The war escalated.

Midway through 1978 the Ethiopian junta launched an all-out offensive to recapture Eritrea, which by then lay almost entirely in guerrilla hands. More than 120,000 Ethiopian troops backed by waves of tanks, rockets, artillery and aircraft invaded the Pennsylvania-size territory on a half dozen separate fronts.

The ELF resistance soon collapsed along the southern border, but the EPLF stopped the government advance by retreating from certain limited positions to reform in the central highlands. Late in the year, Ethiopia opened its second round of fighting, this time with Soviet advisors on the frontlines to guide their strategy and tactics.

Faced with not only a substantial imbalance in weapons and manpower but also the highly sophisticated coordination of Ethiopia's war machine by the Soviet experts, the EPLF went into a large scale retreat. By year's end, they were back in their mountainous northern base area. Ethiopian forces encircled the guerrillas to the south near Afabet and to the east along the Red Sea coast.

But what looked like an Ethiopian victory was undercut by two very important factors. First, the EPLF had maintained its full combat strength and morale by avoiding a face to face defeat and drawing its foe to terrain more favorable to guerrilla war. But more importantly, the leftist guerrillas had failed to compromise their politics for potential Western aid, as the Soviet Union and Ethiopia had loudly predicted.

The following year saw a general stalemate on both the political and the military front, but the initiate was decidedly shifting back toward the Eritreans.

A series of three Ethiopian offensives aimed at the EPLF base area were crushed by the guerrillas. A fourth assault last December turned into an Ethiopian rout. After 15-days of fierce hand to hand fighting, the EPLF had driven the government forces 35 miles backward into Afabet where they are now besieged.

The Political Front

On the political front, 1979 also saw the Cuban forces in Ethiopia refuse to go northward to fight in Eritrea after playing a major role in Ethiopia's border war with Somalia. Though Cuban advisors were reported in Eritrea late in 1978, they were later pulled out, and no military personnel are now with Ethiopian forces there.

Cuba had trained Eritrean guerrillas in the late 1960s, as had Algeria, China, South Yemen and other progressive countries. Most lines up behind Ethiopia in 1977 when the junta aligned itself with the socialist camp, but early doubts about the Derg's policies in Eritrea turned into outspoken criticism as time and the war wore on.

Cuba's reluctance to become involved in the Eritrea struggle was a signal. Last year also saw South Yemen pull its troops out of Ethiopia, after sending them to Eritrea, and both Mozambique and Algerian semi-official media editorialized against Ethiopia's actions in Eritrea.

A regional conference of liberation movements and communist parties-including all the major Palestinian movements-was also held to call for a peaceful solution to the Eritrea struggle based upon the Eritrean people's right to full self determination. And the communist parties of Italy, France and Belgium took similar stands.

At the time of writing, EPLF diplomats are travelling in southern and western Africa to strengthen their support among the anti-imperialist countries of that continent. But in the world at large, the Eritreans remain generally isolated and unsupported.

Soviet support for Ethiopia has cut the EPLF off from many of its natural allies in the socialist camp. Ironically, imperialist opposition to the Marxist guerrilla movement has also blocked the Eritreans from either assistance or even publicity in Western Europe and the US. Despite the size and scale of this bitter war-and despite the Soviet role on the losing side-the US media have all but ignored the struggle.

In the face of this isolation, many find it hard to understand how the Eritrean people-and especially the fighters on the battlefield-have maintained their highly principled adherence to a strategy of national democratic revolution and a firm identification with international socialist and progressive forces.

Yet, for the Eritreans the current situation is nothing new. It is merely a continuation of long-held policies and a deep-rooted commitment to internal popular support as the basis for the waging of the war and the long term struggle for genuine political and economic independence. For those in the midst of the conflict, the proof of the correctness of this line has been the continuity of this popular support and the ability to turn the worst of conditions in their favor.

Today, the EPLF is poised on the verge of a major counter-offensive. The capture of large quantities of heavy weapons and ammunition, the continuing influx of volunteers for the guerrilla army and the highly organized civilian participation are combining with alliances with other progressive forces inside Ethiopia to give the EPLF the edge in the war.

A mark of the EPLF's high morale came for me on a recent trip to the frontlines when I witnessed a cultural presentation by members of guerrilla units outside Afabet. They took a break from the action to assemble in a dry riverbed for songs and dances, beginning with:

Let Marxism develop through our bitter struggle.
The contradiction between the socialist forces is secondary-
We will struggle to correct opportunist mistakes with our blood.
There will be no peace in the world until we all reach communism.

The fighters also sang salutes to the French workers who died in the Paris Commune of 1871, to the emancipation of women as commemorated on International Women's Day and to the ultimate victory of their own long struggle for liberation. The rousing choruses were a testimony to the depth with which the guerrillas identify themselves with the world revolutionary movement.

The EPLF's Revolutionary Practice

But what gives the EPLF its particular internal strength-and its world historical significance-is its thorough grasp of its own immediate circumstances. The revolutionary theory which today guides the front in was and in international diplomacy is rooted in the extensive political practice carried on in the liberated zones over the past decade.

Above all, these years of patient organization and mass mobilization accomplished in conjunction with efforts to transform the daily lives of the oppressed Eritrean workers, peasants and disenfranchised social groups have given the EPLF an abiding faith in the people themselves. The EPLF's political line of self-reliance is a direct outgrowth of this experience.

The obstacles faced by the EPLF today pale beside those that confronted the front at its inception in 1971 after the break with the ELF. At that time, the handful of Marxist guerrillas were opposed by the rival ELF, the full might of imperial Ethiopia and the military power of the US and Israel.

The first task of the liberation movement was to unite the Eritrean people, then divided along tribal, regional, sex, class and political lines. The Eritrean nation itself, only recently out from under Italian and British colonial rule was still a fragile entity, stunned in its natural growth by Ethiopian occupation.

The Eritreans are a people made up of diverse religious and national subgroups. About half are Christians and half Moslems, and there are nine distinct nationalities, each with their own unique language, culture and history. Colonization gave them a single common territory and an integrated economy, but it only partially welded the separate peoples into a social union.

The history of the independence struggle reflects these divisions. The early ELF attempted to draw internal support and external aid on the basis of an appeal to Arab nationalism. At least two expatriate groups today-with no forces inside Eritrea-continue to exploit this false characterization of the struggle to oppose the EPLF and to garner aid from countries like Egypt and Saudi Arabia.

The EPLF fought to resolve this problem by raising a political program in the interests of all Eritreans and at the same time by taking up the specific demands of all the minorities and mediating disputes among them. The front also studied the cultures of all the nationalities and integrated them into their nationwide cultural work.

The fruit of this effort can be seen today throughout Eritrea where all the people have learned dances and songs from each of the nine nationalities. The new Eritrean culture is thus a true melting pot-a synthesis of its various distinct components, rather than a top heavy compromise of the formerly dominant cultures.

A similar lesson obtains with regard to the special oppression of Eritrean women. Today, women play a key role at all levels of the EPLF. They fight on the frontlines, provide political leadership to the liberation army and to the civilian population, teach in the schools, tend the wounded and repair the tanks and trucks in EPLF garages.

But in the beginning, the war involved only men, except insofar as women were called upon to feed and house the fighters. What brought women into the struggle was the assumption of their particular interests and demands by the front in concrete practice.

The EPLF has transformed the social and economic foundations of women's oppression in the civilian society by winning the right of women to own land and by organizing women into political associations at the local level which directly represent them in the newly formed village governments.

The front has also moved to abolish forced marriages, to facilitate divorce and to ban female circumcision, and they have organized an intensive literacy campaign among women through the grassroots political associations.

What is crucial, though, is that the struggle for the emancipation of women is completely bound up with the war for independence. There are no separate women's caucuses or organizations within the EPLF, but at the same time the battle for women's rights has become the daily duty of all the fighters, men and women alike.

Class Struggle And National Independence

While seeking to unite the Eritrean people in the fight for national independence, the EPLF has simultaneously led the class struggle within Eritrea. A class analysis was carried out in 1974 and '75 and political organizers were trained in a series of cadre schools before being located in villages under the control of the front.

These cadre lived among the peasants-learning from them as they slowly won them over, at first individually and then in large numbers. The next step was to organize the people into secret cells for intensive study and then into larger associations of peasants, women and youth.

Each of these was in turn subdivided into smaller sections according to their social class-poor, middle and rich, in the case of peasants. Later, with the capture of many of the Eritrean towns in 1977, new associations were formed of the urban workers and the middle classes. The latter

were subdivided into merchants and traders in one group and professional unions of civil servants, teachers and so on.

In the course of this mobilization, the class struggle intensified,
beginning with extensive land reform targeted at the feudal landlords.
Initially, only the large plots were redistributed, but as experience was
gained, further steps were taken to expropriate more land and set up
cooperatives.

The key aspect to this lengthy process was that these profound
changes in Eritrean life were accomplished by the political associations themselves rather than by the edict of the EPLF. The vast majority of the people were drawn into the social and economic offensives.

Repeated elections were held to sort out the strongest and most
consistent civilian leaders. Specific proposals for reforms were generated within the associations and administered by them. Local militias
were also formed to provide defense for the associations.

And finally, it has been these associations which have provided
the main source of recruits to the all-volunteer EPLF army, as well as
logistical support in all the battles. They prepare food, evacuate the
wounded and often build roads overnight into new areas of combat.

In these and many other ways, the national struggle has become
inextricably linked to the struggle for social revolution. And so too
with the reverse-not one without the other.

It has become a basic democratic questions-the right of the
Eritrean nation to self-determination and independence-that ties it all
together. And it has been through this struggle that all other questions
have been raised.

Thus, what began as a strictly nationalist war in 1961, has steadily evolved into a Marxist-led revolutionary struggle as it became
clearly apparent to those waging it that it could not succeed without
such development.

The current strength and size of the EPLF can be directly attributed to the ability of the Marxist-Leninist core to overcome in practice the external and internal obstacles faced by the national struggle.

For the Eritrean people today, the inconsistent support they
receive from the socialist camp is merely one more in a long series of
barriers to their freedom. There is no sign that their confidence in the
EPLF is wavering.

Life And Death On The Horn Of Africa

The Boston Globe Magazine, July 13, 1980

Deep in Ethiopia, the territory of Eritrea wages a bloody but little noticed war for independence that is a wild card in the big-power competition for influence on the Horn. An eyewitness account.

If a gun discharges in the desert and no one hears it, is there a sound? If forty thousand guns discharge and no one reports it, is there a war?

Philosophers and politicians here may debate this question, but for the people of the Northeast, African territory of Eritrea, the matter has never been in dispute. After almost nineteen years of the bloodiest and most prolonged conflict in the modern history of this turbulent continent, they wonder only at the deafening silence of the world beyond their borders.

The Eritreans are battling Ethiopia for the independence of this former Italian colony, which was annexed in 1962 with US and Israeli backing by their larger and more powerful southern neighbor. In a bizarre and confusing turn of events, they are today locked in a head-to-head confrontation with the Soviet Union, which currently supports Ethiopia. Yet their daily struggle, which has reached almost Vietnam-size proportions, goes all but unnoticed.

The reason for this has little to do with battlefield statistics, more with politics and interests: The little-known Eritrea war falls outside the conventional categories of East versus West, the Soviet Union versus the United States. Led by a left-wing guerrilla movement, the Eritrean People's Liberation Front, the Eritrean challenge to the Soviet Union defies the established wisdom and in so doing is rendered invisible.

Yet this very anomaly is what gives the war in Eritrea its international significance, for it foreshadows a rising trend in Africa and the Middle East: revolutionary nationalism that owes allegiance to neither great power. In this respect, the Eritreans threaten the best-laid plans of both Moscow and Washington. The longer they fight, the more their unique example spreads, and the less stable and predictable is the entire region.

The Horn of Africa has been the scene of great contention between the United States and the Soviet Union for over a decade, swinging from the advantage of one to that of the other with an explosive and erratic rapidity that boggles the mind. Meanwhile, as the stakes and the level of fighting have steadily escalated, both have lost ground. With the area once again headed for a major eruption, more surprises appear to be on the horizon.

In 1968 the Horn was wholly, if weakly, under US influence from the Sudan in the west across Ethiopia to Somalia and south to Kenya. The Eritrea war, which received a low level of support from Soviet allies, was a thorn in Washington's side, but it was being effectively contained by Ethiopia's Israeli-trained army.

Overnight, coups d'etat in Sudan and Somalia changed the big picture in 1969, when those countries swung into the Soviet orbit. With the dramatic collapse of the Haile Selassie regime in Ethiopia and the rise to power of a self-described "socialist" military junta, the Soviet Union appeared to be on the way to controlling the entire region. There was talk of a federation that would even span the Red Sea to include South Yemen.

But a gross underestimation of contending nationalisms by both big powers led to an unexpected twist. The Sudan, already moving away from Moscow, lined up with Washington against Ethiopia. Somalia soon followed suit. And the Eritreans thumbed their noses at everyone with a major escalation of their independence war.

When war broke out in 1977 between Somalia and Ethiopia, the mad scramble for position filled the headlines. In quick succession, US bases were closed in Eritrea and American and Israeli military advisers ejected from Ethiopia. The Russian naval base at Berbera, Somalia, was shut down and the Cuban troops there were ousted.

Over $1 billion in Russian arms and seventeen thousand Cuban troops were sent to Ethiopia to drive the Russian-equipped and Cuban-trained Somali army out of Ethiopia's contested Ogaden region. In the wake of the Ethiopian victory, few observers held out much hope for the Eritreans when the focus of fighting shifted north-ward in their direction, especially because the Eritreans unlike the Somalis, stubbornly refused to ask the United States to bail them out.

As one hundred and twenty thousand newly mobilized Ethiopian troops rolled into the Pennsylvania-size territory behind waves of Soviet tanks and MiG aircraft, the guerrillas retreated from previous-ly captured towns into the surrounding countryside, and both the US and Soviet press issued perfunctory post-mortems for what was described offhandedly as a casualty of history, the victim of larger issues and forces.

As the dust settled, the Russians set about consolidating their hold over Ethiopia and the United States concentrated upon retrenching in Sudan, Somalia, and Kenya. But, against all odds, the Eritreans staged a comeback that has confounded both the pundits and the policymakers. Throughout 1979 they held the Ethiopians to a tense stalemate in a series of fierce battles that cost the Soviet-backed government an estimated twenty thousand casualties. Early this year, the guerrillas turned the tables totally by routing over forty thousand Ethiopian troops on two battlefronts.

Today, the Eritrean People's Liberation Front stands on the verge of a major counteroffensive. Meanwhile, Somali-backed guerrillas in the southeastern Ogaden region are stepping up the fighting there, and recently formed guerrilla movements of other Ethiopian minorities in the south and north are also posing significant threats to the beleaguered Ethiopian junta.

An Eritrean victory could bring down the Soviet-backed government, but the potential alliance of these left-wing national movements could just as easily leave the United States out in the cold. A recent visit to EPLF-occupied areas in Eritrea found the guerrillas and the civilians alike bitter at the great power rivalry that has devastated their small country.

Simply to cover the distance from the guerrilla base areas in northern Eritrea to the densely populated central highlands took five weeks during my recent journey behind the battle lines. I set out late one night with a squad of guerrillas from the EPLF and a half-dozen camels.

We followed ancient footpaths etched into the stone by an endless procession of unshod hooves and bare feet. A small caravan of merchants edged past us on their way north to the Sudan. Then came two families of refugees fleeing Asmara, the Eritrean capital, their tailored slacks and leather shoes a pointed contrast to the mismatched uniforms and patched rubber sandals of the guerrillas.

Day after day we walked, stopping every four hours at small EPLF camps for food and rest. The yellow, scorching midday sun sent rivers of gummy sweat down my chest as we climbed the honeycomb of ridges and crossed freshly plowed terraced farms where peasants sliced narrow furrows in the packed, dry earth with their primitive hand-hewn wooden implements.

After ten days we arrived in the highlands on the outskirts of Asmara, where ten thousand Ethiopian troops were camped in a state of semi-siege. The Eritrean fighters were dug in there in a chain of underground blockhouses on three sides of the city.

Barefoot children played in the village streets with the discarded paraphernalia of war. Empty machine-gun shells were strapped to their chests, webbed belts hugged their bony waists, and some carried wooden replicas of assault rifles. In one town, the youngsters wore green fatigues while drilling in a vegetable garden where they worked each afternoon. They were members of a youth organization known as the Red Flowers, preparing to grow up and join the fight for independence.

Many of the villagers were also members of EPLF-sponsored associations of peasants, women, and teenagers that met weekly for political seminars. Each group was responsible for specific war-related tasks, such as preparing food in time of war, building roads, and repairing bomb damage.

There was talk of the influx of refugees, food shortages, and plans to send donkey caravans to the northern base area for supplies. But there were also accounts of the changes in their daily lives that included the redistribution of land, weekly literacy classes, the provision of medical services, and the introduction of village democracy.

The women, long denied any measure of economic or political freedom under the traditional feudal system, were among the most vocal. "There are none among us who have not buried one who was close to us. Of course we are affected by the war. But now that we have tasted freedom, we will never go back," said one young widow.

As we stood to leave, a 75-year-old farmer added, "We have been struggling for eighteen years. We have been beaten, we have been imprisoned, killed, cut to pieces by the enemy, but this is our land. We don't want anyone else's land, just our own, and even if Russia and Cuba help Ethiopia, we will fight until there is only one man left."

This was a sentiment I heard more than once as we roamed about this area. Said one 40-year-old mother of two EPLF fighters, "I am not afraid. Russia, Cuba, the Derg and their tanks and planes - there is nothing that can defeat us."

I tried pressing them on the question of peace, asking if they wouldn't like to see the war come to an end after all these years, but I was usually met with indignation at the implication of my query.

"As far as I am concerned, I want to finish it now, this night," said Dahab Zereghaber. "But I don't want the war to stop if the enemy does not go out from our country. I want a victory."

It was not merely the abstract wish to raise their own flag over Asmara that motivated these people, but rather the tangible gains they had made in improving their lives under the guerrilla leadership. Ethiopian terror did little to offset this, as we saw on our walk back to the base area.

Shortly after nine one morning, we sat under the checkered shade of an acacia tree, watching a procession of nomadic families, their camels laden with the curved wooden poles of portable huts. The women were perched precariously beneath brilliantly colored straw canopies while the children ran alongside, herding their sheep and goats.

Suddenly, we heard two fighter aircraft overhead. Seconds later, the first explosion echoed off the rocky hills. For six or seven minutes we lay with our noses in the sand, listening to the high-pitched whine of the MiG 21s as they broke into screeching dives climaxed by the sharp cracks of bursting rockets. An eerie silence followed.

By the time we reached the attack site, the only sign of what had transpired was a crimson pool of blood in the sand. Nearby lay a grotesquely twisted steel bomb fragment bearing Russian letters. Two women and a small boy were wounded. Five camels were hurt, one dying.

My guide bandaged the injured people and sent them to an EPLF clinic. Again we moved on, with the civilians behind us muttering epithets at Ethiopia.

If the Soviet Union has won few friends in Eritrea by its all-out support for the Ethiopian government, the past role of the United States here has not been forgotten, either. Stopping for tea in the village of Obel, I was confronted with a grim reminder of my counter's historical part in the war.

A young man in his middle 20s strode into the tea shop and snapped to attention in front of us. He offered his hand all around and generated wild giggles with his caricature of a guerrilla fighter, but one person leaned over to whisper that he was "mental," driven mad in 1967 when he nearly burned to death in his tiny stick hut during a bombing raid by one of Ethiopia's US-made F86 Saber jets.

With the Soviet Union bogged down in Afghanistan and Russian allies refusing to bail them out in Eritrea, the possibility of US reentry here cannot be ruled out. Recent diplomatic moves through neighboring Sudan and Somalia, where the United States now exerts considerable influence, indicate a calculated attempt to displace the Soviets in Ethiopia.

That American weapons and military personnel might also replace the Russians in Eritrea comes as no surprise to the Eritreans. They have learned to expect such turnabouts from a world that has yet to acknowledge consistently even the existence of the war they have been fighting since before many of the guerrillas were born.

Ethiopian Army poised for
new Ogaden guerrilla assault

The Christian Science Monitor (Boston), July 29, 1980

Outside Daghabur, Ethiopia

A David and Goliath battle between the Soviet-supplied Ethiopian Army and the weapon-short nationalist Ogaden guerrillas is looming here in this desolate semidesert region of southeastern Ethiopia.

Ethiopia's Army is rapidly building here for the long expected counterinsurgency campaign against the guerrillas who operate in small units hidden in the Ogaden bush and strike out regularly at supply convoys and small garrisons. They are fighting for the independence of this Somali-speaking region, which neighboring Somalia also claims.

The Western Somali Liberation Front (WSLF), which claims to control most of this area, regularly dispatches squads of 10 to 15 men on their guerrilla operations.

The guerrillas, who ranged in age from about 20 down to 10, could be seen entering and leaving the base here at regular intervals. They carried Russian-made AK-47 assault rifles and RPG-7 grenade launchers. WSLF leaders claimed to have carried out a recent surprise dawn raid against the Qulquul base camp close to Daghabur, inflicting "heavy casualties" and taking 20 rifles while suffering two dead and four wounded.

The guerrilla injured lay in a nearby tent as I interviewed their leaders. "We knew that Ethiopia has sophisticated weapons, and when it comes to numbers, they are more than us, but still we think we can defeat them because we are fighting on our soil and we are ready to die for it," said Omar Nur, a 10-year veteran of the war.

This fervent nationalism directed toward seizing the Ogaden from Ethiopia was echoed by many fighters and civilians with whom I spoke, but a singular problem for the guerrillas is the steady depopulation of the area by the ravages of drought, famine, and war.

Somalia estimates that there are 1.5 million Ogaden refugees now in that country. While 20 percent of these refugees are Oromo peoples from the Ethiopian highlands and a portion of destitute Somalis from inside that state, there were few of them visible in the Ogaden itself.

Simultaneously, the Ethiopian government is trying to resettle non-Somalis here in an apparent effort to change the character of the indigenous population. The guerrillas here acknowledge this and liken their situation to that of the Palestinians of the West Bank in Israel. They add that the loss of their land could provoke tactics of terrorism outside the Ogaden in the event of the stymieing of the war here.

Meanwhile, they hotly deny Ethiopian charges that Somali regulars are involved in the current fighting, and I saw no evidence in the central war zone or along the border to contradict this. In addition, there was a clear sentiment here that the guerrillas wish to lessen their dependence on the Somali state. "Somalia is an independent state and Ethiopia is a colonizer," said Omar Nur, a member of the central committee of the WSLF. "When we get our independence, that does not mean we will join the Somali republic. We just want to get our independence ourselves, with no Ethiopia, no Somalia," he said.

Sporadic fighting takes place here almost daily between the presently besieged government forces and the highly mobile guerrillas. The long-term outlook is for more of the same.

"The Ethiopians are building up, especially around Daghabur, Jijiga, and Harar. They are increasing their armed forces, and it seems they are trying to clear up the Ogaden," said Omar Nur. But he added, "We are ready for them."

The coming months are likely to witness a considerable intensification of this little-known conflict, which has gone on intermittently for close to 20 years and whose human and material cost has reached astronomical figures.

The consequences for Somalia -- which fought Ethiopia twice here in full-scale confrontations in 1964 and 1977 -- and for the entire Horn of Africa have been staggering: thousands killed, hundreds of thousands rendered homeless, and the fragile economies of the region strained to the breaking point. In addition, there is the ever-present threat of a wider war that could easily draw in the Soviet Union and the United States.

At the heart of the crisis here are the efforts by Ethiopia's self-described "socialist" military leaders to hold onto their sprawling northeast African empire against the centrifugal force of a host of armed nationalist challenges. These stretch in a broad arc from the former Italian colony of Eritrea in the north through the western and southern provinces to the ethnic Somalis of Ogaden.

Ironically, all but the WSLF are left-wing movements, though even the guerrillas here received arms from the Soviet Union and training from Cuba, North Korea, Iraq, and Syria before the Russians abruptly changed sides in 1977 to back the newly installed Ethiopian junta.

WSLF leaders, who identify themselves now as Islamic nationalists, say they receive a trickle of aid from Iran, Iraq, and Egypt. But like their tacit allies in Eritrea and elsewhere in Ethiopia, they appear generally isolated from the outside world.

The United States, which is presently negotiating for rights to air and naval bases in northern Somalia at the former site of the Russian base in Berbera, has refused to become embroiled in the conflicts apparently in order to keep open the option of returning to favor in Addis Ababa in the event the Russians are displaced.

The extreme poverty and backwardness of this area make the possibility of a separate Ogaden state seem remote. Pressed on this point, some of the guerrillas indicated that a relationship with either Ethiopia or Somalia was possible, but they were insistent that this would have to base upon a high degree of autonomy.

At the same time, there were indications that there is a high level of tension between the guerrillas in the field and the leadership based on Somalia over this question. One consequence has been the growing relationship between the WSLF and the parallel movements in Eritrea and Ethiopia.

The Oromo Liberation Front operating in southern Ethiopia earlier this year opened an office in Mogadishu in Somalia, and the Eritrean People's Liberation Front followed suit in June.

Should these movements develop ongoing military and political coordination, the base of the present Ethiopian government would shrink to an island of the ruling Amhara nationality in the center of Ethiopia.

This would also lessen the influence of the Somali regime in favor of a broad alliance of political forces generally left but staunchly critical of the Soviet Union, whom they consider to have betrayed them, and also China, whom they blame for sitting on the sidelines.

Civil war threatens in Eritrea

One side of split independence movement
seen seeking pact with Ethiopia

The Boston Globe, September 1, 1980

Araq, Eritrea

Amid widespread reports of a major Soviet buildup in Ethiopia against nationalist guerrillas in the Red Sea territory of Eritrea, there are increasing signs that longstanding divisions within the Eritrean Independence Movement may soon erupt into civil war.

Deserters from the Eritrean Liberation Front (ELF) claim that the declining ELF is seeking a negotiated compromise with Ethiopia and the Soviet Union to end the 19-year war, while mobilizing its members and supporters from a civil war with its larger rival, the Eritrean People's Liberation Front (EPLF).

"Starting from two months ago, our leaders began telling us that Ethiopia is democratic, like ELF, and without fighting there will be a democratic solution to our liberation," said Hadgu Aradom, 20, a four-year veteran of ELF.

According to Osman Ali, 27, the ELF has avoided all combat with Ethiopian forces in Eritrea while agitating against the EPLF. "The ELF taught us more against EPLF than Ethiopia," he said during a recent two-hour interview.

The two men were among six interviewed at a remote EPLF base camp where they had come to join their former rival. More than 830 ELF fighters have deserted to the EPLF over the past six months, according to EPLF sources here, who say the newcomers are given three months of political and military retraining before being assigned to new guerrilla units.

The Eritreans are fighting for the independence of this former Italian colony, annexed by neighboring Ethiopia two decades ago.

The two nationalist organizations have a long history of internal conflict, stretching back to the early 1970s when a split in the original movement broke out into a three-year civil war. They appeared to be making halting progress toward unity after signing a merger agreement in 1977, but this appears now to have collapsed.

While ethnic and religious divisions tended to correlate with the original schism, deep-rooted political differences have long played the primary role in keeping the two organizations apart.

The independent, left-wing EPLF has depended largely on a grass-roots mobilization of peasants and workers for its internal social base, through extensive programs of land reform and social reorganization, while maintaining an international orientation of nonalignment with any big powers.

The ELF, while opposing these radical social programs, ironically has looked to the Soviet bloc for assistance in bringing the war to a halt, the ELF deserters say.

Despite the presence of Soviet advisers on the battlefield here alongside more than $1.5 billion in sophisticated Soviet arms, ELF leaders have argued that the Soviet Union is on the side of the Eritreans, according to the deserters here.

"They said the Soviet Union is on the side of the Eritrean struggle, and we are making an understanding with Russians not to give arms to Ethiopia against the Eritreans," said Hadgu Aradom.

One of the men suggested that a tacit agreement may have been worked out with the Russians to help the Ethiopian army against the EPLF in exchange for recognition of ELF in a later peace agreement, but he could cite no hard evidence.

However, none of the six said he has seen combat with Ethiopia since the summer of 1978, when the ELF suffered heavy losses during the first of the Soviet-backed offensives here. Since then, the EPLF has fought five major conventional battles with Ethiopia to stalemate the counterinsurgency campaign.

The United States has maintained a hands-off policy toward the guerrillas in favor of a so-far unsuccessful effort to achieve a rapprochement with the recently installed Ethiopian junta, which it supported before the 1977 Soviet intervention.

Throughout this period, the ELF has tried to rebuild by avoiding confrontation with Ethiopia and forcibly conscripting peasants, into their army, according to the six deserters.

Solomon Tesfai, 19, claimed he was drafted last year from a village in the Serai district of Southern Eritrea.

"The ELF came to our village and collected the youth. They took 10, but later they released three because their brothers were part of the 10," he said.

"Our parents came and argued against this, but they said this was the call of Eritrea, and they would kill us in front of them if we refused," said Solomon.

The conscription began in March, 1978, according to Hadgu Aradom. "They were taking the youth from market places, from the villages, wherever they could find them," Hadgu said.

"If one escapes and he is caught by the ELF, he is dressed like a woman and forced to tour the village while they beat him with leather whips," he added.

It was also at this time that the ELF began preparing for war with the EPLF rather than Ethiopia, according to Jabhar Abdullah. "They told us to get ready for an assault then, but later they said that EPLF forces were more than ours, so they held off their plans for another occasion," he said.

Meanwhile, according to the men, any open opposition to the civil war policy has been met with severe repression. "Those who ask why we stand against EPLF get lost," said Osman Ali. "Maybe they are arrested or killed-I don't know."

Nationalist groups pose direct threat to Ethiopia regime

The Boston Globe, September 6, 1980

Outside Afabet, Eritrea

When the Soviet Union and Cuba swept into Ethiopia three years ago, the entire balance of power in Africa's strategic horn appeared to be shifting in their favor. Today, however, the situation looks quite different.

The United States has carefully cultivated new relations with a ring of states on Ethiopia's periphery, from Sudan through Kenya to Somalia, effectively encircling the self-described socialist military regime with a network of bases ostensibly aimed at increasing US effectiveness in the Persian Gulf.

But perhaps more important, a growing list of armed nationalist movements linked with neither superpower are providing a direct threat to the Soviet-backed Addis Ababa junta.

Eritrean nationalists have managed to frustrate a series of major military offensives in the Red Sea coastal territory, claimed by Ethiopia, and they now appear to have a slight military edge over the estimated 50,000 to 60,000 Ethiopian troops based there.

A general offensive is now being reported under way in the neighboring providence of Tigray against nationalist guerrillas there, and stepped-up fighting with Somali nationalists in the southeastern Ogaden region has recently provoked charges and countercharges from both Somalia and Ethiopia of border incursions. In addition, a nationalist movement in the southern Oromo region appears to be emerging against the central government.

There are now strong indications that these disparate movements are seeking a formal united front. The formation of such an alliance could mean a formidable combination that could not only threaten the Ethiopian junta but also spell the death blow to Soviet influence in the region.

With the exception of the Somali-backed Ogaden guerrillas, these generally left-wing movements also claim to oppose Western influence, in part because of US involvement against them before the Soviet intervention on behalf of Ethiopia and because the West has since then shunned any moves to help them.

A month-long tour of the Eritrean war zone found the guerrillas here confident that their 19-year war for independence from Ethiopia may finally be turning in their favor, despite the lack of outside support. It also revealed the extent to which the Eritreans now view their protracted struggle from a broader regional perspective.

The Eritrean People's Liberation Front (EPLF) has for the past six months been training and arming thousands of fresh recruits for both the Tigray People's Liberation Front and the Oromo Liberation Front, according to guerrilla leaders here.

They are also in daily radio contact with the Tigrayan guerrillas to coordinate their military operations, and there is talk here of setting up a concrete agreement among the three fronts and other antigovernment forces, which could include clandestine opposition groups within the Addis Ababa capital, according to one high-ranking Eritrean Front leader.

"We are optimistic that we will be able to form a united joint struggle against the junta," said Eritrean Front political bureau member Sebhat Efram during an interview. "We are ready to do anything for the consolidation of this unity," he added.

Meanwhile, the main problem for the Eritreans, and by extension for the other potential Eritrean Front allies, is the continuing disunity within the Eritrean movement itself. Relations between the powerful Eritrean Front and a second smaller movement-the Eritrean Liberation Front (ELF)-have now deteriorated to the point where a small-scale civil war may be imminent.

EPLF leaders charge their declining rival with breaking a three-year-old merger agreement and attacking their forces from the rear. While the ELF makes similar charges against the EPLF, a stream of deserters going both to the Sudan and to the EPLF tends to confirm the EPLF's accusations.

On the Eritrean battlefield, the EPLF appears to hold a decided advantage over the more numerous and more heavily armed government forces, which have been reported preparing for another all-out offensive but have been so far unable to win a series of limited engagements designed to gain a tactical advantage.

Visits to the two main sites of confrontation found the guerrillas holding heavily fortified positions in what appear to be almost impenetrable mountains, while the government forces are bivouacked on low-lying plains.

Under such conditions, Ethiopia's seemingly limitless supplies of Soviet armor artillery and jet aircraft appear to be of severely restricted effectiveness.

Ethiopian deserts interviewed here also say that the Cuban-trained army has serious morale problems in the wake of four unsuccessful attempts to break through guerrilla defenses since early 1979. The last of these resulted in a 40-mile retreat into the government-held town of Afabet, now visible from the EPLF trenches.

Increased fighting in Tigray and in the Ogaden, and the new threat in the southern Oromo region, appear to be affecting the government's capacity to mount a major operation here.

While the conflicts in Tigray and Ogaden now provide the principal military threats to the junta outside Eritrea, the Oromo nationalists may in the long run be the most dangerous of all.

The Oromo people make up over half of Ethiopia's estimated 28 million population, and they constitute a majority of the army. In addition, they occupy the fertile coffee-growing areas that offer the regime its main export crop.

Should the Oromo nationalists achieve the widespread popular support now evident in Eritrea and Tigray, they could not only undercut the armed forces but also cripple the country's economy.

The ruling junta is thus walking a thin line now, and a major military setback on any of the existing war fronts could precipitate its collapse. What appears to sustain them now is only the continuing flow of Soviets arms.

But for the Soviet Union, more is at stake here than a mere military defeat. Ethiopia was seen by the Russians as a key political base for expanded influence in Africa and the Mideast, and the increasingly shaky junta was once portrayed as a model for Soviet-style development.

Instead, it has turned out to be a standard military dictatorship, which has repeatedly chosen military force rather than political means to resolve its multiplying problems.

The fact that most of its opposition comes from the left poses a special dilemma for the Russians. A loss here could discredit them with their closest allies and friends.

Toward this end, the EPLF is also busy at the diplomatic level, with delegates crisscrossing Africa and the Mideast for meetings with pro-Soviet states and movements, according to guerrilla leaders here.

Their aim is to undercut the Soviets in their own backyard. According to one EPLF leader, "We are going to show the Russians that a revolution can be made without them, or against them if that is their choice."

Signs of Eritrean civil war mounting

The Guardian (New York), September 10, 1980

Araq, Eritrea

Amid widespread reports of a pending Ethiopian offensive against nationalist guerrillas in the Red Sea territory of Eritrea, there are increasing signs that long-standing divisions within the Eritrean independence movement may soon erupt into a rear civil war.

Deserters from the Eritrean Liberation Front (ELF) claim that the ELF is seeking a negotiated compromise with Ethiopia to end the 19-year war. At the same time, the deserters say the ELF is mobilizing its members and supporters for a civil war with its larger rival, the Eritrean Peoples Liberation Front (EPLF).

"Starting from two months ago, our leaders began telling us that Ethiopia is democratic like the ELF, and that without fighting there will be a democratic solution to our liberation," said Hadgu Aradom, 20, a 4-year veteran of the ELF.

Meanwhile, according to Osman Ali, 27, the ELF has avoided all combat with Ethiopian forces in Eritrea while agitating against the EPLF. "The ELF taught us more against EPLF than Ethiopia," he said during a 2-hour interview.

The two men were among six interviewed at a remote EPLF base camp where they had come to join their former rival. More than 830 ELF fighters have deserted to the EPLF over the past six months.

The Eritreans are fighting for the independence of this former Italian colony, annexed by neighboring Ethiopia close to two decades ago. The ELF and EPLF have a long history of internal conflicts stretching back to the early 1970s, when a split in the original movement broke out into a 3-year civil war. They appeared to be making halting progress toward unity after signing a merger agreement in 1977, but this appears now to have collapsed.

While ethnic and religious divisions tended to correlate with the original schism, deep rooted political differences, have long played the primary role in keeping the two organizations part.

The independent, left-wing EPLF has depended largely on a grass-roots mobilization of peasants and workers for its internal social base through extensive programs of land reform and social reorganization while maintaining an international orientation of nonalignment. The ELF, opposing these radical social programs, has ironically looked to the Soviet bloc for assistance in bringing the war to a halt, the ELF deserters say. Despite the presence of Soviet advisors and $1.5 billion worth of Soviet arms on the battlefield here, ELF leaders have argued that the Soviet Union is on the side of the Eritreans and holds the key to peace, according to the deserts here.

Meanwhile, the U.S. has maintained a hands off policy toward the guerrillas in favor of a so-far unsuccessful effort to achieve a rapprochement with the Ethiopian junta, which it supported prior to the 1977 infusion of Soviet aid.

Eritrea: Women make gains

The Guardian (New York), September 1980

Nakfa, Eritrea

"The unity of the nine Eritrean Nationalities and the emancipation of women are the backbones of our revolution."

These were the words of Mohamed Nur, political organizer for the Eritrean People's Liberation Front (EPLF) as we attended the marriage ceremony of two guerrilla fighters from different religious and ethnic backgrounds. The wedding, which saw Christians and Muslims joining in celebration, was symbolic of a sharp break with past tradition.

"A woman here had double oppression," according to the 21-year old bride. "She could not even those her own husband, let alone marry someone from a different nationality."

The guerrilla army reflects the degree to which long-standing cleavages in Eritrean society have been overcome. Six of the 13 members of the Political Bureau come from Muslim minority nationalities.

Women Activists

Almost 30% of the rank-and-file guerrilla fighters are women. Women can also be seen playing leading roles in the army, working as political cadre, repairing vehicles and teaching in the EPLF schools.

Ezghaharia Ghilankiel, 20, is the commander of a 50-person guerrilla unit at the frontlines south of Nakfa. She said that she has no problems from the men who serve under her.

A woman in her unit said, "If there is any male chauvinism, I oppose it. If he doesn't listen to me, my comrades, boys and girls, will criticize him. In addition, he is always receiving political education on the subject. With all this, it is easy to eradicate sexual chauvinism."

The participation of women in the war of independence began in 1973. Political Bureau member Sebhat Efrem said that there had been difficulties at first.

"It was hard to politically educate women and to draw them into the people's army because of family pressures, especially from the fathers. Now," said Sebhat, "most of the fathers are proud of their daughters. As a result of all the practical duties done by women in our liberation struggle, men appreciate women's revolutionary contribution."

The destabilizing effect of 19 years of war has enhanced the front's ability to overcome traditional differences between men and women as well as inherited ethnic and religious rivalries. The social cohesion here is striking.

A fervent nationalism has served as the basis for extensive political mobilization by EPLF guerrillas in their protracted conflict with Ethiopia.

Prior to World War 2, Eritrea was an Italian colony. After England's victory over Italy in northeast Africa during World War 2, Eritrea became part of Christian-dominated Ethiopia. In 1961, an armed independence organization-the Eritrean Liberation Front

(ELF)-was formed mainly along religious lines with its base in the Muslin lowlands of western Eritrea.

The growing participation of Christian Eritreans from the highlands later in the decade resulted in a split in the movement into the ELF and the EPLF. The ELF continued to have an Islamic orientation and received support from many Arab countries.

The EPLF, however, downplayed religion in favor of a radical program of social transformation that included land reform and equality for women. By the middle 1970s, the EPLF had organized much of the civilian population into political associations of peasants, workers, women and youth.

These associations served as a recruiting ground for the guerrilla army which now has soared to over 40,000. The EPLF now dominates the military side of the struggle against Ethiopia.

The EPLF has used culture to achieve a high degree of political unity. A starting point has been the traditional songs and dances of the nine Eritrean nationalities. Initially, an EPLF cultural section studied the old cultures and drew on them to write new songs with revolutionary culture incorporates the strengths of all the diverse nationalities.

The marriage ceremony in the village of Felegh was an illustration of how far this process has come, with a cultural group performing before an audience of peasants and nomads. The twilight celebration began with a series of songs and dances from all nine nationalities, broken up by speeches on the political significance of the event.

The bride carried an AK-47

The South China Morning Post (Hong Kong),
OFNS, September 28, 1980

Felegh, Eritrea

Amid a volley of rifle shots and the cheers of guerrillas and peasant farmers, two freedom fighters are pronounced man wife.

The bridegroom is a Moslem from the western Eritrean lowlands, the bride a Christian from the central Eritrean plateau. Both are members of the EPLF-the Eritrean People's Liberation Front which is fighting for independence from the Soviet-backed Ethiopian regime of

Mengistu Haile Mariam.

The wedding emphasizes the "cultural revolution" taking place in Ethiopia as previously hostile ethnic groups unit against the common enemy in Addis Ababa.

"This couple would have been forbidden marriage under past tradition, and their spouses would have been chosen for them at birth by their parents," said Muhammed Nur, the local EPLF commander.

"The unity of the nine Eritrean nationalities and the emancipation of women are the backbones of our revolution."

Now in the 19th year of the war, the Eritreans are fighting for the independence of their strategic Red Sea territory, which was formed out of disparate ethnic groups at the turn of the century under Italian colonization and was annexed by Ethiopia two decades ago.

Divisions between the Moslem and Christian regions of Eritrea plagued the liberation movement for the first 10 years of the war, but the EPLF today claims to represent all sectors of the population.

"Our national democratic programme guarantees freedom of religion to everyone, and we try to show the people this with our practice," Muhammed's said.

By way of example, a group of the predominantly Christian guerrillas prepared special foods for the mainly Moslem civilians who had been fasting all day in observance of Ramadan. At dusk, the people gathered at the local EPLF political office to pray and to eat together.

The wedding guests marched for up to seven hours to get to the ceremony, where they put aside their captured Russian-made AK-47s and feasted on stacks of flatbread and goat meat.

The procedure for guerrilla weddings calls for a formal application to be filled, followed by a three-month waiting period. The couple are allowed a month-long honeymoon and a joint two-week leave at six-month intervals thereafter.

"When I joined the revolution, I forgot everything for myself," said Muhammed Ali, 37, the bridegroom, "I just came to join the war and fight for my country."

He met 21-year-old Mebrak Fituwi in 1976, when they served together in the EPLF's department of political mobilization.

Eritrea: People's Radio

The Guardian (New York), October 8, 1980

Araq, Eritrea

As the first gray streaks of dawn break over this guerrilla base camp, a muffled crackle followed by a few bars of music wafts across the arid valley signaling a resumption of the battle of the air wages here.

Eritrean guerrillas are opening their daily series of radio broadcasts to their own troops, to their civilian supporters and to Ethiopian enemy.

This powerful political weapon is part of an overall propaganda campaign waged by the Eritrean People's Liberation Front (EPLF). It is aimed at building the morale of its followers while undermining that of its Soviet-backed foe, according to Yemane Gebreab of the front's Information Department.

The guerrillas also print newspapers in three languages which are distributed throughout EPLF-controlled areas of Eritrea and inside Ethiopian-occupied towns and military garrisons, according to Yemane.

The Eritrean movement claims to control most of the 40,000 square mile countryside of this strategic Red Sea territory, while Ethiopian government forces hold most of the major urban centers and the main highways.

Now in their 19th year of war, the Eritreans are fighting for the independence of this former Italian colony which was annexed by Ethiopia almost two decades ago.

With the military side of the war bogged down in a stalemate since late 1978, following a massive USSR-backed Ethiopian offensive, the battle for the "hearts and minds" of the civilian population, as well as for the combatants themselves, has assumed a key significance.

As there is no early end in sight for the protracted fighting, morale has become a central factor in the staying power of the two opposing armies, according to EPLF leaders here who say they stepped up their propaganda efforts early in 1979.

During a month-long tour of the war zone, I saw the evidence of this among both guerrillas and civilians as they gathered in small clusters at the frontlines and in remote villages to listen to the twice-daily radio broadcasts.

Interviews with Ethiopian deserters held by the guerrillas also suggested that the propaganda campaign was an important factor in their defection.

Mohamed Beshir, a foot soldier from Ethiopia's Wollo province said that photographs of Soviet tanks captured by the guerrillas and displayed in an Amharic language newspaper helped to convince him that the war was going poorly for the Ethiopian side.

"During the night they were scattered around the trenches we were holding. In the morning we found them," he said, adding "I was convinced because pictures never lie."

Another Ethiopian defector, Mohamed Hassan of Ethiopia's Harrarghe province, also said that photographs of captured Ethiopian soldiers in good physical condition stirred doubts about charges by Ethiopian officers that deserters and prisoners were killed by the guerrillas.

For Wondu Taye of Arusi, however, it was the morning radio program that encouraged him to desert to the guerrillas. "In my mind I hated the junta," said the Ethiopian soldier. "The radio acted as a catalyst in turning me against the system in Ethiopia."

One sign of the impact the guerrilla radio programs are having is the fact that the troops are forbidden to listen to the broadcasts, according to Wondu. "Anyone who listens to the EPLF radio is said to be one with the enemy and is reported," he said.

A visit to the clandestine headquarters of the EPLF Information Department found the guerrillas working through the night to prepare both the broadcasts and the printed leaflets and newsletters.

Radio News Program

In one underground stone building hidden in the mountainous northern Eritrean base area, a young guerrilla sat hunched over a microphone reading the next morning's world news, while two other fighters recorded on a large portable reel-to-reel machine.

A diesel-powered generator hummed in the distance as another group of guerrillas worked a pair of simple photo-offset printing presses under electric lights strung from the low wooden ceilings.

The radio broadcasts are predated in the languages of Tigrinya, Tigre, Arabic, Afar and Amharic, according to Yemane Gebreab who said that the front plans to add programs in the southern Ethiopian language of Oromo soon.

Among the printed materials shown here were a monthly magazine in Tigrinya and Arabic called Vanguard, a 4-page weekly newspaper called Events and two biweeklies in the Ethiopian language of Amharic entitled Truth and Rise Up.

"Our organized members in the towns sneak these into the

Ethiopian garrisons, and our fighters place them in the frontline trenches," said Yemane.

"Sometimes we hide them in cars and deliver them to the houses of Ethiopians in the towns. They have even been put in cigarette packets and sold to Ethiopian soldiers," he added.

Embattled Ethiopia faces insurgents on two fronts

Eritrea rebels active despite Soviet help for Mengistu

The Christian Science Monitor (Boston), October 8, 1980

Outside Af Abed, Eritrea

When the Soviet Union and Cuba swept into Ethiopia three years ago, the entire balance of power in the strategic Horn of Africa appeared to be shifting in their favor. Today, however, the situation looks quite different.

The United States has carefully cultivated new relations with a ring of states on Ethiopia's periphery, from Sudan through Kenya to Somalia. But perhaps more important, a growing list of nationalist movements within Ethiopia itself is providing a mounting threat to the Soviet-backed Addis Ababa regime of Col. Mengistu Haile Meriam.

Eritrean nationalists have managed to frustrate a series of major Ethiopian military offensives in the Red Sea coastal territory, and they now appear to have a slight military advantage over the estimated 50,000 to 60,000 Ethiopian troops based there.

The rapidly spreading guerrilla movement in neighboring Tigre Province also has confronted the central government with a serious military and political crisis. The final straw may prove to be the emergence of a rebellious Oromo movement in northern Ethiopia.

There now are indications that these disparate nationalist movements are seeking a formal united front. Formation of such a front would amount to a formidable alliance that not only could topple the military junta but also would be a heavy blow to Soviet influence in the region.

At the same time, these generally left-wing movements appear to oppose any Western influence, due in part to past United States opposition to movements that might fragment Ethiopia and because the

West so far has shunned any moves to help them.

In a month-long tour of the Eritrean war zone, the writer found the guerrillas here confident that the 19-year war for independence from Ethiopia finally may be turning in their favor. It also showed the extent to which the Eritreans have begun to view their struggle from a regional perspective.

The Eritrean People's Liberation Front (EPLF) for the past six months has been training and arming recruits for both the Tigre People's Liberation Front (TPLF) and the Oromo Liberation Front (OLF), according to guerrilla leaders here. The OLF operates among the Oromos (Gallas) in Shoa Province.

They also have begun daily radio contact with the Tigrean guerrillas to coordinate their military operations, and there is talk of setting up a concrete agreement among EPLF, TPLF, OLF, and other antigovernment forces, which could include the Western Somali Liberation Front (WSLF) in Ethiopia's southeastern Ogaden Desert region, as well as opposition groups operating from the Ethiopian capital of Addis Ababa.

"We are optimistic that we will be able to form a united, joint struggle against the junta," said EPLF political bureau member Sebhat Efram during an interview near the battlefront. "We are ready to do anything for the consolidation of this unity," he added.

Meanwhile, the main problem for Eritreans, and by extension the other potential EPLF allies, is the continuing disunity within the Eritrean movement itself. Relations between the powerful EPLF and a second smaller movement, the Eritrean Liberation Front (ELF), have now deteriorated to the point where a small-scale civil war may be imminent.

Amid continuing reports of a major Ethiopian buildup here, the EPLF appears to hold a decided edge. Visits to the two main sites of confrontation between the EPLF and Ethiopia found the guerrillas holding positions high in what appeared to be almost impenetrable mountains, while government troops were bivouacked on low-lying open plains.

Under such conditions, Ethiopia's vast supplies of Soviet armor, artillery, and jet aircraft ar of little use. The guerrillas are dug into an intricate network of underground trenches and stone-reinforced bunkers from which they routinely bombard their foe with captured artillery and mortars.

Return fire from the Ethiopian side seemed to bounce harmlessly off the hard-packed dirt and shale. Two days of this produced no casualties among the Eritreans who occupied themselves with such tasks as attending classes in mathematics and world geography, preparing food, and strengthening their already complex fortifications.

Increased counterinsurgency activity is also reported by the OLF in the south, though the OROMO nationalists do not appear to be engaging the government on anywhere near the scale of the Eritreans and the Tigreans.

The OLF, however, in the long run may hold the key to the demise of the regime, as over half of Ethiopia's population, and the Army as well, are of Oromo origin.

The ruling Ethiopian junta thus is walking a thin line now, and a major setback on any these war fronts could push them over the edge. What sustains them is only the continuing flow of Soviet arms and military advisers.

For the Soviet Union, more is at stake here than merely military success or failure. Ethiopia was to be a political base for expanded influence throughout the volatile region, and the increasingly unpopular junta was once touted as the new African Bolsheviks.

Instead, they have turned out to be a run-of-the-mill military dictatorship that has turned again and again to armed force to solve their multiplying problems.

Ethiopia bombing 'will lead to famine'

The Guardian (London), October 17, 1980

Khartoum, Sudan

A month-long counter insurgency campaign in Ethiopia's Tigray province, appears to have ended in a military stalemate. But the aerial bombardment of civilian targets, coinciding with the harvest season there has set the stage for widespread famine, according to a guerrilla spokesman.

Leaders of the Tigray People's Liberation Front (TPLF) claim that Ethiopia's Soviet-supplied MiG jets and MI-24 helicopter gunships forced the evacuation of more than 80,000 peasants from remote towns and villages and destroyed large areas of farmland in the depressed region.

A TPLF spokesman, Yemane Kidane, said: "Some kind of famine is imminent. This is a new tactic to demoralize the people, but it will only make them hate the Government more."

The 30-year-old guerrilla called the Government action a "ruthless bombardment," but said that it had little impact on the insurgents.

It is the first time the sophisticated MI-24 attack helicopters have been used in the Horn of Africa where Ethiopia's military junta has been fighting several nationalist movements since it seized power in 1974.

The Tigrayan guerrillas are fighting for what they term "self determination" against the central Government, they are formally allied with independence forces in the neighboring Red Sea territory of Eritrea, and they appear to be seeking closer cooperation with Oromo (Galla) nationalists in Southern Ethiopia and with ethnic Somalis fighting the Junta in the south eastern Ogaden region.

The recent escalation of the air war comes after an apparent failure of the Ethiopian Government to make any headway against the various opposition groups on the ground, despite the presence of frontline Russian military advisors.

The latest five-week campaign in Tigray, which saw more than 40,000 Government troops engaged in five simultaneous drives into the guerrilla-controlled countryside, is now winding down.

Eritrean groups turn on each other

The Irish Times (Dublin), October 25, 1980

[Byline: James Donaghue]

Khartoum, Sudan

Heavy fighting has broken out between rival Eritrean nationalist movements as Ethiopia's Soviet-backed army has begun a series of large-scale assaults on guerrilla positions there, according to usually reliable sources in the Sudan capital.

Early reports indicate that the roughly simultaneous actions pitted the Eritrean People's Liberation Front (EPLF) against mechanized Government forces on two main fronts and against mobile units of the smaller Eritrean Liberation Front (ELF) on a third flank.

EPLF radio broadcasts from inside Eritrea claim that the brigade-size Ethiopian attacks were repulsed along a 25-mile front near the Red Sea coast and near the Government-held town of Afabet within the past two weeks.

Details of the ongoing battles between EPLF and ELF, which began on August 28th, are sketchy as neither front has yet issued a statement. However, informed sources here describe them as the most serious armed confrontations since the three-year Eritrean civil war of 1971-74.

The initial fighting is said to have occurred inside the EPLF's mountainous northern Sahel base area, less than six miles from the heart of their supply and logistical headquarters and only 12 miles from their entrenched anti-Government positions.

EPLF units have since then driven the ELF forces southward into the Barka region where intermittent fighting continues, according to sources here.

The Sudanese Government has attempted to mediate in the dispute, which threatens to become an all-out showdown, but the ELF has so far refused the offer while moving to mobilize its full 6,500-man army for further combat, these sources say.

The Eritreans seek the independence of their former Italian colony which Ethiopia forcibly annexed two decades ago. The two liberation movements have been in a fragile alliance since 1977, but the agreement to merge their guerrilla armies now appears to be a dead letter.

The current outbreak of fighting climaxes a steadily escalating crisis that has been marked by repeated small clashes throughout the three-year unity pact. ELF documents now surfacing here indicate that a plan to abort the agreement existed from the moment it was signed.

The ELF strategy called for stalling on implementing the programme to integrate the two forces in the anticipation that the EPLF would be weakened by a series of frontal campaigns with Ethiopia's numerically and technically superior Soviet-equipped and advised army, according to the internal documents.

When the EPLF failed to succumb to these assaults, the decision was taken to strike at the rear in an effort to divide the EPLF army and to cut its supply lines to neighbouring Sudan, these sources say.

Meanwhile, the ELF has gone through a substantial shift in policy toward the Ethiopian junta and has begun expressing a willingness to accept a compromise short of independence, according to ELF deserters reaching here. Persistent reports of ELF talks with Ethiopian and Soviet officials suggest that moves have already been taken in this direction, but there is yet no hard evidence of direct collaboration between them against the EPLF.

The ELF has long adhered to a Moscow line in both its internal political programmes and in its international diplomacy, despite the massive Soviet intervention on Ethiopia's behalf that forced the guerrillas to retreat from the major Eritrean towns in 1978.

During the past two years the ELF has generally avoided direct combat with Ethiopian forces while trying to consolidate its control of uncontested areas and to limit EPLF's operations to the northern battle zone. Sporadic clashes have taken place at a rate of up to three a month along the boundaries of the two fronts' operational zones while the EPLF faced an estimated 40,000 Ethiopian troops in the Sahel region, according to sources here.

By hemming in the EPLF, the ELF apparently sought to limit its rival's ability to replenish its forces with new recruits as well.

The signal that ELF strategy was undergoing an important change came on July 7th when it withdrew a force of 1,000 men from positions alongside EPLF on the Red Sea coast and began setting up fortified camps in the mountains overlooking the EPLF rear base. By late August the ELF had also moved into place west of the EPLF's Afabet positions, according to sources here. At that moment, the EPLF sent reserve units to drive the ELF out of striking distance.

As the fighting spread southwestward, Ethiopian forces launched attacks near Afabet and on the sea coast, but the Government has been severely weakened by simultaneous fighting with insurgents in the neighbouring province of Tigray and in the southeastern Ogaden region.

These factors, together with a deepening economic crisis in Ethiopia, make it unlikely that the Government will be able to mount an overall offensive against EPLF in the immediate future. While there is a remote chance that negotiations between the warring Eritrean fronts may yet take place, the outlook there is for continued and intensifying combat that could result in the demise of the ELF if present trends hold up.

This would leave the EPLF, which is also engaged in setting up tactical alliances with a number of anti-Government movements within Ethiopia, the sole nationalist force in Eritrea. The result of this could be a powerful constellation of generally Left-wing movements not only opposed to the present Ethiopian Government but also to the dominance of the Soviet Union there.

Eritrean allies at war with each other

The Guardian (London), October 28, 1980

[Byline: James Donaghue]

Khartoum, Sudan

Heavy fighting has broken out between rival Eritrean nationalist movements as Ethiopia's Soviet-backed army has begun a series of large-scale assaults on guerrilla positions there, according to usually reliable sources in the Sudan capital.

Early reports indicate that the roughly simultaneous actions pitted the Eritrean People's Liberation Front (EPLF) against mechanized government forces on two main fronts and against mobile units of the smaller Eritrean Liberation Front (ELF) on a third flank.

EPLF radio broadcasts from inside Eritrea claim that an Ethiopian force of brigade-strength was repulsed along a 25-mile front near the Red Sea coast and near the Government-held town of Afabet within the past two weeks.

Details of the battles between EPLF and ELF, which began on August 28, are sketchy as neither front has yet issued a statement. However, informed sources here describe them as the most serious armed confrontations since the three-year Eritrean civil war of 1971-74.

The initial fighting is said to have occurred inside the EPLF's mountainous northern Sahel base area, less than six miles from their supply and logistical headquarters and only 12 miles from the frontline of the battle against the Ethiopian army.

The first battles took place at Baltat in the mountains overlooking the EPLF base at Arag and at Rora Harar just west of the EPLF-held town of Nakfa, according to sources here.

In a running two-week battle during the first half of September, the EPLF drove ELF units south and west to their rear base at Sherit in the adjacent region of Barka where a 250-ton ammunition depot was destroyed by heavy EPLF bombardment, the sources said.

The ELF retreat ended deep in Barka at Kerkebet, some 50 miles south-west of their deepest penetration of EPLF territory, according to these sources who add the sporadic fighting continues in this region.

The Sudanese Government has attempted to mediate in the dispute, which threatens to become a showdown, but the ELF has so far refused the offer while mobilizing its 6,500-man army for further combat.

With Ethiopian government forces weakened from a month-long counter-insurgency campaign in the neighboring province of Tigray, it appears unlikely that they will be in a position to launch a general offensive to take further advantage of this situation.

In the event, the way is open for a wide-ranging military resolution of the longstanding rivalry between the two nationalist movements unless some last minute negotiations bring a halt to the fighting.

The Eritreans seek the independence of their former Italian colony which Ethiopia forcibly annexed two decades ago. The two liberation movements have been in a fragile alliance since late 1977, but the agreement to merge their guerrilla armies now appears to be a dead letter. The alliance has been breached by minor clashes ever since the pact was signed.

ELF documents now surfacing here indicate that a plan to abort the agreement existed from the moment it was signed.

The ELF strategy called for stalling on implementing the programme to integrate the two forces in the belief that the EPLF would be weakened by a series of frontal campaigns with Ethiopia's numerically and technically superior, Soviet-equipped and advised army, according to the internal documents.

However, in four such conventional confrontations involving as many as 70,000 Ethiopian troops at a time, the EPLF managed by late 1979 to gain ground and expand its forces.

At the same time ELF went into a period of prolonged decline as many supporters deserted both to EPLF and to Ethiopia, with hundreds more fleeing to neighboring Sudan as ELF increasingly concentrated on conflict with EPLF and with the Tigray People's Liberation Front (TPLF) in Tigray province while avoiding combat with the Government, according to deserters now in Sudan.

Faced with the possibility of themselves disappearing through this steady attrition, ELF leaders switched their strategy early this year and began stepping up direct confrontation with EPLF, the deserters say.

Routine high-level contacts between the fronts were broken off during the summer, marking the end of any semblance of cooperation between them and setting the stage for the confrontation that began on August 28, according to sources here. There now appear to be no direct links between EPLF and ELF off the battlefield.

The roots of the conflict lie in sharp political differences which have widened during the past two years. Both fronts project a left-wing image, but their internal policies and international orientations are distinctly separate and often in opposition to each other.

In recent months, differences in the EPLF and ELF's characterization of both the Ethiopian regime and the Soviet role there have become important points of contention. ELF officially denies the Soviet involvement, while ELF deserters say the front has begun describing the Ethiopian junta as a basically progressive regime whose main weakness is on the Eritrea question.

Persistent reports of ELF meetings with Ethiopian and Soviet officials since the beginning of the year lend credence to speculation that some sort of deal may be in the offing.

The most recent of these meetings is reported to have taken place between Ethiopia's Foreign Minister and ELF leaders on August 24 in Beirut.

While there is a remote chance that negotiations between the warring fronts may yet take place, the outlook is for continued and intensifying combat that could well result in the demise of ELF.

Eritrea: Critical juncture

The Guardian (New York), November 12, 1980

Khartoum, Sudan

A compromise between the Eritrean Liberation Front (ELF) and the Soviet-backed Ethiopian government may be in the works following severe ELF military setbacks in fierce fighting with rival Eritrean nationalists, according to usually reliable sources here.

ELF chairman Ahmed Nasser and vice chairman Abdel Idris are now in Damascus for meetings with high level officials from Ethiopia and the Soviet Union scheduled for mid-November, these sources say.

Meanwhile, the ELF guerrilla's army is disintegrating after a 6-week civil war with the larger Eritrean People's Liberation Front (EPLF) in the war-ravaged Red Sea territory, sources in the Sudanese capital report.

Aside from the diplomatic threat of closer ties between its rival and Ethiopia, the EPLF faces the intensive bombardment of its guerrilla base area by Soviet-supplied Ethiopia. The attack, which began two weeks ago is targeting EPLF's guerrilla base in the northern most Sahel region.

The Eritreans are fighting for the independence of that former

Italian colony, which was linked to Ethiopia by a UN-sponsored federation in the 1950s and forcibly annexed by its powerful neighbor in 1962. The two guerrilla movements, conservative nationalist ELF and independent left-wing EPLF, reached a formal agreement to merge in 1977 after a long period of bitter contention, but this unity pact has now apparently completely broken down.

According to reports here, hundreds of ELF guerrillas have either fled to neighboring Sudan or deserted to the rival EPLF or to the Ethiopian army since the outbreak of ELF-EPLF fighting in late August.

One report circulating among Sudanese officials this week place the number of ELF defectors to the Ethiopian government at 1400, while another 800 are said to have gone over to the EPLF.

Relief workers in the Sudanese frontier town of Kassala add that ELF guerrillas are crossing the border there at a rate of up to 85 per day and are disarmed by Sudanese security forces.

Against this backdrop, the reports of ELF negotiations with the ruling Ethiopian junta may not have substantive impact on the long-term situation in Eritrea. They reveal, however, a complex pattern of third party diplomacy set in motion by the Soviet Union to gain an advantage in the otherwise stalemate guerrilla war.

The Soviet Union provided indirect assistance to the Eritrean nationalists during the 1960s and early 1970s against the then U.S.- and Israeli-backed Ethiopian regime of Haile Selassie. When the current ruling junta seized power in 1974, Moscow abruptly changed sides to back Ethiopia. The junta launched a multi-pronged military offensive in Eritrea with the help of hundreds of Soviet advisers and massive quantities of sophisticated arms.

The Eritrean guerrillas were forced to retreat from most of the larger towns and cities they had previously captured, but it was at this point that they took the opportunity to sign the unity pact.

However, the emergence of the EPLF as the dominant military and political force appears to have led the declining ELF to seek its own separate opening to the Ethiopian government, a move which Moscow eagerly exploited through several third parties.

According to published reports, for instance, ELF leaders met with Ethiopian officials for the first time in Rome early this year under the auspices of the Italian Communist Party. Later contacts were facilitated by Nayif Hawatmeh of the Popular Democratic Front for the Liberation of Palestine, culminating in high level meetings in Beirut on Aug. 24 with Ethiopian officials. This meeting coincided with the resumption of diplomatic relations between Ethiopia and Syria, as well as the signing of a friendship meeting between Syria and the Soviet Union.

Fighting between the EPLF and the ELF erupted four days later, but by end October ELF guerrillas were in a chaotic retreat and their entire rear base had fallen to the EPLF, according to sources here.

At the same time, the Ethiopian government began the most intensive aerial bombardment of EPLF positions in the Sahel region in months, according to sources here. This nonstop bombing by Soviet MiG jet fighters is aimed at hidden workshops, transport depots, communications operations and medical facilities, these sources say.

Although Ethiopian forces do not appear to have been prepared for a general offensive at this time, they are now reported to be moving troops into position for a concentrated assault which could come any day, according to sources here. An estimated 7000-9000 infantry troops are now in the Red Sea port of Massawa for rapid deployment to the battlefronts.

The coming weeks are apt to witness a decisive turning point in the delicate balance of forces between the two main contending armies.

Guerrillas may shift alliance

The Financial Times (London), November 14, 1980

Khartoum, Sudan

A realignment of Eritrean nationalist guerrilla forces is now under way, in the aftermath of a two-month civil war.

With the apparent victory of the leftist Eritrean People's Liberation Front over the centrist Eritrean Liberation Front, leaders of the ELF are now negotiating for an alliance with the right-wing ELF-PLF, according to Osman Saleh Sabbe, who heads the small Sudan-based third faction.

An agreement between the ELF and the PLF is expected within weeks, according to Mr. Sabbe.

This new constellation of guerrilla forces represents a strange realignment of the declining ELF, which has been reported to be seeking Soviet intervention to bring about peace talks with the ruling

Russian-backed Ethiopian government. The politically independent EPLF has long dominated the fighting with Ethiopian forces in Eritrea, which has for the past nine months been bogged down in a stalemate.

Eritrea: ELF cadre desert

The Guardian (New York), November 19, 1980

Khartoum, Sudan

Two months of fierce civil war have decimated the Eritrean Liberation Front (ELF) but ELF leaders are likely to continue the conflict against its rival Eritrean People's Liberation Front (EPLF) despite widespread internal opposition, according to ELF deserters here.

Heavy battlefield losses and massive defections have cut ELF fighting strength in half according to two high-level ELF deserters who arrived in the Sudan capital last week disillusioned and bitter at their former guerrilla leaders.

"There is not one who wants the civil war except the leadership," said one 26-year-old former ELF political cadre. "I didn't want to lose my life to defend them so I left," he added.

Steady EPLF advances have also created chaos inside the retreating ELF with large numbers of prisoners-both Ethiopian soldiers and ELF dissidents-unaccounted for and presumed executed, they said.

The ELF is one of two nationalist armies battling Ethiopia's Soviet-backed military government for the independence of the former Italian colony of Eritrea, which Ethiopia annexed in 1962. A 3-year alliance between ELF and EPLF broke down in August after months of minor clashes, and heavy fighting spread across northern and western Eritrea where the two fronts maintain rear bases.

An Unjust War

In a 4-hour interview conducted in English, the two 6-year ELF veterans charged that their leaders sought the civil war to undermine the larger, leftist EPLF while opening negotiations with their former enemy, Ethiopia. "They are trying to prolong their leadership by waging this unjust war," said the political cadre who asked not to be identified in order to avoid reprisals. In the event of further defeats, the ELF is likely to shift to protracted small-scale guerrilla operation against the powerful EPLF, he said adding "They will not stop now."

However, sources here also point out that EPLF units are present throughout the area which may restrain future ELF aggression.

Meanwhile, the ELF deserters said that the declining ELF has resorted to widespread conscription to fill its thinning ranks and that morale among the ELF rank and file was at an all-time low when the civil war erupted.

Forced Conscription

"Most of the fighters are peasants who came by force. They are not volunteers," said one deserter, a former administrator in the ELF's education department. "There are many who want to leave the field, but they cannot get away," he added. Opposition to ELF policies is forcibly repressed, according to the two deserters who said that this has recently led to clashes with the civilian population in ELF-controlled areas as well as large numbers of arrests within the front.

During the past year ELF military units have faced spontaneous peasant rebellions in the districts of Serae, Gash and Dankalia, while more than 100 ELF dissidents have been imprisoned or executed, they said. Among those arrested for opposing current ELF policies were the head of the front's cadre school, identified only as Ghirghis, and revolutionary council member Eyob Gebremeskal, according to the deserters.

The former ELF guerrillas cited preparations for the civil war and secret talks with the Soviet Union beginning in 1978 as the main causes of discontent in the ELF. Meanwhile, the fate of another 50 ELF dissidents and an estimated 300 Ethiopian prisoners of war formerly held in the ELF's northern Barka base is not known, they added. The EPLF overran this region during the fighting in mid-October, according to the deserters.

<u>Africa's twenty-years war</u>
Report From The Eritrean Front
The Nation (New York), October 25, 1980

Somewhere in Eritrea

Random mortar fire rained down on the guerrilla fortifications as we gazed out upon Ethiopian Army positions on the Red Sea coastal plains. "This is normal for us. It is our daily life," said brigade commander Ahmed Chimetti of the Eritrean People's Liberation Front (EPLF). With a sweep of his arm, he pointed out more than a dozen Soviet T-54 tanks hidden in the sparse brush five kilometers away. The charred hulks of two more lay in the open, where they had been destroyed by the nationalist Eritrean guerrillas in the most recent fighting here.

Behind us, small clusters of armed men and women were busily cleaning weapons, mending clothes, preparing food and in one case singing ballads of the long and bitter war. They paid no attention to the sporadic shelling, though the acrid stench of cordite was thick in our nostrils and the exploding missiles were landing only a few score meters away.

It was a typical scene in this small but strategic strip of northeast Africa where a tenacious people have managed to stymie Ethiopia's Russian-backed army in what has become the longest and by far the largest armed conflict in modern black African history. "We have been fighting now almost twenty years. All the men. All the women, even our children are involved. For us there is no choice-it is either independence or death," a soldier named Stefanos Seyoum told me.

More than 40,000 Ethiopian troops have been tied down for the past eighteen months on two main battlefronts in northern Eritrea, with another 20,000 held in reserve in rear-area cities and garrisons. Yet despite a steady flow of sophisticated Soviet arms, they have been unable to mount a single successful advance during this period. A major new Ethiopian offensive had been predicted here since June, based upon reports of shipments of more Russian tanks, helicopter gunships and even a form of toxic gas, but a series of limited Ethiopian attacks during recent months, apparently designed to win a tactical advantage, have utterly failed.

While this has frustrated plans for the generalized counterinsurgency campaign which the guerrillas say is being masterminded by top level Russian strategists, Ethiopia's ruling military committee, the Derg, is fast

losing ground in its highly vulnerable rear. Continuing economic and
political instability are sapping the junta's capacity to prosecute the war
at its present levels, and a host of other nationalist movements are also
pressing in upon it. The recently formed alliance of these movements
threatens not only to topple the beleaguered Ethiopian regime but to alter
the political contours of the strategic African Horn and tarnish the Soviet
Union's revolutionary image throughout Africa. For the guerrillas vow to
"teach the Russians that revolution can be made without them."

Already the Eritrean nationalists have shown some success in
wooing otherwise pro-Soviet movements and states to back their
cause. They have picked up some diplomatic support from
Mozambique, Guinea-Bissau, Guinea-Conakry, Algeria and the
Palestine Liberation Organization, and they are actively courting
Tanzania, Madagascar, Benin and other leftist African countries.
Should this trend continue, the Russians might well find themselves
on the outs with their closest allies here.

During a month's tour of the Eritrean war-front last August, I
found the guerrillas supremely confident that their nineteen-year war
for independence from Ethiopia, which annexed the former Italian
colony in1962, is finally taking a decisive turn in their favor. I also
saw the extent to which the Eritrean nationalists are mounting a successful transition to a regional strategy against the Soviet-backed
junta. During the past six months, the Eritrean People's Liberation
Front (TPLF) and the Oromo Liberation Front (OLF), which operate
in the heart of Ethiopia. They have also given the other movements
captured Russian arms, and are in daily radio contact with the TPLF
in Tigray Province, enabling them to coordinate military and political
operations. In June, the EPLF opened a permanent office in
Mogadishu, the Somali capital where the Western Somali Liberation
Front is headquartered, and there are indications that they are quietly establishing relations with dissident groups in the Ethiopian capital, Addis Ababa. "As far as the future is concerned, we are confident
that we will be able to form a united, joint struggle against the Derg,"
said EPLF political bureau member Sebhat Efram. "We are ready to
do anything for the consolidation of this unity."

Should the various autonomous opposition groups hold together
a working alliance, they would constitute a formidable challenge to
the increasingly isolated Government whose base of power is mainly
in the urban centers where the traditional ruling Amhara nationality
is concentrated. Virtually the only thing keeping them in power today
is the supply of Russian arms. The Tigray front is the fastest growing

of the newer movements and now claims control of 85 percent of
their mountainous northern province despite the 40,000 Ethiopian
troops based there. It is the Oromo Liberation Front, however, that
poses the most serious threat to the junta, for the people in that
southern province constitute more than half of the Ethiopian population and of the army itself. Ethiopia grows most of its coffee in the
fertile Oromo region, and coffee sales to Western countries finance
the purchase of Russian weaponry.

The guerrillas' main strength lies in their popular support. This is
visible in the obviously affectionate day-to-day relations between the
guerrillas and the impoverished peasant farmers and nomadic
herders, and in the flow of contributions to the war effort itself by the
civilians. Each guerrilla brigade has its own cultural troupe which
regularly performs songs, skits ad dances for the villagers and the
fighters. A marriage of two veteran guerrillas in one village prompted a feast of celebration attended by 300 local residents which lasted
until near dawn. "All the people have suffered at the hands of the
enemy," Mohammed Ali, a 60-year-old nomad, told me during the
raucous event. "I have lost two nephews and a niece, but we have suffered most as far as our animals are concerned. They have been trying to kill our camels and almost all the animals we own, but regardless of this we are dedicated to winning our independence."
Afterward, an EPLF cadre conducted an all-night political seminar to
explain its current strategy. The civilians responded by offering scores
of goats and cattle, after which the soldiers distributed second-hand
clothes among the people.

The EPLF has also carried out extensive land reform, and it has
reorganized village society to displace the traditional elite by
installing new committees of poor peasants, women and young militants. These civilian supporters are highly organized in political associations which administer daily life in the villages and provide an
ongoing source of supplies and fresh volunteers for the guerrilla army.

The main weakness of the rebels today is the revival of the long-
standing rivalry between the EPLF and a second, smaller movement,
the Eritrean Liberation Front (ELF). Once the most powerful nationalist army in Eritrea, the ELF has been in a sharp decline since the
1977 Soviet intervention. It now appears that this front has changed
sides and is in collusion with the Russians against the dominant EPLF

The two fronts had signed a merger agreement in late 1977, but
EPLF leaders now charge that the ELF has broken the fragile compact
and begun harassing their units in the rear areas. Both sides are

currently engaged in a war of words that, if continued unchecked, could well touch off a civil war between them. With an armed force of less than 5,000 men, however, the ELF does not appear to be a serious military threat.

Meanwhile, the striking feature of the EPLF is its highly efficient infrastructure. Within their heavily fortified base area, hundreds of kilometers of crude highways have been carved out of the harsh volcanic terrain with picks, shovels and captured land mines which are used to blast through the hard-packed dirt and shale. Possessed of a fleet of 600 captured trucks and Land Rovers, they have become a mechanized army, capable of moving supplies and troops from one trouble spot to another almost overnight.

Each operational zone also has hidden grain mills, small farms, underground repair shops, hospital facilities, supply depots and schools. On a visit to one set of workshops, I found the guerrillas manufacturing spare parts for captured arms, stitching new uniforms, smelting discarded artillery shells and casting hand grenade casings, as well as making school desks artificial limbs for disabled fighters, shovel blades and other tools.

Much of the daily activity of the rank-and-file guerrilla fighters was not directly military. At the Afabet battlefront, the guerrillas started their day in organized political discussions on the issues facing the Oromo front. By 10 a.m. they were studying simple fractions in a third-grade mathematics class. After a lunch of soft flatbread, spicy lentils and hot sugary tea, they fanned out into work teams to chop tress and dig more tunnels in an effort to strengthen their existing fortifications. A complex maze of shoulder-deep trenches winds back and forth along the edge of the ridge in a random and unpredictable pattern that is intended to make precise targeting difficult for Ethiopia's long-range artillery and MiG aircraft.

The terrain and the brutal climate are key factors in this phase of the war. The mountains neutralize the effectiveness of the Russian armor while the scorching temperatures, to which the Eritreans are accustomed, appear to be taking a heavy toll among the Ethiopian troops, who are drawn mainly from the temperate central and southern Ethiopian highlands. The high cliffs are being turned into a labyrinthine fortress with gun emplacements hollowed out of the hard-packed dirt and shale, gun slits open to the valley below. Squads of guerrillas chop the gnarled stubby tree trunks into short thick logs that are stacked by the score in central locations for use in building roofs. Other fighters hack at the ground with pickaxes and shovels.

The deep holes are lined with stone walls a yard thick and covered with layers of wood, rock and dirt, leaving them all but invisible from a short distance away. Weapons include Russian-made AK-47 automatic rifles, RPF-7 grenade launchers and .40-caliber machine guns. On a nearby mountaintop are hidden Soviet T-54 tanks and 120-millimeter artillery pieces, which the guerrillas say they captured in previous battles.

A low ceiling of gray clouds offers some relief from the suffocating heat. When a fierce hailstorm breaks, the soldiers simply halt their work temporarily and huddle together under tattered woolen blankets. Late in the day, the heavy work yields to individual task such as sewing patches on mismatched uniforms, cleaning weapons or studying the morning's lessons. One group of guerrillas descends to the valley for a spirited game of football, and several assemble by a campfire for a round of singing and dancing.

In stern contrast with the almost carefree mood, a young woman works laboriously on a makeshift gas mask. The threat of enemy chemical warfare seems to be taken seriously; guerrillas have made simple masks of cloth, plastic and charcoal. Group seminars have been conducted on the effects of various toxic gases and on measures to take against them, such as special protective clothing, ventilation of underground shelters and rapid dispersal of army units in the event of gas attack, according to guerrilla leaders. Frontline medical teams have also been equipped with scientific kits for collecting samples of gas to enable quick analysis and provide hard evidence for the outside world.

"We are getting ready in a primitive way," squad leader Ezghaharia Chilankiel told me. "We will take some more lessons in the course of the battle, but in the end this can change nothing."

Rival Eritrean Rebels Giving In To Ethiopia?

The Miami Herald, November 6, 1980

Khartoum, Sudan

A belated compromise between the Eritrean Liberation Front (ELF) and the Soviet-backed Ethiopian government may be near after severe ELF military setbacks in fierce fighting with rival Eritrean nationalists, according to usually reliable sources in Khartoum.

ELF Chairman Ahmed Nasser and Vice Chairman Abdel Idris are in Damascus for meetings with high-level officials from Ethiopia and the Soviet Union scheduled for the middle of November, the sources say.

Meanwhile, the ELF guerrilla army rapidly is disintegrating after a six-week civil war with the larger Eritrean People's Liberation Front (EPLF) in the war-ravaged Red Sea territory, according to sources in the Sudanese capital.

Hundreds of ELF guerrillas either have fled to neighboring Sudan or have deserted to the rival EPLF or to the Ethiopian army since the outbreak of fighting in late August, the sources say.

One report circulating among Sudanese officials this week places the number of ELF defectors to the government at 1,400 while 800 more are said to have gone over to the EPLF.

Relief workers in the Sudanese frontier town of Kassala add that ELF guerrillas are crossing the border there at a rate of as many as 85 per day and are being disarmed by Sudanese security forces as they enter.

Against this backdrop, the reports of ELF negotiations with the ruling Ethiopian junta appear to hold little promise of substantive impact on the volatile situation in Eritrea. However, they reveal a complex pattern of third-party diplomacy set in motion by the Soviet Union to gain an advantage in the otherwise stalemated guerrilla war there.

The Eritreans are fighting for the independence of the former Italian colony, which was linked to Ethiopia by a United Nations-sponsored federation in the 1950s and forcibly was annexed by its powerful neighbor in 1962.

The Soviet Union provided indirect assistance to the Eritrean nationalists during the 1960s and early 1970s against the Ethiopian regime of Emperor Haile Selassie, which was supported by the United States and Israel. Among the intermediaries were Algeria, Cuba, Syria, South Yemen and various factions of the Palestinian movement.

When the current ruling junta seized power in 1974, Moscow abruptly changed sides to back Ethiopia, both against former Soviet allies in Somalia and against the Eritreans.

In early 1978, East German envoys attempted to initiate separate talks between the leftist EPLF and the self-described "socialist" Ethiopian junta, but the initial contacts were abandoned when the guerrillas proved intractable on the questions of full independence and the inclusion of the ELF in formal negotiations.

Shortly afterward, Ethiopia launched a multi-pronged military offensive in Eritrea with the help of hundreds of Soviet advisers and massive quantities of sophisticated Soviet arms.

The fronts were forced to retreat from most of the larger towns and cities that they previously had captured, but they also took this opportunity to sign a pact to seek internal unity after years of intense rivalry.

However, the emergence of the EPLF as the dominant military and political force appears to have led the declining ELF to seek its own separate opening to the Ethiopian government, a move that Moscow eagerly exploited through several third parties.

According to published reports, ELF leaders met with Ethiopian officials for the first time in Rome early this year under the auspices of the Italian Communist Party.

Later contacts were facilitated by Nayif Hawatmeh of the Popular Democratic Front for the Liberation of Palestine, culminating in high-level meetings in Beirut on Aug. 24 with Ethiopian Foreign Minister Feleke Woldegiorgis.

This meeting coincided with the resumption of diplomatic relations between Ethiopia and Syria, as well as the signing of friendship treaty between Syria and the Soviet Union.

There is speculation in Khartoum that the Damascus summit was planned then, with the ELF coming under pressure to demonstrate its military viability before the projected November meeting.

Civil war between the EPLF and ELF erupted four days later, but by mid-October ELF guerrillas were in a chaotic retreat and their entire rear base had fallen to the EPLF, according to sources in Khartoum.

Remnants of the ELF army, estimated at less than 3,000 men, now are gathered along the Sudanese border, while many of the front's remaining leaders have fled, the sources say.

Eritrea: Radical realignment

The Guardian (New York), November 26, 1980

Khartoum, Sudan

A radical realignment of Eritrean political forces is now under-way in the aftermath of a bitter 2-month civil war in the strategic Red Sea territory.

The centrist Eritrean Liberation Front (ELF) in September launched military attacks against the larger, leftist Eritrean People's Liberation Front (EPLF). The attacks were beaten back by the EPLF and the now-isolated ELF is reportedly seeking an alliance with the rightist Eritrean Liberation Front-People's Liberation Front (ELF-PLF), led by Osman Saleh Sabbe.

The ELF-PLF has the backing of a number of conservative Arab regimes, although it apparently has no fighting forces on the Eritrean battlefield. A concrete agreement between the ELF and the ELF-PLF is expected within a matter of weeks, according to Sabbe, who this week also called on U.S. President-elect Ronald Reagan to help find a political solution to the 19-year Eritrean war for independence from Ethiopia.

This new constellation of Eritrean forces would mark a startling turnabout for the declining ELF which has been widely reported seek-ing Soviet intervention to bring about peace talks with the ruling Ethiopian junta.

The politically independent EPLF has long dominated the intense fighting with Ethiopian forces in Eritrea which has for the past nine months been bogged down in a stalemate. Civil war with the smaller ELF erupted late in August after a series of minor clashes between the two nominally allied guerrilla armies.

The latest reports from the Eritrea battlefront indicate that fight-ing there has stopped with the ELF camped along the border with neighboring Sudan. This follows a major ELF retreat from areas pre-viously under its control in the Barka region of western Eritrea, according to sources here.

Nimeiri Meets Mengistu

The EPLF has meanwhile taken control of the ELF's former base area but stopped short of pushing the rival forces to the Sudan bor-der, reportedly under pressure from the Khartoum government. Sudan's President Jaafar Nimeiri is this week traveling to Addis

Ababa for talks with Ethiopian Head of State Col. Mengistu Haile Mariam. The meeting is thought to be aimed at starting negotiations between Ethiopia and the Eritrean guerrilla forces, according to officials in the Sudanese capital.

The coincidence of the Nimeiri trip with the disintegration of the once powerful ELF is generating a flurry of political activity here. The events appear to be polarizing the long-divided Eritrean movement into two distinct camps centered around the EPLF and Sabbe's ELF-PLF.

While the EPLF holds unchallenged military superiority inside Eritrea, the ELF-PLF-which has been inactive in the war with Ethiopia since 1978-has considerable financial and diplomatic support among conservative Arab countries.

The potential alliance between the ELF and the ELF-PLF thus appears to be a marriage of convenience with the ELF seeking badly needed external assistance and the ELF-PLF looking to regain a foothold within Eritrea.

Ironically, it was the ELF which drove the ELF-PLF across the border into Sudan two years ago when a brief civil war pitted the two minor armies against each other.

Since that time, the ELF has steadily declined in military strength. It has also seen its external support badly eroded by the diplomatic efforts of the ELF-PLF in the Middle East where most aid to the various Eritrean movements comes from.

Reports that the ELF has been holding a series of compromise discussions with Ethiopian and Soviet officials has accelerated the ELF's isolation both inside Eritrea and abroad.

Against this backdrop, the move to ally with the rightist ELF-PLF represents a sharp about-face for the ELF. Meanwhile, one of Osman Sabbe's first actions upon arriving in Sudan last week was to send a congratulatory telegram to President-elect Ronald Reagan offering to send a delegation to the U.S. immediately. Sabbe warned of "Soviet and communist expansion" in the Horn of Africa and asked the U.S. President-elect to give the ELF-PLF a hearing in Washington. This is necessary the Nov. 8 telegram said because "to help the ELF-PLF means to encounter and curtail communist expansion in this area."

Sabbe also termed the U.S., "morally responsible" for the Eritrean conflict which began in 1961 when then-Ethiopian Emperor Haile Selassie annexed the former Italian colony with U.S. and Israeli backing,

The leftist EPLF, while strongly critical of the Soviet intervention in Eritrea, has declined to seek Western assistance and has long refused to include Osman Sabbe in previous unity talks among the Eritrean movements.

The rising tensions spawned by the Eritrean civil war and shifting political alignments has meanwhile led to violence here in the Sudanese capital. On Nov. 15, two Eritrean guerrilla figures were assassinated on the streets of Khartoum by persons unknown. Shot to death in their car at close range were Osman Agyp and Abdulkader Hamid in an incident marking the first time in over a decade that Eritrean blood has been spilled within Sudan.

All the major Eritrean factions represented here have disclaimed responsibility for the double murder, but there is a growing fear that some kind of retaliation could follow.

Osman Agyp headed a small Eritrean faction that recently broke away from Sabbe's ELF-PLF. His group is backed by Iraq and Egypt himself has been described as extremely close to the ruling Iraqi Ba'ath Socialist Party.

In a related development last week, a member of the EPLF Central Committee defected to the Ethiopian side, apparently with ELF assistance.

Teklai "Aden" Gebremariam had fled the Eritrean war zone in August during what was described here as a "personal crisis" by an EPLF representative. After arriving in Sudan, he first made contact with the ELF and through it, with the Ethiopian Embassy, according to the EPLF.

The 3-year-old guerrilla leader had been experiencing personal problems for several months before he crossed the border into Sudan, the spokesman said, adding, "This was an individual act. It was not politically motivated."

Eritrean leaders offer plan to end 19-year war

The Boston Globe, November 27, 1980

Khartoum, Sudan

Leaders of the Eritrean People's Liberation Front have presented a seven-point plan, including a cease-fire, to end the 19-year Eritrean war for independence from Ethiopia.

At a two-hour press conference Sunday in the Sudanese capital, the Liberation Front's general secretary Ramadan Mohamed Nur, also called for an internationally supervised referendum to decide the fate of the Red Sea territory.

This is the first concrete plan the Eritrean nationalists have put forward to end the fighting there, which has claimed an estimated 100,000 lives and created a million refugees during the last two decades.

The announcement of the proposals in Khartoum coincides with the return of President Jaafar Nimeiri of Sudan from Addis Ababa. He has been in closed door talks with the Ethiopian head of state, Col. Mengistu Haile Mariam, on the Eritrean conflict, among other subjects which have contributed to past hostile relations between the two northeast African neighbors.

In a statement in the Ethiopian capital, Nimeiri announced his intention to mediate both the Eritrean conflict and the long-standing dispute between Ethiopia and its eastern neighbor, Somalia, according to published reports here. While Nimeiri did not specify the form such a settlement might take, his government is in a pivotal position to pressure both sides, since the Eritrean guerrillas supply their armies from here.

The Eritreans have been fighting since 1961 to establish their own state. The former Italian colony was forcibly annexed by the late Emperor Haile Selassie after the collapse of a 10-year United Nations-sponsored federation.

Any mutually agreed upon organization could supervise the ceasefire and referendum the plan calls for said a Liberation Front leader who named the United Nations, the Organization of African Unity, the Arab League and the nonaligned movement as possibilities.

Calls for unrestricted political agitation by all concerned Eritrean parties between the cease-fire and the referendum which would give the voters a choice between full independence, a return to federation with Ethiopia or regional autonomy within the Ethiopian state.

Another key point calls for free, supervised elections after the initial referendum to elect an administration in Eritrea which could serve as a national government or a regional body, depending upon the outcome of the referendum.

This point is aimed at avoiding the thorny question of how to represent the bitterly divided guerrilla movement in the peace process.

The Liberation Front has for the past 11 weeks been engaged in a civil war with its smaller rival, the Eritrean Liberation Front (ELF), and there are several other minor nationalist factions based outside of Eritrea which oppose both guerrilla armies.

The Liberation Front operates in most of rural Eritrea, while Ethiopian government forces are restricted to major towns and highways and the ELF is concentrated along the border between Eritrea and Sudan.

Under the Liberation Front plan, representatives of the government and of all the nationalist factions would be guaranteed access to all areas of the 40,000 square mile territory, regardless of who now controls them militarily.

The initial reaction of ELF leaders here was positive, though they said they would have to study the proposal before issuing and official response. "This is in line with the rights of the Eritrean people to decide their own future," said ELF spokesman Azeyn Yassin.

While the Soviet-backed Ethiopian regime has not yet responded to the Liberation Front proposals, it has since 1976 called for an end to the war based on its own nine-point program for regional autonomy with no option for independence.

The new Liberation Front peace plan represents a significant breakthrough by leaving the main questions to be resolved by the voters, but it is likely to meet strong Ethiopian objections for precisely the same reasons.

Taking their cue from Robert Mugabe's recent electoral victory in Zimbabwe, the Eritrean nationalists appear confident that given the choice, the civilian population will opt for independence. The Liberation Front also appears to feel that it now has majority support for its left-wing policies within the contentious national movement.

Ethiopia, for its part, has long been adamant that it would not consider independence a legitimate choice nor would it allow an outside body to adjudicate the dispute.

The question of external supervision could well become the main obstacle to the present peace proposal but Liberation Front leaders say they are unwilling to compromise on this and they are launching a worldwide diplomatic offensive to gain support for the plan.

Eritrea: Peace plan

The Guardian (New York), December 3, 1980

Khartoum, Sudan

Leaders of the Eritrean People's Liberation Front (EPLF) announced Nov. 23 a sweeping proposal to end the 19-year Eritrean war for independence from Ethiopia.

At a 2-hour press conference in the Sudan capitol, EPLF general secretary Ramadan Mohamed Nur unveiled a detailed 7-point peace plan. It calls for a ceasefire and an internationally supervised referendum to decide the fate of the embattled Red Sea territory. The war is estimated to have claimed over 100,000 lives and created a million refugees during the past two decades.

The release of the proposal here coincides with the return of Sudan's President Jaafar Nimeiri from Addis Ababa where he has been holding closed-door talks with Ethiopian Head of State Mengistu Haile Mariam on Eritrea. This is a subject which has contributed to past hostile relations between the two Northeast African neighbors.

Role for Nimeiri?

In a statement made Nov. 22 in the Ethiopian capital, Nimeiri announced his intention to mediate both the Eritrean conflict and the long-standing dispute between Ethiopia and its eastern neighbor Somalia, according to published reports here.

While Nimeiri did not specify the precise form such a settlement might take, his government is in a pivotal position to pressure both sides as the Eritrean guerrillas supply their armies from here.

The Eritreans have been fighting successive Ethiopian regimes since 1961 to establish their own independent state. The former Italian colony was forcibly annexed by the late Emperor Haile-Selassie after the collapse of a 10-year United Nations sponsored federation.

The EPLF peace plan calls for the formation of a special committee by a major international body to supervise the ceasefire and the referendum. Any mutually agreed upon organization could serve in this capacity, said the veteran guerrilla leader who named the UN, the Organization of African Unity, the Arab League and the Nonaligned Movement as possibilities.

Point number four calls for unrestricted political agitation by all concerned parties throughout Eritrea between the ceasefire and the referendum. The polling would give the voters a choice between full independence, a return to federation with Ethiopia or regional autonomy within the Ethiopian state.

Another key point calls for free, supervised elections after the initial referendum to elect a local administration in Eritrea. This group could serve as a national government or a regional body depending upon the outcome of the referendum. This point is aimed at avoiding the thorny question of how to represent the bitterly divided guerrilla movement in the peace process.

"We don't feel that the question of the unity of the Eritrean revolution has to be a stumbling block to a peaceful solution to the war," said EPLF assistant general secretary Issayas Afwerki, who also attended the evening press conference. "Having the unity of the Eritrean revolution as a precondition to a peaceful solution means we might never arrive at a solution," he said, adding, "The Eritrean people can decide this in their free elections."

The EPLF now operates in most of rural Eritrea, while Ethiopian government force are restricted to the major towns and highways and the smaller, rival Eritrean Liberation Front (ELF)-which recently provoked a bitter civil war with EPLF-is concentrated along the border between Eritrea and Sudan.

Free Campaign Proposed

Under the EPLF plan, representatives of the government and of all the nationalist factions would be given guaranteed access to all areas of the 36,000 square mile territory regardless of who now controls them militarily.

The initial reaction of ELF leaders here was positive, though they said they would have to study the proposal before issuing an official response. "This is in line with the right of the Eritrean people to decide their own future," said ELF political bureau member Azeyn Yassin. (The ELF has been participating in talks of its own with the Ethiopians, and is reportedly ready to accept regional autonomy.)

Osman Saleh Sabbe, who head a small Sudan-based faction known as the ELF-PLF, hailed the EPLF proposal as a positive step, in a Nov. 23 telephone interview. Noting that his follower has also called for a plebiscite to settle the Eritrea war, he said. "The people have to be given a chance to say what they want."

While the Soviet-backed Ethiopian regime has had no chance yet to respond to the EPLF proposals, it has since 1976 called for an end to the war based upon its own 9-point program for regional autonomy with no option left open for independence.

EPLF Confident

The new EPLF peace plan represents a significant breakthrough on several previous sticking points by leaving the main questions to be resolved by the voters. It is likely, however, to meet strong Ethiopian objections for precisely the same reasons.

Taking their cue from Prime Minister Robert Mugabe's electoral victory in Zimbabwe, the Eritreans appear confident that given the choice, the civilian population will opt for independence. The EPLF also appears to feel that it now has majority support for its leftist politics within the contentious national movement.

Ethiopia, for its part, has long been adamant that it would not consider independence as a legitimate choice nor would it allow an outside body to adjudicate the dispute.

The question of external supervision could well become the primary obstacle to the present peace proposal, but EPLF leaders say they are unwilling to compromise on this, and they are now launching a worldwide diplomatic offensive to gain support for the plan.

Sudan expels 2 newsmen; crackdown seen in coverage of Ethiopian rebels

The Boston Globe, November 27, 1980

Khartoum, Sudan

Two Western journalists have been ordered to leave Sudan within 72 hours in what appears to be a crackdown by Sudanese authorities on coverage of opposition movements in neighboring Ethiopia in the wake of talks last week between the heads of state of the two countries.

English freelance writer Nicky Cowan and myself were given the deportation order Tuesday by an official of the Sudanese security.

Originally given only 24 hours to leave Sudan, we were permitted an additional 48 hours after protests were offered by the British and American embassies.

We had been covering the nationalist movements in Eritrea and the Tigray province of Ethiopia from the Khartoum capital, where the guerrillas maintain offices.

The order to expel came as Sudanese authorities stepped up moves to curtail the activities of the guerrillas here, including holding up food, fuel and medicine going across the border to the war zones.

The order was issued a day after the high-level Sudanese delegation returned from Ethiopia, where it had held five days of talks with Ethiopian leaders.

No formal explanation was given for the abrupt deportation beyond "security reasons," but it was apparent that the action was intended to slow the flow of news on the anti-Ethiopian government movements. We had not been reporting on events within Sudan itself.

No mention of the wars in Eritrea and Ethiopia has appeared in the local Sudanese press for months, and requests by foreign journalists to visit the combat areas have not been granted by Sudanese authorities since August. This is the only access to the war-ravaged areas from outside Ethiopia.

Eritrea: Ethiopian offensive

The Guardian (New York), December 10, 1980

[Byline: Gayle Smith]

Khartoum, Sudan

Ethiopian government forces Dec. 2 launched an all-out offensive against independence forces in the Red Sea territory, according to guerrilla leaders here.

Fighting broke out at dawn along a 24-mile front line north of the government-held town of Afabet, said a high-ranking member of the Eritrean People's Liberation Front (EPLF).

By the second day of the attack, however, the EPLF reported repulsing the Ethiopians by inflicting "heavy losses" on the advancing army. "The situation is very favorable to us now," said EPLF assistant general secretary Issayas Afwerki. "Their future to advance initially may abort the campaign," he added.

The opening of the Ethiopian military offensive came after a radio announcement by the EPLF that a cease fire had been reached with the rival Eritrean Liberation Front (ELF).

A bitter civil war erupted between the two wings of the Eritrean nationalist movement in August, but fighting among them is now "completely stopped," said EPLF assistant general secretary Issayas Afwerki today.

"The enemy is trying to take advantage of this situation," he said, but he could give no details on whether or not a firm agreement has been reached with the ELF.

The Eritreans are fighting for the independence of the former Italian colony that Ethiopia annexed in 1962. The war has been bogged down in an uneasy stalemate for close to two years. An estimated 20,000 Ethiopian troops backed by heavy concentrations of Soviet artillery are involved in the current push near Afabet, while another 20,000 are poised to move on the coastal front, according to the guerrilla spokesman.

Although the announcement of the ceasefire between the rival liberation movements appears to have triggered the offensive, guerrilla leaders here say they have been expecting it for several days after receiving reports of stepped-up military activity there.

A concentrated aerial and artillery bombardment of guerrilla positions began last week, and Ethiopian troops have been observed removing landmines from the no-man's land between the opposing forces, Issayas Afwerki said.

Reports of the Ethiopian military drive came as a surprise to many observers here as it follows an announcement that Sudanese President Jaafar Nimeiri was encouraged to mediate the Eritrean conflict during meetings last week in the Ethiopian capital.

EPLF leaders also last week launched a 7-point peace proposal calling for a ceasefire and a referendum to settle the 19-year war.

Eritrea: Guerrilla victory

The Guardian (New York), December 24, 1980

[Byline: Gayle Smith]

Khartoum, Sudan

The Ethiopian army suffered a major setback last week as a general offensive against Eritrean independence forces collapsed after 10 days of heavy fighting in the war-torn Red Sea territory, according to guerrilla leaders here.

Ethiopia's repeated infantry assaults backed by round-the-clock aerial and artillery bombardment failed to break through guerrilla lines near the government-held town of Afabet. This forced the government to abandon its hastily conceived campaign, a high-ranking official of the Eritrean People's Liberation Front (EPLF) told the Guardian.

"All their attempts failed and the positions of both sides are the same now as they were two weeks ago," said EPLF assistant general secretary Issayas Afwerki, in Dec. 14 interview.

Fourth Failure

This marks the fourth failure of the Soviet-backed Ethiopian forces to advance on this 24-mile-long battlefront since January 1979, and it could have drastic repercussions in the demoralized army.

The Eritreans have been fighting since 1961 for the independence of the former Italian colony which Ethiopia annexed two decades ago after a 10-year United Nations-sponsored federation.

A massive Soviet intervention on Ethiopia's behalf in 1978 forced the guerrillas to stage a strategic retreat from most of the major Eritrean towns and cities. The war has been stalemated since then, however.

The guerrillas say that hundreds of USSR military advisers have been directing Ethiopia's successive military campaigns which have involved hundreds of Soviet-supplied T-54 tanks, long-range artillery and MiG jet fighters along with an estimate 40,000 Ethiopian troops spread along two separate 24-mile battlefronts there.

The last major Ethiopian drive came in July 1979 when the EPLF reported inflicting 6000 casualties before repulsing the government assaults.

Renewed fighting has been forecast here since June, but the belea-guered Ethiopian government has apparently been forced to postpone its planned campaign several times. The delay has largely been due to stepped-up fighting with nationalist guerrillas in the southeastern Ogaden region and in the rebellious northern province of Tigray.

The timing of this latest offensive was geared to take advantage of infighting among the guerrillas, who are divided into two separate armies-the EPLF and the Eritrean Liberation Front (ELF) and an Ethiopian diplomatic push to undercut guerrilla support in neighbor-ing Sudan.

Fighting broke out in August when the ELF attacked the EPLF. This provided the government with a long-sought opportunity to con-front a weakened guerrilla defense, as the EPLF hit back and drove deep into the western Eritrean lowlands against retreating ELF.

The opening of the Ethiopian campaign followed by two days the announcement of a tentative ceasefire between the two guerrilla armies.

"The whole offensive relied on the outcome of our clashes with the ELF," said EPLF leader Afwerki. "This offensive began without full Ethiopian preparations because it was assumed that there were loopholes in our defense lines since we had pulled some of our forces during the fighting with ELF," he added.

The offensive itself was concentrated on a single battlefront near Afabet with an apparent plan to stretch the guerrilla lines by repeat-edly assaulting their flanks prior to a breakthrough in the center, according to Afwerki.

The EPLF-lines held, however, and a series of counterattacks on the Ethiopian rear forces Dec. 11 forced the government to withdraw, Afwerki said.

While the battlefield has been quiet since then, the long-term results of the Ethiopian defeat have yet to be measured. There have been persistent reports of dissension inside the Ethiopian army over the lack of progress in the protracted conflict.

This has centered on protests by the peasant-based militia over unequal wages and benefits with the regular army. There is also anger that Ethiopia has reneged on promises of a speedy end to the fighting so the peasants might return to their home villages, according to reli-able sources here.

With this latest blow to army morale, some observers here are predicting mutinies against the Addis Ababa military leadership which could prove more dangerous to the regime than the war itself.

While Mengistu grapples with this potentially explosive situation at home, he is focusing considerable effort on the international diplomatic front as well.

Over the past month, Mengistu has visited Kenya, Sudan, South Yemen and Libya, after a Moscow summit in November. Ethiopian diplomats have also visited several other Middle Eastern states this fall, and there have been an unusual number of bilateral meetings with diplomats and heads of state of these countries in connection with the tense situation in the African Horn.

Leaders Meet

Kenyan President Daniel Arap Moi was last week in Sudan for talks with Sudanese leaders after meeting with both Mengistu and Somali leaders earlier. Bringing "stability" to the volatile region is said to be high on the agenda.

Kenya has been increasingly drawn into this process as reports there have indicated renewed trouble in Somali-speaking northeastern areas of that country. Ethiopia has used this to seek a strengthening of ties with the pro-Western Kenyan regime in an effort to further isolate Somalia, which has long made territorial claims to Kenya's northeast.

Somali leaders, however, claim that Ethiopia is itself provoking the unrest in Kenya as a ploy to gain support. Somalia has meanwhile been backing off from its claims on Kenyan territory and trying to rebuild relations with Nairobi.

Over the past year, the Somalis have noticeably retreated from their sweeping claims to all areas of the Horn inhabited by ethnic Somalis. This includes Ethiopia's Ogaden region, northern Kenya and the former French colony of Djibouti.

Somalia has officially dropped demands for annexation of the three adjacent regions while continuing calls for self-determination in the Ogaden. In effect, Somalia is thus concentrating on the weakest link in the chain, from a more discreet distance of rear guard support for the Ogaden guerrilla movement.

A further impetus for the shift in Somali policy, at least toward Kenya, comes from its drive to win added U.S. military and economic assistance. Hence, the Somalis were dismayed at recent Kenyan charges-also made in private diplomatic approaches to Washington that they were responsible for the current problems in that country, according to Somali representatives here.

In fact, the hand of U.S. policy is increasingly appearing in much of the complex web of diplomatic maneuvering here. Though it is running into many snags created by the conflicting nationalisms in the region. With firm alliances in Somalia, Kenya and Sudan, U.S. strategists apparently believe that a lessening of tensions in Ethiopia, brought about by containing the antigovernment nationalist movements, could result in the Addis regime ousting its Soviet backers.

A key aspect to the U.S. thrust here is the promise of stepped-up economic assistance to the region and to the constituent states, including Ethiopia. Recently, there has been talk here of resurrecting a 1960s plan to expand the now-defunct East African Community to include not only Kenya, Tanzania and Uganda, but also Rwanda, Burundi, Somalia, Ethiopia and Sudan in a broad regional common market.

"It is a far-fetched plan," said one diplomat here, adding, "I don't see it in the foreseeable future." U.S. policy-makers seem undismayed by the negative prospects, however, and they are encouraging bilateral steps in this direction by way of demonstrating its advantages. The recent talks between Sudan and Ethiopia, for example, included plans to set up several joint development projects which are likely to generate significant Western aid to both countries.

Most observers here believe, however, that the most probable short-term effect of such a process would be an Ethiopian move toward a more balanced relationship between the U.S. and the USSR, rather than any drastic shift toward the West. Soviet influence with Mengistu regime could potentially be undercut by these regional developments, but would not be displaced.

Guerrilla Group Calls for
Boycott of Aid to Ethiopia

The Associated Press [via the Cairo bureau], February 2, 1981

Khartoum, Sudan

A guerrilla group fighting in Ethiopia's northern Tigre Province called Monday for a global boycott of military and economic assistance to Ethiopia's Soviet-backed regime.

Yemane Kidane, a spokesman for the Tigre People's Liberation

Front, accused both the Soviet Union and Western nations, including the United States, of propping up Ethiopia's central government.

Kidane said the Soviet Union has provided close to $2 billion in arms to Ethiopia since 1977. He said the West is the principal source of non-military aid, citing a plan by the European Economic Community to give Ethiopia $400 million over the next five years. The Marxist-oriented Tigre People's Liberation Front is one of several ethnic-based groups battling the central government of Lt. Col. Mengistu Haile Mariam, who came to power in 1977 with the overthrow of the late Emperor Haile Selassie.

The Liberation Front claimed that in 1980 it killed or wounded 3,905 Ethiopian soldiers and captured 732.

Kidane said that in a single government campaign last summer, 437 Tigrean peasants were summarily executed and 1,424 imprisoned on suspicion of aiding the guerrillas.

Mengistu's government is in firm control of the Ethiopian capital of Addis Ababa but is being challenged by rebel secessionist groups in about 70 percent of its territory. The rebels claim the government troops are backed by arms and men from the Soviet Union, Cuba and East Germany.

In Eritrea Province, a former Italian colony, Eritreans have been waging a war of independence against Ethiopia since Selassie annexed the area 18 years ago to gain access to the Red Sea.

In 1977 and 1978, Ethiopia fought and won a war with Somalia for control of the Ogaden desert region of Ethiopia, populated by ethnic Somalis, but guerrilla fighting continues.

"The United States gave the junta $28 million last year under the heading of humanitarian relief, but this money is being used to further the war effort," Kidane charged.

The spokesman said the military government has also asked the United Nations for $2 billion in emergency aid. He claimed the money would be used to relocate war victims in government-controlled settlements.

"The junta is hoodwinking the West by hinting they want to get rid of the Russians," Kidane said. "Meanwhile, the Soviet Union makes tremendous profits off their arms sales while taking the opportunity to fully consolidate their control of the regime."

The Tigre People's Liberation Front has been fighting six years to win what it terms "national self-determination" for the 5 million people of the northernmost province. The front claims it now controls 80 percent of rural Tigre while the government holds the major towns and part partially controls the main roads.

Ethiopia: United front?

The Guardian (New York), February 18, 1981

[Byline: Gayle Smith]

Khartoum, Sudan

Nationalist Tigrayan guerrillas on Jan. 30 called for an international boycott of Ethiopia's military government while renewing appears for a united front of internal opposition forces to topple the regime.

In a lengthy statement describing the escalating Tigray insurgency issued here, a spokesman for the Tigray People's Liberation Front (TPLF) accused both the Soviet Union and Western countries of propping up the central government against growing opposition from a wide coalition of nationalist movements.

The guerrilla spokesman cited Soviet arms assistance and Western economic aid as jointly responsible for continuing the conflict there. "Taken together, this is all that keeps the present regime in power," he added.

The guerrilla war in Ethiopia's northeastern Tigray province is the fastest growing antigovernment movement, according to the TPLF spokesman who claimed that the TPLF is now becoming a direct threat to the Addis Ababa government.

"The war in Tigray is sharply escalating with the expansion of operations by the TPLF and a doubling of government forces there to more than 40,000 troops backed by increasingly sophisticated Soviet heavy arms," he said today.

Despite the recent introduction of MI-24 helicopter gun ships and large quantities of armor and artillery, the TPLF claims to have killed or wounded an estimated 3905 Ethiopian soldiers last year while capturing 732 in two unsuccessful counterinsurgency campaigns and 44 guerrilla-initiated actions.

Meanwhile, popular support for the TPLF is also growing as the ruling junta continues to step up random acts of terror against the civilian population, according to the spokesman. He cited widespread bombardment, intentional crop destruction and the arbitrary arrest and execution of suspected guerrilla sympathizers.

"Although neither side is yet in a position to win a decisive military victory, the developing linkage between the TPLF and other nationalist forces and antigovernment opposition groups constitutes a terminal challenge to the narrowly based central government," he said.

'Balance Is Shifting'

"In this respect, the present numerical and arms superiority of the Ethiopian army is deceptive," he cautioned, adding, "The Addis Ababa regime commands a superficially powerful military machine, but it confronts opposition throughout the fragile empire state, and the balance of force is steadily shifting against it."

The TPLF has been fighting six years to win what it terms "national self-determination" for the 5 million people of Ethiopia's northernmost province. The front claims to control 80% of rural Tigray. While the government holds the major towns and partially controls the main highways there.

Although the TPLF lacks substantial external support, it is cementing ties with the independence movement in the neighboring Red Sea territory of Eritrea and with nationalist movements in Ethiopia's southeastern Ogaden and southern Oromo (Galla) regions (see below), along with remnants of formerly urban-based opposition groups.

"The aim of this embryonic united front will be to topple the Soviet-supported central government under a minimum program of mutual support to wipe out feudal exploitation, national oppression and foreign domination," said the guerrilla spokesman. The movements involved are at varying political directions and levels, however, so it is not yet clear how this process will develop.

"With Tigray, the TPLF combines the classic guerrilla tactics of mobile hit-and-run warfare with a political strategy of improving the lives of the predominantly peasant population while providing the people with the means to defend their hard earned gains," he told reporters here.

For its part, the ruling junta attempted major counterinsurgency campaigns in April and in late August. "They managed to retake a handful of minor towns in central Tigray. But they did so at a high cost in men and material, and they have since evacuated all but one of them," said the guerrilla spokesman.

The TPLF says that the present government took power in 1974 by riding a wave of popular but unorganized discontent with the Haile Selassie regime. Instead of fulfilling this mass mandate for change, however, the Mengistu regime has only "made token concessions in the urban areas and the Amhara-populated central Ethiopian countryside while wreaking havoc on the rest of the empire's majority of subject peoples."

"The trend in Tigray and elsewhere in Ethiopia is now unmistakably clear," the TPLF representative concluded. "The Addis Ababa military clique is not only unwilling but incapable of resolving the long-standing grievances of the oppressed masses which are rising up against it.

"The future," he added, "lies with the TPLF and other progressive and democratic forces."

Ethiopia: Oromos fight back

The Guardian (New York), February 18, 1981

[Byline: G.S.]

Khartoum, Sudan

Nationalist Oromo guerrillas claim to be stepping up armed actions in southern Ethiopia against the Mengistu government. They also say there are strengthening ties with other nationalist movements across the sprawling northeast African country.

The Oromo Liberation Front (OLF) carried out over 40 attacks against the government during the past year, according to an OLF spokesman here.

The Oromo nationalists are also seeking closer links with opposition movements in the Somali-speaking Ogaden region of southeastern Ethiopia and Tigray province in the northeast, the spokesman said today. OLF also wants to forge ties with the Eritrean independence movement, fighting in the northeast for nearly 20 years, he added.

"Our organization looks forward to a united front with the other progressive nationalist movements," said OLF spokesman Yohannes Lata.

The OLF is the most recent antigovernment movement to emerge in the turbulent Horn of Africa, but it is potentially the most serious long-term challenge to the Soviet-backed Ethiopian regime. Oromos make up over 50% of Ethiopia's 30-million population and inhabit more than half the territory of the country.

The OLF, like its nationalist allies in Tigray and the Ogaden, describes its aim as "self-determination" from the ethnic Amhara-dominated central government. But the increasing interconnections among these disparate nationalist groupings suggest the possible evolution of a general strategy to topple the Addis Ababa government.

Eritrea: Famine looms

The Guardian (New York), March 25, 1981

[Byline: Gayle Smith]

Khartoum, Sudan

The twin scourges of drought and war now threaten tens of thousands in the embattled Red Sea territory of Eritrea with mass starvation.

Ethiopia, which controls Eritrea, is preparing for a major offensive against guerrillas fighting for the territory's independence. This military move coincides with a severe drought sweeping the already ravaged area, according to diplomatic sources here in the Sudanese capital.

The forthcoming government military campaign will be aimed at closing the border with Sudan to incoming supplies of food, fuel, medicines and ammunition now reaching the guerrillas and the civilian population, these sources say.

Relief officials here are meanwhile reporting the deaths of tens of thousands of animals and the displacement of large numbers of peasant farmers and nomadic herders due to the failure of the annual winter rains this year.

A spokesman for the Khartoum-based Eritrean Relief Association (ERA), which operates in the guerrilla-controlled rural areas, today charged that Ethiopia is trying to blockade Eritrea in an effort to starve the opposition into submission.

French supplies of sophisticated arms from the USSR, which backs Ethiopia, are now being airlifted into Eritrea to reinforce the estimated 60-70,000 Ethiopian troops presently bogged down in a stalemate with the guerrillas, diplomats here say. Ethiopia appears to be moving to interdict the guerrilla supply routes which are also currently being used to ferry nonmilitary goods to the drought-affected areas along the parched Red Sea coast. This could leave over a half-million people without access to outside aid, according to relief officials here.

Journalists have for months been prevented from visiting the affected areas in Eritrea by Sudanese authorities. This is because Khartoum is seeking a rapprochement with Ethiopia in what appears to be a calculated Western attempt to wean Ethiopia away from the Soviet Union. An informal ERA survey conducted in February, however, turned up 104,918 people who reported the loss of livestock and crops in the eastern Eritrean lowlands now under the control of the Eritrean People's Liberation Front (EPLF) according to an ERA representative in Khartoum.

Among the life-supporting animals which perished recently were 48,363 goats and sheep, 7374 head of cattle and 1045 camels, the spokesman said in a March 16 interview.

The relief organization also estimates there are between 500,000 and 600,000 people already displaced by the war, which has continued since 1961. The ERA official said that only a third of them can now be reached by the organization's relief program.

A second, smaller agency, the Eritrean Red Cross and Crescent Society (ERCCS), provides limited assistance to civilian casualties in the western lowlands in cooperation with the Eritrean Liberation Front (ELF), the other independence movement operating in the territory. The Ethiopian government has no relief projects outside the urban areas it controls.

Malnutrition has become endemic throughout Eritrea in recent years leaving the impoverished farmers and nomads subject to a host of major and minor diseases, including tuberculosis, malaria, dysentery, eye and ear infections and other common tropical illnesses from which they are too weak to recover, the ERA spokesman added.

In these circumstances, he concluded, the combination of stepped-up fighting and continued drought could claim the lives of tens of thousands during the coming dry season.

Still question over guerrilla unity

Eritrean rebel groups end feuds to create common front

International Daily News (Rome), March 27, 1981

Rome (Reuter)

The four guerrilla groups fighting for the independence of the Red Sea province of Eritrea have agreed to end their feuding and join forces in their fight against the Soviet-backed Ethiopian government.

Guerrilla sources here said the agreement of the rival factions to cooperate under a single umbrella committee was reached under strong pressure from the Arab League. League member states like Saudi Arabia and Iraq have financed and in some cases armed the rival groups.

The agreement, announced earlier this week in Tunis where the

Arab League council of foreign ministers is meeting, forges the fractious Eritrean movement into a united front to deal with external relations.

But reports by guerrilla sources on the results of the Tunis meeting leave no doubt that many questions remain unanswered about the operations of the four groups within Eritrea itself, notably about the areas which they will control and how they will divide foreign aid.

The outcome of the 20-year-old war, now being waged at relatively low intensity, could affect the strategic balance in the Middle East since Ethiopian control of Eritrea gives their Soviet allies access to Red Sea bases on Egypt's southern flank.

The groups at the Tunis meeting were the Eritrean People's Liberation Front (EPLF), the Eritrean Liberation Front - Revolutionary Council (ELF-RC), the Eritrean Liberation Front - Popular Liberation Forces (ELF-PLF) and the Popular Liberation Forces - Revolutionary Committee (PLF-RC).

It was the first time all four groups had sat down together to try to end their fratricidal disputes.

The latest internal conflict broke out between the EPLF and the ELF-RC last August, ending a three-year effort to merge the two main nationalist factions.

Last year's heavy fighting was apparently sparked by EPLF allegations that the rival faction was holding secret talks with Soviet and Ethiopian officials.

Low-level fighting is still continuing between them in Eritrea, despite a ceasefire declared in December with Sudanese backing, according to diplomatic sources here.

The other two groups, with only a few hundred members in each, are based among the large Eritrean refugee population in neighboring Sudan and are not involved in the internal clashes inside Eritrea, these sources said.

Earlier attempts to unify the main factions, which split apart in 1970, have foundered on ideological and religious grounds.

The Tunis agreement calls for an end to the civil war and to hostile propaganda between the movements, and EPLF spokesman said Thursday.

It also calls for the free movement of all the fronts within Eritrea, he added.

The EPLF at present controls three-quarters of the 117,000 square km territory which has a mixed Christian and Moslem population of two million.

Under the Tunis agreement the secretariat of the Arab League is empowered to setup a committee of its own to monitor the situation in Eritrea. But the precise role of the committee was not specified, the spokesman said.

The unity pact appeared to be loosely patterned on the example of the Palestine Liberation Organization (PLO), an umbrella body made up of representatives of autonomous groups.

At present the ELF-RC operates in the western lowlands of rural Eritrea. The EPLF, the largest guerrilla group, moved into some of the ELF-RC's former territory in last year's factional fighting.

The Ethiopian government controls the major cities and highways, following a Soviet-backed military offensive in 1978 in which it forced the guerrillas to retreat from previously captured towns.

The Eritreans launched their guerrilla war in 1962 when their province was fully integrated into the Ethiopian empire.

The former Italian colony passed to British military rule during World War II and for 10 years, from 1952, formed an autonomous unit within the federation of Ethiopia and Eritrea.

Eritrea: Unity move

The Guardian (New York), April 22, 1981

Rome

Long-time rival Eritrean independence groups are taking the first steps toward establishing a limited united front.

Representatives of four Eritrean organizations met in Tunis March 20-23 to hammer out a breakthrough agreement. The groups are setting up a working committee that will oversee coordination among the forces fighting for independence from Ethiopia and channel foreign assistance into the struggle.

This is the first time all the politically disparate groups have agreed to pool their efforts to defeat the presently stalemated Ethiopian occupation army in the strategic Red Sea territory. The move is taking place in the context of increased contention in the region between the U.S. and USSR.

The agreement follows the emergence of the Marxist-led Eritrean People's Liberation Front (EPLF) as the dominant force within Eritrea over its smaller rivals. These latter groups incline toward one or another superpower, although the Soviet Union is itself supporting Ethiopia in the Eritrea war.

The new pact effectively supersedes a 1977 unity agreement between the EPLF and the Eritrean Liberation Front (ELF). The pact broke down last August when civil war erupted between the two organizations amid reports the smaller ELF was holding secret compromise talks with Ethiopia and the Soviet Union.

Also included in the Tunis agreement are two factions of the pro-Western Eritrean Liberation Front-Popular Liberation Forces (ELF-PLF) which was pushed out of Eritrea into neighboring Sudan by the ELF in a brief 1978 civil war.

The ELF-PLF is led by Osman Saleh Sabbe, a founding member of the original ELF in 1961 who later served as foreign representative of the EPLF, which was formed in 1970. Sabbe was ousted from EPLF in 1976 on charges of seeking personal advantage in clandestine negotiations with the ELF.

The ELF moved against Sabbe's forces in 1978, after entering into a brief alliance, amid accusations that he was trying to engineer a "coup" to take over that front, The ELF-PLF later split again to spawn what is known as the "Revolutionary Committee" of the Popular Liberation Forces (PLF-RC).

While neither of these Sudan-based splinter groups numbers more than a few hundred followers, each receives financial backing from Gulf oil states. The reactionary Arab Emirates appear to be Sabbe's main supporters, while Iraq backs the PLF-RC, whose leader Osman Agyb was assassinated in Khartoum last year.

Leaders of the various Eritrean groups gathered in the Tunisian capital last month at the invitation of the Arab League which played a mediating role among the rival organizations prior to a scheduled conference of Arab foreign ministers.

'Fighting Common Enemy'

Throughout the recent period of infighting among contending nationalist factions, the EPLF has almost single-handedly carried on the war with Ethiopia which ahs been held to a bitterly fought stalemate since early 1979. The Tunis agreement calls for an immediate end to the current civil war and commands the nationalist forces to "direct all weapons against the common enemy."

It also calls for an end to hostile propaganda among the competing groups, and it provides for the "free movement" of all nationalist forces within Eritrea without regard for the de facto boundaries now in effect.

While the vaguely worded agreement, whose content was confirmed by EPLF leaders in Rome, commits the groups to further steps to ward unity, it appears aimed at setting up an umbrella committee or council which will leave the member organizations autonomous. In this respect, it appears to be a more realistic reflection of the internal situation than prior pacts calling for complete mergers.

In addition, the secretariat of the Arab League is empowered to set up an oversight committee of its own to follow up the implementation of the alliance and to insure the end of the current infighting.

The Tunis announcement left several important questions unanswered, chief among them whether the ELF-PLF factions will now try again to establish bases inside Eritrea. There are also the issues of how foreign assistance will be divided and distributed and how the end to the civil war will be monitored.

The decisive factor in bringing the Tunis agreement about is regarded here as the change in the internal balance of Eritrean forces. During the past year the EPLF has strongly rebounded from its 1978 retreat out of the major urban areas it had liberated. The movement increased the size of its operational area by more than 50% during eight months of intermittent fighting with the ELF. The EPLF also successfully withstood a series of attacks by Ethiopian forces while continuing widespread guerrilla actions in Ethiopia's vulnerable rear.

It is this growth which led EPLF to sign the Tunis pact although it had previously refused to cooperate with the rightist splinter groups. It hopes now to receive aid from external parties who had earlier balked at helping the leftist EPLF.

With the EPLF's strength in the field, an injection of foreign aid and an end to the civil war could result in dramatic changes in the independence war. (Informed observers have reported that prior to the Tunis meeting there were signs the ELF was moving to form an anti-EPLF bloc with the other two groups, a situation that would have posed the danger of a renewed and escalated civil war.

The main arena of confrontation between EPLF and Ethiopian forces is in the arid northern mountains of the Sahel region where the guerrillas maintain their principal rear base. An estimated 40-50,000 Ethiopian troops are pinned down there on two long, entrenched battle fronts.

The last time the government was able to mount a full-scale offensive there was in July 1979, when it was soundly defeated by the EPLF. In December of that year, the guerrillas launched a counteroffensive which pushed the Ethiopians out of the mountains onto low-lying plains near the Red Sea coast and outside the town of Afabet where they remain today.

After fighting broke out between the EPLF and the ELF on the southern flank of EPLF's Sahel base last August, the EPLF drove deep into the ELF's neighboring Barka base area, taking full control of northern Barka and setting up a third fixed frontline against potential assaults by Ethiopia from this direction.

Meanwhile the EPLF also moved southeast along the coast to take over former ELF areas in the Danakil region and then inland across Akele Guzai province to the plateau area known as Serae. When a ceasefire was declared in November under pressure from neighboring Sudan, the ELF shifted to small-scale guerrilla operations in central Serae and in the Anseba River area west of the city of Keren.

Progressive Changes

The EPLF's main operations there were centered on political mobilization to consolidate popular support. This involved-and continues to involve today-the carrying out of land reform and the reorganization of traditional village society along democratic lines. This has included the establishment of local militias to defend the social and political gains of the poor and middle peasants.

While the transition period leaves the small EPLF political and military teams vulnerable to hit-and-run attacks in these areas, the grassroots network of popular organization is likely to soon render ELF harassment ineffective, should it fail to be stopped by the Tunis accord.

Perhaps most significantly, the EPLF's substantial expansion into both the coastal and Barka lowlands strikes a powerful blow at efforts by the minor nationalist groups to exploit regional, religious and ethnic divisions to garner support.

In addition, it gives the EPLF increased access to the Sudanese border-and limits the ability of the Sudan to control the movement of supplies-as well as providing larger and more secure areas to establish agricultural and other projects to sustain its forces on a self-reliant basis.

Northern Barka, for example, contains a network of broad, fertile valleys where food can be grown by the EPLF in order to lessen its need to import grain for its standing army in neighboring Sahel.

It would be naïve to think that the loose pact arrived at in Tunis will end the deep-rooted problems in the Eritrean movement which in the final analysis reflects sharp class divisions in the programs and aims of the various groups. But EPLF leaders say the agreement can be a check on them at least for the immediate future.

<u>ERITREA</u>
NATIONALIST FORCES RENEW UNITY EFFORT
Africa News (Durham, NC), April 27, 1981

Rome

[AN] Long-time rival Eritrean nationalist groups are once again taking steps toward establishing a limited united front against the Soviet-allied Ethiopian government—and also against new efforts by Western governments to undermine the 20-year Eritrean independence war.

Representatives of four Eritrean organizations met under Arab League auspices in Tunis March 20-23 to hammer out a breakthrough agreement. They now have a working committee that will oversee coordination of the independence forces and channel foreign assistance to them.

This is the first time all the politically disparate groups have agreed to pool their efforts to defeat the Ethiopian army in the strategic Red Sea territory. The four organizations are:

- The Eritrean Liberation Front (ELF), which as the oldest nationalist group has enjoyed close ties with various Arab countries, particularly Syria in recent years;
- The Eritrean Liberation Front-Popular Liberation Forces (ELF-PLF), which takes a pro-Western stand, is led by Osman Saleh Sabbe, and is backed particularly by the Arab Emirates;
- The Revolutionary Committee-Popular Liberation Forces (RC-PLF), which split from Sabbe's group and is aided by Iraq; and
- The Eritrean People's Liberation Front (EPLF), an independent Marxist-led group which has emerged in recent years as the clearly dominant force within Eritrean nationalist ranks.

The achievement of the loose alliance formalizes the politically independent EPLF's hegemony over the divided nationalist movement at a critical juncture when it is in danger of being caught in a squeeze play between Moscow and Washington, both of which seek a compromise to end the war in favor of Ethiopia.

The new pact effectively supercedes a 1977 unity agreement between the EPLF and the ELF, which broke down last August when civil war erupted between them amid reports the smaller ELF was holding secret compromise talks with Ethiopia and the Soviet Union.

The Tunis agreement calls for an immediate end to this civil war and commands the nationalist forces to "direct all weapons against the common enemy."

While the vaguely-worded agreement commits the groups to further steps towards unity, it appears aimed at setting up an umbrella committee or council that will leave the member organizations autonomous. In this respect, it is a more realistic reflection of the internal situation than prior acts calling for complete mergers.

The announcement left several important questions unanswered, chief among them whether the ELF-PLF and the RC-PLF will now try again to establish bases inside Eritrea (from which they have been excluded since 1978), how foreign assistance will be divided and what influence the donors will try to exert, and how the end to the civil war between the ELF and the EPLF will be monitored.

However, the agreement does appear to preempt efforts by the U.S. to dampen support for the independence movements from Sudan, which controls guerrilla access to external supply and which is now seeking a rapprochement with Ethiopia, evidently with encouragement from the U.S.

Though the new Reagan administration has yet to define a distinctive policy of its own, recent Western strategy in the strife-torn and strategic Horn of Africa has focused on efforts to gain leverage over the Eritrean movement and other internal Ethiopian opposition groups while simultaneously offering significant financial support to the besieged Ethiopian government in Addis Ababa. The thrust of the plan is to enforce compromise settlements on the opposition and to entice Ethiopia to oust the Soviet Union from the area.

Since 1977 the Soviet Union, which once indirectly supported Eritrean nationalism, has provided Ethiopia's ruling military government with over $2 billion in arms. An estimated 1300 Soviet military advisors are also playing key roles in the various counterinsurgency campaigns, but they are having little success outside the southeastern Ogaden region.

Meanwhile, the European Economic Community (EEC) has pledged more than $650 million to Ethiopia over the next five years, and it is now mobilizing to provide another $1.5 billion in emergency relief in response to a UN-sponsored appeal to bail out the hard-pressed Ethiopian economy.

Excluding the Soviet military aid, Ethiopia's major creditors—for a foreign debt of some $700 million—are the World Bank, the International Monetary Fund, and, among individual countries, the U.S., West Germany, China and Libya.

In March, French Foreign Minister Olivier Stirn paid an official visit to Ethiopia, followed in late April by Emilio Colombo, Italy's minister of foreign affairs. Both visits were expected to result in stepped-up bilateral cooperation.

Despite its public posture in recent years of opposing the Ethiopian government and its alliances with the Soviet Union and Cuba, the U.S., too, has channeled funds to Ethiopia through various international agencies, according to U.S. officials in Sudan, who refused to identify the amounts or the routes the money takes.

Western diplomats stationed in capitals in the Horn openly describe the policy as intended to "wean Ethiopia away from the Russians," citing previous realignments in the region by Egypt, Sudan and Somalia as precedents.

The U.S. is also engaged in a major military buildup in the surrounding countries of Somalia, Kenya and Sudan, which apart from wider regional objectives is seen as bringing pressure on both Ethiopia and the guerrilla movements to come to the conference table.

In one possible scenario suggested by a high U.S. analyst during a recent visit to Khartoum, a policy shift in Addis Ababa, perhaps brought about by the ouster of Ethiopian leader Mengistu by "pro-Western" officers, could pave the way for an offer of regional autonomy which the guerrillas would then be forced to accept.

Ironically, this plan is a virtual rerun of Soviet policy when the USSR entered the fray on behalf of Ethiopia in 1977 with a plan to create a federation between Eritrea, Ethiopia and Somalia. It failed then because all three parties refused to accept it.

Since then the Ethiopian government has stuck to its 1976 offer of a severely limited autonomy for Eritrea, while the EPLF has remained firm on demands for independence.

Efforts by the ELF last year to secure an offer of political autonomy through various intermediaries including the Soviet Union, South Yemen, Syria and the Italian Communist Party appear to have collapsed due to Ethiopian intransigence.

There is therefore little reason to believe that the current Western plan could achieve its objective, but it may cause increasing difficulties for the Eritrean movements, especially as the Reagan administration moves ahead with plans to establish a larger U.S. military presence in Sudan.

Sudan is critical because it is the main source of supply for the EPLF and the Tigre People's Liberation Front (TPLF), the strongest of the movements now fighting the Ethiopian government, as well as the most consistently Marxist-oriented.

Within the past year, Sudan's President Jaafar el Numeiry has steadily shifted away from open support for the Eritrean cause and begun a rapprochement with Ethiopia's leader Mengistu Haile Mariam.

Sudanese authorities have recently blocked journalists from visiting the liberated areas of Eritrea and Tigre, and they have periodically harassed the movements within Sudan.

A sign of Sudan's changing policy came at the recent Islamic Conference in Ta'if, Saudi Arabia, where Numeiry stood practically alone in opposing a strongly-worded declaration of support for the Eritrean struggle.

The Tunis conference, backed by the Arab League, can be seen as a counter to Sudan by Arab supporters of Eritrea. and, given the prominent role at the conference which was played by the EPLF, it can also be seen as diluting the divisive influence of the smaller ELF-PLF and RC-PLF, with their independent access to wealthy Arab countries. This result reflects the growing internal strength of the EPLF, which has forced increased Arab recognition and also given the EPLF the confidence to permit the smaller movements a role without being threatened by their influence.

During the past year the EPLF has rebounded from its 1978 retreat out of the major urban areas to become the only viable nationalist force in the field. It increased the size of its operational area by more than 50% during eight months of intermittent fighting with the ELF, while also withstanding a series of attacks by Ethiopian forces and continuing guerrilla actions in Ethiopia's vulnerable rear. An injection of foreign aid to EPLF forces and an end to the war with the ELF could result in dramatically improving the EPLF position against Ethiopia's army.

The EPLF has in recent months established a strong position in the northern Barka area, formerly controlled by the ELF, and it has also moved southeast along the coast to take over former ELF areas in the Danakil region.

In these areas the EPLF's main operations are now centered on

consolidating popular support, by carrying out land reform and reorganizing traditional village society along democratic lines. This strategy has proved successful in the EPLF's own long-term base areas,
and EPLF leaders are confident they can in a similar fashion build a
strong political structure in the new zones.

Aid seen as threat by Eritrean rebels

The Toronto Globe & Mail, August 11, 1981

Washington, DC

As both sides mobilize for renewed fighting in Eritrea's war of
independence from Ethiopia, guerrilla leaders are pleading with the
Soviet Union and Western countries to halt all but humanitarian aid
to that strife-torn nation.

The Soviet Union is supplying massive quantities of arms to
Ethiopia and Western countries are providing the economic aid that
keeps the self-proclaimed Socialist military junta in power, according
to an official of the Eritrean People's Liberation Front.

"This economic aid is stabilizing the Government's economic crisis and allowing them to step up their war effort in Eritrea," Sebhat
Efrem, 32 old a weekend press conference.

He urged the Soviet Union, the United Nations and Western
countries to see that only humanitarian aid for drought and war victims is sent to Ethiopia, and press the regime of Colonel Mengistu
Haile Mariam to begin negotiations to end the war.

He said the Soviet-backed Government forces and the guerrillas
are in the process of preparing for a major military confrontation that
could come in the next several months.

Mr. Efrem's visit to the United States, the first by a top leader of
the leftist EPLF, coincides with a conference of the National Union of
Eritrean Students in North America, being held here to mark the 20th
anniversary of Africa's longest-running armed conflict.

The liberation front is establishing its first full-time office in New
York to lobby United Nations delegates for an internationally supervised ceasefire and a referendum to end the war.

Ethiopia annexed the former Italian colony of Eritrea in 1962 after unilaterally dissolving a 10-year UN-sponsored federation. The United States backed Ethiopia against the insurgents until 1976, when the newly installed military junta abruptly realigned the country with the Soviet Union.

Large scale Soviet intervention in 1978 forced the guerrillas to withdraw from most of Eritrea's previously captured cities. Since then the uneasy stalemate has been marked by periodic outbreaks of civil war among contending guerrilla factions.

According to Mr. Efrem, hit-and-run attacks against Government positions are increasing dramatically. Ethiopia is being forced to redeploy large numbers of troops to defend its rear bases, and several garrisons are now being supplied only by air, he said.

The government is training two fresh divisions and using conscripts to build up its forces in the threatened areas, he said.

Mr. Efrem accused the regime of diverting Western-supplied economic and relief assistance to bolster the war effort.

"This aid from Western countries is helping the Government to intensify its oppression of the Eritrean and the Ethiopian peoples," he said. "Without this aid, the regime would not exist."

While the Soviet Union has provided Ethiopia with more than $2 billion in arms over the past three years, the West remains the country's main trading partner.

Diplomats in Washington say the purpose of economic aid from the West is to undercut the Soviet presence in Addis Ababa in the hope of displacing Soviet influence there.

However, they concede that this is not likely to happen if the war in Eritrea is not ended soon. Instead, the increased Ethiopian need for arms assistance may tighten the Soviet hold.

Ethiopia is also fighting nationalist rebellions in other parts of the country and its confrontation with neighboring Somalia continues. The economy has deteriorated steadily as resources are shunted into the war effort, and this has severely retarded the regime's ability to achieve political stability in rural regions.

The EPLF has recently shown a new openness toward other nationalist factions based among the 360,000 Eritrean refugees in neighboring Sudan.

These groups are meeting in Tunis to forge an alliance under the auspices of the Arab League, Mr. Efrem said. One consequence could be an injection of Arab money into the conflict after years of only lukewarm support.

Tigray minority presses attack on Ethiopia government

The Guardian (New York), October 7, 1981

Nationalist guerrillas in Ethiopia's Tigray province are stepping up attacks on the central government after a 4-month lull in the fighting here, according to a spokesperson for the Tigray People's Liberation Front (TPLF).

The Tigrayan guerrillas launched a series of ambushes against government supply convoys and small outposts in late August and early September. They killed over 240 Ethiopian troops and captured large stores of arms and equipment, according to TPLF Central Committee member Asfaha Hagos.

"We are sharply increasing our military actions after a period of consolidation and growth," said the guerrilla diplomat during a recent interview. Hagos claimed that the TPLF has doubled in size during the past 18 months and now controls over 80% of the 102,000 square kilometer province, leaving government forces isolated in the larger towns and along the major highways.

The TPLF is fighting for national self-determination and a people's democratic revolution, according to the guerrilla leader. The front is also attempting to cement an Ethiopia-wide alliance among other oppressed nationalities and democratic forces, Hagos said.

"We are trying to increase our relations with the Oromo Liberation Front and the Western Somali Liberation Front as well as those who are struggling against the regime in the towns," he said. "The necessity for coordination is paramount."

The TPLF also maintains close ties with independence forces in the neighboring Red Sea territory of Eritrea, annexed by Ethiopia two decades ago after a half century of European colonial administration.

The renewal of offensive guerrilla activity in Tigray coincides with the winding down of a year-long civil war in Eritrea which has left the Eritrean People's Liberation Front (EPLF) in undisputed control of the rural areas there. Leaders of both fronts are now predicting a coordinated effort against government forces in the coming months.

Ethiopia gets it main support from the Soviet Union, yet Hagos said that the largest increases in aid to the beleaguered Addis Ababa government are coming now from Western states in the form of massive economic subsidies. The TPLF leader also said that Ethiopia's growing ties with the U.S. backed Sudanese regime is having the greatest negative impact on the front's military and diplomatic activities. Diplomatic sources say that Ethiopia has threatened Sudan with stepped-up aid to antigovernment forces in the south of the country, which experienced a 17-year civil war between north and south in the early post-war era.

But the U.S. also appears to be involved in pressuring its clients to restrict the activities of the fronts as part of a strategy to win influence in Ethiopia, these sources add.

The Ethiopian regime, for its part, has sought to mask these developments in order to gain time to remobilize new troop strength through an extensive conscription campaign and to solicit Western aid to shore up its crumbling internal economy, according to Hagos.

There are now 60,000 to 70,000 government soldiers tied down in Eritrea, 40,000 in Tigray, 70,000 in the southeastern Ogaden region and 20,000 in the southern Oromo areas, according to Western intelligence.

Ethiopian army morale is plummeting as a result, according to Hagos, who said that one military unit in the town of Humera mutinied in June, while 53 soldiers, including seven officers, defected to the TPLF in August.

Eritrea: New Ethiopian offensive?

The Guardian (New York), November 4, 1981

More than a decade of bitter political rivalry and civil war among contending nationalist movements in Eritrea appears to be over, but there are signs that renewed heavy fighting may soon break out between the Eritreans and the Ethiopian government.

The Marxist-oriented Eritrean People's Liberation Front (EPLF) recently succeeded in driving the smaller, conservative Eritrean Liberation Front (ELF) into neighboring Sudan where its defeated leaders sit in a heavily guarded refugee camp after the failure of diplomatic efforts to end the infighting, according to a high-ranking EPLF spokesperson.

Struggle Advances

Meanwhile, Ethiopian government forces are now mobilizing for

another in a long series of military campaigns to prevent the EPLF
from moving into former ELF areas of operation, said EPLF Central
Committee member Amdemikael Kahsai last week.

Kahsai termed the current situation in the embattled territory
"fluid," but he predicted that it will work to the advantage of the 20-
year Eritrean struggle for independence from Ethiopia.

"We are in a new chapter now," he said in an interview. "This
will mean a major advance for the struggle, both politically and militarily." Kahsai is based in New York to carry the Eritrean case to UN
delegates.

EPLF guerrilla units have begun attacking government garrisons
in the former ELF zones, which had been generally immune from
challenge during the past three years, according to Kahsai. He said
that Ethiopian reinforcements are now moving into these areas.

Five fresh Ethiopian brigades are being deployed in the northern
Sahel province and in the Western Barka lowlands for a possible 2-
pronged attack on EPLF positions, he said, adding that troops have
also been rushed to the southern Serae region of Eritrea.

But the guerrilla leader discounted the possibility of an Ethiopian
success because the EPLF now has substantial increased flexibility of
movement and more forces of its own to throw into any future battle
with the government following the end of fighting against the rival ELF.

The liberation front is stepping up offensive attacks in what could
signal the preparations for a general guerrilla counteroffensive, according
to Kahsai. "We are engaged in broad military operations, selecting the
enemy's weaker points and attacking them in an effort to force them to
concentrate their force in some limited garrisons," he said.

The civil war between the ELF and EPLF had flared up in earnest
in April and lasted until the ELF was fully routed in July and August.
Most of what remains of the disintegrating ELF is now in a single
refugee camp near Kassala in eastern Sudan where the guerrillas have
been disarmed by Sudanese authorities, according to Kahsai.

One small group of 60 to 70 fighters under the command of
Abdullah Idris is still holding out in the nearby hills, and there is an
intense power struggle underway among former ELF leaders in the
refugee camp, Kahsai said. Opposing ELF factions are charging each
other with the responsibility for the civil war and its outcome, while
many ELF guerrillas are currently challenging all the organization's
leadership, he added.

"We are making a general appeal to the fighters to join us," said
Kahsai. "Many of them are patriotic. They were pushed into this war,

and there is every possibility that a big section will join the EPLF."
Meanwhile, the EPLF is moving on several fronts to fill the vacuum
left by the departing ELF inside Eritrea.

"Politically, we are in the phase of arousing the morale of the people
in the areas where the ELF used to operate," the EPLF diplomat noted.
"Economically, we are trying within our capacity to provide them with
some of the basic necessities like medicine, food and education."

"We have already seen some change in the attitude of the people," Kahsai said, adding that the number of new recruits to the EPLF
has jumped considerably in the last two to three months.

"The fact that the ELF has entered Sudan has generally been
regarded by the people as positive for the struggle against the enemy
as a whole."

ERITREA

Changed line-up for next round of fighting

Africa News (Durham, NC), November 16, 1981

[AN] Two wire-service reports filed last week by the same agency
on the same day well illustrate the wide variance of perspective on the
current situation in Eritrea—a variance that makes it difficult to get
a clear idea even of the basic facts. An Agence France Presse correspondent visiting Asmara with Ethiopian authorities reported their
view that the war is practically over, noted markets "bustling with
life," and quoted Ethiopian appeals for reconstruction aid. From
Khartoum, also on November 11, another AFP report relayed news
of a major battle near the Sudan border in western Eritrea, in which
the Eritrean People's Liberation Front (EPLF) claimed as many as
1,000 Ethiopian casualties.

It is impossible, of course, to fully reconcile such conflicting perspectives, and Sudanese government restrictions now limit visits by journalists to areas held by the Eritrean guerrillas, diminishing the number
of firsthand reports. Based on a variety of sources, however, several gen-
eralizations about the status of the Eritrean conflict seem warranted:

- The Ethiopian government does still hold the major centers
  and communication routes, and guerrilla activity affecting

these areas has not been at a high level for some time. On the other hand, Ethiopian troops have not been able to dislodge the strongly dug-in EPLF forces from their base area in the Sahel region north of Nakfa. Occasional major battles, such as a week-long clash at the end of September near Afabet, may have produced many casualties, but they result in little change in the military situation. A similar line-up now seems to be in the making in the Barka lowlands, to the west of Sahel, where in the course of this year the EPLF has almost entirely displaced militarily its rival Eritrean Liberation Front (ELF).

• The movement of relief and military supplies into guerrilla-held areas, as well as the flow of news coming out, is being hampered by Sudan's rapprochement with Ethiopia and the consequent decision to impose stricter border controls. "Sudan is no longer a rear base," Ethiopian Major Dawit Wolde Giorgis, commander in Eritrea, told AFP, though he conceded that in practice the long border could not be sealed.

• Since the last Arab League-sponsored "unity agreement" among Eritrean movements in March (see AFRICA NEWS, April 27), renewed civil war between the ELF and the EPLF has resulted in the virtual exclusion of the former from a military presence within Eritrea. The ELF charges its rival with "destructive military adventures," and with allowing itself to be used as part of an imperialist plot to destroy the ELF. The EPLF, on the other hand, says the ELF was the one to first undermine the unity pact by military action, and that it was defeated because of its lack of organization and popular support in its base areas. Whatever precipitated the latest conflict, however, it does seem that the bulk of the ELF forces still intact have sought refuge in a camp near Kassala in Sudan. The EPLF, accordingly, has a chance to prove its claim that its policy of political mass mobilization can build a solid bulwark against the Ethiopian army in Barka as well as Sahel.

Recently, AFRICA NEWS correspondent Dan Connell talked with EPLF Central Committee member Amdemikail Kahsai, getting his views on the current situation and on the outcome of the conflict with the ELF. Connell's report:

"We are in a new chapter now. This will mean a major advance for the struggle, both politically and militarily," said the EPLF diplomat, who is now based in New York to press the Eritrean case at the United Nations.

In the former ELF zones, according to Kahsai, EPLF guerrilla units have been attacking government garrisons, which had generally been immune from challenge during the past three years. And Ethiopian reinforcements are now moving into these areas.

Five fresh Ethiopian brigades are being deployed in the northern Sahel province and in the western Barka lowlands for a possible two-pronged attack, he said, adding that troops have also been sent to the southern Serai region of Eritrea.

But the guerrilla leader discounted the possibility of an Ethiopian success, due to new EPLF flexibility for maneuver, and the end of the draining fight against the rival ELF.

In fact, he said, the EPLF is now stepping up its offensive capability, attacking the enemy's weaker points and preparing for a possible general counter-offensive. With respect to the ELF, Kahsai, explained that observance of the October 1977 unity pact was always problematic, and that things rapidly went from bad to worse in 1980. The ELF was reported to have held secret meetings with Soviet and Ethiopian diplomats beginning in January of that year. Major clashes with the EPLF took place in June and July. Then on July 17 the ELF pulled back its last military units from joint positions with the EPLF on the Sahel battlefront and set up camps in what appeared to be preparation for a surprise attack.

From December 1979 until the March meeting in Tunis, the EPLF was unable to convene any meetings with ELF leaders, said Kahsai.

Fighting broke out between the two fronts in late August 1980, and it soon spread across Eritrea. A cease-fire was put into effect in November with mediation by officials from neighboring Sudan, but it failed to hold. A buffer zone was established in the Barka region, but, according to Kahsai, small clashes continued in the Sahel and Anseba area.

The March "unity agreement" called for an end to the fighting, and free movement for each group throughout Eritrea. Instead, the civil war flared up again in April and lasted until the ELF was routed in July and August of this year.

According to Kahsai, many ELF guerrillas are now challenging their organization's leadership. "We are making a general appeal to the fighters to join us. They were pushed into this war [between the two groups] and there is every possibility that a big section will join the EPLF."

Meanwhile, he said, the EPLF is moving on several fronts to fill the organizational vacuum in former ELF-held areas.

"Politically, we are in the phase of arousing the morale of the people in the areas where the ELF used to operate. Economically, we are trying to provide them with some of the basic necessities, like medicine, food and education," he explained.

"We have already seen some change in the attitude of the people," he concluded, adding that the number of new recruits to the EPLF has jumped considerably in the last two to three months.

Ethiopia to launch a major offensive, Eritrean rebels say

The Miami Herald, January 17, 1982

Ethiopia's Soviet-backed army is on the verge of launching a general offensive against nationalist forces in the contested Red Sea territory of Eritrea, according to guerrilla sources at the United Nations.

An estimated 90,000 troops are mobilized for the campaign, which could come within the next few days or weeks, according to a spokesman for the Eritrean People's Liberation Front (EPLF), who charged that South Yemen and Libya are providing combat and logistical support for the planned attack.

The guerrilla leader also accused Ethiopia of preparing to use a deadly form of anti-personnel gas in the upcoming campaign. "It's ready now on the front line," Hagos Gebrehiwet said in a telephone interview.

A high-level diplomat at the Ethiopian Embassy in Washington denied the charges, claiming that the 20-year war in Eritrea is all but over. "This is ridiculous," he said. "We're just waiting for them to give up their hands." State Department officials could neither confirm nor deny the military buildup in Eritrea.

If the guerrilla charges are accurate, the drive would be the largest counterinsurgency campaign in the war-torn region since 1978, when a massive Soviet-supported offensive forced the guerrillas to withdraw from most of the territory's main towns.

Since then, the war has been bogged down in an uneasy stalemate, with the Eritrean nationalists holding most of the rural areas and the government controlling the urban areas and the principal roads. The guerrillas are fighting for the independence of the former Italian colony, which Ethiopia annexed in 1962.

Both sides acknowledge that the guerrillas still hold the northern town of Nakfa, under siege since early 1979, and it is this holdout that the Eritrean spokesman claims is the target of current Ethiopian military preparation.

"All their efforts are organized for this. Their plan is to wage this battle for up to 30 days. Their target is again Nakfa," said Gebrehiwet.

South Yemeni pilots have been brought in to fly Soviet supplied MI24 helicopter gunships in the campaign, while Libyan C14 transport planes are providing logistical backup under a central command of five Ethiopian generals in the Asmara capital, Gebrehiwet said.

The alleged Yemeni and Libyan involvement would be a new feature in the stalemated fighting. The two countries signed a mutual assistance pact with Ethiopia last August.

Other factors favoring an Ethiopian assault now include the fact that neighboring Sudan closed the border to guerrilla supply last fall after Ethiopia threatened to back dissidents in the southern part of Sudan and the signing of the treaty with Libya, another Sudanese neighbor. Fighting between Ethiopian forces and Somali-backed nationalists in the disputed Ogaden region also appears to have died down recently.

With supplies cut off, Eritrean guerrillas are fighting with captured Soviet weapons, which include more than 150 armored cars and T54 battle tanks. The guerrillas use the tanks for artillery.

Large troop reinforcements now in Eritrea were moved from the Ogaden, while others are newly trained members of the estimated 250,000 man Ethiopian army, according to Gebrehiwet.

Eritrea: EPLF attacks Asmara

The Guardian (New York), February 3, 1982

The Eritrean People's Liberation Front (EPLF) last week carried out its most dramatic offensive action in four years with a surprise attack on Ethiopian forces in Asmara, the capital of Eritrea.

Guerrilla units controlled one section of the city for 24 hours

Jan. 21. Commandos systematically destroyed Ethiopian jet fighters and helicopter gun ships based at the Asmara International Airport, according to an EPLF spokesman in New York.

The attack came just days after Ethiopian officials had issued a press release claiming the 20-year war in the Red Sea territory was finished. It also followed an EPLF announcement that an Ethiopian counterinsurgency campaign was imminent there (Guardian, Jan. 20).

"This shows that Ethiopia's claims of victory are nonsense, but this is not new. It also shows that we are now capable of attacking them at any time, in any part of Eritrea, even where they are strongest," said Hagos Gebrehiwet in a telephone interview.

The Asmara action is also an EPLF attempt to disrupt Ethiopian preparations for the government campaign forecast for later this month, according to the front's representative.

More than 90,000 Ethiopian troops, backed by an array of Soviet-supplied heavy arms and logistical support, are now deployed throughout the territory for the planned offensive. The aircraft in Asmara were reportedly due to be used in the fighting.

Ethiopian's main concentration of forces is on three battlefronts in the north and west of Eritrea, surrounding the EPLF's main rear base area. Additional forces are dispersed in government-held cities, with the largest garrisons thought to be in Asmara, the port of Massawa and the inland city of Keren.

The EPLF also has substantial forces in the north and northwest where it has held the government to a standstill during a series of major confrontations over the past three years. In addition, the front has large, mobile guerrilla units that range across most of rural Eritrea. The political wing of the EPLF administers this territory.

The recent Ethiopian buildup follows the end of a bitter civil war among rival Eritrean nationalist movements, and it appears to be timed to take advantage of moves by neighboring Sudan to close supply routes to the EPLF over the Sudan border.

But it is also a last ditch effort to contain the continual growth of the EPLF, against a backdrop of increased national revolt in several areas of Ethiopia proper, particularly in Tigray province where guerrillas of the leftist Tigray People's Liberation Front (TPLF) claim to control most of that territory. The TPLF has close ties with the EPLF.

Faced with ongoing political instability and severe economic problems throughout the country, Ethiopia's military leaders badly need a victory in Eritrea, and they appear to have mobilized all available military resources for that purpose.

As a result, the outcome of the upcoming Eritrea campaign may well prove decisive in shaping the political future of the Addis Ababa regime. Ethiopian leader Col. Mengistu Haile Mariam was for this reason expected to arrive in Asmara this week to oversee the opening round of fighting.

The EPLF attack on Asmara by some 2600 guerrillas preempted the Ethiopian plans and set back the campaign to an extent not yet clear. But the blow to Ethiopian morale may be the most important side effect.

Meanwhile, the nature of the assault demonstrated a military sophistication and a level of planning and execution that has long eluded the government despite the assistance of Soviet advisers in Eritrea since 1978.

The surprise raid began early in the morning when EPLF infantry and artillery units opened fire on Ethiopia's 35th Army Brigade headquarters in southeastern Asmara, according to Gebrehiwet.

Two key posts at Selot and Imbeito were taken in heavy fighting as government forces fled deeper into Asmara. During this time, guerrilla units overran the airport and began destroying the MiG jets and MI-24 helicopter gun ships which were to be used in Eritrea for the first time in the war, he added.

No figures were available for the damage, but the EPLF claims to have inflicted heavy casualties on the retreating Ethiopian troops.

"Ethiopia will have to eat its words about the end of the war, because there were many foreigners in Asmara who witnessed this, and it cannot be covered up," said Gebrehiwet

Rebels Say Heavy Fighting Is Under Way In Eritrea

The Boston Globe, February 19, 1982

Ethiopia's Soviet-backed army this week launched the largest military operation in four years against nationalist guerrillas in the Red Sea territory of Eritrea, according to guerrilla sources reached by telephone. The sources charged that government forces are using an unidentified form of disabling gas in the attacks.

Fighting has also spilled over into neighboring Sudan for the first time in the 20-year war, according to a spokesman for the Eritrean

People's Liberation Front (EPLF), contacted by telephone at the United Nations in New York.

Between 90,000 and 100,000 Ethiopian troops and hundreds of Soviet and South Yemeni combat advisers are engaged in the current battles, which also involve large numbers of Soviet-supplied MiG jet fighters, MI24 helicopter gun ships, T54 battle tanks and long-range artillery, according to the spokesman, Hagos Gebrehiwet.

"This is the heaviest, most intense fighting in the history of our struggle because it is concentrated in small areas with all this fire power," he said.

The main combat is centered in the northern mountains of Eritrea's arid Sahel region near the Sudan border where the guerrillas maintain their rear base area, but it has also spread to the densely populated central highlands south of the capital, Asmara, he said.

Ethiopian officials strongly deny the use of chemical weapons in the Eritrea war, but they had no comment this week on reports of renewed fighting there.

[Mohamed Said Barre of EPLF told a news conference Wednesday that Soviet pilots were flying helicopter gunships and South Yemenis were piloting Soviet-made fighter jets against the Eritreans, the Associated Press reported from Khartoum, Barre said that cluster bombs and napalm were being used in the offensive.]

The Eritreans are fighting for the independence of the former Italian colony, which Ethiopia annexed with US backing in 1962. By 1977, the guerrillas controlled most of the strategic coastal territory, but an abrupt realignment of Ethiopia's newly installed military government with the Soviet Union turned the protracted conflict around.

A massive input of Soviet arms and advisory personnel resulted in a series of campaigns in 1978 that forced the guerrillas to withdraw from any captured towns into the rugged countryside, where the war bogged down.

The EPLF claims to have killed or wounded more than 2500 Ethiopian soldiers during the first two weeks of February. Large quantities of Soviet arms and ammunition were also reportedly captured or destroyed in scattered fighting through Feb. 13, with the most serious confrontation occurring along the northeastern coast near Sudan.

Government forces responded with chemical weapons at the coastal base of Turukruk on Feb. 15 and launched the general offensive at dawn the following day, with two brigades attempting a flanking maneuver into Sudan, according to Gebrehiwet.

"Our fighters are reporting symptoms of sneezing and vomiting, but none have died yet from the gas," he said. He said the gas is now being used on other battle fronts as well.

Ethiopia's ambassador to Britain went on BBC radio Wednesday evening in London to deny the use of chemical weapons, but revel leaders say they are collecting samples of brush in the affected areas along with blood tests from disabled to back up their accusations.

Eritreans charge Ethiopia is using gas as new offensive spills over into Sudan

The Miami Herald, February 21, 1982

Ethiopia's Soviet-backed army last week launched the largest military operation in four years against nationalists in the Red Sea territory of Eritrea, according to guerrilla sources who charged that government forces were using disabling gas in the multi-pronged campaign.

Fighting also has spilled across the border into neighboring Sudan for the first time in the 20-year war, according to a spokesman for the Eritrean People's Liberation Front (EPLF), contacted by telephone at the United Nations in New York.

Between 90,000 and 100,000 Ethiopian troops and hundreds of Soviet and South Yemeni personnel are engaged in four simultaneous battles, which involve large numbers of Soviet-supplied MiG fighters, MI24 helicopter gunships, T54 battle tanks and long-range artillery, according to Hagos Gebrehiwet.

"This is the heaviest, most intense fighting in the history of our struggle because it is concentrated in small areas with all this firepower," Gebrehiwet said.

The main combat is centered in the northern mountains of Eritrea's arid Sahel region near the Sudan border, where the guerrillas maintain their rear base, but it also has spread to the densely populated central highlands south of the provincial capital of Asmara, Gebrehiwet said.

Ethiopian officials strongly deny the use of chemical weapons in the Eritrea war, but they had no comment last week on renewed fighting there.

The Eritreans are fighting for the independence of the former Italian colony, which Ethiopia annexed with U.S. support in 1962. By

1977 the guerrillas controlled most of the strategic coastal territory but the abrupt realignment of Ethiopia's newly, installed military government with the Soviet Union turned the protracted conflict around.

Massive Soviet Aid

A massive influx of Soviet arms and advisory personnel resulted in a series of campaigns in 1978 that forced the guerrillas to withdraw from many previously captured towns into the rugged countryside, where the war became a stalemate.

Diplomatic sources in Addis Abba have been reporting a substantial military buildup in Eritrea since late last year for what was termed a "final offensive" against the nationalists, who continue to operate freely in rural areas. However, the government campaign apparently was delayed by a series of pre-emptive guerrilla attacks starting in late January.

The EPLF claims to have killed or wounded more than 2,500 Ethiopian soldiers during the first two weeks of February. Large quantities of Soviet arms and ammunition also were said to have been captured or destroyed in scattered fighting through Feb. 13, with the most serious confrontation on the northeastern coast near Sudan.

Government forces responded with chemical weapons at the coastal base of Gurukruk on Feb. 15 and launched a general offensive at dawn the following day, with two brigades attempting a flanking maneuver into Sudan, according to Gebrehiwet.

Gas Symptoms

"Our fighters are reporting symptoms of sneezing and vomiting but one has died yet from the gas," he said, adding that the gas, which has not been identified, now is being used on other battlefronts as well.

Ethiopia's ambassador to Britain went on BBC radio Wednesday evening in London to deny the use of chemical weapons, but rebel leaders say that they are collecting samples of brush in the affected areas, along with blood tests from disabled guerrillas to support their allegations.

Meanwhile, the extension of current fighting in Sudan threatens to create a major international incident that could draw the Soviet Union and the United States into a confrontation.

While the Eritrean guerrillas do not receive Western backing, the Sudan recently has become an important ally of Egypt and the United States in the volatile region. Under these circumstances, the Eritrea fighting could have serious regional repercussions if the battle inside Sudan continues.

Heavy fighting is reported between Eritrean nationalists and Ethiopian forces at the Sudanese village of Ayet, 15 miles inside the tense border where the guerrillas claim to have interdicted the two government brigades Wednesday morning. Sudan has a small military base about 20 miles away, at Karora.

"They crossed the Sudanese border on Tuesday and the Sudanese did nothing, so we had to defend ourselves by attacking them (the Ethiopians) there," said Gebrehiwet.

"There are only two brigades, which are now cut off from reinforcements and from logistical supplies," he said. "We expect to crush them soon and then to withdraw into Eritrea."

Yemen Sends Help

The guerrillas claim that there are approximately 100 Soviet advisors on each of four battlefronts, and an uncertain number of South Yemeni troops flying the helicopter gunships and playing front-line combat roles.

South Yemen and Libya signed a mutual defense pact with Ethiopia last August, but there are no reports of Libyan forces involved in the Eritrea campaign.

In addition to the two coastal battles near the Sudan border, there is a third attack in progress to the south in the Barka lowlands and a fourth in the plateau area of Serai and Akele Guzai, the guerrilla spokesman said.

MIG21 and MIG23 jets are hitting these areas with cluster anti-personnel and incendiary bombs from dawn to dusk, but there has not been any significant shift of either force yet, Gebrehiwet said.

The guerrillas expect the campaign to last from 20 to 30 days, with potentially decisive results in the long and bitter war, but they offer no precise forecast of the outcome.

Eritrean guerrillas claim major victories

The Toronto Globe & Mail, February 23, 1982

Boston, Mass.

Eritrean nationalists claim to have inflicted substantial losses on Ethiopia's Soviet-backed army in heavy fighting on four simultaneous battlefronts last week across the strategic Red Sea territory and in neighboring Sudan.

A spokesman for the Eritrean People's Liberation Front contacted by telephone at the United Nations in New York said that thousands of Ethiopian troops and an undetermined number of "foreign advisors" were killed or wounded between Feb. 16 and 20 in what he termed the "most intense battles of the war." Meanwhile, the guerrilla spokesman also claimed that EPLF units also attacked the main military and civilian airports in the provincial capital Asmara for the second time in as many months. The control tower, the runway and a dozen Soviet aircraft were "heavily damaged" in the surprise raid last Friday, he said.

"Ethiopia has now engaged its main military forces in the offensive, but the fighting is steadily turning in our favor," said Hagos Gebrehiwet.

Close to 100,000 Ethiopian soldiers are deployed in the 110,000 square kilometer territory for the Government campaign, the largest military action in four years, according to Western intelligence sources.

Sudanese officials in Washington say they have no information about the alleged spread of the war into Sudan, but they express serious concern that such a development could threaten relations between that country and Ethiopia.

The Eritreans have been fighting since 1961 for the independence of the former Italian colony, annexed by Ethiopia after a 10-year United Nations-sponsored federation. The Soviet Union, which once supported the Eritrean demands, has backed Ethiopia since 1977 when the country's newly-installed military junta broke with the West.

The heaviest fighting is now taking place along the northern Eritrean coast, in the western Barka lowlands and across the border in Sudan near the village Ayet, according to Mr. Gebrehiwet.

Eritrean guerrillas reportedly attack key supply facility

The Boston Globe, February 27, 1982

Nationalist Eritrean guerrillas launched a series of attacks on Ethiopia's key supply and logistical facility in the embattled Red Sea territory last week as heavy fighting continued close to the Sudan border, according to guerrilla sources at the United Nations in New York.

The Asmara International Airport was "heavily damaged" on Feb. 19 when rebel units shelled the control tower and the runway and blew up a dozen Soviet aircrafts, according to a spokesman for the Eritrean People's Liberation Front (EPLF) contacted by telephone yesterday. Four days later, the guerrillas entered the port of Massawa to destroy the government's oil storage tanks there, said the spokesman, Hagos Gebrehiwet.

A high-ranking official in the Ethiopian embassy in Washington denied yesterday that a large-scale military campaign was taking place but spokesmen for the State Department confirmed reports of heavy fighting, though they could no provide details.

Meanwhile, the EPLF is claiming over 10,000 Ethiopian casualties in three simultaneous battles that began two weeks ago when the government opened a multi-pronged counterinsurgency campaign aimed at the guerrillas' rear base near Sudan, according to Gebrehiwet.

"Ethiopia has now engaged its main military forces in the offensive, but the fighting is steadily turning in our favor," said Gebrehiwet. "In a few more days, the results of the whole offensive will be known," he added.

Close to 100,000 Soviet-advised and -equipped Ethiopian soldiers are deployed in Eritrea for the campaign, according to Western intelligence sources. The territory has a population of slightly over three million.

While both sides have committed their main forces to a showdown in the arid northern and western mountains of the strategic coastal territory, the guerrillas appear to have held large units in reserve to strike at the government force behind the front lines where it is extremely vulnerable to hit-and-run raids.

The Eritreans have been fighting since 1961 for the independence of the former Italian colony, annexed by Ethiopian then after a 10-year, UN-sponsored federation. The Soviet Union, which once supported the Eritrean demands, has backed Ethiopia since 1977 when the country's newly installed military junta broke with the West.

The government's inability to win a decisive victory has heightened economic and political pressures within Ethiopia, while there have also been reports of morale problems in the armed forces. As a result, the present campaign could have far reaching repercussions in the event of a government failure, even if the guerrillas merely succeed in maintaining the current stalemate.

Meanwhile, the guerrilla spokesman claimed that 7200 Ethiopian troops were killed or wounded and 620 taken prisoner in a five-day battle through Monday in the western lowlands, while an estimated 3700 were put out of action in fighting along the sea coast. He provided no figures on guerrilla casualties.

Five guerrilla battalions were involved in the Asmara airport raid last week when even Soviet MiG fighters, two Antonov transport planes and three helicopter gunships were destroyed, he said adding that an arms depot was also burned and 550 government troops killed during the early morning attack.

Eritrea rebels claim significant victories

The Guardian (New York), March 3, 1982

Eritrean guerrillas claim to have inflicted substantial losses on Ethiopia's army last week in what is being described as the heaviest fighting in the 20-year liberation war.

More than 5000 Ethiopian troops have been killed or wounded in a series of simultaneous battles within Eritrea and across the border in neighboring Sudan since the Soviet-backed government launched an all-out offensive Feb. 16, according to a U.S. spokesman for the Eritrean People's Liberation Front (EPLF).

Five EPLF battalions meanwhile carried out a surprise attack on the territory's main military and civilian airport in the Asmara capital early Feb. 19, knocking out the control tower and destroying a dozen Soviet-made aircraft, said Hagos Gebrehiwet this week.

"Ethiopia has now engaged its main military forces in the offensive, but the fighting is steadily turning in our favor," said the guerrilla representative."In a few more days, the results of the whole offensive will be known," he added.

The EPLF charges that Ethiopia is using the full resources of its powerful arsenal of Soviet and Western arms, including an unidentified form of disabling and possibly lethal gas in the campaign, the largest in four years in Eritrea.

"The symptoms we have observed so far include violent sneezing and vomiting. None have died yet, but we are watching the situation carefully to determine what these weapons are," said Gebrehiwet."

Ethiopian officials strongly deny the use of chemical weapons, but the EPLF spokesman said the guerrillas are collecting samples for analysis, and they expect to provide concrete evidence soon.

Sudanese diplomats in Washington also say they have no information about the spread of the fighting into Sudan, but they express concern that such a development could threaten the fragile rapprochement between that country and Ethiopia.

The Eritreans have been fighting since 1961 for the independence of the former Italian colony, annexed by Ethiopia after a 10-year UN-sponsored federation. The USSR, which once supported the Eritrean demands for self-determination, has backed Ethiopia since 1977 when the country's newly installed military junta broke with the West.

The Soviets have provided Ethiopia with more than $2 billion in modern weapons, but the leftist guerrillas, fighting mainly with captured arms have held the war to a bitter stalemate for the past four years. The government's inability to make significant headway in the war has added to the economic and political pressures within Ethiopia.

Persistent reports of serious morale problems in the armed forces are a reflection of these problems. Under such circumstances, the present Eritrea campaign could have profound effects upon the political future of the regime if it fails to score a decisive victory.

The heavy concentration of troops and arms in Eritrea appears to indicate that this a door-die military campaign for the government of Lt. Col. Mengistu Haile Mariam, who has bucked opposition from within the regime-and reportedly from socialist allies-to attempt a military rather than a political solution to the Eritrean war.

This could explain the apparent Ethiopian desperation in resorting to chemical warfare and to risking relations with Sudan by moving troops across that country's territory. But it is likely to backfire by bringing international attention to the Eritrea conflict.

The heaviest fighting is now taking place along the northeastern coast near the border town of Karora and further south near the government-held town of Afabet, in the western lowlands near the EPLF-held village of Kerkebet and across the border near the Sudanese village of Ayet.

An estimated 370 Ethiopian troops were killed or wounded on the three Eritrean battle fronts, while hundreds more are reported out of action in nearby Sudan where the EPLF now has a full Ethiopian division of 8000 soldiers pinned down.

This is the first time a major battle has been fought on Sudanese soil, and the implications for the entire region are far-reaching. Sudan is a close U.S. and Egypt's ally, while Ethiopia is linked to Libya (another Sudan neighbor) and South Yemen by a mutual assistance pact signed last August.

The Sudanese regime of Gen. Jaafar el-Nimeiri has been walking a political tightrope for months, attempting détente with Ethiopia while singling out Libya as its main regional foe. Sudan's regional policies reflect a strong U.S. influence, but they are also a product of growing internal dissent and a real danger of national economic bankruptcy. This internal disarray has heightened fears of Ethiopian assistance to opposition movements in southern Sudan.

While the continuing battles in northern Eritrea and Sudan constitute the main showdown between the two armies, the EPLF attack on the Asmara airport Feb. 19 suggests that Ethiopia is spread extremely thin in the rest of Eritrea opening the government to the risk of counterattack along its extended supply lines from the rear.

Seven MIG-21 and 23 jets, two Antonov transport planes and three helicopter gun ships were burned in the surprise assault by five EPLF battalions.

Ethiopian leader, Soviet generals
hurt in battle, guerrillas claim

The Miami Herald, March 7, 1982

Ethiopian leader Lt. Col. Mengistu Haile Mariam and two Soviet generals were wounded last week during a battle with nationalist guerrillas in the Red Sea territory of Eritrea, according to a guerrilla spokesman at the United Nations

Ethiopian officials in Addis Ababa immediately denied the reports, which first appeared in the Middle Eastern press on Friday. However, the fiery head of state has not appeared in public since the alleged attack Tuesday morning.

Mengistu and the two Soviet advisers were in the government-held town of Afabet in northeastern Eritrea to assess the rapidly deteriorating military situation there, where guerrillas of the Eritrean People's Liberation Front (EPLF) have repulsed a series of Ethiopian drives over the past three weeks, according to EPLF spokesman Hagos Gebrehiwet.

The three men were wounded in a guerrilla artillery barrage upon government positions along a low-lying plain outside Afabet, where more than 20,000 Ethiopian troops are trying to drive into the mountain stronghold of the guerrillas, Gebrehiwet said Saturday in a telephone interview.

Ethiopian forces launched a four-pronged counterinsurgency campaign aimed at crushing the 20-year-old independence war in mid-February, according to Western intelligence sources, who say that close to 100,000 men were mobilized for the offensive.

Mengistu has been reported spending a great deal of time in Eritrea in recent months, both to oversee the military operation and to emphasize government claims that the rebellious northern province is under control.

Ethiopian officials describe the current campaign, "Operation Red Star," as a combined program of economic reconstruction and guerrilla suppression.

The rebels claim to have inflicted more than 13,000 casualties during the fighting, which has raged across the strategic coastal territory. Ethiopian officials have yet to release any figures on the battles, and no Western journalists have been able to travel to combat areas on either side.

Under the circumstances, an injury to the Ethiopian commander-in-chief could have a profound impact upon the unsettled situation in Eritrea and in Ethiopia as a whole.

The effects on the geopolitically important region—the Horn of Africa—also could be significant because Ethiopia has been a key Soviet ally since 1977, when the East African nation broke with the Western world.

Mengistu emerged that year as the unchallenged winner of a three-year power struggle between rival military leaders who seized the government in a bloodless coup against Emperor Haile Selassie.

The young leader, usually described as being in his mid-30s, is credited with pushing through a series of radical social reforms in the impoverished former feudal kingdom, but he has been intransigent against his political opposition.

More than 10,000 young persons were executed or killed in street battles in the Ethiopian capital during a 1978 crackdown on urban opposition groups, according to Amnesty International, which has repeatedly cited Ethiopia for human rights violations since the military took power in 1974.

The Mengistu government also has taken a hard line against a variety of rural opposition groups among minority nationalities that have demanded a form of autonomy. The Eritreans, who were added to the empire after World War II, seek independence.

The inability of the Addis Ababa regime to defeat the Eritreans has encouraged an increasing dependence upon the Soviet Union, which has provided Ethiopia with more than $2 billion in arms and reportedly is aiding the government with an estimated 400 combat advisers in the current Eritrea battles.

Mengistu is said to have survived more than a dozen assassination attempts over the past five years, but he is also reported to face opposition within the ruling circle of military officers over his refusal to seek a political settlement of the Eritrea war, which is consuming increasingly large portions of Ethiopia economic resources and is running up huge arms debts to Moscow.

Cuban President Fidel Castro also is reportedly displeased with Ethiopia's failure to settle the Eritrea conflict and with the slow pace of the government's attempts to set up a civilian political party.

There are an estimated 13,000 Cuban troops in Ethiopia to protect the government against threats from neighboring Somalia, but Castro has declined to permit his soldiers to fight in Eritrea, according to well-informed sources.

However, whether a serious injury to Mengistu would signal a sharp change in Ethiopian policy would depend upon who took over in Addis Ababa. With a combination of secrecy among the officers close to the top and the absence of a clear line of succession, it is far from clear who would take his place.

Among those often mentioned as a potential rival is Lt. Legesse Asfaw, who leads the organizational department of the committee assigned to develop a political party. Mengistu is committee chairman.

War Crisis Escalates

MERIP Reports, Washington, DC, June 1982

Political developments in the strategic Horn of Africa have lately slipped out of the headlines, but the confrontations brewing there could dwarf earlier conflicts in both military fury and political complexity. The US-backed regimes in Somalia and Sudan each face the possibility of sudden coups d'etat or civil wars. The Soviet-supported Ethiopian government is losing another in a long sequence of campaigns to stamp out nationalist guerrillas in the former Italian colony of Eritrea. Addis Ababa also faces ongoing revolts by three minority nationalities who are increasingly linking up with one another topple the military authorities.

There is dearth of hard information about the actual military and political situation in the area. A brief survey reveals the weakness of analyses that concentrate simply on regional or geopolitical alignments. The more precarious each regime becomes, the more it tends to blame its immediate neighbors for its internal problems, and the more it looks to regional alliances and external aid to compensate for these difficulties. Growing border problems and heightened tensions from the Indian Ocean to the Mediterranean Sea could easily erupt into a full-scale regional war, potentially involving the US and the Soviet Union in a head-to-head crisis.

One alliance links Ethiopia to Libya and the People's Democratic Republic of Yemen (South Yemen), all of which are aligned to some degree with the Soviet Union and are described by Soviet theoreticians as "socialist oriented" or "non-capitalist." On the other side, there are ties between Somalia, Sudan and Egypt, each of which loosely fits the Reagan administration's category of "authoritarian" regimes friendly to Western capital and US policy. Both regional blocs hold their opposite numbers responsible for the unrest within their borders, and these charges are echoed by the world powers which stand behind them.

The US and the Soviets have channeled massive quantities of arms to their respective clients while urging them to consolidate power locally by means of contrasting development models. In both instances, the reliance on military measures far outweighs the emphasis on economic means. Overall arms transfers to the region during the past five years exceed $5 billion, and include a vast array of sophisticated weapons ranging from supersonic jet fighters and helicopter gunships to battle tanks and an assortment of heavy artillery and rocketry. This has not resolved any of the internal crises, but rather set the stage for a "conventional" war between these states of potentially staggering proportions.

A showdown maybe fast approaching. Somali president Siad Barre visited Washington this March in search of additional aid. Ethiopia charges Somalia and Sudan with aiding guerrilla armies in the southeastern Ogaden region and in Eritrea. Somalia accuses Ethiopia and Libya of arming opposition movements in the northern half of that country. Sudan attacks Mengistu and Qaddafi for backing southern dissidents and northern religious and political groups seeking to topple the shaky Nimeiri government. Just days before Anwar Sadat's assassination, the Reagan administration gave Egypt's then-Vice President Mubarak assurances of a US military "umbrella" for any Egyptian military action against Libya.

There is ample evidence to support all of these claims to varying degrees, with all the ramifications they hold at the geopolitical level. But the troubles each government now faces date back more than two decades. Sudan's north-south civil war lasted from 1955 to 1972. The Eritrean war for independence from Ethiopia began in 1961, after a decade of political protest. Somalia incorporated clan and regional political divisions from the moment the former Italian and British Somalilands were joined in 1960. Each of these local conflicts has passed through phases of heightened or muted expression, while regional and international alliances have shifted and swerved with dizzying velocity. During the late 1960s, left-leaning military officers overthrew corrupt pro-Western civilian regimes in Libya. Somalia and Sudan, emulating to some extent the prototypical radical nationalist regime of Gamal Abdul Nasser in Egypt, Ethiopia, under Haile Selassie, was then Washington's strongest African ally. In this period, Israel aided southern Sudan rebels through western Ethiopia. Eritrean nationalists were trained in Cuba, China, Algeria, South Yemen and other progressive states. Ogaden Somalis were helped by North Korea, Iraq and several Palestinian groups.

Charges today by Ethiopia and the Soviet Union that the powerful Marxist-led Eritrean nationalist government is a "pawn of petrodollars" and "Arab reaction" sound as convincing as Sudanese and US claims that "communist subversion" and "Libyan meddling" underlie the problems of the Nimeiri regime. In both cases, the crises are clearly historical and structural. In the most general sense, they are the legacy of the colonial era, complicated by the combination of

economic backwardness and inherited social inequities, and exacerbated by the intrigues of rival neighbors and the opportunism of
external forces.

Beneath their conflicting regional and international alignments,
Somalia, Sudan and Ethiopia share to varying degrees the phenomenon
of narrowly-based military governments which have so far failed to overcome these problems and have slipped into a siege mentality against their
own populations. Each regime seized power on the basis of remarkably
similar programs and self-descriptions. They promised "socialist revolutions" which would bring an end to ethnic, regional, religious and social
injustices. Land reform and widespread nationalizations were at the core of
this orientation. They have constructed mass political associations among
women, youth and peasants and launched statewide literacy campaigns.

The formation of one-party political systems under military leadership was another longer term feature. The undemocratic nature of these
reform governments is not only a striking feature of all these regimes, but
a key to identifying the weaknesses in what are otherwise impressive
attempts to tackle the inherited national and social problems. Individual
circumstances nurtured significant differences in the application and the
consistency of these programs in each country, but these differences make
the similarities over time all the more noticeable. Each successive experiment in what could be termed "socialist-oriented development from
above" has surpassed its predecessor in scope and intensity. Still, even the
sweeping social reforms of Ethiopia's post-1974 military government
have failed to achieve economic and political stability. Instead, the war-
torn empire-state has become the storm center of a dangerously escalating regional crisis zone.

The sequence begins with the seizure of state power by a small
military grouping, usually based in the middle echelons of the armed
forces. In every case, they act in the midst of a generalized political
crisis in which the collaboration of the traditional ruling elite with
imperialism is clearly perceived by large segments of the population.
An alliance of the military and civilian petty bourgeoisie, under strict
control by the military wing, steps forward to create political order
and economic progress with an eclectic, appealing mix of nationalism
and socialism. The regime ruptures its ties with the US and strength-
ens them with the Soviet Union.

Suppression of local civilian left forces comes at an early stage. The
new military leadership shares an interest with the civilian middle class,
the working class and peasantry in dismantling the
remnants of precapitalist and neocolonial economic and social relations.

It plays a forceful and leading role in restructuring the economic base and political superstructure of the country, and reorients the country's foreign policies in a progressive direction. But democratic structures are not built into the social reform process. This leadership also has class and national interests of its own, and seeks to guard its monopoly on state power for the time when it will come into direct conflict with rival class and national forces. Militarism substitutes for political struggle. Scare resources are further drained from reconstruction efforts, and external alliances substitute for declining popular bases. Depending on the conjunction of regional alignments, Western links may become more attractive than Eastern bloc ties.

The Nasser period in Egypt, Somalia's adherence to "scientific socialism," Ethiopia's self-described Marxist-Leninist orientation-each experiment has been described as the one to watch. There can be little doubt that each has brought increased benefits to its people in the sphere of social programs, education, and health care. None, however, has settled the fundamental issues of national and regional disunity.

This failure to build a mass socialist party that would provide a political arena for the resolution of outstanding internal conflicts is both a cause and a consequence of heightening regional and national contradictions. Initial progress in this area marked the early years of both the Siad Barre and the Nimeiri regimes. But the measures to consolidate the Somali and Sudanese nations were uneven and incomplete. This is a key factor in the splintering of the Somali and Sudanese leaderships and their accelerating rightward political and ideological momentum. In Ethiopia, the absence of significant progress on the national question has similarly encouraged a steady narrowing of the leadership and effectively prevented the emergence of any political party to date.

More than a decade of experience in the Horn of Africa and elsewhere in the Third World suggests that the two issues—that of nation-building and party-building—are inseparably and dialectically connected. Together with decisive countrywide action in the social and economic spheres, the struggle to achieve unity and equality among unevenly developed regions and nationalities is a critical arena in which a leading party can be developed. External aid, by propping up narrowly-based military regimes that claim to represent broader class and national forces, encourages shortcuts to this process. These shortcuts have proved to be politically and socially destructive. One can only hope that it will not take greater and more widespread bloodshed in northeast Africa to bring this lesson home.